Africa Yearbook

Africa Yearbook

Politics, Economy and Society South of the Sahara in 2017

VOLUME 14

Edited by

Jon Abbink
Victor Adetula
Andreas Mehler
Henning Melber

BRILL

LEIDEN | BOSTON

Typeface for the Latin, Greek, and Cyrillic scripts: "Brill". See and download: brill.com/brill-typeface.

ISSN 1871-2525
ISBN 978-90-04-36761-6 (paperback)
ISBN 978-90-04-36763-0 (e-book)

This book is printed on acid-free paper and produced in a sustainable manner.

Contents

Preface

In May 2003, the Africa-Europe Group of Interdisciplinary Studies (AEGIS) encouraged some of its member institutions to publish an *Africa Yearbook* with a wider international appeal. The African Studies Centre in Leiden (ASC), the Institute of African Affairs in Hamburg (IAA) and the Nordic Africa Institute in Uppsala (NAI) – all very active AEGIS centres with similar profiles – accepted this challenge and their joint efforts first bore fruit in the initial volume of the series in 2004. In 2007, the Dag Hammarskjöld Foundation in Uppsala (DHF) joined this international project, while the NAI ended its involvement with the fifth volume, published in 2009. As from 2014, the DHF ended its collaboration, and from the 11th volume the NAI re-joined the collaborating institutions, ensuring the *Yearbook*'s continued publication. As from this year, Victor Adetula strengthens the contribution of the Nordic Africa Institute by replacing Sebastian Elischer, one of the team of editors for three years (volumes 11–13) and the Center for African Studies at the University of Florida, one of the institutional collaborators for the last two years. We thank both Sebastian and the Center for their previous support.

As in previous volumes, the country-specific articles cover domestic politics, foreign affairs and socioeconomic developments in the states of sub-Saharan Africa during the calendar year under review. While we recognise the impossibility of finding fully objective indicators for the relative importance of each of the states covered by the *Yearbook*, the length of the country-specific articles aims to reflect the approximate weight of each country. The four sub-regions are also introduced by means of an overview article. Further overviews summarise general continental developments and European-African relations.

The *Yearbook* is based on scholarly work, but is oriented towards a wider target readership, including students, politicians, diplomats, administrators, journalists, teachers, practitioners in the sphere of development cooperation and business people. Without forcing the individual contributions too much into a straitjacket, the volume is primarily concerned with providing factual (though not necessarily neutral) information. Each issue, in focusing almost exclusively on developments during a particular calendar year, provides a completely fresh annual overview of events and thereby adds to the cumulative record of on-going developments.

In November 2012, the *Yearbook* received the prestigious biennial Conover-Porter Award for outstanding Africa-related reference works from the African Studies Association and the Africana Librarians Council in the USA. This was an encouraging sign that the *Yearbook* has become a permanent and appreciated feature in Africanist publishing. The same year, thanks to a generous arrangement by Brill, the Africa Institute of South Africa joined as an African co-publisher, thereby greatly enhancing local distribution on the continent.

This is the fourteenth consecutive volume of the *Yearbook*, and we are proud to add another year to recording African affairs in what we believe is a solid scholarly contribution towards a better understanding of and more knowledge about SSA countries. Brill has since 2016 taken the initiative to publish in addition some country-focused chronologies as a compilation of the *Yearbook* chapters. These testify to the value of information steadily accumulated over time, enhancing accessibility to readers with a main interest in one specific country.

Once again we wish to express our gratitude to all the contributors for their collaboration in this endeavour; to the partner institutions in AEGIS for encouraging us to embark on this ambitious project; to Carol Rowe for her meticulous language editing; to Bas van der Mije for his unfailing coordinating assistance; and to Brill Publishers for their continued commitment. After adding value for nine years, Carol Rowe is retiring with this volume. We wish her all the best. Her reliable support will be missed. And last but not least, we would once again like to thank our participating institutions for their on-going support.

The Editors
Freiburg, Leiden and Uppsala, June 2018

List of Abbreviations

ACP	African, Caribbean, and Pacific Group of Countries (Lomé/Cotonou Agreement)
AfDB	African Development Bank (Tunis)
AGOA	African Growth and Opportunity Act
AI	Amnesty International
APRM	African Peer Review Mechanism
AU	African Union (Addis Ababa)
BCEAO	Banque Centrale des Etats de l'Afrique de l'Ouest (Dakar)
BEAC	Banque des Etats de l'Afrique Centrale (Yaoundé)
CAR	Central African Republic
CBLT	Commission du Bassin du Lac Tchad (N'Djaména)
CEEAC	Communauté Economique des Etats de l'Afrique Centrale (Libreville) = ECCAS
CEMAC	Communauté Economique et Monétaire de l'Afrique Centrale
CEN-SAD	Community of Sahel-Saharan States (Tripoli)
CFAfr	Franc de la Communauté Financière Africaine (BCEAO; BEAC)
COMESA	Common Market for Eastern and Southern Africa (Lusaka)
CPLP	Comunidade dos Países de Língua Portuguesa
DDR	Disarmament, Demobilisation and Reintegration
DFID	Department for International Development (London)
DRC	Democratic Republic of the Congo
EAC	East African Community
ECA	Economic Commission for Africa (United Nations; Addis Ababa)
ECCAS	Economic Community of Central African States (Libreville)
ECF	Extended Credit Facility (IMF)
ECOWAS	Economic Community of West African States (Abuja)
EDF	European Development Fund (Brussels)
EIB	European Investment Bank (Luxemburg)
EITI	Extractive Industries Transparency Initiative.
EPA	Economic Partnership Agreement
EU	European Union (Brussels)
FAO	Food and Agricultural Organisation (Rome)
FDI	Foreign Direct Investment
GDP	Gross Domestic Product
HDI	Human Development Index (UNDP)
HIPC	Heavily Indebted Poor Countries
HRW	Human Rights Watch
ICC	International Criminal Court
ICGLR	International Conference on the Great Lakes Region

IDA	International Development Association (Washington)
IDP	Internally Displaced Person
IFAD	International Fund for Agricultural Development (Rome)
IFC	International Finance Corporation (Washington)
IGAD	Intergovernmental Authority on Development (Djibouti)
ILO	International Labour Organisation (Geneva)
IMF	International Monetary Fund (Washington)
IOC	Indian Ocean Commission (Quatre Bornes)
IORA	Indian Ocean Rim Association (Ebène/Mauritius)
MDGS	Millennium Development Goals
MRU	Mano River Union (Freetown)
NEPAD	New Partnership for Africa's Development
NGO	Non-Governmental Organisation
OAU	Organization of African Unity
ODA	Official Development Assistance
OECD	Organisation for Economic Cooperation and Development (Paris)
OIC	Organisation of the Islamic Conference (Jeddah)
OIF	L'Organisation Internationale de la Francophonie
OPEC	Organisation of Petroleum Exporting Countries (Vienna)
PPP	Purchasing Power Parity
SACU	Southern African Customs Union (Pretoria)
SADC	Southern African Development Community (Gaborone)
SDR	Special Drawing Right (IMF)
SSA	Sub-Saharan Africa
TI	Transparency International
UAE	United Arab Emirates
UEMOA	Union Économique et Monétaire Ouest-Africaine (Ouagadougou)
UN	United Nations (New York)
UNDP	United Nations Development Programme (New York)
UNESCO	United Nations Educational, Scientific and Cultural Organisation (Paris)
UNHCR	United Nations High Commissioner for Refugees (Geneva)
UNICEF	United Nations Children's Fund (New York)
UNSC	United Nations Security Council
USAID	United States Agency for International Development (Washington)
WFP	World Food Programme (Rome)
WHO	World Health Organisation (Geneva)
WTO	World Trade Organisation (Geneva)

Factual Overview (as of 31 December 2017)

West Africa

Country	Area (in sq km)	Population (in m)[a]	Currency	HDI (2015)[b]	Head of State	Prime Minister
Benin	112,622	11.2	CFA Franc	0.485	Patrice Talon	
Burkina Faso	274,122	19.6	CFA Franc	0.402	Roch Marc Christian Kaboré	Paul Kaba Thiéba
Cape Verde	4,033	0.5	Cape Verdean Escudo	0.648	Jorge Carlos Fonseca	Ulisses Correia e Silva
Côte d'Ivoire	322,462	24.4	CFA Franc	0.474	Alassane Ouattara	Amadou Gon Coulibaly
Gambia	11,295	2.1	Dalasi	0.452	Adama Barrow	
Ghana	238,500	28.8	Cedi	0.579	Nana Akufo-Addo	
Guinea	245,857	11.5	Guinean Franc	0.414	Alpha Condé	Mamady Youla
Guinea-Bissau	36,125	1.9	CFA Franc	0.424	José Mário Vaz	Umaro Sissoco Embaló
Liberia	111,370	4.7	Liberian Dollar	0.427	Ellen Johnson – Sirleaf	
Mali	1,240,000	18.9	CFA Franc	0.442	Ibrahim Boubacar Keïta	Soumeylou Boubèye Maïga
Mauritania	1,030,700	4.4	Ouguiya	0.513	Mohamed Ould Abdel Aziz	Yahya Ould Hademine
Niger	1,267,000	20.6	CFA Franc	0.353	Mahamadou Issoufou	Brigi Rafini
Nigeria	923,768	190.9	Naira	0.527	Muhammadu Buhari	
Senegal	197,162	15.8	CFA Franc	0.494	Macky Sall	Mahammed Boun Abdallah Dionne
Sierra Leone	71,740	7.6	Leone	0.420	Ernest Bai Koroma	
Togo	56,785	7.8	CFA Franc	0.487	Faure Essozimna Gnassingbé	Komi Sélom Klassou

a (Population figures are for mid-2017 according to Stiftung Weltbevölkerung, www.weltbevöl kerung.de)

b (Latest data from 2015 according to UNDP hdr.undp.org)

Central Africa

Country	Area (in sq km)	Population (in m)	Currency	HDI	Head of state	Prime Minister
Cameroon	475,442	25.0	CFA Franc BEAC	0.518	Paul Biya	Philémon Yang
Central African Republic	622,984	4.7	CFA Franc BEAC	0.352	Faustin Archange-Touadéra	Simplice Sarandji
Chad	1,284,000	14.9	CFA Franc BEAC	0.396	Idriss Déby Itno	Albert Pahimi Padacké
Congo	342,000	5.0	CFA Franc BEAC	0.592	Denis Sassou-Nguesso	Clément Mouamba
DR Congo	2,344,855	81.5	Congolese Franc	0.435	Joseph Kabila	Bruno Tshibala
Equatorial Guinea	28,051	1.3	CFA Franc BEAC	0.592	Teodoro Obiang Nguema Mbasogo	Francisco Pascual Obama Asue
Gabon	267,667	2.0	CFA Franc BEAC	0.697	Ali Bongo Ondimba	Emmanuel Issoze-Ngondet
São Tomé and Príncipe	1,001	0.2	Dobra	0.574	Evaristo Carvalho	Patrice Trovoada

Eastern Africa

Country	Area (in sq km)	Population (in m)	Currency	HDI	Head of State	Prime Minister
Burundi	26,338	10.4	Burundi Franc	0.404	Pierre Nkurunziza	
Comoros	1,862	0.8	Comoran Franc	0.497	Azali Assoumani	
Djibouti	23,200	1.0	Djiboutian Franc	0.473	Ismail Omar Guelleh	Abdoulkader Kamil Mohamed
Eritrea	124,320	5.9	Nakfa	0.420	Isaias Afewerki	
Ethiopia	1,121,900	105.0	Birr	0.448	Mulatu Teshome	Hailemariam Desalegn
Kenya	569,259	49.7	Kenya Shilling	0.555	Uhuru Kenyatta	
Rwanda	26,338	12.3	Rwanda Franc	0.498	Paul Kagame	Édouard Ngirente
Seychelles	455	0.09	Seychelles Rupee	0.728	Danny Faure	
Somalia	637,600	14.7	Somali Shilling	n.a.	Mohamed Abdullahi Mohamed Musa Bihi Abdi	Hassan Ali Khayre
(Somaliland)	137,600	3.5	Somaliland Shilling	n.a.		
Sudan	2,505,805	40.6	Sudanese Pound	0.490	Omar Hassan Ahmad al-Bashir	
South Sudan	619,745	12.6	South Sudanese Pound	0.418	Salva Kiir Mayardit	
Tanzania	945,087	57.5	Tanzania Shilling	0.531	John Magufuli	Majaliwa Kassim Majaliwa
Uganda	197,000	42.8	Uganda Shilling	0.493	Yoweri Kaguta Museveni	Ruhakana Rugunda

Southern Africa

Country	Area (in sq km)	Population (in m)	Currency	HDI	Head of State	Prime Minister
Angola	1,246,700	28.6	Kwanza	0.533	João Manuel Gonçalves Lourenço	
Botswana	581,730	2.3	Pula	0.698	Seretse Khama Ian Khama	
Lesotho	30,344	2.2	Lesotho Loti	0.497	King Letsie III	Thomas Thabane
Madagascar	592,000	25.5	Malagasy Ariary	0.512	Hery Rajaonarimampianina	Olivier Mahafaly Solonandrasana
Malawi	118,484	18.6	Malawian Kwacha	0.476	Peter Mutharika	
Mauritius	2,040	1.3	Mauritian Rupee	0.781	Ameenah Gurib-Fakim	Pravind Kumar Jugnauth
Mozambique	799,380	29.7	Mozambiquen Métical	0.418	Filipe Nyusi	Carlos Agostinho do Rosário
Namibia	824,269	2.5	Namibian Dollar	0.640	Hage Gottfried Geingob	Saara Kuugongelwa-Amadhila
South Africa	1,219,090	56.5	Rand	0.666	Jacob Zuma	
Swaziland	17,364	1.4	Swazi Lilangeni	0.541	King Mswati III	Sibusiso Dlamini
Zambia	752,614	16.4	Zambian Kwacha	0.579	Edgar Lungu	
Zimbabwe	390,580	16.6	Zimbabwean Dollar	0.516	Emmerson Dambudzo Mnangagwa	

List of Authors

Jon Abbink
Professor of Politics and Governance in Africa, African Studies Centre, Leiden University, g.j.abbink@asc.leidenuniv.nl

Tomas van Acker
Associated researcher, Conflict Research Group/ Department of Conflict and Development studies, Ghent University, tomas.vanacker@ugent.be

Victor Adetula
PhD in Political Science, Head of Research, Nordic Africa Institute, Uppsala, and Professor of International Relations & Development Studies at University of Jos, Nigeria, vadetula@gmail.com

Jean-Nicolas Bach
PhD in Political Science, is director of the French research institute in Khartoum (CEDEJ Khartoum) and coordinator with Roland Marchal (CERI Sciences Po) of the Observatory of Eastern Africa/Observatoire de l'Afrique de l'Est, jeannicolas.bach@cedejkhartoum.com

Alice Bellagamba
Professor of Cultural and Social Anthropology, Department of Human Sciences for Education "Riccardo Massa", University of Milan-Bicocca, alice.bellagamba@unimib.it

Heinrich Bergstresser
Media Consultant, Freelance Research Associate of the Institute of African Affairs in Hamburg and Freelance Trainer of Akademie für Internationale Zusammenarbeit (AIZ) within Deutsche Gesellschaft für Internationale Zusammenarbeit GIZ, Germany, heinrich.bergstresser@web.de

Jesper Bjarnesen
Senior researcher, The Nordic Africa Institute, Uppsala, Sweden, jesper.bjarnesen@nai.uu.se

Mamadou Bodian
PhD (2016) in Political Science, University of Florida, is a Project Coordinator for the Trans-Saharan Elections Programme (TSEP) and a member of the Sahel Research Group, mbodian79@ufl.edu

Yolande Bouka
Visiting Assistant Professor, Elliott School of International Affairs, George Washington University, ybouka@gmail.com

Jennifer C. Boylan
PhD (2016) in Political Science, Managing Editor, Perspectives on Politics, jboylan@ufl.edu

Brett Logan Carter
Assistant Professor, School of International Relations, University of Southern California, blcarter@usc.edu

Clément Deshayes
PhD student, Department of Sociology and Anthropology, University Paris 8 Saint Denis, associate researcher at LAVUE and CEDEJ-Khartoum, deshayes.clement@gmail.com

George Dzimbiri
Lecturer at the Department of Business Administration, the Polytechnic, University of Malawi, gdzimbiri@poly.ac.mw

Lewis Dzimbiri
Professor of Public Administration, Chancellor College, University of Malawi, Deputy Vice Chancellor at Lilongwe University of Agriculture and Natural Resources, Malawi, proflewisdzimbiri@gmail.com

Daniel Eizenga
PhD in Political Science, Post-Doctoral Fellow at the Centre FrancoPaix, Université de Québec à Montréal, Canada, deizenga@ufl.edu

Christine Hackenesch
PhD, Senior researcher, German Development Institute / Deutsches Institut für Entwicklungspolitik (DIE), Bonn, Germany, christine.hackenesch@die-gdi.de

Joseph Hanlon
Visiting Senior Fellow, Department of International Development, London School of Economics, UK and Visiting Senior Research Fellow at the Development Policy and Practice Centre of the Open University, UK, j.hanlon@open.ac.uk

Ketil Fred Hansen
PhD in African History, Professor in Social Sciences, University of Stavanger, Norway, ketil.f.hansen@uis.no

Kurt Hirschler
Freelance Political Scientist, Hamburg, Germany, kurt_hirschler@web.de

Nicole Hirt
Research Fellow, Institute of African Affairs, GIGA German Institute of Global and Area Studies, Hamburg, Germany, nicole.hirt@giga-hamburg.de

Rolf Hofmeier
Former Director, Institute of African Affairs, GIGA German Institute of Global and Area Studies, Hamburg, Germany, gr.hofmeier@gmx.de

Amin Kamete
Senior Lecturer, Urban Studies, School of Social and Political Sciences, University of Glasgow, Scotland, UK, amini.kamete@glasgow.ac.uk

Niels Keijzer
Researcher, German Development Institute / Deutsches Institut für Entwicklungspolitik (DIE), Bonn, Germany, niels.keijzer@die-gdi.de

Christoph Kohl
Research Fellow, Georg Eckert Institute for International Textbook Research, Braunschweig, Germany, kohl@gei.de

Dirk Kohnert
Retired Deputy Director, Institute of African Affairs, GIGA German Institute of Global and Area Studies, Hamburg, Germany, Kohnert@giga-hamburg.de

Janosch Kullenberg
PhD Fellow, Bremen International Graduate School of Social Sciences (BIGSSS), Germany, janosch.kullenberg@oxon.org

Daniel Large
Assistant Professor at the School of Public Policy, Central European University, Budapest, and non-Resident Senior Fellow at the China Policy Institute, University of Nottingham, larged@spp.ceu.edu

Joseph N. Mangarella
Lecturer at the University of Regensburg (Germany), PdD candidate at the Africa Studies Center, Leiden, and at the Institut Français de Géopolitique, Université Paris 8, joseph.mangarella@gmail.com

Richard R. Marcus
Professor and Director, The Global Studies Institute and the International Studies Program, California State University, Long Beach, USA, richard.marcus@csulb.edu

Simon Massey
Senior lecturer and post-graduate course director in the School of Humanities, Coventry University, s.massey@coventry.ac.uk

Andreas Mehler
Director of the Arnold Bergstraesser Institute and professor of Political Science at the University of Freiburg, andreas.mehler@abi.uni-freiburg.de

Henning Melber
Senior Research Associate of The Nordic Africa Institute and Director emeritus of The Dag Hammarskjöld Foundation, both in Uppsala, Sweden Henning.Melber@nai.uu.se

Sanusha Naidu
Senior Research Associate, Institute for Global Dialogue, sanusha.naidu@gmail.com

Anthoni van Nieuwkerk
PhD in International Relations. Associate Professor and coordinator of Security Studies at the Wits School of Governance, Johannesburg, Anthoni.vannieuwkerk@wits.ac.za

Nanjala Nyabola
Independent writer and political analyst based in Nairobi, Kenya, nanjala@gmail.com

Helena Olsson
Political Scientist and Staff Member at the Department of Sociology, Uppsala University, Sweden, helena.olsson@soc.uu.se

Claes Olsson
Political Scientist and Editor at Global Publications Foundation, Uppsala, Sweden, claesolsson@globalpublications.org

Krijn Peters
Associate Professor in Armed Conflict & Post-war Reconstruction, Department of Political & Cultural Studies, Swansea University, UK, k.peters@swansea.ac.uk

Fanny Pigeaud
Journalist, France, Fanny.pigeaud@gmail.com

Marisha Ramdeen
Senior Programme Officer at the African Centre for the Constructive Resolution of Disputes (ACCORD) in Durban, South Africa, Marisha@accord.org.za

Edalina Rodrigues Sanches
Postdoctoral Research Fellow at the Institute of Social Sciences-University of Lisbon and Guest Assistant Professor at ISCTE-IUL, ersanches@ics.ul.pt

Anita Schroven
Researcher at 'Integration and Conflict along the Upper Guinea Coast', Max Planck Institute for Social Anthropology, Halle/Saale, schroven@eth.mpg.de

Jon Schubert
Leverhulme Early Career Fellow, Anthropology Department, Brunel University London, jon.schubert@brunel.ac.uk

David Sebudubudu
Professor of Political Science and Dean of the Faculty of Social Sciences, University of Botswana, sebudubudu@ub.ac.bw

Gerhard Seibert
Associate professor at the Universidade da Integração Internacional da Lusofonia Afro-Brasileira (UNILAB), São Francisco do Conde, Bahia, Brazil, mailseibert@yahoo.com

Tor Sellström
Ph.D.hc (Uppsala 2011), researcher and writer. His latest book is Africa in the Indian Ocean: Islands in Ebb and Flow (Brill; 2015), tg.sellstrom@gmail.com

Roger Southall
Professor Emeritus, Department of Sociology, University of the Witwatersrand, and Research Associate in Political Studies, University of Cape Town, South Africa, Roger.Southall@wits.ac.za

Alexander Stroh
Junior Professor of African Politics and Development Policy, University of Bayreuth, Germany, alexander.stroh@uni-bayreuth.de

Klaas van Walraven
Senior Researcher, African Studies Centre, Leiden, The Netherlands, walraven@ascleiden.nl

Volker Weyel
Consultant, Former Editor-in-chief 'Vereinte Nationen' (1977–2004), Bonn, Germany, volker.weyel@outlook.com

Bruce Whitehouse
Associate Professor of Anthropology, Lehigh University, USA, bruce.whitehouse@lehigh.edu

Douglas Yates
Professor of Political Science at the American Graduate School in Paris, France, douglas.yates@ags.edu

Franzisca Zanker
Senior Researcher, Arnold Bergstraesser Institute at the University of Freiburg, franzisca.zanker@abi.uni-freiburg.de

PART 1

Sub-Saharan Africa

Jon Abbink, Victor Adetula, Andreas Mehler and Henning Melber

Politics were not boring this year, with three long-standing leaders leaving the stage: in the Gambia, President Yahya Jammeh initially refused to vacate the presidency after losing the elections. Concerted efforts on the part of ECOWAS and in particular Senegal forced him in January to leave the country. Angola's President Eduardo dos Santos, after 38 years in power, made way in August for a successor of his choice, who introduced some unexpected corrective measures. Zimbabwe's 93-year-old President Robert Gabriel Mugabe, in power since Independence in 1980, was unceremoniously dismissed in November in an intervention by the military. While the army decided his replacement, the generals remained in denial of all evidence that this was a coup. In contrast, the change in chairing the AU Commission took place according to plan with no surprises.

African economies generally continued to suffer from a volatile world market. Socio-economic disparities and poverty continued and the 'African rising' narrative had reached its sell-by date. Misery among ordinary people, often exacerbated by the effects of climate change, remained the order of the day. Conflict-prone regions continued to be theatres of violence and local residents were victims of terrorist attacks in several parts of the continent. Some good news was the declining rates of HIV/AIDS.

Africa in the World Economy

On the economic front, much happened in Africa. Economic life recovered from a growth slump in 2016, with *continental GPD growth* on average climbing a full percentage point, reverting to some 2.5%, aided by world trade and markets showing an upturn. Real output growth was estimated at 3.6%, although commodity exports did not fully recover. Governments remained active economic actors, buttressed by regular donor fund flows and slightly recovering FDI. Much of the economic activity remained in the informal sphere, which accounted for 30–90% of the non-agricultural economy.

However, as the AfDB noted in its annual report, *structural economic problems* in management, unemployment, agriculture and industrial policy posed a familiar array of challenges, complicated by high population increase constraining economic growth and by limited absorptive capacity. In addition, enduring *environmental-ecological problems* – including the effects of drought and climate change and heavily extractive use of land and water resources – were present in the background, impacting on long-term growth sustainability. While Africa's role

 | DOI:10.1163/9789004367630_002

in the global economy remained of undiminished importance as a source of essential basic products, such as oil, natural gas, gold, coltan, coffee, cocoa and agrarian staples, governance problems and inefficiencies in many national economies remained. It was promising, however, that ongoing technological and ICT innovation was slowly proceeding, especially among the younger generations and returning 'diaspora' migrants, and in new companies and start-ups.

High indebtedness to (inter)national capital markets and (new) 'donor' countries was an issue, in addition to relatively low export revenues (compared with imports), socio-economic inequality and persistent budget deficits. SSA saw a notable rise in public debt: at the end of the year, average public debt stood at some 57% of GDP, representing a 20% increase over the past five years. The continent also remained heavily dependent on foreign sources to finance its current account deficits.

The highest *growth figures* (although again estimates, due to continued inaccuracies in the figures) were realised in Ghana (6%), Ethiopia (8%), Côte d'Ivoire (7.6%), Djibouti (7%) and Tanzania (6.5%) and were lowest (again) in South Africa (0.7%), Nigeria (0.8%) and Chad (0.6%). A few countries, such as Congo-Brazzaville and South Sudan, had negative growth. Despite instability risks, East Africa's GDP growth was higher than other regions', at around 5.4%. In SSA, infrastructure investments again played an important role, although these continued to rapidly raise public debt. Six of the 35 SSA low-income countries were in 'debt distress', i.e., unable to service external interest payment commitments. A further nine were at high risk. Massive investments, although expected to pay off in the long term, were not yet generating sufficient additional tax revenues to repay debts. An example was the Ethiopian Railways Corporation, operating new railways built with Chinese credit to the tune of some $ 3.7 bn, but now heavily in debt by the same sum and without a proper operating budget.

Agriculture continued to be the mainstay of African economies, employing at least 50% of all economically active people, and was seen as having still unrealised potential that could be used to feed a rapidly growing population. Indeed, average food supply per capita via growth in domestic production continued to slowly increase. The president of the AfDB, Dr Akinwumi A. Adesina, in a ceremony in October in Des Moines, Iowa (USA), received the 2017 World Food Prize, awarded for recognising the power of agriculture in creating economic prosperity in Africa. Adesina had long argued for developing African agriculture into a globally competitive business sector. Some experts and African researchers pleaded for the more intensive use of biotechnology in Africa to increase crop yields and stave off declining productivity. Others advocated increasing cropping intensity and serious expansion of irrigated production. Both options were problematic. In addition to agriculture, which inevitably remained central but vulnerable to weather shocks, economic diversification was seen, but did not materialise sufficiently (see Nigeria, Congo-Brazzaville, Angola, Equatorial Guinea, Somalia, or Sudan).

A sign of hope was that *FDI* in Africa was still higher than in other emerging global markets. China expanded its role as Africa's biggest economic partner, investing in and financing infrastructure projects, and as an export destination and source of imports. This was despite the country's growing financial hold on the continent as well as misgivings regarding some of its business practices and rapid resource extraction (not only oil, but also timber, for example, and (illegal) fishing off Africa's coasts, and aggressive fish trading).

An OECD report on *illicit financial flows* published on 20 February stated that Africa lost an estimated $ 50–60 bn to such practices as unauthorised capital export, e.g. via tax evasion, money laundering, trade mis-invoicing, abusive transfer pricing and illegal transport of cash. The sum exceeded government development aid (although not remittances) to Africa. To partly counter this illicit flow, in July Europe introduced new tools, such as the implementation of the fourth Anti-Money Laundering Directive, and measures requiring multinational companies and traders to publish details of their activities on a country-by-country basis, even outside the EU.

The World Economic Forum's *Africa Competitiveness Report* noted that Africa's competitiveness remained largely stagnant, as the overall Africa score was only 5% higher than in 2008. Continued challenges cited were infrastructure deficits, significant skill mismatches, slow adoption of new technologies, weak institutions, weak financial sector development and low levels of regional trade and integration. But there were positive trends in areas such as the quality of macroeconomic policy, human capital development, progress on health and growth of literacy. Some individual countries such as Côte d'Ivoire, Ethiopia, Rwanda and Tanzania improved their competitiveness (despite authoritarianism and lack of freedoms). On the global list of 137, Mauritius was the best placed African country at 45th.

Ongoing research at Oxford University on *multidimensional poverty* (MDI), i.e., measuring more than only daily income, showed that around 36% of poor people under this MDI concept lived in Africa (and 46% in Asia), with the 'poorest regions' being in Chad, Burkina Faso, Niger, Ethiopia, Liberia, Sierra Leone, South Sudan, Nigeria, Uganda (and Afghanistan).

In some countries, ongoing deep *security problems*, such as continuing civil strife or war, regional uprisings and the activities of predatory armed militias, had a major impact on economic activities. Examples were South Sudan, Burundi, Somalia, Mali, Sudan, the CAR, the DRC and West African countries, the last suffering from aggravated armed clashes between (Fulani) pastoralists and settled farmers, which led to the death of thousands of people and multi-million-dollar economic damage, especially in Nigeria. Unpredictable policy approaches in various countries also went on to pose risks for FDI and local private sector investment. Complaints were heard, for instance, in Tanzania, where President Magufuli got things moving but also showed some authoritarian and erratic initiatives that might reduce investor confidence and undermine his broad popularity among the public. Protests and civil strife in Ethiopia slowed down investments and exports.

Political instability threats related to *succession problems* arose in various countries, as, for example, in the uncertainty over who or what might follow Uganda's President Museveni (in power since 1986). This was all the more ironic in that Museveni, in his 1986 inaugural speech, had declared: "The problems of Africa, and Uganda in particular, are caused by leaders who overstay in power, which breeds impunity, corruption and promotes patronage." Similar problems were evident in Congo-Brazzaville, Sudan, Equatorial Guinea and Cameroon, all with (too) long-serving presidents.

African economies' limited absorption capacities – i.e., growth not leading to breakthrough employment growth – and lack of diversification produced an ongoing massive *migrant outflow*, not only of poor and jobless people but also of the trained and educated, seeking better lives. In addition, refugees and asylum seekers were on the move, bringing the outflow to almost half a million.

A report on African Cyber-Security released by the Serianu company in March revealed a somewhat underestimated obstacle to African economic development, notably for banks: *cyber-crime*. It was estimated that banks and companies had lost about $ 3.5 bn due to cyber-attacks – up some 40% from 2016. It appeared that investing in cyber-security and anti-hacking experts was not seen as a priority among African business companies, or was prohibitively expensive for small and medium-sized businesses. Nigerian banks faced the biggest losses, estimated at about $ 650 m.

The AU and the APRM

The AU held its *28th Summit* (officially, the 'Ordinary Session of the Assembly Heads of State and Government of the AU') at its Addis Ababa (Ethiopia) headquarters on 22–31 January. The central theme was 'Harnessing the Demographic Dividend through Investments in the Youth', and the summit discussed (again) youth issues and the further implementation of the 'Agenda 2063' to build an AU of 'self-reliance', economic unity and integration. This summit saw the Chairperson of the AU Commission, South Africa's Nkosazana Dlamini-Zuma, replaced by Chad's Moussa Faki Mahamat. On 30 January, President Alpha Condé of Guinea was elected as the AU's new chairperson, succeeding Chad's Idriss Déby. During this summit, a new initiative was also launched: the Africa Centres for Disease Control and Prevention (Africa CDC), a continent-wide public agency to respond to public health emergencies, to be financed by an annual contribution from the overall AU operating budget. CDC workers were successfully employed in the Ebola crisis and its aftermath in the DRC in June–July.

On 23–28 March, the AU with the ECA held a *Conference of Ministers* in Dakar (Senegal) on 'Growth, inequality and unemployment' within the framework of the of the AU's First Ten-Year Implementation Plan (2013–23) of its *Agenda 2063* and the goals of the 2030 Agenda for Sustainable Development.

The *29th AU Summit* followed on 27 June-4 July in Addis Ababa, with the same central theme as at the January meeting. Many discussions were held, dates for future meetings were set, and documents signed to further policy and implementation of youth training and employment schemes. An *African Youth Fund* was also endorsed. The Summit declared the 2018–27 period as the 'African Decade for Technical, Professional and Entrepreneurial Training and Youth Employment'. During this summit the *2018 AU budget* of *$ 769.3 m* was approved; slightly less than the 2017 budget.

The *Africa Peace and Security Architecture* (APSA), a framework established in 2004 to deal with armed conflict and security problems in Africa, was active via its main pillars: the Peace and Security Council, the Continental Early Warning System, the Panel of the Wise, the African Standby Force (ASF), and the African Peace Fund, and fulfilled mediating roles but did not solve the armed conflicts in Libya, South Sudan or Somalia, where the more than 22,000-strong AMISOM peacekeeping forces were kept in place. Formation and operationalisation of the ASF, the military pillar, continued to face problems of divergences in training and practice between the African national armies and police forces. This inhibited rapid intervention missions, even apart from the political issue of forging a rapid consensus within the AU on major crises. APSA received continued funding from the EU ($ 592 m) under the African Peace Facility programme, but was still hampered by lack of sufficient funds.

On 26 July, the AU Commission and the WFP launched a new report entitled *World Food Assistance 2017*. It showed the humanitarian role of food assistance crises and called (again) for the root causes of hunger to be addressed. It noted that the 17.8 m Africans forcibly displaced (of whom 5.6 m were refugees and asylum seekers, and 13.2 m IDPs) were particularly vulnerable to food insecurity. African governments' policies, despite serious efforts, were not yet successful in tackling this recurring problem.

Controversially, and reflecting its more assertive Africa policy, *Morocco* was allowed to re-enter the AU as the 55th member state, despite its occupation of Western Sahara, where it sabotaged the self-determination decision of the Saharawi people and the establishment of the Saharawi Republic. In her parting speech, Nkosazana Dlamini-Zuma defended the readmission. Morocco also applied to join ECOWAS, following its economic (if not imperial) projection into SSA. The AU's acceptance of Morocco was seen by many as a failure, underlining its political hypocrisy and its giving in to Realpolitik. The decision also thwarted the further development of an AU sub-unit, the 'Arab Maghreb Union'.

The AU sent numerous *election observer missions* to member countries, such as to Angola's general election on 23 August, where the observers reported that they marked "an important step towards consolidation of democracy in Angola" and that the elections were "… generally conducted in line with the national legal framework as well as the international, continental, and regional standards for democratic elections". Rwanda's presidential election (on 3–4 August) was also observed by the AU. Here, as expected, it was concluded uncritically "… that the voting process was conducted in a peaceful, orderly and transparent manner". On 6 April, an AU team observed the National Assembly elections in the Gambia, on 4 May the legislative elections in Algeria, on 3 June the National Assembly elections in Lesotho, and on 16 July elections in Congo-Brazzaville. In all cases, no problems were reported. On 8 August, the first of the Kenya elections was observed. These elections, later annulled by the Kenyan Supreme Court for irregularities and fraud, were given the stamp of approval by the AU mission, which called them 'peaceful', 'transparent' and 'meeting the standards'. Another AU mission was sent to the new election on 27 October. Observation of the legislative elections in Liberia followed on 10 October. All was fine. Additional observer missions were sent to Senegal (22 July–4 August) and Liberia (September).

Numerous other meetings, panel discussions and workshops of the AU and its many departments were held throughout the year. One of the last meetings was the 'Joint Retreat between the Permanent Representatives and the AU Commission Working Methods', held in Cairo (Egypt) on 10–14 December, to review, evaluate and come up with recommendations on the working methods and strategic partnerships within the AU, following up on the Kagame Report and other initiatives to improve the AU's performance and continue its announced reform process.

On the international front, on 17 March the *EU's High Representative for Foreign Affairs and Security Policy* Federica Mogherini, with Commissioner for International Cooperation and Development Neven Mimica, visited AU headquarters in Addis Ababa to meet the new leadership of the AU Commission. The visit was also to discuss security and economic issues and the Joint Africa-EU Strategy, as well as to prepare for the coming AU-EU summit. The *5th AU-EU summit* in Abidjan (Côte d'Ivoire) on 28–30 November, with as a main focus youth (employment) issues, did not deliver much. No joint AU-EU initiative was advanced for stabilising northern Africa and the Mediterranean, and thus the summit did not achieve a breakthrough on managing illegal migration flows from Africa to Europe or on effectively tackling security issues in North Africa. According to the International Organization for Migration, Libya was hosting over 700,000 migrants in very bad conditions and subject to abuse. About 300,000 of them made it to Italy during the year. The AU did not make headway in addressing, let alone solving, the migrant crisis or the Libyan political chaos.

On 7–9 August, AU *finance ministers* met in Addis Ababa to speed up the implementation of earlier decisions by the AU Assembly of Heads of States and Government in meetings of previous summits regarding the *AU's financial autonomy* by 2020. Reflecting Africa's alignment with new 'donors' and partners, on 19 June the 7th Senior Officials Meeting took place of the *AU-Turkey* Follow-up Mechanism at the AU headquarters in Addis Ababa. It assessed the strategic partnership between Turkey and the AU, concluded in 2014. From 5 to 16 June, ministers of trade met in Niamey (Niger) to further discuss the *African Continental Free Trade Area* and conclude the draft Modalities for Tariff Liberalisation and Trade in Services negotiations, and related matters.

Regarding *environmental issues*, the AU co-organised a Global Green Growth Week, under the theme 'Unlocking Africa's Green Growth Potential', on 17–20 October at the UN Conference Centre in Addis Ababa. On 18 September in New York, the AU Committee of African Heads of State and Government on Climate Change had a meeting (on the margins of the UN General Assembly) to discuss the post-COP22 decision at the 28th AU summit earlier in the year to establish three commissions dedicated to the Sahel region, the Congo Basin region and the Island States.

While policies on greening African economies and tackling outstanding environmental problems were declared and partly followed, no radical initiatives or turn-arounds were initiated. Some countries were more active than others, however. For example, the ten countries of the Association for Strengthening Agricultural Research in Eastern and Central Africa (ASARECA) adopted a range of climate change adaptation strategies in agriculture on the basis of its Strategy and Results Framework document for 2017–26, although they were slow in implementing them.

The *APRM* under the new chief executive officer Eddy Maloka from South Africa gained new momentum and resumed visible activities. This was reflected in the recommendations of the *Kagame Report*, presented at the AU Summit in Addis Ababa on 29 January. It suggested that the APRM "could be strengthened to track implementation and oversee monitoring and evaluation in key governance areas of the continent" and thereby play a leading role in the monitoring and evaluation of Africa's 50-year development plan Agenda 2063. As also indicated by Kagame and stressed at a workshop in Cairo in December, the APRM was entrusted with monitoring sustainable development goals (SDGs) implementation on the continent. The extent to which such an expanded mandate required an adjusted APRM questionnaire aligned with the SDG priorities remained a matter for further discussion. Meeting a high-ranking APRM delegation in mid-March, the acting executive secretary of the *ECA*, Abdalla Hamdok, praised the "remarkable partnership" the two institutions had entered into in 2016. He commended Maloka for having achieved the highest rate of external reviews, increased the number of participating countries and enhanced resource mobilisation from member states. He also brought in two more new *strategic partners* with the Mo Ibrahim Foundation and the African Capacity Building Foundation.

At the *APRM Forum*, chaired by Kenya's President Uhuru Kenyatta and held a day ahead of the AU Summit in Addis Ababa on 28 January, Kenya, Djibouti, Chad and Senegal were presented for peer review, while *Namibia* became the 36th country to join the APRM. Announcing the decision, Namibia's President Geingob claimed in his speech to have always supported the APRM, but argued that "Namibia and Botswana were considered worldwide as good examples of democracy in Africa and we therefore decided to abstain from joining the APRM as we did not want to be used as a point of reference to be used against our fellow African countries."

An *APRM review* mission took place in Liberia from 4 to 20 April. A second-generation peer review was also undertaken in Kenya. By year's end, 20 of the 36 countries that had so far acceded to the APRM had gone through self-assessments and the peer review, while Liberia, Uganda and Sudan had completed the self-evaluation and were expected to be evaluated in 2018. The country review reports for Chad, Djibouti and Senegal were, however, not publicly released within the stipulated six-month period after completion. With the re-emergence of the APRM as an active institutionalised body there was also discussion as to whether it should become a suitable *conflict prevention tool*. The fact that some of the APRM reports took up to seven years to be released might indicate difficulties in providing a flexible response to any necessary short-term intervention. Instead, short-term reviews on burning issues were considered as possible options to be introduced.

Democracy and Elections

As part of the 'wave of democratisation', several dictatorial and authoritarian governments, mostly in response to internal pressures, but with reasonable support of the international community, embarked on *political reform programmes* that ushered in an era of transition to liberal democracy. Periodic elections based on universal suffrage and other requirements and conditions for free and fair elections had gained ground. Although there seemed to be a general lack of public confidence in the electoral system, Africans by their actions acknowledged elections as a key democratic institution and preferred to use "regular, open and honest elections" rather than "other methods" to choose leaders. These responses no doubt pointed all vital stakeholders to the need for broad-based political reform programmes, which should target, among other things, electoral systems and other democratic institutions, currently very weak and undeveloped in Africa.

SSA maintained an impressive record of elections and *transfer of power*. In Ghana, the ruling party was ousted in a keenly contested presidential election. In the Gambia, the dictator Yahya Jammeh, defeated in the 2016 elections, was eventually forced, including by pressure from the international community, to leave the country. However, there were observable gaps in Africa's democratic experiments as regards whether and when democracy was seen to extend beyond holding periodic elections to include such issues as good governance and a functioning state able to undertake the task of effective and efficient delivery of public goods to the majority of the population. A central concern was why democracy had not led to an improved standard of living for the general population, despite the experience of an impressive number of elections and peaceful transfers of power since the 'third wave of democratisation'.

Generally speaking, the democratic governments that littered the African political landscape claimed to be more respectful of human rights and civil liberties, but they in fact continued with previous policies, which were marked by distraction of the attention of the masses away from fundamental aspects of democracy, especially the issue of better living conditions. Thus, in spite of the installation of electoral politics, democracy, expressed in terms of *regime responsiveness* to its citizenry and political empowerment of the people, was still some time and distance away in many African countries, although many so-called free and fair election campaigns promised improved living conditions for the people. In spite of the success of celebrated periodic elections, calls for a 'democracy dividend' remained very loud in almost every part of the continent and, in the most recent Kenyan elections, disputes over the result triggered violence. These experiences highlighted the need to re-examine the essence of liberal democracy and its chances of promoting democratic development. For instance, while some saw elections as critical to democratic development, the rise of hybrid regimes during the 'third wave of democratisation' gave others reason to criticise reductionist conceptions of democracy that exaggerated the role of elections in democratic development. It was argued that elections added some value to democratisation, including the claim that democratic performances are associated with electoral cycle. Thus, the idea that the mere repetition of elections strengthens the quality of democracy was celebrated in many official circles, and in some cases with the support of key members of the international community. In Africa, however, elections have on the contrary produced fraudulent leadership, erosion of legitimacy and corruption, usually starting with fraudulent election and bad governance.

Presidential and general *elections* were held in Somalia, Lesotho, Rwanda, Kenya, Liberia and Somaliland. Parliamentary and legislative elections were also held in the Gambia, Congo, Senegal, Angola and Equatorial Guinea. From the preparations to the actual ballot casting, these elections were major political engagements that involved a wide variety of actors, including some members of the international community who were providing democracy assistance and, in some cases, sponsoring election observation missions. These elections produced varied outcomes that had implications for democracy and governance. In Somalia, President Hassan Sheikh Mohamud lost the election to the former prime minister Mohamed Abdullahi Mohamed, who was declared president in a peaceful transition of power after the incumbent conceded defeat and congratulated the victor. President Paul Kagame sought and got another seven-year term in Rwanda. The Kenyan elections presented another high-stakes election, resulting in a win for the incumbent, President Uhuru Kenyatta. In Angola, President Jose Eduardo dos Santos stepped aside and worked for his successor's victory in the long-awaited election. After ten years in office, it was time for Ellen Johnson-Sirleaf of Liberia, Africa's first female president, to leave office. George Wean, a former footballer, won the election and took office.

Because of the critical status and role of elections in Africa, considerable attention was given to issues relating to the process and outcomes and some instructive *lessons* were learned. Issues of legal and constitutional provisions for election processes and procedures, the role of the judiciary and other democratic institutions, election security and the involvement of diaspora communities and other external actors, including the international community, were all relevant factors. The role of electoral management bodies also came under serious scrutiny in many circles. On the evidence of 2014/2015 Afrobarometer data from 36 African countries on public perceptions of electoral management institutions and the quality of elections, trust in the electoral management bodies in many African countries decreased significantly with successive elections. While a majority of citizens said their most recent elections were mostly free and fair, some expressed serious concerns about the fairness of vote counts, corruption during elections and the safety of voters during campaigns and at the polls. In many instances, appeals by opposition parties were focused primarily on irregularities in electoral procedures arising from the actions and inactions of the electoral management bodies, which were generally not perceived to be objective and independent by the general public in many countries. In addition, they were accused of lacking the required technical skills and competence and were generally underfunded by governments that may have wanted to exercise considerable influence over how they executed their mandate.

Elections in some countries were generally marred by *violence*, ranging from verbal attacks to outright killings. Electoral contests produced undesirable outcomes that threatened peace and security, and the domination of the political landscape by 'godfathers' and money-bag politicians further complicated the trends in electoral violence. The political environment in many countries was characterised by underdeveloped structures and institutions, which presented extraordinarily wide opportunities for political corruption, patronage politics and electoral violence. Electoral politics generated a lot of contradictions for most of the African democracies that were now experiencing mixed political outcomes, often including violent political conflicts. Disputes over the outcomes of elections often intensified and led to a large-scale violence that attracted international responses.

The expansion of the mandate of *regional bodies* to include the promotion of democracy and good governance paid off in some respects. In West Africa, under the Revised Treaty, ECOWAS scaled up its normative instruments and institutional arrangements to anticipate and confront challenges to peace and security in the region, particularly with regard to conflicts and political governance. The ECOWAS Protocol on Democracy and Good Governance included provisions on zero-tolerance for ascension to power through unconstitutional means, as did the AU's Charter on Good Governance and Elections at the continental level. With these initiatives, African regional bodies were able to partially engage with the election-related processes on the continent, including by sending election observation missions and settling election-related disputes. An example was the AU mission led by Thabo Mbeki to observe and monitor the conduct of elections in Kenya.

Unconstitutional Rule, Coups and Armed Conflict

The *Gambia* was the scene of a return to constitutional rule after a brief period of confusion. On 1 December 2016, incumbent President Yahya Jammeh had been defeated by Adama Barrow in the presidential election. After initially conceding defeat, Jammeh later rejected the result. He had taken power by force in 1994 before winning barely competitive elections in 1996, 2001, 2006 and 2011, thereby scrupulously respecting the electoral calendar. Jammeh could not resist an attempt to hold on to power, and thus declared that he had lost confidence in the electoral process. An intense phase of diplomatic negotiation and more influential outright pressure started from there. ECOWAS, very intent to maintain its commitment to preserve democracy, threatened military intervention if Jammeh did not step down by 19 January. Though the UNSC backed ECOWAS in its diplomatic moves, it did not endorse military action. Nevertheless, Senegalese troops prepared for intervention. Jammeh declared a state of emergency on 17 January and urged the Gambian Congress to allow for a three-month extension of his term. Senegal allowed Barrow to be sworn in at the Gambian embassy in Dakar (Senegal). On 19 January, Senegalese troops invaded Gambia with Nigerian Navy and Air Forces backing the intervention. Faced with the prospect of a military advance, Jammeh finally stepped down on 21 January and fled the country for Equatorial Guinea, one of the toughest autocracies on the continent. Democratically elected President Barrow took up office on 26 January, thereby ending two months of political crisis. ECOWAS announced that about 4,000 of its troops would remain stationed in the country to ensure security: the mandate of the troops was extended for one year on 5 June.

The most spectacular removal of an – undoubtedly, if 'badly' – elected president occurred in *Zimbabwe*. The most important precursor was a crisis within the ruling ZANU-PF party triggered by President Robert Mugabe himself when he fired First Vice President Emmerson Mnangagwa. Mugabe's move was most likely motivated by his wife Grace Mugabe, who had aspirations to succeed her elderly husband.

Clearly, not only the creeping palace coup, but also the triggering event were not in the least conformity with the spirit of a republican constitution. Mnangagwa, as one of the main historical figures of the liberation war, had a solid base within ZANU-PF; Grace Mugabe had built her own faction within the party. A power struggle unfolded within the dominant party between these two factions. Mnangagwa first had to flee the country, but then managed to call for members of ZANU to abandon Mugabe. The support from within the army was the most decisive endorsement and turned the balance in favour of Mnangagwa. On 14 November, army units gathered around the capital, Harare, and seized control of the broadcasting network plus key parts of the city. It might still have been possible for Mugabe to stay in power if he had made some core concessions at this point. Finally, on 19 November, Mugabe was expelled from his own party after an internal vote and removed from his position as president and party chairman, which he ignored. An ultimatum to resign or see himself impeached in parliament was then issued. After initially ignoring the deadline for resignation, Mugabe finally resigned on 21 November and Mnangagwa stepped in as interim president and leader of ZANU-PF. This unexpected turn of events signalled the end of 37 years of ruthless autocratic rule and sent shock-waves to other regimes on the continent. It was also a headache for SADC and the AU, where Mugabe had had solid support over decades. The AU's Commissioner for Peace and Security, Smail Chergui, said that this was "not a coup according to AU rules", which would have inevitably provoked much sharper reactions. It seemed that the comparatively smooth end of Mugabe's rule was at least not the worst outcome of the crisis. However, it left in place a regime with little popular legitimacy.

The enduring crisis in *Burundi* following the controversial 2015 re-election of Pierre Nkurunziza continued to linger, but the president seemed increasingly in control of all essential sectors in the power apparatus. However, Minister for Water, Environment and Planning Emmanuel Niyonkuru was assassinated on 1 January on his way home from a New Year's celebration, adding another name to the long list of political assassinations since 1961 (when Prime Minister Prince Louis Rwagasore was killed). The UN renewed sanctions against Burundi for another year on 23 October, citing ongoing human rights violations, but it was probably not by chance that the same occurred in the *DRC*, where President Kabila also held on to power, despite being in a dubious position regarding constitutional rule. The effectiveness of such sanctions, however, could not be immediately proven. One assumption was that this was a matter of size and power: in contrast to the smaller Gambia, the DRC was much more difficult to influence in a certain direction. On the other hand, Burundi is comparable in size to the Gambia. This allows for a different interpretation: it was rather the influence of the sub-region or immediate neighbours that decided the effectiveness of external instruments in preserving a constitutional order (and democracy).

The Boko Haram insurgency with its epicentre in Nigeria, al-Shabaab in Somalia and ongoing decentralised *theatres of armed conflict* in the DRC and the CAR cost many lives. In addition, intercommunal conflicts escalated in Ethiopia between Oromo and Somalis and in Nigeria between pastoralists and farmers, resulting in sizable casualties. A mixture of direct attacks and terrorist acts were signs of 'asymmetrical' warfare with insurgents in a weaker position. Nevertheless, governments were not able to restore full control over sizable areas on the outskirts of the countries affected, and had to be moderately afraid of strikes, even in their capital cities. The escalation of violence between the anglophone minority and government forces in Cameroon added to the already sobering balance sheet of peace and conflict on the continent.

Al-Shabaab militias in Somalia continued to pose a threat to the fragile government as well as to peacekeepers. In one spectacular incident, fighters stormed a military base in Af-Urur village near Bosaso on 8 June, killing dozens of soldiers and civilians. This came after five al-Shabaab members captured in April were sentenced to death. Less than a week later, on 14 June, al-Shabaab militants attacked Somalia's capital Mogadishu, killing 31 people. Worse was to come: on 14 October, over 300 people were killed and hundreds more were injured in a terrorist double car bomb attack in Mogadishu. Finally, after two more bombs were set off on 28 October, gunmen entered a hotel frequented by security officials and politicians, killing 23 people and injuring at least 30. The gunmen were besieged by security forces for 15 hours. All these incidents showed that the government and its international allies were not in control. However, on 21 November, a US air raid killed more than 100 al-Shabaab fighters near Mogadishu, showing that retaliation could also be of spectacular dimensions.

A large part of the international engagement to control violence was devoted to *military missions*. One of the biggest and most complex operations was in *Mali*, where the peace process had stalled. At least 23 UN peacekeepers with the Multidimensional Integrated Stabilization Mission in Mali (MINUSMA) were killed in attacks by Islamist armed groups. While al-Qaida in the Islamic Maghreb (AQIM) continued to kill government officials in the north and carry out suicide attacks, government forces excelled in extrajudicial killings and torture. *Burkina Faso* was also targeted when two terrorists killed 18 in a café in the capital on 18 August. The gunmen fired on customers on a terrace before making their way inside, resulting in a siege that lasted until early morning. Both gunmen were killed. In a controversial move (mostly within ECOWAS and particularly Nigeria), and with the support of France, five Sahelian states had launched their *G5-Sahel initiative* (Mauritania, Mali, Burkina Faso, Niger and Chad) in 2015 and had started to build up a Joint Force, which became operational in the triangle area of Burkina Faso, Niger and Mali in October. Command and Control Headquarters were equipped and staffed. Besides fighting terrorism, the G-5 Force was meant to restore state authority, combat transnational criminal networks and have a role in the return of refugees and IDPs.

The Nigerian government felt immediately isolated by this turn of events and tried to bolster an alternative multinational framework for its own purposes. The Islamist *Boko Haram* sect continued to pose serious threats to security in northeast *Nigeria*, although the overall number of deaths went down from about 3,000 in 2016 to 2,150. Actions by the security forces also fueled the conflict. On 17 January, a Nigerian jet fighter bombed an IDP camp, mistaking it for a Boko Haram encampment near the Cameroonian border, killing 52 people. Among the most spectacular acts of violence was an attempt by the security forces to free people held hostage by Boko Haram; more than 40 people were killed in this operation on 27 July. On 15 December, Nigerian troops confirmed that they had arrested on islands in Lake Chad over 400 people who were suspected of being associated with the group, including fighters, wives and children. The operation took place over a period of two weeks. It was difficult to rate the overall effectiveness of security forces and other measures. On the one hand, around 82 schoolgirls ('the Chibok girls') were freed on 5 May after extensive negotiations, ending three years of captivity for some of the hostages. On the other, the number of suicide bomb attacks perpetrated by children went up from 30 in 2016 to 83. Renewed activities by *Biafran separatists* alongside the increased number of violent encounters between pastoralists and farmers further exemplified Nigeria's problems in preserving peace and security.

Cameroon also clearly remained in the focus of Boko Haram attacks. The deadliest of these was on 12 July in Waza (once a tourist attraction because of its natural park, but now a no-go area for foreigners), when 16 were killed and at least 36 injured. Nigeria, Cameroon, Chad and Niger, all members of the CBLT with its more developmental and ecological missions, had formed together with Benin the Multi-National Joint Task Force (MNJTF) – outside both ECOWAS and the African Peace and Security Architecture pursued by the AU. While the G5-Sahel clearly angered Abuja, the MNJTF as a partly Nigerian initiative had similar problems; it did not have the blessing of the AU headquarters in Addis Ababa but, like the G5-Sahel, the MNJTF also attracted support from France, the EU, the US and UN organisations. Cameroon's Northwest and Southwest regions also became the scene of civil war-like situations when there were clashes between security forces and anglophone protesters, including increasingly violent separatists. Although international concerns arose and UN Secretary-General António Guterres officially asked the authorities to conduct an investigation into the violence, no further international involvement was visible.

The major *peacekeeping missions* operating south of the Sahara were – in order of size – the AU Mission in Somalia (AMISOM), with around 22,000 personnel, the UN Organization Stabilization Mission to the DRC (MONUSCO; nearly 21,000), the hybrid UN/AU Mission in Darfur (UNAMID) and the UN Mission in the Republic of South Sudan (UNMISS), each with around 17,000 personnel, MINUSMA with nearly 15,000 and the Multidimensional Integrated Stabilization Mission in the CAR (MINUSCA) with 14,000 personnel. Besides these substantial peacekeeping operations, the UN Interim Security Force for Abyei (UNISFA) continued to operate with about 4,800 personnel, as did the scaled-down UN Mission in Liberia (UNMIL) with under 1,500 personnel remaining. The UN Operation in Côte d'Ivoire (UNOCI) terminated its mission on 30 June. The number of UNAMID staff was reduced gradually over the year.

A new theatre of violence within the *DRC* appeared in Kasai Central province, where a coalition of militias started to challenge security forces after they killed a critical traditional chief. Two UN experts sent to the region to investigate human rights abuses were abducted on 12 March and killed in unexplained circumstances. The number of casualties in these battles was difficult to confirm, but could be as many as 4,000. Further to the east, a new coalition of Mai-Mai militias operated in a large territory ranging from South Kivu and Tanganyika to Maniema province.

One of the main zones of turmoil in the *CAR* stretched from the centre of the country to the south-east. Here, two factions of the former rebel Séléka alliance plus the Christian anti-Balaka militias, repeatedly clashed. In addition, in the north, further Séléka components clashed during the year with either anti-Balaka groups or a locally important militia. Overall, some 1,000 people may have been killed in the CAR.

Piracy worldwide continued on the general downward trend seen over the last several years, with the number of attempted and actual incidents down to 180, from 191 in 2016. Within Africa, Nigeria remained a hot spot for piracy and number two worldwide behind Indonesia, with 33 cases of attempted or actual attacks. In Somalia, 39 crew members were taken hostage, and 65 crew members were kidnapped in Nigeria.

Epidemics and Disasters

At the AU Summit at the end of January, leaders endorsed the Addis Ababa Declaration on Immunisation to advance universal access to immunisation, but the poverty-related dire standard of living of many people, especially among slum-dwellers in overpopulated urban areas with inadequate sanitation and other unhygienic conditions, were again a fertile breeding ground for the spread of a variety of preventable *infectious diseases*. Most spectacularly, Madagascar reported in August a deadly outbreak of airborne plague, of which close to 2,000 cases were suspected during the year with around 100 fatalities. By year's end, the outbreak had been contained. Uganda confirmed on 17 October an outbreak of the deadly Marburg virus in the border area with Kenya, though it was limited to very small numbers of victims.

Guinea battled to contain a large-scale measles epidemic, and an outbreak was reported in Ethiopia too. During a meningitis epidemic in northern Nigeria, 14,473 cases (including 1,158 deaths) were reported, of which over 50% involved children under the age of 16. Cholera hit Nigeria in June and Chad in August, while Kenya had reported close to 4,000 cases (including 76 deaths) by the end of November. Cases of cholera and diarrhea decreased in Ethiopia and Somalia but remained a concern. The DRC was the most cholera-affected country, with 88% of recorded cases (55,000 and 1,200 deaths) in West and Central Africa. Yellow fever spread through Angola's capital Luanda to Kinshasa in the DRC, but was eventually extinguished. A marked increase in lifestyle-related health issues such as obesity was also recorded.

The latest *HIV/AIDS* statistics (for 2016) presented by UNAIDS estimated the number of people living with HIV in East and Southern Africa as the world's most affected regions at 19.4 m (more than half of the worldwide total of 36.7 m), with 790,00 new infections (43% of the global total) and 420,000 AIDS-related deaths. Over one-third (270,000) of the new infections were recorded in South Africa and 59% of those infected were women and girls. In West and Central Africa, 6.1 m people were living with HIV (56% women), with an estimated 370,000 new infections, and 310,000 deaths from AIDS-related illnesses.

As before, *floods* left an impact on parts of the continent. Cyclone Enawo caused devastating damage when it hit the north-east coast of Madagascar in early March, killing more than 80 people and destroying the homes of close to 250,000. Unregulated settlements and urban encroachment into hillsides led to *mudslides* emerging as a new main factor in so-called natural disasters (exacerbated by climate change and other effects of human activity). It was estimated that during August alone, as a result of intense rains and subsequent mudslides, at least 1,240 people were killed – about 25 times more victims than those of hurricane Harvey in Texas. In Liberia's capital Freetown alone, an unofficial death toll suggested more than 1,000 casualties and hundreds more missing after a devastating mudslide on 14 August. Torrential rains and severe flooding destroyed hundreds of homes and killed more than 40 people in Niger's capital Niamey at the end of August. Over 200 people were believed to have died from a mudslide in a fishing village in the Ituri province of the DRC in mid-August, while intense rains displaced more than 1,100 people in Nigeria's Benue state.

Early the year, the Horn of Africa faced one of the worst *drought*-related crises in decades. At least 17 m people faced hunger across eight countries (Somalia, Ethiopia, Kenya, Djibouti, Eritrea, South Sudan, Sudan and Uganda). In Somalia, some 40% of the population were affected, resulting in massive drought related internal displacements of mainly young people. In December, the UN Office for the Coordination of Humanitarian Affairs estimated that more than 15 m people in the region were facing severe food insecurity. Early in the year, the office's chief, Stephen O'Brien, described the crisis to the UNSC as the largest since World War II, with $ 4.4 bn needed "to avert a catastrophe". The continuing loss of water in the area around Lake Chad (estimated at 90% of its original volume) affected the livelihoods of some 7 m people in parts of Nigeria, Cameroon, Chad and Niger. While the El Niño effects of the previous year had eased, parts of Southern Africa remained drought stricken too. In particular, the Eastern Cape in South Africa had become a region where people had to live with water shortages on a constant basis. International attention was paid to the water crisis escalating during the second half of the year in Cape Town, a prominent international holiday destination. Such selective focus distracted once again from the ordeal millions of common people faced all their life in most parts of the continent in a daily battle for survival.

PART 2

African-European Relations

Christine Hackenesch and Niels Keijzer

The year's agenda was packed with an EU-AU summit and the launch of a European External Investment Plan (EIP), as well as Africa featuring on the G7 and the G20 agendas – both chaired by European countries. The year also marked the tenth anniversary of the Joint Africa-EU Strategy, which had been welcomed at the time as a fundamental shift towards a more equal partnership, and a move from *"aid to trade and investment"*. It is telling that ten years later the EU's discourse was advocating a similar shift, with the EU's High-Representative for Foreign and Security Policy arguing in September that the EU had made a shift from doing things "for" to doing things "with" Africa, or put differently "from the aid perspective to the partnership perspective".

More than ever before, such statements gave the impression that Africa's external partners were more impatient to develop Africa than was the continent itself. After introducing new initiatives to help create decent jobs, the G20 leaders stated in their outcome document that they would welcome *"African ownership"* and offered to align their initiatives with African regional strategies and priorities. These statements testified to the strong presence of strategies and initiatives for cooperating with Africa, in which a key challenge is not related to ownership, but rather to translating these strategies into reality. Moving ahead with new leadership in pursuit of a reform agenda set out under Rwanda's President Kagame, the AU, increasingly assertive as an organisation, now needed to radically move away from this image of 'policy evaporation'. One opportunity in this regard would be offered by the negotiations on the future of EU-ACP cooperation after the expiry of the Cotonou Partnership Agreement, for which the AU convened an internal working group in October to advise on an all-Africa position.

At the continental level, relations between Europe and Africa continued in damage control mode, i.e. the ongoing search for an easy-going heads of state summit without prior political controversy (like that caused by Mugabe's attendance in 2007, for example). At the regional level, relations were similarly 'laissez faire': In contrast to its earlier assertiveness of its own principles, the EU did not take a firm line against problematic developments on the African continent, such as Uganda's development into a quasi-monarchy, Zimbabwe's salon coup or the acute political crisis in the DRC. Where it did act, it did so in close consultation with the regional authorities concerned. This was the case with a region that maintained strong and close links with the EU – the five Sahel countries: Burkina Faso, Chad, Mali, Mauritania and Niger (or G5 Sahel) – in the adoption of a *Rapid Action Plan*, which – as the EU emphasised – was to be implemented in "full ownership and under the

 | DOI:10.1163/9789004367630_003

primary responsibility of the countries concerned". Observers wondered whether those were signs of a break with an interventionist past and a move towards a future when the EU would work 'with the grain' of its African partners.

AU-EU Summit

In November, the fifth AU-EU summit took place. The regular summit process had been set in motion by the inaugural summit in Cairo in 2000. Seven years later, the Joint Africa-EU Strategy (JAES) was adopted, accompanied by an action plan to guide exchange and cooperation in the periods between the following summits. The starting point of the JAES had been an EU strategy for Africa adopted in 2005, which reflected above all the EU's desire to address Africa as one entity for the first time. Despite covering everything from basic education to space travel, the implementation of the JAES did not reflect the ambition it had generated. Two key factors explain the gap between intentions and results: (1) limited engagement of member states of both the EU and the AU, and (2) lack of its own means of implementation. Instead, the partnership in practice shrank to a 'Commission to Commission' relationship and relied on the EDF, an inter-governmental fund linked to the Cotonou Partnership Agreement.

EU High Representative and Commission Vice-President Federica Mogherini visited the AU on 17 March and discussed preparations for the summit with AU Chairperson Moussa Faki Mahamat. This was the first of three visits Mogherini made to Africa; she also attended the G5 Sahel ministerial meeting in June and the AU-EU summit in November. During her speech at the AU, Mogherini stressed that the AU and EU had a relationship of close cooperation, particularly with regard to peace and security, and that the EU was committed to intensifying its support for investments through the External Investment Fund.

At the summit on 29–30 November, the EU sought to move away from the JAES and open a new chapter in the partnership. Influenced by Rwandan President Kagame's report on AU reform, a key signal was given by the AU when it requested the EU to change the name of the summit from Africa-EU summit to AU-EU summit. The EU complied and a new logo and accompanying social-media hashtag were issued. On the EU's side, the official discourse strongly claimed that the above-mentioned ambition of the Cairo summit had been realised. As Mogherini had argued in September, "the European Union and the African Union have moved to a different kind of relationship, not donor recipient, but two political partners covering all aspects of our relationship".

But had they really? An International Crisis Group report detected *strong feelings of frustration* within Africa over the EU's frequent assertion of an equal partnership whereas in reality the relationship remained asymmetrical: the summit was used to discuss African challenges and opportunities, while the EU did not allow discussion of its own, such as Brexit and the democratic challenges in some of its member states. The report also noted that the two groups had fundamentally different views on migration: the EU focused on preventing irregular migration and returning migrants, while the AU was mainly interested in increasing legal migration. Moreover, AU members were disappointed both by the size of the EU's Emergency Trust Fund for Africa, and by the tying of projects to European implementation organisations.

The *succession to AU Commission Chair* Nkosazana Dlamini-Zuma, whose critical stance towards the EU's colonial past had strained relations, by Chad's Moussa Faki Mahamat was regarded by the EU as an opportunity to strengthen relations. In his inaugural speech to the AU, Faki identified the EU as its main strategic partner. Although high-level relations improved, preparations for the summit were not much different from earlier ones, being mainly dominated by EU institutions, with ideas for the summit revolving mostly around expressing positive views about the partnership and launching new initiatives.

The summit itself, however, did not go according to plan at all. Despite the new AU-EU label, both regional organisations had great difficulty in orchestrating their membership. Instead, member states dominated the proceedings, with North African states blocking civil society organisations from taking the floor, and some EU member states presenting hawkish views on migration. Since the summit took place in Africa, the AU was in charge of uploading the *summit conclusions document*. It delayed doing so for a full week, to the frustration of the EU, which had to report back to several European Council working groups in Brussels before receiving that core document. It was even suggested that the AU had unilaterally changed the following sentence in a hard-fought paragraph about the readmission of migrants by including a reference to its own constitutive act: "We underline the importance of working jointly and swiftly on all aspects linked to irregular migration, in accordance with international law, the AU Constitutive Act, its regulations and instruments, including return, readmission and reintegration of own nationals in accordance with international law and standards, the principle of nonrefoulement [i.e. the practice of not forcing refugees or asylum seekers to return to a country in which they are liable to be subjected to persecution] and applicable due international legal processes." Since the AU had already uploaded and circulated the document, there was nothing the EU could do about it. The EU was taken aback by the strong pushback from AU members, even though this could be seen as being part of the equal partnership they had desired for so long.

EU-Africa Cooperation on Migration

Throughout the year, the EU strengthened its cooperation with African countries on migration. On 25 January, the European Commission published a Communication on "Migration on the Central Mediterranean Route: managing flows, saving lives" to urge member states to take action in order to curb the likely increase in uncontrolled migration flows during spring and summer. The Communication called on EU institutions and member states to coordinate their actions and cooperate more closely. In particular, the EU and member states should increase support for the Libyan coast guard, enhance the fight against smugglers and human traffickers, strengthen support for the protection of migrants, particularly those who returned voluntarily, increase efforts to secure the EU's southern borders and intensify cooperation with North African countries.

During an *informal summit in Malta* on 3 February, EU leaders discussed the external dimension of the EU's migration policy and, in particular, cooperation with Libya. In the Malta declaration, EU leaders emphasised that they aimed to take additional measures to reduce migration flows, which increased further in spring and summer, and to cooperate more closely with the Libyan authorities in this regard.

On 13 June, one year after the establishment of the EU's *migration partnership framework*, the European Commission published the fourth progress report on its implementation. The EU highlighted that cooperation on migration with all five pilot countries (Ethiopia, Mali, Niger, Nigeria and Senegal) had intensified, and pointed out that cooperation with Niger in particular had made progress: border controls had been enhanced, smugglers arrested, and human trafficking reduced, and voluntary returns of migrants from Niger to their countries of origin had increased. Independent research pointed out that in other cases, particularly Ethiopia, the EU's insistence on (a small number of) returns had not led to tangible results but had instead soured relations. The better results of the partnership framework in the case of Niger were explained by differences in interests. Niger was mainly a country of transit, not of origin of migrants, and so its incentives to cooperate with the EU were different from those of the countries of origin.

A specific Action Plan "to support Italy, reduce pressure and increase solidarity" was published by the European Commission on 4 July. The objective of the Action Plan was to accelerate efforts by the European Commission, EU member states and Italy itself to manage the increasing number of migrants arriving through the Mediterranean route. The fifth progress report on the migration partnership framework, published on 6 September, highlighted intensified cooperation with North and West African countries and a reduced number of deaths in the Mediterranean Sea.

The EU *Emergency Trust Fund for Africa* (EUTF) scaled up its activities throughout the year. According to the EUTF's annual report, 40 new programmes were approved for North Africa, the Sahel and the Lake Chad region, as well as the Horn of Africa. Even though the EU acknowledged that challenges in project contracting remained, the impressive sum of € 900 m had been contracted to project implementers during the year. Resources from the EU's budget to the EUTF (mostly from the EDF) increased by € 525 m to € 2.9 bn. EU member states, together with Switzerland and Norway, also slightly increased their contributions from € 152 m in 2016 to € 340 m by December. Member states' contributions were mostly directed towards the North Africa window, as for legal reasons the EDF funds were earmarked to SSA and could not be spent in North Africa.

Peace and Security

The EU supports peace and security in Africa and elsewhere through missions and operations as part of the EU's Common Foreign and Security Policy. There were eight missions and operations deployed in Africa – three of them in the Sahel region, three in the Horn of Africa, one in the CAR and one in Libya. Most of them were military training missions or civilian capacity building missions.

The EU's financial support for peace and security in Africa remained a contentious issue throughout the year. The EU passed amendments to its Instrument contributing to Stability and Peace (IcSP) to allow for financing Capacity Building in Support of Security and Development (CBSD) measures. The revised regulation now allowed the EU to provide financial support for providing training, equipment and infrastructure to military actors in African countries. This move was criticised by civil society actors, researchers and European Parliamentarians, who cautioned that the reform of the regulation would contribute to a *securitisation* of the EU's development policy. The EU was also criticised because CBSD might further bolster security forces in authoritarian regimes.

In December, during a meeting of the Foreign Affairs Council, Mogherini proposed the creation of a new European Peace Facility (EPF). She did not explain the proposal in more detail, but experts assumed that the EPF would be an off-budget instrument to provide financial support for peace support operations and capacity building in African countries (and beyond) that could be a successor to the African Peace Facility (APF) in the next EU-Multiannual Financial Framework. The APF was funded through the EDF and represented the EU's most important instrument to provide financial support to African-led peace and security operations. Since 2004, the EU had channelled about € 2.4 bn through this instrument, by far the greater part of it to AMIS in Darfur and AMISOM (about 90%). Another challenge for the APF had been to provide long-term predictable funding for African-led missions. From the EU's perspective, one challenge faced by the APF was that it could only fund African regional operations and not military actors in individual African countries (e.g. to support African members of the G5 Sahel initiative). Mogherini's initiative to develop an EPF could therefore be seen as a response to the critical debates around the IcSP as well as a response to some of the shortcomings of the APF.

West Africa

The EU adopted the Rapid Action Plan for the Sahel in June, to be implemented under the aegis of Burkina Faso, Chad, Mali, Mauritania and Niger. The G5 Sahel agreed to take action on four priorities: 1) Preventing and countering radicalisation, 2) Creating appropriate conditions for youth, 3) Migration and mobility, 4) Border management, including the fight against illicit trafficking and transnational organised crime. The EU pledged funds for the five countries of around € 8 bn, albeit managed through a wide range of programmes and instruments (including the Trust Fund for Africa), and expressed strong support for and priority to the countries concerned. On 4–5 June, at a ministerial meeting in Bamako (Mali) of G5 countries, Mogherini emphasised that "Ensuring the security, stability and development of the countries of the Sahel is in the interest first of all of the local populations but also of European citizens."

Towards the very end of the year, West Africa continued to be the "African region of European hope" when the opposition candidate George Weah won Liberia's run-off presidential elections. Following the positive example set in response to the Gambian presidential elections in 2016, this was an important result for the region and its governance standards. This may have concealed the EU's lack of engagement in relation to *Togo*, where protests intensified against President Faure Gnassingbe, who had been ruling Togo since 2005 (after his father had run the country from 1967).

The EU Election Observer Mission (EU EOM) in the *Gambia*, one of only three EU EOMs in Africa in 2017, was deployed on 13 March with about 50 observers from EU member states, Norway and Switzerland to observe the parliamentary elections. The mission's final report, released on 1 October, urged the Gambian authorities to conduct extensive legal reform, enhance the independence of the Electoral Commission and strengthen civic and voter education in order to improve democratic development in the country.

The EU also sent 74 election observers to monitor the election in *Liberia* on 28 December. The chief observer, Member of the European Parliament Maria Arena, said that the election day was "calm and benefited from organisational improvements made by the National Electoral Commission".

Central Africa

The EU took a distinctly non-interventionist approach to *Cameroon* and its long-term ruler Paul Biya, following the increasingly tense situation in the Anglophone north-western and south-western parts of the country. A 93-word EU statement was issued in September, calling for abstention from violence and an open and inclusive dialogue. No direct EU mediation was offered.

Shortly after the Brussels donor conference on the *CAR* on 17 November 2016, violence there had intensified. The EU, together with the CEEAC, AU, OIF and UN, published a joint statement on 19 February to express its concern regarding the security situation, particularly in the prefectures of Ouaka and Haute-Kotto. The statement condemned the violence committed by the 'Front Populaire pour la Renaissance de Centrafrique' and its allies, as well as by the 'Mouvement pour l'Unité et la Paix en Centrafrique', and called for an immediate end to the violence. The EU and its partners highlighted the importance of the initiative for peace and reconciliation led by the AU, CEEAC and ICGLR. On 25 July, the EU General Court rejected a case brought by the Badica and Kardiam diamond dealing companies, who had challenged the UN sanctions list implemented by the EU and its condemnation of the illicit trade in diamonds mined in the CAR in defiance of the export ban imposed as part of the Kimberley process.

The EU continued to follow closely the situation in the *DRC*. Political tensions had been on the rise since President Kabila had overstayed his second presidential term without preparing a date for the next presidential elections and despite the fact that the Constitution only allowed for two terms. A political agreement for a transition period leading to the holding of peaceful and credible elections by December had been signed on 31 December 2016. This deal broke down, however, following the unexpected death in February of opposition leader Étienne Tshisekedi, who had been set to oversee the transition of presidential power. In response to the situation, the EU, together with the AU, UN and OIF, issued a joint statement on 16 February, reaffirming the need for all parties to rally behind the mediation efforts led by the 'Conférence Episcopale Nationale du Congo' (CENCO) and calling on all parties to implement the agreement that had been reached in December 2016. On 6 March, the EU's Foreign Affairs Council stated that the EU remained seriously concerned by the DRC's political situation, given the stalemate in agreeing a date and timetable for presidential elections and the disproportionate use of force in some parts of the country. The Council further expanded the EU's Common Foreign and Security Policy sanctions against the DRC and, on 29 May, decided to expand the list of restrictive measures to be implemented against high-level Congolese officials and added nine individuals to the list. The EU had first introduced restrictive measures against seven Congolese individuals on 12 December 2016 in response to their obstruction of the electoral process and implication in human rights violations. The Council stressed that the EU was seriously concerned by the crisis in Kasai Province, the deteriorating security situation and the disproportionate use of force and human rights abuses by the Congolese security forces.

The Electoral Commission finally announced on 5 November that presidential elections would take place on 23 December 2018. In response, the EU Foreign Affairs Council issued a statement on 11 December stressing that the Congolese government and the Electoral Commission were responsible for implementing the agreed measures and ensuring that the new election date would be respected.

East-Africa / Horn of Africa

The EU's relations with *Ethiopia* continued to be tense. The upsurge in demonstrations against the Ethiopian government since the end of 2014, which accelerated in 2016 and 2017, indicated strong popular dissatisfaction with government policies, a level of public dissent, and increased ethnic tensions. The government's violent response illustrated the extent to which the regime was shaken by the protests. According to human rights organisations, several hundred people were killed. The situation hardly improved after the government formally ended the state of emergency at the end of August. On 17 March, Mogherini visited Ethiopia and met with Prime Minister Hailemariam Desalegn. During her visit, she emphasised the EU's readiness to help to address the humanitarian crisis and the drought, as well as EU-Ethiopia cooperation on migration. She also lauded the government for establishing a political platform and entering into dialogue with the opposition, while avoiding open criticism of the Ethiopian authorities for their violent response to the anti-government protests. The European Parliament adopted a resolution on 18 May, highlighting the strategic importance of Ethiopia while urging the Ethiopian government to cease human rights abuses against members of the Oromo community and other ethnic groups. On 12 December, the EEAS spokesperson highlighted that the EU was deeply concerned about violent clashes that had taken place at universities and called on the Ethiopian authorities to investigate the incidents and work towards an inclusive political dialogue with all stakeholders.

On 23 October, the Council of the EU renewed its sanctions against *Burundi* for another year. These measures were taken in the context of the EU's Common Foreign and Security Policy and included a travel ban and asset freeze against four high-level Burundian politicians whose engagement was deemed to be undermining democratic governance and the search for a peaceful political solution. On this occasion, the EU called again upon all parties to refrain from any acts of violence and instead to end the cycle of impunity of perpetrators. In addition, the EU maintained the suspension of parts of its development aid in the context of the Article 96 mechanism of the Cotonou Partnership Agreement. While members of the European Parliament sought to table a resolution to condemn Burundi's authoritarian turn at the 22nd session of the EU-ACP Joint Parliamentary Assembly on 19–21 June, the ACP parliamentarians did not agree to sign the critical statement.

In *Rwanda*, President Kagame secured a third term with a landslide victory of 98.8% of the votes at the presidential elections in August – a third term only made possible by an amendment to the Constitution in 2015. While Rwanda's relations with the EU and other parts of the international community were tense after Kagame's amendment of the Constitution, the EU did not come out with a strong statement after the August elections. The EEAS spokesperson noted that the elections went off peacefully and were well organised but that Rwanda should improve the inclusiveness and transparency of the process and take steps towards achieving a level playing field, in line with recommendations of the AU EOM.

The elections in *Kenya* provided an uncomfortable reality check for the EU EOM. Two days after the 8 August elections, the EU's chief observer presented the mission's preliminary statement and commended all the parties who had contributed to the electoral process. The statement further noted that election result forms were still being processed, and the EOM urged the losing candidate to accept defeat graciously, and/or use legal means to challenge the process and outcome when appropriate. Though in effect legitimising the election, the statement did call for a critical assessment of the benefits and challenges of using digital technology in the process. The statement was immediately challenged by Kenyan stakeholders, and in October became a cause of controversy when the High Court annulled the election. The subsequent withdrawal of the opposition candidate delegitimised the process even further, and the EU EOM could do no more than issue a one-page statement calling on all parties to enter into dialogue and redress grievances using legal means. The final report was not completed by the end of the year, and the case of Kenya may inform reflection in the EU on how to adjust observation processes to both new technologies and political crises resulting from elections.

The EU remained deeply concerned by the deteriorating security situation in *South Sudan*. The EEAS spokesperson stressed on 7 November that the EU firmly supported IGAD in its efforts to promote peace and bring all actors to the table during the so-called High Level Revitalisation Forum. The EU welcomed the convening of the High Level Revitalisation Forum on 17 December and used the opportunity to stress that the EU was ready to support the peace process in various ways. Furthermore, the EU would not refrain from using restrictive measures (read: sanctions) against South Sudanese individuals who obstructed progress in the peace process.

Southern Africa

On 17 February, the EU extended its sanctions on *Zimbabwe* for another year. The measures mainly included travel bans and an asset freeze for seven high-level individuals who were responsible for human rights violations and obstruction of democratic reforms. The November AU-EU summit was the first in more than a decade where the question of Mugabe's attendance was no longer a dominant issue – for the simple reason that Mugabe was no longer president. Following the coup d'état in all but name, the EU could do little more than issue a brief statement calling for an orderly transition and inclusive dialogue. While the EU had already lifted its travel ban and restrictive measures against the new President Emmerson Mnangagwa in 2016, he was still subject to US sanctions.

In general terms, the EU had not come up with a comprehensive strategy to respond to the deteriorations in the governance situation in Southern Africa. In most Southern African countries, the *liberation movements in power* had recently been under severe pressure and had often responded by restricting political spaces for the opposition, civil society and the media. While in *Angola* the (peaceful) change of president in the August elections could be interpreted as a small positive sign, the security and governance situation in *Mozambique* deteriorated during the year. The mid-term implications of the change of presidents in Zimbabwe and tensions around the succession to President Zuma in South Africa were not yet clear. Even though there was recognition that political regimes in Southern Africa were entering a critical stage, the EU was left with few instruments and little sense of strategy to support democratic reforms across the region.

International Criminal Court

In 2016, South Africa, the Gambia and Burundi had sent letters of withdrawal from the ICC. The Gambia and South Africa withdrew these letters in October. In the same period Namibia, Kenya and Uganda threatened to submit such notifications, but in the end did not. Discussions continued at the level of the AU on this sensitive topic in Africa-EU relations. In January, the AU adopted a non-binding resolution urging its member states to withdraw from the ICC, but (not uncommonly for AU resolutions) there was no follow-up. While heads of state and government avoided addressing the issue at the AU-EU summit, it was likely to come up again during discussions on the future of ACP-EU cooperation, given the inclusion of an expression of support for the ICC in the Cotonou Partnership Agreement.

Africa as the New EU Investment Frontier?

The international discourse on the need for a 'quantum leap' in investment in Africa proved to have strong direct influence on EU cooperation with Africa too. A key initiative that was introduced at the very beginning of the Juncker administration concerned the Investment Plan for Europe ('Juncker Plan'), which sought to improve the investment environment and dramatically expand private investment within the EU, combining reforms of the regulatory environment, advisory services to increase awareness of investment opportunities, and new funding to stimulate investment. In his 2016 State of the Union address, Juncker had announced the creation of an "external sister" to the plan, in the form of an ambitious *Investment Plan for Africa and the Neighbourhood*, which had the potential to raise € 44 bn in investments. The plan was to follow the same logic, orienting around the use of public funding as a guarantee to attract public and private investment to create real jobs.

The negotiations towards operationalising this plan claimed a substantial portion of the agenda of the key stakeholders in EU development cooperation: the EU Commission, member states, Parliament, national development banks and the EIB. Following the practice of the EUTF that had been launched in 2015, months of intense negotiation that ended in the summer did not involve any serious direct exchange with the intended investment subjects in Africa. This approach to developing the investment plan reflected a broader trend in which the EU was pursuing its interests towards Africa more directly, but the key question remained of the extent to which this relative neglect of 'ownership' among African recipients (or rather the assumption of ex-ante presence) would lead to effective cooperation.

EU Member States

Among the EU's member states, *Germany*'s interest in cooperation with Africa continued to be high throughout the year. Within the G20 Finance Track, German Finance Minister Wolfgang Schäuble proposed developing 'Compacts with Africa' aimed at improving the business environment in selected African countries and thereby attracting FDI. Compacts were prepared by the World Bank, IMF and AfDB. During a meeting of the G20 finance ministers in Baden-Baden in March, five countries expressed interest (Côte d'Ivoire, Morocco, Rwanda, Senegal and Tunisia). During the G20 Africa Partnership Conference on 12–13 June, another two countries joined – Ethiopia and Ghana – and, at the annual meetings of the IMF and the World Bank in October, Benin, Egypt and Guinea expressed interest in signing a compact. The G20 leaders' declaration signed during the G20 summit in July highlighted that G20 countries intended to foster "sustainable and inclusive economic growth and development, in response to the needs and aspirations of African countries, contributing to create decent employment particularly for women and youth, thus helping to address poverty and inequality as root causes of migration". In parallel to the G20 Compacts with Africa, German Minister for Economic Cooperation and Development Gerd Müller presented a 'Marshall Plan with Africa' with the objective of supporting long-term sustainable development on the continent. The plan, which was published in January, put a strong emphasis on Europe-Africa cooperation. The document developed three pillars for cooperation with Africa: economic relations, trade and development cooperation; peace security and stability; and democracy, rule of law and human rights. Through the Marshall Plan, Germany provided financial and technical assistance to some of the Compact countries to support their endeavours in complying with the Compact requirements. German Chancellor Angela Merkel expressed her continued interest in strengthening relations with the continent by joining the AU-EU summit in Côte d'Ivoire despite being in the midst of complicated discussions on forming a new coalition government at home.

In July, his first visit to Africa brought the new French President Emmanuel Macron to Mali, where French troops continued to fight Islamist terrorists. Macron implemented one of his election campaign promises in August by setting up a special council on Africa, composed of young business people with ties to *France* and Africa. The special council on Africa was meeting on a regular basis and was meant to advise Macron on how to improve France's image on the continent. In November, Macron used his attendance at the AU-EU summit in Côte d'Ivoire to make a visit to neighbouring Ghana and Burkina Faso. He deliberately did not travel to Senegal but to Burkina Faso in order to emphasise his intention to give a fresh start to French-African relations. Particularly in Burkina Faso, his visit was accompanied by tensions. Youth protests and grenade attacks on French troops hours before Macron's arrival in Ouagadougou highlighted the challenges in developing a new approach in French-African cooperation.

Cooperation with Africa remained important for *Italy*, particularly as a result of the high number of migrants and refugees constantly arriving in the southern parts of the country. During its G7 presidency, Italy made cooperation with Africa an important subject, indicated not least by the symbolic choice of the venue for the summit in Sicily, where refugees and migrants were arriving in large numbers due to its proximity to North Africa. During his opening address, Italian Prime Minister Paolo Gentiloni called for a new partnership between the G7 and Africa with a strong focus on investment and aid. Heads of state and government from Ethiopia, Kenya, Niger, Nigeria and Tunisia, as well as the AU chairperson, AU Commission president and AfDB president took part in the meeting. The summary of the outreach session on Africa highlighted the importance for the continent of peace, security and investment. The only concrete initiative that emerged from the meeting was Italy's announcement of a "G7 Exchange and Empowerment Program for Emerging African Innovation Leaders", which was intended to contribute to innovation and science cooperation.

The New European Consensus on Development

At the annual European Development Days in June, the EU issued a new *European Consensus on Development* – a tripartite statement signed by the Council of the EU and the representatives of the governments of the member states meeting within the Council, the European Commission and the European Parliament. The new European Consensus replaced the previous Consensus adopted in 2005 and set out a vision for the development policies of the EU institutions and member states. This earlier 2005 document had been important for the negotiation of the current generation of EU financial instruments, as well as informing the development policies of the countries that joined the EU after 2004 as part of their accession trajectories.

While the statement was of a horizontal nature and not exhaustive in setting out regional priorities, SSA continued to receive most of the EU's development funds. The Consensus aimed at aligning EU development policy with the 2030 Agenda for Sustainable Development and its 17 Sustainable Development Goals. The Consensus put the Agenda centre stage and discussed in detail how European development policy should contribute to the 'five Ps' – People, Planet, Prosperity, Peace and Partnership. Moreover, having one strategy for the EU and its member states was an important step forward from the 2005 version, which was split into two parts, with a separate chapter for the EU institutions. However, while ensuring that all actors' interests were well represented, the new Consensus failed to set clear priorities for where the EU should concentrate its efforts to support African and other developing countries in implementing the 2030 Agenda.

The Future of EU-ACP Relations

This year saw continuing preparatory discussions in both the EU and the representation of the ACP in the run-up to negotiations about how to govern relations between the EU and the states concerned after the Cotonou Partnership Agreement expires in 2020. In the EU, these discussions were mainly guided by a policy proposal ('Communication') that had been issued by the European Commission and the European External Action Service in November 2016. This Communication made the case for continuing to legislate the EU's relations with ACP and non-ACP countries separately, as had been the practice since the first Lomé Convention was agreed to in 1975. Where the Cotonou agreement of 2000 reformed the partnership by 'decentralising' trade relations into bilateral and regional trade agreements as well as unilateral EU trade preference schemes, the 2016 proposal suggested a major reform in terms of strengthening regional dynamics.

While EU member state diplomats discussed with the EU throughout the year what the proposal's implications for the future partnership might entail, the EU delayed publishing its detailed recommendation for a negotiating mandate until 12 December. That proposal described and proposed the basis for a new international agreement consisting of an *'all-ACP' foundation* and attached protocols setting out cooperation priorities and process towards Africa, the Caribbean and the Pacific. As the agreement stipulated that negotiations were due to start in August 2018, at the end of the year the EU was facing a considerable challenge to elaborate a negotiating mandate in half a year on the basis of an EU recommendation that was detailed on status quo, but silent or sketchy on reform. On the ACP side, a Council of Ministers meeting in Brussels could have adopted an all-ACP position that would build on the 2016 summit of heads of state, which argued for continuity in the relationship. It had in previous years prepared and deliberated on several studies on the future of the group and its cooperation with Europe. However, it was decided that a special session of the Council would convene in Togo on 27 May 2018, when such a position could be adopted.

PART 3

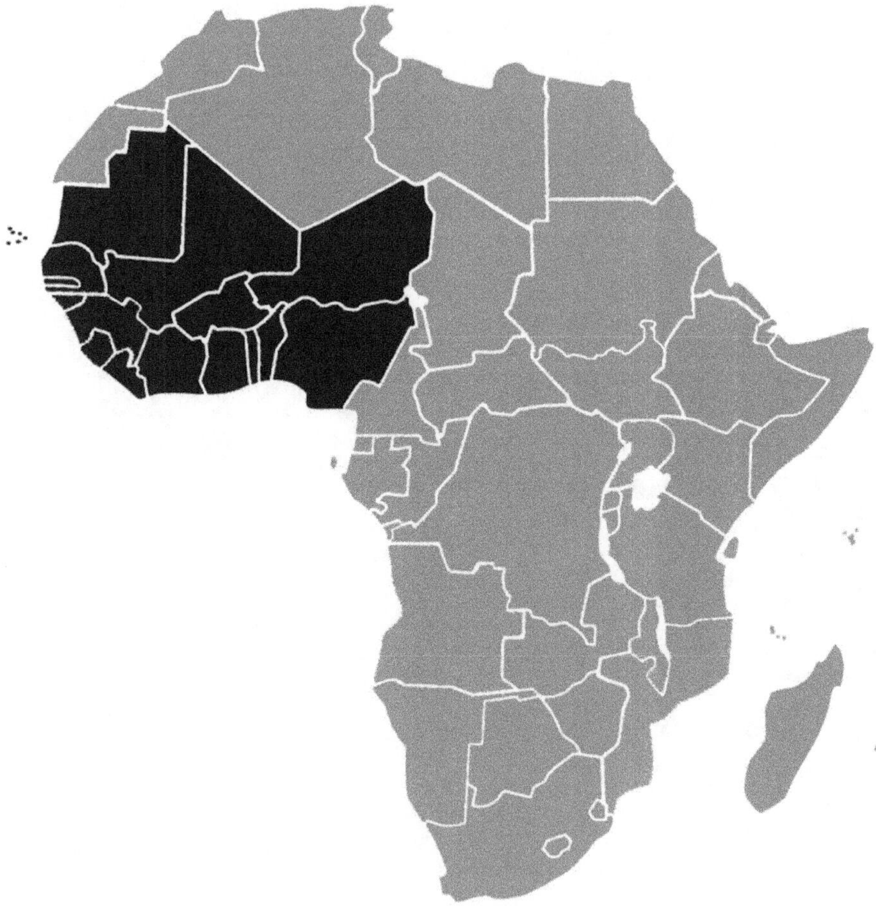

West Africa

Victor Adetula

The sub-region witnessed significant developments in both the political and economic spheres. A number of governments embarked on economic reform programmes, which produced varying outcomes. Some of the results generated public outcry and other forms of civil action including protests, demonstrations and strike action. The general trend for opposition parties to come to power through elections continued and there were cases, as in the Gambia, where the opposition defeated the incumbent in relatively peaceful elections. However, there were concerns that change in government did not result in improved living conditions for the majority of the population.

The sub-region also faced many security challenges. Insurgent groups, cross-border crime and violence associated with disputes over election results were major sources of insecurity. Insurgencies spread across the Sahel to the Lake Chad Basin. An example of the growing threats to security, was Mali, where this was the deadliest year since the emergence of instability five years before. Regional dimensions of insecurity were most felt where the effects of conflicts in one country easily spread to others and this partly explained the coming together of the G5 Sahel countries to form a regional security and development organisation. Even so, many security challenges, in the form of terrorist attacks, cross border crime, drug smuggling and human trafficking, continued to hit the general population, particularly in Mali, Burkina Faso, Côte d'Ivoire, Niger and Nigeria. Both the old and new governments in the sub-region emphasised economic development in their foreign policy and adopted various forms of economic diplomacy, which helped them to explore the opportunities and benefits of close relations with old and new global economic powers.

Regime Dynamics and Human Rights

Election-related issues, security challenges, conflicts and conflict resolution processes dominated the socio-political landscape. These variables interacted with each other to influence the direction of events and development. More than half of the countries in the sub-region either held or were preparing for elections and some countries, unsurprisingly, had to deal with election-related problems and disputes that had links to the challenge of insecurity and instability in the region.

 | DOI:10.1163/9789004367630_004

In *Ghana*, early in the year and following the results of the December 2016 election, a new government was formed led by President Akufo-Addo, whose party had previously been in opposition.

In *Liberia*, the first post-war elections resulted in the emergence George Weah as president, replacing Ellen Johnson Sirleaf. It was not a smooth ride, but came nowhere near the upheaval in the *Gambia*, where the refusal of Yahyah Jammeh to leave office following his defeat by Adama Barrow in the December 2016 presidential election. This resulted in a political impasse that would have degenerated into a political crisis but for the timely intervention of ECOWAS. Troops from Nigeria, Ghana and Senegal were deployed to their borders with the Gambia under the auspices of the *ECOWAS Mission in Gambia* in collaboration with the AU and with the endorsement of the UN. It was indeed a case of 'African solutions for African problems'. Although former president Jammeh had become a 'bad guy' of West Africa, the leaders were committed to a peaceful resolution of the crisis, evidently guided by the lessons of the experiences of Liberia, Côte d'Ivoire and Sierra Leone.

In *Sierra Leone*, preparations for the 2018 elections dominated the political life and every step in the electoral process attracted considerable attention, both domestically and internationally. Possibly because of the relatively impressive performance of its national economy, Sierra Leone was generally more respected by some influential actors in the international community than at home.

In *Nigeria*, the Islamist insurgency of Boko Haram in the North East zone, activities of militants in the Niger Delta, secessionist agitation for a Biafran state by the Igbo in eastern Nigeria, violent conflicts between herders and farmers in central Nigeria, which quickly spread to other parts of the country, and a growing number of armed robberies and kidnappings worsened the security situation. The capacity of the security and defence structures was challenged, despite claims by the government that it was on top of the situation. There were allegations of human rights abuse, excessive use of force and extra-judicial killings by the Nigerian security services in the handling of the Boko Haram insurgency and the Biafra agitators. *Islamist insurgencies* in Niger, Mali and Bukina Faso compounded the problem of insecurity in West Africa.

Protest politics became prominent and gained more ground as a form of political participation. The raised level of social and political protest suggested the persistence of a 'democratic deficit'. Citizens were frequently on the street protesting against state policies and programmes, and calling for improved public service delivery using various informal mans of communication, including social media. In Benin, reform programmes that included constitutional amendments and economic liberalisation were met with resistance in parliament and from the labour unions, who carried out a number of protests and demonstrations to resist economic liberalisation and privatisations. Similar events occurred in Nigeria. In Togo, civil society organisations, including faith-based groups, in collaboration with the opposition, organised several demonstrations, which put the government of President Faure Gnassingbé under pressure. Côte d'Ivoire experienced protest actions of a different kind. Dissatisfied soldiers organised military mutinies that almost turned into widespread strikes and protests. Economic hardship in countries like Guinea led to protests throughout the year and political tensions between trade unions, opposition parties and the government. Senegal also witnessed recurrent strikes, which undermined the social sector, including education.

The expectation that expansion of the democratic space would improve the *human rights* performance of democratically elected governments in West Africa was not fully realised. Electoral democracy did not have a significant impact on the standard of human rights and civil liberties in many countries across the sub-region. The commitment to and compliance with the rule of law by governments and their official agencies was still clearly at a very low level. As part of their economic reform programmes, some governments put in place legal frameworks for the protection of contracting parties in business and commercial agreements and other necessary legal procedures with the aim of creating an attractive business climate conducive to foreign investment. However, the same governments paid little attention to the political and social rights of the population that are associated with political participation, freedom of expression, freedom of association, media rights, and so on.

While there were efforts to redress the poor human rights situation in the Gambia after the ousting of President Jammeh, there were concerns in many quarters that the sub-region did not demonstrate significant improvement in respect for human rights and civil liberties. In many countries, there was little progress in dealing with human rights violations, and the impunity of security forces. Complaints about restrictions on press freedom and harassment of opposition groups still persisted in some countries. In Guinea-Bissau, positive economic development was recorded, but incessant conflicts among members of the country's political class intensified and almost degenerated into a political crisis and intra-party conflicts obstructed the smooth running of government. There was political tension and cases of human rights violations and attacks on both the opposition and the media were on the increase across the country. In Togo, institutional and electoral reforms generated reactions and responses from civil society, mainly in form of protests, demonstrations and other forms of civic action. Various civil society groups joined the opposition to put pressure on the government and called for an alternative to the Gnassingbé regime, whose record of human rights violations was a great concern. In Guinea, the persistence of high-profile human rights violations and the impunity of the security forces remained a major concern. In Mauritania, never free of abuse of civil liberties and human rights violations, the government tightened the blasphemy law and restricted freedom of expression, thereby increasing political repression.

Regional Cooperation and Foreign Affairs

The domestic configurations in the various states, commitment to pan-Africanism and some global changes and developments continued to influence the conduct of external relations. ECOWAS, the AU and the UN were the key platforms for conducting multilateral diplomacy. There were concerns about developments in the global *trade regimes*, including the EPAS and AGOA, depressed world commodity markets, discriminatory protection and debt crises. While ECOWAS as a body had signed up to the EPA, Nigeria and Gambia remained adamant in their refusal to sign the agreement. They expressed concern and fear about the effects of unrestricted access to their markets for products from developed countries. The EU had dismissed this fear as unfounded.

The challenge of border insecurity, irregular migration, maritime insecurity, human trafficking and other forms of *cross-border criminality* continued to draw attention and a number of key players in international bodies had shown marked interest in helping the sub-region address these challenges. For example, as the activities of insurgents spread across Nigeria to other countries in West and Central Africa, the United States and some European powers, notably France and the United Kingdom, provided support and assistance to Nigeria to enable the government to combat terrorism. The EU, France and other key members of the international community extended significant assistance and support to the G5 Sahel countries (Chad, Niger, Burkina Faso, Mali and Mauritania), which certainly helped the G5 Sahel counter-terrorism joint task force to become effectively operational.

West African countries had always exhibited a strong commitment to *regional integration* as a development strategy and Nigeria had always provided the required leadership and support within both the ECOWAS and AU frameworks. The ECOWAS platform was of immense importance to all West African countries and every country looked to exert influence over its mandates. However, one of ECOWAS's challenges was the lack of adequate funding, made worse by member states' lack of commitment to their financial obligations. The event of the 52nd ECOWAS summit in Abuja (Nigeria) where Cape Verde lost the election for the rotating presidency of the ECOWAS Commission to Côte d'Ivoire, possibly due to the debts owed by the former, was quite illustrative. At the same time, some read politics into the activities and operations of ECOWAS. For example, most international attempts to mediate in the Togolese crisis failed because the mediators proposed by ECOWAS were not considered neutral.

Nevertheless, West African countries were generally supportive of initiatives towards peace and stability in the sub-region and increased intra-Africa trade within the framework of the *ECOWAS trade liberalisation scheme*, and the ongoing efforts of the ECA and the AU towards the establishment of a *Continental Free Trade Area*. However, Nigeria cautioned against rushing ECOWAS's integration agenda, warning against pushing for a single currency by 2020 without taking into consideration some of the region's fundamental particularities. In November, the fifth triennial *EU-AU summit* was held in Abidjan (Côte d'Ivoire) under the theme 'Investing in Youth for Accelerated Inclusive Growth and Sustainable Development'. Apart from highlighting the importance of serious engagement with the youth question, the summit provided an opportunity for Europe and Africa to jointly address the Mediterranean migration crisis that had been dominating EU-AU relations.

Apart from ECOWAS's intervention in the Gambia to avert large scale violence, the expansion of its membership to *Morocco* was another issue that attracted attention. Morocco regained its membership of the AU in January, and later in the year applied to join ECOWAS. Morocco's application was accepted in principle by the ECOWAS Summit. However, the details of its operationalisation were yet to be worked out. Morocco's interest in ECOWAS generated debate in many West African countries, the argument in some circles included the question of why Morocco would want to benefit from both North Africa and West Africa in clear disregard for the geographical definition of 'region'. The fall of Kadhafi in Libya in 2011 had created a vacuum in North Africa with respect to who would promote North Africa's links with the rest of the continent. It seemed that Morocco aspired to take over the role of promoting *Afro-Arab cooperation* by seeking opportunities for active engagement with Africa beyond the *Maghreb*. Morocco's soft-power diplomacy in West Africa paid off, achieving, for example, partnership with Nigeria in major projects in agriculture and gas exploration. Morocco's perception that it is surrounded by unfriendly neighbouring countries made close association with friendly countries immediately outside the Maghreb a foreign policy objective. There was therefore a sense in which Morocco's desire for ECOWAS membership was linked to its geopolitical interests, security imperatives and 'new' policy towards the rest of Africa.

ECOWAS continued to be by far the best-functioning regional integration scheme in Africa, particularly in the areas of conflict management and support for democracy. North Africa's lack of a properly working regional forum for cooperation might have been the reason for *Tunisia*'s application for ECOWAS membership as an observer and Mauritania's wish to re-join after withdrawing in 2000. The extension of ECOWAS to include North African countries might also help address ongoing conflicts in the West African Sahel, many of which had links to the north.

The West Africa sub-region continued to provide Nigeria with opportunities to operationalise its vision and aspiration as a hegemonic power. Nigeria's vision of becoming one of the 20 largest economies in the world by 2020 and joining the

G-20 club of nations were indicators of its aspirations beyond its traditional sphere of diplomatic influence. Of course, its domestic economy and politics posed some challenges. Notwithstanding, no other country in the sub-region, and very few in Africa as a whole, could compete with Nigeria in terms of economic and military capabilities. The country's military ranked fourth-largest in Africa, and 36th in the world, with military expenditure of $ 1,723 m (0.4% of the country's GDP) in 2016. The administration of President Muhamadu Buhari made some efforts to redirect Nigeria's foreign policy to address its immediate challenges, which in turn informed government priorities. These included curbing the Boko Haram insurgency, revamping the national economy, clamping down on all forms of corruption, theft, abuse of power and privileges, and working to recover looted funds. Nigeria and her neighbours Cameroon, Chad and Niger, plus Benin, worked together to address the threat of Boko Haram within the regional framework of the Lake Chad Basin Commission.

Apart from Nigeria, Senegal and Ghana also sought to project themselves as diplomatic powers in the sub-region. The peaceful power transition in Ghana made the country a model for Africa's democratic experiment and therefore an attraction to members of the international community. Senegal had always hosted many diplomatic missions and international non-governmental organisations, which had helped its self-projection as a diplomatic power. The election of *Côte d'Ivoire to the UNSC* was not only an endorsement of the country's international standing and a recognition of its successful efforts at post-conflict recovery and stability, but also secured more visibility for West Africa within the context of Africa's growing interest in the UNSC reform.

The change of government in the *Gambia* significantly affected the style and direction of the country's external relations. Jammeh's era of shaky diplomatic relations with many countries including neighbouring Senegal ended and the new administration did much to overhaul the country's international relations generally. President Barrow promised to improve the country's bilateral relations with Senegal and, at the multilateral level, announced plans to overturn the previous administration's decision to withdraw the country from the *Commonwealth* and the *ICC*. The Gambia started reaping the results of the some of the foreign policy actions taken to reverse the diplomatic misdeeds of the Jammeh administration. Both the EU and the US demonstrated commitment to end the *diplomatic penalties* imposed on Gambia during Jammeh's reign. The EU pledged to provide € 75 m ($ 80 m) in *development assistance* to the new government. The African Export-Import Bank committed $ 500 m for projects in tourism, infrastructure and agriculture and the IMF approved the disbursement of financial assistance of $ 16.1 m to the Gambia under a rapid credit facility. The US response to the new development in the Gambia included the readmitting the country to the AGOA trade programme and giving it duty-free access and investment opportunities in US markets. In addition, the travel restrictions imposed on government officials, key businessmen and their families were lifted, and the US government decided to issue passports to some 2,000 Gambians living in the US who had been awaiting deportation.

Socioeconomic Development

Average *GDP growth* in West Africa rebounded to 2.5% after the remarkable decline in the regional average toward the end of 2016. However, the performance and experience of individual countries varied. Nigeria, with the largest economy in the sub-region and on the continent, accounted for 70% of regional GDP and was the 13th-largest oil-producing country in the world in 2016. Oil constituted about 75% Nigerian government revenue, but the rapid economic growth was found mostly in the non-oil sector. Disruptions in the oil sector coupled with foreign exchange, power and fuel shortages had caused output to contract by 1.5 % in 2016. Notwithstanding, output in Nigeria was projected to grow by 0.8% in 2017, as a result of a recovery in oil production, continued growth in agriculture and higher public investment.

The *emergent global powers*, notably China, India and other BRICS countries, demonstrated continued interests in West Africa, with its large market and huge natural resources. New and rapidly expanding markets in West Africa, such Côte d'Ivoire, along with old and establish markets like Nigeria, were major attractions to foreign investors. The involvement of China and others in the mining sector seemed to have pointed a number of governments to the need to come up with adequate policies and regulations for the mining sector. Despite this courting of new friends, the old and traditional friendship with the West remained. In addition to preserving closer ties with Europe, West African countries were committed to strong economic ties with the US. It was partly for this reasons that the annual AGOA meeting was held in Lomé (Togo) in August. The importance of the event cannot be overemphasised in view of the seemingly negative attitude of President Trump towards Africa, and the drop in American imports from Africa in recent years (from $ 26.8 bn in 2014 to $ 18.7 bn in 2015, i.e. down 30%), mainly due to the fall in African oil exports.

The popular narrative about Africa's *economic growth* was clearly expressed in the performance of West African economies in 2016. In 2017, however, a number of countries in the sub-region subscribed to free trade, foreign investment and effective taxation measures. Their serious efforts towards sustaining and improving their GDP were well-received and supported by international financial institutions, notably the World Bank and the IMF, and also the AfDB. This subscription, although at varying levels, to a free market economy and the adoption of neo-liberal economic policies and reform programmes seemed intended more to gain the support of leading members of the international community, especially the key global financial institutions, but were only by default beneficial to ordinary people. Growth rates recorded in the sub-region for most of 2016 suggested satisfactory performance before the setting in of economic *recession* towards the end of the year, and this downward trend continued in 2017, resulting in low performance, with the exception of a few countries, notably Cote d'Ivoire and Senegal, which continued with the impressive economic growth and relative political stability of recent years.

Recent electoral contests in West Africa took place in the context of debate on the *performance of the national economies*. Accusations and counter-accusations focussed on the management of the national economy by the incumbents as well as the feasibility of the alternatives offered by the opposition. Unsurprisingly, therefore the management of national economies was accorded top priority on government agendas. In Nigeria, the Buhari administration finally gained momentum. The government launched programmes focusing on the energy sector, food production and development of infrastructure towards a full recovery of the country's economy, and a lot was done to get the country's economy out of the woods. In Ghana, the administration of President Akufo-Addo embarked on major economic restructuring programmes that resulted in economic growth, with a marked decrease in national debt and successful job creation. However, there were concerns that the benefits of Ghana's economic growth were not felt by ordinary people. Similarly, in Benin, while the new government's reform programmes were generally well received internationally, particularly by global financial institutions, the policies and programmes of President Patrice Talon's administration were not popular among the population. In addition, the Akufo-Addo administration in Ghana adopted the 'Ghana Beyond Aid' strategy to help the country pursue self-reliance, with focus on industrialisation, trade and foreign investment. It was not the same, however, for many other countries in the sub-region, whose development was essentially driven by foreign aid and assistance. A number of countries received substantial *technical support and financial assistance* for the development of the energy sector and infrastructure. The case of Togo was illustrative, with significant budgetary aid from the EU, France and Germany. In 2016, the EU's budgetary aid for Togo was $ 16.5 bn. When added to the German aid package of $ 60 m, this represented an approximate 50% increase in aid since 2014. The EU, France and Germany agreed to harmonise their aid to Togo, which amounted to about € 715 m in total for the period 2014–20.

In Nigeria, the administration of President Buhari adopted the National Economic Recovery and Growth Plan (2017–20) to enable the country to come out of economic recession and the adverse effects of the global economic downturn by restoring economic growth, investing in Nigerians and building a globally competitive economy. A wide range of reforms was embarked upon including the creation of an enabling environment for FDI. In March, as part of the initiative of the Presidential Enabling Business Environment Council, a 'visa on arrival' policy was introduced. Nigeria's overall business climate showed noticeable improvement.

According to the World Bank's *Doing Business 2017: Equal Opportunity for All*, Nigeria ranked 169th of 190 countries. One impressive result of the administration's economic strategy was the success of eurobond sales.

Anti-corruption measures and efforts to promote transparency, accountability, probity and good governance were consciously pursued generally across the sub-region but especially in countries where the previous government had been accused of corruption and fiscal indiscipline. Nigeria, Ghana and Benin were at the forefront of the *war against corruption*. Among the indices of improvement in Nigeria were its rating by TI, its growing economy and the improved environment for FDI. Nigeria was ranked 136th of 175 countries in TI's 2016 Corruption Perceptions Index. As part of efforts towards strengthening the country's anti-corruption campaign, the Buhari administration sought bilateral partnerships with international agencies and individual countries to confront crime and corruption. Nigeria used international multilateral platforms to campaign for an international legal framework to enforce anti-corruption measures and strengthen existing international institutions to effectively deal with corrupt practices. The country remained committed to the EITI.

In Togo, President Gnassingbé had set up the High Authority to Combat Corruption and made it operational almost two years after it was created by law. However, the opposition doubted the integrity of its members and their ability to control corruption effectively. Some inadequacies and limitations in the various strategies adopted by governments in the fight against corruption made them appear as deliberate sanctions on the opposition rather than carefully designed anti-corruption measures. This was widely rumoured in Nigeria and Ghana and other countries where government anti-corruption measures did not receive much popular support.

Benin

Alexander Stroh

Politics remained focussed on President Patrice Talon's activities, despite his attempts to delegate public appearances to government members. Talon, who had assumed office in 2016, continued with ambitious reform projects including constitutional amendments and economic liberalisation. These project met resistance in parliament and from labour unions. The economy received tailwinds from increased agricultural production and economic recovery in neighbouring Nigeria, as well as from regional and global financial institutions that trusted in the new government's reform capacities.

Domestic Politics

Elected in 2016, President Patrice Talon promised to reduce corruption and significantly strengthen the country's economy. The proposed ways of doing so, however, were contested in the second year of his presidency. Talon had been a successful businessman before assuming the presidency and pushed for *economic liberalisation and privatisations* once in office. Labour unions were able to mobilise thousands to

 | DOI:10.1163/9789004367630_005

protest against these policies and go on strike on 20–22 June. The organisers spoke of more than 10,000 demonstrators on the streets of Cotonou on the first day. Official figures were unavailable. Towards the end of December, parliament passed a law that limited the right to strike in some parts of the public sector, which was the major formal employer. The law was taken to the Constitutional Court but no judgement emerged before the end of the year.

One of Talon's political priorities stalled in early April. *Constitutional amendments* were supposed to reform the country's institutional framework, but parliament decided unanimously on 24 March that the reform project should not pass as a matter of urgency which would have limited the assembly's margins of influence. On 27 March, the magistrate's union went on strike against the reform because it would "undermine judicial independence", as union leader Michel Adjaka was quoted as saying. On the same day, Defence Minister Candide Azannaï – a long established politician known for his individualistic attitude – resigned from his post over the constitutional amendment bill. On 4 April, the reform project even fell short of the three-quarters majority in the National Assembly required to discuss the amendment in the regular legislative process. The presidential proposal won 60 out of 83 votes. This result mirrored the rather loose coalition building in parliament, which was hardly based on durable party structures. Sixty members of the Assembly supported the president and formed the 'Majoritarian Bloc in Parliament', while the rest positioned themselves in the 'Minority Bloc in Parliament'. Talon made no observable efforts to create a party organisation that would include his supporters, although, one-and-a-half years into his term, this was no reason to be overly surprised. None of Talon's predecessors had been backed by even an established, much less strongly organised, party when voted into office. Presidents Kérékou and Yayi took years before loose party alliances were transformed into a single party organisation. The only special feature of Talon's party policy was that party politicians were not urged to form an official alliance with a catchy name.

De facto political alliances changed over the course of the year but generally the president's broad support remained intact. On 27 October, Talon followed up on his conflict with former ally Sébastien Ajavon and carried out a *cabinet reshuffle*, replacing three ministers considered to be close to Ajavon. The latter, who came third in the 2016 presidential race, had supported Talon against then President Yayi's preferred candidate, Lionel Zinsou. However, Ajavon and Talon had been rivals in business and observers had considered their political alliance to be unstable from the very beginning and Ajavon had been prosecuted for drug crimes shortly after Talon moved into Marina Palace, the presidential office. The prosecutor later dropped the charges, but Ajavon still sued the Republic of Benin before the African Court on Human and Peoples' Rights in February. He felt ill-treated by the authorities and saw his reputation and business damaged. The court case was pending at the end of the year.

Through the October reshuffle, the cabinet grew from 21 to 23 members. The senior minister in the Presidential Office Pascal Koupaki, Senior Minister for Economic Planning and Development, Abdoulaye Bio-Tchané, Talon's former lawyer and then Minister of Justice Joseph Djogbénou and most other key cabinet members retained their posts. *Modeste Kérékou* was the most notable entry into government. He received the portfolio for small and medium enterprises and employment promotion. The younger son of former long-term president Matthieu Kérékou, in office 1972–1991 and 1996–2006, brought with him the positive image and, presumably, the still influential network of the Kérékou family, now unmistakeably allied to the president.

In the 2016 election, the Soglo family – highly influential in politics since Nicéphore Soglo had been elected as the country's first democratic president after the 1990 national conference – had supported Linoel Zinsou. Consequently, the 'Renaissance du Bénin' (RB) party headed by Nicéphore's son *Léhady Soglo*, the mayor of Cotonou, went into opposition. Léhady intended to use the municipality of the country's economic capital as his political powerhouse, similar to his father's. Nicéphore Soglo had been the mayor of Cotonou when his fierce political rival Matthieu Kérékou had served as Soglo's democratically elected successor in Marina Palace. However, the geographical area of the city of Cotonou equals that of the department of Littoral and departments were governed by prefects, appointed by presidential decree and representing the central authority of the state, whereas mayors were elected and departments exercised supervisory authority over the municipality. President Talon appointed an energetic and vocal young prefect for Littoral, Modeste Toboula, who had already started to challenge the municipality in 2016 and presented himself as a strong law and order administrator. Mayor Léhady Soglo did not accept the implied criticism. But instead of raising his profile through this opposition, he suffered political defeat at several levels. On 21 May, his party, the RB, split into factions. The party's executive council, officially called the 'politburo', dismissed Soglo from his post as party president. Soglo challenged the process but was unable to unite the party under his leadership. On 26 July, Prefect Toboula summoned the mayor over an allegation about his financial management brought by members of the municipal council. The meeting took place on 28 July. The same day, the minister for administrative decentralisation and local government suspended Soglo. On 2 August, the mayor was finally suspended from office. Soglo contested this decision before the Supreme Court. The case was pending at year's end and the first deputy mayor was serving ad interim.

Joint action taken by Minister of the Interior and Religious Affairs Sacca Lafia and Prefect Toboula fuelled a discussion about the government's respect for *freedom of religion*. The minister and the administrator in charge of public security strictly implemented the government's new urban clean-up programme, not only by removing unauthorised small roadside businesses but also, on 27 January, by demolishing roadside sunshades erected for Friday prayers. Devout Muslims often occupied public spaces in front of overcrowded mosques but the new policy would not tolerate any systematic use of public space for religious gatherings. Representatives of the Islamic community met with cabinet ministers and the president on 1 and 4 February, respectively, to discuss the situation. President Talon generally confirmed the public order policy and alluded to countries such as Algeria, where Friday prayers were not allowed to affect public order. At the same time, the government underlined that the measures were in no way directed against religious groups. Instead, the new policy sought to reinforce public security and to bring order to chaotic urban roads. Since public pressures continued to rise, the president allowed the exceptional use of public space after the meeting with the dignitaries until new spaces for religious activities could be arranged with the help of the state. On 3 March, Catholic clergy sought clarification from the government. The ministers of the interior and of justice dispelled the bishops' concerns about occasional religious events. Processions and other public events would be permitted as usual.

On 29 June, a court in Cotonou began the trial of 20 defendants in the *'ICC Services' case*. This company had been accused since 2010 of defrauding ordinary citizens, small scale investors who had trusted in a hidden Ponzi scheme. When it came to light, the scandal grew into the country's biggest known financial scandal; it put heavy pressure on the then government of President Yayi, and caused the resignation of his minister of finance. Domestic journalists reported that tens of thousands of victims were awaiting compensation.

Rumours about *President Talon's state of health* and physical capacities spread when he left the country for medical treatment in Paris in the beginning of June. Talon disappeared from public view for about two weeks but then presented himself in good shape. Marina Palace announced that he had undergone successful surgery on the prostate and the digestive system. Talon went back to Paris for a check-up on 30 June and returned on 4 July according to media reports.

Given the campaign promises concerning *press freedom*, journalists expected improving working conditions and an end to the legalistic harassment that Benin's critical media had increasingly deplored during President Yayi's rule. International observers from Freedom House to 'Reporters sans Frontières' (RSF) and the US State Department's human rights section confirmed the country's decline in press freedom under President Yayi. Contrary to promises and expectations, this situation did not change and RSF reported further deterioration. The international media watchdog joined with many other observers, including the American diplomatic service, in highlighting the ambivalent role of the High Authority for Audio-visual Media and Communication (HAAC), which was responsible for protecting press freedom and punishing misconduct. Media outlets close to the opposition that had been shut down in 2016 were hindered from returning to air. In particular, Sikka TV, which even obtained a favourable court order, had its operations restricted. Following massive journalist protests in mid-January, HAAC lifted the broadcasting ban on Radio Soleil FM, E-Tele and Eden TV on 26 January. The US State Department's human rights report on Benin recalled another factor that increased the vulnerability of journalism from the economic perspective: "It was possible to purchase and thus influence the content of press coverage." Many journalists continued to be underpaid or insufficiently trained.

Foreign Affairs

Foreign politics largely focussed on regional and sub-regional affairs. Most of President Talon's official visits abroad were in an *economic context*. On 11 January, he attended meetings at the AfDB headquarters in Abidjan, where he also met with *Côte d'Ivoire*'s President Alassane Ouattara. On 10 April, Talon saw Ouattara again, this time in the latter's capacity as chairperson of the UEMOA, which held an extraordinary meeting of the heads of state and government in Abidjan.

On 10–11 May, Talon was in *Kenya* to discuss bi-lateral trade and business opportunities. The programme included talks with President Uhuru Kenya and Talon's participation in a round-table at the 17th general assembly of the African Commercial Insurance Agency, and followed up a working visit by the Kenyan minister of foreign affairs to Benin in January. On 21 May, Talon represented Benin at the Arabo-Islamic and American summit in Riyadh (Saudi-Arabia), where US President Donald Trump was present. Talon continued his Asian trip to Ahmedabad in India, where he joined the 52nd annual assembly of the AfDB Group, highlighting once more that he prioritised economic issues.

Relations with *Europe* continued to be good. On 13 July, the Swiss Federal President Doris Leuthard visited Benin. During a visit to France on 2–9 October, President Talon was unable to meet with French President Emmanuel Macron or Pierre Gattaz, president of the French federation of entrepreneurs, but he used the journey for business-related talks and to meet the Beninois diaspora. On 29–30 November, President Talon joined the 5th *AU-EU summit* in Abidjan. In general, close working relations between the government and its European partners did not require major political events such as state visits; it was a matter of business as usual with positive connotations.

On his way home from France on 9–11 October, Talon paid courtesy calls on his *sub-regional peers*: President Kaboré in Ouagadougou (Burkina Faso), President Ouattara in Abidjan, President Akufo-Addo in Accra (Ghana) and President Gnassingbé in Lomé (Togo). Togolese media outlets reported that Talon was frequently in touch with Gnasingbé over the domestic political crisis in *Togo* and that he tried to mediate in the conflict and even returned discretely to Lomé on 18 October, but no significant easing of the Togolese crisis had emerged by year's end.

Benin continued to play a minor role in the *sub-regional security* architecture. Situated at the geographic margins of the Sahelian and Nigerian crisis zones, Benin was contributing by year's end 412 troops and police to the UN Multidimensional Integrated Stabilization Mission in Mali (MINSUMA) and an unreported number of garrison support troops to the Multinational Joint Task Force that united military contingents from Nigeria and all its neighbours to fight Boko Haram in the Lake Chad Basin. Benin was the only partner whose territory was not directly affected by jihadist terrorism. Though it was part of Benin's foreign security policy to keep a low profile, the country also continued to provide troops to other UN missions, in particular the mission in Congo, with 461 personnel contributed at the end of the year. Other contingents of between one and 22 staff supported missions in the CAR, Haiti, Liberia and Sudan.

In December, the Assembly of State Parties of the Rome Statute elected Beninese citizen and former law professor Reine Alapini Gansou as one of the four African judges serving the *ICC*. She had held several international posts before, including the chair of the African Commission on Human and People's Rights. Also in December, the secretary general of the *OIF* visited Benin, giving particular attention to SèmèCity, a government lighthouse project in the digital industries sector.

Socioeconomic Developments

Benin was affected by the economic slowdown in Nigeria, Africa's biggest market. The weak oil price had taken Nigeria's economic growth into negative figures but 2017 saw a recovery from this recession. In parallel, Benin's *growth* had also dropped in 2016 and recovered slightly in 2017, with the AfDB reporting 4% and 5.5% growth, respectively. Despite an increase in the public debt quota due to higher spending related to the implementation of the *government's action programme*, the country's financial partner institutions remained confident that the programme's positive effects would pay back in the near future. IMF's Managing Director Christine Lagarde visited Cotonou on 10–11 December and confirmed this confidence, but also pointed to challenges. The IMF and AfDB both hailed the government programme's focus on modernising the agricultural sector and the political stability in Benin, but they also highlighted unpredictable market vulnerabilities related to climate change, cotton prices and economic developments in Nigeria. They urged Benin to continue to improve the business climate and to promote the private sector – a message that trade unions generally did not welcome.

At first glance, the *cotton* sector results proved the optimists correct. The production of the country's major export crop surged by 73% compared with the 2016 harvest to 450,000 tonnes, significantly exceeding early forecasts. After years of public control over the industry, the 'Association Interprofessionelle de Coton' (AIC), of which President Talon had been one of the founders, managed the 2016–17 season for the first time since 2011–12. The increase in production needed to be seen in context, however, as the previous season marked a five-year low. Compared with 2015, the 2017 record high corresponded to a more moderate rise in output of 12.5%. Forecasts for the 2017–18 season, which started in November, estimated further growth to up to half a million tonnes. More generally, *agricultural production* developed very favourably. According to Xinhua news agency, government officials disclosed on 13 April that overall growth in the sector reached 13.2%, with close to average results for domestic staple food crops such as cassava and yam.

The macroeconomic optimism of Benin's financial partners did not always translate into high levels of trust between clients and companies on the microeconomic ground. On 17 November, the Ministry of Interior ordered the South African general director of MTN Benin to leave the country within a week. MTN was a South African *mobile telecoms* company which also offered mobile banking. Clients panicked when the news quickly spread across the social media networks that the administration had accused MTN's Benin branch office of failing to pay fees exceeding € 200 m. Mobile banking users feared they would lose their money, but this did not happen.

On 27 September, the government and the Danish-led consortium BWSC/MAN signed an international contract to fight Benin's massive shortage of *electric power*, with the parastatal water and electricity company SBEE as the main domestic technical partner. The signatories agreed on the construction of a geothermal power station at Maria-Glèta. The first phase of the project would guarantee the production of 120 MW, equivalent to one-fifth of the government's commitment for 2021. Development Minister Abdoulaye Bio-Tchané announced that construction would take 18 months and that the complete Maria-Glèta power plant should produce 480 MW after the conclusion of several project phases. The government also announced that a further 100 MW would be available by 2021 through solar and other renewable energies. Costs of the first construction phase were estimated at CFAfr 106.9 bn (approx. € 163 m), funded by the Islamic Development Bank, the West African Development Bank, the ECOWAS Bank for Investment and Development and the Republic of Benin. The state would also be responsible for compensation to people who had to leave the construction area, amounting to some CFAfr 2.6 bn (approx. € 4 m). Official estimates were that 400 jobs would be created directly at the power plant.

The government-driven project 'Bénin Taxi' was launched mid-year to provide new *traffic* solutions in the city of Cotonou, which suffered from too much personal vehicle use and related environmental risks. The new company sought to become the first to provide reliable and large-scale taxi services in the country's biggest city. Earlier attempts by the municipality to introduce a low-price bus system had failed. The population of Cotonou continued to prefer the personalised services of so called Zémidjan motorbike taxis. Since the new yellow cabs only started business in July, no reliable measures of their success were available by the year's end, when the fleet amounted to over 250 taxis, according to national television reports.

On 26 December, the National Assembly passed a law banning the production, importation, exportation, commercialisation, storage, distribution and utilisation of *plastic bags* (Law No. 2017–39). The national government had announced this move in 2016, just before Talon's state visit to Rwanda, which had introduced a total plastic bag ban years before. Benin's law came at least a year later than the government had promised but implementation was expected by as early as August 2018. The law stipulated drastic punishments, including substantial fines and imprisonment for three to six months for just discarding non-degradable plastic bags. In order to create perfect legal certainty and to avoid a political defeat among the public with this highly symbolic project, President Talon requested the Constitutional Court to check the bill's constitutionality. The Court had no objections (decision DCC 17–255).

Burkina Faso

Daniel Eizenga

Terrorist activities grew in 2017, particularly in the northern Sahel region where dozens of small-scale attacks targeted security forces, schools and local traditional leaders. An attack also took place in downtown Ouagadougou, claiming the lives of 18 individuals and marking the second such attack in the capital in less than two years. The military joined those from Mali, Niger, Mauritania and Chad to form the newly operational G5 Sahel counter-terrorism joint task force, which conducted its first mission in the Liptako-Gourma region where the borders of Mali, Niger and Burkina Faso meet. President Kaboré also sought to strengthen ties with several bilateral partners during the year. During many of his foreign trips, Kaboré highlighted the economic growth that Burkina Faso had experienced in 2016 and 2017. However, the opposition and several labour unions challenged the government during the year, expressing their frustrations with the lack of qualitative change, despite strong economic growth. The 25th bi-annual Pan-African Film and Television Festival, FESPACO, took place in Ouagadougou, once again attracting travellers and movie-goers from around the continent and the world.

 | DOI:10.1163/9789004367630_006

Domestic Politics

Throughout the year, terrorism and *growing insecurity* in the north factored into domestic politics. The security situation remained challenging, given the numerous asymmetrical attacks on small communities, security forces and government buildings in the north near the border with Mali. The worsening insecurity led President Roch Kaboré to appoint Colonel-Major Oumarou Sadou as the new army chief of staff replacing General Pingrenoma Zagré, who had successfully ended the 2015 attempted coup d'état. It also resulted in large-scale efforts to reform the security sector with the aim of improving security throughout the capital and on major thoroughfares. These efforts failed to prevent a *terrorist attack on 13 August*, carried out in downtown Ouagadougou, which targeted the popular Aziz Istanbul restaurant, leaving 18 people dead and dozens wounded. By the end of the year, no one had claimed responsibility for the attack, but it had several similarities with the terrorist attack on 15 January 2016 that had targeted the Cappuccino restaurant and Hotel Splendid, located less than 500 metres from Aziz Istanbul.

Several different groups claimed responsibility for *smaller scale attacks* that took place primarily in the north. However, one group that emerged as particularly important in northern Burkina Faso was Ansar al-Islam, sometimes spelled Ansarul Islam or Ansaroul Islam – the first active terrorist organisation known to be led by a Burkinabè citizen, Ibrahim Malam Dicko, and believed to be comprised principally of Burkinabè fighters. Ansar al-Islam's activities were heavily concentrated in Dicko's home province of Soum, part of the Sahel region of Burkina Faso, which borders Mali and Niger. Under Dicko, the group attacked security forces several times, assassinated local leaders suspected of cooperating with Burkinabè security forces, and *threatened school teachers*, demanding that they incorporate Qur'anic education into their curricula. During the first three months of the year, the security situation in northern Burkina Faso deteriorated so significantly that local officials closed public schools in Soum, Loroum and Oudalan provinces. By the end of the year, the group had been responsible for the deaths of security forces and civilians in Nassoumbou, Baraboulé, Petega, Tongomayel, Pogwol, Dowoulé and Djibasso.

While facing the challenge of growing insecurity in the north, the government also confronted an *increasingly hostile opposition*. Seeking to stir public debate and incite popular discontent with the government after its first year in office, the political opposition published in February a memorandum titled, 'A Year Lost for Burkina Faso', denouncing a politicised cabinet, rampant corruption and the three politicians most closely associated with the ruling party, the Movement of the People for Progress (MPP): President Roch Kaboré, Speaker of the National Assembly Salifou Diallo, and Minister of Security and the Interior Simon Compaoré. In April, the opposition organised a political rally against the ruling party which brought together some 3,000 demonstrators protesting against the declining state of the nation under the current government.

Kaboré and the MPP sought to regain the support of voters through the legislature with proposed reforms to the electoral code and the laws regulating procedures for public-private contracting, and even drafting an entirely new constitution to break with the former regime. The *draft constitution* went through a series of revisions and was the subject of debates held both by the Constitutional Commission and by judicial institutions across Burkina Faso's 13 regions, before the president of the Constitutional Commission, Halidou Ouedraogo, submitted the draft to President Kaboré. After Kaboré requested a series of revisions, Ouedraogo submitted a third draft to the president on 27 December, though it remained unclear when or even if a referendum would be scheduled to approve the new constitution.

The government also sought to bolster its standing with voters by demonstrating progress toward *national reconciliation* following the popular uprising of October 2014 and the subsequent failed coup d'état of September 2015. Several highly anticipated trials were scheduled to begin during the year, including the case against former president Blaise Compaoré and his government, a military case against the leaders of the 2015 failed coup, and the case against the former foreign affairs minister, Djibril Bassolé, who was accused of helping to orchestrate the failed coup. However, very little progress was made on these cases and none had reached a verdict by the end of the year.

After several postponements, the *trial of the final Compaoré-led government* began on 4 May. The former members of Compaoré's government, 31 ministers including Compaoré himself as minister of defence, were to be tried on charges related to the popular insurrection that ousted Compaoré from power in October 2014, including complicity in voluntary homicide and deliberate assault. The High Court of Justice suspended the trial, however, in response to the defence's argument that Compaoré and several of his former ministers were being tried in absentia. Faced with this constitutional complication, the legislature drafted and approved a bill reforming the composition and functions of the High Court of Justice in an attempt to strengthen the guarantee of a fair trial, the rights of the defence and the rights of victims. In practice, the law would enable defendants to appeal against a conviction if they were tried in absentia. Compaoré remained in exile in Côte d'Ivoire throughout the year.

Bassolé, who had been imprisoned following the failed coup, was hospitalised in late January, which led to several of his supporters appealing for his temporary release. In April, the Office of the UN High Commissioner of Human Rights (UNHCRC) judged that his imprisonment and detention were arbitrary and called for his immediate release. The *military tribunal* overseeing his case granted Bassolé provisional release in October, but stipulated that he remain under house arrest.

The UNHCRC repeated its call for Bassolé's release in December, noting that, while his condition may have improved, he continued to be deprived of his liberty. The trial of others facing charges related to the failed coup was postponed until 2018.

Distinguished politician, former minister and ambassador, speaker of the National Assembly and chairman of the ruling party, *Salifou Diallo*, passed away on 19 August in France. Presidents, politicians, diplomats and other leaders from across the African continent visited Burkina Faso to pay their respects to this eminent political figure. Diallo was replaced as speaker of the National Assembly by Alassane Bala Sakandé on 8 September and was buried in his hometown of Ouahigouya the capital of Burkina Faso's Nord Region.

Foreign Affairs

In June, the UNSC unanimously adopted Resolution 2359 (2017) authorising the deployment of the *G5 Sahel military joint force*, which brought together troops from Mali, Niger, Mauritania, Burkina Faso and Chad and was tasked with combatting terrorism and organised transnational crime in specific trans-border zones. An official map of these zones designated the shared borders between Burkina Faso and Mali, and Mali and Niger, but, notably, the map did not include the border between Burkina Faso and Niger within these zones. French President Emmanuel Macron called on a number of Western countries and their allies to provide financial support to the joint force, which had an initial budget of $ 523 m, but much of the budget remained unmet by the end of the year. The five member states of the G5 each agreed to contribute $ 10 m, while EU members pledged a total of $ 143 m, the United States committed $ 60 m, Saudi Arabia promised $ 100 m, and the UAE agreed to provide $ 30 m.

In addition to its financial commitment, Burkina Faso was to provide 550 soldiers and 100 police/gendarmes to the G5 Sahel force, which would eventually total 5,000 soldiers. Burkinbè troops participated in the G5 Sahel's *first military mission*, operation 'Haw Bi' or Black Cow, which took place in early November and sought to establish control of the Liptako-Gourma region, which comprises parts of northern Burkina Faso, Mali and western Niger. 2,900 Burkinabè soldiers were already deployed to other UN peacekeeping missions, including the Multidimensional Integrated Stabilisation Mission in Mali, considered the most dangerous UN peacekeeping mission and to which Burkina Faso was one of the largest troop contributors.

A number of *Malian refugees* continued to seek safety in Burkina Faso at the two refugee camps located in the Sahel Region. These troop commitments and the continued need to support regional security efforts placed a heavy strain on the country's resources. However, France's President Macron aimed to reassure the five countries of the G5 Sahel that the necessary financial support for the force would be obtained and that France would contribute an additional $ 1.5 bn in funds for development in the Sahel over the next five years.

Relations between *France* and Burkina Faso remained strong throughout the year. In April, the French Agency for Development announced that it would commit roughly $ 100 m to Burkina Faso's national plan for sustainable development and, in October, the French ambassador to Burkina Faso delivered several military vehicles and other equipment to aid counter-terrorism efforts. This followed the trial of a French special forces *soldier accused of molesting two Burkinabè girls* in June 2015, which began in the Paris Criminal Court in April. The accused soldier, referred to as Sebastien L., had been deployed to Burkina Faso as part of Operation Barkhane, the French counter-terrorism mission in the Sahel. He admitted to sexual contact with the girls, aged three and five at the time of the incident, but was unable to offer any explanation for his behaviour, blaming his actions on alcohol and the stress of the mission. The court sentenced the soldier in June to one year in prison and a one-year suspended sentence and ordered him to pay the family roughly $ 18,500.

Relations also appeared tense during *President Macron's visit* to Ouagadougou in November. The visit was intended to display the strong connection between the two countries and Macron did indeed use the occasion to announce that France would *declassify its intelligence files* on the assassination of former president Thomas Sankara. Macron said that the files would be made available to the Burkinabè justice system in an effort to shed light on the unsolved investigation of Sankara's murder. It was widely speculated that Blaise Compaoré had collaborated with the French military to organise the assassination of the leftist revolutionary president in 1987. However, the announcement was overshadowed by comments Macron made to an audience of students at the University of Ouagadougou on 28 November. Several members of the *media criticised Macron* for making patronising comments and directing inappropriate humour at President Kaboré. The criticisms forced Macron to respond in an interview with French media representatives after his return, despite the fact that Kaboré agreed that the remarks were a demonstration of respectful fraternity.

President Kaboré also sought to establish and strengthen several *other bilateral relationships* while promoting development initiatives for his country. Despite increasing pressures and a $ 50 bn enticement from Chinese affiliated companies, Burkina Faso continued to recognise and maintain diplomatic ties with Taiwan. The specific effects of the decision remained unclear, but Burkina Faso and Swaziland were the only two countries on the African continent that continued to recognise Taiwan as a separate nation. Kaboré travelled to Qatar, Egypt and Switzerland and met with the president of Benin in Ouagadougou, all in an effort to strengthen bilateral ties around the world. While the specific initiatives discussed during these trips varied, they primarily focused on the development objectives laid out by Kaboré's government in the national plan for sustainable development. Burkina Faso also signed an agreement with Equatorial Guinea, which outlined plans for the importation, storage and transportation of a supply of liquefied natural gas from Equatorial Guinea to Burkina Faso.

Relations between *Côte d'Ivoire* and Burkina Faso also remained strong, despite temporary problems at the border. Hundreds of thousands of Burkinabè continued to migrate to Côte d'Ivoire for employment and goods transit between the two countries continued to be responsible for a significant portion of Burkina Faso's imports and exports. The transportation of goods was temporarily halted in May during an Ivoirian mutiny. The renegade soldiers blocked dozens of trucks carrying goods bound for Burkina Faso for days and in some cases the soldiers forced the drivers to pay bribes for the release of their vehicles.

In September, following the terrorist attack on the Aziz Istanbul restaurant in Ouagadougou and worsening insecurity in the north of the country, the US Embassy *evacuated its Peace Corps volunteers*. Peace Corps programmes in the country were subsequently suspended indefinitely as a security precaution. In November, following reports that black African migrants were being auctioned off in slave markets in *Libya*, Burkina Faso recalled its ambassador to Libya. Libya's ambassador to Burkina Faso responded by calling on the international community to support Libya in finding a lasting solution to the escalating migration crisis.

Socioeconomic Developments

Burkina Faso continued to rank amongst the poorest countries of the world according to several indicators, such as the UNDP's Human Development Index, which placed it 185th out of 188 countries and territories. Nevertheless, the *economic outlook* presented by most forecasters at the end of the year remained positive. After experiencing less economic growth in 2014 and 2015, it became clear that the economy had seen a rebound, with a recorded 5.8% growth in 2016 and an estimated 6% growth in 2017. Forecasters optimistically predicted growth accelerations to 6.3% for 2018 and 2019. Burkina Faso's two largest sectors, agriculture and mining, both appeared strong at the end of the year.

Cotton remained the primary economic driver in the *agricultural sector*. Fears of a cotton collapse had peaked in 2016, when the Ministry of Agriculture discontinued the use of genetically modified cotton supplied by seed maker Monsanto. However, the 2016–17 harvest yielded roughly 750,000 tonnes of raw cotton compared with the previous year's 600,000 tonnes and the cotton reportedly maintained a higher quality than the discontinued genetically modified variant. The strong harvest and government efforts to maintain high farm-gate prices for cotton producers led economic forecasters to predict strong agricultural production in 2018 and 2019.

The *mining sector* also contributed to the renewed growth. Under the new government, and by the end of the year, more transparent regulations and greater policy clarity had become norms in the mining sector, which in turn contributed to several plans to open new gold mines such as the Natougou mine, scheduled to become fully operational by 2019. These changes to the regulations encouraged companies such as the Australian based Vital Metals to invest in exploration over the next several years. Burkina Faso was the fourth largest producer of gold in Africa in 2017.

Another economic cause for optimism related to improvements in the overall supply of energy. In addition to the deal struck with Equatorial Guinea for a supply of natural gas, the Zagtouli *solar power plant* came online. The plant employed roughly 200 Burkinabè workers, was financed by the EDF and French Agency for Development, was the largest operating solar power plant in West Africa, and could produce 33 MW of power from its 55 ha of solar panels. The plant was an ambitious step forward by the government, which hoped to meet up to 30% of its power needs through solar energy by 2030. Burkina Faso was currently importing a significant portion of it power needs from its neighbours in Ghana and Côte d'Ivoire.

Despite these promising economic outlooks, *several strikes* disrupted daily life. In February, the truck drivers' union went on strike, shutting down transportation for days and causing thousands to descend on petrol stations, thus creating an artificial fuel shortage. In April, police officers staged a protest and strike against internal and high-level corruption within the police force. In June, judges and court clerks organised a strike in protest against all violent acts against members of the judiciary. Two days earlier, protesters in Manga, roughly 100 km from the capital, had damaged a judicial building during demonstrations for the release of a detainee. During the ruling party's 2nd Ordinary Congress, held in late June, it became clear that these strikes were disrupting the government's efforts as several members spoke out against the "recurrence of repetitive off-the-cuff strikes", which party members claimed hampered the country's economic progress. However, the union of truck drivers opted to strike again after security forces beat truck drivers who refused to pay a check point tax in Tenkodogo in August. Burkina Faso has a long history of union activity and strikes as well as other forms of *political activism*, which have routinely frustrated and harassed administrations.

Another example of the *public activism* that typifies Burkinabè civics could be observed during the annual 13 December march commemorating the death of investigative journalist *Norbert Zongo*. Nineteen years after his death in 1998, hundreds gathered in Koudougou, Zongo's hometown roughly 100 km west of Ouagadougou, calling for justice for his unsolved murder. The case had been dismissed by former president Blaise Compaoré's administration in 2003 and reopened following Compaoré's fall from power in 2014. On 5 May, an *arrest warrant* was issued for Blaise Compaoré's brother, who was charged with inciting Zongo's murder. He was then arrested in France in October. At a hearing on 13 December, officials at the French Court of Appeals asked François Compaoré if he would consent to be judged in Burkina Faso, but he refused to be tried under the Burkinabè judicial system and the French Court of Appeals scheduled his next hearing for March 2018.

The 25th bi-annual Pan-African Film and Television Festival, known by its French acronym *FESPACO*, took place from 25 February to 4 March. The festival, always held in Ouagadougou, was established in 1969 and continued to be the largest of its kind on the continent. The government went to great lengths to *increase security measures* before and during the event due to fears over the terrorist-related insecurity in the north of the country. Two small-scale attacks, the first targeting a police station and the second a school, occurred in the north during the event, but the increased security in the capital prevented attacks from disrupting the festival. The organisers selected 150 films from more than 1,000 entries to compete and roughly 100,000 people from around the world attended the event. Five feature-length films from Senegalese directors were in contention for the top prize known as the Golden Stallion of Yennenga. In the end, the Senegalese-French director Alain Gomis took the *top prize* for his film 'Felicité', while Beninois director Sylvestre Amoussou received the silver stallion for 'Un Orage Africain', and the bronze stallion went to 'A Mile in My Shoes', by Moroccan director Said Khallaf. The Moroccan film, 'Hyménée', by Violaine Maryam Blanche Bellet, won best short film and best documentary went to 'Nubuke', by the Ghanaian Aryee Bismark. A Rwandan short film titled 'A Place for Myself' won the new Thomas Sankara prize, inaugurated to commemorate the revolutionary leader and former Burkinabè president.

Finally, Burkinabè *architect Diébédo Francis Kéré* received recognition for his work in London, where he was asked to design the 2017 Serpentine Pavilion in Hyde Park. Kéré was the first African architect to be commissioned to design the Serpentine Pavilion, a temporary pavilion designed annually by world famous architects. Born in Gando, Burkina Faso, Kéré had emerged as one of the world's most renowned architects for his designs using elements from the environment to promote sustainable or green architecture. Despite the fact that his projects are sited in many countries across Africa and Europe, one of his most celebrated designs is his first, a primary school in his hometown. Also in 2017, Kéré received recognition for his design of Lycée Schorge, a secondary school on the outskirts of Koudougou (Burkina Faso). The school's design utilised locally sourced materials in innovative ways to diffuse natural light, ventilate the rooms and protect from dust, helping students and teachers to reach new levels of educational excellence.

Cabo Verde

Gerhard Seibert

In January, the ruling 'Movimento para a Democracia' (MpD) re-elected Prime Minister Ulisses Correia e Silva unopposed as party leader. In the same month, and despite having lost two consecutive elections in 2016, Janira Hoppfer Almada was also re-elected unopposed as leader of the opposition 'Partido Africano para a Independência de Cabo Verde' (PAICV). The government authorised the heavily indebted national airline 'Transportes Aéreos de Cabo Verde' (TACV) to take out three loans from commercial banks to cover operational and current expenses. In August, TACV's domestic flights were taken over by the Canary airline Binter Cabo Verde, while Icelandair assumed the management of the airline's international flights. As in previous years, the tourism sector continued to grow significantly.

Domestic Politics

In the MpD's direct party leadership elections on 8 January the incumbent *Prime Minister Ulisses Correia e Silva was re-elected unopposed* with 99% of the valid votes. The turnout was 65% of the 29,449 registered party members. At the same time,

 | DOI:10.1163/9789004367630_007

294 of 300 party delegates were elected, while six delegates in the United States were elected on 21 January. On 3–4 February, the 300 delegates participated in the MpD's 11th convention. The delegates rejected new statutes proposed by the party leadership that introduced rules on incompatibilities and ineligibilities between party functions and senior positions in the public administration and state enterprises, because they were considered discriminatory to the rights of MpD members compared with members of other parties. Instead, the delegates only approved a resolution that made the exercise of party functions incompatible with executive positions in the public administration, public enterprises and NGOs financed with public funds. Correia e Silva promised to submit a bill on the incompatibilities to parliament. The delegates also approved the principle of gender parity. Miguel Monteiro was elected as the party's new secretary general.

In the PAICV's direct leadership elections on 29 January, *Janira Hopffer Almada was re-elected unopposed*, with 97% of the more than 20,000 votes cast, out of 34,720 registered voters. The PAICV's 15th ordinary congress, held in Praia on 17–19 February, was attended by 413 delegates. In her opening speech, Hopffer Almada assumed full responsibility for the party's defeats in the legislative and municipal elections. She appealed for internal unity to strengthen the party and promised to continuously improve the party's structures and capacities and to pursue a strong and constructive opposition to government action. Humberto Brito, a former minister of tourism, was elected chairman of the 50-member National Council, with 93% of the votes. Manuel Portugal was elected chairman of the seven-member National Council of Jurisdiction and Supervision. In turn, the National Council elected Julião Varela as the party's secretary-general, while Hopffer Almada assumed the chair of the 21-member national Political Commission. The congress was marked by the absence of the 'Grupo de Reflexão', the about 20 opponents of Hopfffer Almada's leadership.

On 28 April in the National Assembly, the opposition parties PAICV and 'União Cabo-verdiana Independente e Democrática' (UCID) rejected a bill on the incompatibility between party functions and senior public jobs submitted by the MpD government. The 39 votes of the ruling party in favour of the law were insufficient to reach the necessary two-thirds majority of 72 deputies. Correia e Silva declared that, despite the rejection, the rule would be maintained that senior positions in the public administration could not be held simultaneously with leading party posts. PAICV leader Hopffer Almada declared that her party had voted against the proposal because the MpD had rejected her party's proposal to award public sector jobs only through a public application process.

On 20 December, Prime Minister Correia e Silva announced an *expansion of the government* by the appointment of two new ministers and six assistant secretaries of state. The Ministry of Economy and Employment headed by Jose Gonçales was dismembered into three new ministries. Alexandre Monteiro became the head of the new Ministry of Industry, Trade and Energy, while Gonçales assumed another two portfolios, the Ministry of Tourism and Transport and the Ministry of Maritime Economy. The latter moved to Mindelo in São Vicente on the grounds that several administrative units related to the maritime economy were located in the city. Júlio Herbert was appointed deputy prime minister for regional integration, a portfolio that was withdrawn from the Foreign Ministry. The new assistant secretaries of state were Gilberto dos Barros (finance), Edna Oliveira (administrative modernisation), Pedro Lopes (innovation and vocational training), Paulo Lima Veiga (maritime economy), Carlos do Cano Monteiro (ministry of state) and Amadeu da Cruz (education). The purpose of the restructuring of the government was to improve its efficiency and strengthen political coordination.

Foreign Affairs

Portugal, the EU and ECOWAS dominated the diplomatic agenda. ECOWAS denied Cabo Verde the rotating presidency of its Commission. On 10 January, President Jorge Carlos Fonseca attended in Lisbon in the funeral of Mário Soares (1924–2017), the former Portuguese prime minister and president. In his message of condolence, Fonseca stressed the importance of Soares for Cabo Verde's Independence in 1975. In December 1974, as foreign minister, Soares had headed the Portuguese delegation that negotiated the terms of the archipelago's decolonisation.

During the *4th Portugal-Cabo Verde Summit* held in Praia on 21 February, the two countries signed the Strategic Cooperation Programme 2017–2020, worth € 120 m, twice the value of the previous programme of € 56 m. At the meeting, Portugal's Prime Minister António Costa declared that his government was analysing a proposal for the resolution of Cabo Verde's debt of € 200 m arising from the social housing programme 'Casa para Todos' that was due for completion in 2021. The housing project, implemented from 2010, had accumulated liabilities of $ 664 m by the end of 2015.

On 9–12 April, *Portugal's President Marcelo Rebelo de Sousa paid a state visit* to Cabo Verde, seven years after the last presidential visit from the former colonial power. He was accompanied by Foreign Minister Augusto Santos Silva and six parliamentarians from various Portuguese parties. The official visit started in Fogo Island, where the Portuguese visited a local winery. On the second day, in Praia, Sousa was received by President Fonseca and Prime Minister Correia e Silva. The renegotiation of the special partnership with the EU was among the matters discussed. Later that day, Rebelo de Sousa gave a speech in the National Assembly, where he praised the archipelago's democracy as an example in the African context. On the third day, in São Vicente, Rebelo de Sousa addressed the local Municipal Assembly and met with students and lecturers at the University of Cabo Verde

(Uni-CV). On 22–27 November, President Fonseca made a reciprocal visit to Portugal to further strengthen bilateral relations. Fonseca was received by his counterpart Rebelo de Sousa, visited the headquarters of the CPLP and had lunch with Prime Minister António Costa. In addition, he was received by the Portuguese parliament and met with businesspeople in Porto. He was also awarded an honorary doctorate by Lisbon University.

On 10 May, José Manuel Pinto Teixeira, the EU representative in Cabo Verde, announced that, in addition to the € 55 m national financial programme for 2016–20, the country would for the first time receive $ 10 m from EU Regional Funds for ECOWAS countries to finance energy, competitiveness and transport projects. A project that received € 2 m in funding was the regional Centre for Renewable Energies and Industrial Maintenance (CERMI), implemented in partnership with Luxembourg's development agency.

On 10 July, Foreign Minister Tavares was in Brussels to present his country's *proposal for an extension of the Special Partnership with the EU* signed in 2007. The EU approved the proposal, which included the three new sectors of investment, growth and employment, ocean management and maritime economy, and institutional reforms. On the same day, President Fonseca held talks with the president of the European Council, Donald Tusk, and the following day was received by the president of the European Parliament, Martin Schulz, and the president of the European Commission, Jean-Claude Juncker.

On 19 June in Praia, Foreign Minister Tavares and Luxembourg's Minister of Cooperation and Humanitarian Action Romain Schneider signed two agreements worth € 48 m for cooperation projects as part of the IV Indicative Cooperation Programme (PIC) for 2016–20. The first project was intended to strengthen the management of renewable energy, while the objective of the second was to increase sanitary facilities in 100 schools. The principal areas of Luxembourg's PIC were employment and employability (€ 32 m), water and sanitation (€ 12.3 m) and renewable energy (€ 4.5 m).

On 24 September in Washington DC, Prime Minister Correia e Silva signed a new Status of Forces Agreement (SOFA) on *military cooperation with the United States* that enabled the presence of American troops in the archipelago. The SOFA allowed the two countries to strengthen security cooperation in several areas, including maritime security, combatting trafficking, and provision of humanitarian assistance. During his official visit to the United States, the prime minister visited the Massachusetts Military Academy, where he agreed to sign in 2018 an agreement on the training of marines and agents of the coast guard. In addition, he visited the US Naval Academy, the National Democratic Institute and Bridgewater State University, where he sought to strengthen the existing partnership with Uni-CV.

On 16 December, at the 52nd ECOWAS summit in Abuja (Nigeria), allegedly due to being $ 25 m in arrears with membership contributions, *Cabo Verde lost the election for the rotating presidency of the ECOWAS Commission* to Ivory Coast, although it was Cabo Verde's turn. Fonseca, who intervened six times in favour of his country at the summit, repudiated the election process and attributed the defeat to political arrangements. Foreign Minister Tavares described the decision as a defeat for ECOWAS, which had disrespected its own statutes. He argued that the debts had not been a justification, since other member states also owed contribution payments of up to $ 400 m.

Socioeconomic Developments

On 3 March, the *Binter Cabo Verde airline* inaugurated regular flights to Boa Vista, the fourth island after Sal, São Vicente and Santiago served by the Canary company. On 15 April, and 16 and 17 June, the domestic airline inaugurated regular flights to Fogo, Maio and São Nicolau, respectively. On 1 August, Binter received the monopoly on domestic flights when TACV ceased operating inter-island flights. At the same time, the government announced that by June 2018 it would acquire a 49% stake in Binter, of which 30% would be in the form of the commercial concession and 19% would be in return for a payment of $ 1.4 m. At a later stage, the state's shares would be made available for purchase by private investors. On 3 June, the Azorean airline SATA Internacional inaugurated a regular flight from Ponta Delgada via Praia to Boston. The new air connection was considered important both for the Cabo Verdean community in the United States and for the promotion of the country's tourism.

On 11 May, the government decided to *privatise the international operations of TACV*, which had accumulated debts of € 110 m. In the process, 260 employees, about half of the personnel, would lose their jobs. On 15 June and 25 July, respectively, the government authorised TACV to borrow $ 3.3 m and $ 2 m to meet urgent financial obligations. On 10 August, the government signed a one-year renewable management contract for TACV Internacional with Loftleidir Icelandic, a subsidiary of Icelandair. Loftleidir announced that it would operate from Amílcar Cabral International Airport in Sal and increase the TACV fleet to three aircraft immediately, to five by the end of 2018 and to 11 within three years. The government expected Loftleidir to develop Cabo Verde as an airport hub linking four continents. The government paid € 100,000 in the first month, and € 75,000 for every other month during the contract period to cover TACV's operational costs. The government expected to conclude the company's privatisation by 31 December 2018. In September, TACV cancelled its international flights due to engine damage in its only Boeing aircraft. Only some of the passengers were transferred to other airlines. From 29 September to 5 November, TACV rented two aircraft to transport international passengers. The aircraft damage caused losses of $ 2.5 m. On 12 October, the government authorised

TACV to take out another bank loan of $ 16.8 m. On 5 and 7 November, the first two Icelandair aircraft arrived in Praia to operate the TACV flights to the United States, Brazil and Portugal.

On 8 March, the central bank 'Banco de Cabo Verde' announced that the 'Caixa Económica de Cabo Verde' would absorb the assets of the dissolved Novo Banco. Finance Minister Olavo Correia declared that the *dissolution of Novo Banco* could cost the treasury a total of $ 20.2 m. Central bank governor João Serra reassured Novo Banco's 13,200 account holders that their deposits would be transferred in full to the Caixa Económica. Novo Banco had been created in 2010 by the government in partnership with the 'Banco Português de Gestão' with a stock capital of $ 3.4 m with the object of providing microcredits to combat poverty, but every year it generated financial losses, despite being recapitalised four times between 2012 and 2017. On 28 April, 34 of the 60 bank employees were dismissed, while the other 26 lost their jobs in May and June.

On 27 November, Prime Minister Correia e Silva declared in the National Assembly that the *2018 national budget* of $ 681.7 m was in line with the government's strategic sustainable development plan focusing on economic growth, connectivity, job creation and local and regional development. The budget increased government staff costs by 9% and the total salary bill by 7.6%. The average public sector salary was expected to rise by 2.5%, while the national minimum monthly salary was increased to CVE (escudo) 13,000 ($ 145). The public debt was expected to reach 132.2% of GDP. PAICV leader Hopffer Almada fiercely criticised the budget as one of postponed promises that would impoverish the country and increase social inequalities and regional asymmetries. On 12 December, the budget was approved with 34 votes of the MpD and 25 against, 22 from the PAICV and three from the UCID.

Tourism continued to expand. According to the annual hotel inventory for 2017, the country had 275 hotel establishments, 42 (18%) more than in 2016. Hotel accommodation capacity was 12,463 rooms and 20,421 beds, an increase of 9.0% and 11.1%, respectively. Santo Antão had 68 establishments (24.7% of the total), followed by Santiago with 50 hotels (18.2%), São Vicente with 45 (16.4%), Fogo with 32 (11.6%) and Sal with 31 (11.3%). In terms of numbers of beds, Sal had 48.2% of the total, followed by Boa Vista (27.6%), Santiago (9.9%) and São Vicente (5.5%). The sector employed 8,825 people, 14% more than in 2016. Over the year, Cabo Verde received 716,775 visitors, 72,246 (11.2%) more than in 2016. The main countries of origin were again the UK (23.6%), Germany (11.2%), Belgium/Netherlands and France (9.7% each), and Portugal (9.5%).

Côte d'Ivoire

Jesper Bjarnesen

Côte d'Ivoire continued its overall trend from recent years of impressive economic growth and relative political stability. Productivity in all major industrial sectors continued to rise; recent legislative elections and political reforms were consolidated; and additional initiatives to restructure and streamline the economy were taken. Despite these overall indications of an encouraging post-conflict recovery, 2017 began in tumultuous fashion, as military mutinies threatened to evolve into more widespread strikes and protests. These events unfolded while the country's first ever vice president was appointed, and a new government was announced. Although the protests of dissatisfied solders continued to cause concern through most of the year, the government was relatively successful in negotiations with the mutineers and retained a constructive dialogue with the disgruntled parties. In combination with declining cocoa prices, the military mutinies added pressure on the Ivorian authorities to implement much-needed security sector reform, in their efforts to lead the country towards the stated goal of becoming a middle-income country by 2020. At the same time, the election of Côte d'Ivoire to the UNSC was seen as a further confirmation of the country's international standing as having

 | DOI:10.1163/9789004367630_008

consolidated its post-conflict stabilisation internally, and directing its ambitions outwards, towards multi-national diplomatic as well as military collaboration.

Domestic Politics

Following the legislative elections held on 18 December 2016, the political year began with a series of new appointments to key government positions. On 10 January, President Alassane Ouattara named outgoing Prime Minister Daniel Kablan Duncan as the country's *first vice president*. Duncan had served as minister of finance when Alassane Ouattara was prime minister in the early 1990s, and had been appointed prime minister in 1993 when Ouattara resigned after losing a power struggle to Henri Konan Bedié following the death of the country's first president, Félix Houphouët-Boigny. Duncan had joined Ouattara's government as minister of foreign affairs in 2011, and been appointed prime minister in November 2012. All major political actors welcomed his appointment as vice president, in part because of his long and loyal service to the country and also because he was generally perceived not to be interested in running for president in the potentially highly competitive elections in 2020. The new post of vice president was set up under constitutional changes voted by referendum and approved in November 2016, along with the establishment of a second legislative chamber, the first ever *Ivorian Senate*, to which one-third of its 99 members are appointed directly by the president.

The task of replacing Duncan as prime minister was bestowed upon the former secretary-general to the president's office, and long-standing councillor to Alassane Outtara, Amadou Gon Coulibaly. Prime Minister Coulibaly announced his *new government* on 17 January, with only minor changes to the previous composition. Coulibaly was also assigned responsibility for the ministerial portfolio of the national budget on 19 July. Guillaume Soro, the former leader of the 'Forces Nouvelles' (FN) rebel movement, who had served as prime minister for five years until 2012, was re-elected speaker of parliament on 9 January.

In the days preceding these high-level political appointments, a series of *army mutinies* raised fears of a military coup or a return to armed conflict. On 6 January, armed soldiers broke into an armoury in the central town of Bouaké and took to the streets, shooting into the air, taking control of local police stations and setting up roadblocks, effectively shutting down most of the main entry points into the city centre. Within a day, mutinies had spread to Abidjan, Korhogo and several smaller towns across the country. In addition to concerns about a potential destabilisation of the country, there was also speculation that the mutinies might be politically motivated, as the appointment of the new vice president and prime minister had yet to be announced. These initial fears were laid to rest when the demands of the soldiers were made public and primarily concerned payment of salaries and other financial compensations. It also became clear that the protesting soldiers were former rebel fighters from the 'Forces Armées des Forces Nouvelles' (FAFN). They had been integrated into the Ivorian armed forces following the 2010–11 post-electoral crisis but were demanding financial recompense as well as a clarification of their military ranks and improvements to their conditions of service. Many of these soldiers had been involved in similar mutinies in 2014.

The mutinies ended on 8 January, following a statement on national TV by President Ouattara in which he urged the soldiers to return to their barracks and promised to address their demands. Following a day of gunfire across Bouaké, the leaders of the mutiny accepted the government's conditions, which included the promise of a one-time remuneration of CFAfr 12 m, equivalent to approximately € 18,000, to be paid out to 8,400 former rebels in the armed forces in two instalments. In the aftermath of these negotiations, Ouattara relieved Chief of Staff General Soumaila Bakayoko, Senior Commander of the National Gendarmerie Gervais Kouassi and Director General of Police Bredou M'Bia of their duties.

On 18 January, the agreement between the government and the mutineers proved to have stirred resentment in other sections of the armed forces, as shots rang through several cities once more, this time from members of the *gendarmerie* (military police), blocking parts of the port authority in Abidjan and of the city centre of Bouaké, and taking to the streets in other parts of the country. The gendarmes were reacting to the initiation of payments of instalments of CFAfr 5 m (roughly € 7,500) to the mutinying soldiers on 17 January, and their protests added to the threats of a general strike by public officials, which had begun on 9 January, with claims for similar financial compensation for unpaid salaries. In the administrative capital of Yamoussoukrou, mutinying gendarmes were confronted by some of the soldiers behind the earlier mutiny, resulting in the deaths of at least two gendarmes. To appease the mutineers and public officials, the government promised to oversee all demands and prepare wide-reaching reforms.

On 8 February, a group of Ivorian Special Forces in the south-eastern town of Adiaké, which housed the army barracks of these elite units, took to the streets and fired into the air. These protests were widely seen to emulate the January mutinies, with the intention of attaining a similar deal of a one-off sum to compensate for unpaid salaries. Following talks with the army leadership, the mutinying Special Forces accepted a return to barracks, with a promise that the government would oversee a wide-ranging restructuring of the armed forces.

New mutinies erupted on 11 May in Bouaké, spreading to Abidjan, when some of the payments promised to the former rebels within the armed forces had failed to materialise. A new agreement was reached on 15 May, with a new promise that the equivalent of around € 11,000 would be paid to each soldier, but the agreement did not succeed in appeasing all parties in the mutinies. On 24 May, four people were killed in a confrontation between police officers and ex-combatants from the FAFN who were among the approximately 6,000 fighters that had not been integrated into the Ivorian armed forces, and who claimed similar financial compensation for their past services to Ouattara during the 2010–11 post-electoral crisis.

Although it was the outstanding payment of salaries and other aspects of the conditions of service that motivated the mutinies within the armed forces, the government's lack of control over certain factions within the army reflected a broader pattern of a *divided Ivorian polity* post-conflict. The mutinies exposed the underlying three-way split within the army between former FAFN combatants, soldiers loyal to Ouattara, and those loyal to former president Laurent Gbagbo, reflecting a broader pattern of political animosity that became clearer during the year. The new chief of staff, General Sekou Toure, articulated these divisions within the armed forces on 31 May, during a visit to the troops behind the January mutinies in Bouaké. Toure, appointed on 9 January after the initial mutinies, stated that reconciliation between these three factions within the armed forces was necessary for a genuine integration of the former FAFN fighters.

In terms of the underlying patterns of political animosity, speculation about growing *tensions between former rebel leader Guillaume Soro and the president* dominated national media throughout the year, with suggestions that the 2020 elections would see these two central characters in Ivorian politics become increasingly competitive. Although both Ouattara and Soro insisted that their collaboration was as strong as ever, their supporters exchanged accusations throughout the year. Soro's supporters accused the president of having pushed for constitutional reforms in order to exclude Soro from the presidential race. Ouattara was also accused of having purged the security forces and public authorities of known Soro sympathisers. Finally, many saw the arrest in mid-May of Soro's right hand man, Souleymane Kamagaté Koné, also known as 'Soul-to-Soul', as an indirect attack by the president on Soro. Koné was eventually charged with high treason, after a weapons cache was discovered in a villa belonging to him in Bouaké. In an open letter posted on Soro's website, Koné – who held the title of Chief of Protocol for the Speaker of Parliament – claimed that his arrest was planned by the president to get to Soro, and suggested that it was meant to prevent Soro from running for president in 2020.

Supporters of President Ouattara, as well as some external observers, estimated that Soro had staged the military mutinies as a show of force, demonstrating his control over former FAFN fighters within the armed forces. Such commentaries also emphasised that Soro's supporters extended to the former civilian branch of the FN, and that many former FN officials had been integrated into the 'Rassemblement des Républicains' (RDR), strengthening Soro further.

The building *tension within the ruling coalition*, the Rally of Houphouëtists for Democracy and Peace (RHDP), also included former president Henri Konan Bédié, whose party, the 'Parti Démocratique de la Côte d'Ivoire' (PDCI), had allegedly been promised the right to appoint the coalition's unified presidential candidate for the 2020 elections. The tensions within the RHDP also reflected the ongoing negotiations around Ouattara's proposal to transform the coalition into a unified party. The indications by the end of the year that the two main parties of the RHDP, Ouattara's RDR and Bédié's PDCI, would contest the 2018 senatorial elections individually, rather than as a unified coalition, suggested that the unification of the two was not on the immediate horizon.

In addition to the high-level political tussles and continuous mutinies, domestic politics continued to be challenged by localised clashes in the south-western cocoa producing regions, primarily due to disagreements over access to cultivable land. *Land-related conflicts* had plagued Côte d'Ivoire for decades, and had been central to the build-up of the armed conflict in the early 2000s. They were exacerbated by the persistent contractions within national land tenure legislation, as well as the deliberate exploitation of these tensions by political actors on local, regional and national levels. In mid-October, seven people were killed and several thousand fled their homes during clashes over a 9,000 ha cocoa plantation outside the western town of Guiglo in the Cavally region. The clashes only ended when the security forces intervened. This incident was the most violent of a series of confrontations in the same region.

On 28 March, the former first lady, *Simone Gbagbo* was acquitted of charges of war crimes and crimes against humanity at the Ivorian criminal trial court ('cour d'assises') in Abidjan, due to irregularities in the proceedings and lack of evidence. Although the ICC had indicted her following the 2010–11 post-electoral crisis, the Ivorian authorities had refused to transfer her to The Hague, where the trials of her husband, Laurent Gbagbo, and his close collaborator, Charles Blé Goudé, were still on-going at the end of the year.

The Ivorian Special Investigative and Examination Cell had indicted several high-ranking officers from the FAFN who had fought against the Gbagbo regime in 2010–11 but none of them appeared in court during the year. Indeed, on 26 January, some of the indicted officers received promotions, raising concerns that their cases would be unlikely to go to trial. The ICC continued its investigation into suspected crimes committed by pro-Ouattara forces but were still to issue arrest warrants at the end of the year. The lack of progress in the prosecution of crimes committed during the post-electoral crisis, particularly on the side of the forces loyal to Ouattara, continued to inspire fears among Gbagbo supporters and international observers alike of relative impunity and a lack of transitional justice under Ouattara's leadership.

Foreign Affairs

Despite concerns over the escalation of domestic instability, international confidence in the consolidation of peace remained strong. On 30 June, the UN Operation in Côte d'Ivoire (ONUCI) ended its mandate after a 13-year presence as the primary peacekeeping mission since the failed coup d'état in September 2002. Although the *dismantling of UNOCI* coincided with the upsurge of mutinies within the armed forces, leading some observers to raise concerns of renewed destabilisation in the absence of the UN peacekeepers, the departure confirmed the overall impression of a gradual normalisation of the country's post-conflict political landscape. The UNSC confirmed this assessment in a joint statement. Meanwhile, *French troops* remained in the country under the mandate of a permanent military base, charged with supporting the national consolidation of peace after the 2010–11 armed conflict, but also with a role in military operations in other parts of the continent, such as the anti-terror operations in the Sahel region.

In May, the Ivorian armed forces contributed 150 troops to the *peacekeeping and anti-terror operations* under the UN Multidimensional Integrated Stabilization Mission in Mali (MINUSMA), established by UNSC Resolution 2100 of 25 April 2013 to support the country's political stabilisation following the military coup of 21 March 2012. MINUSMA's forces totalled 11,267 in August, and Côte d'Ivoire's commitment may be seen as an intention to play a more significant regional diplomatic role. Some analysts suggested that investing in similar deployments could be part of a strategy to alleviate the divisions within the Ivorian armed forces and facilitate the envisioned security sector reforms by providing new challenges for restless soldiers and, potentially, professionalising the army further through its involvement in UN-lead peacekeeping operations.

On 2 June, the UN General Assembly elected Côte d'Ivoire as one of the non-permanent members of the *UNSC* for the 2018–19 two-year term, along with Equatorial Guinea, Kuwait, Peru and Poland. The coinciding of the end of the UNOCI mission with the election of Côte d'Ivoire to the UNSC was not lost on President Ouattara, who stated that the appointment marked a "new phase in our strategy of diplomatic repositioning".

Côte d'Ivoire's positive standing with international actors was further illustrated by Ouattara's warm reception by French President Emmanuel Macron in Paris on 31 August. Macron vowed to work to strengthen bilateral cooperation between *France* and Côte d'Ivoire, emphasising sustainable development, education and security as three key priorities for France. He also stated that the planned EU-AU summit in Abidjan in November would be an opportunity to strengthen the partnership between Africa and Europe, with a particular focus on the youth.

On 29–30 November, Ouattara hosted the high-profile *EU-AU summit*; the fifth triennial summit within the framework of the Joint Africa-EU Strategy, adopted at the inaugural summit in Lisbon in 2007. The theme of the Abidjan summit, 'Investing in Youth for Accelerated Inclusive Growth and Sustainable Development', was an ambitious agenda to invest in the future of the continent's youth, highlighting sustainable employment opportunities, echoing the forward-looking optimism that had characterised Emmanuel Macron's statements in Paris in August. In addition to a reaffirmation of the principles of the joint strategy, a new EU external investment plan for Africa was presented. The plan's primary goal was to "trigger € 44 billion investments in Africa by 2020, thereby creating new job opportunities for young people across the African continent". A more specific roadmap for achieving this goal was not achieved.

The *Mediterranean migration crisis* continued to dominate EU-AU relations, as it had consistently in the aftermath of the 2014 European refugee crisis. Ivorian nationals had been amongst the casualties and detainees for several years and more than 13,000 Ivorian migrants arrived on EU territory by sea during the year. At the same time, the majority of Ivorian migrants continued to move to countries within West Africa, such as Ghana, Senegal and – increasingly – Burkina Faso, or to travel by air to destinations further afield, primarily the US and Europe but in increasing numbers towards the Middle East, China and Australia.

Socioeconomic Developments

Côte d'Ivoire continued its impressive economic performance of 2016, when the IMF classed it as the fastest growing economy. The estimated *GDP growth* rate for 2017 was 7.6%, which continued the trend of a slight decline over the past five years but still represented one of the ten fastest growing economies worldwide. This continued growth was credited in large part to the fiscal and monetary policies of the administration, coupled with on-going reforms designed to improve conditions for the private sector and facilitate mutually beneficial collaboration between public and private actors. Despite this positive outlook overall, both structural and short-term factors raised concerns that the Ivorian economy could face tougher times ahead. Most fundamentally, inequality indexes continued to rank Côte d'Ivoire among the least inclusive economies worldwide, with a Human Development Index ranking of 171 out of 188, and the same negative ranking in the *gender inequality* index. The persistent lack of gender equality prompted the World Bank to focus its fifth report on the Ivorian economy on this theme, with the alluring subtitle, 'How Côte d'Ivoire could make at least 6 billion dollars'.

In the expanding *energy sector*, average crude oil output was estimated at 54,000 b/d, representing an increase of 8% from an average of 50,000 b/d in 2016, while average gas production slowed significantly during the year. Productivity within Côte d'Ivoire's main agricultural sectors was encouraging. *Cotton* production increased slightly in the 2016–17 growing season, by 5.7%, from 310,177 tonnes in 2015–16 to 328,090 tonnes, as reported by the chairman of the 'Conseil du Coton et de l'Anacarde' (CCA), Mamadou Bamba. Cotton production generated approximately CFAfr 87 bn (or € 133 m) in revenue, which, due to a more favourable bargaining price, represented an increase of more than 12% from CFAfr 77.2 bn (€ 116 m) during the 2015–16 growing season. The outlook for the sector remained positive, as a public support fund worth CFAfr 21 bn (€ 32 m) was established to weather unforeseen crises during the growing season. CCA Director-General Adama Coulibaly stated that this support fund would assist the cotton-producing sector in becoming self-reliant and independent of government subsidies. As an illustration of the optimism surrounding cotton production, Bamba estimated that production would reach its pre-war levels of 400,000 tonnes within the next two growing seasons.

In terms of productivity, even the Ivorian *cocoa production* showed positive signs, as the world's largest producer increased its harvest by 28.5% to a record 2.15 m tonnes for the 2016–17 growing season. However, the continued reliance on cocoa production as the cornerstone of the economy had proven historically to expose the Ivorian economy to the fluctuations of the global market, risking not only drops in immediate revenue but also the secondary effects of increased smuggling of cocoa beans to neighbouring Ghana, where state subsidies ensured price stability for its producers, leading in turn to a fall in Ivorian revenues. These dynamics threatened to hit the Ivorian economy once more in 2017, as prices dropped from around $ 3,000 per tonne in August 2016 to around $ 2,000 in March 2017; a reduction of approximately 40%. This dramatic fall led the Ivorian administration to cut its guaranteed price to cocoa farmers by 36% in April, which in turn – in addition to the economic consequences facing cocoa producers – led to concerns that as much as 20% of the crop, or approximately 400,000 tonnes, might be lost to smuggling. Specifically, the Ivorian regulating body for cocoa and coffee prices, the 'Conseil du Cafe-Cacao' (CCC) urged the administration in neighbouring Ghana to lower its prices to reduce the incentives to Ivorian producers to smuggle their crops across the border.

According to President Ouattara, the 40% drop in cocoa prices led to a net loss of CFAfr 150 bn, or roughly € 230 m, at a time where the military mutinies and strikes among public sector workers were creating uncertainty about continued productivity. The government's promises to remunerate an ever-increasing number of mutineers with one-off payments seemed to put additional pressure on the economy, with Ouattara eventually stating that this combination of challenges had put the government in "an impossible situation". In April, the government reduced its annual budget by 10% and in May, it announced a $ 1.1 bn *loss in export earnings*. Despite lowering prices, its stabilisation fund had diminished by CFAfr 300 bn (€ 46 m) as of October.

Ironically, these dramatic fluctuations occurred while the *International Cocoa Organization* was completing the transfer of its headquarters from London to Abidjan in a stated effort to bring the organisation closer to the realities of its largest producers. As the two leading producers on the global market, Côte d'Ivoire and its eastern neighbour, Ghana, account for two-thirds of the world market, and the sudden drop in cocoa prices led to intense activity between the CCC and its Ghanaian equivalent, Cocobod (Ghana Cocoa Board). President Nana Akufo-Addo of

Ghana was reluctant to go back on his electoral promise to ensure domestic cocoa prices, which would have provided a short-term measure to stem smuggling from Côte d'Ivoire to the more profitable Ghanaian market. However, the two parties seemed to be working towards a closer collaboration in order to impose sterner demands with regard to international terms of trade. During an official visit to Côte d'Ivoire in early May, Akufo-Addo insisted that a change was needed to the way the world's two most important cocoa producing countries had left their producers in the hands of investors outside the continent.

On 16 October, Ouattara returned the courtesy with a two-day official visit to Accra (Ghana), when the two presidents confirmed their commitment to finding solutions resistant to the volatility of the cocoa producing sector, citing two avenues for structural reform. First, there was talk throughout the latter half of the year of revitalising a long-standing idea of establishing a cocoa sector equivalent to the crude oil sector's OPEC; in other words, an association of the world's primary cocoa producers intended to give them a more decisive role in determining the global terms of trade. Second, the intentions of both leaders with regard to investing more in domestic processing industries primarily focussed on producing cocoa paste and butter. The meeting was also seen as a diplomatic gesture in response to the verdict of the International Tribunal for the Law of the Sea, which had ruled in favour of Ghana on 24 September in a case regarding rights to offshore *crude oil extraction*. Following the verdict, both parties were unequivocal in their stated commitment to respect its findings and continue to strengthen the partnership between the two countries.

By the end of the year, immense challenges were still towering over the Ivorian authorities. Nevertheless, there was *reason for optimism* on account of a number of positive development indicators in Côte d'Ivoire's macro-economic performance. The new National Development Plan (NDP) adopted for 2016–20 envisioned the ascension of Côte d'Ivoire to the status of a middle-income country by 2020 by consolidating its economic growth and sectorial reforms, and by reducing the poverty rate significantly. Added to these were the determined efforts of the Ivorian authorities to handle crises relating to the military mutinies, and the country's cordial relationship with some key members of the international community including the Bretton Woods institutions. In April 2016, donors had pledged $ 15.4 bn in grants and loans to support the NDP. The World Bank Group committed to doubling its support over the next four years to approximately $ 5 bn. These commitments provided the Ivorian economy with some measure of counter-balance to the troubling developments in 2017.

The Gambia

Alice Bellagamba

The Gambia entered 2017 amidst uncertainties that overshadowed the political landscape following the 2016 elections. A week after the out-going President Yahya Jammeh had accepted the results and conceded defeat to President-elect Adama Barrow, he reneged on his concession, citing electoral irregularities. Jammeh was adamant, despite the condemnation of his actions by members of the international community and threats by ECOWAS that they would use all necessary means to enforce the mandate of the Gambian voters. This political deadlock put the country on the brink of generalised violence, resulting in massive population displacement, with 50,000 people estimated to have crossed into neighbouring Senegal. Diplomatic interventions, essentially by ECOWAS, which also deployed its regional forces to the Gambia, and the support of the AU and the UN helped calm the emerging political the crisis, and on 19 January Jammeh fled the country, making way for the new government.

 | DOI:10.1163/9789004367630_009

Domestic Politics

On 1 December 2016, the election of Adama Barrow had ended the 22-year tyrannical rule of President Yahya Jammeh. The election was the first *peaceful transfer of political power* in the country since Independence over 50 years before. As the official presidential inauguration day drew closer, there was increased tension in the country because of the rejection of the election result by Jammeh and his party in January. Several diplomatic negations were on-going at various levels. The diplomatic interventions by the ECOWAS were the most visible, among other efforts to ensure peaceful transfer of power. The ECOWAS intervention was led by President Muhammed Buhari of Nigeria. As these processes continued, President-elect Barrow left the country to attend a regional summit in Bamako (Mali) and later flew to neighbouring Senegal. He was subsequently sworn into office in Dakar on 19 January by the president of the Gambia Bar Association, while ex-president Jammeh was still in state house negotiating the terms of his departure. During this critical period, security matters were in the hands of the Gambian security forces, although ECOWAS member states were monitoring developments and troops from a number of member states that were on alert ready to be deployed to the Gambia.

After weeks of intense diplomatic mediation, civil society lobbying and resignations of high government officials, 21 January turned out to be the decisive day. As forces of the *ECOWAS Mission in Gambia* (*ECOMIG*) advanced towards the Gambian border, Jammeh and a sizable entourage of family members and a few loyalists were escorted by Gambian security forces to Dumdum Airport, where he boarded a plane and left the country for an undisclosed destination. Gambians were to discover later that he had fled to *Equatorial Guinea*, where he was granted political asylum.

President Barrow returned home to form a *coalition government* with a cabinet that comprised members of the six political parties that had formed the opposition coalition: the United Democratic Party (UDP), the National Reconciliation Party (NRP), the Gambia Moral Congress, the People's Democratic Organization for Independence and Socialism (PDOIS), the People's Progressive Party (PPP) and the Gambia Party for Democracy and Progress. To the surprise of many, the PDOIS voluntarily opted not to take any cabinet positions. Fatoumatta Jallow Tambajang, a political activist and staunch critic of the Jammeh administration, was appointed as the vice president and minister for women's affairs. All regional governors appointed by Jammeh's Alliance for Patriotic Reorientation and Construction (APRC) government were replaced. Cases of sabotage and political infighting were reported that might have undermined the effectiveness of the coalition government but, unlike the Jammeh government, known for constant cabinet shuffles, the new administration seemed committed to ensuring stability in public services. The only major *cabinet reshuffle* came on 10 November, when Minister of the Interior

Mai Ahmad Fatty was relieved of his appointment. The government gave no reason for this dismissal.

Jammeh was reported to have stolen about $ 11 m from the state coffers. This and other related cases of *corruption* prompted the new government to launch a Commission of Inquiry to investigate the financial activities of the former president, his associates and family members. In addition, the government launched investigations into the death of Solo Sanding (a leading member of the UDP who had been tortured to death in April 2016) and other cases of extra-judicial killing, enforced disappearance and state-organised torture by the Jammeh administration. In some cases, the investigation involved exhuming bodies from secret graves, mostly in rural areas including some villages in the Western Region. Some security personnel, intelligence officers and members of Jammeh's dreaded hit squad, popularly known as the 'Jungulars', were arrested in connection with various incidents of state violence. In March, Barrow's government announced the establishment of a *truth commission* to investigate abuses allegedly committed by the Jammeh administration.

Parliamentary elections took place in April, and were deemed peaceful and transparent. The UDP won 31 of the 53 seats in parliament; the APRC won five seats; the NRP five; Gambia Democratic Congress five; PDOIS four; the PPP two; and one seat was won by an independent candidate. *Landmark legislation* included the Constitutional Review Commission Act 2017, passed on 11 December; the National Human Rights Commission Act 2017, passed on 13 December; the Truth, Reconciliation and Reparations Commission Act 2017, passed on 13 December and the 1997 Constitution (Amendment) Act 2017, passed on 29 February.

Political stability remained fragile. On 2 June, loyalists of the ousted president clashed with ECOMIG forces in Kanilai – Jammeh's home village. One person was killed, six seriously wounded and a dozen more culprits were detained. Generally, the presence of ECOMIG forces ensured relative peace and stability. In June, the military mission of the 500 ECOMIG troops was extended by another year to support security sector reform and training.

There was a notable departure from the practices associated with the previous regime, particularly in the *relationship between state and religion*. The new administration reversed the name of the country from the Islamic Republic of the Gambia back to its secular name – Republic of the Gambia. President Barrow maintained a cordial and impartial relationship with the religious institutions and leaders. The Supreme Islamic Council became less vocal and political than it had been during the Jammeh era. Barrow appointed an independent advisor on all religious matters, ensuring the separation of state and religion and reducing the influence and function of imams and clergy in mosques and pulpits. This was a key change from past years, when religion and the imams were used as instruments of political power and manipulation. The Barrow administration also declared religious tolerance, which was welcomed by religious minorities such as the Ahmadiyya Muslim sect, which had had a fractious relationship with the previous regime and the Supreme Islamic Council.

Foreign Relations

The government of former president Jammeh had had shaky diplomatic relations with many countries including neighbouring *Senegal*, which often led to border closures. With the coming of a new administration, Barrow promised to improve the country's international relations, and he and his counterpart President Macky Sall of Senegal met in March and expressed the urgent need to forge closer diplomatic ties and strengthen bilateral cooperation. The two countries, which share deep cultural and religious ties, signed a number of agreements to support reciprocal economic growth. This improved cooperation was notable in the areas of security, electricity supply and the construction of the *Trans-Gambia Bridge* across the River Gambia to facilitate commerce between the two countries.

The president also announced plans to overturn Jammeh's unilateral decision to withdraw the country from the *Commonwealth* and the *ICC*. The Gambia's disregard for human rights and the rule of law had severely strained its relations within the regional and wider international community under the Jammeh administration. The country had suffered a host of *diplomatic penalties*, including losing benefits from AGOA in 2015, the imposition of a US travel ban on the Gambia government in 2016 and the withholding of EU development funds. Progress made by the new government in strengthening the rule of law and promoting human rights and political participation significantly improved the country's diplomatic isolation and led to an increase in aid inflows.

In February, the EU pledged to provide € 75 m ($ 80 m) in *development assistance* to the new government. The African Export-Import Bank also committed $ 500 m for projects in tourism, infrastructure and agriculture. In June, the IMF approved the disbursement of $ 16.1 m in financial assistance under a rapid credit facility. The 2016 US travel restrictions imposed on government officials, key businessmen and their families were lifted following the government's decision to issue passports to some 2,000 Gambians living in the US awaiting deportation. In a similar vein, in December, the Gambia was readmitted by President Donald Trump to the AGOA trade programme, giving it duty-free access and investment opportunities in US markets. Building on the 2016 Global Magnitsky Human Rights Accountability Act, an Executive Order signed by Trump in December provided for the US Treasury to announce a global freeze order on Jammeh's assets, and other international investments related to the exiled dictator.

In August, an agreement on establishing a consultation mechanism between the Ministry of Foreign Affairs of the People's Republic of *China* and the Gambia's

Ministry of Foreign Affairs, International Cooperation and Gambians Abroad was signed by the two foreign ministers at a ceremony held at the office of the Chinese Foreign Ministry in Beijing. During his visit, Foreign Minister Darboe and the Chinese Minister of Commerce Qian Keming also signed an agreement for RMB (renminbi) 82.85 m ($ 12 m) of debt relief. China also gave a *grant* of RMB 300 m for the construction of an International Conference Centre in the Gambia.

Socioeconomic Developments

Jammeh's refusal to step down impacted significantly on the *tourism* sector. Throughout the period of the elections and up to his eventual exit, the country was considered insecure. Tourist occupancy rates in all Gambian hotels dropped significantly and most hotels and restaurants were operating at below capacity. The hospitality industry recorded a remarkable revenue loss estimated at over $ 200 m. The negative impact of the political impasse was also felt on the country's supply chain and all macro and micro levels of the economy. Cross-border trading at weekly open-air markets along urban and rural border villages experienced recession during the political deadlock through January. After the January crisis, however, the return to democratic rule boosted the tourism and hospitality industry and high tourist receipts led to full occupancy in local hotels.

According Minister of Finance and Economic Affairs Amadou Sanneh, January was a *challenging period*. The interest rate stood at 24% and inflation at 9%. Unemployment was very high and state-owned enterprises were in a critical situation. Sanneh announced the standing national debt to be in the sum of GMD (dalasi) 48.3 bn ($ 1.1 bn; about 100% of GDP in 2016) and international reserves to be about $ 27 m (just 0.7 months of import cover). The raised local food prices were attributed to growing foreign currency constraints and slow recovery from the 2015 Ebola crisis, which continued to hamper economic growth in the sub-region.

Drastic *reductions in government expenditure*, and a drop in domestic borrowing made possible by increased donor support, fiscal consolidation and the recent pick-up in domestic revenue, contributed to the decline in interest rates. The government announced a set of cutbacks especially in the government's fleet of vehicles. The Gambia's debt to GDP ratio fell to 112% from 120% in 2016. In the exchange rate market, the dalasi depreciated to an estimated annual average of GMD 46.1: $ 1.

The Ministry of Finance announced a government reduction in the price of *petrol, diesel and kerosene* at the pump. The new price for petrol was set at GMD 47.00 per litre, diesel at GMD 46.00 and kerosene at GMD 40.00, down from GMD 50, GMD 47.27 and GMD 43, respectively. The Ministry of Finance urged oil marketing companies to abide by the new prices, and the minister promised that he would continue to monitor developments in the global oil market and make appropriate adjustments when necessary. The drop in the prices of petroleum products also prompted the Ministry of Transport, Works and Infrastructure to release a statement announcing a new tariff, reducing fares on passenger vehicles across all destinations.

Barrow's administration planned to focus on strengthening agricultural productivity, improving the energy sector, reducing unemployment and increasing capacity development and wages for civil servants. Investor confidence drew *investment* interest and inflows into the country faster than expected, as was evidenced in clearance delays at the *Banjul Sea Port*. China proposed to the government a € 140 m ($ 160 m) plan to redevelop and increase the capacity of the port. It was estimated that the upgrade would take about three months to complete. There were also discussions in the mineral sector regarding *oil* exploration and drilling. Government sources confirmed that talks with Oslo-listed African Petroleum over an extension of the firm's oil exploration rights in the Gambia ended with no deal reached.

Ghana

Jennifer C. Boylan

With the election of Nana Addo Dankwa Akufo-Addo as President of Ghana in the December 2016 elections, the New Patriotic Party (NPP) was back in power for the first time in eight years. The transition from National Democratic Congress (NDC) to NPP rule dominated the political scene. From taking control of national and district offices to rolling out the new administration's social and economic platforms, 2017 was a year of major overhauls. These restructuring efforts decreased Ghana's debt, generated economic growth and created jobs. The year also saw several controversies surface, including national issues involving the Delta Force vigilante group, the Ministry of Finance, and the Electoral Commission (EC). The extent to which Ghana's economic growth was felt by everyday Ghanaians was also of concern, particularly given the increases in the price of petrol throughout the year.

Domestic Politics

Nana Akufo-Addo was sworn into office on 7 January as the fifth president of Ghana's Fourth Republic. The inauguration was attended by *influential African leaders*

 | DOI:10.1163/9789004367630_010

including Nigeria's Muhammadu Buhari, Côte d'Ivoire's Alassane Dramane Ouattara, Liberia's Ellen Johnson Sirleaf, and Ethiopia's Prime Minister Hailemariam Desalegn. The new NPP government had its work cut out, given the abundance of campaign promises made in 2016, including turning the economy around, building a new factory in each of the 216 districts, $ 1 m development funding in each of the 275 constituencies, free senior high school (SHS) education across the country, and a dam in every village. The *governance tasks* were divided so that Vice President Mahamudu Bawumia and Minister of Finance Ken Ofori-Atta would focus on economic strategy and financial reforms, while President Akufo-Addo would focus on judicial reforms, foreign policy and education.

On 4 January, the then President John Mahama helped kick off an initially smooth political transition to the NPP by inviting the new administration to tour Flagstaff House. Just after Akufo-Addo was sworn-in as president, however, *NPP-affiliated vigilante groups* (including Invisible Forces, Delta Force, etc.) began forceful takeovers of state assets and public facilities, including the administration of school feeding programmes, toll booths, pay-to-use public toilets, and even sensitive government offices including the passport office, Tema Port and Harbour, and National Disaster Management Organization (NADMO) and National Health Insurance Scheme (NHIS) offices. The NPP's reaction was mixed; while some leading members condemned the takeovers, and encouraged police to prosecute the perpetrators, others defended the seizures and pointed out that they were meant to protect state institutions and state resources.

To be sure, there were numerous reports of items missing from government offices, including Flagstaff House, which were presumed to have been taken by members of the former administration. Missing items were such a problem that an *official task force* composed of officials from various government agencies was formed to investigate these issues. However, when news came out that 208 *luxury vehicles* were missing from the state house and that Akufo-Addo was having to use his own personal vehicle for transport, the takeovers escalated and armed 'macho men' began confiscating suspected government cars from the residences of former government officials. One of the most brazen of these attempts, reported on 1 February, occurred when 15 armed security personnel, dressed in military uniforms and accompanied by Driver and Vehicle Licensing Authority personnel, stormed the private residence of NDC National Organiser Kofi Adams and took custody of five luxury vehicles incorrectly believed to be state-owned.

Civil society groups issued statements denouncing the unlawful behaviour in general, and Akufo-Addo's State of the Nation address on 21 February condemned the *lawlessness*. In that speech, the president also claimed to have instructed the inspector general of police to apply the law irrespective of perpetrators' political affiliations.

Then, on 24 March, dozens of members of the NPP-affiliated Delta Force group arrived at the office of newly appointed Ashanti Region Security Coordinator

George Adjei. The crowd pulled Adjei from his office, caused significant property damage and physically assaulted him in a disagreement about the appointment. The perpetrators turned themselves in to police on 27 March. Twenty of them were arrested, but seven were discharged for lack of evidence. On 31 March, Akufo-Addo visited the Ashanti Region as part of his national 'Thank You Tour', and met with the Asantehene and other political leaders, again emphasising that lawlessness would not be tolerated.

Dramatically, on 6 April, the 13 charged suspects were in court when a group of 'macho men' stormed the court, overwhelmed security and freed the suspects. The news horrified the nation and drew strong condemnation from *civil society groups* and the UN. When the suspects again turned themselves in, they avoided jail sentences and were given lenient fines in a 17 October ruling, causing further dismay. The Center for Democratic Development (CDD-Ghana), a civil society group, issued a statement on 24 October highlighting that the case fostered distrust in the justice system by indicating "that incumbent party members and affiliates who break the law ... [will] not face the full rigors of the law".

Other than these issues with vigilante group violence, the transition to NPP governance was smooth. Akufo-Addo acted swiftly to install the new government in order, as he claimed, to speedily attend to the ailing economy. The team of ministers and deputy ministers were selected and quickly approved with the help of the NPP's *75-seat majority* in parliament after the 2016 elections. Despite profuse promises to protect the public purse, however, Akufo-Addo also nearly doubled the number of ministerial appointments. With a total of *110 appointed ministers* distributed between 36 ministries (including six new ministries), Akufo-Addo's government became the largest and the most expensive in Ghanaian history.

At the district level, the appointment of metropolitan, municipal and district chief executives (DCEs) was controversial, and sometimes violent, as usual. Akufo-Addo had made campaign promises about introducing elections for DCEs, but this was not implemented ahead of his own 2017 nominations. One mechanism that did further complicate the typically turbulent DCE appointment process was that Akufo-Addo had also promised that 30% of his appointees would be women. Given a sparsity of female candidates, districts felt in some cases that the nominated person was imposed on them in cases where the candidate was not well-known locally as compared with other grassroots candidates. In the end, 36 of the 212 nominated persons were women (~17%), as compared with 19 (or 9%) female DCEs in the previous NDC administration.

Akufo-Addo had also pledged to appoint women to 30% of state jobs. The most prominent female appointee was arguably Gloria Akuffo, who became attorney-general. The 2016 election had seen 36 women elected to parliament, or 13.1% of total seats, as compared with 30 (11%) elected women MPs in 2012. This increase made Ghana 138th out of 192 countries worldwide in terms of female representation. A February report released by the National Media Commission showed that media coverage of women candidates in the 2016 elections had been low compared with their male counterparts.

As for the principal political opposition, early in the year, the NDC was still recovering from its 2016 election losses. A *13-person committee* was assembled to assess why the NDC had lost, and they toured the country to engage with different communities, often encountering less-than-happy crowds of supporters when they arrived. The NDC also began something of a constituency-level house-cleaning exercise, given reports from around the country of NDC executives who had been either suspended or otherwise reprimanded for being 'rebellious' against the party (which often meant they had backed an independent MP candidate who lost in 2016).

Nationally, the former NDC administration faced heavy criticism for failing to account for GH¢ (cedi) 7 bn it had spent while in office, as well as for a $ 14 m uncompleted vice presidential state house in the Cantonments neighbourhood. With regard to the house, the NDC claimed the original price was $ 5.9 m, but that the contractor had overrun the amount. Still, this *unaccounted expenditure* was money spent in excess of the GH¢ 43 bn approved in the 2016 Appropriation Act and, because Ghana was in the last year of a three-year Extended Credit Facility (ECF), there was great concern that the IMF would impose a fine, as it had on the Kufuor administration in 2001 for missteps by the former J.J. Rawlings government. Ultimately, the IMF did not issue any fines, though the overspending prompted a February visit from IMF officials to assess the damage.

Other political developments related to campaign promises included first steps toward creating new regions, enacting a free SHS policy, carrying out of a digitisation campaign, and implementing the Representation of the People's Amendment Law (ROPAL), passed in 2006. First, a nine-member Commission of Inquiry was created to consider six petitions for *new regions* that had been received: two from the Northern Region, two from Brong Ahafo, one from Western, and one from Volta. Chaired by retired Supreme Court Justice Stephen Alan Brobbey, the Commission held its first hearings in November at Osu Castle, Accra.

The long-awaited *free SHS policy* was enacted but only included first-year students in the initial stage. The policy would follow this and subsequent class years through to graduation. The fact that this staggered enrolment process was not initially made public caused some distress, particularly for families with children already enrolled in secondary school. Also of concern was that the government did not announce specific plans to handle increased enrolment, particularly with regard to school infrastructure, teacher-to-student ratios, and ensuring that quality learning outcomes remained high. Finally, even the inclusion of first-year students alone stretched the national budget to the limit, sparking questions about the feasibility of further extensions of the programme.

As part of the NPP administration's goal of formalising the economy and reducing the cost of business, *digital systems* were introduced for a wide variety of government services. This included the implementation of an e-business registration system, a digital port clearance system, a street address system accessible through an app, a mobile interoperability system, national ID cards, and an online passport application system that utilised biometric data. Sub-national governments were also encouraged to make use of digital processes. On 7 November, for instance, the Accra Metropolitan Assembly began a digital process of re-valuing all the properties within the capital in the hope of increasing tax revenues.

Though passed in 2006, *ROPAL*, which would allow Ghanaians living abroad to vote in national elections, had never been implemented. Akufo-Addo had made campaign promises to enforce this law and, while on an official trip to Togo in May, Akufo-Addo revealed that his government would begin talks on implementation with the EC. On 5 July, Akufo-Addo reaffirmed this commitment at the Diaspora Homecoming Summit held in Accra.

The transition to NPP rule was affected by some lingering issues from the previous administration. First, though the 2016 election results were largely accepted, on 4 January, the NPP alleged irregularities and challenged the results in three constituencies: Asuanfo South, Banda and Pru West. Next, in August, reports surfaced about questionable contracts that the Ministry of Local Government and Rural Development had signed with the Jospong Group. In this case, a four-month single-sourced GH¢ 98 m contract had been signed with the conglomerate company to carry out fumigation, although Zoomlion Ghana Ltd already had a contract for this work. An investigation commenced toward the end of the year. Third, *allegations of illegal behaviour* were aimed at EC Chairperson Charlotte Osei via a July petition compiled by staff members and sent to Akufo-Addo. Numerous charges of supposed single-handed cancelling and awarding of contracts and money missing from the EC's endowment fund resulted in the formation of a corruption investigation committee, which summoned Osei and her two deputy chairpersons, Amadu Sulley and Georgina Amankwa, to appear. The committee was to begin sitting in January 2018.

Turning to the newly-installed NPP administration, a controversy arose from the April purchase of a $ 2.25 bn government domestic bond by a company with ties to prominent government officials. The claim was that Franklin Templeton Investment Ltd, a US-based investment firm, had colluded with the government, and particularly the Finance Ministry, to secure the purchase of 95% of the bond in the largest single-day bond sale ever by an SSA country. The matter was taken up by Ghana's Commission on Human Right and Administrative Justice, the enforcement division of the US Security and Exchange Commission, and by Luxembourg's 'Commission de Surveillance de Secteur Financier'. The investigations continued through the end of the year.

On 2 November, the Colleges of Education Teachers Association of Ghana (CETAG) went on strike because of salary arrears owed to them since October 2016. CETAG appealed to the National Labor Commission, which came back with a

4 October ruling that the teachers were to be paid within two weeks. This deadline was not met and the 38 public colleges of education in Ghana were closed for three weeks. The strike was called off following assurances that the government would pay the arrears by April 2018.

Foreign Affairs

Akufo-Addo developed the use of a catchphrase, *'Ghana Beyond Aid'*, to describe the administration's new focus on industrialisation, trade and investment in place of reliance on foreign aid. In October, Vice President Bawumia gave a keynote address at a 'Ghana Beyond Aid'-themed forum organised by the Embassies of Denmark, Norway and the Netherlands, where it was announced that these countries would phase out their development aid to Ghana by the end of 2020.

The 'Beyond Aid' policy framework could fundamentally change Ghana's relationships with both foreign nations and international agencies. Exemplifying the potential for change, during French President Emmanuel Macron's visit to Accra on 30 November, Akufo-Addo gave an answer at a press conference in which he somewhat provocatively argued that Western aid to Africa was unsustainable and that Western preferences (he particularly emphasised the power of the individual 'French taxpayer') should not dictate policies in African nations. The video of the response went viral.

In defence of the 'Ghana Beyond Aid' strategies, the president and other officials also routinely stated that they would not turn away aid and that the approach was merely a strategy to get *beyond Ghana's aid dependency*. Indeed, Ghana continued to accept aid, including a one-year extension of the IMF's $ 918 m ECF, a $ 1.2 bn three-year deal with the World Bank's IDA in May, and development assistance from the EU, China, the US, and many European nations, among other aid sources. In February, the UK also announced that it would maintain its £ 130 m annual aid package after previously threatening to suspend it because of Ghana's *laws against homosexuality*. World Bank figures showed that Ghana had received an estimated $ 1.3 bn in ODA in 2016.

Related to the pursuit of trade over aid, on 4 January, Ghana became the 104th member of the WTO to ratify the *Trade Facilitation Agreement* (*TFA*). By 22 February, the necessary two-thirds WTO-member ratifications had been achieved. The TFA was designed to expedite trade and reduce trade costs for WTO members, with the greater portion of the benefits reportedly to be received by developing country members.

Regionally, Ghana's first involvement of the year with *ECOWAS* included former president John Mahama's involvement in failed efforts to persuade Gambian President Yahya Jammeh to step down from power. ECOWAS threatened military intervention to uphold the Gambian election results and Jammeh eventually resigned. In February, Ghana sent a nine-member delegation to the ECOWAS parliament meeting in Abuja (Nigeria), where Ghana was only allocated eight seats. The speaker of the parliament refused to swear in the *Ghanaian delegation*, resulting in an embarrassing gaffe for the nation. The former vice president of Sierra Leone, Alhaji Chief Sam-Sumana, took refuge in Ghana after being dismissed by Sierra Leone's president. Sam-Sumana reached out to former president J.J. Rawlings for help but, after a 28 November ECOWAS court ruling that his sacking was illegal, Sam-Sumana returned to Sierra Leone.

The Akufo-Addo administration also took strides to bring itself closer to two of its neighbours: *Togo and Côte d'Ivoire*. In early May, Akufo-Addo met with Togolese President Faure Gnassingbé on an official visit. The two leaders resolved to deepen bilateral ties in security and other sectors. They visited the unfinished joint border post at Noepe and Akanu, stressing the need to complete that project and the Sogakope-Lome drinking water supply project.

While a September maritime ruling in Ghana's favour against Côte d'Ivoire could have shaken the relationship between the two nations (discussed in Socioeconomic Developments below), Akufo-Addo and President Alassane Ouattara had been friends for years and had a mutual interest in working together to *stabilise the price of cocoa*. The two countries collectively produce 60% of the world supply and the two leaders announced they would build a joint-venture cocoa processing factory and curb cocoa prices using voluntary restrictions on production in a buffer stock plan colloquially nicknamed 'Chocpec'.

Outside of the West African region, two countries that featured prominently in Ghana's foreign affairs in 2017 were France and China. Akufo-Addo had spent almost two decades working at a law firm in *France* and his administration took obvious steps to bring itself closer to the French government and its former colonies in West Africa. In February, Air France commenced direct flights from Paris to Accra. In March, Akufo-Addo attended a sod-cutting ceremony for a new French embassy in Accra, where he thanked France for its security assistance and the implementation of development projects. During Akufo-Addo's two-day trip to Togo in early May, he criticised the inability of Ghanaians to speak and write French, and announced plans to make French language classes compulsory from elementary to secondary school. Finally, though some commented on the apparent discomfort of President Macron throughout Akufo-Addo's press conference rejoinder during Macron's one-day trip to Ghana in November, it was significant that he had opted to visit Ghana as one of three countries in his first tour of Africa (not including his trip to Mali in May).

Ghana's interest in deepening its relationship with France and its neighbours was also probably due to security concerns. Though Ghana did not face specific threats, the presence of jihadist groups in the Sahel, piracy in the Gulf of Guinea, and recent terrorist attacks in Côte d'Ivoire (in 2015 and 2016) and Burkina Faso (in 2017) made better *regional coordination* a priority for Ghana's foreign policy. A May rocket attack on a UN compound in Mali, where more than 100 Ghanaian soldiers were stationed, sent shock waves through the country until it was confirmed that no Ghanaian soldiers had been killed in the attack.

The relationship between Ghana and *China* took some interesting turns. As part of the government's campaign against illegal small-scale gold mining ('galamsey'), illegal Chinese miners were arrested in April. (See further below, under Socioeconomic Developments.) Chinese involvement in galamsey mining had long been a sensitive issue, particularly given large Chinese investments in Ghana. These arrests, and resulting media stories about China, including a series of popular cartoons by Bright Tetteh Ackwerh, prompted Chinese officials to call on the government to stop distorted media representations of the Chinese and warned that the arrests could damage the countries' bilateral relations. Ghana's information minister dismissed the 'China threat' in a public interview, which suggested a shift in the government's approach. But then in May, China offered to pay $ 10 m to help begin Ghana's Multilateral Mining Integrated Project (MMIP) programme to provide illegal small-scale miners with alternative livelihoods in the mining industry.

Socioeconomic Developments

The NPP administration promised an overhaul of the economy and *national-level financial indicators* certainly improved. Despite Ghana having had the fastest growing economy of the year in 2011, GDP growth rates had been as low as 3.9% in 2015 and 3.3% in 2016, the lowest growth rate since 1990. Estimates put 2017 GDP growth at 7.9% by the end of the year, greatly aided by industry sector growth of 17.7%. The debt-to-GDP ratio had risen to as high as 73.4% in 2016, but fell to about 70% at the end of 2017, and was predicted to drop to 66.1% in 2018. The fiscal deficit grew to a whopping 9.5% at the beginning of the year, but was reduced to 5.6% by year's end and projected to drop to 4.5% in 2018.

Bank of Ghana (BoG) interjections into the economy also helped generate greater economic stability. The bank cut *interest rates* five times, from 25.5% to 20% by year's end, to boost consumer spending, increase business investments and encourage payments on otherwise non-performing loans, among other goals. The *inflation* rate slowed through the year from a high of 17.5% to a low of 11.8%, while the value of the cedi also began to stabilise.

The *mechanisms used to achieve this growth* included: addressing the debt in the energy sector; expansions in the energy sector, the oil industry and farming;

restructuring the debt; removing ghost names from government payroll; formalising the economy; and lowering the cost of doing business to foster foreign investment and start-up projects. Still, the extent to which this economic growth was felt by everyday Ghanaians was questionable, particularly since an 11.8% interest rate was still very high and Ghanaians were also rocked by *fuel price increases* in 12 of the 24 pricing periods during the year. Reports also showed that migration from Ghana to Europe was high and increasing.

The BoG reported that over $ 2 bn (about GH¢ 8.7 bn) in *remittance payments* had been sent to the country in 2016, dwarfing the GH¢ 183 m collected by the Ghana Revenue Authority as tax revenue in that year. Yet Ghana was also one of the most expensive African countries to send remittances to, with charges at over 12%. This encouraged individuals to remit money in other ways, increasing the likelihood that the government was losing out on a crucial source of tax revenue. The government announced a plan to reduce remittance charges to 5% by 2020, with the help of a $ 2.6 m grant from the Swiss State Secretariat of Economic Affairs.

Akufo-Addo began the year by revealing the *energy sector*'s suffocating $ 2.4 bn debt in his 8 February state of the union address. This debt was both large and convoluted, with Ghana Gas owed $ 400 m by the Volta River Authority (VRA), the VRA owed millions by the Electricity Company of Ghana (ECG) and the ECG unable to pay its debt in part because of a GH¢ 1.5 bn debt owed to it by government ministries and agencies. On top of this debt, Ghana's underperforming thermal power plants and restrictions on hydropower generation imposed because of the need to conserve water, meant that Ghana continued to import electricity. Electricity provision did improve overall but, in early December, customers in Accra neighbourhoods nearly rioted after machine breakdowns left some without power for days.

On 2 March, Finance Minister Ofori-Atta told parliament that the Energy Sector Levy Act, passed in 2015, had brought in about GH¢ 100 m more revenue than expected in 2016, putting total revenue at GH¢ 3.3 bn. With consumer costs still high, however, on 4 April parliament passed an *Energy Sector Levies Amendment Bill* reducing the special petroleum tax by 2%, the national electrification scheme levy by 3%, and the public lighting levy by 2%. This reduction was expected to cost the government GH¢ 308 m in revenue.

To increase its power options, the NPP government ramped up a rapid *power sector expansion* in the hope of making existing supplies more reliable. Construction on the Bridge Power Project, the world's largest liquefied petroleum gas-fired power plant, began in Tema on 29 April. At 400 MW, the project would provide electricity equivalent to up to 17% of the country's current capacity. In August, Ghana secured a 15-year liquefied natural gas (LNG) deal with Equatorial Guinea, which also included the building and operation of an LNG regasification terminal in Takoradi. The government also offered attractive waivers to woo renewable energy independent power producers, in the hope of reducing the country's large debt burden from the importation of crude oil to power thermal plants. The Energy Commission likewise began a National Rooftop Solar Project to decrease costs for households wishing to switch to solar power. Ghana's renewable energy capacity stood at 1% throughout the year.

In April, the NPP administration also renegotiated the Ghana Power Compact deal signed in 2014 with US-based Millennium Challenge Corporation. Power Compact II was amended so that Ghana retained majority ownership (at 51%) and the potential for future layoffs was eliminated. The $ 498.2 m deal would contribute toward six projects, including $ 350 m to the ECG. Despite the new terms, the deal still contained a controversial Article 7.1 stipulation that the implementation of the agreement would not be subject to Ghanaian law.

With regard to Ghana's *primary exports*, gold prices somewhat improved during the year, global oil prices dropped in the first half of the year, but began to improve in the latter half, while cocoa prices dropped and remained low.

On 15 November, as *gold* prices improved, Newmont Africa began construction of the new Subika underground mine at its Ahafo operations, including plans to expand processing operations by more than 50%. The $ 300–380 m project was expected to produce 1.8 m ounces of gold over the next 11 years.

The three primary *petroleum* extraction sites in Ghana continued to be the Jubilee Field, the TEN Fields, and the Offshore Cape Three Points (OCTP) integrated oil and gas project. Production from the Jubilee Oil Field had been declining in recent years and was shut down during the second half of the year to allow for the completion of repair works on the floating production storage and offloading vessel after a fault developed in 2016. Production at the TEN oilfields had begun in October 2016, though at a reduced production rate. On 23 September, the International Tribunal of the Law of the Sea unanimously ruled that Ghana, and not Côte d'Ivoire, had the rights to the oil discovered in the TEN oil fields and production increased to 80,000 b/d after the ruling.

The Sankofa field, located within the OCTP project, began producing oil ahead of schedule in May, after UK Export Finance in January provided the last $ 310 m funding piece to GE Oil & Gas necessary for the project to fully develop. The terms of the Sankofa oil and gas deal, with 'Ente Nazionale Idrocarburi' (Italy) and Vital (Netherlands), were generally understood to be detrimental to Ghana's economic interests. The total private sector commitment for OCTP was $ 7.9 bn, the biggest investment in Ghanaian history. Overall, Ghana's state oil revenues more than doubled from $ 93.4 m by mid-2016 to $ 191.3 m by the first half of 2017.

The *smuggling of petroleum products* became an important issue, with the National Petroleum Authority estimating that smuggling was costing the nation GH¢ 850 m. The Association of Oil Marketing Companies warned that up to 4,000 workers could be laid off because of the profit loss.

A Ghanaian oil firm, Quantum Oil Terminals Ltd, opened a $ 41.3 m suit in the Accra High Court against both the World Bank's IFC and the OPEC Fund for a breach of contract related to an IFC loan. In May, a London High Court ruled against the case being heard in Ghana but, on 1 November, a Ghana Court of Appeal ruled that the proceedings in London would not stop the case in the Accra High Court. The case remained pending at year's end.

In May, the CEO of the Ghana Cocoa Board (COCOBOD) announced that about 33% of the country's *cocoa* trees were more than 30 years old, and thus unproductive, and that the government would begin destroying old trees, planting new trees and providing hybrid cocoa seedlings for free. The administration began biometrically registering cocoa farmers, introduced input subsidies on fertiliser and insecticides for cocoa farms, paid farmers higher prices for their cocoa, promised that COCOBOD scholarships to wards of cocoa farmers, and reintroduced mass spraying of insecticide. Measures were also promised to enable Ghana's 12 cocoa-processing companies to operate at full capacity. To help pay for these investments, Ghana borrowed $ 1.3 bn ahead of the October harvest, $ 500 m less than in 2016.

Another government initiative designed to help the cocoa industry was an energetic campaign to stamp out *galamsey* (illegal mining), which destroys farm land, causes soil erosion, and poisons water, among other detriments. With support from traditional leaders (the government doubled the monthly salary to chiefs and queen mothers), farmers, members of the Media Coalition (via a *#StopGalamsey-Now media campaign*), the Ghana Water Company and the Mineworkers Union, the Ministry of Lands and Natural Resources was tasked with ending galamsey. On 29 March, the minister issued a three-week ultimatum for illegal miners to halt their activities or face arrest. A GH¢ 100 m per year MMIP project was launched to enforce mining regulations and provide individuals with alternative livelihoods in the legal minor sector. Chief Justice Georgina Woode designated 14 courts to handle illegal mining cases, the issuing of small-scale mining licenses was suspended and a ban was placed on small-scale mining. OccupyGhana, a civil society pressure group, organised National Red Friday on 21 April to rally citizens against galamsey. A 28 November Afrobarometer Dispatch reported that 74% of Ghanaians "say no citizen should be permitted to engage in illegal small-scale mining for any reason", while 80% also believed that the government was responsible for providing illegal miners with alternative livelihoods.

The NPP government also sought to save money in two primary ways. First, it began to decrease the amount Ghana owed by *restructuring debt* (i.e. replacing more expensive loans with less expensive loans). Second, in April, it used a biometric verification database of government workers, as part of a broader digitisation plan, to delete 26,589 *'ghost workers'* from the government payroll. This would make an estimated saving of GH¢ 433 m per year. Partially in response to an overcrowded banking sector, the BoG also issued new banking regulations such that the minimum capital requirement for operation was increased from GH¢ 120 m to GH¢ 200 m. The BoG also put 15-year tenure limits on banks' CEOs, time limits on other positions, and size limits on banks' boards of directors.

A wide range of *development projects* were initiated. First, the Ministry of Food and Agriculture launched a five-year '*Planting for Food and Jobs*' programme in April focusing on maize, rice, soybean and sorghum. In its first year alone, the flagship programme created 745,000 jobs, especially in rural areas. The programme was supported by Canada ($ 150 m) and the US ($ 225 m). Second, the first phase of the *Takoradi Container Terminal*, an inland clearing depot to decongest Takoradi Harbour, located about 6 km from the harbour, began accepting containers in April. Total project costs were estimated at $ 65 m, with a $ 350 m second phase scheduled to begin in 2018. Third, a $ 21.5 bn *Railway Master Plan* was announced, involving 4,000 km of new track connecting Accra to the Upper East Region. Spearheaded by German-French Railway Consortium, construction on the first phase of the project, the Accra-Tema-Kumasi line, began in December.

On 28 June, Ghana signed a $ 10 bn *bauxite* project with China, which would include the construction of alumina refineries and railway infrastructure to transport the commodity. Ghana reportedly has 960 m tonnes of bauxite, which is refined into alumina and then smelted to become aluminium. A ten-year Ghana *Housing Redevelopment Plan* was announced under which the government would work with three private partners to provide 15,000 affordable homes with one to four bedrooms, costing between $ 30,000 and $100,000. The project was expected to create at least 18,720 direct and indirect jobs. However, the Parliamentary Select Committee on Works and Housing also found that the Ministry of Works and Housing already owed contractors GH¢ 1.3 bn.

On 15 November, construction work began on a $ 30 m cement factory, 90% financed by Iran. The remaining 10% would be financed by the Ghanaian government. Annual production would be about 600,000 tonnes of cement, sorely needed for the increased development. The Ghana Investment Promotion Center (GIPC) registered more than 49 new projects, worth more than $ 3 bn, in the first quarter of 2017 alone. Total FDI for 2017 stood at $ 4.9 bn, as compared with $ 2.4 bn in 2016 and $ 2.7 bn in 2015.

Start-up projects attracting major investment included a $ 4.8 m investment into LOGIQUE, a Ghana-based tech accelerator company working to modernise technology systems in Africa, the start of Ghana's first meal kit service for busy professionals, HomeCho, and over $ 11.6 m of investment in MPharma, an Accra-based start-up that manages prescription drug inventory for pharmacies and their suppliers in four African countries.

The first-ever *malaria vaccine* was announced, along with plans to roll out real-life trials in Ghana, Kenya and Malawi beginning in 2018. The vaccine had taken

30 years to develop, with funding from the Bill and Melinda Gates Foundation and the PATH Malaria Vaccine Initiative.

Despite Ghana being a safe and stable democratic nation, with no longstanding violent ethnic or religious conflicts, many Ghanaians continued to risk their lives to travel to Europe. The International Organization for Migration reported that 27% more Ghanaian *migrants* had landed in Italy by boat in 2016 than in 2015. Many migrants were reportedly from the Brong Ahafo Region, noted as the epicentre of Ghana's struggling poultry industry. In April, it was announced that Ghana accounted for the highest number of applications for the US 'green card lottery' system: 1.73 m Ghanaians, or roughly 7% of the Ghanaian population, had applied in 2015. On 28 November, a report in 'The Guardian' found no evidence that the widely-reported 'fake US embassy' operating in Accra had ever existed. Rather, the arrest of an individual issuing counterfeit US visas from his apartment may have given rise to the story.

Guinea

Anita Schroven

After economically challenging years, Guinea experienced economic consolidation as a result of FDI in bauxite mining. The population remained in dire conditions, which led to protests throughout the year and political tensions between trade unions, opposition parties and the government. Little progress was made to deal with high-profile human rights violations, and the impunity of security forces remained a major concern. President Condé earned recognition on the international level but became increasingly beleaguered during the year due to strikes, the delay in holding local elections and his refusal to comment on his succession.

Domestic Politics

The early months set the tone for the rest of the year. Between the end of January and 20 February, *students and teachers held demonstrations*, calling for better education, which halted all activity in this sector. The protests later expanded into a general strike across the country. On 13 February, the government responded by closing all schools for 12 days and installing road blocks in Conakry to prevent

 | DOI:10.1163/9789004367630_011

protesters from marching towards the seat of government in Kaloum. After a deal on improved working conditions and salaries had been struck between the government and the unions on 20 February, many teachers continued their protests, demanding more improvements, which lead to two more days of violence, leaving eight dead and many more injured in Conakry alone. Seven human rights activists attached to 'Voice of the People' were arrested for their participation in the protests, which were declared to be a "disturbance of public order".

In response to the strikes, President Alpha Condé undertook a *cabinet reshuffle* on 27 February. Former teacher and trade unionist Ibrahima Kalil Konaté replaced Ibrahima Kourouma as tertiary-level education minister. Minister for Civil Service Sékou Kourouma was replaced by his advisor Billy Nankouma Doumbouya and Environmental Minister Christine Sagno was replaced by Nafissatou Baldé. In November, a new *teachers' strike* began and continued till year's end, asking for better working conditions and increased salaries, which had not materialised after the February agreement. Strikers were determined to carry on their protests into the new year. Students joined in across the country to call for better learning conditions and for the government to meet the teachers' demands, so that schooling could finally continue. Armed confrontations with security forces left at least four students dead. These strikes and the broad popular support they received indicated the frustration with which Guineans were waiting for an improvement in living conditions and their frustration with the political elite in general.

At the end of January, the government postponed *local elections* (overdue since 2005) due in February without giving a new date, claiming that there was insufficient time for preparations. The opposition called for a national strike in February, alleging that the government was not respecting the internationally mediated joint electoral accord of October 2016. After *popular protests*, government and opposition parties agreed on the electoral code on 24 February and projected local elections for June. Opposition parties and civil society groups took to the streets in July, demanding the elections and accusing the government of mismanaging public resources. In August, opposition members were killed and some seriously injured when they protested for the elections to finally be scheduled. A new accord was struck between the main political parties under the leadership of personal councillor to the president, Tibou Kamara, a close personal friend of Cellou Dalein Diallo, the leader of the main opposition party, the 'Union des Forces Démocratiques de Guinée' (UFDG). On 25 September, the new election date was announced as 4 February 2018. Nevertheless, two days later the opposition held another rally to underline its lack of trust in the government's promises and to demand more accountability. A week later, two persons were killed in another round of protests, which resulted in more protest marches on 4 October, this time demanding that the police abandon the use of firearms during protest marches. The anniversary of the 2016 election accord on 12 October was again used by the opposition to highlight the government's shortcomings in implementing the election deal and respecting the rule of law.

In December, many *independent candidates* and electoral lists registered with the 342 local-council-level election committees, amongst them many young candidates with civil society or media backgrounds. This evolution surprised the established parties and made predictions of electoral outcomes more difficult. At the same time, these elections were seen as a measure of Condé's popularity and his chances for a third – unconstitutional – term. Speculation on the succession was already causing tensions within the ruling party, the 'Rassemblement du Peuple de Guinée'.

Ibrahima Kassory Fofana, long-time politician and former finance minister under Lansana Conté, had kept his position as state minister at the Presidency for investments and public-private partnerships, and was juggling for position as a potential successor to the president in 2020. Fofana's strongest rival, Ousmane Kaba, also a former finance minister, despite seeming too removed from the party base, had managed to reconcile with President Condé at the beginning of the year and was welcomed back into the party fold. Important voices, such as that of former minister Alpha Ibrahima Keira, General Director of Police Bangaly Kourouma and the governing party's national coordinator Nantou Chérif Konaté, called for a change in the Constitution to prolong Condé's presidency by a potential third term. Condé himself made no contribution to this debate, but his constant silence was taken as an implicit statement of interest in a third term, which was already in August stirring up public debates and raised tensions between Condé and the president of the Constitutional Court, Kéléfa Sall.

While Cellou Dalein Diallo of the UFDG had long been regarded as the unofficial leader of the *opposition*, his position became contested during the year. He seemed to lose control of the more extreme sections of his party's base and at the same time was seen to be weakened by the improved public performances of other opposition parties' leaders, especially businessman Mamadou Sylla of the 'Union Démocratique de Guinée', Faya Millimono of the 'Bloque Libéral' and former prime minister Lansana Kouyaté of the 'Partie de l'Espoir pour le Développement National'. Diallo continued to be beleaguered by court cases against him. In October, he and his wife did not appear in court to serve as witnesses in the case of the 2016 murder of journalist Koula Diallo.

Press freedom came under increasing government pressure, which impeded journalists' work and research and the free circulation of information. On 23 February, television journalist Hassan Sylla was charged with 'gross misconduct' and suspended for six months, supposedly for his involvement in the school strikes. Four journalists working for Gangan TV were arrested in October on charges of offending the head of state and spreading false rumours. When at least 18 journalists came to their support, they were attacked, mistreated and imprisoned without charge. Most of them were released by November, but charges of spreading false rumours were levelled against their leaders, indicating a stricter interpretation of libel laws and laws protecting the presidency at a time when criticism of his and his government's performance were voiced increasingly publicly. In July, journalist Alia Camara was suspended for criticising the performance of the country's school system. In the same vein, the private radio station Espace FM was closed down for one week in November for allegedly publishing sensitive information affecting national security and troop morale. On 25 November, on the occasion of the annual meeting of the Francophone Press Union, President Condé hinted at the lack of professionalism within the Guinean press and warned journalists to respect the laws of the land and standards of their profession so as to avoid confrontations with state authorities. Freedom House ranked Guinea as 'partly free' but noted that the press was 'not free'.

Guinea's struggle with the *impunity of the security forces* continued. On 10 January, Aboubakar Sidiki 'Toumba' Diakité was to have been extradited from Senegal to Conakry for his alleged implication in the 2009 *stadium massacre* known as 'Bloody Monday' and the assassination attempt on then-president Dadis Camara. Only on 12 March did this extradition take place. In the course of the following months, Diakité declared that some of his co-accused were innocent, while his lawyers complained about his detention conditions at Conakry's main prison and accused the president of influencing the courts. In November, the independent panel of judges investigating the 2009 stadium massacre concluded its inquiry. More than 14 suspects were accused, including current and former high-ranking officials such as former president Dadis Camara, former vice president Mamadouba Toto Camara, and Aboubakar 'Toumba' Diakité. They were all officially charged on 10 November. However, doubts were voiced about the legal system's capacity, and indeed the political will, to actually hold the trials. The government had turned to the USA and the EU to shore up the necessary funding. A civilian class-action suit of victims and their families had joined the proceedings, which had been supported by the ICC and the International Federation for Human Rights.

The Guinean judiciary continued to labour under more *high-profile political cases*. In March, the Supreme Court revoked the guilty verdicts passed on three individuals, Commander Alpha Oumar Diallo, Officer Jean Guilavogui and business woman Fatou Badiar Diallo, who had been accused of plotting the 2011 attack on President Condé's private home. On 22 August, former soldier and trade unionist Jean Dougou Guilavogui was arrested and not released on bail till 21 December for allegedly participating in an unlawful assembly. The trial of high-ranking members of the military charged with abusing civilians in 2012 was further delayed to 2018, when the main accused, former governor and military commander Sékou Resco Camara failed to attend his court hearing. Similarly, there was no progress in the legal cases against security forces involved in human rights violations during demonstrations in Conakry between 2011 and 2017, in Zogota in 2012 and Womey in 2014.

These cases indicated the limited authority that Guinean courts had over the military and the facility with which political interests could be pursued in the judiciary.

Foreign Affairs

Condé's government fared better internationally than domestically. At the end of January, he took over the *Presidency of the AU*. He launched the 'Afro-Champions Initiative' to support the growth of African multinational companies through harmonised investment and tax measures across the continent. A joint import tax of 2% was seen as a key element to advance business across the continent. In April, as part of his AU tenure, Condé received representatives of the AU Commission, including Idris Déby, Paul Kagame and Moussa Mahamat Faki, in Conakry to prepare for the next AU summit in Kigali (Rwanda) in July.

In January, Condé successfully negotiated for *Gambia*'s President Jammeh to leave office after he lost the presidential elections and both ECOWAS and the AU had threatened a military intervention. While Condé had served as ECOWAS negotiator, bilateral relations soured and, in October, Prime Minister Umaro Sissoco Embalo of Guinea Bissau visited Condé to improve relations.

In March, Guinea hosted the *'African Initiative for Renewable Energy'*, which brought together donors, third-party funders and African leaders to explore the possibilities of renewable energy for the continent. With a 6,000-MW hydroelectric potential, Guinea was indexed as an important power exporter for the subregion. Similarly, the West African Power Pool project of sharing electricity in the MRU, with an estimated budget of $ 460 m, received major funding from the AfDB in June. Guinea had been cooperating with Sierra Leone and Liberia to create a private regional airline to facilitate much-needed travel within the region and thereby encourage economic growth and improved infrastructure, a process especially relevant for Forest Guinea, which is infrastructurally isolated and economically neglected.

On 8 June, an attack on the UN mission in *Mali* (MINUSMA) killed four Guinean soldiers and two more were gravely injured. With 863 soldiers, Guinea was one if the main contributors to MINUSMA and had lost 12 soldiers so far. In December, Guinean and Malian officials came together to clarify border conflicts resulting from artisanal gold panning in the border region, which had increased with the economic downturn of the previous years. This saw Guineans from other regions come into the gold-rich region of Siguiri. In the on-going border conflict, four Malian gendarmes had allegedly been killed by Guinean villagers.

In November, Guinea held a two-day *investors' meeting in Paris* to find private and public investments opportunities for its 'National Economic and Social Development Plan 2016–20', a € 13 bn plan consisting of 53 projects laid out by Minster of

Planning Kanny Diallo. The World Bank committed $ 2.35 bn and prepared a new partnership framework to cover its increased commitment in the country. These announcements came after World Bank Vice President for Africa Makhtar Diop had visited Conakry in July to assess potential for investment by the Bank.

During the year, President Condé remained in the good books of major *international players* such as George Soros and Bill Gates, who supported him throughout the mining sector reform and beyond, which opened the country to international mining corporations and FDI.

Socioeconomic Developments

After a few years of economic decline, Guinea's gross economic figures were improving slightly, with increased FDI, stabilised inflation (8.2–8.4%) and overall *GDP* growth of 4.3%, with $ 6.9 bn in GDP. Real GDP growth was projected at 6.7%, but remained lower at 6.4%, partly due to the increased costs of imported goods. Cautious fiscal policies led to a budget deficit of only 0.4% of annual GDP. With FDI increasing in the mining sector, imports skyrocketed in the course of the year, resulting in a *trade surplus* of $ 181 m for the second quarter. The World Bank's Debt Sustainability Analysis assessed the country to be at moderate risk of debt distress with increased vulnerability due to its high economic dependency on global mineral prices. The World Bank's Doing Business report ranked Guinea 153rd, a significant rise of ten places. The HDI ranked Guinea 183rd (of 188 countries), with a gender development index of 0.784. TI ranked Guinea 148th (of 180 countries) in its Corruption Perception Index, maintaining the index rate of 27 of 2016.

In January, the *mining* giant Rio Tinto announced that they were abandoning their Simandou iron ore projects in the south-east of the country, handing over shares to the now majority holding Chinese government-owned Chinalco, which announced that it was waiting for world prices of iron ore to improve significantly before developing the project, which stalled Guinea's hopes for jobs, income and development in that region. Chinalco was demanding lowered government options (those beyond the 15% stipulated by law), the abandonment of a trans-Guinean railway to export the ore and the clarification of Guinea's conflict with a previous Simandou owner, the Israeli Beny Steinmetz Group Resources, whose owner had been detained for questioning on multiple occasions for supposed bribery of Guinean government officials to secure Simandou blocs 1 and 2.

In May, a former minister of mines, Mahmoud Thiam, was found guilty by a US court of money laundering, corruption and embezzlement of more than $ 8.5 m in the course of his interactions with Chinese businesses during his ministerial tenure. *Bauxite exports* continued to be Guinea's main revenue source, with Emirates-owned Guinea Alumina Corporation expected to become the largest bauxite exporter of the year, surpassing 'Compagnie des Bauxites de Guinée' and French-Chinese-Singaporean-run 'Société Minière de Boké'. The latter was joined by French 'Alliance Minière Responsable' in June to expand its Boké's production to 5 m tonnes per year.

April saw *public unrest* in Boké, leaving at least five dead, when workers and the population demanded improved working and living conditions and the curbing of bauxite-related pollution. The area's public infrastructure contrasted starkly with that of other mining facilities, which had reliable electricity and running water. During Guinea's fifth mining symposium, held in May, President Condé put pressure on the companies to respect environmental and social standards in their conduct. In September, Boké saw more than ten days of public protests, which shut down the mine, with people demanding electricity and water. At least two protesters died, and tens were injured. State symbols such as military barracks and defunct health centres were attacked and partially destroyed. In particular, the inhabitants of Kolaboui, an important road and rail crossing point in the area, were increasing the pressure on both government and multinationals to provide a minimum level of public services and employ local staff instead of foreigners. Elders of the area intervened as negotiating partners since central government did not see fit to participate in the negotiations. In the same region, the abandoned bauxite site of Friguia at Fria was now being revived by the new Russian proprietors with the expectation of improving the crumbling public service infrastructure, which the government had not supported since the mine had shut down years before.

The increase in *Chinese economic interests* was underlined by a $ 20 bn cooperation deal between the two governments in September. China would invest in infrastructure, including roads and hydro-electricity, and was to be repaid in mining concessions and permits for its state-run bauxite and iron companies.

Siguiri's AngloGold Ashanti *gold* mine received an expansion of its power supply to further expand operations of the open-pit oxide mines, of which the government held a 15% interest. While the area was rich in diamonds and gold, the company held expansive concessions that both local and West African miners had been violating for decades in their traditional open-pit and gold panning activities. In May, many of these artisanal miners were arrested in an effort to protect AngloGold Ashanti's interests.

With income from mineral exports, Condé aimed to make Guinea agriculturally self-sufficient by the end of his mandate in 2020, but with the poor quality of rural infrastructure and lack of large investments in *agriculture*, his goal appeared to be unattainable. In April, the price of a standard 50-kg bag of imported rice increased from the state-subsidised FGn (franc) 250,000 to FGn 285,000, leading to popular protests in Kouroussa.

Guinea had become a significant country of origin for *Mediterranean migrants* arriving in Italy, whether adults (7% of total arrivals) or minors (10%). The

International Organization for Migration also reported that Guineans were among the leading groups in south-south returns to countries of origin, returning for example from Morocco, Libya and Niger.

Against the background of the 2013–16 *Ebola virus outbreak*, Guinea hosted several vaccine trials, one of which was declared successful in January by WHO and the director of the National Agency for Health Security, Sakoba Keita. In May, 300,000 doses of this vaccine were stockpiled by the Global Alliance for Vaccines and Immunisation in case of a new Ebola outbreak. In the aftermath of the outbreak, the Red Cross had announced that over $ 5 m had been stolen from emergency and humanitarian funds, reflecting the structural problems of transparency and accountability in Guinea. WHO and UNICEF mounted their largest campaign ever to eradicate polio in Guinea. Conakry's *waste management and sanitation* challenges were highlighted in August, when a garbage dump dissolved into a landslide due to the rainy season, killing at least ten persons and destroying many homes in Hamdallaye.

Guinea was named UNESCO's *World Book Capital 2017*, and hosted the main cultural events in Conakry during April. Conakry's public spaces benefitted from cleaning, painting and improvements in traffic and waste management for this occasion, and it highlighted the country's cultural production, which contrasted, however, with its low literacy rate of 25%.

With the high-profile religious marriage of Cellou Dalein Diallo to his second wife, the debate on the *legalisation regarding polygyny* was re-launched in June. While polygamy was forbidden with Independence in 1958, an estimated 50% of marriages in Guinea continued to be polygynous and the call for legal recognition aimed to improve the legal status of religiously or traditionally married wives and their children. Others feared further disadvantages for women and girls in Guinea's patriarchal society if polygyny were legalised.

Guinea-Bissau

Christoph Kohl

Throughout the year, Guinea-Bissau continued to be dominated by a conflict between President José Mário Vaz and his party, the 'Partido Africano da Independência da Guiné e Cabo Verde' (PAIGC), led by the former prime minister, Domingos Simões Pereira. Parliamentary work remained blocked because the PAIGC prevented the election of the presidentially appointed prime minister, Umaro Sissoco Embaló (PAIGC). Human rights, the opposition and the media came under pressure. The political crisis contrasted with a positive economic development.

Domestic Politics

The *conflict between the president and PAIGC-dominated parliament* continued: in January and February Prime Minister Embaló failed to present his government programme within the constitutional time limit because the PAIGC-dominated parliament bureau refused to discuss it. The bureau blocked an alternative majority that would favour Embaló's cabinet, consisting of all 41 'Partido para a Renovação Social' (PRS) parliamentarians and 15 rebel members of parliament excluded from

 | DOI:10.1163/9789004367630_012

the PAIGC. Although the Constitution stipulated that President Vaz should dismiss Embaló, he remained in office without a legal basis. Attempts by the PAIGC to reintegrate the 15 renegade parliamentarians failed. Interior Minister Botche Candé's (PAIGC) plans to replace parliamentary security guards in January gave rise to suspicion; the step was interpreted by parliament as exceeding his powers. The ransacking of the office of the speaker of parliament, Cipriano Cassamá (PAIGC), on 24 January was conceived as part of a plan to attack parliament by former presidential candidate Nuno Gomes Nabiam ('Assembleia do Povo Unido – Partido Democrático da Guiné-Bissau', APU-PDGB), while on 21 April, Vaz in turn accused undisclosed political circles of planning to assassinate him. In October, supporters of the 15 rebel parliamentarians attacked the PAIGC headquarters.

Throughout 2017, the *Conakry Accord*, signed on 14 October 2016 to end the political deadlock, was not implemented because Vaz had failed to appoint a consensus prime minister and continued to play for time, despite international pressure. In February, Embaló strongly criticised the ECOWAS mediator, Guinean President Alpha Condé. ECOWAS, in turn, threatened to accelerate the withdrawal of its peacekeeping Mission in Guinea-Bissau (ECOMIB). In March, Embaló also attacked the president of the ECOWAS Commission, Beninese politician Marcel Alain de Souza. On 25 April, ECOWAS threatened to impose sanctions but a 30-day deadline expired without any action; instead, Vaz was granted an additional three months. During an ECOWAS summit in Abuja (Nigeria), on 16 December, sanctions were back on the agenda after participants had become frustrated by Vaz's erratic attitude.

Well attended *protest rallies* organised by the 'Movimento de Cidadãos Conscientes e Inconformados' (MCCI) against Vaz and his allies, demanding compliance with the Conakry Accord, took place throughout the year, starting on 23 February. On 13 April, the movement's leader, Lesmos Monteiro, was beaten by unidentified men. A demonstration on 27 May was violently dispersed by the police, leaving 20 injured, after about 2,000 protestors had peacefully approached the presidential palace. Opposition rallies reached new peaks in October and November. Again, police broke up a peaceful rally on 16 November, leaving ten protestors injured. The 'Liga Guineense dos Direitos Humanos' (LGDH) criticised the disproportionate use of force. A rally announced for 30 November was postponed when the police were unwilling to guarantee security. The authorities restricted freedom of assembly. Another rally was stopped by the police on 7 December. In contrast, demonstrations in favour of Vaz organised by the movement '*O Cidadão*' lacked mass support.

Human rights were ailing. When an arrested adolescent was found dead in police custody in January, the LGDH complained that police impunity was widespread. Seven police officers were arrested. The poor state of prisons was a cause for concern in TI's report released on 22 January. A group of 19 child labourers known as 'taliban children' were repatriated from Dakar (Senegal), where they had been forced to beg and work in the streets to earn money for their Muslim marabouts. In

August, Embaló's plans to detain any taliban children found in Guinea-Bissau drew severe criticism from human rights organisations. On 23 June it was reported that advocate Ruth Monteiro had accused the deputy director of justice of having mistreated her. The LGDH accused Embaló of not understanding the function of the state after he ordered the Ministries of the Interior and Defence on 26 September to detain anyone who insulted the president or other state institutions. It was reported on 14 October that the director of the 'Instituto Nacional de Estudos e Pesquisa', Leopoldo Amado, had been dismissed after he organised debates on the political crisis. As in previous years, Freedom House's Freedom in the World index issued in January classified Guinea-Bissau as 'partially free'.

The *media* came under pressure. On 30 March, the country's regulatory body, the 'Conselho Nacional de Comunicação Social', accused politicians of trying illegally to control the media. On 26 June, Vaz reminded Bissau-Guinean journalists not to damage the country's reputation, provoking harsh criticism from the media. On 30 June, the government suspended radio and television broadcasts by public 'Rádio e Televisão de Portugal' (RTP) and activities of the news agency 'Lusa', accusing the Portuguese government of violating a bilateral agreement. The decision was heavily criticised. The Portuguese government emphasised RTP's independence and spoke of an "attack on freedom". RTP and 'Lusa' resumed services on 10 November. In early September employees of 'Televisão da Guiné-Bissau' presented a petition to the government, demanding an "end of censorship". In the year report presented by Reporters without Borders on 26 April, however, Guinea-Bissau's position improved by two places, to 177th. Freedom House's Freedom of the Press index, published on 28 April, classified Guinea-Bissau as 'partially free'.

In TI's Corruption Perception Index released in January, Guinea-Bissau had fallen by ten points from 2016 to rank 168th. On 24 January, 24 civil servants were convicted of *corruption*. The justice police announced on 14 June that it had discovered a corruption scheme within the national hospital as well as a network that had embezzled taxes paid by commercial banks to the Finance Ministry. On 18 September, authorities blocked the payment of the salaries of about 4,000 civil servants suspected to be ghost workers.

Perversion of justice increased. In January, Attorney-General António Sedja Man (PRS) took action against Nabiam, who was questioned on his public statements about hypothetical plans to attack the parliament. In May, Man summoned independence war veteran and leading PAIGC member Manuel 'Manecas' dos Santos after he had made hypothetical statements on a coup. He was arrested on 19 June and detained for one day. This led to fierce criticism from the lawyers' bar association, which accused Vaz of using the justice apparatus to persecute people. Eventually, on 14 November, Man was replaced as attorney-general by former justice police director, Bacar Biai (PRS). The fight against corruption was used by Vaz and Man as a means to intimidate the opposition: on 6 January, Vaz accused Pereira and his former government of having embezzled € 100 m. The parliament bureau refused to waive Pereira's immunity. He and the PAIGC declared that Vaz and Man had tried to seize him, using accusations of corruption as a pretext. On 21 June, the attorney-general accused three former ministers in the former Pereira PAIGC government of corruption; the case against former transport and telecommunications state secretary João Bernardo Vieira was closed in early August.

With regard to *security concerns*, the residence of Energy Minister Florentino Mendes Pereira (PRS) was burgled on 16 January and the premises of 'Lusa' and RTP were robbed on 15 March. The Bissau Regional Court postponed on 29 May its judgement in the case of former army chief of staff José Américo Bubo Na Tchuto, who had been accused of attempting a coup in December 2011. The recruitment in August of 750 new soldiers aged 18–25 and a report on 3 December that spoke of 1,600 new recruits were met with astonishment, as there had been international attempts to encourage the downsizing the armed forces. Six soldiers were arrested on 16 December for allegedly planning to assassinate General Chief of Staff Biague Nantan.

On 5 January the government replaced all *regional presidents* and the mayor of Bissau. They had been appointed by the PAIGC-led government in 2014–15.

Foreign Affairs

On 14 February, the UNSC extended the mandate of *UNIOGBIS* (United Nations Integrated Peacebuilding Office in Guinea-Bissau) for one year up to 28 February 2018. A delegation of the UNSC Committee visited Bissau in mid-June to revise sanctions imposed against military officials following the military coup of April 2012. On 20 December, the UNSC Committee de-listed one officer, former general chief of staff António Indjai, but others remained on the list.

ECOWAS postponed the withdrawal of *ECOMIB*, as agreed in December 2016 due to the ongoing political crisis. Sixty-five officers out of a total contingent of about 500 left Bissau on 4 June. ECOWAS eventually extended its mission beyond 30 June by 90 days. In September, the UN and AU asked for an extension of ECOMIB's presence and the peace force remained in Guinea-Bissau at the end of the year.

On a state visit to *Serbia* on 21 November, Prime Minister Embaló revoked Guinea-Bissau's diplomatic recognition of Kosovo, which had been signed in 2011 by then president Malam Bacai Sanhá.

President Macky Sall of *Senegal* was declared persona non grata by the oppositional MCCI shortly before his planned visit to Guinea-Bissau on 20 April, and his visit was postponed. Senegal was regarded as a protégé of Vaz and as "dark force" with geostrategic interests in Guinea-Bissau. Another date agreed for a visit in December was also cancelled.

On 23 November, human rights activists organised a vigil in front of the Libyan Embassy in Bissau, protesting against slavery in Libya. About ten Bissau-Guinean migrants had been rescued from *modern forms of slavery in Libya* two months earlier. Dozens of Bissau-Guineans were reportedly held captive there and some women had allegedly been forced into prostitution, although the International Organization for Migration denied the presence of Bissau-Guineans in Libya.

The political crisis in *Gambia* at the turn of 2016–17 affected Guinea-Bissau: about 1,000 Gambians, mostly women and children, had sought refuge since December 2016. They returned after the situation had normalised by late January.

Guinea-Bissau's first ever participation in the *Africa Cup of Nations* football championship in Gabon in January triggered popular excitement.

Socioeconomic Developments

An IMF team that visited Bissau on 10–19 May conducted discussions on the third review of the IMF-supported programme under the ECF. The mission praised significant progress in public financial management and tax and customs administration. As a result, the IMF approved a $ 4.1 m disbursement on 7 July. In June, the World Bank endorsed the Country Partnership Framework for 2018–21 as a full country strategy for Guinea-Bissau; the bank's development aid was therefore expected to double. On 12 September, Guinea-Bissau signed an agreement to settle debts with China's Exim Bank dating from 1990 by 90% to $ 5 m. On 3 October, an IMF mission described *economic activity* as "buoyant" while GDP growth was projected at 5.5%, with inflation of about 2% for the year. The IMF called for diversification of the economy as much of the positive development depended on the export of cashew kernels. The IMF completed the fourth review on 11 December, approving the disbursement of a further $ 4.3 m. The fiscal deficit was expected to fall below 2% by year's end. This positive outlook was reflected in the conservative Heritage Foundation's Index of Economic Freedom, presented on 16 February: Guinea-Bissau rose from 145th in 2016 to 119th. In the World Bank's Doing Business Index published on 1 November, however, Guinea-Bissau fell four places to rank 176th. In the Mo Ibrahim Index of African Governance, also published in November, the country dropped one place to rank 43rd.

In March, President Vaz estimated that 90% of *fishing* in Guinea-Bissau's Exclusive Economic Zone was illegal. Four ships were stopped for various infractions in that month alone. To improve maritime security, Spain donated two patrol vessels in February-March. Negotiations between the government and the EU on 26–28 June on a new fisheries agreement were not concluded. On 25 July, it became known that China would donate $ 26 m to construct a new fishing port and related installations in Bissau.

With regard to *energy and water*, in January, environmentalists criticised the planned construction of a hydroelectric power station in the Cufada National Park. According to the environmentalists, corruption was responsible for endangering the national park. Meanwhile, the 'Organisation pour la Mise en Valeur du Fleuve Gambie' announced on 26 January that it was launching a feasibility and environmental impact consultation concerning the construction of a 20 MW hydroelectric power station in the nearby Saltinho area of the Corubal River. The project was supported by the AfDB, UNIDO (UN Industrial Development Organization), ECOWAS, and the Austrian Development Bank. The construction of a 30 MW biomass power plant in Mansôa by a Chinese corporation started in March. In May, the World Bank granted $ 7 m to improve the water and electricity supply in Bissau. In June, reports said that a new contract worth € 10 m to expand the construction of two substations and a power line by a Portuguese enterprise on the outskirts of Bissau was under way. In August, it was reported that a French enterprise would construct a 15 MW thermal power station in Bissau, financed by a $ 28.7 m West African Development Bank grant. Investments in the energy and water sectors were necessary: from the middle of the year, Bissau was hit by a water and energy shortage caused by a lack of generator fuel and technical breakdowns. In October, the Arab Bank for Economic Development in Africa granted a loan worth $ 11 m for the construction of a power plant in Bissau; the government and a financial entity would fund the remaining $ 10.75 m.

The marketing campaign for *cashew* kernels, the country's main cash crop, was very successful due to increased international demand, which led to record prices being paid to farmers by agents from India, China and Mauritania. Prices soared to up to € 2.30 per kg and exports reached 200,000 tonnes. As one of the main cashew producers, Guinea-Bissau took part in the inaugural meeting of the Consultative International Cashew Council in Abidjan (Côte d'Ivoire) on 17 November.

It was reported on 24 January that the AfDB would support a *rice* value chain development project with a loan and a grant worth $ 5.7 m. The remaining 5% of the costs were to be provided by the government and beneficiaries. The project was expected to run for four years and was aimed at reducing the annual rice deficit of more than 80,000 tonnes of the staple food.

In *transport* developments, on 2 April, the Gambia Transport Service Company launched a non-stop bus service between Gambia and Bissau. In the same month, a ship connection that linked the islands of Bolama and Bubaque, Bissau, and the Quinará Peninsula was inaugurated.

With regard to *telecommunications*, on 17 July the government announced the creation of a consortium supported by the World Bank to the tune of $ 35 m to initiate within 18 months the country's access to a submarine cable that linked Africa with Europe. The state held 49% of the shares, while the French provider Orange and the South African MTN held the remainder. In September, the Swiss Cajutel telecommunications company became active in Guinea-Bissau.

According to Interpol, the Bijagós Archipelago was vulnerable to *drug-trafficking*. The director of the local Interpol office, Martinho Camará, voiced his concern in February that Guinea-Bissau might transform from a transit to a consumer country. The 'Observatório Guineense da Droga e da Toxipendência' said in July that at least 25% of incoming drugs were already consumed locally, particularly by adolescents, and the US State Department continued to list Guinea-Bissau as a narco-state. On 12 May, a suspicious plane was reported to have passed by in the remote southern part of the country.

As in previous years, various economic sectors were hit by *strikes* over unpaid or low wages and poor working conditions. Postal workers went on strike in January, demanding the payment of salaries due from the past seven years. Justice sector employees demanded permanent employment and improved conditions. Even the salaries of parliamentarians were in arrears in March, as a result of political motives. Teachers went on strike in May, September, October and November. During the strike, parents paid the teachers' salaries. Government spending on education was very low. Civil servants were on strike in July, and health workers at the national hospital in August.

In the Human Development Index released by the UN on 21 March, Guinea-Bissau ranked 178th. It was one of the countries with the highest child mortality, according to a UNICEF report disclosed in October. A WHO and World Bank report in December assessed that Guinea-Bissau had one of the lowest levels of health care.

Liberia

Franzisca Zanker

Presidential and legislative elections were the main political event in Liberia in 2017. The stakes were high as these would be the first post-war elections for which the Liberian security sector was solely responsible. They were hotly contested, with 20 presidential candidates and over 980 candidates for the 78 seats in parliament. The process went well, with disputes resolved in court rather than on the streets. Populist George Weah was elected president.

Towards the end of her tenure at the end of the year, President Johnson Sirleaf's domestic legacy came increasingly under question, but internationally she retained much political clout. Liberia strengthened its relationship with neighbouring Côte d'Ivoire and hosted the regional ECOWAS summit. The estimated real GDP growth stood at 2.5%, certainly an improvement from –1.2% in 2016, though still far off the 8.7% of 2013. The budget for the fiscal year 2017/18 was at $ 526.6 m, a 12.3% reduction on 2016/17.

 | DOI:10.1163/9789004367630_013

Domestic Politics

The main political event of the year was the *presidential and legislative elections*, held on 10 October, with a second presidential run-off on 26 December. The stakes were high, since these elections would bring about the first peaceful and democratic transfer of power since 1944. They were also the first post-war elections for which the Liberian security sector was solely in charge of ensuring security, the UN Mission in Liberia (UNMIL) having formally handed over responsibility for security matters in mid-2016.

The elections were hotly contested, with 20 presidential candidates and 986 candidates vying for the 73 seats in the House of Representatives, from a total of 26 political parties. The high number of candidates can be explained not least by the political and financial gains at stake. The publically unpopular 2012 Democracy Sustainability Act stipulated that the political parties or coalitions that came first, second and third in the presidential elections would receive an annual sum of $ 2 m, $ 1 m and $ 500,000, respectively, from the national budget. Legislators would also receive high salaries. The proliferation of parties and candidates did not translate into concrete party politics, however, and voters were yet again left to choose primarily on the grounds of regional bases, patronage and personalities rather than of specific issues. Issues that all contestants addressed, irrespective of party, included poverty reduction, the maintenance of peace and security, the elimination of corruption and revitalising the Liberian economy. The number of female contestants was low, amounting to fewer than 20% of those standing for the legislature and there was only one female presidential candidate, Macdella Cooper, who went on to win a slim 0.7% of the votes.

Candidates for the legislature had to take a simple majority to win, and only 26 representatives were able to retain their seats, with 64% of seats taken by newly elected officials. In the last senatorial elections in 2014, only two of the 15 senators had been able retain their seats, indicating that representatives may be better able than senators to present their local campaign promises, though there was also a notable difference in election turnout (see below). The Congress for Democratic Change (CDC) became the strongest party in the House, with 21 seats (an astounding gain of ten), out-doing the Unity Party (UP), which retained 20 seats (losing five compared with 2011). The Liberty Party (LP) lagged behind with only three seats (losing four). Highlighting the weakness of political parties, 13 seats were won by independent candidates (up from nine in 2011), with no parties apart from the CDC and UP taking more than five seats. Nine women were elected, one more than in 2011, but making up only 12% of the House of Representatives. An Equal Representation and Participation Bill from 2016, which created five seats reserved for female politicians in the House of Representatives, as well as one for youth and one for people with disabilities, was not promulgated in time for the 2017 elections.

The three main *contenders for the presidency* were Joseph Boakei (UP), George Weah (CDC) and Charles Brumskine (LP). *George Weah*, a former international football star-turned politician, won 38.4% of the vote in the first round and 61.5% in the second, making him the president-elect. He had no overtly distinct policies and did not appear at either of the two presidential debates that took place (see below). As a populist candidate with an anti-establishment message appealing to young voters, his campaign stood in contrast to Boakai, who was over 70 years old. Weah was the only candidate to win wide support nationally and not only in his home county and had already carved out a political career, including a stab at the presidency: in 2005, when he lost to Ellen Johnson Sirleaf in the run-off, and as vice presidential running mate to Winston Tubman in 2011. He became senior senator for Montserrado County in 2014. This time round, Weah formed unlikely alliances with the National Patriotic Party (NPP) and the Liberia People's Democratic Party (LPDP). The latter was led by the former speaker of the House of Representatives, J. Alex Tyler, who had been the subject of persistent corruption allegations, including legal proceedings. More surprising, however, was his running mate from the NPP, senior senator Jewel Howard Taylor (from Bong County), the ex-wife of Charles Taylor. Weah had previously been a strong critic of both Charles Taylor and his party, the NPP. Both Howard Taylor and Weah rejected repeated claims that Charles Taylor, serving a 50-year prison sentence in the UK for war crimes committed in neighbouring Sierra Leone, was influencing the election. Weah did, however, admit in March to taking a phone call from him, which resulted in international condemnation of Taylor's attempt to influence the Liberian election process.

The vice president before the elections, *Joseph Boakai*, was the so-called 'pseudo-incumbent' candidate, a safe choice known for his relatively austere lifestyle and an absence or the corruption scandals that had tainted many other UP members. The increasingly visible rifts between him and Johnson Sirleaf, including over who his running mate should be, and the fact that the latter's own domestic legacy was being increasingly called into question, meant that his incumbency status was not so politically relevant, however. Renowned for napping at public events, the 73-year-old had the nickname 'Sleepy Joe' and won 28.8% of the first round votes and 38.5% in the run-off. *Charles Brumskine*, a lawyer and former president pro tempore of the Liberian Senate under Charles Taylor, came third with a much lower 9.6% of the vote. He had previously contested elections, coming third in 2005, and fourth in 2011. Faced with the prospect of yet again not making it to the run-off, he contested the election results, making allegations of fraud (see below).

Other notable contenders included former Coca-Cola chief executive Alexander Cummings, as standard bearer for the Alternative National Congress (ANC), a splinter faction of Weah's CDC. He quickly gained grassroots popularity, bringing a fresh face to Liberian politics and was the only candidate to attend both presidential debates (see below). He came fifth with just over 7% of the vote and the ANC failed to gain a single seat in the legislature. Another newcomer to politics was an entrepreneur, Benoni Urey of the All Liberian Party. Though he had not held any major elected office, he had been firmly aligned politically with Charles Taylor. Once the head of the then Bureau of Maritime Affairs, he had been the subject of a UN travel ban and assets freeze list for a number of years. Though rich enough to finance a solid election campaign, he had no major campaign bases and only took 1.6% of the vote. Another contentious but politically established face was former warlord turned senator (from Nimba County), Prince Johnson, of the Movement for Democracy and Reconstruction, who came fourth with 8.2%.

The presidential run-off, originally scheduled for early November, was delayed when Brumskine and the LP brought a formal *challenge to the first round election results*. When the National Elections Commission (NEC) rejected his allegations of irregularities, the LP appealed to the Supreme Court. In what Liberia's leading newspaper, 'FrontPage Africa', dubbed the "bedfellows of political convenience", Boakai, Cummings and Urey all joined Brumskine in his fraud allegations. The Court agreed to delay the run-off but went on to decide that the claimants had delivered insufficient evidence to warrant new elections, so the run-off took place before the end of the year.

Voting went well in both rounds with no major incidents, though there were long waiting times at a few polling stations, poor crowd control and some issues with the electoral roll because polling staff had received inconsistent training. *Turnout* was higher than previous elections, at 75.2% for the presidential and legislative elections, and 55.8% for the presidential run-off on 26 December. This contrasted with the 25.2% turnout for the senatorial elections in 2014, which were marred by the Ebola epidemic, and the presidential run-off in 2011, with a turnout of 38.6% due to a boycott by the opposition.

Election observer missions, including ECOWAS, the AU, the EU and organisations such as the Carter Center, all lauded the elections, which, despite some shortcomings including incidents of hate speech and harassment, were generally peaceful and transparent. The Liberian judiciary was seriously put to the test during the election process, with international observers congratulating them for implementing due process, while acknowledging the multitude of challenges they faced, including the lack of preparation (and training) for the lawyers involved, which led to delays in judgements.

The *NEC* also faced numerous challenges, not least due to doubts as to its legitimacy. Previous elections in 2011 and senatorial elections in 2014 had been marred by difficulties caused by an opposition boycott and the Ebola epidemic, respectively. This time round, despite a budget shortfall, continuing challenges in registering and educating voters in some barely accessible parts of the country, the NEC managed the process well on the whole, as election observers across the board agreed. Threats that the election process would be derailed included allegations in

March that the NEC chairperson Jeremy Korkoya was an American citizen, in contravention of the Liberian Constitution. He was sued unsuccessfully several times over this matter, and faced further calls to step down over his handling of the presidential run-off in December, but managed to remain in office.

In addition to such disputes over citizenship and residency rules embedded in the Constitution, another stormy legal wrangle in the run-up to the elections arose over the *Code of Conduct* for Public Officials and Government Employees, issued in 2014, which inter alia stipulated that all presidential appointees should resign two years (or three for tenured positions) before running for elected office. The Supreme Court upheld the constitutionality of the Code of Conduct in March. Though the aim was to deter potential candidates from exploiting public office, a widely held perception was that it restricted popular and appropriately experienced candidates from running. Given the division even within the court – with a narrow three-to-two ruling – and the controversies surrounding the implementation of the Code, President Johnson Sirleaf appointed a three-member Ombudsman in April to help enforce implementation. The Code was confirmed by the legislature in June, with some amendments, but by July, further appeals to the Supreme Court allowed some candidates to bypass the Code and stand, despite having held public office during the previous three years.

The NEC registered over 2.1 m voters between 1 February and 14 March, an increase on previous elections. Despite some gaps on the final register and technical glitches, related not least to the absence of a civil registry and the difficulty of registering voters because of the terrain and the lack of citizen education and technical capacities, election monitors deemed the exercise credible. The NEC allowed *campaigning* to start on 31 July and to continue until 8 October. Differences in financial resources undermined the equality of opportunity for the presidential and legislative candidates, as rules on campaign finance were insufficiently enforced. This also applied to media coverage, with much of the media sector reliant on political sponsorship in return for coverage. No free airtime was given on the state broadcaster. UNMIL Radio gave each of the presidential candidates two hours of free airtime, which just over half of them used. In essence, this meant that most media coverage – including print, radio and television – was given to the incumbent UP, and to the CDC and the LP, the second and third largest political parties, respectively. Two *presidential debates* sponsored by Liberian civil society activists took place in August and September, with only a fraction (four and three, respectively) of the 20 candidates attending. Weah did not attend either. Apart from media coverage, financial resources were a constraint in other respects. Financial hand-outs to communities as part of the election campaign, whilst illegal, were noted in complaints made to observer missions, but were rarely sanctioned.

In contrast to the 2011 elections, *no election-related violence* took place. Twenty political parties signed the 'Farmington River Declaration' on 4 June, committing themselves to a peaceful transition of power and violence-free elections, The peaceful election represented a feat for the Liberian security sector, which was solely responsible for the elections for the first time in the post-war period. An election security task force was set up in January and 555 police officers were trained in community policing and election security.

Sporadic violent incidents including armed robberies, land disputes, mob violence and presumed ritual killings occurred during the year, and the Liberia National Police (LNP) was not always able to respond due to limited staff and equipment, especially in rural areas. By June, there were 5,127 police officers, 75% of them based in Montserrado County. The Armed Forces of Liberia (AFL), with 2,000 personnel, also struggled to maintain operations beyond Montserrado and Margibi Counties. The relationship between the security sector and local communities continued to be fraught. In one incident in early January, after the discovery of the body of an 18-year-old girl, apparently killed for ritual purposes, around 500 persons stormed the local LNP station in Buchanan, Grand Bassa County, demanding that the suspect be handed over. The situation was contained after reinforcements arrived from the Police Support Unit. In May, 17 AFL soldiers assaulted a group of civilians in Wainsue, Bong County, injuring over a dozen. Five of the soldiers were arrested and military investigations were ongoing at year's end.

Overall, Liberia remained stable in the first full year since the official *UNMIL handover* in 2016. By the end of February, only 434 UNMIL military and 310 police remained in the country, mostly in Monrovia, with military observers conducting regular patrols throughout the country. By July, only field offices in Voinjama and Zwedru and a communications hub in Gbarnga remained outside Monrovia. In late 2016, the UNSC had requested the UN Secretary-General to provide a peacebuilding plan for Liberia, which was unveiled in in March. The plan was developed in close cooperation with Liberian stakeholders and was in its first phase. In addition, a revised national Liberian security strategy aimed at building peace, security, stability and development through the accountable and effective coordination of the security sector was further consolidated and was submitted for review to members of the National Security Council in May. A public expenditure review of the justice and security sector, scheduled to take one year, was launched in the same month.

The *human rights record* was mixed. The high level of pre-trial detention remained a problem, with over 65% of the prison population awaiting trial in overcrowded prisons. There were at least nine prison escapes during the year. Poor sanitation, inadequate nutrition and limited medical care added to the human rights violations experienced by prisoners. Sexual and gender-based violence continued to be rampant, not least because of widespread impunity. A domestic violence bill was passed in the Liberian legislature, but President Johnson Sirleaf failed to sign it by the end of the year. The 2017 Global Gender Gap Report ranked Liberia 107th of 144 countries with the highest gender equality gap, making it one of the worst places for women in the world. Relatively high scores for women's political empowerment (based on the legislature in place before the elections) and economic participation were pulled down by poor scores for educational attainment, health and survival.

Though not all electoral candidates had equal access to *media* (see above), there was critical reporting of the election campaigns and elections throughout the year, especially by newspapers. Incidents of harassment of journalists by government officials were sporadically reported throughout the year, and Freedom House continued to rate Liberia as 'partly free'. Though some newspapers had online editions, excessive costs and poor infrastructure meant Internet access was limited to a small number of Liberians.

Despite 2017 being the final year of President Johnson Sirleaf's tenure, the Liberian *governance reform agenda* continued to advance at a snail's pace. Additional decentralised service centres for issuing documents such as birth certificates and drivers' licences were put in place outside Monrovia, but a Local Government Bill and Land Rights Bill were not approved by the senate before the year's end. In her annual state of the nation address in January, Johnson Sirleaf promised to prioritise fighting corruption, but the General Auditing Commission released at least 20 reports implying fraud and/or misappropriation at government ministries and agencies. Several cases were passed on to the Ministry of Justice for further investigation and prosecution. In the meantime, those accused of corruption, including Alex J. Tyler, continued to hold prominent political roles with no obvious restrictions. Since its inception in 2008, the Liberian Anti-Corruption Commission had brought just two prosecutions.

Foreign Affairs

In June, the UN Operation in Côte d'Ivoire (UNOCI) rapid reaction force at the border between Liberia and *Côte d'Ivoire* officially ended its operations, and it became up to the two countries to continue to facilitate the return of the remaining Ivorian refugees from Liberia and to carry out joint cross-border security operations. By late August, the two countries had signed several agreements aimed at strengthening cooperation and bilateral relations as well as re-launching a Joint Commission, originally created in 1972, which met for the first time in 39 years. As of August, official figures showed that 11,896 refugees were still living in Liberia (down from over 200,000 refugees in 2011), with voluntary returns still occurring, albeit at a slower pace than in 2016. Many refugees, sceptical about returning to Côte d'Ivoire, were hoping to integrate locally in Liberia.

Elsewhere, Liberia continued to be involved in *international peacekeeping operations*, by contributing 78 AFL troops to the UN Multidimensional Integrated

Stabilization Mission in Mali (MINUSMA). One Liberian peacekeeping soldier was killed during an indirect attack on a MINUSMA camp in May.

In early June, Liberia hosted the 51st session of the *ECOWAS Heads of State and Government Summit.* President Johnson Sirleaf had been the ECOWAS chairperson in the year preceding the summit. In her opening remarks, she highlighted the democracy consolidation in the region – particularly referencing the peaceful transition in the Gambia and elections in Ghana, fighting terrorism in the Sahel region, freedom of movement and prioritising agriculture and infrastructure projects. The Farmington River Declaration, whereby 20 political parties had committed themselves to peace (see above), was signed during the summit and witnessed by the regional leaders, a symbolic act highlighting the efforts at maintaining peace and security in the region. During the judicial impasse before the run-off of the presidential elections in Liberia, Guinean President Alpha Condé (as chairman of the AU) and Togolese leader Faure Gnassingbé (the new ECOWAS chairperson) engaged in mediation efforts to make sure the process was not derailed.

Several Liberians were indicted and convicted outside the country for *crimes committed during the Liberian civil wars.* In June, the British Metropolitan Police's war crimes unit arrested Agnes Reeves Taylor, another former wife of Charles Taylor, and charged her with torture committed during the first civil war. In October, former rebel leader Mohammed Jabbah was found guilty on four charges of fraud and perjury in relation to his asylum and later permanent residence application by a federal court in Philadelphia. The case included testimonies about his war crimes. Other investigations in Switzerland and Belgium against former commanders remained ongoing. The fact that these cases were only brought to court outside the country highlighted the elevated levels of impunity for war crimes still persistent in Liberia.

The inauguration of American President Donald Trump had the potential to affect the traditionally strong *bilateral relationship between the US and Liberia.* President Johnson Sirleaf had a close relationship to the previous administration, especially to Secretary of State Hillary Clinton and National Security Advisor Susan Rice. Johnson Sirleaf was reserved in congratulating Trump after his election, in contrast to Weah, who was quick to comment positively. As an anti-establishment figure himself, he was sometimes called 'Africa's Donald Trump'. By the end of Johnson Sirleaf's tenure, her domestic legacy was certainly questionable, but internationally she still had much political clout.

Socioeconomic Developments

The lingering impact of the global decline in commodity prices and the Ebola outbreak of 2014/15 continued, albeit it with a slight upturn. The estimated real *GDP growth* was 2.5%, certainly an improvement from -1.2% in 2016, though still far off the 8.7% of 2013. The UNMIL drawdown was believed to have adversely affected the surprisingly bad macroeconomic performance in 2016. The fact that there were no major security issues in 2017 (despite the elections), combined with a slight pickup in gold exports, led to the improved growth. *Inflation* remained a problem, standing at 12.5% by the end of the year. The depreciation of the Liberian dollar against the US dollar continued, rising by over 20% since 2013, and the Central Bank of Liberia took a stronger stance on regulating the exchange rate between the two currencies. Many Liberians continued to depend on US dollars for their daily lives. Dependency on imports (especially rice), coupled with weaker exports of Liberia's main commodities – iron ore, rubber and gold – further hindered economic development. Efforts to diversify the economy, especially through the Agricultural Transformation Agenda showed only limited results so far. The *budget* for the fiscal year 2017/18 was signed by the president in July, after approval by the legislature, at $ 526.6 m, a 12.3 % reduction on 2016. At $ 298 m, government salaries accounted for 59% of total expenditure, an increase from 2016 explained in part by payments to election staff. Expenditure on security and the rule of law ($ 86 m) and the health sector ($ 77.1 million) was lower than in 2016.

A newly amended *tax law* took effect from January, which included an increase in General Sales Tax on items such as telecommunications, as well beverages, such as drinking water. The same law saw tax breaks for members of the legislature and the Supreme Court. The leaked Paradise Papers in November 2017 saw Ellen Johnson Sirleaf listed as a director of a Bermuda company between 2001 and 2012. As over 60% of Liberians continue to live below the poverty line, and inequality was one of the main root causes of conflict, economic development continued to be a politically contentious topic.

Mali

Bruce Whitehouse

Unprecedented levels of insecurity and violence, primarily fomented by jihadi insurgents, combined with heightened inter-community tensions continued to disrupt the lives of millions of residents in Mali's central and northern regions. Although the Malian state, led by President Ibrahim Boubacar Keita, worked with international partners to contain these threats, intensified activity by and coordination among jihadi groups based within Mali's borders posed a grave threat to Mali and its neighbours. Implementation of the peace process between the Malian government and Tuareg separatist movements remained sluggish as pressure mounted abroad to levy sanctions against those blocking implementation. Despite these challenges, Mali's leaders cultivated closer relations internationally, agricultural production was up, and the overall economy expanded throughout the year.

Domestic Politics

Insecurity rose to ever-greater heights in Mali, making 2017 the deadliest year since the country's slide into instability had begun five years earlier. Over 700 deaths were reported, including those of some 350 civilians, nearly 300 members of Mali's

 | DOI:10.1163/9789004367630_014

security forces and 45 UN peacekeepers; a further 546 people were wounded. Most of these were casualties of violence perpetrated by *armed jihadi groups* primarily in the northern regions of Gao, Timbuktu and Kidal, but also extending into the central regions of Segou and Mopti. Jihadi activity against government and foreign military targets as well as civilians continued to mount, especially near Mali's borders with Burkina Faso and Niger, and added to its already significant transnational dimensions. In January, French troops in the Timbuktu region arrested a man suspected of involvement in a 2016 terrorist attack in neighbouring Côte d'Ivoire that had killed 19 civilians. In March, the western Sahel's main jihadi groups – al-Qaida in the Islamic Maghreb, Al-Mourabitoune, Ansar Eddine and the Macina Liberation Front – announced their fusion into a new organisation dubbed the 'Jama'a Nusrat al-Islam wa-l-Muslimin' (JNIM), or Group to Support Islam and Muslims. Led by Ansar Eddine's founder, Iyad Ag Ghaly, the group declared its hostility to all Western military forces, to West African secular states and to the peace process seeking to reconcile the Malian state with Tuareg separatists. JNIM claimed responsibility for multiple attacks, including one in June on a tourist resort on the outskirts of Mali's capital city, Bamako, in which two attackers, four civilians and one Malian soldier were killed. It also continued to hold for ransom foreigners and Malian soldiers captured in previous years. Jihadis kidnapped a Colombian nun from the south-eastern town of Koutiala in February, but later released their two longest-held foreign hostages, a Swede and a South African who had been in captivity since 2011. In October, several Malian soldiers captured by JNIM were reportedly killed in a French military airstrike against a jihadi camp in the Kidal region. The same month, jihadi fighters based in Mali and affiliated with the Islamic State in the Greater Sahara (ISGS) ambushed a joint Niger/US military patrol in western Niger, killing four American and four Nigérien soldiers. In December, JNIM and ISGS announced that their organisations were uniting to coordinate operations against French, US, UN and regional government forces.

The *government's response to growing security threats* included plans to recruit 5,000 additional troops and coordination with neighbouring governments to set up *a regional counterterrorism force*. Known as the G5 Sahel joint force, this initiative was intended to secure Mali's volatile eastern border zones and was projected eventually to field 10,000 troops. In November, it carried out its first combat operation, involving some 750 soldiers from Burkina Faso, Chad and Niger alongside 180 French personnel, in the Gao region. To inhibit insurgents' mobility, civilian travel by motorcycle was banned in areas of central Mali. The government also extended the state of emergency (in effect since 2012) for another year in October. UN and French forces working with Malian troops were granted new powers to monitor flows of people and vehicles and to seize weapons.

A different kind of violence escalated in the form of deadly *clashes between sedentary and nomadic populations*. These conflicts, primarily pitting ethnic Bambara farmers against Fulani herders, increased insecurity in the central regions of Segou and Mopti. Members of the Malian security forces were sometimes implicated in these conflicts and accused of committing human rights abuses against Fulani civilians. Meanwhile, limited progress was made in implementing the *peace process between the government and Tuareg rebels*. This process suffered a major setback in January, when a suicide bomber killed dozens of rebel fighters and government troops gathered at a staging ground for joint security patrols in the northern city of Gao. Joint patrols were later initiated and interim civilian authorities were set up under the terms of the 2015 peace accord signed by Mali's President Ibrahim Boubacar Keita and representatives of the main consortium of northern Tuareg rebel groups, the 'Coordination des Mouvements de l'Azawad' (CMA). A conference of national understanding stipulated by the same accord concluded in early April after an initial CMA boycott. Nevertheless, renewed skirmishes broke out between CMA and pro-government militia fighters near Kidal and Ménaka for several days in July as implementation of the accord's other provisions – including demobilisation and disarmament of armed groups – lagged behind schedule.

In April, President Keita formed a new cabinet and appointed Abdoulaye Idrissa Maïga, previously defence minister, to the post of prime minister. In June, the National Assembly approved *revisions to the 1992 Constitution*, to include the creation of a new senate and other changes called for by the peace accord, as well as broadened powers for the executive. In July, a well-known Malian journalist and blogger critical of government corruption survived an assassination attempt. In August, following weeks of massive public protests in Bamako and other cities against the draft constitutional changes, Keita announced that he had indefinitely suspended the revision initiative, which would have required approval by referendum. His government also dropped its prosecution of the popular anti-corruption activist and radio host Mohamed Bathily, widely known as 'Ras Bath', following months of court battles in the wake of Bathily's 2016 arrest on charges of 'inciting troop disobedience'. In December, former president Amadou Toumani Touré visited Mali for the first time since his resignation in the immediate aftermath of the March 2012 coup d'état. After spending six days in Bamako, Touré returned to Dakar (Senegal), where he continued living in exile. Following the December resignation of Prime Minister Abdoulaye Maïga, another former defence minister, Soumeylou Boubèye Maïga, was appointed prime minister. The government postponed regional elections, originally scheduled for December, until April 2018 due to continuing insecurity, and began preparations for presidential elections to be held in July 2018.

Foreign Affairs

President Keita upheld an *active foreign policy* agenda, undertaking a total of 32 trips abroad; these included attending 20 summits and multilateral meetings and making ten official visits. He also made an additional two private visits to France, one of them for medical care. His government hosted the Franco-African summit in January, attended by leaders of 35 countries, as part of a broader effort to promote foreign investment to aid Mali's stabilisation.

Mali's worsening security problems meant that the country remained a concern for the *UN*. MINUSMA, the UN's peacekeeping mission in Mali since 2013, continued to be its deadliest mission in terms of casualties sustained by peacekeepers, 150 of whom were killed between the onset of the mission and the end of 2017. MINUSMA fielded nearly 15,000 personnel, including over 11,700 troops, 1,700 police and 1,500 civilian staff. Its forces were strengthened by the arrival of a new contingent of troops and attack helicopters from *Germany*. In New York, the UNSC adopted sanctions targeting unnamed individuals and entities threatening Mali's peace process amid growing international perceptions that multiple parties to Mali's conflict were resisting full implementation of the accord. The UNSC also hosted deliberations over the creation of the regional counterterrorism force, and passed Resolution 2359 to authorise the establishment of this joint force within the *G5 Sahel* framework for regional cooperation between *Burkina Faso, Chad*, Mali, *Mauritania* and *Niger*. As plans for the force expanded from 5,000 to 10,000 troops, pledges in support of its annual budget (estimated at € 423 m) came from various donors including *Saudi Arabia*, the *UAE* and the *EU*, although the full amount had yet to be secured by year's end. The EU extended its Capacity Building Mission in Mali, launched in 2014 to train Malian police and paramilitary personnel, for two years beginning in January. It also kept up its Training Mission (EUTM), established in 2013 in the town of Koulikoro, to train elements of the Malian armed forces. In addition, the EUTM began preparing officers from Mali and its neighbours to lead the G5 Sahel joint force.

France continued to operate its own counterterrorism mission, Operation Barkhane, with approximately 4,000 troops in the Sahel, including 1,000 based in Mali. In May, Mali hosted French President Emmanuel Macron's first official trip outside Europe; during his one-day visit, Macron visited French troops deployed as part of Barkhane and met with President Keita. In November, Barkhane's commanding officer accused unnamed signatory groups to Mali's peace accord of colluding with jihadi movements. An international summit organised in December by President Macron helped secure additional political and financial support for the G5 Sahel force.

The *US* continued a gradual resumption of development assistance to Mali, which had been curtailed after the 2012 coup. USAID signed agreements with the Malian government to fund projects in agriculture, health, good governance and conflict resolution for a total of $ 47 m. *Switzerland*, another major bilateral donor, pledged to spend some € 83 m from 2017 to 2020 on rural development, education, governance and other priorities.

Within the West African region, Mali's foreign affairs were dominated by multilateral efforts to create the G5 Sahel force. Mali signed up to legal conventions with Chad and Niger to combat cross-border terrorism, and hosted an *ECOWAS* summit in Bamako, attended by President Faure Gnassingbé of *Togo*, to inaugurate a regional counterterrorism early warning network. President Keita also hosted a visit by President Nana Akufo-Addo of *Ghana*, during which the two men agreed to strengthen their countries' relations in the areas of trade, agriculture and security.

Socioeconomic Developments

The *economy grew* by an estimated 5.3% over the year and inflation remained low. In November, representatives of the IMF declared Mali's state budget to be in line with its fiscal goals. Insecurity caused major *social and economic disruptions* for many Malians, especially in the country's central and northern regions. At least 500 *schools* either remained closed or were newly closed due to pervasive violence and threats to state employees. The crisis also had a negative impact on agricultural production and the distribution of food in affected regions, leading to *food insecurity* for an estimated 3.8 m people, some 20% of Mali's population. The UN found evidence of growing malnutrition among Malian children, estimating that 142,000 of them faced severe acute malnutrition and that this number would continue to rise. Other disruptions stemmed from workers' *strikes* in the state health and higher education sectors, and from persistent corruption and abuse of public funds. The state auditor general issued a report in October estimating that *corruption* had cost the Malian treasury some € 100 m in 2015. The government announced a crackdown on illicit enrichment by civil servants, requiring state employees to declare their financial assets by the end of the year. The Ministry of the Economy and Finance announced a € 3 bn ten-year plan to improve access to basic social services and infrastructure for residents of conflict-affected northern regions.

Northern insecurity notwithstanding, Mali's *agricultural sector* was buoyed by a record *cotton* harvest of 645,000 tonnes in the 2016/17 season, allowing Mali to overtake Burkina Faso as SSA's largest cotton producer. By the end of December, cotton harvests for the 2017/18 season had already surpassed those of the previous year, in part due to the use of additional land for cotton cultivation. Since cotton is only grown in Mali's southernmost regions, this crop was little affected by the ongoing troubles further north. Production of *rice* continued to rise, up some 300% over the previous decade, to nearly 3 m tonnes. Government subsidies helped fuel this growth, which increased Mali's rice production levels to twice its domestic consumption.

In the *mining sector*, industrial production of *gold* (which accounts for most of the value of Mali's exports) amounted to 49.6 tonnes for the year, an increase of 5% over 2016. Three new gold mines were in development to offset older mines coming to the end of their production lives. Artisanal gold production resumed in October following a three-month suspension for restructuring imposed by the Ministry of Mines. Artisanal gold output was estimated to match industrial output for the year.

Prospects for *energy* generation were boosted by support from Algeria for plans to generate electricity from new wind and solar plants, and to build new 40-MW hybrid power plants in Timbuktu and Gao. A 33-MW solar energy plant was announced for the Segou region with funding from the AfDB and the IFC, and a commercially funded 90-MW thermal plant was announced for the Kayes region. Mali secured € 40 m from the Islamic Development Bank to underwrite energy imports, and € 71 m from the AfDB to fund construction of an electricity transmission line linking Mali with Guinea.

New *transportation infrastructure* initiatives included the development by Dubai-based DP World Group of plans for improved shipping and customs logistics. The World Bank disbursed € 64 m for the rehabilitation of rural roads in the southern regions of Koulikoro and Sikasso, with the aim of facilitating farmers' access to local markets. The government also spent some € 7.6 m toward the re-establishment of passenger rail service on the line connecting Bamako and Dakar. In *telecommunications*, Mali's newest mobile network operator, Telecel, began service in Bamako after making an initial investment worth over $ 200 m, with hopes of attracting 3 m new mobile phone subscribers nationally. Telecel is the country's third network after Orange Mali and Malitel.

Mauritania

Helena Olsson and Claes Olsson

The political climate remained fragile owing to the fragmented state of the political opposition and the open split in the Senate within the ruling party, the 'Union pour la République' (UPR) over President Aziz's proposal to change the Constitution and replace the Senate with new regional councils. The UPR nevertheless increased its concentration of power and executive responsibility. The death of the high-profile opposition leader, Ely Ould Mohamed Vall, on 5 May removed one of the most respected opponents to Aziz. Before his death, Vall had been expected to play an influential role in the referendum campaign on the constitutional changes. The government's decision to tighten the blasphemy law restricted freedom of expression and thereby increased political repression. Aziz continued efforts to promote a 'national dialogue process', despite the fact that the most recent round of National Dialogue in October 2016 had been boycotted by the main opposition coalition, the 'Forum National pour la Démocratie et l'Unité' (FNDU). The threat of radicalisation, violent extremism and terrorism continued to jeopardise prospects for security and development.

 | DOI:10.1163/9789004367630_015

Domestic Politics

Divisions within the ruling UPR came to the fore when 24 of its members in the Senate on 18 March voted against President Mohamed Ould Abdel Aziz's proposal to abolish the Senate, the High Islamic Council and the High Court of Justice and to replace them with new regional councils. International media reported that a total of 33 of the 56 senators voted against the proposal while the official news agency, 'Agence Mauritanienne d'Information', reported that 30 senators had voted against, with one abstention and two absentees. The rejection in the Senate was apparently unexpected and Aziz accused senators opposed to his proposed reforms of being 'traitors'. His response was to announce that he would seek approval for the proposed *constitutional reforms* by using Article 38 of the current 1991 Constitution, which provided for a referendum.

The president's decision was contested by, among others, four former chairmen of the 'Ordre National des Avocats' (the National Bar Association), Diabira Maroufa, Yacoub Diallo, Mahfoudh Ould Bettah and Ahmed Salem Ould Bouhoubeiny, who claimed that Article 38 was subservient to other parts of the Constitution, according to which each of the two chambers, the National Assembly and the Senate, had to approve the proposed amendments with a two-thirds majority before a *referendum* could be held. The timing of the referendum – in August – was also questioned. It was in the middle of the rainy season in the south and many opposition-supporting southern villagers would be occupied in the fields, which was expected to encumber opposition efforts to get them to vote against the proposal. *Changing the national flag* was also included in the reform proposal; it was proposed that two horizontal red stripes would be added to the green flag with a yellow crescent moon and star to symbolise the blood shed in the 1960 independence struggle.

On 10 July, eight opposition parties, including the FNDU and the moderate Islamist party Tawassoul (which had not boycotted the 2013 parliamentary elections), as well as the leading anti-slavery movement 'Initiative pour la Résurgence du Mouvement Abolitionniste en Mauritanie' (IRA – Mauritanie), signed a declaration of 'boycott actif' against the referendum, which was scheduled to take place on 5 August. Daily protests against the referendum, in which more than 1.4 m Mauritanians were eligible to vote, started on 21 July and were occasionally reported to have been violently suppressed by the security forces. On 3 August, the final day for campaigning, police and opposition activists clashed in Nouakchott and three other regions. Ravina Shamdasani, spokesperson for the UN High Commissioner for Human Rights, expressed concern about the unrest, particularly the "apparent suppression of dissent and use of excessive force by the authorities against protest leaders". According to the official statement made by the 'Commission Electorale Nationale Indépendante' on 7 August, the turnout was 53.7%, with 85.6 % of voters supporting the change. President *Aziz abolished the Senate* on 15 August, in accordance with the referendum result.

'Reporters sans Frontières' described the harassment faced by *journalists* covering protests against the referendum, several of whom were interrogated. Harassment continued even after the referendum: according to local media, on 25 August, police arrested four journalists – Moussa Sambasy, editor-in-chief of 'Le Quotidien de Nouakchott', Jedna Ould Deida, director of the news website 'Mauriweb', Babacar Baye Ndiaye, editor-in-chief of the news website 'Cridem', and his publisher Aminata Houdou, known as Rela Ba. The journalists were questioned about their critical coverage of the detention of the opposition senator Mohamed Ould Ghadda, who had been arrested on 10 August and was one of the Senate members who had voted against the constitutional amendments initiated by the president. Ghadda was interrogated about financial support he allegedly received from Mohamed Bouamatou, a Mauritanian pro-opposition businessman. Ghadda was detained again in October for two months on vague corruption charges. The chairman of the 'Syndicat des Journalistes Mauritaniens', Mohamed Salem Ould Dah, denied that the journalists had been interrogated in connection with their journalistic activities. Local media reported that, on 17 October, the 'Haute Autorité de la Presse et de l'Audiovisuel' ordered the five privately owned news stations ('Dava', 'Sahel TV', 'Chinguitt', 'al-Watania' and 'Al-Mourabitoun TV') to cease broadcasting because of "failing to fulfill their financial agreements". The move was seen as an additional sign of suppression of the independent press. Mauritania was ranked 55th out of 180 countries in the Press Freedom Index.

On 25 August, the American Federation of Labor and Congress of Industrial Organizations urged the US administration to remove Mauritania from the list of approved countries since "The government of Mauritania routinely fails to conduct investigations into cases of *slavery*" and "harasses and imprisons anti-slavery activists and will not publicly acknowledge the continued existence of slavery". On 8 September, a group of US anti-slavery activists were denied entry to Mauritania. This was first reported by a local anti-slavery organisation, 'SOS-Esclaves', and later confirmed by the US Embassy. On 10 September, Minister of Culture Mohamed Lemine Ould Cheikh confirmed that the Mauritanian government had notified the US Embassy that the visas had not been granted because the visit had not been "subject of consultation with the Mauritanian authorities as is customary". On 2 December, with the international focus on Libya, where many sub-Saharan refugees were being sold as slaves, President Aziz admitted that Mauritania still had its own long-standing problem with slavery. He reiterated Mauritania's commitment to combat slavery in the same way as the country had combatted terrorism and organised crime, and to revise the legislation whenever necessary.

Mauritania remained a key ally of the West in countering *Islamist extremist groups* in the region. On 12 December, NATO announced its intention to continue its support for the National Crisis Management Centre (inaugurated in November 2016) through the four regional operational coordination centres across the country, located in Nouakchott, Nouadhibou, Rosso and Néma. The system was intended to facilitate local awareness in the various provinces, improve operational watch and early warning for the population of threats and risks, and to enhance preparedness for crises affecting national security.

The impending return of radicalised combatants from war zones such as Iraq and Syria increased the potential risk of terrorist attacks. However, on 21 March, the French Ministry of Foreign Affairs relaxed its security advice, widely seen as more general guidelines for the international community. The Adrar-region, with historical oasis towns such as Chinguetti and Ouadane, was re-categorised from a 'red zone' to an 'orange zone', as was the Senegal River valley farming belt in the south, around Kaédi and Sélibabi. This was expected to facilitate the establishment of foreign business relations and to help international organisations and non-governmental organisations to implement agricultural and poverty reduction programmes.

On 16 November, the government tightened the *blasphemy and apostasy law* through revision of Article 306 in the Penal Code, which states that any Muslim, man or woman, who insults religious symbols, will be sentenced to death. The revised law, unlike the original, would apply even to those who expressed repentance. ("Chaque musulman, homme ou femme, qui se moque ou outrage Allah ou Son Messager [Mahomet] – Paix et Salut sur Lui – ses anges, ses livres ou l'un de ses Prophètes est passible de la peine de mort, sans être appelé à se repentir. Il encourt la peine capitale même en cas de repentir.") The decision followed the judgement by the appeal court in Nouadhibou on 9 November to reduce Mohamed Mkhaïtir's death penalty for apostasy to two years' imprisonment and a fine. In 2014, Mkhaïtir had criticised in his blog those who used religion to marginalise "certain groups" in society. The decision of the appeal court caused clashes and outrage in the country. While human rights activists welcomed the court's decision, thousands of demonstrators demanded Mkhaïtir's execution. President Aziz's decision to tighten the blasphemy law was regarded as a response to this public reaction intended to regain the support he had lost after the referendum in August.

Foreign Affairs

President Aziz intended to play an active role in unblocking the constitutional crisis in *Gambia* and, on 18–19 January, he met Senegalese President Macky Sall and

Gambia's president-elect Adama Barrow, and on 20 January Gambia's President Yahya Jammeh in Banjul. However, the issue of regional security threats arising from al-Qaida-linked groups in *Mali* and beyond dominated Mauritania's relations with neighbouring countries. Mauritania was hosting more than 50,000 Malian refugees and, together with Burkina Faso, Chad, Niger and Mali, continued to participate in the G5 Sahel, a regional security and development organisation made up of Mauritania, Mali, Niger, Chad and Burkina Faso.

Migration, the fight against terrorism and organised crime, relations between Mauritania and the EU, and regional forums such as the G5 Sahel, dominated relations with the EU and the US. On 6 January, Minister for Foreign Affairs and Cooperation Isselkou Ould Ahmed Izid Bih met his Spanish counterpart Alfonso Dastis and, in March the Spanish Special Naval Warfare Force participated in 'Operation Flintlock' in Mauritania. The exercise was organised by the *US* Special Operations Command for Africa (SOCAFRICA), which was in turn under the umbrella of the US Africa Command (AFRICOM). On 27 January, US President Donald Trump signed an executive order restricting entry into the United States for refugees and nationals of seven Muslim countries, but Mauritania was not included.

On 10 February, the presidents of the G5 Sahel countries decided to create a joint force to combat terrorism and drug trafficking in the *Sahel region*, but the lack of funds was a challenge. An annual budget of € 400 m was estimated to be needed for the force to be fully operational. On 5 June, the EU announced it would give € 50 m ($ 56.4 m) to the force, while the G5 Sahel countries contributed € 50 m ($ 56.4 m) and France pledged € 8 m ($ 9.3 m). The US opted out of the multilateral approach, but Secretary of State Rex Tillerson announced on 30 October that the US would contribute $ 60 m via bilateral agreements in the Sahel region. The US, however, rejected proposals to allow cooperation between the UN Multidimensional Integrated Stabilisation Mission in Mali (MINUSMA) and the G5 Sahel joint force. This lack of coordination was expected to hinder the creation of a coherent *security* infrastructure in the region, especially given the weak capabilities of the G5 Sahel constituent armies, the faltering implementation of the peace process in Mali, the porous borders and the highly mobile groups of fighters in 'hard-to-patrol' terrain.

On 6 June, Mauritania joined Saudi Arabia, Bahrain, Egypt, the UAE, Yemen, Libya and the Maldives and broke diplomatic ties with *Qatar*, accusing it of supporting Islamist militants, which Qatar vehemently denied.

Mauritania attached major importance to its relations with *China*. On 19 May, President Aziz met Chinese Foreign Minister Wang Yi in Nouakchott. Aziz expressed his willingness to support China's international initiatives, including China's stance on reform of the UNSC and the One Belt and One Road Initiative. China's policy of non-interference in the domestic politics of its African partners was regarded as favourable to Aziz, who often faced pressure from European partners over human rights issues. On 30 October, Minister of Fisheries and Maritime Economy Nani Ould Chrougha and his Chinese counterpart, Yu Kangzhen, signed a revised intergovernmental agreement on fisheries cooperation. The partners reached a consensus on fishing quotas adjustment and fishing zones and discussed the export of Mauritanian aquatic products to China, where Mauritania had the longest cooperation in fisheries of all African countries. The discussions resulted in five Chinese enterprises being authorised to carry out fishing operations in Mauritania, using a total of 200 vessels.

On 23 May, Japan decided to contribute $ 6 m, through the WPF, to assist local communities and *Malian refugees* in the Hodh Ech Chargui region in south-eastern Mauritania. Japan's contribution allowed WFP to provide a comprehensive nutrition and livelihood support to 50,000 Malian refugees in Mbera camp, and also to assist some 22,500 vulnerable Mauritanians living around Mbera. On 28 December, Canada, the EU/European Civil Protection and Humanitarian Aid Operations, Germany, Japan, Spain and the USAID Food for Peace programme, decided to contribute $ 11.7 m to assist both Malian refugees and host Mauritanian communities living in Hodh Ech Charghi.

On 8 November, the Mauritanian Minister of the Interior and Decentralisation Ahmedou Ould Abdallah and his *Algerian* counterpart Noureddine Bedoui signed an accord in Nouakchott to open the first crossing point on the *Algerian*–Mauritania border. The Mauritanian side of the 460 km desert frontier has been declared a military zone. No opening date was proposed for the crossing, which would be located at Chegga, in the north-east of Mauritania, with Tindouf the nearest town on the Algerian side. Opening the border post was expected to boost bilateral trade and make the area more secure.

On 20 December, both international and regional media reported that President Aziz had appointed a new ambassador, Mohamed Lemine Ould Abeye, to *Morocco*, although this was not confirmed by official Mauritanian sources. During the previous five years, Mauritania had been represented in Morocco by a chargé d'affaires, because of the latent tension between the two countries. Nouakchott criticised Rabat for hosting Mauritanian regime critics, such as Mohamed Bouamatou, and Morocco did not regard favourably the rapprochement between Nouakchott and Algeria, or the fact that Mauritania was one of the countries to have recognised the Saharawi Arab Democratic Republic.

Socioeconomic Developments

The government was expected to work in line with the IMF's macro-economic recommendations (article IV consultations, see *Africa Yearbook* 13) in order to secure further funding. The National Commission against Corruption ('Comité National de Lutte contre la Corruption') continued their work, but little progress was reported and Mauritania was ranked 143rd out of 180 countries in TI's corruption index.

Consumer price *inflation* was estimated at 2.5%. Real *GDP growth* was estimated at 3.4% and continued to depend heavily on mining, construction and agriculture. A prolonged decline in global *oil and metal* prices had exposed the weaknesses of a development strategy over-reliant on mining and oil. Estimates suggested that Mauritania needed an iron ore price in excess of $ 100/tonne to guarantee the profitability of its key export commodity, but prices averaged just below $ 60/tonne.

A new *agriculture* partnership agreement worth $ 21 m between IFAD and Mauritania was signed on 18 January. Poultry farming, goats' milk and non-timber forest products were included in the first phase of the project. The agreement was expected to boost nutrition for nearly 300,000 farmers in six regions of the country and to reduce their dependence on imported staple foods. On 6 February, the World Bank Group and the Global Agriculture Food Security Program committed to an investment of € 3.5 m each to modernise, expand and diversify Tiviski SARL, a family-owned enterprise and Mauritania's biggest employer in the dairy sector, with 160 staff; it was also creating an additional 3,000 jobs and promoted opportunities for female-owned milk suppliers.

Mauritania's *fishing* industry was estimated to have contributed 25% to public revenue, up to 5% to GDP, and to have generated 53,000 jobs nationwide, approximately 30% of which were for female workers. However, women were mainly active in the local market where demand was limited and the highest quality fish were reserved for wholesalers in the male-dominated export sector.

On 27 February, the ECA initiated a *technical assistance* mission to establish a partnership with the 'Office National de la Statistique'. Expected results included improving GDP calculation methods and monitoring the country's progress in implementing the Sustainable Development Goals and Agenda 2063.

On 4 December, ExxonMobil Exploration and Production signed production sharing contracts with Mauritania for three *deep-water offshore blocks* located an average of 124 miles, or 200 km, offshore from Mauritania, together measuring nearly 8.4 m acres.

Niger

Klaas van Walraven

Mahamadou Issoufou continued his second term as president unopposed, exploiting his political advantages to the full. With the country squeezed between Islamist insurgencies, Issoufou remained a favourite collaborator for Western powers. His profile as interlocutor on migration and terrorism issues delivered funds to prop up budgets stretched by security spending and depressed commodity prices. Issoufou also made use of the impotence of the opposition, which had disintegrated in the wake of the 2016 elections. The price was embittered opponents, who had to leave meaningful opposition to civil society groups (relatively strong in Niger), who took to the streets, focusing discontent on the 2018 budget bill. Security threats remained substantial, notably because of the power vacuum in parts of Mali and Burkina Faso, with which the government tried to improve cooperation. Insurgent groups staged various attacks from Malian territory. In one incident casualties included four members of US special forces. The war against Boko Haram was marked by a fall in civilian casualties but could not prevent occasional attacks and kidnappings of civilians, including dozens of girls and adolescent boys from a village north-east of Diffa. Relations with France, under new President Macron, remained close, centring on security concerns. Economic growth, which had suffered from low uranium

 | DOI:10.1163/9789004367630_016

and oil prices as well as recession in Nigeria, recovered somewhat. Infrastructural improvements were impeded by budget constraints and other difficulties. Heavy rains led to the worst floods since 2012, while resulting in good harvests.

Domestic Politics

Politically, President Mahamadou Issoufou had a free hand to pursue his second-term agenda. The opposition remained marginalised as the ruling 'Parti Nigérien pour la Démocratie et le Socialisme' (PNDS) dominated the National Assembly, with the presidential majority boosted further by a range of lesser parties. On 8 January, in response to an opposition-sponsored march in protest against poor living conditions the previous December, pro-government supporters staged a counter-*demonstration* in the capital Niamey. Some 20,000 people, led by Mohamed Bazoum (PNDS chair and interior and security minister), shouted slogans in support of President Issoufou.

Prime Minister Brigi Rafini undertook two minor *cabinet reshuffles*, one in April and the other in October. The first involved the appointment of Yahouza Sadissou as minister for higher education, following violent student protests; he was replaced at the Ministry of Labour by Mohamed Ben Omar. The reshuffle on 30 October concerned the replacement of Omar Tchiana, a member of a minor party, who left the Department of Transport in protest at the suspension of measures against a transport company involved in a road accident that caused 29 fatalities. He was replaced by a PNDS minister, Mahamadou Karidjo. The portfolios of industry, population and public works also changed hands.

The transport minister's departure may have pointed to the government's self-serving tendencies, and the government was also downgraded from 'hybrid' to 'authoritarian' in international rankings as a result of its repressive reflexes. However, on 2 April, Issoufou said he would not try to modify the Constitution to create the possibility of a third term. He nevertheless remained vindictive towards his principal opponent, Hama Amadou, the leader of the opposition 'Mouvement Démocratique Nigérien' (Moden-Lumana), who remained in exile avoiding prosecution for his alleged involvement in a *baby trafficking scandal*. The long-running case, which had political connotations, led to the trial on 13 February of several accused, including Amadou. Niamey's Appeals Court sentenced Amadou in absentia on 13 March to a one-year prison term for complicity in the trafficking. The same fate befell Abdou Labo, a member of the opposition 'Convention Démocratique et Sociale' (CDS), who had been defeated as a candidate in the 2016 presidential race. Although Niger has the benefit of a relatively independent judiciary, Amadou's lawyer claimed the objective was to prevent his client from standing in the 2021 elections. This bizarre case helped to poison relations with the opposition further.

As the formal opposition was largely ineffective, NGO leaders such as firebrand Nouhou Arzika and the more reasonable Moussa Tchangari filled the void. The latter organised an anti-government march in Niamey on 13 January. It proved to be the start of a series of *protest gatherings*, which exploited disappointment over the government's failure to fulfil socioeconomic promises made during Issoufou's first term. Slogans centred on corruption, bad governance, prestige infrastructure projects, higher education and the presence of foreign troops (a sensitive issue in Niger). On 18 March, thousands of people in Niamey protested against the cost of living and called for investigations into an alleged corruption scandal concerning uranium sales; 11 opposition parties took part. On 5 April, a civil society leader involved in a lawsuit over the uranium scandal received a two-week prison sentence. On 10 April, students demonstrated in several cities. Grievances centred on study conditions and grant payments. The gathering in Niamey degenerated into fighting with riot police. One student died (there were rumours of another fatality), more than 100 students and 21 policemen were injured, and hundreds of people were arrested. The university campus, situated on the more peripheral south bank of the river, was closed. However, police violence was filmed and aired on social media. On 16 April, the authorities announced the arrest of three police officers on charges of assault. They were sentenced to jail. On 10 May, a demonstration planned by civil society groups in Niamey was banned and dispersed by the authorities. An activist who protested at the last-minute banning order was put in detention three days later on charges of inciting violence.

In the second half of the year, discontent crystallised around the *2018 budget bill*, which demonstrators deemed 'anti-social' (it involved limitations on civil service salaries, a rise in power charges and the introduction of new taxes). A demonstration involving over 1,000 people on 29 October got out of hand. Groups of protesters were blocked on their way to the National Assembly, after which fighting broke out in adjacent districts. Twenty-three policemen were wounded, vehicles and a police station were burned, and the headquarters of the Election Commission was vandalised. Three protest leaders were detained; they were released on 24 November. A consumer association involved in the march was banned, while Interior Minister Bazoum accused Moden of complicity. Finance Minister Hassoumi Massaoudou defended the 2018 budget bill, arguing that it imposed taxes on the rich. Protests did not stop after the National Assembly approved the bill on 26 November, however. On the last day of the year, thousands of people marched through Niamey.

As the handling of some of these demonstrations showed, the administration occasionally succumbed to *authoritarian reflexes*. On 17 July, journalist and union leader Baba Alpha and his 70-year-old father were sentenced to two years in prison and fines for carrying false papers. Of Malian origin, they were deprived of their citizenship. 'Reporters sans Frontières' claimed the sentence was politically motivated. Earlier, on 14 May, police detained human rights activist Abdourahamane Insar. He was sentenced to six months in prison for inciting people on Facebook to revolt. He was released on 8 June. Although his case was taken up by AI, Interior Minister Bazoum claimed Insar and others had called for violence and that they were Moden activists abusing the decriminalisation of press offences. (Admittedly, not all opposition and civil society forces were necessarily democratically inclined themselves.)

Security remained on the government agenda. Issoufou said that 10% of national resources went into staving off insurgent challenges. Attacks by *Boko Haram fighters* continued in the south-east, although the previous year's counter-insurgency operations diminished the extent of the violence. On 1 January, two or three army soldiers were killed and seven wounded in an attack in Baroua, west of Lake Chad. This came after the surrender of dozens of fighters the previous week. An unconfirmed report claimed a dozen insurgents were killed. The exchange took place at a time when another 20–30 fighters had surrendered, which was accompanied by a presidential appeal to Boko Haram to lay down their arms. On 9 April, however, insurgents clashed with the army near Gueskérou and 57 jihadists were reportedly killed, including one of their leaders. They had arrived from Nigeria with motorbikes and vehicles. The rest of the fighters, who were reported as well-trained and informed about army positions, were pushed back over the Komadougou-Yobé, the frontier river. The army captured vehicles, munitions and arms (including a vehicle-mounted machine gun that had been stolen in a fierce attack on Bosso near Lake Chad the previous year). A dozen soldiers were injured.

The assault ended the relative calm that had set in after the surrender by Nigérien Boko Haram fighters (totalling 130–150 by April). On 28 June, two female suicide bombers set off explosives in an IDP camp in Kabélawa (south of Nguigmi), killing two other people and wounding a dozen. It was the first attack on such a camp on Nigérien soil. Like the attack on Baroua, it took place further away from the Nigerian border. On 2 July, insurgents arrived on foot in the village of Ngaléwa (close to Kabélawa), known to be hostile to Boko Haram. They slit the throats of nine people and adducted 37, all young girls and boys – the first *mass kidnapping* in Niger. On 5 July, one of Niger's jet fighter planes killed 14 displaced farmers by mistake in the village of Abadam, straddling the border with Nigeria. Having returned to tend to their fields, two Nigériens and 12 Nigerians perished in the attack; this was not the first incident of its kind, the Nigerian army having made similar mistakes in the past. A Nigérien journalist said that the army had been nervous about recent attacks. During July, a further 7,000 refugees left the region, crossing into Chad. On 21 August, the army reported having killed 40 Boko Haram fighters, but Niger's strategic position deteriorated in October as a result of the withdrawal of hundreds of Chadian troops in response to fiscal problems. It was reported, moreover, that traders in the regional capital Diffa, whose businesses were suffering from a ban on the trade in food and fuel, were compensating for their losses by trading with the enemy. On 15 October, Diffa's governor warned that the offer of an amnesty would expire on 31 December. UN figures in August mentioned a total of 540 civilian victims in Niger so far, including those killed, wounded and abducted. Civilian fatalities had dropped, however, from 227 in 2016 to 141.

Fighting in the north-west was fiercer. On 22 February, an army patrol ran into an ambush near In Tirzawane, close to the border with Mali. A dozen or more military were killed and 19 wounded. The insurgents, allegedly of a jihadist group led by Adnane Abou Walid al-Sahraoui, formerly a member of the Polisario front, who had sworn allegiance to Islamic State, captured seven vehicles and burnt four. The assault demonstrated the striking power of the several dozen insurgents, who arrived heavily armed and equipped with motorbikes and vehicles from the Malian Ménaka region, evading French, Malian and Nigérien intelligence. In response, France announced its willingness to station counter-insurgency troops (50–80 men) to provide aerial guidance to the Nigérien military. On 6 March, three days after the declaration of a *state of emergency* in the Tillabéri and Tahoua regions, a gendarmerie post was attacked in the Gourma region, close to the borders with Mali and Burkina Faso. Five gendarmes were killed. Two French Mirage fighters stationed in Niamey intervened, as well as French helicopters from Gao (Mali). The insurgents, possibly from the 'Mouvement pour l'Unicité et le Jihad en Afrique de l'Ouest' (MUJAO), were driven off. In mid-September, the government extended the state of emergency for a further three months.

These measures could not prevent an attack near the village of Tongo Tongo on 4 October, again staged from the Ménaka region. The ambush drew publicity as the victims included four members of *US Special Forces*, one of whom appeared to have been executed. Four Nigériens died, while two Americans were injured. The American forces, present to train Nigériens in counter-insurgency operations, were 12 in total and were patrolling the border together with 30 Nigérien military. The troops were allegedly lured into extended discussions with village elders, allowing 50 fighters to lay an ambush. The insurgents, who, according to the International Crisis Group, had recruited youngsters from the local Fulani community, were described by the Americans as associated with Islamic State. Locals suggested al-Sahraoui. The US-Nigérien operation appeared poorly prepared, as troops were lightly armed and unaware of the risk of attack. Lacking back-up personnel, they had to be rescued by French forces in Mali. The US Africa Command (AFRICOM), started an inquiry whose results were not expected before year's end. Niger's government declared three days of mourning. A Tongo Tongo elder was arrested for complicity, and President Issoufou convened a session of the 'Conseil National de Sécurité'. Nevertheless, another attack took place on 21 October. The insurgents arrived in vehicles and were armed with rocket launchers. They attacked a gendarmerie post at Ayorou, capturing a large stock of weapons, ammunition and vehicles. Thirteen gendarmes were killed and another five injured. In an ominous sign of the gradual escalation of the insurgency, the government announced on 4 November that it would allow the US to arm its surveillance drones. Moreover, it became clear that the American involvement in the fighting at Tongo Tongo in October did not represent an isolated incident, when it was confirmed early in 2018 that US Special Forces, in conjunction with Nigérien military, had also fought militants on 6 December. Eleven jihadists, reported to be aligned to Islamic State, were killed. US and Nigérien forces suffered no casualties.

Foreign Affairs

With Niger playing a key role in sub-regional security, relations with *France* remained close. President Issoufou held separate talks with his new French counterpart President Emmanuel Macron at the G7 summit in Sicily on 26 May. On 2 July, the two men met at the Bamako summit of the G5 Sahel countries (Chad, Niger, Burkina Faso, Mali and Mauritania) and at a similar event in New York on 18 September. On 13 December, Issoufou flew to France, meeting the French president in multilateral discussions on G5 military cooperation. On 22–23 December, Issoufou welcomed Macron, his defence minister and the French chief of staff in Niamey, where the French president celebrated Christmas with the 500 French troops stationed there. The Niamey base hosted Mirage jet fighters and drones. Like the Americans, whose air facility is in Agadez, the French decided to arm their surveillance drones before 2020.

Niger also tried to improve military cooperation with *Mali and Burkina Faso*, as the faltering peace process in Mali was leading to a worsening power vacuum in the border zone. On 24 January, the three countries announced they would share intelligence and operational resources to combat insecurity in the Liptako-Gourma region, where the borders of the three countries meet and jihadists had taken refuge. The force would be modelled on the four-nation 'Force Multinationale Mixte' (FMM) of Nigérien, Chadian, Nigerian and Camerounian troops fighting Boko Haram. On 9 May, Niger signed an accord on judicial cooperation with both Mali and *Chad*, facilitating the sharing of intelligence and extradition procedures.

More broadly, Niger participated in the security cooperation of the *Sahel G5*. On 6 February, the five nations met in Mali and resolved to establish a joint force to combat terrorism and drug trafficking (a kindred decision had already been taken the previous year). Pushed by the French, it was now rumoured that the force would number 10,000 (5,000 during a first phase). The summit in Bamako (Mali) on 2 July discussed the issue of funding. With a requirement estimated at € 423 m, the G5 countries announced a joint contribution of € 10 m, while the EU pledged € 50 m and France € 8 m. Thus, while having the FMM in mind (which also had a long gestation period), the project proved financially daunting. President Issoufou proposed that the G5 force become a brigade within the UN peacekeeping mission in

Mali, MINUSMA, whose € 1 bn budget could then be involved. The headquarters of the force were established in Sévaré (Mali) on 9 September and it became operational on 1 November While Morocco pledged logistical and training assistance, the financial issue continued to bedevil the project as the US remained lukewarm about integration in MINUSMA for fear of increasing UN peacekeeping costs. At discussions in France on 13 December, Saudi Arabia pledged € 100 m for the force, followed by the UAE (€ 30 m) and the Netherlands € 5 m). The US eventually pledged € 60 m.

On 3 March, members of the UNSC began a tour of the three countries hit by the Boko Haram insurgency, starting in Cameroun. The *EU* meanwhile tried to stem the outflow of migrants via the Sahara by providing Niger with a grant worth € 610 m. With Agadez the main transit point for West Africans en route to North Africa, it was hoped this money would help Niger to improve *migration* policing. The European Border and Coast Guard Agency Frontex resolved to set up a base in Agadez before year's end so that EU officials could process migrants there. In previous years, the government had set up transit centres financed by the EU and the International Organisation for Migration in Niamey, Arlit, Agadez and Dirkou to assist migrants willing to return home. While the government claimed that the number of migrants passing through had dropped by 80%, many of these now avoided Agadez and other checkpoints by navigating the more dangerous desert routes. On 17 July, the EU announced that it had released € 10 m for the Nigérien government, with a further € 10 m to follow before year's end. The amounts would be used to tackle the deeper causes of migration. At a conference in Paris on 28 August to discuss migration issues, President Issoufou and his Chadian counterpart pointed out to Western partners that, if they wished to eradicate the problem, African countries required more assistance in terms of development aid. The conference agreed to a proposal put forward by President Macron to provide Niger and Chad with official powers to register and process legal migrants to Europe.

Socioeconomic Developments

Rains were heavy, boding well for the country's cereal harvest. However, they also led to the *worst floods since 2012*. In September, it was estimated that nearly 200,000 people were affected. Fifty people died, mostly in the Niamey region, more than 12,000 ha of agricultural land was destroyed and over 15,000 head of cattle drowned. The principal regions affected were Tillabéri, Maradi, Zinder and Dosso. The government developed an assistance plan.

Economic growth improved somewhat and was estimated in November at 5.2%, but this was insufficient to keep up with population growth and could not alleviate Niger's budget difficulties either. Faced by disappointing sales to recession-struck

Nigeria (which would normally absorb one-fifth of Niger's exports), the government had already cut less important expenditure in 2016. Public debt had escalated from 26% of GDP in 2012 to 48% in 2016. The 2018 budget of € 2.9 bn (a 2.5% increase) foresaw tax increases, reductions in expenditure and the scrapping of tax exemptions. The *IMF* applauded the measures. On 23 January, it approved a three-year ECF credit of $ 134 m, with an immediate disbursement of $ 19.2 m. An IMF mission to Niamey on 6 November deemed Niger's macroeconomic performance as generally satisfactory. According to the World Bank's 'Doing Business' index, the *business environment* had improved (Niger rose from 164th to 150th of 190 countries). This could not prevent a deterioration in the legal battle waged with *Africard*, a Lebanese-owned company that had won a contract with Salou Djibo's military government in 2011 for the production of passports. Having cancelled the € 53 m contract later, Issoufou's government vainly pleaded its case before various tribunals. Africard now proceeded with the seizure of government property in France and the US.

Construction of the *Niger-Benin railway* continued to be mired in problems similar to those with Africard. On 29 September, the Supreme Court of Benin confirmed judgements in favour of a Beninese company claiming to be the owner of the contract, to the detriment of French conglomerate Bolloré, Niger's favoured partner, which had built the railway section between Niamey and Dosso. Issoufou's government continued to refuse to deal with the Beninese company or a Chinese alternative proposed by Benin in an effort to resolve the deadlock. Without the section between Dosso and Parakou, the railway, which was intended to link Niamey with Cotonou, remained inoperative. On 2 April, President Issouofu opened a 100 MW *power plant* near Niamey. Despite the slogan 'electricity for all', the country still suffered numerous power cuts, notably in the hot months of April and May when air conditioners work around the clock. On 24 November, the AfDB agreed to provide $ 107 m for the upgrading of the road linking Niger with Burkina Faso. Additional funding came from the EU, Japan and the Burkinabé government.

The government banned *artisanal gold mining* in two regions. In the Djado plateau in the north-east, it imposed a shutdown in February, fearing gold mining could become a source of revenue for insurgents and increase trafficking (artisanal mining had exploded since discoveries in 2014). On 15 July, a ban was imposed in the Liptako region close to Burkina Faso, where more than 20,000 people had been mining deposits for several decades. The government justified this measure with allegations of anarchy on the mine sites.

Despite efforts to curb *illegal migration* across the Sahara, the outflow of (West) Africans via Niger continued unabated. Opting for the more dangerous desert routes to avoid checkpoints (since 2015 traffickers also risked severe penalties), numerous people paid with their lives. On 21 May, 44 bodies, including of babies, were recovered near Agadez. The victims' vehicle had broken down and people had died of thirst. Only six managed to reach safety. Earlier that month, eight Nigérien migrants, including five children, died on their way to Algeria. In mid-June, the army rescued a group of 100 persons abandoned in the desert by their trafficker – a regular occurrence and one that brings a certain death sentence. On 25 June, the army rescued 24 people from a group of 70 abandoned in the Ténéré sand desert en route for Libya. The others were assumed to have perished. With the economy and population of Agadez having grown significantly from this gruesome trade, the government invested more than € 60 m in the city's infrastructural development in an effort to revamp its tourist potential. In September and October, Algeria expelled 7,800 West Africans to the border with Niger, where they faced difficult conditions. It was estimated that some 100,000 people from SSA were living illegally in Algeria. Public opinion was shocked by reports of migrants being sold into slavery at auctions in Libya. A group of 25 from the Horn of Africa was evacuated to Niger on 11 November. Niger summoned the Libyan ambassador for talks on 19 November.

There was no let-up in terms of the deeper causes of these problems. One issue, Niger's *demographic situation*, received renewed attention, however. President Issoufou expressed an aim to bring the population growth rate down from 3.9% to 3%. The government wanted to end child marriage by making education compulsory for girls up to the age of 16. The current population growth meant that women bore an average of 7.6 children, at which rate Niger would have a population (currently around 19 m) of 25 m in 2025 and 90 m in 2050. The average age was 15. On 11 July, Minister for Population Christelle Rakiatou Jackou announced that the use of contraception showed a slight increase (from 5% in 2006 to 12%), adding that she aimed to raise the figure to 50%. There was UN assistance for a programme of family planning to attain this goal, besides legislation to provide free contraceptives. On his visit to Niger on 23 December, President Macron announced that France would provide funding to boost girls' school enrolment to reduce early marriage and pregnancies.

On 8 April, Minister of Education Daouda Marthé reported that the state had been paying € 7.3 m a year to thousands of so-called 'ghost teachers'. With 80% of teaching staff made up of contract workers, the 'Haute Autorité de Lutte contre la Corruption et Infractions Assimilées' had systematically checked schools and their payrolls (salaries for temporary staff were in the range of € 114 to € 152 a month – considerable sums in Niger).

Nigeria

Heinrich Bergstresser

The ill-health and absence of President Muhammadu Buhari, which lasted for months, the on-going Islamist insurgency in North East zone, the precarious situation in North Central, organised crime and the country's slow recovery from the worst recession for 30 years set the political and socioeconomic scene. The president's advanced age and poor health led to further debates during the second half of the year and at year's end, when the issue of succession and questions about Buhari's achievements and his capacity to lead the country were prominent, and the forthcoming elections in early 2019 did nothing to dampen these debates. Despite the many challenges, Vice President Yemi Osinbajo, a lawyer and former commissioner of justice in Lagos, handled the most dangerous threats in a professional and far-sighted manner, thus convincing the elites and the public that the democratic institutions were more stable than was widely assumed. However, the government eventually sealed a deal with the new US administration under President Trump, which was ready to sell military hardware to combat terrorism. Beyond that, the battered economy slightly began to recover.

 | DOI:10.1163/9789004367630_017

Domestic Politics

President Muhammadu Buhari left Nigeria on 19 January, after informing the leadership of both houses of the National Assembly that he was going on a ten-day vacation and routine medical check-up in Britain, and that Vice President Yemi Osinbajo, in accordance with the *Constitution* would take over as acting president. It soon became apparent that the president's absence would last longer than first announced, and this caused widespread uncertainties about the impact of Buhari's state of health on the political system, but on 10 March, Buhari returned to Nigeria, admitting that he had never been so ill, and, with some self-imposed restrictions, he eventually resumed his duties.

Less than two months later, on 7 May, after receiving the 82 Chibok girls who had been released from captivity by Boko Haram, the president again left for Britain for further consultations with his physicians. For the second time during the year, and the fourth time since the Buhari administration came to power in 2015, the *vice president took over as acting president.* It soon became clear that, this time, the medical trip would last much longer than before and the debate over a possible succession gained momentum. On 19 August, however, Buhari returned to Abuja and, obviously physically weak, he addressed the nation in a national broadcast the following day. Against the backdrop of the crisis in the Igbo-heartland in the east and a growing debate in several parts of the country about the devolution of powers and the restructuring of the entire political system, he underlined his commitment to Nigerian unity which, he said, was not negotiable. In addition, on 21 August, he notified the National Assembly of his resumption of duties as president.

Despite the president's poor health during the year, he used his executive powers to appoint and remove several chairmen and board members of the numerous *state agencies and federal parastatals*; these short-term lucrative positions served first and foremost to redistribute huge financial resources to the political elite. It was estimated that NGN (naira) 1.985 tn, more than a quarter of the federal budget, were allocated to about 480 federal agencies in the 2017 budget.

In early January, the president approved the appointment of Major-General Emmanuel Bassey (rtd) and former assistant controller-general of immigration, Ado Abdullahi Ja'afar, as commissioners of the Civil Defence, Fire, Immigration and Prisons Services Board. On 13 April, he removed the heads of 23 federal government agencies such as the National Agency for the Prohibition of Trafficking in Persons (NAPTIP), to which Julie Okah-Donli was appointed director general. On 30 June, another woman, Patience Oniha, replaced the long-serving director general of the Debt Management Office, Abraham Nwankwo, who retired after two five-year terms in office.

For the rest of the year, *appointments* followed in their dozens, including top positions in the state-owned media. By the end of the year, Buhari had appointed more than 1,400 persons to fill positions on the boards of the agencies and parastatals of several federal ministries. After a lengthy investigation, he sacked the secretary to the government of the federation, Babachir David Lawal, on 30 October, and replaced him with Boss Gida Mustapha. The director-general of the National Intelligence Agency, Ayodele Oke, was also sacked, and, towards year's end, a senior foreign affairs adviser to the Presidency, Ahmed Rufa'i Abubakar, was short-listed as his replacement.

The most important appointment, however, was made by acting president Osinbajo who, on 7 March, swore in Walter Onnoghen as Nigeria's *17th substantive chief justice*. For months it seemed that the issue hung in the balance after Buhari had sworn him in only in an acting capacity in November 2016. More was to come, and Osinbajo used his temporary powers to make other far-reaching appointments. On 29 June, he appointed 14 new resident electoral commissioners and assigned the chairmanship of the Independent Corrupt Practices and Other Related Offenses Commission to Bolaji Owasanoye.

Against the backdrop of a generally precarious situation in which the armed forces were fighting at least *14 security threats across the country*, the military redeployed their upper echelons. This they did at frequent intervals, a scale of deployment that had not been seen before in the Fourth Republic, and it was a clear indication that all was not well in the military, particularly with respect to the ongoing fight against the insurgency in North East zone. On 9 January, the first batch of more than a dozen brigadiers and major generals were redeployed, including Major General Enobong Udoh, who became general officer commanding (GOC) 6 Division in Port Harcourt. In early May, in a radical strategic review of the security challenges, the army appointed further top commanders. Major General Ahmed Mohammed Dikko took over as GOC 1 Division, in Kaduna, Brigadier Ibrahim M. Yusuf emerged as acting GOC 7 Division, garrisoned in Maiduguri, and Major General Ibrahim Attahiru was named commander of 'Operation Lafiya Dole' in North East zone. At a quite early stage, however, on 7 December, Attahiru was replaced by Major General Rogers Ibe Nicholas, after the military suffered several setbacks against the Islamist insurgents. More redeployments were undertaken and Major General Peter J. Dauke was posted as GOC to 81 Division in Lagos, while Brigadier Benjamin I. Ahanotu took over his position as acting GOC 3 Division in Jos. Eventually, another brigadier, Stevenson O. Olabanji, emerged as acting GOC 8 Task Force, garrisoned in Maiduguri and Major General Leo Irabor moved to the Multinational Joint Task Force. The brigadiers belonged to the batch of 45 who were promoted to two-star generals on 20 November.

Earlier, mid-July saw the most *far-reaching military shake-up* in recent years, with 49 major generals and brigadiers and almost 600 officers from the rank of colonel down to lieutenant affected. But more was to come, when, on 29 December, another round of redeployments took place, involving almost 400 officers. Among them was

Major General Musa S. Yusuf, who took over as GOC 6 Division in Port Harcourt, replacing Major General Enobong Udoh. The latter was transferred as GOC 81 Division and Major General Okwudili F. Azinta was named GOC 2 Division in Ibadan.

Shortly before, in an unprecedented move, the tenure of four service chiefs, Gabriel Olonisakin (defence), Tukur Buratai (army), Ibok-Ete Ekwe Ibas (navy) and Sadique Abubakar (air force) was extended for a second time, although all but Buratai had already been due for retirement a year before.

The cases of two major generals, Ibrahim Sani and Patrick Falola, who were to have faced *courts martial* in 2016 for misconduct and dereliction of duty, took another twist. Falola, who had been demoted to brigadier, took his case to the Court of Appeal and, at the end of March, the army council eventually restored his rank and he withdrew his case. However, in July, Sani was demoted to brigadier for misappropriation and was ordered to return NGN 23 m, and subsequently had to accept compulsory retirement. He challenged his retirement in court and, on 12 December, the Court of Appeal ordered the army not to retire him until the case before the court had been determined. The hearing was set for 15 March 2018.

The *police force*, with a strength of some 370,000 and rated by the World Internal Security and Police Index International the 'worst' globally in terms of its ability to handle internal security challenges, also underwent some changes, mainly focusing on promotions. In the course of the year, close to 10,000 senior police officers were promoted. On 19 April, it was announced that plans had been concluded to recruit 30,000 personnel annually in order to enhance community policing, with the bulk of the 150,000 recruits over a period of five years expected to serve in their own communities.

A further change was seen in the *privatisation of security organisations*, a trend that gained momentum throughout the year. In November, the National Assembly passed an establishment bill for the National Peace Corps under the command of the controversial Dickson Akoh, despite sharp criticism from the security forces. By year's end, however, the president had not yet signed the bill into law.

On 11 May, the National Assembly released details of *Assembly expenditure* of NGN 125 bn for the current year, the equivalent of some $ 400 m. For years, public pressure had been relentless and, as expected, the document confirmed that the income of the parliamentarians, their aides and the management was impressive, to say the least.

On 26–27 July, both houses of the National Assembly voted on 33 *amendments to the Constitution*, which would usher in a number of sweeping changes. However, only towards the end of November was the shortened list of revised amendments forwarded to the 36 state assemblies for ratification. To the disappointment of many women's organisations and civil society and business circles, some of the amendments were dropped, including the deletion of the controversial land-use act, the transfer of parts of the executive legislative list to the concurrent legislative list, the guarantee of a married woman's right to choose her state indigeneship by either birth or marriage, and finally, the 35% affirmative action for women in government and other state institutions. At year's end, the amendments had still not been ratified, although only 24 state parliaments were required to ratify them before they could be sent to the president for his approval.

Statutory *gubernatorial elections* were conducted in Anambra state on 18 November, which the incumbent, Willie Obiano of the All Progressives Great Alliance, won by a clear margin; the party was popular in parts of the Igbo-heartland but only in Anambra was it successful at the polls. A number of unresolved court cases concerning past gubernatorial elections were finally decided during the year in favour of the incumbents.

The slightly improved *security situation* in the crisis-ridden North East zone suffered a number of setbacks, which cost the lives of dozens of security personnel and hundreds of innocent citizens and Islamist insurgents. As in previous years, Borno state was the main target of suicide bombings, mostly carried out by young girls. Other deadly assaults constantly reminded the public that the *Islamist insurgency of Boko Haram* was far from over, although the security services arrested members of the sect in their dozens. Most of the attacks were repelled, however, and a number of attempts were foiled by the security services.

Several attacks in January heralded yet another year of the insurgency, if on a smaller scale. On 8 and 10 January, half a dozen soldiers, including an officer, lost their lives when members of Boko Haram invaded two suburbs, Cinki Gundu and Old Marte, on the outskirts of Maiduguri. Shortly afterwards, on 16 January, two bombs were detonated on the university campus, killing half a dozen persons, including Professor of Veterinary Medicine Aliyu Mani while observing the dawn (*fajr*) prayer. This deadly attack was just the beginning of a chain of *suicide bombings at Maiduguri's university*, including an attack on 25 June that killed some 16 persons.

The accidental bombing by a military jet of an IDP camp in Rann, a village in Kala-Balge local government area in Borno state, shocked the general public and further lowered the *reputation of the security services*. Over 230 people were killed. On 9 February, half a dozen soldiers lost their lives in a battle along the Maiduguri-Dikwa road. Against the backdrop of the ongoing insurgency, Borno state governor, Kashim Shettima, claimed on 13 February that, over the years, the insurgency had resulted in almost 100,000 fatalities and some 2.1 m persons had been internally displaced, although most sources suggested much smaller numbers.

On 1 March, the military claimed to have arrested close to 7,900 suspected insurgents and killed some 50 others in previous weeks. Barely two weeks later, seven Boko Haram suspects were arraigned for the abduction and killing of a dozen foreigners from construction sites in Kebbi and Bauchi states in 2011 and 2013, respectively. Soon afterwards, in an event clearly aimed at demonstrating leadership and strength, Minister of Defence Brigadier Mansur Dan-Ali (rtd), on behalf of the president, launched the Nigerian Army Small Arms Championship at the newly established shooting range in the former Boko Haram stronghold of Sambisa Forest.

On 1 April, Bulama Kailani Mohammed Metele, a high-ranking member of the Mamman Nur Faction, and listed 253rd on the list of most wanted terrorists, surrendered. This was only one of many such capitulations in the months that followed. By mid-April, the government acknowledged on-going negotiations with Boko Haram splinter groups to free the *Chibok school girls* who were still in captivity. Eighty-two were eventually released on 6 May in exchange for some imprisoned Boko Haram suspects, but some 100 were still missing and it was reported that some of them did not wish to be released. Prior to that, on 18 April, troops had rescued more than 1,600 captives in Kala-Balge local government area.

Bombings and killings continued unabated and, on 8 June at the Bakasi Camp in Maiduguri, acting president Osinbajo unveiled a new plan for the effective delivery of relief supplies to IDPs. However, even the IDP camps were targeted by suicide bombers: Dalori 1 and 2 camps, on the outskirts of the Borno state capital, were attacked on 23–24 July and at least four persons were killed. On 25 July, one of the worst incidents took place in the Lake Chad Basin: about 40 oil exploration workers, including ten academic and technical staff of the University of Maiduguri, contracted by a subsidiary of the Nigeria National Petroleum Corporation (NNPC), and security operatives and members of the civilian joint task force were ambushed by insurgents, led by Abu Musa al-Barnawi. All were killed except for the three university staff, who appeared on video three days later, pleading to be rescued and for their captors' demands to be met. At the end of the year, their fate was still not decided.

This *renewed upsurge in attacks* threw the military off balance, as was evident when, on 11 August, soldiers invaded the premises of the local UN Office for the Coordination of Humanitarian Affairs, claiming to be searching for hidden arms. Only two days later, the federal government apologised and assured humanitarian agencies that it would respect and safeguard their diplomatic status.

On 2 September, in a new onslaught, the *air force bombed* alleged hideouts in the Sambisa Forest to neutralise remnants of the Islamists and intensified the bombardment in early November. On 1 October, in an effort to overcome the growing frustration among the combat units, President Buhari joined the military in Maiduguri to celebrate Independence Day. However, contrary to several announcements, the military failed for the umpteenth time to hunt down Boko Haram's self-proclaimed leader, Abubakar Shekau.

Neighbouring *Adamawa was also a key target* of the insurgents, although not on the scale seen in Borno. The state was caught between attacks by Islamist insurgents and deadly conflicts between farmers, herdsmen and security services. The worst attack took place on 21 November in a mosque in Mubi, when, during the early morning prayer, a boy detonated an explosive device, killing himself and more than 50 worshippers. In neighbouring Yobe state, the military suffered a serious setback when, on 24 October, Islamist insurgents attacked a base near the state capital Damaturu, killing several troops. On 20 November, Adamawa suffered heavy losses among local farmers and police when Fulani settlements in Numan local government were raided, allegedly by ethnic Bachama militants, leading to the death of at least 50 persons, including women and children. Soon afterwards, on 1 December, the police force lost half a dozen staff during a *battle with suspected herdsmen* in the same area, which prompted the military to take over the entire area.

The on-going crisis in North East zone persuaded Buhari to approve the establishment of a naval base on Lake Chad on 27 March and, soon afterwards, to upgrade the army institute of technology and environment in Biu to a university. Finally, on 25 October, he assented to the North-East Development Commission (Establishment) Bill 2017.

The already *precarious security situation in the eastern Middle Belt region* worsened and the region became a veritable battlefield, affecting neighbouring northern and southern states, such as Adamawa, Kaduna, Delta, Enugu and Cross River. Cattle rustling, disputes over grazing rights and fertile land, and organised crime led almost daily to deadly skirmishes and to the deaths of scores of herdsmen, peasants, security personnel and innocent civilians. As before, Benue was a focal point of hostilities when fighting broke out around 22 January, allegedly between Fulani herdsmen and local farmers in Ohimini local government area, killing more than ten. In a similar incident in Buruku local government area on 10 March, several persons fell victim to the attackers. In a ghastly attack on the yam market in Zaki Biam on 20 March, unknown gunmen invaded the market and shot more than 50 persons. Further attacks on several other communities followed, so that, towards year's end, four IDP camps in Logo local government area alone were hosting some 80,000 refugees. At the turn of the year, another massacre triggered by herdsmen in Guma Logo local government area, cost the lives of more than 70 persons.

Several *deadly assaults in Plateau state* were recorded, including a wave of attacks in Bassa local government in September and October. In Riyom local government area, about ten traders were ambushed and killed, allegedly by Fulani herdsmen, as they returned from the weekly village market in Makera on 7 November.

There was a similar *precarious situation in neighbouring Kaduna state*, particularly in the south, where a spell of violence claimed hundreds of lives. On 19–20 February, Kaura and Jama'a local government areas suffered deadly attacks, allegedly by Fulani herdsmen, who gunned down 20 people. The Miyetti Allah Cattle Breeders Association (MACBAN) blamed most of these atrocities on Fulani from outside Nigeria who were using the international grazing routes as a haven. Although MACBAN could not substantiate this claim, it maintained that, over the previous two years, no fewer than 600 herdsmen had been killed, several others kidnapped for ransom and some 2 m cattle rustled. On 16 March, Kaura was hit again and an estimated 100 persons were killed and, on 15 April, a dozen more were killed in local farming communities in Jema'a.

The on-going killings in this region compelled the security forces to start a new campaign to end the attacks and atrocities. On 19 April, the chief of army staff inaugurated '*Operation Harbin Kunama II*' ('Operation Shooting Scorpion'), which was supposed to cover southern Kaduna and neighbouring states, such as Zamfara and Katsina. In fact, this did not prevent further violence, as was borne out by further carnage in Kajuru local government in mid-July, which claimed close to 40 lives. But this time mostly herdsmen were killed.

The issue of *grazing reserve centres* and the prohibition of open grazing, which had re-surfaced the previous year, gathered momentum in July, when Taraba state, another focal point of hostilities, passed the Open Grazing Prohibition and Ranches Establishment into law. In September and November, Ekiti and Benue states followed suit. More states in the Igbo- and Yoruba heartlands in South East and South West zones, such as Imo, Ebonyi and Ogun, were debating similar laws, trying to control the growing threat. On 7 April, the federal government had vowed to demarcate 6,000 km of cattle routes without delay, but no progress had been reported by year's end.

More states in the south felt the impact and, in addition, *communal clashes* with quite a noticeable ethnic and sectarian undercurrent gave more cause for concern. The worst incident happened in South West zone in ancient Ile-Ife in March, when Yoruba and Hausa clashed, triggering mayhem in which scores died and close to 100 persons were injured. In November, however, in Ikorodu in Lagos state, home of the notorious 'Badoo Cult', 500 members gave themselves up to the police.

Calls for an independent Biafra by advocacy groups in the Igbo heartland, such as the Indigenous People of Biafra (IPOB), the Movement for the Actualization of the Sovereign State of Biafra, the Biafra Independence Movement and the Biafra Zionist Movement, continued undiminished through the year. The somewhat self-proclaimed chief promoter, Nnamdi Kanu of IPOB, arrested for treason in 2015, was eventually released on bail on 28 April on tough bail conditions. Kanu's address to a crowd of his supporters was put on the Internet on 28 May, violating a court order banning him from giving interviews or addressing rallies, but no action was taken by the authorities. In mid-September, the military conducted a four-week operation named Egwu Eke II ('Python Dance') to tackle separatist agitation in South East zone. This was considered a needless provocation and caused widespread unease, underlining the reputation of the security services for their heavy-handed management of sensitive political situations, as was amply demonstrated in skirmishes with IPOB members on 10 and 13 September, and the siege of Kanu's residence in Abia's capital, Umuahia, where he was put under house arrest and dozens of his supporters were arrested. By imposing a four-day dusk-to-dawn curfew, Abia's Governor Okezie Ikpeazu only added fuel to the fire. On 15 September, the governors of South East zone banned all IPOB activities, and the Nigerian defence headquarters controversially declared IPOB a terrorist organisation. When President Buhari signed a presidential proclamation proscribing IPOB on 18 September, it was challenged in court but to no avail. On 17 October, there was high drama in the federal high court in Abuja when Nnamdi Kanu did not appear to face trial. The judge warned the three persons who stood surety for him that they would lose their bail bonds of NGN 100 m each if they failed to produce him in court. The judge adjourned the case, but Kanu had gone underground and local observers suspected that he was somewhere in the Niger Delta.

By mid-November, Buhari, who for years had conspicuously shied away from the Igbo heartland, made his first visit to the region since assuming power. He focussed on Ebonyi state, where he reiterated his firm stand on a united Nigeria. On 18 October, as a gesture of goodwill, he had approved the payment of pensions for retired Biafran policemen who had been granted a presidential pardon in 2000, and subsequently agreed to pay victims of the civil war NGN 88 bn in compensation.

Despite the incidence of *piracy, kidnappings and killings in the volatile Niger Delta*, there was tangible improvement in the security situation. On 16 January, acting president Osinbajo began the first leg of a fact-finding tour of the Niger Delta, trying to re-establish trust in the government's development and security efforts. Within the next few months, more trips to the region followed. Around the time of his first visit, however, a crew of seven Russians and one Ukrainian were taken hostage after their ship, sailing under the flag of Antigua and Barbados, was attacked. In another incident at the end of April, at least eight Nigerians on board a supply vessel were kidnapped. There were more cases of piracy and killings, such as on 15 May in Delta state, where four policemen patrolling the river were killed. The federal government and the security services responded to the challenges with a carrot-and-stick approach. In mid-February, Minister of State for Petroleum Resources Emmanuel Ibe Kachikwu unveiled a 20-point agenda aimed at establishing permanent peace in the oil – and gas-producing region, of which one significant measure was the creation of job opportunities for youth. The government released an additional NGN 35 bn to enhance the existing amnesty programme, which had already been allocated NGN 20 bn in 2016. On the other hand, on 7 October, the security services, under the leadership of the GOC 6 Division, began a concerted exercise in six Niger Delta states, code-named 'Operation Crocodile Smile II', and another but much shorter one about three weeks later, named 'Operation Octopus Grip'. However, given the poor human rights record, many stakeholders and residents of the coastal areas discounted any good intentions, and accused the security forces of high-handed behaviour. In mid-November, the chief of naval staff announced that, since beginning of the year, more than 1,000 illegal refineries had been destroyed, and dozens of suspected oil thieves had been arrested.

Throughout the year, *organised crime* persisted, although the security situation in Greater Lagos and neighbourhoods tangibly improved – thanks to private capital subsidising the local police force. However, murder and the lucrative business of *kidnapping* for ransom remained frequent, although several notorious gangs were smashed and hundreds of perpetrators arrested or killed. On 13 January, kidnappers struck at the Nigeria-Turkish International School, taking a handful of students and staff hostage. After 12 days in captivity, they were released physically unharmed. On 31 January, a UN monitoring team demarcating and delineating the Nigerian-Cameroon border was attacked and five of them were killed, including a Kenyan and a Cameroonian. Two German archaeologists from Frankfurt University, Peter Breunig and Johannes Behringer, working with the national commission for museums and monuments, were abducted in southern Kaduna state on 23 February. They were released two days later but two Nigerian staff working with them were killed during the raid. Kidnappings were recorded in several federal states, involving ordinary citizens, politicians, public servants, business people, clerics, traditional rulers, students, academic staff, security personnel and foreigners. To cite a few examples: on 9 April, the commissioner for water resources in Cross River state, Gabriel Odu-Oji, was kidnapped and set free a month later, but Olamide Odimayo, a chieftain of the All Progressives Congress in Ondo state, was not so lucky. He was found dead one week after his abduction on 15 June. Even policemen were targeted, such as an assistant commissioner who was taken hostage together with his family along Birnin Gwari-Funtua highway in Kaduna state on 27 September. All were released a few days later. One of the worst incidents took place on 6 August during Sunday mass in St Philip's Catholic Church in Ozubulu in Anambra state, when gunmen, allegedly belonging to a crystal meth drug cartel, raided the church and shot scores of worshippers. On 13 October, the four members of a British missionary and optical medicine charity team were kidnapped from a clinic in Delta state. The visiting optician, Ian Squire, was eventually killed, while the others were released after a three-week ordeal. And on New Year's Eve, Chief Etum Numana, his wife and some others were shot in Sanga local government area in southern Kaduna state. The number of kidnappings and killings was unknown but, on 3 November, the inspector general of police, Ibrahim Kpotum Idris, disclosed that up to 3,000 suspected kidnappers were being held in custody. Given the large number of victims, the president, on 29 December, assented to a bill making the treatment and care of victims of shooting incidents compulsory, thereby ending years of legal wrangle.

Deficiencies in legal and security proceedings came into sharp focus when, on 27 January, gunmen stormed the Owerri High Court in Imo state and rescued the notorious criminal Henry Chibueze, alias Vampire, and two other defendants. Chibueze was killed in early March in a gun battle with the police in neighbouring

Rivers state. He was one of many criminals apprehended or killed by security forces, including the gang leader, Chukwudubem Onwuamadike, alias Evans, who for years had terrorised South West zone and was finally arrested in Lagos on 10 June.

As in previous years, the government's *anti-corruption campaign* did not yield too many results. In early January, however, the federal high court in Lagos ordered the temporary seizure of some $ 153 m from the former minister of petroleum resources, Ms Diezani Alison-Madueke, who had moved to Britain and allegedly siphoned money from the NNPC and deposited it in Nigerian banks. In August and October, some of her luxury properties in Nigeria were confiscated. In addition, in August, at the request of the Nigerian authorities, the British National Crime Agency (NCA) froze some of Ms Diezani Alison-Madueke's assets in London, allegedly worth £ 10 m. Interestingly, at the end of the year, the EFCC had still not taken any legal steps to have her extradited from Britain. Patience Jonathan, wife of former president Goodluck Jonathan, also came under severe scrutiny and, in April, a court in Lagos ordered the interim seizure of some $ 5.8 m on the grounds that there was sufficient evidence that it was the proceeds of unlawful activities. The Court of Appeal had still not heard her case at year's end. In the northern metropolis Kano in February, a court impounded close to $ 10 m of former NNPC group managing director Andrew Yakubu.

More was to come, and former top echelons of the military, including Alex Badeh, Umar Dikko, Adesola Amosu and Dele Ezeoba were indicted for *money laundering and procurement fraud* involving millions of dollars. The most prominent case concerned the involvement of the former national security advisor, Colonel Sambo Dasuki (rtd), in a $ 2.1 bn arms procurement scandal and it dragged on with no verdict in sight; meanwhile, Olisah Metu, spokesperson of the People's Democratic Party, who was allegedly also involved, had been in custody since early 2016. This trial was considered a test of the government's ability to present sufficient evidence against high-ranking officials and have them convicted. The first high-profile corruption ruling since the change of power came to naught: even though the former governor of Adamawa state, James Bala Ngilari, was sentenced on 6 March to five years' imprisonment without the option of a fine, the Court of Appeal in the state capital Yola discharged and acquitted him on 6 July. On 5 April, a court in Abuja had already cleared the federal high court judge, Adeniyi Ademola, his wife Olabowale and the senior advocate of Nigeria Joe Agi of all charges of fraud brought against them. The cases against the judges Sylvester Ngwuta and Rita Ofili-Ajumogobia for money laundering were still pending at year's end. The emergence of the 'Paradise Papers' in November – like the 'Panama Papers' in 2016 – which listed top Nigerian politicians and business people did not seem to have an impact. The ease with which politicians could evade the consequences of unlawful behaviour was proved yet again by lawmakers who had lost their seats following Supreme Court verdicts but refused to refund any salaries and allowances received.

As in previous years, the security situation in several parts of the country, as well as the government's systematic and willful disregard of court orders, had grave consequences for *human rights*. Ibrahim El-Zakzaky, founder and leader of the *Islamic Movement of Nigeria*, also known as Muslim Brethren or Shiites, arrested in December 2015, was still in custody at year's end, despite his serious ill-health and a court order granting him bail and ordering the federal government to provide him with accommodation in Zaria or any northern town of his choice. The government maintained that it was unable to build a house for him and the sect was declared a security threat, like Boko Haram. The former national security adviser, Dasuki had also been kept in detention since December 2015. Appeals for the implementation of the bail orders reached the Supreme Court which, in December, set the hearings for March 2018.

Against the backdrop of on-going kidnappings, more states such as Lagos and Bauchi passed a bill prescribing the *death penalty* for hostage takers whose victims died in captivity. Other states initiated comparable legislative measures. Such decisions were in accord with the upholding of the death sentence for capital offences, which were handed down not only to criminals but also to security agents: on 9 March, a court in Abuja passed a verdict on two police officers who had been indicted for the murder of two Igbo traders in Apo district in June 2005; Police Sergeant Lucky Orji was found guilty on 31 July of the murder of a student in Port Harcourt; and in December, a court-martial in Maiduguri found Lance Corporal John Godwin, who had served in 'Operation Lafiya Dole', guilty of killing five rescued civilians. Despite the growing number of death sentences, however, no executions were reported during the year.

Courts in Lagos and Bauchi passed two *noteworthy verdicts for rape*. On 24 March, in Lagos, a man was sentenced to 14 years' imprisonment for raping a virgin and, on 6 December, two men in Bauchi were sentenced to life imprisonment for raping and crippling a middle-aged woman.

The *overpopulated prisons* forced several states to release dozens of detainees, reflecting the findings of the 18-member inter-ministerial presidential committee on the decongestion of prisons nationwide, chaired by the chief judge of the federal Capital Territory High Court, Ishaq Bello, and inaugurated by Minister of Justice and Attorney General of the Federation Abubakar Malami on 31 October. Even the military released hundreds of people who had been detained in illegal camps such as 'Giwa Barracks' in Maiduguri, and were eventually cleared of having ties with Islamist insurgents. In September and October, however, more than 2,300 Boko Haram suspects were tried in secular courts behind closed doors. In the first phase of the trials, about 45 were convicted and sentenced to varying prison terms while over 460 were released.

Even though the military set up an inquiry into allegations of human rights abuses in June, and the acting president inaugurated a further panel in August, accusations of *excessive use of force and of extra-judicial killings* continued, particularly in North East zone and in the Igbo heartland. Despite the climate of allegations and indictments, the military simply rebuffed these accusations. In contrast, in December the police force responded to similar criticism and ended the Special Anti-Robbery Squad's regular stop-and-search operations, with an announcement that the unit would undergo fundamental reform.

Foreign Affairs

As in previous years, relations with the *United States* were to a large extent shaped by the Islamist insurgency of Boko Haram and the volatile situation along the Nigerian shores of the Bight of Biafra. In January, the then director of the Defence Intelligence Agency, Lieutenant General Vincent Stewart, visited Nigeria to lend support in the fight against the terrorists, which was confirmed by General Thomas Waldhauser, commander of AFRICOM, during a two-day visit in February.

The administration of the incoming US president, Donald Trump, did not delay in indicating its readiness to provide *weapons to combat terrorism*, a clear departure from Barack Obama's approach. In March, military and security cooperation was fostered by an international maritime exercise, 'Obangame Express 2017', along the West African coast, sponsored by AFRICOM, with the Nigerian phase taking place from 24 to 28 March, but it was not till December that the US announced that it would sell 12 Super Tucano A-29 planes worth $ 593 m.

Towards the end of August, an eight-member US Congress delegation on a tour of West Africa, led by Democrat Senator Christopher Coons, made a four-day stop in Nigeria to get first-hand information about the situation in the North-East. On 19–20 November, Deputy Secretary of State John Sullivan participated in the *bi-national commission*'s meeting in Abuja.

A Nigerian hacker, Obinna Obioha, was sentenced to more than four years imprisonment for embezzling $ 6.5 m from businesses in the US and elsewhere. He had coordinated the fraud in Nigeria but local and US police forces had traced him and arrested him in 2016 on his arrival in the US.

Nigeria's relations with *Britain* were shaped once again by various legal and security issues. In January, Nigeria's top policeman, Ibrahim Kpotum Idris, made an official visit to the London Metropolitan Police. Around the same time, a British court ruled that Shell could not be held responsible in the UK for the devastating oil spills in Nigeria.

The James Ibori saga finally came to a close when, on 3 February, he left Britain after his release from prison in December 2016, having served many years for corruption and money laundering. He received a rousing welcome at his Oghara country house in Delta state the following day. On 24 August, a British citizen of

Nigerian origin, Josephine Iyamu, was arrested in London upon arrival from Lagos and charged under the *Modern Slavery Act*, but no verdict had been reported by year's end. A 36-year-old Nigerian drug smuggler, Patrick Udensi, who had made millions of pounds from his illegal trade, made the headlines when he was ordered by a judge in Britain to hand over £ 1.2 m or to have seven years added to his 15-year sentence. The NCA had discovered that he had valuable assets in Nigeria.

On a more constructive note, a six-week training exercise for Nigerian Air Force personnel took place in mid-year, led by dozens of Royal Air Force instructors, and, in August, the *BBC World Service's Pidgin service* was launched, focusing on West Africa, and with an estimated audience of some 100 m listeners.

Economic cooperation with *China* was furthered by securing long-term loans to the tune of over $ 7.5 bn, with generous conditions, for ambitious rail and energy projects. After years of delay and wrangling, the Mambilla hydroelectric power plant finally took off when, on 10 November, both sides signed an agreement with a consortium of three Chinese companies to build the 3,050 MW power project in Taraba state within six years. In April, it was reported that Jigawa state, in the crisis-ridden far north, had handed over 12,000 ha of fertile land to Chinese investors, who intended to expand large-scale sugar cane farming, although this was considered by locals to be a severe threat to small-scale subsistence farmers and their families. Meanwhile, China and other Asian countries, including Indonesia, Malaysia and Thailand, had thousands of Nigerians in detention, and at least 300 were on death row.

Relationships with other African countries were largely shaped by the crisis in *Gambia*. At the start of the year, Gambia's President Yahya Jammeh was unwilling to concede defeat after being voted out of office some weeks before. ECOWAS had mandated the Nigerian president to lead a regional delegation to persuade Jammeh to hand over the reins of government to the elected President Adama Barrow. The diplomatic approach failed. By 11 January, military action by ECOWAS was on the cards and, on 19–20 January, *ECOWAS troops under ECOMIG* (ECOWAS Military Intervention in The Gambia) under the command of Nigerian Air Commodore Tajudeen Yusuf entered the tiny country. That action prompted Jammeh to back down, and he left for good on 21 January, after a 'golden handshake' from ECOWAS, and finally settled in Equatorial Guinea.

Another factor in Nigeria's African foreign policy was Nigerians facing problems in *other African countries*. During the year, many Nigerian migrants stranded in Libya on their way to Europe were airlifted out by the coordinated efforts of the International Organization for Migration and the National Emergency Management Authority. Those brought back to Nigeria numbered about 6,600 by year's end. According to NAPTIP, at mid-year a further 5,000 Nigerians were waiting to be rescued from Mali. In March, close to 100 Nigerians were deported by South Africa, and the Nigerian Ministry of the Interior acknowledged that about Nigerian

400 citizens had been jailed there for various offences, including prostitution and drugs. Increasing numbers of Nigerians in the diaspora, like other African communities in their various host countries, were the target of *xenophobic attacks*, a situation that was sharply criticised by Nigerian politicians.

On 16 December, the 52nd ordinary session of ECOWAS took place in Abuja, after being originally scheduled to be held in Togo. It was overshadowed by the unfolding crisis in English-speaking south-east *Cameroon*, which caused thousands to flee across the Nigerian border, and, towards year's end, about 10,000 were registered in Cross River state.

Relations with the *EU* were shaped by the rising number of African refugees and migrants and by human trafficking into Europe. The bodies of 26 young Nigerian women who had attempted to cross the Mediterranean in November were retrieved and the corpses buried in Italy. They were believed to be victims of sex trafficking rings and two North Africans were eventually prosecuted in Italy for trafficking and skippering one of the sunken boats. By mid-year, more than 12,000 Nigerians had crossed the Mediterranean and landed in Italy. At year's end, about 6,600 were registered in Germany alone, a significant reduction on previous annual numbers. However, the EU, including Britain, frequently deported dozens of Nigerian migrants and, in April, Germany even expelled a young Nigerian born in Germany, who was suspected of being a member of the so-called Islamic State. On 28–29 November, the 5th AU-EU summit took place in Abidjan and President Buhari attended in person.

Despite his ill-health, Buhari kept a fairly busy travel schedule. He attended the 72nd session of the *UN General Assembly* on 19 September and US President Trump received him and other African leaders the following day. Barely a month later, Buhari attended the 9th *D-8 summit* in Istanbul and held bilateral talks with the Turkish government.

Socioeconomic Developments

Oil and gas prices gradually improved from $ 53 per barrel of Nigeria's high-quality crude oil at the start of the year to slightly above $ 60. The increase heralded further price rallies. The production level was kept above 2 m b/d, securing a level of foreign currency inflow not seen since the oil price plummeted in 2014. But that did not prevent a serious fuel shortage over the Christmas period, which almost brought social life in Nigeria to a standstill.

Foreign reserves increased from $ 28 bn at the start of the year to $ 38 bn towards year's end. In addition, over the course of the year, the exchange rate on the parallel market rebounded from over NGN 500: $ 1 to about NGN 360: $ 1, thanks to massive interventions by the Central Bank, which frequently injected huge amounts of dollars into the forex market. In the first six months of the year alone, close to $ 10 bn were allocated, even though the Central Bank kept its own exchange rate to NGN 305: $ 1.

As in previous years, the Central Bank regularly issued bonds and treasury bills worth several billion dollars. Not surprisingly, the already precarious *domestic debt* situation worsened and, at the end of September, the federal government was indebted to the tune of $ 40.8 bn, while end of June figures for the indebtedness of the 36 federal states and Abuja put the figure at over $ 10.4 bn. *External debt* did not cause much concern because, of the overall debt of only $ 15 bn, the federal government owed $ 11.1 bn, so the second tier of government was externally indebted by only $ 4 bn. In November, however, reports indicated that seven states, including Abia, Kano and Ogun, had secured approval to take on external loans of $ 1 m, while three other states in the north were waiting for the go-ahead to borrow an additional $ 500 m. This would bring the states' external debts to an estimated $ 5.5 bn.

The state governments claimed that, under the allocation of the *external debt service* between 1995 and 2002, they had been overcharged, and they had for years wanted to be refunded. The federal government under former president Olusegun Obasanjo, which had reached a final agreement for debt relief with the Paris Club in 2005 and later with the London Club, had refused to compensate the states. At the end of 2016, however, President Buhari released the first tranche of an estimated NGN 1 tn, to be followed by subsequent payments in July. Towards year's end, the final tranche – of an undisclosed amount – was paid. Nevertheless, apart from Lagos and a few other southern states, the state governments' poor performance in generating internal revenues resulted in frequent financial challenges, a situation that was not helped by endemic corruption.

As in previous years, the signing of the *2017 federal budget*, totalling NGN 7.4 tn ($ 24 bn) based on a benchmark of $ 44.5 per barrel of crude oil, production of over 2 m b/d and an exchange rate of NGN 305: $ 1 was significantly delayed. Only on 12 June did acting president Osinbajo assent to the budget, which had been passed by the National Assembly on 10 May and showed a projected deficit of NGN 2.3 tn, expected to be financed largely by loans and by recovering ill-gotten gains. Interestingly, and contrary to the president's proposal, the lawmakers increased the budget by NGN 143 bn.

Due to recurrent wrangling over the budget proceedings, the Presidency and the legislature eventually agreed to pass forthcoming budgets before the end of the calendar year, which corresponds to the fiscal year. On 7 November, President Buhari punctually submitted his 2018 budget proposal of NGN 8.6 tn ($ 28.2 bn) but the National Assembly let the deadline pass, causing further delay and uncertainty. However, the president's proposal was based on a projected oil output of 2.3 m b/d at an assumed price of $ 45 per barrel. Once again, the *deficit spending* was considered within the scope of NGN 2 tn and the expected growth rate was put at 3.5%, a considerable increase over the meagre 1.5% recorded in 2017.

In line with the *Economic Recovery Growth Plan* 2017–2020, launched on 5 April and endorsed by the IMF, the newly established Development Bank of Nigeria, tasked with supporting small businesses, defined by size and not by sector, received $ 1.3 bn start-up capital from international creditors. Prior to that, on 15 September, the vice president inaugurated the presidential council on Sustainable Development Goals (SDGs) in order, inter alia, to stimulate the N-Power programme, which tallied with some of the SDGs. The N-Power programme had already secured NGN 30,000 monthly stipends for at least 174,000 volunteers. Despite this programme, which was earmarked for youth with a reasonable level of *education*, the mushrooming of private universities and the low enrolment in the commercialised sector forced the joint admissions and matriculation board in August to lower the minimum cut-off mark for Nigerian universities in the 2017/18 academic session. The Ministry of Education acknowledged in September that 63 m adults were illiterate and 11.5 m children were not attending school.

On 26 January, literary icon Buchi Emecheta, known for championing women and girls in her writings, passed away at the age of 72 in London, where she had lived for most of her life. After winning 1–0 in Zambia on 7 October, the 'Super Eagles' sealed a place in the *FIFA World Cup 2018* in Russia.

Senegal

Mamadou Bodian

Domestic politics was dominated by the holding of the 30 July elections and the subsequent victory of the ruling BBY coalition, which retained its majority in parliament due to a fractured opposition. While this victory bolstered President Sall's prospects for re-election in 2019, restrictions on political freedom and, in particular, the trial of the Mayor of Dakar, Khalifa Sall, who was detained for allegedly embezzling public funds, provoked divisions in national politics and charged the post-election political climate. In matters of foreign policy, Senegal sought to project itself across the world and through international organisations as a diplomatic power, while adopting measures to attract foreign investment. Although a favourable macroeconomic outlook seemed to keep Senegal on a sustainable path, the country remained a least developed country, with almost half of the population living below the poverty line. The context of recurrent strikes undermined the social sector, including education.

 | DOI:10.1163/9789004367630_018

Domestic Politics

Legislative elections were initially scheduled for 2 July but were postponed until 30 July. An electoral victory for the ruling 'Benno Bokk Yaakaar' (BBY) coalition ('United in Hope' in Wolof) would allow it to maintain a majority in the National Assembly and bolster President Macky Sall's prospects for re-election in 2019. A series of controversial *electoral reforms* marked the pre-electoral period. On 2 January, MPs passed a bill that increased the number of seats in parliament from 150 to 165. Of these, 15 were allocated to the Senegalese diaspora, estimated at 3 m people and considered a significant economic force. Subsequently, 60 MPs would be elected on a national list based on a proportional system using the largest remainder method. The rest would be directly elected by a simple majority. More specifically, 90 seats would be decided by multi-member constituencies based on Senegal's 45 départements, while 15 seats (almost 10% of seats in parliament) would be determined in the eight newly created constituencies representing the diaspora. Although these changes to the electoral code directly responded to a constitutional amendment adopted by referendum on 20 March 2016, some opposition MPs (from the 'Parti Democratique Sénégalais' [PDS] and 'Rewmi' in particular) unsuccessfully pushed to keep the size of the National Assembly at its current level of 150 to avoid an extra financial burden. On 27 February, after several rounds of negotiations between the ruling majority, the opposition and the non-aligned political parties, the Ministry of Interior and Public Security set at CFAfr 15 m the deposit to be paid by candidates/lists to participate in the July legislative elections, down from CFAfr 20 m in 2012.

The various political parties or coalitions had until midnight on 30 May to file their lists. On 29 May, attempts to form a unified opposition coalition under the leadership of former president Abdoulaye Wade, former prime minister Idrissa Seck, and the mayor of Dakar, Khalifa Sall, who was in custody for allegedly embezzling public funds, failed because of disputes over who should lead the joint national list. On 9 June, *final lists of candidates* were published and, of the 49 party/coalition lists that the Ministry of the Interior received, 47 were confirmed, compared with 24 in the 2012 legislative elections. They included the ruling BBY coalition, looking to retain its majority in parliament. Despite his advanced age (91 years), former president Abdoulaye Wade headed the list for 'Wattu Senegal', which was principally made up of members of the former ruling party, the 'Parti Démocratique *Sénégalais*' (PDS). Khalifa Sall was leading the national list of another coalition, 'Manko Taxawu Sénégal', from prison.

The registration of a record number of lists/candidates raised fears that voting might be too complicated, given that voters might have to take 47 lists into the polling booth. On 15 July, despite the initial refusal by the political opposition, which created a 'Non' coalition to oppose the electoral amendment, the National

Autonomous Electoral Commission (CENA) and contending parties/coalitions eventually reached an agreement whereby voters would be able to choose a minimum of five ballot papers. A week before the 30 July *legislative elections*, tension mounted in response to the slow distribution of biometric *identity cards* used to vote. The social movement 'Y'en a marre' ('We're fed up') waged a campaign with the slogan 'Ma carte, je vote' ('My card, I vote') to criticise the government for poor election logistics, while Abdoulaye Wade called for a rally the next day in downtown Dakar to demand better distribution of the cards. In response to these demands, President Sall appealed to the Constitutional Council, which relaxed voting rules, allowing citizens without the biometric cards to use their old identity cards or passports to cast their ballots – along with proof they had applied for the new ID card. This decision was rejected by Wade's campaign, which accused the ruling majority of preparing the ground for ballot rigging.

On 30 July, 54% of the 6.2 m registered voters cast their ballot. The ruling *BBY coalition won* with 49.5% of the votes cast and secured 125 of the 165 seats. Adboulaye Wade's 'Wattu Senegal' coalition won 19 seats and Khalifa Sall's coalition, 'Manko Taxawu Sénégal', took seven. Although international observers considered the elections reasonably transparent, the post-election period did not pass without hiccups. Several coalitions disputed which party won the election in Dakar while awaiting the official publication of the results. The 'Manko Taxawu Sénégal' coalition made an appeal to the Constitutional Council for the annulment of the results, accusing the administration of delivering the new biometric cards selectively to favour the ruling BBY coalition. On 15 August, the Constitutional Council rejected all appeals and officially confirmed the BBY victory. A total of 14 parties is now represented in parliament, including the 'Parti de l'Unité et du Rassemblement', which surprisingly secured four seats, and the 15 MPs representing the Senegalese diaspora for the first time.

The legislative victory of the ruling majority gave a boost to President Sall's prospects for second term in 2019. On 11 September, Wade, who was seen as a threat to the regime, announced his resignation from the National Assembly. In a letter addressed to the secretary-general of his party, he concluded that "his mission" had come to an end. A major controversy that created a schism in national politics arose from the *trial of Khalifa Sall*, mayor of Dakar since 2009. He was a member of the 'Parti Socialiste', which was part of the ruling BBY coalition, but was widely considered a potential challenger to Macky Sall in the 2019 presidential election. On 7 March, he was placed in pre-trial custody for allegedly embezzling $ 2.85 m of city funds. While awaiting trial for what supporters considered politically-motivated charges, he campaigned from jail and was elected as an MP. On 17 August, his lawyers filed for his release from prison and for parliamentary immunity, arguing that, according to the Constitution, a deputy cannot be prosecuted or detained while serving the state. The ruling majority and other legal scholars challenged this opinion on the ground that Khalifa Sall had been elected in the midst of the judicial process. To cut the controversy short, the National Assembly lifted his parliamentary immunity on 25 November, paving the way for his trial. The trial opened on 14 December but was eventually postponed because – as Court President Maguette Diop argued – the conditions for it were not fully in place. The trial was scheduled for 3 January 2018, in a special hearing that would be exclusively devoted to Khalifa Sall's case.

Although the government supported efforts to reinforce public confidence in institutions and ensure respect for the rule of law, there were some *restrictions on political freedom* and freedom of speech. On 23 February, Toussaint Manga, a member of the PDS and the leader of the 'Union des Jeunesses Travaillistes Libérales', was released after a preventive detention of more than ten months for "public order offences, acts of vandalism and destruction of state property". On 20 June, after several years of discussions and negotiations over media law reform, parliament adopted a *new Press Code* to regulate the operations of media organisations and the practice of journalism. The new Code, made up of 233 articles, was welcomed as progressive as it established a coherent legal framework that guaranteed fair competition between the various media players and equitable access to the media for all. However, it drew sharp criticisms from many who considered its adoption (following the use of an urgency procedure and without thorough parliamentary scrutiny) a missed opportunity for Senegalese law to be made consistent with international standards on freedom of expression. While the draft Code initially promised to decriminalise press offences, it provided for many restrictions on freedom of speech and contained many provisions that penalised the work of journalists.

The victory of President Sall's BBY coalition in the July elections resulted in a minor *cabinet reshuffle* on 7 September. While the reshuffle emphasised continuity – as Prime Minister Mahammed Boun Abdallah Dionne and most major portfolios remained unchanged – the new team of 39 members included eight women (two more than in the previous cabinet) and a new Ministry of Oil and Renewable Energies following recent discoveries of oil and gas on Senegal's Atlantic coast. Abdoulaye Daouda Diallo, who had been sharply criticised by the opposition for poor organisation of the legislative elections, was replaced as minister of the interior by Aly Ngouille Ndiaye, a member of the 'Alliance pour la République' (the president's party).

Although limited resources restricted the capacity to adequately control Senegal's borders, the authorities developed transnational collaborative *security and intelligence efforts*, sometimes leading to substantial results. On 29 March, agents of the Air and Border Police arrested two Moroccan nationals suspected of being linked to the Islamic State (IS) at Dakar's Leopold S. Senghor International Airport. On 1 April, police arrested a Nigerian suspect known to Nigerian intelligence services to be a recruiter for Boko Haram. He had been in Mauritania for some months before coming to Senegal. Despite security threats, the 25th Saint-Louis jazz festival took place on 25 April. Hundreds of security guards were deployed to ensure security. On 11 October, two suspected Algerians terrorists were arrested in Rosso, a border city near Mauritania, thanks to collaboration with Turkish and Algerian authorities. The two men, who had arrived in Senegal on 2 June from Turkey, were suspected of fighting for IS. On 19 October, the US Embassy warned its citizens of a 'credible threat' of a terror attack in Dakar. The embassy advised all staff members to stay away from seaside hotels and to take special care when visiting popular places in the capital. Radicalism and violent extremism preoccupied scholars and ulemas of the 'Wassatiya Forum in Africa'. On 7 October, they held a scientific congress in Dakar to reflect on the subject: 'La Wassatiya: enjeux et contribution à la paix et à la stabilité en Afrique'. The Wassatiya forum had been founded in 2009 in Mauritania with the objective of bringing together Islamic associations and scholars from 15 African countries, including Senegal, Mali, Morocco, Sudan and Mauritania.

Two *major incidents* caused a number of fatalities. On the night of 12 April, a fire broke out at the 76th spiritual retreat of Medina Gounass in southern Senegal, resulting in 30 deaths and about 87 injuries. The retreat, commonly known as Daaka, attracts thousands of pilgrims every year from various countries in the Sahel region. On 24 April, 21 of 72 passengers (mostly women) died after their boat capsized on the Sine Saloum River in the Fatick region (in central Senegal). According to an official report, they had been on their way to fish along the coast. The cause of the accident remained unclear, but reporters presumed that violent winds and an overloaded boat were to blame.

Foreign Affairs

Senegal sought to maintain a comparative advantage as a *diplomatic power in Africa* and to project this power across the world and through international organisations. On 7 September, the former minister of justice, Sidiki Kaba, was appointed minister of foreign affairs and the Senegalese diaspora in a cabinet reshuffle. On 9 October, he began a ten-day diplomatic tour across neighbouring countries including Mali, Guinea-Bissau, the Gambia, Guinea-Conakry, Cabo Verde and Mauritania, as part of a foreign policy approach that emphasised good neighbourliness.

Senegal's previously dysfunctional relationship with the *Gambia* under Yahya Jammeh took a decisive turn after Senegal, as a key ECOWAS mediator, played a vital role in the post-election impasse there. With former president Jammeh refusing to accept defeat in the country's presidential election on 1 December 2016, Adama, who was declared the winner, sought refuge in neighbouring Senegal. On 19 January, he was sworn in at the Gambian Embassy in Dakar. Two days later, international pressure – including the threat of regional military intervention – prompted Jammeh finally to concede victory and he flew into exile in Equatorial Guinea, allowing Barrow to return home. On 18 February, President Sall was the guest of honour at the Gambia's Independence Day celebrations and on 2 March, President Barrow made his first official trip to neighbouring Senegal. Several lines of cooperation were discussed and agreed between the two countries on matters such as defence and security and other outstanding issues, including the building of the Trans-Gambia Bridge that would span the River Gambia. Work on this Trans-Gambia Bridge – funded by the AfDB along with other multilateral and bilateral donors – had begun in late 2015 to early 2016, but eventually stopped due to complications between the former Gambian president Jammeh and President Sall. If completed, the bridge would usher in a new era in Gambia-Senegal ties and facilitate the movement of people and goods between the south and north of Senegal.

Senegal continued its efforts to strengthen bilateral relations with *other African countries* in various sectors. On 13–15 October, Burkina Faso's President Roch Marc Christian Kaboré paid an official visit, culminating in the signing of several partnership agreements in the areas of education, vocational training and culture. On 23 October, President Sall went to Cape Town (South Africa) for a three-day state visit. He took part in the signing of a memorandum of understanding in areas such as tourism and a business forum organised to improve business opportunities and economic cooperation between the two countries. On 15 May, President Nana Akufo-Addo of Ghana arrived in Dakar for a three-day working visit, as part of the second phase of his official working visits to the countries of the ECOWAS region. He discussed with President Sall the opportunity to strengthen cooperation between the two countries, especially in the education sector, and reiterated Ghana's full commitment to enhancing ECOWAS.

Diplomatic relations with the *Middle East* and the Arab world took many twists and turns. On 4 June, Israel's Prime Minister Benjamin Netanyahu and President Sall met on the sidelines of the 51st ECOWAS Summit in Liberia. They announced the resumption of full diplomatic ties, which had been frozen after Israel recalled its ambassador to Dakar and cancelled its foreign aid programmes in Senegal on 23 December 2016, in retaliation for Senegal's cosponsorship of UNSC Resolution 2334 against Israeli settlements. On 7 June, following the diplomatic crisis in the Gulf, Senegal recalled its ambassador to Doha, joining the list of countries (including Saudi Arabia, the UAE, Bahrain and Egypt) that severed relations with Qatar. However, on 22 August, the Ministry of Foreign Affairs announced the return of Ambassador Mamadou Sally Sall to Qatar. In a statement to the press, the Ministry noted that Senegal strongly encouraged ongoing initiatives between the two countries and would contribute to a peaceful settlement of the crisis between Qatar and its neighbours.

President Sall invited private sector actors in *developed countries* to explore the opportunities offered by the 'Plan Sénégal Emergent' (PSE), especially in its public-private partnership dimension. On 20 March, he left Dakar for a three-day official visit to Switzerland at the invitation of President Doris Leuthard Hausin. The two leaders exchanged views on cooperation in various areas, including the Pilot Program for the Promotion of Technical and Vocational Education in Senegal. President Sall took part in the CEO Africa Forum, a platform for dialogue between public sector decision-makers and business leaders to encourage investment in Africa, and was also awarded the title of Doctor Honoris Causa by the Geneva School of Diplomacy and International Relations at a ceremony held in his honour. On 12 April, President Sall spoke at a joint press conference with Portugal's President Marcelo Rebelo de Sousa, who was in Dakar for a two-day official visit to boost bilateral cooperation through the intensification of trade, investment and partnership on issues of common interest. On 18 April, Senegal and Russia signed in Moscow a memorandum of understanding aimed at developing cooperation between the two countries in priority sectors such as the maritime industry, the aviation industry, the chemical industry, metallurgy and mechanical transport.

Senegal and *France* maintained close cultural and political ties and worked closely together on West African regional issues. On 12 June, President Sall met with French President Emmanuel Macron during his visit to France. They reaffirmed their commitment to the fight against terrorism, to preserve the Paris Climate Agreement, and to jointly promote private investment in Senegal. On 30 June, they spoke on the telephone about the situation in the Sahel region, on the eve of the G5 Sahel (G5S) Summit in Bamako (Mali) that took place on 2 July. This discussion extended previous exchanges on 12 June between the two presidents and talks that took place between French Foreign Minister Jean-Yves Le Drian and his Senegalese counterpart, Mankeur Ndiaye, during a joint press conference in Dakar on 15 June. On 19 October, Prime Minister Dionne and France's Prime Minister Édouard Philippe held the third Franco-Senegalese intergovernmental seminar, which set out roadmaps for the enhancement of bilateral relations in areas such as transport, economic development, schooling and higher education, health, and a joint approach to regional security.

On 25 September, President Sall presided over the opening ceremony of the third session of the *Investing in Africa Forum*, initiated in 2015 by the Chinese Development Bank, with the approval of the Chinese government, and supported by the World Bank Group and several African countries as a global platform to foster multilateral cooperation and to identify new investment opportunities in Africa. The meeting ended with several memoranda of understanding in the energy, agriculture and education sectors. On 12 June, President Sall travelled to Berlin to attend a meeting on the G20 Compact for Africa, a consultative framework promoted by the German G20 presidency to boost investment in 54 African countries.

Senegal sought to position itself on the *regional and world stage* as a diplomatic power. In January, Senegal's UN Special Representative Prof Abdoulaye Bathily lost in the elections for the position of chairperson of the AU Commission held at the 28th Ordinary Session of the AU Assembly in Addis Ababa (Ethiopia). On 17 May,

President Sall was appointed by his peers as president of the Conference of Heads of State and Government of the 'Organisation pour la Mise en Valeur du Fleuve *Sénégal*' (OMVS), during their 17th conference in Conakry (Guinea), succeeding the President Alpha Condé of Guinea, who had led the organisation for two years. On 17 May in Malabo (Equatorial Guinea), Minister of African Integration, NEPAD and the Promotion of Good Governance Khadim Diop attended the summit of the AU's Committee of Ten Heads of State and Government on the reform of the UNSC. On 16 October, Senegal was elected, with the support of the AU, ECOWAS and the OIC, to serve a three-year term on the UN's Human Rights Council.

Terrorist attacks in recent years in four of the eight UEMOA member countries had sparked the need to establish a 'watch and early warning mechanism' and adopt a framework cooperation agreement on *security and intelligence*. This concern was at the heart of the third meeting of the UEMOA High-Level Committee on the Implementation of the Common Policy in the Fields of Peace and Security, opened in Dakar on 27 October. The meeting was led by President Sall as chairman of the committee responsible for the implementation of the project 'Peace and Security in the UEMOA Space'. The fourth Dakar Forum on Peace and Security was held on 13–14 November under the theme 'Current security challenges in Africa: for integrated solutions'. Nearly 800 people – military personnel, experts, diplomats and others – took part in what had become, since 2013, an annual strategic meeting of decision-makers involved in Africa on security issues on the continent.

An important challenge was associated with *migration* management. On 5 March, the US Immigration and Customs Enforcement agency deported 130 Senegalese in an irregular situation. The deportees accused the Senegalese government of pocketing the $ 25,000 given to each of them by the US government. In response to these accusations, the American Embassy in Senegal firmly denied that they had been offered any compensation. On 21 November, Foreign Minister Sidiki Kaba summoned the chargé d'affaires of the Libyan Embassy in Senegal to notify him of the "profound indignation" of President Sall over the sale of SSA migrants on Libyan soil. On 5 December, Prime Minister Dionne revealed that 2,500 young Senegalese migrants had been repatriated from Libya. On 22 November, the US Department of Justice arrested former Senegalese foreign minister Cheikh Gadio. He was charged – alongside Hong Kong's former home secretary, Patrick Ho Chi-ping – with bribing Chadian and Ugandan authorities, and international money laundering. After ten days in federal custody in New York, the former Senegalese diplomat was placed under house arrest until the first hearing of his trial, due in early 2018.

Socioeconomic Developments

Senegal had one of the best performing economies in SSA. Political stability, gradual progress in structural reforms, and favourable external factors contributed to sustaining a *high 6.5% growth* rate in 2016 and 2017, which was mainly attributed to more substantial contributions from the secondary and tertiary sectors. The budget deficit narrowed from 4.2% of GDP in 2016 to 3.7%, as a result of government efforts to increase tax revenues and rationalise current expenditure. According to the African Financial Markets Initiative, the average rate of *inflation* remained low at 1.7% in mid-2017, well below the UEMOA ceiling of 3%.

While the macroeconomic outlook looked favourable, public debt continued to grow as a result of increasing state investment projects in support of PSE. On 16 May, Senegal issued a CFAfr 660 bn *eurobond* (approximately $ 1 bn), at a rate of 6.25%. According to banking sources, the transaction involved Citigroup, JP Morgan, Natixis and Société Générale. The funds were meant to finance infrastructure projects to increase the country's growth to above 7% from 2018. Senegal retained the confidence of donors and international financial institutions. On 28 June, the IMF Executive Board approved the fourth review of the country's economic performance under a programme supported by the Policy Support Instrument (PSI) and approved a one-year extension of the PSI arrangement. The programme aimed to implement economic policy and structural reforms to achieve growth and macroeconomic stability as part of the PSE.

Senegal had a promising *business environment.* According to the latest World Bank annual ratings, the country moved up from 147th in 2016 to 140th in 2017, out of 190 economies in the Ease of Doing Business report. Since 2014, the government had sought to maintain a level playing field for foreign investors to participate in various sectors. A plan to attract Chinese companies shifting low-end manufacturing to Africa started, with the construction of four new factory buildings in a $ 138.6 m project in Diamniadio, on the outskirts of Dakar. On 11 December, Chinese ambassador to Senegal Zhang Xun announced that Chinese investment had amounted to $ 66 m in the first eight months of the year. The government also set a goal for accelerating financial returns to Senegal through multinational hydrocarbon companies. On 2 May, the CEO of French oil company Total, Patrick Pouyanné, met with President Sall and Prime Minister Dionne to confirm oil exploration deals that had initially began in December 2016. They signed two agreements permitting Total to search for oil and gas in offshore Senegal. On 8 May, British oil company BP and its partner, Kosmos Energy, announced a significant discovery of roughly 15 tn ft^3 of natural gas off Senegal's coast at the Yakaar-1 exploration well site.

While these discoveries of natural resources might help economic growth to accelerate and propel Senegal into a newly industrialising and middle-income country, *petroleum* exploitation activities presented governance challenges. On 2 May, President Sall fired Energy Minister Thierno Alassane Sall over disagreements regarding oil contracts with Total and Kosmos Energy. Prime Minister Dionne was entrusted with the government's energy portfolio, alongside his other functions, until 7 September following the creation of a new Ministry of Oil and Renewable Energies.

Despite confident performances, the economy suffered from a weak *power grid.* Although the government set targets to achieve 60% access, demand for electricity grew faster than supply. Energy output had risen from 898 MW in 2015 to 1,168 MW in 2016, and increased sharply in 2017 as Senegal's first two renewable energy projects totalling 50 MW were connected to the grid early in year. A further 94 MW project was under construction. On 13 October, the government issued an open tender for solar projects with a combined capacity of 100 MW as part of the Scaling Solar initiative led by the IFC. On 20 November, VINCI Energies was awarded a contract to build eight photovoltaic solar power plants, with a total capacity of 17 MW, over a period of ten months.

Senegal also worked to improve *infrastructure and transportation* services to support production. On 25 May, the World Bank Group approved the financing of the Dakar Express Bus Rapid Transit System Pilot Project (BRT) at over CFAfr 184 bn. The BRT was intended to facilitate the urban mobility of 300,000 passengers per day and reduce by nearly half the duration of journeys in public transport in Dakar. After a ten-year construction process, the Blaise Diagne International Airport was officially opened on 7 December in Diass, a rural town 40 km from Dakar. The new airport replaced Dakar's Léopold Sédar Senghor International airport and had an initial capacity of 3 m passengers per year.

Senegal was still among the world's least developed countries with almost 46.7% of the population living below the *poverty* line. Non-monetary indicators suggested that inequality had stagnated, although progress in poverty reduction had been rather modest. According to the national employment survey, the *unemployment* rate for people aged 15 and over was estimated at 10.8% in the third quarter of the year, compared with 12.5% in the previous quarter. This rate was slightly more noticeable in urban areas, where 13.8% of the active population were unemployed compared with 7.6% in rural areas. Unemployment varied according to gender and women were more affected (16.5%) than men (5.9%).

Despite investment in *education* and training, Senegal had yet to realise human capital objectives to achieve fundamental transformation goals. Repetitive crises and strikes in the education sector constituted a significant handicap. On 7 June, the 'Syndicat Autonome de l'Enseignement Supérieur' held a march to demand the implementation of the commitments signed by the government in May 2016: the two parties had signed a memorandum of understanding covering the modification of the National Pension Fund, the introduction of a supplementary pension and a monitoring process for the pension system. On 5 July, the French Baccalaureate exams were cancelled following reports that the exam papers had been leaked. The French, History and Geography tests were postponed until 10 July. The Board of the National Baccalaureate Office opened an investigation into the leaks, saying that the credibility of the examination had been undermined. On 2 October, the government closed all Yavuz Selim schools, which were reportedly linked to the

US-based Turkish Islamic preacher, Fethullah Gülen, accused by the Turkish government of orchestrating the 2016 attempted coup in Turkey. Protests broke out in the streets as some 3,000 students, many of them belonging to the elite families of Dakar, found themselves barred from attending their classes. The Ministry of Education responded to the outrage of students and their parents by establishing a provisional school administration involving Senegalese administrators and the Parents' Association of Yavuz Selim.

A series of unfortunate incidents undermined the reputation of the public *health* sector. On 5 February, the country's only radiotherapy machine at Aristide Le Dantec hospital was shut down for more than a month due to various technical problems. The failure of this now out-dated machine, given to Senegal by France in 1989, endangered the lives of many cancer patients. On 17 October, the death of a 12-year-old girl at a hospital in Pikine (a department of the Dakar Region) sparked public outrage at the bad quality the public health service. The director of the hospital rejected the parents' accusation of "non-assistance to a person in danger".

Resistance to the CFAfr *currency* grew to become a subject of debate among intellectuals, raising justified questions regarding the history of the CFAfr and its link to Senegal's independence, economy and politics. On 25 August, Kemi Séba, a Franco-Beninese activist and founder of the NGO 'Urgences Panafricanistes', was arrested in Dakar for burning a CFAfr 5,000 banknote in an anti-colonial rally over the regional CFA franc on 19 August. A few days after the court released him, Kemi Séba was deported to France on 7 September, despite the fact that several human rights groups – including AI Senegal and the Senegalese League of Human Rights – asked the Senegalese authorities to delay the expulsion.

Sierra Leone

Krijn Peters

Preparations started to take place ahead of the March 2018 elections. These included registration of voters, a visit by an ECOWAS delegation and, most importantly, the selection of presidential candidates by the various political parties. The two main parties nominated their candidates in November. Economically, the country continued to perform reasonably well, with a GDP growth figure of around 5.5%. Two exceptionally large diamonds were discovered, both in the Kono district. In August, Freetown was struck by a natural disaster, when the side of one of its hills collapsed following relentless rains, and as a many as 500 people were killed in the mudslide. Deforestation and the uncontrolled construction of dwellings were to blame.

Domestic Politics

In preparation for the March *2018 multi-tier elections* (presidential, parliamentary and local councils), the registration of over 3 m people took place in April. For the first time, a *biometric registration system* was used for the entire process. However, questions were raised as to whether the National Electoral Commission (NEC) would be ready in time, with staff in its ICT department struggling with the

 | DOI:10.1163/9789004367630_019

new system. The deputy majority leader of parliament, Hassan Sherriff, stated that more about 300,000 names were missing from the register. The Governing Board of the ECOWAS Network of Electoral Commissions (ECONEC) met on 6 and 7 July in Abuja (Nigeria) to prepare for its Needs Assessment and Solidarity Mission, among other things. The mission would be used to assess where ECONEC, created in 2008 from the electoral bodies of the 15 ECOWAS member states, could support the election process. The five-day mission took place mid-July and ECONEC board president, Mahmood Yakubu, met with a number of stakeholders, such as the national security coordinator, the inspector general of police, the NEC, various political parties, civil society organisations and the Sierra Leone Association of Journalists. On 12 October, ten judges were appointed to sit on electoral courts mandated to investigate *electoral offenders*. The creation of these special courts followed an earlier announcement by Chief Justice Abdulai Cham in response to a request by the NEC. Offenders, such as those who registered more than once, faced either a $ 70 fine or two years in prison.

On 31 August, the NGO National Election Watch pressed the need for an independent inquiry to look into a fire at the Alliance Democratic Party's (ADP) headquarters. The ADP's leader, Mohamed Kamarimba Mansaray, stated that on 29 August two persons on a motorcycle had driven by and thrown several Molotov cocktails at the building.

Throughout the year potential *candidates for the presidency* moved in and out of favour of the two main political parties. On 5 September, Kandeh Kolleh Yumkella resigned from the Sierra Leone Peoples Party (SLPP) – the main opposition party to the governing All People's Congress (APC) – following the suspension of his bid for the presidency in July. Andrew Keili announced his resignation as the frontrunner on 14 September. Yumkella – who was the former director-general of the United National Industrial Development Organisation – and Keili subsequently created the National Grand Coalition. They and former vice president Dr Joe Demby accused the SLPP of violating rules, betrayal, manipulation and other malpractices. This left Brigadier-General Julius Maada Bio (rtd), a former military head of state, as the SLPP's presidential candidate, and he was confirmed on 15 November during the party's national convention in Freetown. This was Bio's second attempt to win the presidency.

During the APC's convention in Makeni, held on 15 November, *President Koroma handpicked his successor*, Foreign Minister Samura Kamara. The party's chosen vice presidential candidate was deputy speaker of parliament Chernor Maju Bah. Koroma continued to act as chair of the APC, but was barred from running in next year's election, as he had served the maximum two terms permitted by the Constitution.

On 27 November, an ECOWAS court ruled that Sam-Sumana, who had served as vice president under Koroma, had been unlawfully dismissed by his boss in March 2015 and was entitled to benefits and backdated pay. In response to the ruling, the

Office of the Attorney General issued a statement: "The government of Sierra Leone refused to participate in the proceedings and now therefore does not accept nor recognise the decision of the ECOWAS Court in respect of the specific judgement."

Foreign Affairs

Former warlord-turned-president *Charles Taylor*, serving a 50-year prison sentence after being indicted and found guilty by the Sierra Leone Special Court for aiding and abetting Sierra Leone's rebel Revolutionary United Front, was found to have made a phone call from inside a UK maximum security prison on 28 January. This was somewhat embarrassing for the British authorities and worrying for Sierra Leone and particularly Liberia, as Taylor was still seen as having considerable influence in the region.

On 17 May, President Koroma attended the *AU Committee of Ten Heads of State and Government* on the UNSC Reforms (C-10) Fourth Consultative Summit in Malabo (Equatorial Guinea). He was chairman of the C-10, which had been initiated by an AU ministerial meeting in Swaziland in 2005. The objectives of the summit and the C-10 more generally included to: develop a strategy to canvass and advance the common African position; examine the evolution of the UNSC reform process thus far, including the progress of the intergovernmental negotiations; and assess the current state of play in the intergovernmental negotiation process and suggest a way forward for consideration and endorsement by the AU Assembly of Heads of State.

Socioeconomic Developments

According to a prognosis published by the AfDB in January, Sierra Leone would see a near doubling of real *GDP growth* from 3.9% to 6.9%, suggesting that the country was expected to bounce back from the economic damage done by the 2014/15 Ebola crisis. In September, the World Bank reduced this prognosis to 5.6%. Between 14 and 28 March, an IMF team visited Freetown to discuss the possibility of an ECF arrangement with the government. John Wakeman-Linn, the IMF's team leader stated: "Sierra Leone's economic reforms of the last three years have been largely successful. The economy proved resilient in the face of two major exogenous shocks: the Ebola epidemic and collapse of iron ore prices and associated loss of production 2014–2015." Following an increase in inflation – to 17.4% – and growth of the fiscal deficit – to 8.2% by the end of 2016, the World Bank team underscored the importance of the government's aim to safeguard macroeconomic policy in order to achieve the targets set out in the UN's Sustainable Development Goals and in

Sierra Leone's Agenda for Prosperity. This would be challenging because, although iron-ore prices had picked-up again, donor support for the country was reduced. On 5 June, the IMF approved $ 224 m under its *ECF arrangement* to support policies aimed at reducing inflation, strengthening the government's social safety net and boosting domestic investments and revenues. $ 53 m was immediately disbursed. It was anticipated by the team that the ECF arrangement would be used for investments in infrastructure and social spending, with the latter directly benefitting vulnerable segments of society and contributing to poverty reduction. The aim was to create more inclusive growth by prioritising public investment. To reduce inflation to single digits in the medium term – *inflation* stood at 12% by the end of the year – the Bank of Sierra Leone embarked on a programme focused on building reserves, limiting external interventions in the exchange rate and promoting exchange rate flexibility.

In January, Sekou Drame, the CEO of the *mobile phone* company Sonatel/Orange, announced that they would continue to invest in Airtel Sierra Leone, which was wholly owned by Sonatel/Orange. $ 33 m would be invested across the course of the year to improve customer experience and modernise Airtel's network. Fewer and fewer mobile phone 'black-spots' remained in the country and the various networks covered most rural areas, enabling crucial services for rural dwellers. Nevertheless, the quality of Sierra Leone's mobile networks was not necessarily meeting minimum standards. On 30 August, three mobile phone operators – Orange, Africell and Sierratel – were fined a total of $ 1.4 m by Sierra Leone's national telecommunication commission (NATCOM) because of expensive data and call charges, weak data services and poor or dropped voice calls. In addition, NATCOM called for the three companies to give their subscribers 72 hours of free talk time, although only 18 hours were given in the end. This became the ground for the threat of a class action – unique to Sierra Leone's judiciary – by the civil society group Native Consortium and Research Centre. On 21 September, it threatened both NATCOM and the three mobile phone companies with legal action. On 19 October, Orange launched in Sierra Leone, rebranding Airtel Sierra Leone (which it bought in 2016) as Orange Sierra Leone.

At the start of the year, FAO published its *Crop Prospects and Food Situation* report. It raised the alarm for 29 African countries, including Sierra Leone, and stated that, while global food supply conditions were robust, specific circumstances such as armed conflict and drought posed a risk to food availability. For Sierra Leone, FAO stated that the impact of the *2014–15 Ebola outbreak* was still noticeable, estimating that nearly 160,000 people were still in need of food assistance.

The country had struggled over the years with illegal *fishing* practices by foreign nations in its territorial waters. The announcement by the World Bank on 1 March that it would provide $ 4 m to strengthen the regulatory and legal frameworks in the fishing sector was welcome news. The funds, from the World Bank's Global

Environment Facility, were also to be used for monitoring the sector and for institutional development. Given that the sector employed as many as 100,000 people directly and provided 10% of the population with indirect employment opportunities, it was important that a significant part of the money would go to support coastal communities. At a regional scale, protection of Sierra Leone's maritime domain and that of other West African countries received a boost when, on 4 May, ECOWAS accepted support from the German government in the form of technical equipment. The equipment would help ECOWAS's Multinational Maritime Coordination Centre, based in Cotonou (Benin), which monitors and enforces policy in the Gulf of Guinea, with countries belonging to one of three zones. Sierra Leone was in Zone F, together with Ghana, Burkina Faso, Côte d'Ivoire, Guinea and Liberia.

Under the AfDB's 'New Deal on Energy for Africa', the continent should see universal access to energy by 2025. On 16 February, DfID, the AfDB and the government of Sierra Leone started a $ 13 m upgrade and extension of the *electricity* distribution system between Kenema (eastern province) and Bo (southern province). It would involve part upgrading and part construction of a 33 kV electricity line between the two provincial capitals. Access to electricity was part of the country's post-Ebola recovery programme, launched by the president. On a rather larger scale, and while attending the ECOWAS Heads of State summit in Liberia on 4 June, the four countries making up the MRU – Côte d'Ivoire, Liberia, Sierra Leone and Guinea (CLSG) – saw their electricity interconnection project approved by the AfDB. The costs of the project were estimated to be $ 460 m and it was anticipated that it would be completed by the end of 2019. The project would involve the construction of substations and a 1,303 km 225 kV transmission line across the CLSG countries. Following this first phase, a second phase would see the strengthening of national electricity utilities under the West African Power Pool (WAPP) Master Plan, to be finalised by a third phase, which would see rural communities benefitting from electrification along the transmission line. Once realised, it would allow Sierra Leone to purchase part of its electricity needs from neighbouring countries, rather than having to rely on expensive and environmentally unfriendly diesel generators.

The presence of *diamonds* in Sierra Leone had been blamed by many for having fuelled the decade long civil war (1991–2002), if not for causing it in the first place. On 13 March, a very large 709 carat diamond was discovered in Kono District, with the happy finder indicating that he wanted to use some of the proceeds for the development of his local community. Emmanuel Monoh, a pastor and artisanal diamond miner, found the stone, which had an estimated value running into the tens of millions of dollars, in the village of Koryadu. It ranked among the 15 largest diamonds ever found and the largest stone discovered in Sierra Leone for half a century. And Monoh would have to share the proceeds of the sale with the government, which would take 4% of the cost of valuation and export, a percentage kept deliberately low to deter illegal cross-border smuggling. Bidding for the diamond was first set for April, but when only six offers were received, it was extended to 10 May, only to be postponed again. An auction then took place on 4 December in New York and the 'Peace Diamond' was eventually sold for $ 6.5 m to British jewellers Laurence Graff. The price was considered somewhat disappointing, with a spokesman for the group that hosted the auction, Martin Rapaport, stating "perhaps we're dealing with the price of transparency", referring to the Sierra Leone government's pledge to keep the whole process transparent. Following the sale, the government collected a 30% income tax and another 15% of the proceeds of sale. A second large diamond (the 29th-largest in the world) was discovered on 11 November, again in Kono District, this time by a mining company – Meya Mining – rather than by an artisanal miner. The 476 carat rough diamond, named the 'Meya Prosperity', was again purchased by Graff in the final days of the year for $ 16.5 m, indicating that it was of higher quality than the 709 carat stone.

Although Freetown is plagued by deadly *floods* every year during the peak months of the wet season, on 14 August, three days of intense rains triggered a landslide in the hilly outskirts of Freetown. Initial estimates put the death toll at at least 312 people. A mortuary assessment put the figure as high as 400 and this was later revised upward to more than 500. A whole flank of Mount Sugar Loaf in the Regent area collapsed and buried hundreds of people, leaving at least 10,000 homeless. The landslide was ranked as among the worst flood-related disasters on the Africa continent for 20 years. Urbanisation pressures, lack of urban planning and increasing deforestation – either from firewood collection or to make space for building plots – resulted in large sections of the 'protected' Freetown Peninsula Mountains now being vulnerable to these kinds of 'man-induced' natural disasters. An additional factor was the erratic rainfall patterns attributed to climate change. The 2012 National Protected Areas Act had hardly been enforced in the hilly area preferred by more affluent Freetown inhabitants. Visiting the area the day after the disaster, President Koroma said the devastation "was overwhelming us" and called for international support. In response, the government of Israel pledged blankets, medicines, clean drinking water and other essentials. The International Organisation for Migration released $ 150,000 in emergency funds while the UN was busy assessing humanitarian needs. Particular concern was expressed over the possibility of an outbreak of water-borne diseases. Every year during the rainy season, Sierra Leone witnesses an outbreak of cholera and UN feared that this would happen again, but on a larger scale. According to its spokesperson Stephane Dujarric, other potential diseases included typhoid and diarrhoea. The day after the disaster about 150 burials had already taken place, but it was feared that some bodies might never be recovered. On 29 August, the authorities in neighbouring Guinea reported that they had found along that country's shoreline the bodies of at least 19 people who they suspected had fallen victim to the floods and been swept into the sea, washing up some 250 km away from Freetown. On 28 August, the World Bank's country manager, Parminder Brar, said that his organisation would make $ 500 m available over the next three years for disaster preparedness and $ 13 m for immediate support for environmental safety projects.

In early November, the Red Cross confirmed that more than $ 2 m of its *Ebola funds* had not reached the victims but had instead been skimmed off by Red Cross staff colluding with local bank workers. A total of $ 5 m had been lost across the three affected countries through salaries for 'ghost' workers, fraudulently inflated prices and fake custom bills. The Red Cross had been one of the leading organisations fighting the Ebola outbreak.

Towards the end of October, the Union Trust Bank Sierra Leone (UTB), Sierra Leone's only private indigenous bank, received a line of credit worth $ 3 m from the AfDB to support mainly female-owned small and medium-sized enterprises (*SMEs*). The money would enhance private sector development, showing the profitability of SMEs in rural areas.

On 27 October, the AfDB approved a total of € 48 m, consisting of a loan of €26.62 million and a grant of €21.4 million to improve the Guinea section of the road towards the border with Sierra Leone, with further support coming from the EU and the government of Guinea. This route leads to Sierra Leone's main crossing point to Guinea and is essential to connect to both Conackry and part of the *Trans Africa Coastal Highway* network, which connects Sierra Leone to neighbouring countries and others further afield.

Law enforcement responded violently to a *demonstration at Njala University*, near Bo, killing one secondary school student and injuring several others. Lecturers were on strike for several months because wage and pension payments had not been forthcoming. The deadly protests started on 23 March, and took place in Njala, Kenema and Freetown. Police officers, who used life ammunition, arrested 35 people.

On 5 July, new legislation under the Citizenship Amendment Act allowed women to pass on their nationality to their children for the first time in Sierra Leone's history. The amendment was seen as an important achievement for *gender equality* and particularly important for the Sierra Leonean diaspora community.

Togo

Dirk Kohnert

The demand for political change, initiated by institutional and electoral reforms, constituted the major contentious issue between the government and the challengers to the Gnassingbé regime throughout the year. Civil society organisations and representatives of the Christian church supported the demands of the opposition. The notoriously divided opposition gathered new momentum from August, when the lead was taken by a hitherto hardly known opposition party and its charismatic leader, Tikpi Atchadam. He organised huge demonstrations by all 14 opposition parties in the second half of the year, which put the government increasingly under pressure. Foreign affairs were dominated by the impact of increased aid from the international donor community. Socio-economic affairs were marked by diminishing human development and economic freedom.

Domestic Politics

The controversy over *institutional and electoral reforms* to initiate political change after nearly 50 years of rule by the Gnassingbé regime continued to dominate

 | DOI:10.1163/9789004367630_020

domestic politics. Right at the start of the year President Faure Gnassingbé nominated two advisory bodies: a Commission of Reflection on Political, Institutional and Constitutional Reforms and a High Authority to Combat Corruption. He established the former on 3 January, but the opposition regarded this step as another attempt by Gnassingbé to call into question the compromise on institutional reforms that had been reached in 2006, mediated by the international donor community, within the framework of the Global Political Accord. On 6 January, he nominated the seven members of the High Authority to Combat Corruption, which had been created by law in July 2015 but had never become operational. Again, the opposition doubted the neutrality and independence of the chosen members as well as their ability to control corruption effectively.

Six months later, in August, a hitherto hardly known opposition party, the 'Parti National Panafricain' (PNP), founded in 2014, thoroughly shook up the stale domestic politics by organising *huge demonstrations* by all 14 opposition parties. This was facilitated by a new approach to politics taken by PNP's charismatic leader, Tikpi Atchadam, a 50-year-old former student leader and lawyer by profession, who originated from a village near Sokodé, Central Togo. His use of social media to spread his message, as well as DVDs of his passionate speeches, distributed even to the remotest villages, contributed to his success. His outspoken language motivated the discontented to come out en masse and demonstrate for a speedy end to the autocratic reign of the Gnassingbé dynasty. Simultaneous anti-government demonstrations in the urban centres of Lomé, Atakpamé, Kara and Sokodé on 19 and 20 August were violently repressed by the security forces, leading to at least two deaths, several injuries and the conviction of 14 out of 27 demonstrators accused of rebellion, violence and aggravated theft, including the general secretary of the PNP. Big anti-government marches with over 100,000 participants in Lomé on 6–7 September aroused special attention, especially since social media networking had been systematically hindered by the government's blocking WhatsApp, mobile phones and the Internet.

Meanwhile, the government followed its own strategy to continue the process of national reconciliation. It organised a new *delimitation of municipal borders* and with it of local constituencies. This was apparently deemed necessary to win the envisaged local elections, which had been postponed time and again since 1987. At the end of the year, local elections were predicted for June 2018, together with general elections, which were similarly pending. On 23 June, the parliamentary majority of the ruling party, the Union for the Republic (UNIR) voted in a draft law on the creation of 116 municipalities. The opposition denounced the method of border definition as a tribal exercise that allegedly had the major aim of assuring the maximum number of constituencies in favour of the Gnassingbé regime. For example, relatively more municipalities were created in the sparsely populated north, considered to be the traditional fiefdom of the ruling party, compared with the densely populated south, held to be the stronghold of the opposition.

A little later, the *church took sides with the opposition*. On 18 September, the Bishops Conference of Togo urged the government to carry out the reforms requested by the people in accordance with the 1992 Constitution, which had been revised by the late General Eyadéma in favour of the Gnassingbé regime in 2002. The Conference also denounced the wave of repression and the excessive use of force against fellow citizens, sometimes even in their homes. Last, but not least, it urged the Army to adopt a republican attitude of political neutrality in accordance with the Constitution and advised the regime to refrain from inciting ethnic hatred in the media and on social networks.

In response to growing popular pressure, the UNIR majority in parliament adopted a proposal one day later (19 September) for the review of the 1992 Constitution. The proposal excluded crucial points of difference with the opposition, such as the introduction of a retroactive presidential term limit in order to end the 50-year rule of the Gnassingbé regime immediately. However, the government did not get the required majority (four-fifths of the deputies of the National Assembly) because the opposition boycotted the vote. Gnassingbé therefore resorted to a constitutional *referendum* on the law to be held on an as yet undetermined date in 2018.

At the end of October, the ruling UNIR held a party congress at Tsévié (32 km north of the capital), the first congress since the party's inception in 2012. The major aim of the convention was the renewal of party organs and personnel, including women members and the young Turks of the party. At the end of March, the government had already nominated Ingrid Asade, known as Togo's 'Iron Lady', a close follower of Faure Gnassingbé, as the new head of the national social security fund, the 'Caisse Nationale de Sécurité Sociale (CNSS). The opposition suspected the replacement to be a strategic manoeuvre in view of the upcoming 2018 elections. The CNSS had allegedly often been used in the past as a covert war chest for the Gnassingbé clan to finance election campaigns.

Human rights violations continued to be a great concern. In January, 11 Ghanaians were shot dead and beheaded in northern Togo near the Benin-Togo border. They were believed to be victims of 'modern day slavery' from northern Ghana who were returning home from Nigeria. Ghana was said to be a source, transit and destination country for children and women trafficked for the purposes of forced labour and commercial sexual exploitation. In addition, member states of the UN Human Rights Council, as well as AI in its annual report on Togo, published in February, were alarmed about continuing impunity, excessive violence on the part of police and gendarmerie, arbitrary arrests and restriction of freedom of expression. On 28 February, for example, the security forces in Lomé dispersed demonstrations against the rise in petrol prices with live ammunition, killing one person and wounding several others. On 18 October, four people were shot dead (one in Lomé and three in Sokodé), several injured and about 60 arrested in the course of violently suppressed anti-government demonstrations. The demonstrations in Sokodé had been triggered by the imprisonment of an imam close to opposition leader Tikpi Atchadam. The imam had openly denounced the violence used by military personnel against opponents of the regime. Earlier, on 20 September, one child had been shot dead and 25 people injured during unauthorised demonstrations in Mango, in the extreme north of the country. Three days later, the families of the victims brought charges at the ICC against the army commander responsible, General Damehane Yark, one of the old stalwarts of the Gnassingbé regime.

On 6 February, the High Authority for Audiovisual and Communication (HAAC) shut down a private radio station and a TV station, 'City FM' and 'La Chaine du Futur', both belonging to the Sud-Médias group, for allegedly breaching licensing rules. In early June, the HAAC suspended the newspaper 'La Nouvelle' for one month for breach of journalistic ethics. The HAAC statute did not provide any possibility of appeal against these decisions. Increasing *encroachment on Internet media freedom*, taking various forms from subtly increasing regulatory powers over social media to wholesale Internet shutdowns to thwart huge anti-government demonstrations in early September, gave reason for growing concern. The Economy Intelligence Unit (EIU) democracy index 2017 for Togo ranked media overall as 'unfree'. Government interference with the Internet and mobile phones was of special concern in view of the growing reliance on digital information and communication technologies in the context of participatory development approaches of international donor agencies. Nevertheless, Reporters without Borders' World Press Freedom Index ranked Togo 86th out of 180 countries, a rise of two places from 2016.

Harsh *prison conditions* remained a problem, notably overcrowding, with over 4,200 prisoners in the country's 12 prisons, which were designed to hold 2,720. The congestion was mainly due to the abnormal length of pre-trial custody. In May, 63.8% of prisoners were awaiting their judgement, several of them having been in detention for years, as the National Commission for Human Rights, in collaboration with the Ministry of Justice, revealed on Africa Pretrial Detention Day. Apart from this, there prevailed a general mistrust on the part of the general population vis à vis the Togolese justice system. According to a survey (published in May) by an independent Togolese NGO, only 37% of a representative sample of interviewees admitted to trusting the system. An additional 48% cited problems of corruption and the long delay of cases.

All in all, Togo was still classified as 'partly free' according to Freedom House's overall 'Freedom in the World Rating', the same as in 2016 (Aggregate Score: 48/100). The EIU Democracy Index ranked Togo 142nd out of 167 countries worldwide, down ten places from 2016. With an overall score of 3.32, Togo was still classed as an 'authoritarian' regime.

Foreign Affairs

At the 51st ordinary ECOWAS summit, held in early June in Liberia for the first time in 30 years, President Gnassingbé was elected on 4 June as the new chairperson for one year. The decision was hailed by, among others, Israel's Prime Minister Benjamin Netanyahu, who was a speaker at the summit. The renewed Israeli interest was mainly due to its desire to secure Africa's diplomatic backing on *Israel*-related issues in international forums such as the UN. In addition, Israel offered cooperation in counter-terrorism and economic development. Togo had long standing friendly ties with Tel Aviv, including close cooperation with Israel's security services (Mossad), which had provided sophisticated advice and computer hardware and software since the reign of the late General Eyadéma. Togo was also one of the few developing countries that voted with the USA against the UN resolution condemning President Trump's decision to recognise Jerusalem as the capital of Israel at the end of the year. However, there was a controversy about the expediency of an Israel-Africa summit planned for October in Lomé. Member states of the OIC, to which Togo had belonged since 1997, furiously demanded reprisals against Togo, but Gnassingbé, who had visited Jerusalem in September, succeeded in persuading most his peers to hold the summit. It took place in Lomé on 24–26 October, with 30 of 55 African states represented, but most international attempts to mediate in the Togolese crisis failed because the mediators proposed by ECOWAS were apparently not neutral.

France, the former colonial power in Lomé, was also concerned about the Togolese crisis and, as Togo's biggest supplier of arms, was reluctant in May to proceed with the delivery of five French military helicopters. At the end of November, President Emmanuel Macron called for freedom of expression and for an electoral framework that would guarantee free and fair elections.

The annual *AGOA* forum took place in Lomé on 8–10 August. The prospects of this deal were gloomy in view of the bearish attitude of President Trump vis à vis Africa and decreasing American imports from Africa in recent years (from $ 26.8 bn in 2014 to $ 18.7 bn in 2015, i.e. – 30%), mainly due to a fall in African oil exports.

In contrast, the *EU* approved disbursements of $ 16.5 bn in budgetary aid for Lomé in February, which was complemented by a generous German aid package of $ 60 m signed during a five-day visit (8–13 June) by Gnassingbé to Berlin. This aid package corresponded to a 50% increase in aid since the last government negotiations in 2014. On 22 June, the EU, France and Germany agreed in Lomé to harmonise their aid to Togo, which amounted to a total of about € 715 m for the period 2014–2020. Thus, Europe remained Togo's most important development cooperation partner.

China, another influential partner, provided for the construction of a modern TV complex for the state-run Togolese television station and Radio Lomé. The controversial construction of the joint Benin-Togolese Adjarala hydropower dam on the Mono River at the joint border, contracted by the Chinese company Sinohydro and financed with credits from the China Exim Bank to the tune of $ 551.1 m, which had stalled in 2016 because of financial problems, apparently continued. It was meant to increase electricity generation by a significant 147 MW. However, environmental, economic and social impacts on the local population were a concern. Approximately 21,000 people would be affected on both sides of the border, including 12,000 people or 1,800 households in Togo.

Togo continued to participate in peacekeeping missions in the sub-region, with about 1,400 soldiers and policemen, especially in Mali.

Socioeconomic Developments

At the beginning of the year, the government signed two new *credit deals*, with the IMF (18 January, $ 238 m for ten years) and the World Bank (31 January, $ 350 m for three years, 2017–20). Both agreements were guided by the National Development Plan (NDP) for 2018–22, which had still not been officially released by the end of the year. The NDP focused on more robust, inclusive and sustainable growth (4.8%), taking into account the low inflation pressure (estimated -1%) and the high, though slowly falling poverty rate (55%), and weak governance, which together led to alarming consequences for the current account deficit and debt. Huge public infrastructure investments in previous years had contributed to a rise in public debt from 48.6% of GDP in 2011 to an estimated 81.5% in 2017, as well as to a high current account deficit reaching 9.8% of GDP (2016), largely due to investment-related imports. The IMF therefore advised an austerity programme. The first IMF-financed three-year ECF, which had replaced the Poverty Reduction and Growth Facility, had expired long ago (in 2011). A new ECF had been delayed till January, when a staff-level agreement with the government for a three-year ECF of SDR 176 m (about $ 238 m), or 120% of Togo's IMF quota, was negotiated.

This fell in line with the policies of other aid donors. In September, the World Bank presented its new *Country Partnership Framework* (CPF) for the four-year period July 2016 to June 2020, the first medium-term strategy since the resumption of IDA financing in 2008. The increased poverty orientation of the new IDA's 18 replenishment, which provided increased support for fragile states, resulted in the doubling of IDA resources for Togo, which rose to $ 230 m, available during 2018 to 2020. This amounted – together with the $ 113 m IDA financing already approved in 2017 and other resources from the sub-regional IDA envelope – to a total of over $ 350 m for the CPF period. The restructuring of the two weak public banks ('Banque Togolaise pour le Commerce et l'Industrie' and 'Union Togolaise de Banques') that had been delayed several times, but was envisaged by, amongst others, the most recent IMF ECF arrangement, was still under way at the end of the year.

The AfDB assisted the government in coping with another serious problem – man-made *coastal erosion.* In the middle of the year, it approved a $ 41 m loan to Togo and Benin for the construction of 28 groynes to stabilise the shoreline. According to expert estimates, the Togolese coastline receded by an average of 10 m. per year, and even by up to 20 m. per year east of the deep-water harbour of Lomé, constructed in 1968. Two national roads along the coast had already been washed away, and the former coastal colonial capital Anecho was threatened with submersion by 2030. Apart from the negative effects of the construction and extension of the port of Lomé, with its impact on sedimentary accumulation by the change produced in sea currents, other human interference had accelerated coastal erosion too, notably, the illegal harvesting of sand and gravel along the shore for construction purposes.

The low and falling ranking of Togo in the annual HDI, published in March for 2016, showed that economic growth did not necessarily bring about improved human development. Togo's HDI ranking had decreased by -52.0 units, from 114.0 (1990) to 166.0 (2015), taking it to the bottom of the 188 countries surveyed.

According to official data presented by the government at the end of January, the *unemployment* rate had fallen from 6.5% in 2011 to 3.4% in 2015, 55.1% of whom were considered poor. However, these figures were questioned as being rather politically motivated in view of reference levels of unemployment in neighbouring countries such as Ghana (12%) and Nigeria (13%). In addition, the rate of under-employment had increased from 22.8% (2011) to 24.9% (2015), making a total of 28.3% un- and under-employed, mostly young people. The National Agency for Volunteers, which had tried to tackle this problem in the previous five years by mobilising 11,189 young people, succeeded getting only 2,284 young unemployed into work.

Phosphate production, the major export industry, was boosted by the completion of a $ 1.4 bn project to mine 5 m tonnes of phosphate rock per year. The production was managed by the 'Société Nouvelle des Phosphates du Togo' (SNPT) and supplemented by the construction of a phosphoric acid and fertiliser plant, built by Elenilto, an Israeli mining company. According to the African Investigative Publishing Collective (based in Accra, Ghana), phosphate production was informally administered directly from the offices of President Gnassingbé by the Moroccan-Israeli family of Raphael and Liron Edery. Evidence suggested that this special arrangement could have facilitated corruption. In 2016 and 2017, for example, close to 90% of Togo's phosphates had been bought at well below world-market prices by 'privileged clients', i.e. the Indian family of shippers Gupta-Kalyan. Ashok Gupta had been already under investigation by the Australian Federal Police in another case for bribing politicians for access to phosphate resources.

Of similar importance to aid from the international donor community were *remittances from Togolese migrants*. According to the most recent IFAD data, published on 15 June, remittances totalled $ 287 m in 2016, or 9.1% of GDP. Apart from the trans-Sahara route of migration, ships under Togolese registration were also reported to have carried clandestine migrants to Turkish and European harbours. In February, the national body responsible for state action at sea (ONAEM-Togo), created in 2014, revealed in its second annual report that, of 566 vessels registered in Togo by the end of 2016, about 200 had to be deleted from the list because they had tarnished the image of the country and acted illegally.

In July, the government concluded a contract with the English enterprise Bboxx to provide 300,000 domestic solar-home-kits to be distributed in rural areas in the next five years within the framework of the 'CIZO' ('enlighten', in the local language Mina) initiative, at an estimated cost of about $ 117 m. This was meant to bring the *electrification* rate in rural areas up from the current 6% to 35% in 2022. The government was to provide about $ 15 m and the remaining $ 102.5 m would have to be secured from private investors, i.e. using popular mobile payment solutions for the sale of the kits via mobile payments (PAYGO).

The new *budget for 2018* was adopted in parliament at the end of the year as usual, on 20 December. Totalling CFAfr 1,321.9 bn, it represented a 7.7% increase on the 2017 budget, with 44% allocated to expenditure on health, education and grassroots socio-economic development. Opposition deputies boycotted the vote en bloc and were notably scathing of the opacity of budget management and the violation of the financial law (LOLF), which stipulated the balancing of the previous budget before voting on the new one. However, the National Assembly had not yet balanced the budgets for 2016, 2015 or 2014, apparently because the audit court had reported inconsistencies concerning the implementation the 2014 budget, which had not yet been cleared up. In addition, the opposition complained about impunity with regard to tax fraud, mismanagement of parastatals such as Togo Telecom, SNPT, the autonomous port of Lomé and the two state-owned banks, etc.

Aggregated indicators of Togo's *economic freedom* showed stagnation or even regression. In economic freedom, as measured by the Heritage Foundation's Economic Freedom Index 2018, published in November. Togo fell from 137th (2016) to 144th (score: 67.2) of 183 countries surveyed. In short, Togo's economic freedom too retained the overall status of 'mostly unfree'.

PART 4

Central Africa

Andreas Mehler

Overall, the year combined an accelerated economic crisis for most countries of the sub-region with on-going heavy violence touching three countries, with Cameroon, a new-comer, seeing severe armed confrontation. Heads of state of the CEMAC area finally cleared the way for the free movement of people within the community, but doubts remained about whether this would have game-changing effects in a space exhibiting little complementarity of national economies.

Democracy and Elections

Central Africa arguably remained the SSA sub-region whose regimes and rulers could be called democracies and democrats with the least credibility. Dinosaurs like Obiang Nguema, Paul Biya and Sassou Nguesso – all of whom were already presidents in the 1980s – competed with the also 'well experienced' Idriss Déby and dynastic leaders Ali Bongo and Joseph Kabila for the title of most resilient autocratic regime. It was difficult to rate the popularity of leaders, but open contestation grew nearly everywhere.

National elections were only held in two of the seven countries of the sub-region and both were anything but democratic: In Congo (Brazzaville) the legislative elections were overshadowed by alleged fraud; calls for a boycott of the elections were at least partially successful. While the overall legitimacy of the elections was severely limited, this also applied to opposition representation in parliament: in the end, only 16 out of 153 elected members were not from the presidential majority. Equatorial Guinea's municipal and legislative elections were termed equally unfair by most commentators. The dominant 'Partido Democrático de Guinea Ecuatorial' and its allies won all 75 seats in the Senate and 99 of the 100 seats in the lower house. The ruling alliance was also able to win in all the municipal mayoral elections. Elections were due in the DRC but, as in Gabon (with legislative elections), they were again pushed to 2018. Some controversies over the electoral commission were even recorded in São Tomé and Príncipe, the sub-region's most democratic country. This meant that the already palpable crisis of representation grew across the board and was the basis of increasingly violent protests.

Potentially most severe was the steep decline of political rights in Cameroon. Here, Internet access in the two anglophone regions was cut for 93 days (this technique was used also in other countries, such as the DRC). 1 October, which marks the anniversary of the declaration of Independence for former Southern Cameroon

 | DOI:10.1163/9789004367630_021

by anglophone activists, not only saw the killing of more than 20 people by security forces but also the arrest of at least 500 protestors. A quarter of a century after the popular revolts of the early 1990s against authoritarian regimes in the sub-region, *pro-democracy activists* were not ready to give in to repression and delay tactics. In the DRC, demonstrators took to the streets throughout the year and in several parts of the country to protest against the endless push-back of elections.

The inability or unwillingness of the Cameroonian government to guarantee minority representation for anglophones not only pushed the country to the brink of civil war, but also had clear consequences for its international respectability. The Freedom House Index ranked seven out of eight countries in the sub-region as 'not free' (and only São Tomé and Príncipe as 'free'); Gabon's political rights sub-index fell by one point.

Instability, War and Peace

2017 was another dramatic year in terms of widespread violence in the sub-region. Most of this violence happened within the confines of given states as a result of politically motivated conflict, but some also had transnational dimensions, as with the Boko Haram rebellion (whose epicentre is in Nigeria, but which also affects Cameroon and Chad), and the activities of the Lord's Resistance Army (originally from Uganda, but operating inter alia in the CAR) and to some extent in eastern DRC, where some groups allegedly received support from actors across the border while the government also drew support from irregular fighters in the region. Porous boundaries enabled protagonists in the various battlefields in the CAR to maintain their cross-border networks. However, it was significant that violent opposition to regimes in the DRC, Congo and Cameroon came from within the country.

Anglophone separatists in the two English-speaking regions of *Cameroon* turned to more violence after the regime showed no signs of compromise. With the upheaval in Cameroon in full swing (with the aim of building 'Ambazonia' out of the combined North-West and South-West provinces, if necessary by a full war of liberation), continuous calls for secession of Katanga (DRC) and less prominent but not entirely forgotten ideas to create a 'Republic of Logone' (in the CAR), *separatism* looked like a more realistic political option than ever before to more and more political actors in Central Africa. Considerably less clear were the separatist plans within further DRC provinces (Bas-Congo and the Kivus) or for the island of Bioko in Equatorial Guinea. Whatever the prospects of such movements, their existence pointed to the absence of dialogue between periphery and centre and/or deficits in the institutional structure of states. The way decentralisation – portrayed as a major reform since the 2000s in many countries – was pursued in the sub-region hardly produced the effects its architects had claimed it would.

Central Africa was, in fact, the scene of many armed conflicts. In the *DRC*, ongoing violence in the east was noted, despite continuous efforts of both the army and international peacekeepers to extinguish rebellion. Here, a more decentralised pattern of fighting between ethnic militias was observed. But, in parallel, a new coalition of movements comprising at least 11 Mai-Mai factions started to operate in a large area from South Kivu and Tanganyika to Maniema province. With President Joseph Kabila still unwilling to provide the basis for free elections, the entire political system lacked any legality or legitimacy. In the CAR, the pattern of decentralised confrontations in several parts of the country (North, Centre, East) shifted only in terms of the actual geography of hostilities. The elected government was no more capable of providing stability than the previous transitional government. The UN peacekeeping mission was able to stabilise some areas, but even the capital, Bangui, was not exempt from violence.

Continuously high numbers of refugees and IDPs were a clear consequence of such on-going large-scale violence. Again, the DRC, the CAR and Cameroon had to deal with particularly high numbers. The DRC alone had a "total number of concern" of nearly 4.8 m people, of whom 4.6 m were IDPs, returned IDPs and returned refugees, representing roughly 6.6% of the total population. UNHCR statistics indicated that the CAR alone was the source of about 534,000 refugees in the region. When adding the number of 886,000 people of concern within the country (IDPs, returned IDPs/refugees), some 30% of the population were either on the run or only recently resettling. Cameroon's recent wave of armed conflicts, mostly in the anglophone province, produced over 220,000 IDPs, Congo's post-electoral violence some 107,000. Moreover, hosting nearly 250,000 refugees from the CAR and 85,000 from Nigeria made Cameroon a further important target of UNHCR activities. At the same time, Cameroonian soldiers were reported to be forcing Nigerian refugees onto trucks – after manhandling them – to deport them back to Nigeria. The most important host countries for refugees after Cameroon were the DRC (around 180,000), Chad (100,000) and Congo (30,000). This negative trend was set to continue with the outburst of more violence in the CAR since December.

On 1 June, the US government sanctioned General François Olenga (DRC) in the context of his oversight role over the Republican Guard, which was a main force in quelling protests. Only three days earlier, the EU had sanctioned eight officials close to President Kabila for "planning, directing, or committing" severe human rights violations.

Human Rights and Transitional Justice

On the same occasion, the EU targeted the government's spokesperson Lambert Mende for his involvement in repressive media policies. It was hardly surprising that war-like situations led to massive human rights violations. The authorities harassed journalists who covered the protests and also occasionally shut down the Internet. In the DRC, security forces used live ammunition and tear gas in several incidents to repress anti-regime demonstrations. Potentially more shocking was that in both 2016 and 2017, security forces covertly recruited fighters of the defeated M23 rebellion, now in Rwanda and Uganda, to crush civilian protest, mostly between May and July; this was reported by HRW.

The repression excesses on 1 October in anglophone Cameroon also targeted prominent legal personalities such as Paul Aya Abine, a magistrate at the 'Cour Suprême', whose house in Akwaya was stormed by uniformed armed men; fortunately, he was absent. The 'Fédération Internationale des Droits de l'Homme' issued several reports on the intimidation and temporary arrest of human rights defenders in the context of the anglophone crisis.

AI issued a report with the title 'Between Recession and Repression: The Rising Cost of Dissent in Chad', which documented the threats and harassment received by human rights defenders and journalists. In one incident, the director of publication of a popular newspaper received more than a dozen anonymous calls openly threatening him after he published an article critical of President Déby.

Not only state forces were responsible for severest human rights violations. Most of the abuses documented in the CAR were committed by factions of the former Séléka alliance and their arch-enemies, the so called Anti-balaka forces. In a special report on the CAR, HRW documented 305 cases of sexual violence by members of armed groups. Some women were first raped and subsequently held captive as sex slaves for up to 18 months, and forced to cook, clean and collect food and water for their torturers.

Without precedence in the sub-region, a Special Court was created as a tool of transitional justice for the CAR (such as had been in place in Sierra Leone in the 2000s). This hybrid tribunal was to be integrated into the national justice system, but would employ international and national staff and apply a mix of national and international law. In June, most of the tribunal's magistrates and the special prosecutor were sworn in.

This development must be put in perspective with the latest developments in the trial(s) of Jean-Pierre Bemba at the ICC. In a process related to his trial for crimes against humanity and war crimes, Bemba and some co-accused were indicted for witness tampering. He was sentenced in March to a one-year prison term and a fine of € 300,000. However, Bemba had already appealed against his sentence in the main trial in 2016 (for fair trial issues) and it was unclear when the victims of 2001 would ever get a material compensation for their suffering. While the ICC stepped up its presence in Central Africa in this calendar year with field missions to the CAR and the DRC, it hardly looked effective in fulfilling its core task.

Socioeconomic Developments

This was the second crisis year for most countries in the sub-region. The estimated overall growth rate of 0.9 % (AfDB figures, up from 0.1% in 2016) documented the disappointing progress of Central Africa's economies, also compared with Africa as a whole (+3.6%). The AfDB deplored the limited diversification of the economies and a "lifeless" private sector. Labour productivity had declined over the last two years. The IMF's World Economic Outlook (published in April 2018) could only report modestly satisfactory *GDP growth* rates for the CAR (estimated at 4%), the DRC (3.4%) and Cameroon (3.2%). According to the same source, GDP, imports, exports and government revenues all declined in Chad, Congo, Gabon and Equatorial Guinea. The AfDB's African Economic Outlook provided, as always, different figures based on domestic authorities as well as the AfDB's own estimates, but stated quite dramatic losses in GDP per capita for Congo (–4.0%) and Equatorial-Guinea (–7.3%). Economic activity further slowed down in most of the sub-region. The effects on the public purse were, logically, also heavy, and led most countries to conclude adjustment programmes with the IMF (see below).

The Index of *Economic Freedom* (Heritage Foundation) reflected minor progress in Cameroon and Chad that could not outweigh a declining trend overall: four (rather than five in 2016) countries were now in the 'mostly unfree' category (the DRC – with declining ratings, Gabon, São Tomé and Príncipe, and Cameroon) and four (rather than three) in the worst category of 'repressed' economies: the CAR, Chad, Equatorial Guinea and Congo, ranked between 162nd and 177th (of 180 countries). The World Bank's 'Doing Business' report provided a similar picture: Cameroon ranked best (163rd), followed by Gabon, Sao Tomé and Príncipe, Equatorial Guinea and Congo. Chad, the DRC and the CAR were again at the very bottom of the world-wide ranking (at 180th, 182nd and 184th of 190 countries, respectively).

At an estimated 10.1%, the overall *inflation* rate was once again well above the 3% threshold fixed by CEMAC. This reflected the rather unfavourable conditions of the world market for the sub-region's most important export, namely – mostly – oil. For the six countries of the CEMAC zone combined, some 70% of the value of exports was based on oil products. The ongoing low price levels for oil products on the world market was clearly bad news for half of countries in the sub-region (Equatorial Guinea, Chad, Congo and Gabon).

Sub-regional Organisations

In view of all these dismal developments, one might have expected a new push for intra-regional cooperation and an intense search for joint solutions. However,

Central Africa's main sub-regional organisations did not develop a strong dynamism. This was particularly true of *CEEAC*, which did not hold a summit despite – or because – of the severe political crisis in its biggest member state (the DRC). CEEAC foreign ministers met to discuss the crisis in the CAR on 21 October in Libreville (Gabon); potentially the strongest conclusion was to urge CEEAC's secretary-general to speed up the elaboration of a multidimensional programme for stabilisation and reconstruction in the CAR. Marginally notable was also the start of an internal reform process with an expert meeting held in Libreville on 29–30 November.

In contrast, *CEMAC* produced diverse headlines, mostly linked to the need for a new round of fiscal and economic reform in most of the CEMAC states. Following the December 2016 extraordinary summit in Yaoundé (Cameroon), which had decided to start negotiations with the IMF at shortest notice, four countries (Cameroon, Gabon, the CAR and Chad) concluded *adjustment programmes* as early as October with the Bretton Woods organisation in order to get much needed budgetary support. In total, CFAfr 1,044 bn (€ 1.6 bn) were earmarked for the period to 2020, but neither Congo nor Equatorial Guinea were ready to sign up to such programmes. The fiscal impasse there was potentially more severe, but all governments were frantically looking for ways to cut expenditure while developing new sources of funding, particularly by raising tax revenue. The ambivalent social and political effects of earlier structural adjustment programmes started in the late 1980s were not forgotten, and it remained to be seen whether both sides had learned from this earlier period.

The most spectacular move by CEMAC in years hardly received any attention in the face of the deep economic crisis. On 31 October, an extraordinary summit in N'Djamena (Chad) endorsed the *free circulation of people* in the sub-region after taking note of the ratification of the relevant agreement by all member-states. This was achieved more than 15 years after the first discussions on this principle. In 2013, the governments of both Equatorial Guinea and Gabon had even temporarily suspended the project out of fear of a mass influx of migrants. On 1 November, with Cameroon the last country lifting visa requirements for citizens of all other member states, the free movement of people within the CEMAC zone (though limited to a stay of only three months) was officially established. Requirements to enter a different CEMAC country still varied, with some countries asking for biometric documents. Whether the legendary harassment by Cameroonian frontier police would suddenly stop with the new regulation was another open question. More generally, it was unclear whether, in the context of conflict and dysfunctional state services, this new move could become a catalyst for economic dynamism, which was clearly what the CEMAC summit hoped. The summit also urged the Commission to examine the modalities of strengthening the consumption of goods originating from within CEMAC by first producing an inventory of products available – a sign that almost nothing had been achieved on this front before. The eternal competition between Libreville and Douala (Cameroon) as site of the sub-regional Stock Exchange was apparently resolved, giving Libreville the oversight body of financial markets and making Douala the actual location of the Exchange. The summit was attended by the heads of state of Cameroon, the CAR, Chad and Equatorial Guinea as well as the prime ministers of Congo and Gabon.

Internally, CEMAC renewed its personnel. In February, heads of state or their representatives had met in Djibloho (Equatorial Guinea), mostly to decide on some key positions within the organisation or its adjunct institutions. A former prime minister of Gabon, Daniel Ona Ondo, was made chairman of the CEMAC Commission while Fortunato Ofa Mbo from Equatorial Guinea became director general of the 'Banque de Développement des États de l'Afrique Centrale' (BDEAC) – despite the protest of Cameroonian Prime Minister Philemon Yang, who pleaded for the principle of an alphabetical rotation by country, which would have made a Cameroonian the successor to the Chadian Abbas Mahamat Tolli. Tolli was nevertheless promoted to be governor of BEAC.

In February, a four-day council of defence ministers of *CBLT* member states was held in Abuja (Nigeria), also attended by non-member Benin. It was obvious that CBLT's original mission was no longer the main concern of the member states, which had turned to security issues. The ministers adopted a number of decisions, including adjusting the force's capacity requirement, the organisational structure of the office of the head of mission, the organisational structure of the Multinational Joint Task Force (MNJTF) (to incorporate the military, police and civilian components) and the relocation and reshaping of some of the military sectors. At the margins of the meeting, the AU and CBLT signed two memoranda of understanding to boost the fight against Boko Haram. One was meant to mobilise additional support for the MNJTF. Defence ministers, chiefs of staff and heads of the intelligence service met for a second security-focused gathering on 14 December in N'Djamena. Within the CBLT's proper field, the African Development Fund decided to cover some of the costs of a CBLT rehabilitation programme with credits and grants in August. On 6 October, CBLT's Executive Secretary Sanusi Imran Abdullahi and the UNDP representative in Chad, Carol Flore Smereczniak, signed a convention on a $ 240 m programme meant to bolster resilience against climate change and reduce pressure on eco-systems in the area for the period 2017–22.

Cameroon

Fanny Pigeaud

The crisis between the government and the country's two English-speaking regions that had begun in late 2016 worsened over the months and turned into an armed conflict involving guerilla attacks on the security forces. These acts of violence became President Paul Biya's main problem as he appeared to be preparing to run for the presidential election of 2018. In the northern part of the country, the militant group Boko Haram continued its sporadic attacks against the civilian population. On the economic front, oil production declined. Though less affected by the fall in commodity prices than the other countries in the region thanks to the diversification of its economy, Cameroon was forced to conclude a loan agreement with the IMF.

Domestic Politics

The crisis that had set the government and the country's two English-speaking regions – the Southwest and the Northwest – in opposition since 2016 gradually

 | DOI:10.1163/9789004367630_022

worsened over the months. While the authorities refused to return to the federalism demanded by the anglophone leaders, they did agree to open negotiations. These talks led to the creation, in late June, of a *National Commission for the Promotion of Bilingualism and Multiculturalism*, then, in February, to the suspension of a strike call issued by several teachers' trade unions, and finally to a resumption of classes in certain schools in the two regions in question. Just as it was holding talks, however, the government declared two organisations illegal: the Cameroon Anglophone Civil Society Consortium, established in December 2016 as an association of lawyers, teachers, and members of the English-speaking civil society, and the Southern Cameroons National Council, a political party that had been calling for the independence of the English-speaking regions since 1995. The authorities also asked Internet access providers to suspend their services in the two crisis areas from 17 January onward, as they feared that online social networks could be used to encourage and organise protest movements. This radical decision had an adverse effect: it increased the tensions and the resentment of the English-speaking minority, roughly 20% of the total population, against the central government. It also focused the attention of the international media on Cameroon. The American whistleblower Edward Snowden was one of those who spread the hashtag #BringBackOurInternet, which was widely used in social network news feeds. The suspension measure was not lifted until 20 April, at the demand of President Biya.

In the meantime, activists campaigning for the anglophone cause had, in early March, announced the creation of a new movement named Southern Cameroons/Ambazonia Consortium United Front, which presented itself as "a broad-based movement that unites all organisations which seek the restoration of the statehood of Southern Cameroons", i.e. the former English-speaking Cameroon.

The second half of the year was marked by *outbreaks of violence*. In August, private and public schools in Southwest and Northwest were set on fire by alleged supporters of the secession of both regions. In late August, only a few days before the beginning of the school year, the government attempted to calm things down by ordering the release of some 70 leaders and activists of the anglophone cause who had been arrested in late 2016. Classes were able to begin but some schools remained closed in Southwest and Northwest, while a number of parents were threatened with reprisals if they sent their children to school.

On 1 October, the anniversary of the official reunification of the English and French-speaking parts of Cameroon, radicals defied the authority of Yaoundé: they 'proclaimed' the birth of a state called *Ambazonia*, corresponding to the former English-speaking Cameroon. This led to renewed demonstrations: for instance, between 30,000 and 50,000 people demonstrated in Bamenda, the capital of Northwest Region, where the government had deployed a large number of security personnel. This first day of October was marked by heavy violence: human rights organisations claimed that 17 persons were killed in clashes between demonstrators and police. According to the local UNHCR Office, these events forced more than 3,000 people to flee to neighbouring Nigeria.

Condemning the violence and calling for dialogue, President Biya, in the days that followed, dispatched the English-speaking Prime Minister Philemon Yang to Bamenda in an attempt to revive talks. But to no avail: in November, the crisis turned into an armed conflict. Three gendarmes and one soldier were killed in attacks by separatists in Southwest and Northwest. Improvised bombs also exploded in Bamenda, including one in the vicinity of the Mobile Intervention Group, a police unit comprising the largest contingent of policemen in the region. There were no casualties, but a curfew was immediately imposed in Bamenda. Access to the Internet again became difficult in Southwest and Northwest.

Furthermore, a number of media also reported that the government had issued *international arrest warrants* against some ten secessionists, including members of the Southern Cameroons Ambazonian Governing Council, a kind of unity government. The most militant secessionists, of whom at least some lived abroad, made extensive use of online social networks to communicate and, in particular, to explain that the police and gendarmes deployed in their regions constituted "colonial forces" of occupation which must be resisted by force of arms. Pictures of men in uniform also circulated, the latter being presented as members of the Ambazonia Defence Forces commanded by Ayaba Cho Lucas. Over the months, the militants of the anglophone cause appeared increasingly divided and split into three groups: those calling for more justice but not challenging the institutional organisation of the state, those advocating a return to federalism, and those actively militating in favour of secession. A number of political players estimated that the government, by stepping up its military presence in the two English-speaking regions and having 'moderate' leaders arrested, had only strengthened the most extremist fringe groups.

Between late November and late December, the separatists mounted new *attacks against members of the security forces*. On 1 December, Biya blamed "a band of terrorists claiming to be part of a secessionist movement" and announced that all steps would be taken "to end these criminals' ability to do harm". Immediately afterwards, the Rapid Intervention Battalion, an elite army unit reporting directly to the president and known for its ruthless methods, was deployed to Manyu division, where the attacks were concentrated. In the following days, its soldiers made at least one incursion into Nigeria, where some of the secessionist fighters had a rear base. The military authorities also intensified the surveillance of the railway line connecting Yaoundé to the northern city of Ngaoundéré, as it feared that anglophone 'separatists' might attempt to carry out acts of sabotage. By late December, nearly 20 members of the security forces had been assassinated in the space of two months. In his end-of-year speech, President Biya again took a firm stand, reiterating his resolve that all those who had taken up arms "should be fought relentlessly and held accountable for their crimes before the courts of law".

Even though the 'anglophone crisis' dominated the news and ranked prominently in the concerns of many Cameroonians, it was never debated in the *National Assembly*. This remained so until late November, when a scheduled plenary review of the draft budget law for 1918 was interrupted by deputies of the Social Democratic Front (SDF), the main opposition party that had been founded in 1990 in Bamenda, who called for a debate on the issue. Their colleagues from the presidential party, the Cameroon People's Democratic Movement, expressed their opposition to this idea by walking out of the plenary assembly, while the parliamentarians of the SDF sang a song hostile to President Biya. On 11 December, the deputies of the SDF again prevented the Assembly from carrying out its work – this time by using vuvuzelas to make themselves heard, but to no avail.

As the anglophone crisis grew in intensity, the armed group *Boko Haram* remained active in the north, mounting sporadic attacks against civilians. In late September, eight persons were killed by a suicide bomber in the village of Ouro-Kessoum, 2 km from the Nigerian border, in Far North Region. One month later, 11 more people had their throats cut in Gouderi, while a suicide attack carried out by a young girl resulted in the death of five children in Zamga, 2 km from the border. A UNICEF report published in April stated that 27 children had been forced to carry out suicide attacks in the region between January and March, compared with nine in the corresponding period of 2016. Since 2014, according to the NGO International Crisis Group (ICG), Boko Haram was believed to have killed 2,000 civilians and soldiers, and to have kidnapped 1,000 persons in Far North Region. In September, HRW, for its part, accused the Cameroonian authorities of having forcibly deported 4,000 refugees to Nigeria in the course of the year, on suspicion of being linked to Boko Haram. The UNHCR also condemned these deportations as a violation of the agreements signed by Cameroon within the framework of the protection of refugees. The Cameroonian government dismissed all these charges. In July, it also issued a protest following the publication of a report by AI that, as in the previous year, accused the security forces of having committed war crimes and acts of torture in the context of the war against Boko Haram.

The *presidential election* scheduled for October 2018 was regularly brought up for discussion throughout the year. President Biya, aged 84 and in power for 35 years, gave no clear indication of his intentions, but the probability that he would run for the presidency was deemed to be high: in two speeches, he thus referred to an event planned for 2019 as if it were clear that he would still be in charge at that time. Although the 'anglophone crisis' was never debated in the National Assembly, it was used as an argument by those who wished to see him step down from power as well as by those who supported him. For the former group, this conflict – like the one involving Boko Haram – demonstrated that Biya, whom his party had long presented as a guarantor of peace, had become a destabilising factor and that it was time for him to step down. The president of the Episcopal Conference of Cameroon, Archbishop Samuel Kléda, also issued a statement to this effect at year's end. For the second group, Biya was still the right man for the job: active in the corridors of political power since 1962, he was, according to them, the one who was best qualified to come to terms with the country's complexity, having succeeded in containing Boko Haram within a confined area. On the opposition side, a number of personalities expressed their readiness to run for the presidency, including the lawyer Akere Muna, a native of Northwest and the son of the former prime minister Solomon Tandeng Muna, the jurist Maurice Kamto, president of the Cameroon Renaissance Movement and former minister-delegate to the minister of justice, and the agronomist and civil society activist Bernard Njonga. The SDF, for its part, did not disclose its plans: it remained unclear whether its chairman, John Fru Ndi, would run at all, having already been a candidate in 1992, 2004 and 2011.

One of the rare positive events of the year for Cameroon, the victory of the national football team (the Indomitable Lions) at the *Africa Cup of Nations* ('Coupe d'Afrique des Nations'; CAN) on 5 February was able to revive the feeling of belonging to a united country, though only for a few days. After winning the trophy, the goalkeeper Fabrice Ondoa, hero of this CAN and a French-speaking native of Yaoundé, proclaimed first in French and then in English, and in explicit reference to the anglophone crisis: "It is thanks to our unity that we were able to achieve this (sentence originally in French) … My brothers, I am from Bamenda. Bamenda, I love you!"

Foreign Affairs

With regard to Cameroonian diplomacy, the year witnessed an extensive shift of personnel which, in early November, affected the central administration and many of the country's diplomatic missions abroad. These changes had been expected to take place for many years. The media noted that they occurred in a context in which *Canada and Great Britain* had asked Yaoundé to recall the Cameroonian diplomats serving in those countries, where they were accused of engaging in activities inconsistent with their status.

President Biya's foreign policy was largely concerned with the anglophone crisis. On 25 November, he thus dispatched Minister of Territorial Administration and Decentralisation Emmanuel René Sadi to *Nigeria* with a "special message" for President Muhammadu Buhari. Sadi was received by Vice President Yemi Osinbajo. A few weeks earlier, thousands of Cameroonians from Northwest and Southwest Regions had crossed the border to seek refuge in Cross River State in south-eastern

Nigeria. On 7 December, President Biya then received the high commissioner of Nigeria to Cameroon, Lawan Abba Gashagar, again to discuss the anglophone crisis.

The conflict in the English-speaking regions was also the subject of several statements on the part of Cameroon's Western partners. In July, on the occasion of the French national holiday, the ambassador of *France* to Cameroon addressed it in a speech in which he advocated dialogue. UN Secretary-General António Guterres, for his part, asked the Cameroonian authorities to conduct an investigation into the acts of violence that had taken place on 1 October. In late October, after visiting the CAR, Guterres made a brief stop in Yaoundé, where he met with Biya, although the subject of their conversation was not made public. In November, furthermore, the UN Regional Office for Central Africa (UNOCA) declared that it was "particularly concerned by the upsurge of violence, especially against the civilian population and state agents" in the English-speaking regions. It reiterated the commitment of the UN to the territorial integrity and unity of Cameroon and invited the various parties to resolve their differences through peaceful means. In late December, Patricia Scotland, secretary-general of the Commonwealth, of which Cameroon is a member, paid a four-day visit to the country. She met with the country's main political leaders as well as with representatives of the political parties, civil society and the business community. She attended an official diner with President Biya, at which she expressed her "great sadness" over the events in the English-speaking regions. She also called upon Cameroonians to "preserve peace and unity, and to encourage in all circumstances genuine dialogue."

In late October, after the publication of an *ICG* report on the anglophone crisis, the government announced that it was barring the ICG from conducting activities on its territory. Minister of Communication Issa Tchiroma Bakary accused the ICG of being a "destabilization organization defending the interests of the secessionist movements veiled with unconfessed interests whose sole dream is to install chaos" in Cameroon.

Two cases pertaining to *freedom of speech* were also widely commented on abroad, especially in France. They both came to a close at year's end. The first involved the journalist Ahmed Abba, a Hausa-speaking correspondent of the French public radio station Radio France Internationale (RFI): he was released on 22 December after spending 29 months in pretrial detention. In 2016, he had been sentenced in the first instance to ten years' imprisonment for condoning acts of terrorism. Having appealed against this verdict, he was finally acquitted by the military tribunal of Yaoundé but sentenced to 24 months' imprisonment for "non-denunciation of terrorism". The management of RFI, which operates under the auspices of the French Ministry of Foreign Affairs, became very active in this matter, which in turn generated considerable tension with the government. In December, the American-Cameroonian writer Patrice Nganang was arrested and imprisoned for three weeks before being released and deported to the United States. He was prosecuted for "apology for crime" and for posting "threats" on Facebook, where he said that he would like to "put a bullet right in Paul Biya's forehead".

As in previous years, the security situation remained poor on the border with the CAR. In July, the Cameroonian authorities decided to close the border for several weeks due to clashes between armed groups in the CAR. On 11 September, presumed rebels from this neighbouring country led an incursion into the territorial department of Boumba-et-Ngoko, 58 km from the city of Yokadouma. These armed men assaulted the employees and ransacked the equipment of a French logging company, the 'Compagnie Forestière du Cameroun'. Disturbances also occurred on the border with Equatorial Guinea: in late December, the Cameroonian police detained some 30 persons transporting arms and military uniforms who were about to cross the border, coming from the city of Kye-Ossi. The military security service and the local police in Ebolowa opened an investigation into this matter.

Not accustomed to taking part in regional or continental events, President Biya nevertheless attended the 5th AU-EU Summit in Côte d'Ivoire in late November. One month earlier, he had travelled to Chad to attend an extraordinary CEMAC summit.

Socioeconomic Developments

Balanced in terms of expenditure and revenue, the fiscal *budget* for the year amounted to CFAfr 4373.8 bn (€ 6.6 bn), 3.3% higher than the budget for 2016. Domestic assets amounted to CFAf 3143.3 bn (71.8% of the total amount, an increase of 9.6% over the current fiscal year), while the external assets (loans and donations) were estimated at CFAfr 625 bn. Remaining cautious in its calculations, the government banked on an oil price of $ 40 per barrel and hoped to take CFAfr 495.1 bn in oil revenues, an increase of 12% over 2016. To improve its fiscal revenues, Yaoundé also relied on the increase of a special tax on oil products and on the reintroduction of customs duties on non-pulverised cement (clinker). These duties had been suspended in 2009 in order to combat the high cost of living following the sociopolitical unrest of February 2008. At the time, only one cement factory was in operation, the 'Cimenteries du Cameroun' (Cimencam), compared with four in 2017. The other suspensions of customs duties that had been agreed in 2008 (notably on imported wheat) were maintained. With regard to non-tax revenues, the state hoped to raise CFAfr 1297 bn, including CFAfr 585 bn in loans from development partners, CFAfr 560 bn raised on the financial markets, and CFAfr 85 bn from donations. On the expenditure side, the budget earmarked 47.1% of total expenditure for the functioning of the state and 36.3% for investments (an increase of 4% over the previous budget).

The government reckoned on an *economic growth* of 6% and an inflation rate of 3.3%. These predictions exceeded those of the IMF, which expected a growth of

4.2% and an inflation rate of 2.2%. According to the IMF, it was actually 3.6%. This growth was driven by ongoing infrastructural projects. However, the implementation of these large projects was necessarily linked to increased import needs, so that the trade balance remained in deficit.

At the end of the year, the 'Société Nationale des Hydrocarbures' (SNH) announced that Cameroon had sold 16.9 m barrels of *crude oil*, compared with 20.5 m in 2016. According to the state-owned corporation, this decrease was due to the decline in domestic production, which amounted to 28 m barrels by the end of the year, down 16.4% from 2016. While production was mainly from offshore fields located in the coastal drainage basins (Rio del Rey and Douala/Kribi Campo), the SNH hoped that mapping the largely unexplored areas on the mainland would lead to the discovery of new oil reserves. In June, it accordingly initiated a procedure to map the sedimentary basins in Southwest (Mamfe) and North (Garoua/Koum). It also signed a contract with the American company Noble Energy, in which it agreed to share 4 bn m^3 of natural gas and 18 m barrels of gas condensates in Cameroon's Yoyo Block, located in the Douala/Kribi Campo basin. The exploitation of natural gas reserves could partly compensate for the projected fall in oil revenues. The production of natural gas was on the rise anyway, reaching 335 m m^3 on 31 October, which represented an increase of 15.5% compared with the same period in 2016. It was expected to reach 445.1 m m^3 by the end of the year.

The 'anglophone crisis' had an economic impact that was still difficult to assess at year's end. The *suspension of Internet services* in Southwest and Northwest Regions proved costly for local businesses, especially in Buea. Businesses operating in the field of new technologies were forced to relocate to Douala in order to continue their activities. On the whole, economic activity was sluggish all year round in these two regions. In addition, it became apparent that the disturbances had the effect of increasing the fraudulent exports of cocoa to Nigeria.

In June, following the conference of the heads of state of CEMAC, held in Yaoundé in December 2016, the government and the *IMF* agreed on an economic programme supported by an ECF of $ 666.2 m. A few months later, in September, the deputy managing director of the IMF visited Yaoundé. He stated that the economic health of Cameroon was relatively better than that of its neighbours but contended that the pre-crisis levels of economic growth were unsustainable. He explained that it was necessary to reduce government spending by focusing on the elimination of wasteful or superfluous expenditure. He assured everyone that the salaries of civil servants would not be lowered and that spending would be increased in the health and education sectors. He advocated a reduction of administrative formalities, a simplification of the fiscal system, and greater participation of the private sector in the main sectors of the economy. He also announced that the services of the IMF would offer assistance in the field of revenue administration, the modernisation of taxes and customs, budget management, and budget risk management.

There was modest progress in the realisation of *construction projects* aimed at creating new infrastructure: at year's end, a new bridge over the River Wouri was opened to traffic in Douala, thereby reducing the road traffic problems that had been having a crippling effect on the economic capital. The deep-water port of Kribi, on the other hand, was not put into service, and the work to improve the condition of the road connecting Douala and Yaoundé was interrupted. In December, the AfDB granted Cameroon a loan of € 150 m for the construction of the Nachtigal hydroelectric dam, with a production capacity of 420 MW. Located 65 km to the north of Yaoundé, on the Sanaga River, this power plant should boost Cameroon's power production capacity by 30%. Expected to cost € 1.1 bn, the dam would be built by the Nachtigal Hydro Power Company, a joint venture of the Cameroonian state (40%), the 'Electricité de France" Group (40%) and the International Finance Corporation, a subsidiary of the World Bank (30%). Construction would begin in 2018, and the dam was scheduled to become operational in 2022. In 2015, the *electricity* generation capacity of Cameroon, with one of the highest potentials in Africa in terms of electric energy, was estimated at 1,289 MW, with hydroelectric energy representing 59% of the total. Roughly 48% of the Cameroonian population had access to electricity. In late October, the American Hydromine Company announced that it planned to invest $ 3 bn (CFAfr 1,500 bn) in the construction of the Grand Eweng hydroelectric dam, also to be located on the Sanaga River, near the villages of Kan, in the territorial department of Sanaga Maritime, and Dibang, in Nyong-et-Kéllé. This dam (1,800 MW) could be finished by 2025. Hydromine would carry out this project with private funding. On 26 October, the governor of Centre Region and the managing director of the Hydromine branch office in Cameroon began marking out the construction site in Dibang.

There were no changes in the *mining* sector. However, an NGO called 'Forêts et Développement Rural' (FODER) implicated Chinese mining companies in numerous accidents that occurred at open mining sites in East Region, claiming that 43 persons died in 2017 as a result of landslides. The mining companies were accused of not protecting the sites they had exploited, leaving them open to ill-equipped local craftspeople working without any kind of safety precautions. Between 2012 and 2014, according to FODER, 250 mining sites were thus opened and not protected by 65 different companies in East Region, known for its rich gold deposits.

In May, President Biya surprised everyone by publishing the conclusions of the administrative commission of inquiry that had been set up in the immediate aftermath of the *Camrail train accident* of 21 October 2016, which officially claimed the lives of 79 people and injured at least 600, in addition to an undetermined number of disappearances. The fact that Camrail is a subsidiary of the French Bolloré Group, omnipresent in Cameroun and often considered to be all-powerful, had led many to believe that the authorities would prudently set the issue aside until it was forgotten. The commission established that "the responsibility for the derailment of the

Intercity train no.152", which connected Yaoundé and Douala, "lay mainly with the rail carrier, the Camrail company". The causes of the accident, which occurred in the small town of Eséka, were determined to have been "excessive speed (96 km/h)", "non-compliance with certain safety rules", "severe anomalies and defects" and "use of passenger cars with partly defective brake elements". The presidency, which had until then always protected the interests of the French industrial group, announced that it had requested an audit of the concession contract signed by Cameroon and Camrail in 1999. According to experts, the terms of this agreement were particularly unfavourable to the state and created the conditions that led to the accident.

Central African Republic

Andreas Mehler

The population faced another disastrous year with the number of IDPs and refugees continuing to increase as a result of renewed fighting in various parts of the country; food insecurity hit nearly half of the population. The elected government in conjunction with international actors managed to secure the vital Bangui-Douala corridor, but fully controlled only the south-west. In the centre, the south-east and the north-west, new deadly confrontations, often involving unexpected coalitions of armed movements, could not be prevented, even by international peacekeepers who sometimes faced outright popular hostility. Efforts to prepare the justice system to deal with past crimes against humanity were taken, but did not yet yield results.

Domestic Politics

President Archange-Faustin Touadéra met with criticism from many quarters when he had little to show in terms of economic progress and security after one year in office. Faced with half a dozen policy guidelines, some observers wondered what

 | DOI:10.1163/9789004367630_023

the government's vision for restoring stability was and raised doubts as to whether there even was one. A core issue was the official attitude towards the numerous armed movements that continued to threaten peace and rarely behaved responsibly. Touadéra clearly favoured an inclusive approach, potentially because he did not have the means to confront rebel groups effectively. On 12 September, he carried out a *major reshuffle* of his government, appointing 16 new ministers and raising the number of portfolios within the cabinet from 23 to 34. The return of Marie-Noëlle Koyara, who had been the first female minister of defence during the transition period, to that same post was potentially a positive surprise. More significant, however, was the fact that some new ministers were linked to armed movements: Energy Minister Gontran Djono Ahaba, the nephew of former warlord president Michel Djotodia, and Water and Forestry Minister Lambert Mokove Lissane were clearly seen as representatives of the Ex-Séléka movement within government. Equally represented was now the opposing anti-Balaka movement with Government Secretary Jean-Alexandre Dedet and Culture and Tourism Minister Jacob Mokpem Bionli. Retaining his position, Prime Minister Simplice Sarandji was quoted as saying, "For me they are all Central Africans", to justify the inclusion of rebels in the government. As a side-effect of this move, government expenditure was clearly set to rise.

In fact, both government and UN peacekeepers were unable to prevent or stop *on-going armed conflicts*, at first in the centre of the country. Since November 2016, two former components of the Séléka alliance, the 'Front Populaire pour la Renaissance de la Centrafrique' (FRPC) and the 'Union pour la Paix en Centrafrique' (UPC), had repeatedly clashed in or around Bambari. The FPRC was seen as completely opportunistic in its choices of partners, who included its former opponents, the Anti-Balaka movements, while the UPC was clearly linking up with sometimes very vulnerable, and sometimes violent and armed Fulani groups. On 12 February, the UN Multidimensional Integrated Stabilization Mission in the CAR (MINUSCA) intervened to halt the advance of the FPRC coalition, killing the FPRC chief of staff, Joseph Zoundéko. MINUSCA obtained the withdrawal of militia structures from the city, including the UPC headquarters under Ali Darassa, and the local anti-Balaka chief, Gaétan Boadé, also left Bambari. MINUSCA then declared Bambari a "city free from armed groups". Violence declined in this key city, but the moves resulted in a *transfer of conflict further east*, with several attacks recorded on Bakouma, Nzako and Zémio. An upsurge in violence was recorded in May, hitting mostly the provincial capitals of Bangassou (with more than 100 killed) and Bria, but also Alindao (188 died here alone according to HRW, which also documented 25 cases of rape), Mobaye and later again Zémio, often against armed Fulani cattle herders and Anti-Balaka groups loosely allied to the FRPC. In Bria, in-fighting between the factions of this alliance resulted in an upsurge of 73,000 IDPs in May and June. Between 20 and 23 June, over 80 civilians died in these battles. In a particularly bloody confrontation in the town of Gambo in early August, Anti-Balaka elements attacked

UPC and armed Fulani individuals, who retaliated by targeting a local health centre; more than 100 civilians were killed, including International Committee of the Red Cross volunteers. On 18 October, Anti-Balaka militia attacked the Fulani village of Pombolo, killing at least 26 civilians; this was preceded by an attack on Kembe eight days earlier resulting in a similar death toll.

The second most dangerous zone was the area between Batangafo and Kaga Bandoro (in the north). Here the 'Mouvement Patriotique pour la Centrafrique' (MPC) and Anti-Balaka groups fought for control of Batangafo. In December, two villages in the vicinity were largely destroyed by MPC troops, leading to the displacement of some 24,000 civilians. Further to the west, at the end of the year the newly established 'Mouvement National pour la Libération de la Centrafrique' (MNLC; a recent MPC splinter group) clashed with the locally strong 'Révolution et Justice' (RJ) movement in and around Paoua. RJ and the hitherto rival Anti-Balaka fighters joined forces to counter the MNLC, but also targeted civilian Muslim communities, killing four civilians; the MNLC burned down entire villages in retaliation. Tens of thousands of people were internally displaced and up to 500 people were killed.

But tensions were also high in many other places. While autochthony discourses and interreligious animosity played some role in individual outbursts of violence, it was rather the *competition for access to valuable natural resources or trade routes* that remained the key driver of violence among the armed groups. Even within the armed movements, significant violence was used to settle scores between local commanders, On 7–8 December, rival factions of the FPRC clashed in Ippy (in the centre of the country), resulting in an undetermined number of casualties and the displacement of over 15,000 civilians. This terminated a phase of relative peace that had prevailed after the 'Rassemblement des Républicains' (RDR), an Anti-Balaka faction, had signed an agreement with the FPRC, MPC and UPC in October. In mid-December, UPC elements reportedly killed Gaétan Bouadé, the RDR leader.

In contrast, the security situation in the capital *Bangui* improved somewhat after the last escalation in February, when a local militia leader was killed, leading to further killings in retaliation. It was mostly in the third arrondissement of Bangui that militia members clashed in internal power struggles and competition over illegally imposed taxes; in one obscure event a grenade exploded on 11 November, killing four people.

Although pilot projects were started, the *implementation of DDR* made little progress – to no one's surprise in the circumstances. The FPRC, one of the most important movements, even suspended its participation. The government and the donor community, with MINUSCA as the main implementer, engaged in all sorts of DDR, while in parallel working to build up new and reliable national security forces. In November, MINUSCA removed the mostly Fulani 3R ('Retour, Reclamation, Rehabilitation') forces under the command of General Sidiki Abass from Bocaranga and the MPC from nearby Bang. On 30 October, Defence Minister Koyara issued a concept paper for the training of the national armed forces by the EU Military Training Mission (EUTM-RCA) and, on 18 November, President Touadéra signed two decrees on the organisation of the 'Forces Armées Centrafricaines' (FACA) and the general staff. Seventy FACA soldiers trained by the EUTM-RCA were deployed to Obo in November as a first detachment, and 72 further FACA soldiers were sent to Paoua to work alongside MINUSCA.

Considerable efforts were deployed to reach an inclusive *peace agreement*. The Catholic Sant'Egidio community organised intensive talks in Rome and Foreign Affairs Minister Charles Armel Doubane and President Touadéra's political advisor, Georges-Isidore-Alphose Dibert, eventually signed a so-called 'Entente de Sant'Egidio' on behalf of the government, as did representatives of 13 armed movements. Of the important players, only the 3R movement was not present. It is worth noting that four of the major civilian political parties co-signed the document along with the vice president of the National Assembly. The document called, inter alia, for an immediate ceasefire, respect for the elected authorities and the acceptance of the political-military groups as part of security sector reform and the reconstruction process. The possibility of an amnesty was alluded to, in stark contrast to the peace roadmap presented by the National Assembly to the government in May, which had excluded amnesties for war crimes. The document was clearly not worth the paper it was written on: only a day after the signing of the agreement, nearly 100 people were killed in Bria in clashes between the FPRC and Anti-Balaka fighters. Taking the fragmentation of groups into account, it was much more realistic to engage in local peace agreements as those signing a paper would then also commit to their words. An agreement between the 3R and local Anti-Balaka groups was signed in Bouar on 15 December, and local authorities in Bria, supported by MINUSCA, launched a road map for peace in Haute-Kotto on 19 December.

The (re-)establishment of *state authority* was one of the main goals of both the government and MINUSCA. The progressive deployment of trained FACA battalions was only one element of this strategy. On 8 September, a concept note was published and four days later Touadéra appointed new prefects to all 16 prefectures, nine of them with a military background (and none of them Muslim). In October, he corrected that balance somewhat: among the 71 sub-prefects (i.e. district officers), various rebel movements and the Muslim community were represented. At year's end, 14 of the 16 prefects and 63 of the 71 sub-prefects were installed. The FPRC and MPC were initially opposed to the redeployment of state authorities in Bamingui-Bangoran, Vakaga and Nana-Grebizi prefectures. In some cases, extensive consultation with armed groups preceded the deployment, showing the nature of the local balance of power.

Fighting impunity was another important challenge; both a restoration of the formal *justice system* and establishing internationally sponsored transitional justice organs were on the agenda. On 23 February, President Touadéra signed a decree naming a military judge from the neighbouring DRC, Colonel Toussaint Muntazini Mukimapa, as the prosecutor of the Special Criminal Court (SCC). In May, two female international investigating judges were appointed, as were five national judges, but the SCC was still not operational by year's end. In parallel, 19 of the 24 first instance and appellate courts started to function, though with reduced capacity. In the last two months of the year, eight Anti-Balaka members were sentenced by a court in Bouar (in the west) to up to 20 years' imprisonment for criminal association, unlawful possession of homemade arms, murder and theft. On 11 September, President Touadéra created a preparatory committee for a truth, justice, reparations and reconciliation commission, which had been asked for in the aforementioned Sant'Egidio declaration. On the other hand, the government did little to implement an asset freeze for a number of individuals, who were still able to receive their state salaries despite being under international sanctions.

The *Lord's Resistance Army* (LRA) continued to pose a threat in the south-east. In late October, the group stepped up its attacks on villages. AI, referring to other NGOs, calculated that there were 113 attacks, 12 civilian casualties and 362 kidnappings over the year. The withdrawal of Ugandan forces (which had officially fought the LRA) ended in August, and this also enabled various Ex-Séléka factions to gain ground in the south-east.

Foreign Affairs

In the competition for international public attention, the CAR again fell into the background compared to other crisis areas including Syria and Mali, but arguably also Yemen and Myanmar (with the Rohingya crisis), which had consequences for levels of assistance. Potentially, it was in this context that UN Under-Secretary-General for Humanitarian Affairs Stephen O'Brien repeated the warning of precursors to *genocide*, although no criteria for genocide were given, and neither was this a mainly interreligious conflict. It was true that in individual cases mosques and Muslim traders were targeted by some armed groups: in one instance, Anti-Balaka attacked a mosque in Bangassou on 13 May, killing the town's imam, amongst others. The Catholic Church in the town subsequently hosted 1,500 Muslim civilians in their premises. But there was certainly not any systematic move to kill entire religious or ethnic groups on a national scale.

At the margins of the UN General Assembly session, UN Secretary General António Guterres co-presided with President Touadéra and the chairperson of the AU at a high-level meeting on 19 September on the political, security and humanitarian situation in the CAR. At a press conference, Touadéra deplored the departure of France's Operation Sangaris in 2016, and also the withdrawal starting in April–May of about 2,000 US and Ugandan forces that formed part of the AU-led Regional Task

Force that was fighting the LRA. Guterres also visited the CAR on 24–27 October as the first country in a series of further visits to peacekeeping operations worldwide.

MINUSCA peacekeepers continued to be met with hostility and were not unopposed even within government. The local population in Bangui repeatedly attacked staff and property. On 10 May, Anti-Balaka allegedly kidnapped and killed peacekeepers in the deadliest attack on a MINUSCA convoy since the establishment of the mission. Five peacekeepers were killed and ten were injured on the road between Bangassou and Rafai. On 24 November, a crowd threw stones at UN vehicles after a fatal road accident attributed to MINUSCA: three peacekeepers were injured and three MINUSCA vehicles destroyed in the event. On 9 December, a rocket was launched into the MINUSCA camp in Kaga Bandoro, probably as part of the protest against the arrival of the new prefect; nobody was killed or injured. Facing the upsurge of violence, the UNSC renewed the MINUSCA mandate on 15 November for another year and authorised an increase of the troop ceiling by 900 to a maximum of 11,650 military personnel in order to bolster one core task in particular – the protection of civilians. Accusations of misconduct remained common. Most significant was that, in June, Congo was pushed to withdraw its 629 troops in response to sexual abuse allegations. A leaked memo stated that six accusatory letters had been sent to the battalion commander regarding not only alleged sexual abuse, but also fuel trafficking and lack of discipline. Several allegations of sexual abuse dating back a number of years involving French forces deployed under Operation Sangaris were dismissed by French judicial authorities.

In search of international support, Touadéra did not limit himself to the CAR's traditional partners. A state visit to *France* on 25 September did not bring about new prospects of military cooperation. He also met with *EU* High Representative Federica Mogherini and President of the European Parliament (EP) Antonio Tajani in Brussels on 22 November ahead of the EP conference 'Towards a renewed partnership with Africa', in which he also participated. At the margins of the event Touadéra called for material support for the SCC.

Less conventional was his meeting with Russian Foreign Minister Sergei Lavrov on 9 October in Sotchi (Russia). In November and December, *Russia* lobbied the UNSC to lift the arms embargo on the CAR in order to equip the FACA with small arms and light weapons. This had been a constant request from Bangui authorities during the transition period but it had not been favourably received by most international partners, who did not trust the FACA. This assessment clearly changed with the progressive training of new FACA personnel by the EUTM-RCA and an exemption to the arms embargo was granted after reinforced security on warehouses was promised. Russia began almost immediately with the first shipment of arms for 1,300 soldiers including, inter alia, 900 pistols, 5,200 assault-rifles, 840 Kalashnikovs and 270 missile-launchers, plus ammunition. Russia also signalled its readiness to train the FACA on these weapons.

Within Africa, Touadéra made notable visits to neighbouring countries that had at least tacitly supported some rebel movements in the past. Most prominent was a trip to *Chad* on 29 June, where he met also AU President Alpha Condé of Guinea and the chairperson of the AU Commission Moussa Faki Mahamat (from Chad) alongside Chad's President Déby. There was press speculation that Touadéra was put under pressure on this occasion to issue amnesties to rebel leaders. A new *African Initiative for Peace and Reconciliation* in the CAR, established at the AU summit on 30–31 January, led to the adoption of a new 'roadmap to peace' by a ministerial conference held in Libreville (Gabon) on 17 July. The document was signed by representatives of the CAR government (Foreign Minister Doubane), the AU, CEEAC, ICGLR, Angola, Chad, Congo and Gabon. The roadmap was quite vague and did not provide for clear milestones. It claimed to include the contents of the previous (failed) attempt to establish a peace accord by Sant'Egidio in Rome, but clearly was meant to put African actors in the driver's seat for future negotiations. Subsequently, France affirmed that the African Initiative and this roadmap would constitute the main framework for a political solution, while the UN stressed the need for coordination with MINUSCA. All those efforts looked sterile as long as all the armed movements remained internally fragmented – self-nominated leaders could often speak only for a battalion of fighters. Chad was a key player in this new turn of events. In November, a National Assembly delegation went to N'Djamena and signed a parliamentary cooperation agreement. Touadéra participated at the CEMAC summit in N'Djamena on 31 October and he also visited *Sudan* on 10–11 December. Together with the presidents of Niger and Djibouti, Touadéra was one of the few African heads of state to come to Kigali for Rwandan President Kagame's inauguration ceremony on 18 August. On his return trip, he was accompanied by 40 of the 200 FACA soldiers trained by the Rwandan army. Touadéra, accompanied by Defence Minister Koyara and Chief of Staff General Luc Ngaifei visited *Equatorial Guinea* at the end of the training phase of 144 FACA soldiers on 28 October, mostly to witness a demonstration of their newly acquired military skills in the presence of President Obiang Nguema Mbasogo.

Socioeconomic Developments

GDP growth was slower than expected at around 4% (IMF projection), so that the losses resulting from years of turmoil (2012/13) were still not recovered. The ongoing violence in parts of the country significantly hampered agricultural production. Insecurity and repeated displacement led to a 58 % decline in crop production and increased food prices. Roughly every second person was in a food-insecure situation. The rare good news was that the economically central Bangui-Douala (Cameroon) corridor remained open, enabling a projected growth in export volume of 17.7%. Timber, cotton and official diamond exports saw significant increases. Nevertheless, there was little reason for optimism.

The upsurge of violence, first in the south-east and towards the end of the year in the north-west, led to an increase in the number of *IDPs*, bringing the total to 688,700 – a 60% increase compared with 2016. The number of *refugees* increased by 26% to over 545,000 hosted in neighbouring countries, although 45,000 refugees from earlier episodes of war returned to their villages of origin. This meant that, by year's end, the overall number of those forcibly displaced was higher than ever. Humanitarian assistance was stepped up, but the official humanitarian response plan of the UN's Office for the Coordination of Humanitarian Affairs was underfunded (61.3 % of the needs were not covered). One particular problem was the dangerous work environment for humanitarian assistance: during the year, 14 aid workers were killed and 297 humanitarian workers were temporarily relocated because of the lack of security.

On 15 December, the IMF's executive board completed the third review under the *ECF* arrangement. Most importantly, this exercise enabled the disbursement of SDR (special drawing right) 28.41 m (about $ 40.2 m). The difficulties of running a reform agenda in parallel with efforts to gradually restore security in additional urban centres – and not only Bangui – were acknowledged. Overall, the IMF expressed satisfaction with the authorities' efforts in many fields, which even led to the approval of an augmentation of the ECF by SDR 38.99 m (about $ 55.1 m). As important was the assessment of needs as part of the national strategy for recovery and peace, as well as for a more solid backing of economic growth.

One source of concern was the high risk of *debt distress*. An updated so-called debt sustainability analysis suggested that the government should rely on grant financing with strict limitations on highly concessional financing for critical projects only.

State *revenue growth* in 2016 and 2017 was lower than projected, close to the African average of 2.2% of GDP. The state was able to reduce some of its domestic debt arrears. However, it was clear that only a higher productivity and income from taxes and customs would help matters. On 22 June, Global Witness published a report ('A Game of Stones') that described the continued possibilities for smuggled *diamonds* to fund armed movements in the CAR. The government rejected the report only a few days later and stressed the importance of diamond exports for economic recovery. In fact, many sources in the report predated the newly established policies, but it was undisputed that a good part of the diamond production left the country illegally. The readmission of diamond exports produced in so-called green zones under government control also led to a slow upturn in legal diamond exports as part of the processes foreseen in the so-called Kimberley Process. The World Diamond Council, an important body of the worldwide diamond industry, officially reaffirmed its support for efforts to prevent the trade in conflict diamonds originating from the

CAR. The Ministry of Mining and MINUSCA undertook a joint mission to Berberati, a green zone designated by the Kimberley Process, to explore possibilities for national oversight and taxation of income generated by the illicit exploitation of natural resources. On 20 July, the General Court of the EU upheld an asset freeze imposed on two Belgian-based diamond companies that had procured diamonds from the CAR. It was clear that the main stakeholders in the war economy could count on partners outside the country.

Chad

Ketil Fred Hansen

Déby's regime remained superficially stable by keeping to its practice of frequently changing its top personnel. Relative peace prevailed in the heartland of the country. Effective repression by a heavily militarised regime with additional military support from France and the US managed to control insurgent movements in northern Chad/Southern Libya. Chad's diplomacy was very active during the year and succeeded in bringing about the election of a Chadian as chairperson of the AU. The low price of oil on the world market caused a fiscal crisis.

Domestic Politics

Chad's fully personalised style of politics had unintended consequences. Speculation around *President Idriss Déby's health* was widespread, with rumours in N'Djamena insisting that he could die at any moment. The fact that his prime wife and Chad's first lady, Hinda Déby, obtained *French citizenship* for herself and their five children on 15 January was interpreted as a sign of serious illness as it meant Déby would have provided security for his loved ones before his death. The fact that he was not present at the opening of the UN General Assembly in September was also taken as a sign of his ill health. Déby made numerous private trips to see his

 | DOI:10.1163/9789004367630_024

doctor at the American Hospital in Paris, but there were no reliable reports that his health deteriorated during the year.

Déby continued to *rule by decree*, deposing and nominating ministers, governors, prefects and CEOs of state-owned businesses at will. His first significant cabinet change came on 6 February, when he replaced Foreign Minister Moussa Faki Mahamat, just elected as chairperson of the AU, with Hissein Brahim Taha, who was at that time Chad's ambassador to France. A more unexpected change was the nomination of the award-winning filmmaker Mahamat Saleh Haroun as minister of culture and tourism. Haroun had been living in France since fleeing Chad during the civil war in the early 1980s and was without political experience. Numerous minor alternations in the government occurred before the last important reshuffle took place on 24 December, when Déby reduced the size of the government from 38 ministers and state secretaries to 23. Thus, 15 ministers and state secretaries lost their positions and were not replaced. Some well-known figures such as Minister of Public Security Ahmat Bachir and Minister of Justice Ahmat Mahamat Hassan were simply dismissed. The new government was composed of 18 men and five women.

On 30 July, Déby changed four of the country's 23 governors. On 5 September, he replaced 31 prefects and 62 sub-prefects and dismissed Mohamed Ibni Oumar Saleh as CEO of the state-owned cotton company CotonTchad. Son of the main political opposition spokesperson Ibni Oumar Mahamat Saleh, who had been taken by Déby's secret police on 3 February 2008 and had not been seen since, he had been rewarded with the CEO position in October 2016, for which he returned from exile in France. CotonTchad was the second most important employer in Chad with more than 2,000 employees. In the first week in October, Déby dismissed the governor of Borkou region together with the prefect of Faya and a military commander as he found their response to rebellions there inadequate.

Trade unions – on strike since the end of 2016 – signed a memorandum of understanding and strikes terminated on 8 April. However, numerous shorter *strikes* by teachers, lawyers, doctors and other public sector employees followed throughout the year, in protest against unpaid salaries and reductions in bonuses. Three trade unions, the 'Union Nationale des Syndicats du Tchad', the 'Syndicat National des Enseignants et Chercheurs du Supérieur' (Synecs) and the 'Confédération Indépendante des Syndicats du Tchad', collaborated closely in most strikes. While workers' unions were allowed to strike, members of associations and social movements saw their right to demonstrate and protest heavily reduced by the regime.

On 13 January, the newly created 'Mouvement pour l'Eveil Citoyen' (*MECI*, founded on 29 December 2016) was formally banned, accused by the regime of being closely connected to the rebellion in the northern parts of the country. Denying any connection to any rebellions, MECI argued that it was not a political party or association and so it could not be banned under the current law. In their own words, MECI was only a coalition of political parties, civil society organisations and individuals interested in restoring democracy. The secret police interrupted their first annual assembly arranged at the Al Mouna centre in downtown N'Djamena on 27 May. On 6 April, Nadjo Kaina, the leader of the young, anti-regime citizen movement *IYINA*, was arrested for public disorder. He encouraged people to wear red clothes as a sign of protest to mark the anniversary of President Déby's fifth re-election in 2016, red being a symbol of the blood shed during the war against French colonial rule. He was released without charge a month later, on 4 May. On 12 April, Dingamnayal Nely Versinis, the head of the '*Collectif Tchadien Contre la Vie Chère*', a consumer protection organisation, was arrested after encouraging small traders at the Millet Marked in N'Djamena to protest against an increase in market fees. The public prosecutor released him on 27 April.

On 26 February, agents of the National Security Agency arrested Daniel Ngadjadoum, a journalist with 'Tribune Info' and a well-known opposition figure in N'Djamena, for writing an article critical of President Déby; he was released without charge on 1 March. On 17 October, Juda Allahondoum, a journalist on the staff of the weekly newspaper 'Le Visionnaire', was arrested after publishing an article on fraud in the aviation sector. He was released without charge a month later, on 16 November. Other journalists and owners of publishing houses received threatening phone calls and visits. Even so, press freedom was improving, according to Reporters without Borders, compared with previous years.

Both Timan Erdimi (an ethnic Zaghawa) and General Mahamat Nouri (an ethnic Daza-Tubu) trained troops, or rather armed civilians, in Southern Libya/North-Eastern Chad. Based in Qatar since 2009, Erdimi still controlled the *politico-military group* 'Union des Forces de la Résistance' and was aiming at removing his uncle, President Déby, from office. Nouri had led the politico-military group 'Union des Forces pour la Démocracie et le Developpement' from his home in France for years, also with the ultimate goal of toppling Déby. In addition, Mahamat Mahdi Ali, roughly 50 years old and always a rebel leader, also from the Daza-Tubu clan and living in France but out of sympathy with Nouri, commanded the 1,500 strong '*Front pour l'Alternance et la Concorde au Tchad*' (FACT), which trained in the same region. On 18 January, at Chad's request, French authorities froze all Nouri's and Mahdi's bank accounts on suspicion that they were financing the rebellions against Déby. The amounts frozen were, however, utterly insignificant. Believing then that *Qatar* was funding the rebels, on 23 August Déby ordered the closure of the Qatari embassy in N'Djamena and its staff to leave Chad within ten days. At the end of November, four colonels in the Chadian army defected and joined FACT, together with some 20 soldiers. However, as long as the Déby regime was backed by France and the US, the chances for the rebel movements to make a successful coup were believed to be minimal.

According to TI, *corruption* was rampant in Chad. Though ranked as 165th out of 180 countries on the corruption perception index, Chad officially took combating corruption seriously. In July, the Ministry of Finance established a free phone number – 700 – which citizens and businesses alike could call to report acts of corruption on the part of civil servants. At the same time, Déby himself was accused of having received payments of $ 2 m from the company China Energy in one of his private accounts in the United States. Efforts to combat corruption were in reality sometimes used to get rid of political adversaries. For example, on 13 July, Laoukein Médard was sacked as mayor of Moundou, the second most important town in Chad, and accused embezzling the equivalent of € 40,000, for which he was detained in prison. He was only released on 24 November, after the charges were dropped.

In an attempt to turn the focus away from domestic fiscal problems, Déby voiced his intense opposition to the CFA franc and, in an interview with 'Jeune Afrique' in June, called the device a colonial legacy. He argued that, without a sovereign national currency, economic policy-making was difficult and still dependent of the will of Chad's former colonial master.

Foreign Affairs

While internal security and increased controls reduced the number of attacks by Boko Haram in Chad, the group still threatened parts of the population around Lake Chad. However, Boko Haram killed more Chadian soldiers than civilians. In October, Chad reduced the number of troops fighting Boko Haram, partly in response to this high death rate and the high cost of the operations. Hundreds of troops were pulled out of the Diffa region in *Niger* to be deployed in the Tibesti area in northern Chad. While Déby officially stated that the transfer of troops was due to an increase in rebel activities in the frontier region with Libya, there was speculation that the reduction was intended to speed up the process of establishing the G5 Sahel joint force that had been started in February.

To be precise, on 6 February, the *G5 Sahel* (Mauritania, Mali, Burkina Faso, Niger and Chad) had decided to set up a joint force of up to 5,000 troops to increase security and fight terrorism in the region. This decision was endorsed first by the AU on 17 April and then, on 21 June, by UNSC resolution 2359. Present at the G5 Sahel conference in Bamako (Mali) on 2 July, President Déby stated that European countries should release the cash already pledged to fund the force and increase their funding. On 13 December, all the G5 Sahel heads of state, including Déby, met outside Paris together with representatives of the international donor community to expedite the financing and complete setting up the 5,000-troops joint force.

Chad was also an active participant in the 11,000 strong MINUSMA (UN Multidimensional Integrated Stabilisation Mission in Mali). As a reward for its important role in *Mali*, former Chadian Minister of Foreign Affairs Mahamat Saleh Annadif, assumed the leadership of MINUSMA operations in January. At the end of 2017, some 1,550 Chadian troops were still participating in MINUSMA, a force estimated to cost more than $ 1 bn per year to operate; only Bangladesh and Burkina Faso had more troops involved than Chad.

N'Djamena was the home of France's *Operation Barkhane*, which by year's end involved some 4,000 troops, five drones, eight jetfighters, 17 helicopters and some 600 support vehicles and armoured cars. While some of the equipment and troops were operative in Mali and Niger, France also had temporary military bases in the towns Faya and Abeche in Chad. The annual costs of the operation for France were estimated to be around € 600 m.

Chad, which had one of the largest, best-equipped and best-trained armies in Africa, was among the Sahelian states that hosted AFRICOM's (United States Africa Command) annual Flintlock exercise for Special Operation Forces at the beginning of the year. Some 2,000 Special Forces from Africa, Europe and North America trained in Chad for three weeks starting on 27 February.

Active in both the AU, CEMAC and the G5 Sahel, along with other *regional organisations*, Chad also signed a long list of bilateral agreements. Two of them were the 9 May agreement between Chad, Niger and Mali to cooperate in legal matters concerning the fight against terror and trans-border smuggling, and a bilateral agreement signed in late October to allow nationals from the UAE to make visa-free visits to Chad. CEMAC member countries also adopted visa-free travel arrangements for each other's citizens on 31 October at a summit in the Chadian capital. However, all Chadians were denied visas to the US when, on 24 September, the Trump administration put Chad on the list of countries whose citizens were not welcome. This was heavily criticised by the AU, the Chadian authorities and many international embassies, apparently including the US embassy in N'Djamena, but the US Homeland Security administration did not repeal the travel ban for Chadian nationals.

On 30 January, after a lengthy voting procedure ending with 39 votes in favour and 15 abstentions, African heads of state elected Chad's Foreign Minister *Moussa Faki Mahamat as chairperson of the AU Commission*. This was an indication of Chad's standing among its peers in Africa and Faki Mahamat took office in Addis Ababa (Ethiopia) on 14 March.

Déby continued his *frequent visits abroad*, to Europe, the Middle East and various African countries. *France*'s President Macron, in office from 14 May, received Déby in Paris on three occasions, on 11 July, 28 August and 13 December. According to press reports, the fight against terror in the Sahel was always the main issue discussed. Macron never travelled to Chad, however, and this was interpreted in N'Djamena as a sign of a weakened relationship between France and Chad, although many French public figures and ministers did visit. French Minister of the Environment Ségolène Royale made an official visit on 29 January to discuss issues concerning Lake Chad after signing the day before in Paris a convention to restore the ecosystem and planting of trees around the lake, and promising € 1 m to support the project. French Minister of State for Development Jean-Marie Le Guen made two official visits, on 14–15 February and 9–11 April, and Minister of Defence Jean-Yves Le Drian visited on 26–27 February. During the French presidential election campaign, Marine Le Pen, the candidate of the 'Front National', made a visit to Chad on 21 March to discuss security and counter-terrorism with Déby. Finally, Minister of the Armed forces Florence Parly visited on 30–31 July. On 23 March, four unidentified men kidnapped a French citizen employed in the mining sector near the town of Goz Beida in the south-east part of the country. He was released in Sudan on 7 May through the coordinated efforts of the French, Sudanese and Chadian intelligence services.

Déby also received numerous other official visitors in N'Djamena, including *China*'s Vice President Li Yuanchao, whom he welcomed on 9 May to discuss commercial cooperation, *Egypt*'s President Abdel Fattah Al-Sisi, received on 17 August to discuss the fight against terror, and *Turkey*'s President Recep Tayyip Erdoğan, received on 27 December to sign a number of trade deals and confirm increased cooperation. A more controversial official visit was that by *Sudan*'s President Omar al-Bashir, whom Déby invited specially for the celebration of his 27 years in power on 2 December. The international arrest warrant issued by the ICC in 2009 was still in force, and thus Chad went against international law by not jailing him.

On 24 December, a group of mainly Chadian mercenaries headed by Mahamat Kodo Bani, attempted a coup against President Teodoro Obiang Nguema in *Equatorial Guinea*. The coup failed and ended with the arrest of some 50 Chadian coup plotters, who were imprisoned. Chadian diplomacy tried hectically to convince the Equatorial Guinean administration that Déby's regime had not played any role in the coup attempt. Although Kodo Bani had been a general in Chad's National Army in the 1990s, he was among those who had abandoned the Déby camp and joined the military opposition in the mid-2000s.

Chad was very active in promoting the signature of a formal peace accord in the neighbouring *CAR*, but was variously suspected of putting pressure on Bangui to issue amnesties to Muslim rebel leaders seeking support from N'Djamena. It was clear that Déby continued to exercise considerable political clout in the CAR.

Socioeconomic Developments

Some 70% of *government revenue* came from oil. With the international price varying from \$ 42/barrel to \$ 66/barrel during the year, Chad faced a serious fiscal crisis. While tax revenues had made up close to 15% of GDP in 2013, this was estimated to have fallen to some 6% in 2017. A more than five-year positive trade balance was turned into a negative balance in 2016 and 2017. In June, an agreement was reached between Chad and Exxon over a high court ruling in 5 October

2016 that the oil company should pay duties and fines totalling $ 74 bn, representing some 30 years of oil production at today's prices. Exxon paid $ 200 m to resolve the conflict and continue exploring and exporting crude oil. The US was by far Chad's biggest customer, buying close to 60% of Chad's exports, mostly oil. France, formerly a very important buyer, was overtaken by both India and China, but was still the most important supplier of imported goods, at close to 20% of all imports.

The oil deal between Chad and the Swiss company *Glencore* created a scandal when the accounts published in June revealed that, of the $ 271 m oil sales revenue, the Chadian state had to pay $ 231 m in debt-service costs. Déby acknowledged publicly that the deal was a "fool bargain" and "an irresponsible step". Glencore produced close to 2.5 m barrels from the Mangara and Badila oilfields over the year and lent $ 312 m to the Chadian regime to help it cope with the country's economic crisis, while the Chadian authorities started re-negotiating the Glencore contract; negotiations were still on-going at the end of the year.

Food *prices* fluctuated heavily during the year and between different parts of the country. In most areas, basic cereals such as millet and sorghum were cheaper than in 2016 due to a better harvest. However, it was impossible to generalise this to a decrease in overall food prices throughout the country. As an example, a two-year-old ram was sold for CFAfr 17,000 in March in Moundou (down from CFAfr 25,000 in 2016) but was sold in the same month for CFAfr 22,000 in Sahr (down from CFAfr 42,000 in 2016), and in Goré for CFAfr 19,000 (unchanged from 2016). Overall, malnutrition was reduced from some 50% of the population to 43%, according to the World Hunger Index 2017. The state-set price of gasoline increased from CFAfr 5.23/litre to CFAfr 5.68/litre on 14 January, giving rise to massive protests by the drivers of both registered taxis and clandestine motorcycle taxis.

Chad relied on *foreign funding* to cover humanitarian needs, the functioning of the state and long-term development. On 24 February, an international *donor conference* took place in Oslo for the Lake Chad region and pledged some $ 672 m to combat famine and fight terror in the region. According to the UN, $ 1.5 bn was necessary to cover humanitarian needs in the region. On 30 June, the IMF approved a three-year arrangement under the ECF for about $ 312 m. The aim was to restructure commercial debt, make debt sustainable and stabilise Chad's fiscal position in order to make it possible to finance public goods such as schools and hospitals. Apparently none of the 16 measures set out in August 2016 had yet taken effect and the new agreement included a clause requiring their implementation. Higher taxes for everyone and a reduction in state employees' salaries and allowances reduced many people's income. With inflation at close to 4% and a fall of 7% in GDP in 2016, Chad's economy was under heavy pressure.

On 6–8 September, an international donor meeting in Paris, organised by the Chadian government to support Chad's newly adopted National Development Plan, received pledges of $ 20 bn, including around $ 1 bn from the World Bank, close to another $ 1 bn from the EU and a little more than $ 500,000,000 from the AfDB.

In December, the AfDB signed a $ 77 m deal to finance the long-planned bridge over the Logone River, connecting the Chadian town of Bongor with the Cameroonian town of Yagoua. Until the construction is finished, more than 2,000 commuters and merchants a day would have to continue to use rough and ready boats or make long detours.

Many of the *IDPs* in Chad were living very close to home. In Kanem region, on the north-eastern flanks of Lake Chad, some 90,000 of the 130,000–160,000 IDPs lived in their sub-prefecture of origin. They had had to move because of insecurity caused by Boko Haram. Chad also hosted some 320,000 refugees from Sudan in the four regions bordering Sudan and some 75,000 from the CAR in the three regions bordering that country. Many of them had been in Chad for more than ten years. In addition, some 8,000 refugees from Chad were living in east Sudan. On 18 December, the UNHCR started to repatriate the first 300 of them from the Um Shalya camp in Darfur, where most of them had been living for more than ten years.

A case of *cholera* was discovered in the Sila region in south-east Chad on 14 August and the disease spread. By 22 October, when the health authorities declared the end of the epidemic, 50 persons had died in the Sila region, and 19 more in the neighbouring Salamat region. The main source of the cholera was contaminated water in the Bahr Azoum River.

Congo

Brett L. Carter

On 16 July, citizens in the Republic of Congo were called to the polls to elect a new National Assembly, the fourth legislative election since President Denis Sassou Nguesso reclaimed power in 1997. The elections occurred in the midst of the worst crisis since 1990, which had compelled Sassou Nguesso to convene the National Conference and ultimately permit Congo's first democratic elections in 1992. Certain the legislative elections would be fraudulent, citizens registered their frustration by refusing to participate. Sassou Nguesso responded to citizens' frustrations by continuing the campaign of repression that he had begun in the run-up to the constitutional referendum of October 2015. Several opposition leaders and journalists were imprisoned, others remained incarcerated, without trial, and one political prisoner died in police custody. Abroad, Sassou Nguesso sought financial and military support to buttress his weak domestic position. As global oil prices remained

 | DOI:10.1163/9789004367630_025

low, existing oil fields reached maturity and Sassou Nguesso's massive infrastructure programme failed to generate sustainable economic growth, the government's debt/GDP ratio spiked to nearly 120%. The government slashed domestic spending, causing per capita GDP to fall sharply.

Domestic Politics

Sassou Nguesso began the year by incarcerating André Okombi Salissa, his ally during the 1997 civil war, a government minister from 1997 to 2012, and a deputy in the National Assembly since 2002. Okombi Salissa had publicly opposed the constitutional referendum of October 2015 and had contested the March 2016 presidential election. When fellow opposition leader and presidential candidate General Jean-Marie Michel Mokoko had been arrested in June 2016, Okombi Salissa had gone into hiding. Sassou Nguesso's security services discovered him in Brazzaville in January. He was detained and both he and General Mokoko were still being held in prison without trial at year's end – only the two most prominent of about 100 *political prisoners*, according to AI.

In January, Sassou Nguesso also arrested two prominent *journalists*: Christ Dongui Nganga and Ghys Fortuné Dombé Bemba. Dongui Nganga was arrested for filming the National Assembly's vote to strip Okombi Salissa of his parliamentary immunity, enabling Sassou Nguesso to proceed with criminal proceedings. Ostensibly public, the vote was even filmed by 'Télé Congo', the state-run television station. Ndongui Ganga's arrest outraged many Congolese citizens. Dombé Bemba, publisher of the 'Talassa' newspaper and one of Congo's most highly regarded journalists, was arrested for covering a series of human rights violations committed by Sassou Nguesso's military in the Pool region surrounding Brazzaville.

The scale of the military's *human rights violations* became clear in February, when the 'Observatoire Congolais des Droits de l'Homme' (OCDH), Brazzaville's most prominent human rights NGO, released its annual report. Entitled 'Governance by Terror', the document was scathing, and received media coverage around the world. OCDH released a second report just six weeks later, in mid-April, entitled 'Repression behind Closed Doors'. Since April 2016, when military operations had commenced, some 30,000 residents of Pool had been displaced by fighting; the government blocked access to affected areas and so the true death toll remained unclear. Although the Sassou Nguesso government claimed to be pursuing the Ninja militia, most observers, including OCDH, regarded the military operation as an attempt to intimidate citizens into accepting the results of the obviously fraudulent presidential election of March 2016. The OCDH reports were later corroborated by the US State Department's human rights report, released in March.

In addition to military atrocities in the Pool region, OCDH documented the scale of Sassou Nguesso's mass incarceration programme and the frequent use of *torture*.

This was underscored in February, when Colonel Marcel Ntsourou, a regime dissident who was once a senior official in Sassou Nguesso's domestic surveillance apparatus, died in police custody. He had been declared healthy by a doctor just before his death, and many citizens suspected that he had been poisoned. After initially blaming his cousin, Franck Mbani, with whom he shared a prison cell, the regime claimed Ntsourou died of natural causes. Sassou Nguesso forced the Ntsourou family to forgo an autopsy, which could have shed light on the cause, and a public funeral in Brazzaville, which would have provided frustrated citizens with an occasion to protest. The government's mistreatment of political prisoners emerged again in August, when opposition leader Modeste Boukadia, who had been in prison since January 2016, was released in failing health. He was immediately evacuated to France for treatment and was still there at year's end.

The *opposition* harnessed widespread frustration with repression and with the consequences of a severe financial crisis by organising a series of mass protests in May and June. On 8 June, the opposition held a memorial ceremony for the victims of the military assault on Pool. In response, Sassou Nguesso security forces arrested participants and surrounded the homes of opposition leaders. On 10 June, the National Day of Reconciliation, the opposition called on citizens to wear a sign of mourning. Brazzaville was placed on 'lockdown', according to Charles Bowao, a former government minister turned opposition leader.

Sassou Nguesso was forced to prepare for July's legislative elections amidst widespread protests. He again responded with repression. In February, the National Assembly made it illegal for political parties to accept private funding, a provision that citizens widely believed would be applied only to opposition parties. On 31 May, Congo's embassy in Paris announced that it would issue no more visas until further notice. On 11 June, the *Internet* went down. Sassou Nguesso's spokesman claimed a fishing vessel off the coast of Pointe-Noire had snapped a fibre optic cable, separating Congo from the West Africa Cable System. The government claimed that repairs would take between two and seven weeks, ending comfortably after the July elections, but offered no evidence to corroborate its explanation, and it was unclear which 'fishing vessel' was responsible. Citizens suspected the Internet shutdown was a deliberate attempt to block opposition protests or to prevent media coverage of the government's violent response.

The first round of the *legislative elections* took place on 16 July, and the second on 30 July. The primary opposition coalition, the 'Front Républicain pour le Respect de l'Ordre Constitutionnel et l'Alternance Démocratique – Initiative pour la Démocratie au Congo' (FROCAD-IDC), announced an electoral boycott on May 26. "No elections," they declared, "until the end of the war in Pool [and] the liberation of all political prisoners." On 19 June, Mathias Dzon, another former presidential candidate and Sassou Nguesso minister, called the exercise an "electoral farce". The elections were rejected across the country, including in Sassou Nguesso's supposed northern strongholds. Citizens ransacked polling stations, lit fires outside them and barricaded streets in front of them. This response was unprecedented in Congolese history. In the event, the dominant 'Parti Congolais du Travail' (PCT) claimed a massive victory, as everyone knew it would. Opposition parties were awarded just 16 of the National Assembly's 153 seats, with fully 10 seats, or 6% of the entire Assembly, allocated to Sassou Nguesso's relatives. The AU observer mission claimed that campaigning had been carried out normally, causing widespread outrage.

The year concluded much as it began. Opposition leader Paulin Makaya, who had been arrested in November 2015 for organising a series of protests against Sassou Nguesso's constitutional referendum, completed his 24 months' prison sentence, but Sassou Nguesso simply refused to release him. He remained in prison at year's end.

Foreign Affairs

Sassou Nguesso's foreign policy was dominated by his efforts to secure financial and military support amidst his range of domestic crises. He flew from Palm Beach, Florida, to Brazzaville on 31 December 2016, after his failed bid to meet President-Elect *Donald Trump*. Although the potential meeting was shrouded in secrecy, by May it was clear that it had been arranged by Sassou Nguesso's son Denis Christel, longtime American lobbyist and former felon Jack Abramoff, and US Congressman Dana Rohrabacher of California, commonly referred to as Russian President Vladimir Putin's 'favorite congressman' and suspected by fellow Republicans of accepting illicit financial transfers from the Russian government. As a face-saving measure, in January Rohrabacher lead a congressional delegation to Brazzaville, where he gave several interviews on Sassou Nguesso-owned media outlets.

Corruption trials in foreign courts continued to dominate Sassou Nguesso's foreign policy. In January, Philippe Chironi, a French national, was convicted by a *San Marino* court of laundering nearly € 70 m on Sassou Nguesso's behalf between 2006 and 2011. With Lucien Ebata, Chironi had co-founded Orion Oil, widely regarded as a front company for Sassou Nguesso's money laundering apparatus. Chironi was also administrator of Forbes Afrique Media Holding, which Ebata had founded with Sassou Nguesso capital. In March, the president's nephew Wilfrid Nguesso was indicted in *France* for public corruption, as were his daughter Julienne Sassou Nguesso and son-in-law Guy Johnson in June. After Teodorín Obiang, Equatorial Guinea's vice president and the son of its president, was convicted of public corruption by French courts in October, observers predicted that Sassou Nguesso's family would be targeted next. In March, in an attempt to block further damaging revelations, Sassou Nguesso ordered the arrest of two Italian journalists who were investigating his Italian son-in-law's role in oil sector corruption. The government blocked Internet access in Pointe-Noire to prevent the journalists from transmitting incriminating information to Rome, and then confiscated their computers. The event caused a minor diplomatic crisis with *Italy*.

Sassou Nguesso made a series of bilateral agreements with foreign governments, most of which sought to diminish his exposure to European sanctions. In January, the government announced that Beijing would assume primary responsibility for the construction of the Pointe-Noire Special Economic Zone (SEZ), the centrepiece of the government's efforts to diversify the economy away from oil. The Chinese and Congolese governments held several ministerial meetings throughout the year. Days after the SEZ announcement, Sassou Nguesso's son Denis Christel laid the first stone of the *Université Privée de Marrakech* (UPM), located in Oyo, the president's home village of just 5,000 residents. Many suspect Oyo was selected in exchange for Sassou Nguesso's support for *Morocco*'s bid to rejoin the AU. In March, Sassou Nguesso undertook a state visit to Algeria, though it apparently yielded no major financial commitments from President Abdelaziz Bouteflika. A week later, Sassou Nguesso announced new *military accords with the Russian government*, which agreed to train the Congolese military. Given Sassou Nguesso's ongoing military operation in the Pool region, most citizens reacted with frustration.

Socioeconomic Developments

Congo's *GDP*, adjusted for purchasing power parity, was estimated to have contracted by roughly $ 1 bn for a second consecutive year and reached $ 29.2 bn by year's end, a contraction from $ 30.3 bn in 2016 and $ 31.1 bn in 2015; its growth rate for 2017 was −3.6%. The fall in per capita GDP was even more pronounced: from $ 7,500 in 2015, to $ 7,100 in 2016, and finally to $ 6,700 in 2017.

By April, the extent of Congo's *financial crisis* was fully apparent. When global oil prices dropped in 2014 and 2015, the government had funded its massive infrastructure budget by reverting to the oil-backed loans used throughout the 1980s, but this strategy had been forsworn to secure debt relief from the IMF and the World Bank in 2010. In March, just six years after receiving that debt relief, the government announced that the debt/GDP ratio had reached 77%, exceeding the 70% limit imposed by CEMAC. In fact, as the *IMF* forced Brazzaville to concede in October, the government's debt/GDP ratio was nearly 120%. The government had committed roughly four years of future oil revenue, and was now technically in default to Glencore and Trafigura.

In May, Sassou Nguesso began working with an Abu Dhabi investment firm to float a $ 4 bn Eurobond, equivalent to roughly half of Congo's annual GDP, measured in current US dollars. The scheme fell through, and Sassou Nguesso redoubled his efforts to secure a bailout from the IMF. During its first visit, in March, the IMF pressed the government to accept a series of transparency measures, including an audit of the state-owned oil company 'Société Nationale des Pétroles du Congo' (SNPC). Sassou Nguesso resisted. Discussions continued during the year, although his negotiating team drew substantial criticism. The team was lead by Lucien Ebata, a key figure in Sassou Nguesso's money laundering apparatus. He also hired Dominique Strauss-Kahn, former managing director of the IMF and a former French finance minister, to help cover up evidence of major corruption. Despite the ongoing financial crisis, citizens organised a series of protests against IMF intervention, believing it would prop up the failing Sassou Nguesso government. The *#SassouFit Collective*, a civil society organisation, launched a social media campaign called 'Don't Save the Tyrant' directed at Christine Lagarde, the IMF's managing director.

This financial crisis, in turn, caused a fuel crisis in Brazzaville and Pointe-Noire. The state-owned oil refinery satisfied just 20% of Congo's domestic demand for fuel. The rest was imported, and SNPC enjoyed a monopoly on these imports. The SNPC had long been dominated by Sassou Nguesso's son, Denis Christel, so the monopoly on fuel imports effectively belonged to the president's family. Since the SNPC was bankrupt, it was unable to purchase enough fuel on the international market to satisfy domestic demand. Rather than abandon the monopoly – and hence forgo monopoly profits – Sassou Nguesso chose to subject his citizens to a fuel shortage. As cover, the government blamed "technical difficulties" at Congo's oil refinery. Massive queues outside fuel stations became so common that even Sassou Nguesso's propaganda apparatus – normally insistent on providing positive news – was forced to cover them.

This economic contraction had three broad causes. First, the *oil sector* generally accounted for more than 60% of GDP, 75% of government revenue and 90% of total exports. With global oil prices persistently low and existing oil fields reaching maturity, the government was losing its chief source of revenue. In November, Prime Minister Clement Mouamba acknowledged that, since 2015, total government revenue had fallen by 31.3% and revenue from the oil sector alone had fallen by 65.1%. The substantial drop in revenue and the government's failure to curtail spending generated a massive spike in the debt/GDP ratio. This caused the government to briefly default on a $ 478 m Eurobond debt payment in August, which prompted a further credit rating downgrade. Second, faced with this financial crisis, the government was forced to make a drastic cut of more than $ 1 bn in planned spending. Since its construction budget constituted a substantial share of non-oil GDP, the *sharp drop in government spending* exacerbated the crisis. Third, most major infrastructure projects, after receiving debt relief in 2011, were riddled with *inefficiencies* and, as a result, did little to foster growth or improve living standards. The government had invested more than $ 1.6 bn in the Imboulou Dam Project and the *Centrale Électrique du Congo* (CEC), but achieved no improvements in electricity access. The *unemployment* rate remained at 36%.

In February, the government announced it was unable to afford vaccines, but then in March announced the opening of a state-of-the-art hospital in Oyo, Sassou Nguesso's native village, to serve only 5,000 people. The hospital, which cost $ 21 m, was more an expensive monument to Sassou Nguesso's late daughter – whose name the hospital bore – than an investment in public health.

The government hoped that the Moho Nord oil field, which began production in March, would provide some financial relief. It may in the medium term, as production was expected to reach 350,000 b/d in 2019 – an increase of 25%, making Congo sub-Saharan Africa's third-largest crude producer.

Democratic Republic of the Congo

Janosch Kullenberg

The last minute agreement of 31 December 2016 gave many people hope that the country's political deadlock could be resolved in 2017. However, instead of implementing the agreement, President Kabila undermined its stipulations and used the time foreseen for the transition to outmanoeuvre the opposition and consolidate his power. The resulting loss of legitimacy provoked more political and armed resistance. The regime responded to these forms of opposition with excessive force and arbitrary arrests. There are strong indications that it also staged insecurity and deliberately exacerbated violence in order to further delay the organisation of the elections. Together, these factors exacerbated local dynamics of violence throughout the country and led to an acute humanitarian crisis.

Domestic Politics

The delayed elections and the question of whether President Joseph Kabila would continue to cling on to power were the most important political issues of the year. Kabila, who had reached the end of his second constitutionally limited term,

 | DOI:10.1163/9789004367630_026

should have stepped down in 2016. Under considerable international and domestic pressure, he agreed somewhat surprisingly to many of the opposition's demands on 31 December 2016. The *Comprehensive and Inclusive Political Agreement*, commonly referred to as 'L'accord de la Saint Sylvestre', stipulated that elections were to be organised in 2017, but also that Kabila would not attempt to change the Constitution and run for office again. Until the elections, he would lead an interim government together with a prime minister from the opposition. A monitoring body, the 'Conseil National de Suivi de l'Accord' (CNSA), under the leadership of opposition veteran Etienne Tshisekedi, would supervise the process and function as a platform for discussions.

Despite the hope that a valid solution for the country's political impasse had been found, the implementation of the agreement proved contentious. First, as the deal had literally been struck at the last minute, the formal signature process for all parties continued well into 2017. Subsequently, conflicts emerged over the implementation of the agreement's stipulations and particularly over the distribution of ministries and the process for selecting the prime minister. While the presidential majority demanded that the opposition would provide a list of candidates from whom Kabila would choose, the opposition perceived this as a stratagem for him to handpick the prime minister.

The death of 84-year-old opposition veteran *Etienne Tshisekedi* on 1 February considerably weakened the opposition. As founder and president of Congo's first opposition party, the 'Union pour la Démocratie et le Progrès Social' (UDPS), Tshisekedi has been a central political figure since the 1980s. Having defied long-term dictator Mobutu and subsequently Kabila, he possessed unique moral authority. With his passing, the opposition lost its capacity to mobilise the masses and, therefore, its ability to put the government under pressure. The demise of this unifying figure also intensified the opposition's disintegration. When Tshisekedi's son Felix was designated to lead the UDPS and the 'Rassemblement' (alliance) opposition platform, some of his father's long-term companions in the struggle for democracy contested the monarchist style of the succession. Dissident groups formed, such as the 'Rassemblement Kasa-Vubu' under the leadership of Joseph Olenghankoy and several UDPS factions, including under the party's deputy-secretary, Bruno Tshibala.

Out of frustration with the short-sightedness and self-interest of Congolese politicians, the 'Conférence Épiscopale Nationale Congolaise' (CENCO) – the representative body of the Congolese Catholic Church that had led the negotiation of the 31 December Agreement – stepped back from its role as mediator on 27 March. The presidential majority continued to skilfully exploit and exacerbate the tensions in the opposition by co-opting and integrating its members. On 7 April, President Kabila unilaterally appointed Bruno Tshibala as *prime minister* without solving the on-going dispute over the nomination process. This selection formally fulfilled a central criterion of the Sylvester Agreement, as Tshibala was officially an opposition figure. However, as he now belonged to dissident factions of both the 'Rassemblement' and the UDPS, it also increased the fragmentation of the opposition. In response, the 'Rassemblement' called for mass demonstrations on 10 April. The turn – out was low and the mass protests turned into a general strike because the authorities banned public demonstrations and heavily deployed security forces. Given the high risks to their safety, opposition followers were discouraged from participating, particularly as Felix Tshisekedi himself immediately left the country for Addis Ababa (Ethiopia) after calling for the popular uprising. On 9 May, five weeks after his nomination, Prime Minister Tshibala presented his 59-member transitional government. Most members were recycled from the previous government and key ministries remained in the hands of Kabila's associates. A few new nominations emerged from Tshibala's circle of 'Rassemblement' defectors.

Subsequently, the presidential majority and several smaller parties, including the 'Union pour la Nation Congolaise' (UNC), agreed on special arrangements for the implementation of the Sylvester Agreement. On 22 July, Kabila designated Joseph Olenghankoy as the president of the monitoring mechanism, the CNSA. Although officially made by parliament, this nomination was another violation of the agreement, as it should have been made by consensus with the opposition and this post was designated for the president of the 'Rassemblement'. Like the new prime minister in April, Olenghankoy was formally an opposition member but, as a 'Rassemblement' dissident, he no longer represented it. Kabila thus continued to *split the opposition* and to further hollow out the agreement.

Meanwhile, the government further delayed *the elections* by withholding the election budget and conducting half-hearted voter registration. Citing alleged technical and logistical issues, central stakeholders repeatedly made tentative statements in order to test whether an additional extension would be accepted. For instance, on 15 February, Minister of Budget Pierre Kangudia stated that, given the country's total annual budget of $ 5.2 bn, it would not be possible to spend the $ 1.8 bn foreseen for organising the elections. Meanwhile, insecurity disrupted voter registration and gave the government an excuse for further delays. On 9 May, the president of the 'Commission Électorale Nationale Indépendante' (CENI), Corneille Nangaa, stated that *violence* in the Kasai region was delaying the election process. Kamuina Nsapu fighters had allegedly looted six CENI offices and beheaded three election workers, stalling the registration process in the region. On 7 July, Nangaa announced in Paris that, given these security-related delays, elections could not be organised before the end of the year. On 10 October, Nangaa then announced that elections could not take place before April 2019, because finalising the voter registration in the unstable Kasai region would take another three months and an additional 16 months would then be needed to organise the polls. Many saw this as an exaggeration and hence as a political move by the director of the officially 'independent' CENI.

After eight provincial assemblies had passed no-confidence motions against their governors and while the electoral calendar had not been developed, the CENI was forced to improvise *gubernatorial elections* in Bas-Uélé, Haut-Katanga, Haut-Lomami, Kwilu, South Kivu, Sud-Ubangi, Tshopo and Tshuapa provinces. As the first round on 26 August did not lead to the required majorities in three provinces, a second round became necessary. The level of competition sparked hope for a genuine democratic process and real change. However, results were sobering as seven of the eight elected governors belonged to the presidential majority party or were supported by it.

Civil society organisations engaged in several initiatives against Kabila. A prominent figure was Sindika Dokolo, a Congolese businessman, the husband of the richest woman in Africa, the daughter of former Angolan President José Eduardo dos Santos. With apparent Angolan backing, Dokolo regularly denounced Kabila on Twitter and signalled his support for opposition candidate Moïse Katumbi. Congolese authorities reacted on 13 July, by sentencing him in absentia to one year in jail for alleged fraud. However, this attempt to intimidate him seemed to harden Dokolo's stance. On 10 August, he started an intense social media campaign against Kabila, entitled 'Les Congolais Debout!'. On 17 August, after a three-day meeting in Paris, Dokolo and civil society organisations, including Lucha and Filimbi, launched the 'Manifesto of the Congolese Citizen'. Referring to Article 64 of the Constitution, the document called on Congolese to engage in non-violent protest, should elections not be held by the end of the year. Civil society organisations increasingly pushed for a transition phase without Kabila. Dr Denis Mukwege, a popular gynaecologist and founder of the Bukavu based Panzi hospital, was widely discussed as a transitional, non-political head of government during such a transition phase.

A week after US ambassador to the UN, Nikki Haley, had demanded during her visit that elections take place in 2018, CENI, finally published the *electoral calendar*, setting the election date for 23 December 2018. Although, the publication could be seen as a concession to Haley's resolute demands, many observers criticised it for legitimising the regime's delay tactic. Furthermore, there were justified concerns that this calendar, like previous ones, would not be upheld and would only serve to buy more time for the government to find an (extra) constitutional method of remaining in power. While opposition parties, such as the UDPS, UNC and 'Mouvement pour la Libération du Congo' had each individually rejected the calendar, reiterating their demands that President Kabila leave office by 31 December, international bodies such as the UNSC and the AU accepted the calendar, while highlighting the importance of its timely implementation.

Another step towards the elections was progress in *voter registration*. After the security situation in the remaining provinces of Kasai, Kasai Central and Lomami improved, voter registration recommenced on 4 September. As soon as 9 September, the CENI president announced that approximately 99% of estimated voters had been registered. Opposition and international watchdogs criticised the process as being flawed for producing unusually high numbers in some areas, and very low ones in others. In addition, a lack of funds, legislation and logistical support – whether real or perpetuated by the government – risk further delaying the elections. CENI estimated the cost of the elections at $ 1.3 bn, while international observers estimated at least $ 500 m. Both estimates were beyond the means of the Congolese government in these times of economic downturn. Meanwhile, international donor support for the elections remained at only 6% of the agreed $ 123.3 m, because of concerns over an illegitimate election process.

The government continued with the *repression of the political opposition*, severely limiting basic human rights, such as the right to peaceful assembly, free expression and physical integrity. The UN Joint Human Rights Office in the DRC (UNJHRO) reported 1,375 violations of democratic space (with 2,543 victims) during the year, committed mostly by state agents. Given the pressure demonstrators were able to exert on the government, the latter attempted to 'professionalise' its security forces through better pay, training, management and equipment. A priority for Kabila – who was notoriously scared of being killed like several members of his family, including his father, grandfather and aunt – was to control the army and police by repeatedly reshuffling their leadership. In addition to better command and control structures, essential contingents were paid regularly. Recent European training and equipment allowed security forces, who were previously working mainly with guns, to repress demonstrations without resorting to deadly means. Throughout the year, the police and army disrupted demonstrations by blocking off streets, intimidating activists and arresting leaders. Radio, Internet and telephone services were blocked during critical periods to hinder critics' communication and organisational capacity. In combination with the credible threat of deadly violence, the approach proved fairly successful in discouraging protesters. Consequently, opposition and civil society groups, who were no longer able to motivate people to risk their lives, resorted to organising general strikes, so called 'villes mortes' (dead cities). These were observed to varying degrees in the country's major cities throughout the year.

Presidential candidate Moïse Katumbi was not able to return to the DRC after fleeing the country when he was convicted in 2016. An investigation by the CENCO into his two convictions – for recruiting mercenaries and fraud – was leaked to the press on 4 May and confirmed the political nature of the cases. In response, the government opened a third case against Katumbi on 13 May for alleged tax evasion. A month later, the UN Human Rights committee ruled that the Congolese government should take all necessary steps for Katumbi to return safely to the DRC and participate freely in the presidential elections. However, it remained unclear how the UN would implement its decision, particularly since the peacekeeping mission showed no appetite for confronting the government. Three days later, Katumbi announced his imminent return to DRC at a press conference in Paris but, despite this and similar statements, he had not returned by year's end.

As the year reached its conclusion and the extension period granted by the Sylvester Agreement gradually expired without elections, the dynamics of protests changed again. A secular coordination committee associated with the Catholic Church, the 'Comité Laic de la Coordination de l'Eglise Catholique du Congo' – called for nation-wide protests on 31 December. Against heavy repression and open threats, Sunday protests succeeded in mobilising tens of thousands for the first time since September 2016. In response, security forces shot tear gas and live ammunition, including within parishes and churches, killing at least eight, injuring 46 and arresting over 140, including priests and altar boys. The *violence against peaceful protesters* provoked heavy domestic and international criticism. In a subsequent speech, the archbishop of Kinshasa, Cardinal Monsengwo criticised the security forces and called for the country's "mediocre" leadership to step down. This prompted a wave of mockery of the government on social media and reignited the country's political debate.

The *security situation* deteriorated to the point that the authorities eventually cancelled the annual Independence Day parade on 30 June. In addition to an escalation of low intensity conflicts in the volatile east of the country, violence also spread to formerly peaceful areas in the Kasai region and Congo Central province. As usual, the population bore the brunt of these developments. The UNJHRO reported 6,495 human rights violations over the year, representing an increase of over 25%. State agents routinely committed 60–65% of these abuses. Nevertheless, armed groups continued to prey on civilians. Of all the non-state armed actors, the 'Forces de Résistance Patriotique de l'Ituri' (FRPI) reportedly committed the most (7%) human-rights abuses. After the withdrawal of the US supported Regional Task Force in March, the security situation seriously deteriorated in north-western Haut Uele and the northern part of Bas Uele Provinces. Small splinter groups of the *Lord's Resistance Army* (LRA) continued attacks in remote areas, along the border with the CAR, particularly in the Garamba National Park. Attacks were aimed at facilitating poaching and obtaining supplies by robbing local communities, often abducting civilians to carry the pillaged goods. Towards the end of the year, the LRA reduced its activities after the poaching season in Garamba National Park ended.

Ethnic violence intensified as community-based militias carried out reprisal killings against other armed groups and their assumed supporters. In North Kivu, the tit-for-tat killings between Hutu-based militias, such as the Democratic Forces for the Liberation of Rwanda (FDLR) and Nyatura, and self-proclaimed autochthones Hunde, Nande, Nyanga and Kobo groups were significant. For instance, on 17 February, Mai-Mai Mazembe and Nduma Defence of Congo (NDC)-Guidon killed 27 Hutu civilians in Nyanzale, Rutshuru territory. In Tanganyika Province, violence between the *Luba (Bantu) and Twa* (Pygmy) communities continued. The traditional hunter-gatherer Twa were still considered second-class citizens by the land-owning Luba. Twa are often paid exploitative wages and their livelihoods are threatened by deforestation, mining and the expansion of Luba farmlands. On 5 January, a Twa militia allegedly killed 15 Luba near the town of Manono, injuring 37 civilians and burning down 65 houses. By the end of February, the conflict had spread to five of the province's six territories, displacing nearly half a million people. In response, MONUSCO reinforced its presence in Manono, supported community-based conflict resolution and facilitated the deployment of the 'Forces Armées de la République Démocratique du Congo' (FARDC) to Moba, Monde and Nyunzu territories. After a ceasefire had been mediated by a peace forum in February, the conflict reignited in March and April. Luba and Twa militias clashed in Kalemie territory following allegations that the latter had conducted raids on Luba crops and cattle. During the fighting, four people were killed and hundreds of homes were burned. Members of the Twa community also attacked FARDC positions and clashed with Bafuliro and Banyamulenge in the Bendera area of Kalemie territory, reportedly resulting in six civilian deaths, including a Twa chief. In August, fighting between the two groups in Kalemie territory led to the deaths of 75 people and injured dozens. The conflict spilled over to Pweto territory in Haut-Katanga province. In October, Twa militias attacked the prison in Pweto town and freed 52 prisoners.

Besides older grievances and long-standing animosities, the Congolese government also played a significant role in these conflicts. Kabila's growing illegitimacy resulted in an intensification of armed resistance. Armed insurgencies increasingly became politicised, albeit in a somewhat superficial manner. The rhetoric of armed mobilisation shifted from the traditional animosity against Rwanda to a much more pronounced stance against Kabila. Most armed groups now explicitly attacked state symbols and agents, while the army itself was vulnerable because of overstretch and a drop in the value of salaries (due to fixed exchange rates).

Armed groups sometimes formed *alliances* against the government. Most prominent was the 'Coalition Nationale du Peuple pour la Souveraineté du Congo' (CNPSC), also referred to as 'l'Alliance de l'Article 64', in reference to the article in the Constitution setting out the duty of citizens to oppose anyone who violates the Constitution. The CNPSC comprised at least 11 Mai-Mai factions under the leadership of veteran commander William Amuri Yakutumba and operated in a large area from South Kivu and Tanganyika to Maniema province. On 3 July, fighting between Mai-Mai Yakutumba and FARDC in Fizi forced the mining company Banro to stop all activities and evacuate its staff from the Namoya gold mine. Twenty-three mining trucks were caught in cross fire near Lulimba and Yakutumba. Rebels temporarily held 24 Tanzanian and Kenyan drivers. On 27 September, the Mai-Mai coalition attacked Uvira with heavy weapons, first from the hills and the next day by boat. The attack almost succeeded in taking the province's second largest town and only decisive intervention by MONUSCO, including by sinking some of the attacking boats with helicopter fire, brought their advance to a halt. In Tanganyika, elements of this alliance, Mai-Mai Malaika, Mai-Mai Hapa na pale and Twa militias, killed 15 army soldiers during nine attacks between 7 October and 14 November.

The government reportedly also *staged insecurity*. The police and army, notorious for their corruption and involvement in illicit trading in military resources and equipment, were unable or unwilling to prevent attacks. Opposition and civil society groups even saw them as responsible for permitting and facilitating attacks. One particularly worrying trend was the extraordinary spate of at least four prison raids within six weeks. Most spectacularly, Kinshasa's Makala central prison was attacked by alleged followers of the 'Bundu Dia Kongo' (BDK) religious sect on 17 May, freeing the group's leader Ne Muanda Nsemi along with 4,600 other inmates. It was questionable whether the BDK possessed the organisational capacity for such a high profile target in the capital. On 11 June, unidentified heavily armed men attacked Beni prison, freeing the majority – 930 of 966 – of the inmates and killing at least eight guards. Another attack, on a high profile prison in Beni on 22 June, was repelled by FARDC and MONUSCO troops. At least nine people were killed during the fighting.

Similarly, the re-emergence of the *M23* rebellion, whose members had been languishing in Ugandan demobilisation camps since the end of the rebellion in November 2013, raised many questions. Warnings by North Kivu Governor Julien Paluku in November 2016 about the possible return of M23 elements had been widely viewed as political scaremongering. However, in mid-January, approximately 200 rebels reportedly briefly took control of Ishasha village, in Rutshuru territory. The Ugandan government, which denied as late as mid-January that former M23 fighters had left their camps in Uganda to return to the DRC, eventually admitted that the rebel group had become active again and responded by deploying Uganda People's Defence Force (UPDF) troops to the border. On 19 January, Ugandan security forces detained more than 100 former M23 members attempting to return to the DRC, worn down by the fighting. The ex-combatants were captured in the western district of Mbarara. On 27 January, two Congolese military helicopters on a reconnaissance patrol targeting the M23 crashed in unclear circumstances near the Mikeno and Karisimbi mountains in Rutshuru territory, close to the Rwandan border. Although two FARDC soldiers and three Russian crewmembers were rescued, two Russian crewmembers and a Congolese colonel died in the incident. The M23 claimed to have captured at least one Russian pilot. In response, the Congolese government increased its operations and deployed 700 additional troops in North Kivu Province – with apparent success. On 30 January, 30 M23 members fled the DRC to Rwanda. Similarly, in February, the Ugandan authorities arrested an additional 44 fighters who were returning from the DRC after clashes with Congolese troops in Rutshuru territory.

The Congolese government subsequently stated that the re-emergence of the M23 rebellion could make the organisation of the elections difficult. Members of the opposition cautioned that the reactivation of the rebel group might be an attempt by Kabila to distract attention away from the DRC's political crisis and further delay the elections. An investigation by HRW suggested that there had been at least some collaboration between the former adversaries. HRW reported in September that the government had recruited former M23 rebels in camps in Uganda and Rwanda and deployed them to crack down on protesters in Kinshasa and Kalemie.

Local and national politicians were widely suspected of exacerbating dynamics of violence to further delay the elections and gain relevance as guardians of (in) stability. A prominent example was the handling of the *Kamuina Nsapu* rebellion in the Kasai region. After the government refused to recognise the authority of the traditional leader Kamuina Nsapu and security forces killed him in subsequent clashes, an armed rebellion had intensified under his name in 2016. Kamuina Nsapu militia groups conducted attacks against security forces, government institutions and civilians, including their own. On 24 March, for instance, suspected Kamuina Nsapu ambushed a truck and beheaded 42 police officers on the Tshikapa-Kananga road. The rebels also attacked civilians, including from their own group, for perceived disloyalty.

The government responded with ruthless *military operations* against the militia and associated members of the Luba community. UNJHRO reported that in the first half of the year, FARDC soldiers had conducted arbitrary arrests and summarily executed suspects, killing at least 428 people, including at least 17 women and 140 children. In February, a video on social media showed Congolese soldiers indiscriminately firing on a group of unarmed Kamuina Nsapu followers. Although the authenticity of the video could not be independently verified, it appeared to be consistent with UN reports of Congolese military operations against the militia and was further corroborated by the gradual discovery of at least 87 mass graves in the area of operations. As the conflict developed, the government also mobilised other ethnic groups against the Luba and Lulua, who formed the ethnic base of Kamuina Nsapu. The army reportedly armed and supported 'Bana Mura' militias from the Pende, Tetela and Tshokwe minorities to commit gruesome violence against suspected followers of Kamuina Nsapu.

Since the beginning of the insurrection in August 2016, at least 3,300 people had been killed and 1.4 m displaced. The government nevertheless denied the systematic application of excessive force and only tried those soldiers directly involved in the video. Two members of the *UN panel of experts* on the DRC, who attempted to investigate the large-scale human-rights abuses in Kasai-Central Province, were kidnapped in March. Two weeks later, villagers found the bodies of the US expert Michael Sharp and the Swedish expert Zaida Catalán. Communication Minister and government spokesperson Lambert Mende quickly blamed the Kamuina Nsapu militia for the deed, although it was counter-intuitive that the militia would kill investigators of government violence. While government and UN investigations were flawed, Radio France International (RFI) published an exclusive investigation into the murder of the two UN experts on 13 September, suggesting that they had been killed in a government ambush.

During the second half of the year the violence in the Kasai region abated. The army had stifled resistance. In August, MONUSCO finalised the deployment of three companies in Kananga, Mbuji-Mayi and Tshikapa, which also appeared to have a stabilising effect. Accordingly, some of the 31,700 Congolese refugees in Angola were gradually returning, resulting in new inter-ethnic tensions as communities of origin had restructured ethnically during the violence. Returnees were also encountering an acute humanitarian crisis, as the violence had deterred the population from going to their fields. Ironically, the humanitarian need increased after the conflict itself had calmed down and 2.8 m people in the Kasai region were facing critical levels of food insecurity at the end of the year.

Foreign Affairs

International criticism of the prolonged delay of the elections and the destabilising behaviour of the Congolese government steadily increased. On 15 June, for instance, Kofi Annan and the group of elder statesmen called for peaceful transition and expressed concern over the destabilising effect an escalation of the crisis would have on the wider region. The international community also resorted to sanctioning individuals responsible for repression and excessive violence, particularly in the Kasai region. On 29 May, the EU imposed *sanctions* on nine key members of the Congolese regime for "obstruction of the electoral process and related human rights violations". They included Deputy Prime Minister (and former minister of interior) Evariste Boshab, Interior Minister Ramazani Shadary, the Head of the Intelligence Service Kalev Mutond, and Communication Minister (and government spokesperson) Lambert Mende. Like seven others already listed in December 2016, they were sanctioned with travel bans and asset freezes in the EU. On 1 June, the US followed suit and imposed sanctions on Kabila's top military adviser, General François Olenga, freezing his assets and banning American businesses from interacting with him. These sanctions increased the pressure on the government and demonstrated that everybody could be held responsible for their actions. However, staying under the critical threshold, the sanctions failed to alter the government's rationale. Determined to stay in power by all means, Kabila's team did not change its behaviour. Civil society and human rights organisations demanded an extension of sanctions to people in Kabila's inner circle, who held much sway but not necessarily official functions. EU and US repeatedly alluded to further sanctions but did not follow through. EU member states were divided on the issue, reportedly because of French and Spanish business interests.

The administration of *US* President Donald Trump showed, unsurprisingly, less constant interest in the DRC. It did not appoint an ambassador to Kinshasa or a new Special Envoy for the Great Lakes region. However, US ambassador to the UN, Nikki

Haley, took a personal interest in the country after a short visit, including to an IDP camp in Kitshanga, at the end of October. She subsequently insisted on the organisation of the election in 2018 and maintained pressure on Kabila to fully investigate the murder of the two UN experts. On 22 December, the US declared sanctions against Israeli businessman Dan Gertler, a close friend of Kabila and responsible for corrupt business deals. Gertler's corrupt and opaque arrangements had cost the country $ 1.36 bn in revenue in 2010–12 alone. Given that Gertler had provided Kabila with illicit funds since 2001, these sanctions could mean that Kabila might run into difficulties maintaining the solid war chest required for dealing with the challenge of elections.

Meanwhile, the government pushed back strongly against international interference. Bilaterally and within multilateral bodies such as the UN, the government stressed the DRC's national sovereignty as a fairly effective response to criticism. Given its outspoken position, former colonial power *Belgium* bore the brunt of this push back. For instance, when on 8 April, Belgian Foreign Minister Didier Reynders stated that the nomination of Bruno Tshibala as prime minister violated "the letter and spirit of the 31 December agreement", the Congolese government responded by suspending its military cooperation with Belgium.

In addition to emphasising national sovereignty, the Congolese government also engaged in clever diplomacy with its *African neighbours*, who proved receptive to arguments of African solidarity and sovereignty, and tended to prefer constructive engagement to the more punitive approach of sanctions. Concerned about the influx of Congolese refugees from the Kasai region, the government of *Angola* – a long time friend and ally of Joseph Kabila and his father Laurent before him – nonetheless increased the pressure on President Kabila. On 12 May, it publically called for all Congolese stakeholders to "immediately cease violence, acts of extremism and political intolerance". However, given that the influx of refugees has been curtailed and Angola's new president had first to deal with many domestic challenges, relations seemed to stabilise. Kabila was also able to count on other old supporters in South Africa and Zimbabwe. On 20 August, during its 37th summit and under the leadership of South African President Jacob Zuma, *SADC* formally accepted delaying the elections beyond 2017.

The government kept hindering the work of *journalists* and human rights investigators by not allowing them access to conflict areas, such as the Kasai region, as well as hospitals and mortuaries. In mid-July, government spokesperson Lambert Mende announced that Kinshasa-based journalists would need written permission to travel outside the capital. The government continued to expel critical international experts, such as HRW Central Africa Director Ida Sawyer, RFI Kinshasa correspondent Sonja Rolley, Reuters journalist Aaron Ross and Belgian Congo expert Kris Berwouts. In addition, the government continued to cut the signal of radio RFI for most of the year, and blocked Internet and telephone services during protest periods.

The UN Organization Stabilization Mission in the Democratic Republic of Congo (*MONUSCO*) had a particularly challenging year. The DRC's political crisis, the preparation of the elections and the escalation of violent conflicts in scale and type required the mission to take on new tasks while covering a wider area. In addition to supporting the preparations for the elections, which included air lifting 4,000 tonnes of registration materials, the mission redeployed some of its troops to respond to the violence in the Kasais and protect civilians threatened by electoral violence in Kinshasa. However, instead of being supported to face these numerous challenges, MONUSCO suffered heavy budget and *troop reductions*. The cuts – a counterintuitive move in the current volatile environment – followed intense political pressure from the new US administration. During the negotiations in New York, Nikki Haley had stated that UN peacekeepers were supporting a (Congolese) government that was "corrupt and preys on its citizens". Instead of taking on MONUSCO's request to increase the number of police to protect civilians against politically motivated violence in urban environments, the UNSC reduced MONUSCO's troop ceiling from 19,815 to 16,215. As there were de facto only 16,893 troops deployed, the reduction through MONUSCO's new mandate on 31 March was largely symbolic. However, it meant that the mission had to cut over 600 troops. MONUSCO was thus forced to repatriate a full battalion of Indian peacekeepers by August. Specifically, this meant that MONUSCO closed five company-sized operating bases in North Kivu province: Bunyapuri, Masisi, Nyabiondo, Luofu and Walikale. Then, in June, the UN General Assembly decided to cut MONUSCO's budget by almost a $ 100 m (8%), which arguably contradicted the extensive tasks of the UNSC's mandate. The peacekeeping mission responded by repatriating four additional companies (960 troops) in October, cutting civilian posts and reducing the travel (movement) budget. It also changed its protection approach from a static deployment in many local peacekeeping bases, to closing additional bases and having a more agile force that could engage in more patrols and short-term deployments. Although the success of the new "protection through projection" approach still had to be evaluated, some contradictions became apparent: contingents that hade not been responsive to alerts in close vicinity, often for political reasons, were not likely to become more pro-active from a greater distance. This was particularly unrealistic as the closure of bases meant that alert and information gathering systems would not be maintained at the same level. It was also foreseeable that the peacekeepers could hardly become more mobile with a reduced travel budget.

The greatest obstacle to the achievement of MONUSCO's mandate was, however, the *Congolese government*. It was very difficult for the mission to cooperate with authorities that repressed their own population and committed massive human rights abuses. As a result, cooperation with the administration and security forces was reduced or cancelled. Without the Congolese partners, however, MONUSCO had little chance of carrying out its tasks and fulfilling its mandate. The government even intimidated the peacekeeping mission with demands to reduce the troop ceiling and the threat of withdrawing host nation consent. In the eyes of many, MONUSCO was too guarded in its approach towards the Congolese government. The mission shied away from confronting the government's destabilising policies, which increased the suffering of the Congolese population and endangered MONUSCO's mandate.

The UN also increasingly became a target of armed attacks. In the first quarter, joint FARDC-MONUSCO *military operations against the Allied Democratic Forces* (ADF) in Beni territory interrupted the activities if the militia, which had initially been established against the Ugandan government. MONUSCO was able to establish forward operating bases near Beni town and Mamudioma, in the ADF's traditional area of operations, known as the 'triangle of death'. After a lull in fighting during which the ADF had largely avoided confrontation, the group shifted its strategy to directly attacking FARDC and MONUSCO troops. On 12 August, well equipped ADF elements in army fatigues attacked four FARDC positions approximately 30 km from Oicha. At least 14 soldiers were killed and three more wounded. On 17 September, one Tanzanian peacekeeper was killed and another injured by presumed ADF elements during a joint MONUSCO-FARDC patrol on the road to Mamudioma. On 7 October, the ADF attacked four army positions and killed at least 25 travellers on the Mbau-Kamamga road. On 9 October, the same group reportedly attacked the peacekeeping base in Mamudioma, 30 km northeast of Beni town, killing two Tanzanian soldiers of MONUSCO's Force Intervention Brigade (FIB).

Most dramatically presumed ADF elements attacked the Semuliki peacekeeping base, killing 15 Tanzanian Peacekeepers on 7 December. This constituted the worst attack on UN peacekeepers since 1993 and the deadliest ever in the DRC. The UN almost immediately blamed the ADF although investigations were on-going and the circumstances of the attack were not fully resolved. Reportedly, coordinated attackers surprised the badly prepared Tanzanian FIB contingent at dawn. The attackers took out their communications capacity after a distress call was made. However, MONUSCO reinforcements only arrived the next morning, apparently because they were unable or reluctant to conduct flight operations at night. It remains unclear what prompted the UN to immediately declare the ADF responsible for the attack. The style of this attack – coordinated, over several hours and with heavy weapons – did not match the ADF's, whose fighters normally operated with machetes and AK47s. Accordingly, experts assumed that the ADF must have been equipped and supported by a third party. This corresponded to an investigation by the Congo Research group at New York University, which reported that the ADF had colluded with other local groups and the FARDC in the mysterious killings of over 800 civilians in the Beni region in 2014–16.

In response to the attack, the Congolese army and the *UPDF* declared a joint military operation against the ADF. Between 22 and 27 December, the UPDF announced that it had destroyed eight ADF camps and killed more than 100 fighters in the Congolese-Ugandan borderland through air and artillery bombardment. However, MONUSCO was unable to confirm any traces of shelling. There was speculation that the Ugandan engagement, however active in practice, was intended to demonstrate regional power and relevance. Others pointed towards a possible attempt to securitise this area in light of increasing oil exploitation in Western Uganda.

Partly in response to these issues, UN Secretary-General Antonio Guterres, appointed a *new MONUSCO leadership*. On 1 November, he appointed the Canadian Kim Bolduc as his new Deputy Special Representative in charge of humanitarian affairs and, on 27 December, he nominated Leila Zerrougui as his Special Representative and new head of MONUSCO. This choice raised hopes for improvements as Zerrougui was widely respected for her expertise and skills. She had previously served as deputy head of mission on the DRC (2008–12) and special representative for children in armed conflict (2012–16), and had co-developed many of MONUSCO's protection tools.

Socioeconomic Developments

The *humanitarian crisis* worsened throughout the year. In October, the UN declared the highest level of humanitarian emergency. By the end of the year, a staggering 43 m people were internally displaced and an additional 622,000 Congolese refugees were registered in neighbouring countries. Approximately 16% of the population was in need of humanitarian aid, of whom 7.7 m people were facing acute hunger – an increase of 30% from 2016. Dilapidated infrastructure, insecurity and government restrictions continued to obstruct humanitarian access in the central and eastern parts of the country. Despite these challenges and growing needs, humanitarian funding remained insufficient. At year's end, only 57% of the requested $ 812.6 m had been provided.

Destabilisation increased the risk of *epidemics* and further reduced the capacity of state institutions to respond to them. On 12 May, WHO declared an Ebola outbreak in a remote area of north-eastern Bas-Uele province. This first outbreak since 2014 was quickly brought under control and resulted in the death of only four of nine infected patients. On 13 June, WHO confirmed two separate outbreaks of polio in Haut-Lomami and Maniema provinces. The outbreak appeared to be vaccine-derived. WHO assessed the risk of spread of the disease as high on the national level and low on the international level. The rainy season increased the prevalence of waterborne diseases. Cholera spread to 20 of the 26 provinces and particularly threatened the Kasai region, where violence related to the Kamuina Nsapu insurgency exacerbated the already poor sanitary conditions. By mid-September, at least 528 people had died in the epidemic.

Humanitarian problems were compounded by more structural factors and *macro-economic developments*. Low commodity prices continued to negatively affect growth. On 26 May, the government lowered its estimate of *GDP* growth from 4.9% to 3.9%. The Economist Intelligence Unit gave an even lower estimate of 2.2%. By the end of the year, consumer price *inflation* had reached 49.6%, the highest level since the early 2000s. The Congolese franc depreciated by 30% over the year and stood at FC 1,614: $ 1.

While the government managed to stabilise the exchange rate, diminishing purchasing power resulted in *strikes* in the public sector. After medical personnel and professors went on strike during July and teachers threatened to follow suit, the government agreed to raise the exchange rate for public sector salaries to FC 1,130: $ 1 from the previous FC 930. However, the combination of rising prices and low – often unpaid – salaries, considerably increased the risk of plundering and misbehaviour on the part of security forces. Pressured by quickly *decreasing foreign currency reserves*, Prime Minister Tshibala requested international financial assistance to overcome the economic crisis. After a visit in July, the IMF denied this request, given the government's lack of will to address the political crisis and conduct reforms. The IMF's decision highlighted inherent instability and thereby further increased the country's difficulty in attracting investment and aid funds.

Rising commodity prices and higher production resulted in stronger *economic growth* towards the end of the year and led to more positive forecasts for 2018. Global oil, copper, cobalt and gold prices were expected to rise further. Positive effects were likely to be limited by high services imports, higher profit repatriation by *mining* firms and lower aid inflows. The government was in the process of revising the 2002 mining code, proposing to shift the focus from attracting investors through favourable conditions, to increasing profits from existing production. Proposed changes included higher taxation of mining profits from 30% to 35%, an increase in government shares for new projects from 5% to 10% and an increase of royalties for strategic resources from 2% to 10%. This reform would have the double effect of increasing Kabila's bargaining power through Western strategic interest (notably in cobalt), and maximising Congolese revenues. Given the corrupt structure of the mining sector, much of the increased revenues would be appropriated by Kabila and his cronies, providing them with the means to deal with the election challenge.

Equatorial Guinea

Joseph N. Mangarella

As President Teodoro Obiang Nguema Mbasogo turned 75 and remained the longest serving republican head of state in the world, prominent members of the ruling Essangui clan jostled for strategic control. Vice President Teodoro Nguema Obiang Mangue ('Teodorín'), his father's likely successor, drew negative international publicity and complicated efforts to reboot the faltering energy sector. The government clung to gas production in the hope of rebalancing the economy and warding off allegations of human rights abuse.

Domestic Politics

The Equatoguinean regime had perennially relied on a mix of political patronage, repression of civil liberties and the crude instillation of fear. 2017 was no exception, but for the increasing instances of 'palace intrigue' surrounding the potential successor to President Obiang. In late March, the president concluded a nationwide tour following his landslide electoral victory in 2016, during which he thanked his voters and publicly attributed 'economic reform' to political stability.

 | DOI:10.1163/9789004367630_027

The ruling party, the 'Partido Democrático de Guinea Ecuatorial' (PDGE), recorded similarly sweeping victories in unfair *parliamentary and municipal elections*. During the week that 273,502 registered voters took to the polls, the government blocked messaging services such as WhatsApp, Facebook and Twitter, followed by a total Internet firewall. When voting booths opened on 12 November, the government banned private vehicles on roadways and systematically arrested opposition members. The US-based EG Justice reported that, in mainland Bata, Diosadado Esono, a member of the 'Convergencia para la Democracia Social' (CPDS), had been arrested for destroying a ballot box on the grounds that voters had been influenced by the intimidation from government officials. Outside a polling station in Bata, civil society activist Raimundo Bernabe Nnandong Abeso ('Ruso') was arrested after attempting to take a photo with a family member. Esono, Ruso and several other members and observers of the CPDS and the 'Ciudadanos por la Innovación' (CI) were arrested for allegedly disturbing the electoral process, although they were released without charge on 15 November. On 20 November, the National Electoral Commission announced that an 84% turnout had given the PDGE and its 14 allies all 75 Senate seats and 99 of the 100 seats in the lower house; CI retained one seat with 5.8% of the vote. All mayoral posts were won by the ruling alliance. The promises of the national political dialogue (2014) would therefore remain unfulfilled.

Palace politics, not lopsided electoral campaigns, would prove to be more determinative of the country's power structure. The year saw a deepening schism between two rival factions: those in favour of the presidential succession of Teodorín, son of First Lady Constancia Mangue Nsue de Obiang, and those supporting Gabriel Mbaga Obiang Lima, son of President Obiang's former wife and the long-standing minister of oil. After removing several of Lima's ministerial advisors in 2016, Teodorín continued his campaign to disrupt his half-brother's oil licensing rounds throughout the first half the year, notably through key funding cuts to Lima's outreach programmes with the assistance of close allies in Prime Minister Francisco Pascual Obama Asue and Jeronimo Osa Osa Ecoro, head of the PDGE. Despite Lima's retention of former advisors in unofficial capacities, Africa Energy Intelligence reported that the ever-influential First Lady Constancia had in mid-August pushed through the creation of a post for her niece and former singer, Candida Okomo Nsue Mensa. As the deputy managing director of the cash-glutted state oil company GEPetrol, 'Candy' Nsue was given the helm when the former managing director loyal to Lima, Antonio Oburu, unexpectedly quit on 12 November. Upon the latter's departure, former deputies were purged and replaced with Teodorín loyalists. Lima would thereafter have to count on newly elected allies in the legislature, as well as on the support of presidential adviser, Julian Abia Biteo.

The ruling family's perceived vulnerability probably contributed to the regime's draconian responses to free expression and dissent. On 17 April, Enrique Asumu and

Alfredo Okenve of the leading development NGO 'Centro de Estudios e Iniciativas para el Desarrollo' (CEID) were subjected to a week's unlawful detention for violating an indefinite suspension of CEID's activities, which included its advocacy as a member of EITI's national steering committee. A taxi strike on 17 May led to several arrests, including that of Benjamin Ndong, a rapper who had released a song in support of the strikers. On 23 June, two journalists covering a meeting of the CPDS had their equipment and records confiscated. Four days later, Joaquin Elo Ayeto of the human rights group Somos+ was detained and released without charge for purportedly inciting violence. Yet no detention garnered more international reprobation than that of political cartoonist *Ramon Nse Esono Ebale* on 16 September. A critic of the regime, he was sent to the infamous Playa Negra prison but had not been charged as of December, despite urgent appeals for his immediate release by AI, PEN International, and HRW.

On 29 December, 'Jeune Afrique' revealed through sources in Malabo that, on 27 December, 31 Chadian and Central African mercenaries had been arrested in Cameroon near the Equatoguinean border with alleged plans to stage a coup against President Obiang. The reports shied away from certitude, however, and added that a contingent of mercenaries led by an Equato-Chadian general with ties to CI had apparently been summoned by authorities in the border town of Evinayong. On 30 December, President Obiang publicly called for "vigilance" after amassing troops near the freshly closed Cameroonian border.

Foreign Affairs

Wanton human rights violations and corruption continued to strain the country's relations with the West. In addition to the EU's condemnation of the legislative elections and international outrage over arbitrary detentions, *France*'s years-long prosecution of Teodorín for *ill-gotten gains* dominated the headlines and portended a difficult presidential succession. After Teodorín's lawyers successfully had his trial adjourned on 1 January for want of preparation, President Obiang unsuccessfully attempted to solicit the intervention of French President François Hollande, who, despite greeting President Obiang at the 27th Africa-France Summit in Bamako (Mali), politely rebuffed the request to circumvent his country's judicial independence. In absentia proceedings recommenced in France's 'Tribunal Correctionnel' in late June, and the wishes of French prosecutors were partially granted by the tribunal on 27 October, when Teodorín was found guilty of embezzlement, money laundering, corruption and breach of trust. The court sentenced him to a suspended three-month jail term and a € 30 m fine. The next day, the PDGE released a statement on state television condemning the ruling as "politically motivated" and an "abuse of power". Although Teodorín immediately launched an appeal, pleading diplomatic immunity, he would continue to face litigation elsewhere, notably in *South Africa*, where the Western Cape High Court seized his assets on 1 September after plaintiff Daniel Janse van Rensburg successfully sued for his wrongful detention in 2015.

It made both political and economic sense, then, for the government to continue its pursuit of non-Western allies, energy partners and influence in multilateral fora. More notably, Equatorial Guinea applied to join *OPEC* in January, after the government had aligned its oil production cuts with the cartel in late 2016. During a bilateral economic forum organised in Jeddah (Saudi Arabia) on 10 May, Gabriel Lima reportedly pressed the country's case behind closed doors. The lobbying bore fruit on 25 May, when Equatorial Guinea was admitted as OPEC's 14th member. Lima hoped that the newly acquired partners would encourage new and diversified investment in the country's stagnating energy sector, which was deemed responsible for waning Chinese interest. In bids for political legitimacy on a global stage, the regime fronted its own candidate for the *AU* chairmanship, Foreign Minister Agapito Mba Mokuy. Though unsuccessful, Malabo hosted the C-10 summit on 17 May and obtained the AU's endorsement to run for one of the region's two non-permanent seats on the *UNSC*, which it won on 2 June. Equatorial Guinea's first two-year tenure would begin on 1 January 2018, despite public admonitions from human rights watchdogs such as the UN's HRW representative.

On the regional level, efforts to build energy-based alliances and continental influence were enhanced and showed more progress than years prior. At least four memoranda of understanding based on energy cooperation were signed with regional counterparts. On 20 March, Oil Minister Lima and his South Sudanese counterpart agreed on terms for the training of oil executives in Juba by Equatoguinean counterparts. On 7 April, the president visited Maputo in *Mozambique* and reached an agreement with President Felipe Myusi to lend assistance to Mozambique's fledgling hydrocarbons sector, seemingly in exchange for greater influence in the CPLP. Two months later, in June, Lima signed an agreement with his Ghanaian counterpart to supply *Ghana*'s ports with Equatoguinean liquefied natural gas (LNG). During a state dinner held in Malabo on 21 August, Ghanaian President Akufo-Addo announced the recommencement of the Permanent Join Commission of Cooperation between the two countries begun in 2010. The year's *gas diplomacy* was rounded off in mid-September in Ouagadougou, when Oil Minister Lima agreed to supply gas to Burkina Faso through the Ghanaian port of Tema.

The strategy of strengthening regional ties as a bulwark against external and economic threats was made more apparent in October, when the government lifted visa requirements for *CEMAC* members and ratified the bloc's free movement convention, after 15 years of dithering alongside Gabon. At the same time, the government advertised itself as a refuge for regional autocrats by offering sanctuary to *Gambia*'s ex-President Yahya Jammeh after his resignation on 22 January. Since Equatorial

Guinea was not a party to the ICC, Jammeh was potentially able to escape extradition. In addition, President Obiang hosted *Uganda*'s President Yoweri Museveni on 25 August and awarded him the country's highest honour (the Great Collar of Independence) for his contributions to the pan-Africa cause. In April, the two heads of state had signed bilateral agreements on energy and diplomatic cooperation.

Socioeconomic Developments

Oil production continued its years-long slide as oilfields declined with age and, as a consequence, economic output fell to an estimated nominal GDP of $ 11.4 bn, representing a real *GDP contraction* of 5.3%. Since the *oil industry* still contributed 90% of government revenue, at least 94% of export earnings and at least 80% of GDP, a spike in the benchmark price of crude from June through December slowed the pace of contraction (8.9% in 2016) and attenuated the rise in external debt, which totalled roughly $ 1.39 bn. Per capita income, an estimated $ 24,243 (PPP), remained among the highest in sub-Saharan Africa. Nevertheless, foreign currency reserves continued to be depleted to service deficits, and in June the government sought the assistance of the IMF. In addition, income inequality in Equatorial Guinea remained among the highest in the world, with a stubbornly high poverty rate of roughly 80%.

The government's approach to the *IMF* for debt financing signalled a fiscal desperation unseen since before the oil boom of the mid-1990s. In an apparent effort to secure financing, the government took perfunctory steps to institute economic diversification and fiscal transparency. One initiative targeted the country's dire business climate, ranked 173rd of 190 in the World Bank's Ease of Doing Business Assessment; in July, the government announced a one-stop shop business window in an effort to reduce the 17 administrative procedures required for starting small and medium-sized businesses, which included the assent of the prime minister. In September, the forest and environment minister abruptly cancelled all timber-felling permits in a supposed attempt to curtail illicit trade and bring the industry within the government's domain. In August, the director-general of EGPetrol announced the national oil company's publication of 'La República', an industry newspaper meant to diversify the company's portfolio and signal efforts towards greater transparency.

These few initiatives, however, were unlikely to meaningfully sway the IMF or address economic decline. Not only had income inequality remained an issue, but the regime *mismanaged expenditure* in a way that neglected to support a thriving base of taxable citizens. There was no evidence to suggest that the regime had increased spending on health and education, estimated at 2%–3% of the budget in previous years. EG Justice reported that schools lacked proper facilities, while grade retention and dropout rates remained abysmally high. Vaccination rates and access to safe drinking water remained shockingly low. In September, electricity outages in hospitals led to the death of Casimira Pilar Ayecaba during a routine C-section in Bata. Instead, public funds were characteristically diverted to infrastructure (roughly 80% of the budget) and projects contracted to members of the ruling clan. In February, the government moved to its *new capital city* of Oyala in the newly-created province of Djibloho for a three-month trial period. Although the city's rainforest location made it more defensible and came with promises by the state of socio-economic benefits, its $ 7 bn price tag, five-star hotel and expansive golf course led to criticisms of wastefulness. The vast majority of builders and labourers were foreign.

As in previous years, more serious efforts were allotted to reviving the hydrocarbons sector to replenish state coffers, and more precisely *gas production* to replace oil, which fell to roughly 200,000 b/d (compared with peak production of 350,000 b/d in 2004–2006). The eventual construction of the country's most promising joint venture, the much publicised *Fortuna floating LNG* facility, made halting progress. Set to process 2.2 m tonnes of gas per annum by 2020, the Ophir Energy-operated FLNG would be the first of its kind in Africa. But negotiations between London-based Ophir and the state appeared to stall a final investment decision. In January, Ophir and the government haggled over tax rates, while in March state-owned Sonagas demanded its own shares in the project. In addition, financing for the $ 2 bn project had not been finalised by year's end, though on 18 December the company had announced a possible $ 1.2 bn agreement with unnamed Chinese investors. Despite the setbacks, the government proceeded to line up gas sales to Ghana and Burkina Faso.

At the same time, the government worked towards its goal of boosting oil production to 300,000 b/d in the mid-term. Despite Teodorín's obstructionism and distaste for Western majors, Oil Minister Lima succeeded in auctioning up to 30 offshore blocks as part of *EGRonda 2016*. The winners were announced on 5 June in Cape Town during Africa Oil and Power 2017, and included mainstays such as ExxonMobil, Ophir, Taleveras and Atlas Petroleum, as well as newcomers such as the Irish firm Clontarf, the Israeli Elenilto and the Nigerian Offshore Equator Oil and Gas. More good news for the regime emerged in December, when ExxonMobil struck oil in block EG-06, which straddled the once-highly productive Zafiro field. It was unclear, however, whether the reserves were commercially viable. As evidenced by the withdrawals of PanAtlantic in early February and Hess in late October, industry experts remained sceptical that the country's oil production could ever be substantively revived.

Gabon

Douglas Yates

In response to mounting tensions, President Bongo endeavoured to fight corruption, reform the Constitution and conduct a national dialogue with his opponents. But his real challenger was the world commodity crisis, as low prices for oil and other primary exports increased the burden of his costly Gabon Emergent programme.

Domestic Politics

In January, President Ali Bongo started the year by distancing himself from his powerful former cabinet director *Maixent Accrombessi*, whose corrupt system of clientelism had become something of an embarrassment. Victim of a cerebral vascular attack a few days after the presidential elections, Accrombessi had been evacuated on 18 August 2016 to convalesce in London. During that time he was replaced by Martin Boguikouma, a former governor of Ogooué-Maritime province. In an effort to reduce corruption and dwindling government revenues, Bongo launched Operation Mamba, an *anti-corruption campaign* in January, leading to the arrest of 90 individuals, mostly from Accrombessi's inner circle, such as former super-minister

 | DOI:10.1163/9789004367630_028

Magloire Ngambia, who had been in charge of investments, public works and territorial development, and former petroleum minister Etienne Ngoubou, who were both detained in Libreville's central prison. In March, several other 'Accrombessi boys' were locked up, including general director of the infrastructural public works agency, the 'Agence Nationale des Grands Travaux d'Infrastructures', Landry Patrick Oyaya, and two of Magloire Ngambia's key advisers, Christian Nkero-Capito and Grégoire Bayima. On 24 April, the general director of the merchant navy, Léon Ndong Nteme was also detained.

Bongo cynically also used his anti-corruption campaign to threaten investigations into the accounts of several *opponents* who had previously been ministers under his father, Omar Bongo, including adversaries *Jean Ping*, Didjob Divungui di Ndinge, Guy Nzouba Ndama, and Zacharie Myboto. They all spent the year challenging the legitimacy of his 2016 re-election. On 22 February, Bongo offered to hold talks with moderate opposition leaders in an apparent bid to ease tensions. But his main political rival, Ping, rejected this call for dialogue, branding the talks a 'masquerade' in which he said he would not participate. Ping accused Bongo of cheating to win re-election in the August 2016 elections and of using security forces to violently suppress protests in the weeks that followed. On 27 April, Alexandre Barro Chambrier, a 'Parti Démocratique Gabonais' (PDG) deputy from Libreville and former government minister, who now presided over his own party, 'Heritage and Modernity', gave an interview on the French public channel 'TV5 Monde' in which he mocked the president's dialogue as a 'monologue' intended to convince the international community that the situation in Gabon had been normalised. Calling for a boycott of the talks, Chambrier declared that the majority of people supported Ping's resistance.

Defying these staunch critics, Bongo spent € 18.2 m on his 'national dialogue' with the opposition, which commenced on 28 March and ended on 27 May. In a public display of his willingness to work with opponents and hear their calls for change, Bongo announced that he would reshuffle his cabinet, dismiss corrupt ministers Yves-Fernand Manfoumbi (agriculture) and Paul Biyoghé Mba (social and family development) and, to get around Ping, offer cabinet posts to the moderate opponents who participated in his dialogue, including Fang leader *Casimir Oyé Mba*, a former prime minister under Omar Bongo and member of the 'Union Nationale' who had supported Ping in 2016, and René Ndemezo'o Obiang, another former baron of the Omar Bongo era and 'Union Nationale' opposition coalition member. Obiang was promised a portfolio in reward for serving as vice president of Bongo's national dialogue. Any moderates who participated in the dialogue also had to accept the rescheduling of legislative elections, which had already been moved from December 2016 to July 2017, and were now pushed to the spring of 2018.

On 28 June, two days after Bongo reorganised his presidential staff, the surprise return of Maixent Accrombessi to Gabon confirmed suspicions that Bongo's time for dialogue with opponents was over, and his regime would now return to business as usual. On 25 August, Bongo named Brice Laccruche Alihanga, a man in Accrombesi's circle, to head his presidential cabinet, displacing a loyal member of the president's ethnic Téké from Bongoville, Alain-Claude Bilié By Nzé. This marked the return of Accrombessi's men to the centre of power, despite signs during the first half of the year that they would all be purged.

On 21 August, a *new 38-member cabinet* was presented. Prime Minister Emmanuel Issoze-Ngondet kept his post. This cabinet reshuffle was ostensibly aimed at better reflecting the country's *ethnic balance*. For example, Ali Bongo named Punu 'southerner' and former opposition leader Pierre Claver Maganga Moussavou as his vice president as a reward for the latter's participation in the national dialogue. A four-time candidate in the presidential elections of 1993, 1998, 2009 and 2016, Moussavou had challenged the president's father, Omar Bongo, three times for the presidency (but eventually became one of his political clients) before unsuccessfully challenging his son (but then accepting positions in his subsequent governments).

On 28 September, the government adopted a bill in the council of ministers for a *revision of the Constitution*, touching notably on the role of the president and parliament. Decried by the opposition as a "monarchical project" and a "constitutional coup d'état", the bill was scheduled for debate in the two legislative chambers by year's end. Zacharie Myboto, head of the 'Union Nationale', complained that the propositions would "concentrate all power in the hands of the head of state, reducing the prime minister's role to that of a foreman". Alexandre Barro Chambrier called the reform "a democratic retreat". According to a version obtained by 'Jeune Afrique', the text proposed adopting a two-round majoritarian ballot for presidential elections, and gave the president an indefinitely renewable seven-year mandate, in effect opening the door for Ali to become 'president-for-life' (like his father Omar Bongo, who had ruled Gabon for 42 years). The reform proposed reducing the mandate of senators from six to five years, and the number of mandates for members of the Constitutional Council to a single, non-renewable, nine-year term. In addition, it proposed giving the president the power to "take charge of government policy" in case of a "change in the majority" in the National Assembly. It also required officials to swear an "oath of loyalty" to the head of state and "respect the confidentiality" of all dossiers and information acquired both during their service and after leaving office. Finally, it proposed protecting President Bongo from any criminal charges of high treason by a proposed 'Haute Cour de la Justice' (a special French-style tribunal independent of the judicial branch designed to try members of the executive without violating the separation of powers doctrine): "The president of the republic," the text proposed,"who has ceased exercising his functions, cannot be charged, pursued, searched, arrested, detained, or judged for acts defined by this organic law on the High Court of Justice." This would effectively shield Bongo from any charges of embezzling public revenues, were he ever to step down from office.

On 14 December, the National Assembly adopted these constitutional reforms. (The Senate approved an amended text on 11 January 2018.) The contents of the amended text were not made public. Thus, Gabon's Constitution was amended in an occult fashion by a legislature 98% dominated by the ruling PDG party. At the end of December, in preparation for the 2018 legislative elections, it was reported that Malika Bongo, the president's eldest daughter, had been chosen to run as the PDG candidate in the Bongo clan fiefdom of Haut-Ogooué, foreshadowing the possibility of a third generation of dynastic rule in Gabon.

Foreign Affairs

From 14 January to 5 February, Gabon hosted the 31st *Africa Cup of Nations*, which was won by Cameroon for the fifth time. Both the tournament hosts and the defending champions, Côte d'Ivoire, were eliminated after failing to win any of their games. On 21 January, a Russian hacking group, New World Hackers, claimed to have taken down the official 'Confédération Africaine de Football' (CAF) website in response to CAF's decision to choose Gabon as host nation. "We did this in protest against Gabon," said an e-mail claiming to be from one of the hackers. "They are running the Africa Cup in a country where the dictator Ali Bongo is killing innocent people!" Gabon's image as an exceptional oasis of peace and stability in the region apparently suffered from the regime's use of violence to suppress democratic opponents.

Relations with *France* were strained during the first half of the year. The socialist government of President François Hollande had been critical of Bongo's re-election. Prime Minister Issoze Ngondet met with France's Foreign Minister Jean-Marc Ayrault on 24 March, but this did not resolve the impasse. On 6 July, the public television station 'France 2' broadcast, at prime time, a documentary about 'Le Clan Bongo' that caricatured Ali as a "diabolical and heartless" man who lavished money on personally directing the London Symphony Orchestra at Abbey Road studio while his people lived in squalor. After the election of President Emmanuel Macron in May ended socialist control in France, Bongo tried to repair his reputation by supporting Macron's efforts to fight global climate change. On 12 December, Bongo represented the AU at the One Planet Summit in Paris, an effort by Macron to sustain the COP21 Paris Climate Change Accords abandoned by the new US President Donald Trump.

Relations with the *United States* hardly improved after the departure of Barrack Obama and the election of Donald Trump to the White House. Invited by King Salman to Saudi Arabia with 11 other Islamic heads of state to participate with President Trump in a 20–21 May summit in Riyadh, Bongo had hoped for closer relations with the new American president. But Bongo suffered a diplomatic rebuff in New York, after proudly displaying a 'selfie' taken with Trump on the margins of the UN General Assembly meeting, when he was not invited to the 20 September working lunch for African leaders at Trump Tower, organised by the White House. On

16 December, a knifeman stabbed two Danish journalists in Libreville in retaliation for what he called US "attacks on Muslims" and Trump's recognition of Jerusalem as Israel's capital.

Strategic relations between the US and Gabon continued unabated, however, as members of the 13th Expeditionary Sustainment Command, 101st Airborne Division, and 79th Sustainment Command, under the auspices of the US Africa Command (AFRICOM), staged Operation Judicious Activation 17–2, on July 24–30, which set up a small command outpost in Libreville. This new quarterly exercise, in its first year of existence, aimed at testing American capabilities to deploy to a forward location in central Africa and set up an early entry command post able to manage logistics before the main element of troops were deployed and long-term structures were put in place.

Gabon's relations with *Great Britain* were pursued less publicly by the president, whose youngest children had been sent to elite English boarding schools in recent years. He conducted private personal business in Britain, being outside of France's sphere of influence. On 14 October, for example, at the Royal Albert Hall, with over 4,000 Freemasons from 136 Grand Lodges around the world present, Bongo was knighted by the United Grand Lodge on the 300th anniversary of the England-based Freemasons organisation. Such personal contacts remained important to Bongo's below-the-radar foreign affairs.

Relations with *China* continued to improve as Bongo redirected Gabon's reliance away from its traditional Western partners. On 26 May, during an official two-day visit to Libreville to discuss bilateral trade and investments, Ji Bingxuan, the vice president of the Standing Committee of the National People's Congress, formally announced that China would rebuild Gabon's charred National Assembly building, which had been set ablaze during post-election protests in 2016. It was not clear whether the Chinese would reconstruct the building (which was originally built by Chinese Overseas Engineering Company in 2002) at a cost or for free, as the Chinese had recently done in neighbouring Congo (Brazzaville). In another gesture of diplomatic good will, on 1 October a Chinese naval hospital vessel called the 'Peace Ark' arrived at the Port of Owendo for a week-long visit to the capital, providing medical services to 6,092 patients, accepting 18 hospitalised patients, and performing 43 operations on the vessel. On 9 October, Bongo boarded the vessel and spoke highly of the free Chinese medical services provided as a concrete step toward implementing the consensus reached during his official state visit to Beijing the previous year.

Socioeconomic Developments

According to the World Bank, *oil* accounted for 80% of Gabon's exports, 45% of its GDP, and 60% of government revenues. So the global slump in oil prices led the

Bongo government to trim its budget to $ 4.23 bn, and his Mamba anti-corruption campaign led to the government purging questionable oil projects. One of these, negotiated by the state-owned Gabon Oil Company (GOC) and Touchstone Oil & Gas, had allowed that Canadian firm to take over Remboué field. But, six months after his appointment on 3 January, Jacob Thaty Tsioba, the new head of the public 'Direction Générale des Hydrocarbures', had not signed it off. Tsioba had been an oil-sector auditor with Steward International before taking up the post. The management of GOC had been embarrassed by an audit two years before that revealed that some of its executives were earning exorbitant monthly salaries of more than € 30,000. Pascal Houangui, named oil minister in January, failed to manage an explosive oil workers strike situation and was replaced on 22 March by Vincent de Paul Massassa, who on 25 October announced that the struggling GOC would be taking a majority share in the 'Société Gabonaise de Raffinage' (SOGARA). On 7 November, Noël Mboumba was appointed as the refinery's new head. Such reshufflings of petroleum regulatory posts in the first half of the year reflected the instability brought about by the Mamba anti-corruption campaign.

Several foreign oil businesses that had been losing money in the wake of falling commodity prices announced their *withdrawal from Gabon*, notably *Shell Gabon*, which had been operating in the country over 56 years. On 13 January, 400 Shell Gabon workers went on strike, fearful about the firm divesting its assets from the country. On 7 March, Carlyle said it would buy Shell's fields. On 28 July, chief executive officer David Roux announced that Assalla Energy, a portfolio company of Carlyle Group, would go forward with the purchase of Shell oilfields. On 1 November, Shell completed this sale of its entire Gabonese oil operations to Assala for $ 628 m.

Shell was not the only firm divesting. Houston oil company *Vaalco*, which had refocused its attention on Gabon with the acquisition of supplementary interests in Etame Marin oil block and had dramatically reduced expenses to generate profits of $ 2.9 m in 2016, compared with losses of $ 31 m in 2015, proved unable to compensate for continued low oil prices and, no longer able to cover its debt, or to make the investments necessary to improve operations, asked a business bank to find a buyer for all its Gabonese oil assets on 5 December. Vaalco Gabon's primary source of revenue had been its 31.1% interest, via a production sharing contract, in operations in the 3,000-km² offshore Etame Marin block.

On 10 May, highly indebted Bouygues Energies & Services also announced that it would end its operations in Gabon, causing problems with the soon-to-be-unemployed union members of 'Syndicat des Agents de Bouygues Energies & Services Gabon'. On 22 November, the company announced that it would be going into liquidation.

Not all business news was bad, however. On 2 June, Singapore conglomerate Olam announced it would launch a new mining terminal at Owendo to capture *manganese* currently treated by the 'Compagnie Minière de l'Ogooué' (Comilog).

And on 10 June, French businessman Vincent Bolloré buried the hatchet with the government about his mismanagement of the Port of Owendo. In November 2016, Bolloré Transport and Logistics had purchased 49% of the 'Société de Terminaux des Conteneurs du Gabon', which runs the port in Gabon's Special Economic Zone. Manganese production, representing 15% of Gabon's exports, reached a new record of 5 m tonnes, with Comilog claiming 4 m tonnes and two other firms, the Chinese 'Compagnie Industrielle et Commerciale des Mines de Huazhou' and 'Nouvelle Gabon', claiming the remainder. Gabon was set to become the world's largest manganese producer in 2019.

With $ 160 m in *debt* maturing in December, and growth only estimated to be 1%, the recent wave of borrowing on private sovereign bond markets led Gabon to become one of the continent's most indebted nations, having issued $ 3.3 bn of bonds to fund Bongo's'Gabon Emergent' development programme. The IMF estimated the debt-to-GDP ratio at 62%, up from 31% in 2008. Investor interest increased after Gabon reached an agreement with the IMF on 19 June for a $ 642 m arrangement, which allowed it to refinance, on 8 August, $ 200 m of its eurobonds maturing in 2025.

São Tomé and Príncipe

Gerhard Seibert

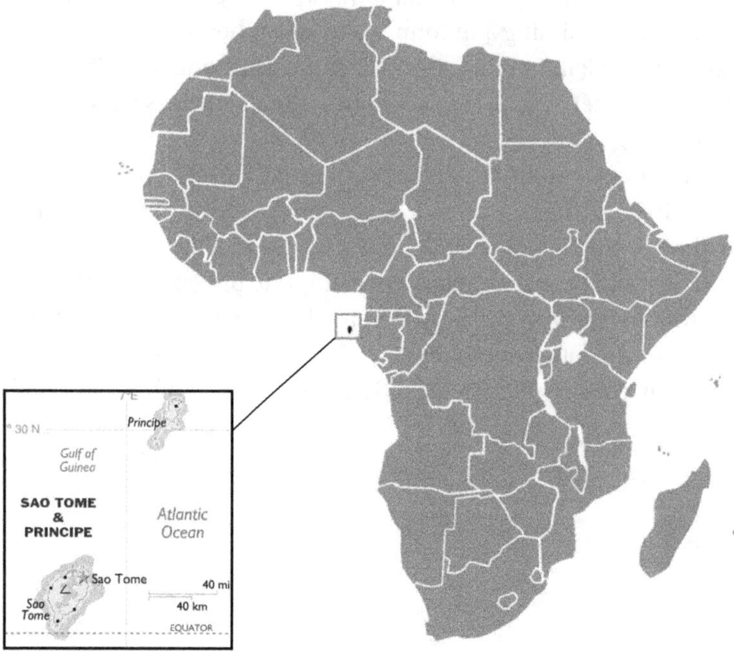

The three opposition parties fiercely contested the presence of military instructors from Rwanda and legislation on the establishment of a new independent Constitutional Court and a restructured 'Comissão Eleitoral Nacional'. Newly established relations with Beijing resulted in the signing of a five-year cooperation package worth $ 146 m. While the development assistance promised by China covered many areas, Beijing denied São Tomé funds for the construction of a deep-sea container transhipment port, which had for years been the Trovoada government's top priority for local infrastructure development.

Domestic Politics

Opposition parties were increasingly weary of many government actions that could be interpreted as efforts to curtail civil liberties and the country's overall democratic standing, and the court system was the most important battle ground. On 19 April, the Supreme Court decided to readmit five lower court judges, who had

 | DOI:10.1163/9789004367630_029

been suspended in May 2016, arguing that the suspension had been illegal. Their suspension had been prompted by an external review of professional performance in 2015, which had classified the five judges as mediocre. At the time, Prime Minister Patrice Trovoada had publicly defended the suspension, saying that if they were unfit as judges they had better work elsewhere in the civil service. On 26 April, judge counsellor Manuel Silva Gomes Cravid was elected with three of the votes of his peers as president of the five-member Supreme Court, replacing José Bandeira, who had been elected in 2013. The election of Gomes Cravid, considered an opponent of Trovoada, was interpreted as a setback for the prime minister. On 5 June, a three-month strike by judiciary staff for higher salaries and better working conditions ended after the government agreed to increase salaries from 1 January 2018.

On 15 August, the 'Acção Democrática Independente' (ADI) majority in the National Assembly approved a bill on the establishment of a *new autonomous Constitutional Court* against the votes of the opposition parties. The law provided for the election of the five judges by a simple majority, favouring the ADI, which had 33 seats in parliament. Opponents of the project argued that the law violated Article 157 of the Constitution, which stipulates that judges be elected by a two-thirds majority. However, the ADI countered that this provision only applied to the previous situation, where the Supreme Court functioned as Constitutional Court. In addition, the opposition considered the establishment of an autonomous Constitutional Court as an attempt by Trovoada to prevent possible unfavourable future decisions by the Supreme Court acting as the Constitutional Court. As it was the prerogative of the Constitutional Court to approve final election results, the opposition feared that future election results might be manipulated by a court controlled by the ADI.

In the same vein, the ADI majority approved on the same day a *bill to restructure the 'Comissão Eleitoral Nacional'* (CEN) against the votes of the three opposition parties. Under the new law, the mandate of the CEN was extended from four to seven years. While the new CEN was composed of nine members, of whom six came from all the parties represented in the National Assembly, the new CEN was made up of three commissioners elected by the National Assembly. Two commissioners, acting as the president and the secretary, were to be designated by the majority parliamentary group, while the third, i.e., the vice-president, was to be appointed by the second-largest parliamentary group. The opposition viewed the establishment of the new CEN as another measure that would enable the ADI to rig elections.

On 1 December, Supreme Court President Gomes Cravid accused his ex-assessor Justino Veiga, a former minister of justice, of *attempted bribery* at the request of the businessmen and parliamentarians Delfim Neves ('Partido da Convergência Democrática'; PCD) and Osvaldo Vaz ('Movimento de Libertação de São Tomé e Príncipe/Partido Social Democrata'; MLSTP/PSD). Veiga was detained by the police on 4 December, but released by the investigating judge the following day. The alleged bribery attempt was related to a legal dispute over the Rosema brewery and was supposedly an effort to take it away from Nino Monteiro (MLSTP/PSD), its owner since 2009, to return it to its previous owner, the Angolan businessman Melo Xavier. Neves, a personal friend of Veiga, denied the accusations, which he described as a political conspiracy by the government based on mere rumours. On 10 December, the accusations prompted Osvaldo Vaz, MLSTP/PSD vice-president and hitherto party leader Aurélio Martins' right-hand man, to resign from his post. Monteiro, who had accused Vaz of involvement in the scandal, was also a major financier of the MLSTP/PSD. After this episode, Trovoada announced that two judges, two public prosecutors and two agents of the Judiciary Police from Portugal would be integrated into the local judiciary to combat corruption within the institution.

On 14 December, opposition members of parliament asked the existing Constitutional Court for a preventive constitutionality check of the law on the new autonomous Constitutional Court. Nevertheless, on 27 December, President Evaristo Carvalho promulgated the controversial *law on the new Constitutional Court*. The following day, Gomes Cravid, president of the Supreme Court acting in its function as the Constitutional Court, declared Carvalho's action unconstitutional and void, since he had disregarded the legal 25-day term for the preventive constitutionality check that would have ended on 8 January 2018. Unimpressed, on 30 December, Carvalho announced the dismissal of Gomes Cravid as president of the old Constitutional Court on the grounds that the autonomous Constitutional Court had taken over this function. In turn, the opposition parties 'União dos Democratas para a Cidadania e Desenvolvimento' (UDD), PCD and MLSTP/PSD fiercely criticised the president's conduct as unconstitutional.

The opposition and the government had clashed earlier over the presence in the country of Rwandan military instructors. On 6 May, at the invitation of the Trovoada government, 20 Rwandan military instructors arrived in São Tomé to train 90 state security forces personnel, including 30 members a newly created 'Unidade de Protecção dos Dirigentes do Estado' (UPDE) to counter threats to national security and provide protection for political leaders against terrorist attacks. Their presence was fiercely contested by the three opposition parties, the MLSTP/PSD, PCD and UDD because of the absence of any defence cooperation agreement with Kigali. In addition, Danilson Cotu, the PCD's parliamentary leader, declared that, under the Constitution, the entry of foreign troops was only possible with the president's permission after consultation with the Council of State. Moreover, the opposition considered Rwanda's military assistance unnecessary, since São Tomé was already receiving military assistance from the United States, Brazil, Portugal, Morocco and Angola. Nevertheless, the National Assembly approved the Rwandan military presence by 30 votes of the ruling ADI against 16 votes of the opposition parties.

Foreign Affairs

São Tomé's bilateral relations focused on China and, to a lesser extent, *Rwanda*, while multilateral relations were related to the search for development funds. On 6 January, Rwanda's Foreign Minister Louise Mushikiwabo and her local counterpart Urbino Botelho signed in São Tomé two agreements, one on political-diplomatic consultation to coordinate their countries' involvement in the AU, and the other on air transport and migration. During her 24-hour visit, Mushikiwabo was also received by President Carvalho and Prime Minister Trovoada. From 9–12 March, Foreign Minister Botelho and Natural Resources Minister Carlos Vila Nova headed a government delegation to Kigali. During the visit, bilateral cooperation agreements were signed on civil aviation, tourism, a mutual visa waiver and memoranda of understanding on cooperation in agriculture, livestock and fishing, as well as a preferential trade agreement. From 22 to 26 March, a large Rwandan business delegation visited São Tomé in search of investment opportunities. On 8 May, Trovoada and his wife were received by Rwanda's President Kagame in Kigali when they attended the Transform Africa Summit 2017 on ICT as a transformative agent. On 18 August, Trovoada attended Kagame's inauguration for another seven-year term.

Less than four weeks after São Tomé and *China* re-established full diplomatic relations, on 19 January, a Chinese multi-ministerial delegation headed by Zhou Zhaoming, director general of the Chinese Ministry of Trade's Department for West Asia and Africa, arrived in São Tomé to define areas of development cooperation, with priority given to the agriculture, health, energy and infrastructure sectors. Zhaoming, who was received by Prime Minister Trovoada, announced that the Chinese development cooperation programme would start soon. Ten days earlier, a Chinese medical mission had visited São Tomé to draw up working areas in the local hospital for Chinese medical doctors, who were expected to arrive in February.

On 6 March, Lin Songtian, director-general of the Chinese Foreign Ministry's Department African Affairs, headed another delegation to São Tomé. Songtian, who was received by Foreign Minister Botelho and Prime Minister Trovoada, promised *Chinese assistance in transforming the archipelago's advantages into resources*, but also criticised the establishment of relations with Taiwan in 1997, which had violated the internationally recognised one-China principle. On 29 March, São Tomé was admitted as a full member of the Forum for Economic and Trade Cooperation between China and Portuguese-speaking Countries (Macao Forum) established in 2003.

On 3 April, 20 years after its closure, the *Chinese embassy in São Tomé* was officially reopened in the presence of various government ministers and members of the small local diplomatic corps. In his address, Foreign Minister Botelho indicated health, energy, transport and agriculture and livestock as future areas of bilateral cooperation. On 28 July, Beijing's ambassador handed over to São Tomé's Foreign

Ministry a donation of five Chinese Hawtai cars worth $ 75,550 to mitigate the transport problems of the foreign ministry's protocol service. In late August, the ambassador handed over 1,000 tons of rice in Chinese food aid.

During *Trovoada's first official visit to China* from 10 to 17 April, he was received by both Premier Li Keqiang and President Xi Jinping. His delegation included Foreign Minister Botelho and Finance Minister Américo Ramos. Premier Li declared that China was ready to open a new chapter of bilateral relations by engaging in mutually beneficial cooperation and cultural exchanges with the archipelago. Both premiers witnessed the signing of several five-year cooperation agreements on tourism, services, agriculture, fisheries, infrastructure construction, student scholarships and medical assistance worth $ 146 m. Trovoada, who for many years had defended his country's relations with Taiwan, piously affirmed that his people had never forgotten the support provided by the Chinese people and gave assurances that São Tomé firmly adhered to the one-China policy.

From 8 to 16 May, President Carvalho paid an official visit to *Portugal*, where he was received by President Marcelo Rebelo de Sousa and Prime Minister António Costa. In addition, Carvalho, who was accompanied by Foreign Minister Botelho, visited the Calouste Gulbenkian Foundation, the Instituto Marquês de Valle Flôr, the Portuguese naval base in Almada, and the local Sãotomean immigrant community in Lisbon. On 13 May, together with Rebelo de Sousa, he participated in the commemoration of the 100th anniversary of the apparitions of the Virgin Mary at Fátima, celebrated in the presence of Pope Francis. On 31 May, during a four-day visit to São Tomé, Portugal's Secretary of State for Foreign Affairs and Cooperation Teresa Ribeiro signed an agreement for a credit line of € 10 m for private sector investment and imports from Portugal.

On 19 January, the resident *EU* ambassador in Libreville (Gabon) and Foreign Minister Botelho signed in São Tomé a finance agreement for € 6.75 m for a four-year project to promote the production of *cocoa, pepper and coffee for export*. On 23 February, the head of cooperation at the EU delegation in Libreville, and Botelho signed five agreements worth € 3.5 m for infrastructure rehabilitation projects as part of the 10th EDF.

On 17 February, Zahira Virani, the local UN representative in São Tomé, and Foreign Minister Botelho signed a finance agreement worth $ 13 m for governance improvement, social cohesion promotion and economic growth as part of the UN Development Assistance Framework programme for 2017–2021. On 23 February, Minister of Finance, Trade and Blue Economy Américo Ramos announced that the *World Bank* and the *EIB* would provide a grant of $ 16 m and a soft loan of $ 13 m, respectively, to finance the government's Energy Sector Recovery Project, including the rehabilitation and extension of the Contador hydroelectric dam and the improvement of the public utility 'Empresa Nacional de Água e Eletricidade' to improve the quality of life of 90,000 beneficiaries.

Socio-economic Developments

On 30 January, the National Assembly approved a *national budget* of € 132 m with the votes of the ruling ADI. During the parliamentary debate, Prime Minister Trovoada admitted that the foreign grants included in the budget had not yet been received and that it was not guaranteed either that the listed amounts would be fully disbursed. At the request of the IMF, on 27 July the National Assembly approved a revised budget of € 129 m in an attempt to reduce the primary fiscal deficit to 1.8% in 2017. The austerity measures included reductions in fringe benefits for civil servants and in public administration expenses for fuel and phone calls.

Some developments were recorded in the *oil sector*. Between 21 January and 23 August, the French geoscience company CGG Services SA carried out 3D seismic surveys in the exclusive economic zone (EEZ) blocks 5, 6, 11 and 12, where the US Kosmos Energy and the Portuguese Galp Energia were the operators. On 3 October, following a request by a consortium of British Petroleum (BP) and Kosmos to open negotiations for the direct acquisition of exploration rights for EEZ blocks 10 and 13, the 'Agência Nacional de Petróleo' (ANP) called on other companies to express their interest in the two blocks within 15 days. From 20 October to 22 December, the ANP held a restricted auction for the two blocks with the participation of BP/Kosmos and a second consortium comprising the French Total and Galp Energia.

On 25 August, Hélio Almeida, governor of the Central Bank, presented six new bank notes and five new coins in denominations with three fewer zeros to be put into circulation on 1 January 2018 as part of a *currency reform*. The new, STD (dobras) 5, 10, 20, 50, 100 and 200 bank notes were designed and printed by the British company De La Rue. The redenominated currency series depicted endemic wildlife and included innovative anti-counterfeiting features. The new money replaced the STD 5,000, 10,000, 20,000, 50,000, 100,000 bank notes and STD 2,000, 1,000, 500, 200 and 100 coins that had previously been in circulation. From January 2018, the new fixed rate of exchange would be STD 24.50: €1.

On 27 September, the South African investment company Here Be Dragons (HBD) and the Regional Government of Príncipe started the relocation of 130 families, a total of 500 people (6.6% of the island's population), from their dilapidated 1920-constructed accommodation in the Sundy estate in Príncipe to new homes elsewhere on the small island. The *resettlement project* was conceived by UN Habitat as a participatory process and was financed by HBD, which held the concession for Sundy as an integral part of its engagement in the development of eco-tourism in Príncipe.

PART 5

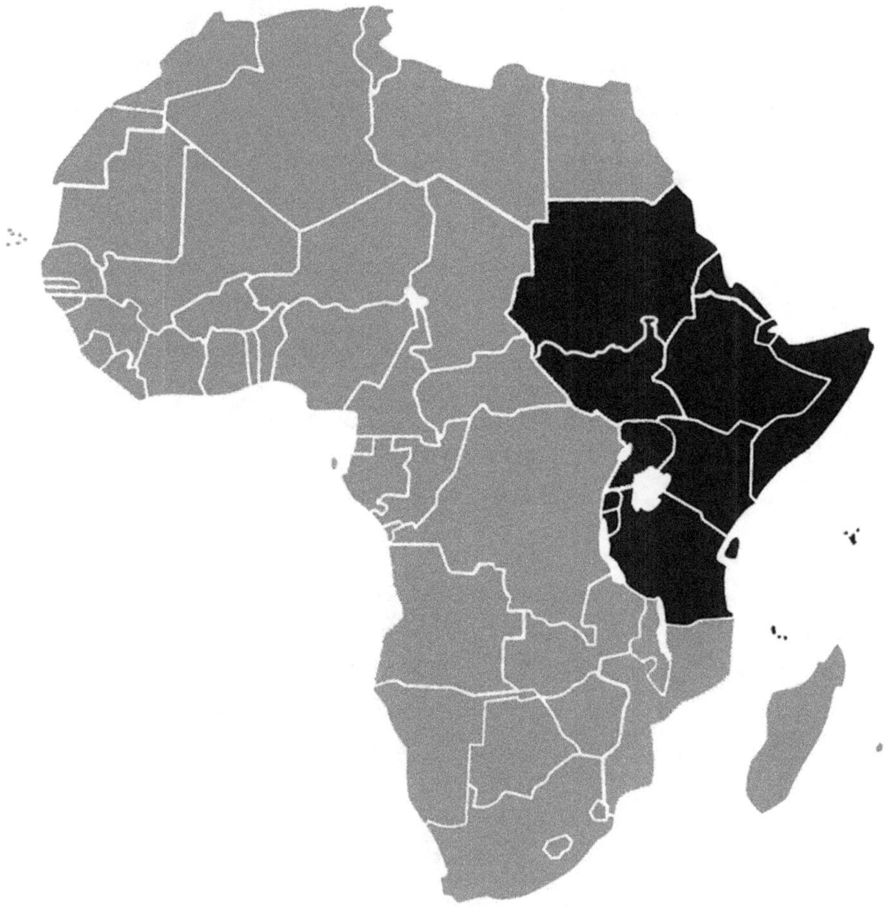

Eastern Africa

Jon Abbink

Eastern Africa remained a turbulent area, marked by political volatility and unrest, but it was nevertheless the region in Africa with the highest average economic growth rates. At the same time, socio-economic inequities and regional strife continued, and major development ventures such as dams, large-scale energy projects and commercial mega-plantation schemes remained contested. Resentment about long-ruling presidents and dominant parties increased, notably among the restive youth, who felt blocked from employment and advancement. Income growth and opportunities were largely reserved for a minority of well-educated and connected urban young people. Some countries, such as Burundi, Somalia and South Sudan, struggled with (post-) conflict economic crises. Environmental and demographic developments did not help to mitigate the picture, despite state initiatives to tackle the problems of rapid population growth, drought, food insecurity and ecological constraints. Green energy initiatives were discussed and implemented here and there. International players such as the UN and the EU kept up their commitments with various countries in the region to development and security cooperation, poverty reduction and control of outmigration, the last being seen as having a major impact on population movement and conflict instability.

Political Developments

Overall, politics in Eastern Africa retained its strongly authoritarian character under long-dominant ruling parties or autocratic presidents, but *elections* were held in Kenya, Rwanda, Somalia and Somaliland, including, in the last three countries, for the presidency. The Kenyan parliamentary elections took place twice, because the 8 August round was marred by serious irregularities and was rejected by the Kenyan Supreme Court. The re-run on 29 October confirmed the incumbent, President Uhuru Kenyatta, in office. The elections in Rwanda were highly problematic due to the undermining of the electoral process and, as predicted, kept President Paul Kagame in power with a suspect 98.8% of the vote. In Somalia, a contested presidential election, manipulated by all kinds of moneyed interests and an indirect clan-based voting system, produced an unexpected winner, Mohamed Abdullahi 'Farmajo', although he was not a newcomer to Somali politics (having previously been a prime minister). The only credible election was the presidential polls in Somaliland, although the candidate of the ruling party Kulmiye came out victorious.

 | DOI:10.1163/9789004367630_030

Some countries, such as South Sudan and Sudan (Darfur and the Nuba mountains), saw undiminished levels of *armed conflict*, with civil strife and demonstrations continuing in Ethiopia, Djibouti and Burundi. Citizens in countries such as Eritrea, Ethiopia and Rwanda suffered under ongoing intrusive surveillance and the stifling of political and civic life.

In *Burundi*, although the open violence triggered by President Pierre Nkurunziza's pursuit of a third presidential term in 2015 subsided, tension remained, as his presidency beyond the constitutional term limit continued to be resented. Nkurunziza nevertheless strengthened his position by bringing the ruling party CNDD-FDD more into line and suppressing civil, political and armed opposition. There was talk in the media of addressing the long-standing issue of constitutional reform and also preparations for the 2020 elections, but the president's politics remained highly contested by opposition groups and the younger generation.

In neighbouring *Rwanda*, nothing changed, despite the elections: President Kagame continued as before, having made sure that no one could effectively oppose him. Government policies and measures could not be criticised or challenged by the population without repercussions. The human rights record continued to be challenged by international human rights organisations and even the UN. Donor countries, unable to learn from the examples of, for instance, Egypt and Ethiopia, were again soft on him and condoned his authoritarianism, perhaps due to Rwanda's GDP growth and the country's role as leading troop and police contributor to peacekeeping operations.

In *Somalia*, the delayed presidential elections produced Mohamed Abdullahi 'Farmajo' as the new president, a candidate who found broad acceptance, despite somewhat dubious and externally influenced elections. He announced reforms, offered amnesty and talks to al-Shahaab (which were rejected) and tried to forge more consensus. A turn-around in the country's political and socio-economic path was not achieved, however. The Somali Federal Government remained a problematic outfit, not expanding its political-territorial control or governmental authority over the country much, and marred by corruption and too much dependency on donor funding, remittances and other (Middle Eastern) interference. AMISOM peace-keeping forces continued combatting al-Shabaab, who committed the worst car bombing in Somali history, killing 512 people in Mogadishu.

Somaliland showed much more stability and also had presidential elections, which were orderly and credible and yielded a new candidate, Muse Bihi Abdi, from the ruling Kulmiye party.

Elections in *Kenya* were fraught with difficulty in a somewhat chaotic and violent political landscape. First-round results triggered protests and violent police reprisals in the days after their announcement, and at least 37 people in opposition strongholds in Nairobi and western Kenya were killed by police. In some places, such as Laikipia, the election reignited tensions over land ownership between local communities and the significant community of European origin. An opposition petition to the Supreme Court led to its annulling the August result (in a 4–2 vote), with a statement that "the elections had not been conducted in the spirit envisioned by the Constitution". The second election round on 29 October, as noted above, returned President Kenyatta to power. Protests were to no avail this time.

Uganda's President Yoweri Museveni, consolidated in power in 2016 after another term extension and election, also carried on business as usual, still with no clear succession trajectory outlined. The constitutional age limit for tenure of the office of president was definitively scrapped. The plan had led to public protests and violent scenes even in parliament, but it eventually became law and created the opportunity for the incumbent to extend his tenure for the foreseeable future. The political atmosphere in the country deteriorated, with the president's political opponents, civil society organisations and the media on the receiving end.

Tanzania's President John Magufuli, in his second year in office, pursued a more authoritarian leadership style, which narrowed existing democratic space and curtailed critical public debate. Freedom of assembly and of expression by opposition groups were frequently restricted by the authorities, and political rallies were banned outside of election periods. Opposition politicians were frequently arrested, interrogated and intimidated, critical media were closely scrutinised and there was increasingly less tolerance of dissenting opinions in general. The political system – with the dominant, long-ruling CCM ('Chama cha Mapinduzi', or Revolutionary Party) able to control all spheres of public life and enjoying the support of the majority of the population – was not under threat, despite a clear deterioration in the general political climate. Magufuli further consolidated his grip on the CCM, suppressing discontent within party ranks. Semi-autonomous Zanzibar remained relatively calm on the surface, but the long-standing confrontation between the CCM and the opposition CUF remained acute.

The small island state of *Seychelles* remained generally stable politically and economically, and had the highest per capita GDP in Africa. After the 2016 elections, the long-ruling 'Parti Lepep' still controlled the executive (government), but the legislature was dominated by an opposition coalition of three parties.

The other archipelago, the densely populated *Comoros*, also showed overall stability, although its politics remained divided due to a lack of unified 'identity', and the issue of the separate status of Mayotte Island was a challenge (its population wanted to remain French and not be politically part of Comoros). President Azali Assoumani had his first year in power after his election in 2016 and drew on his political experience to consolidate his rule at home and renew relationships with bilateral partners and international organisations.

Politics in *Sudan* remained as authoritarian and tense as ever. Media control and harassment continued and hundreds of political prisoners remained in jail. President Omar al-Bashir announced the formation of a new Government of National

Accord, emerging from the so-called National Dialogue process. The composition of and participants in this government were far from representing a solid basis for peaceful political competition. Social and political tensions in society were unrelenting, with student movements contesting and (armed) groups active in peripheral regions. Tensions reached a peak in Darfur in May, when a joint attack was launched by rebel groups based in Libya (SLA/Minni Minawi) and South Sudan (SLA/Transition Council). They were repelled but the attack sent a message to the international community that the Darfur war (ongoing since 2003) was not over.

South Sudan had perhaps the worst humanitarian and political problems in Eastern Africa, with untold human suffering, deep food insecurity, violent ethnic 'revenge' actions and a spectacularly incompetent government. It gave official declarations of a ceasefire but went on with military campaigns and a deliberate counter-insurgency policy. A controversial National Dialogue initiative did not work out. Armed opposition remained fragmented, despite efforts to achieve greater unity. The ongoing fighting led to declarations of famine in two parts of Unity State in February.

Djibouti saw what could be called 'political stability' but of the same authoritarian and repressive kind, under veteran President Ismaïl Omar Guelleh and his 'Union pour la Majorité Presidentielle' (UMP). They dominated the political realm, with little space for opposition or civil society activities. For example, in October, a demonstration in Tajourah, in the Afar-inhabited north, was violently dispersed by security forces. In this area, the 'Front pour la Restoration de l'Unité et de la Démocratie' (FRUD) had been active in previous years, but was relatively passive due to an Ethiopian military presence.

Eritrea was another story of stifling, authoritarian 'stability', with virtually no progress on any front, and a regime still dominated by Isayas Afewerki, its first and only president since Independence in 1991. The country's militarised command-economy was maintained and the human rights situation was again very precarious. Political apathy reigned and out-migration of the young went on steadily, although in diminishing numbers. There was a crackdown on some remaining schools that offered religious education as part of their curriculum, and in one instance (an Islamic school) this triggered the first student demonstration in Asmara since 2001.

Ethiopia's political scene was marked by insecurity and growing disagreement on the way forward within the ruling party EPRDF (in power since 1991). Demonstrations and street actions by youths across Oromia and Amhara Regions continued, despite a reinstated state of emergency, and took on a grim character. The ruling party struggled to find answers and addressed the issues in several long meetings at the end of the year. There was a feeling that the regime had run out of options.

The *political opportunity structures* in Eastern Africa in general were not conducive to inclusiveness, freedom, rule of law or human security. Life remained precarious for large parts of the population, including socio-economically, and political activities continued to be high risk. Democratic culture and transparent, accountable government still had a long way to go, as in most countries political freedoms and judicial independence were at risk or not developed, usually on the basis of the idea that the 'development process' needed a strong and authoritarian government. The Freedom in the World report by the US-based watchdog Freedom House stated that democracy was on a "downward trend" during the year, with unreformed autocracies maintained in Rwanda, Eritrea, Ethiopia, Sudan and South Sudan (worst), and Uganda, Kenya and Tanzania having a 'partly free' status. Burundi's political rights and freedoms after the controversial 'election' and reinstatement of President Nkurunziza, remained very subdued and the country was considered 'not free'. Positive exceptions were Somaliland and Seychelles. Insecurity and mistrust marked the political process in most countries, fed by allegations of corruption and elite power abuse.

The Afrobarometer surveys – an ongoing comparative series of public attitudes measuring projects on democracy, governance, and economic conditions in Africa now in their 7th round – were carried out in several countries, including Togo, Zambia, Ghana and Zimbabwe. Results revealed citizens' ongoing scepticism and lack of trust in their governments, serious disappointment over (access to) judicial systems, general public service provision and employment, and resentment of the lack of political accountability and transparency, despite progress being noted in fields such as education, poverty reduction and basic services.

On the *political indexes* drawn up by global monitoring agencies regarding civil rights and political and media freedoms – to be interpreted with caution because of a certain lack of context appraisal – Eastern Africa was not doing very well: for instance, the World Press Freedom Index (of 180 countries) gave Comoros the highest position of Eastern African countries, at 49th, but all other countries in the region were placed below 85th. Lowest but one was Eritrea. Similar pictures of (lack of) political rights were drawn by HRW, the Human Freedom Index (of the Fraser Institute), Reporters without Borders (but with a slight improvement over 2016, except in Tanzania and Eritrea) and the Mo Ibrahim Index of African Governance. The last showed what many observers already knew: that progress in governance improvement as shown in the past decade had stagnated and in some countries had reversed, including, among others, Somalia, Burundi, South Sudan, Djibouti, Eritrea and Sudan. Overall, a state of political misery and insecurity continued across the region.

TI's Corruption Perception Index (180 countries) showed little change in the rankings of Eastern African countries on *corruption*, which is important to measure because of its overall corrosive impact on politics, public administration, economic life and public morality. South Sudan and Somalia were on the lowest places, with Sudan 175th, Eritrea 165th, Burundi 157th and Uganda 151st. Eastern Africa was disproportionately low on this scale. TI's new measure, the 'Bribery index' of institutions (on a scale of 0–100) saw Rwanda as the least bribery-prone country in the region and Burundi as the most. Notably bribery-prone were the police, the judiciary and education sectors. But not all countries in the region were measured, and it was noted that reporting of corruption by citizens to the authorities in Eastern Africa was very low. Fundamental transformation towards political liberalisation, well-regulated open economies and governance and conflict management in the sub-region did not really occur.

Transnational Relations and Conflict Configurations

General issues in international relations between the countries of Eastern Africa were the perennial Nile water question (Ethiopia-Sudan-Egypt), major trans-border infrastructure investments (e.g., in Uganda-Kenya, Ethiopia-Sudan and Ethiopia-Djibouti) and violent conflict and terrorist threats in the region, as in South Sudan, Somalia, the Eritrea-Ethiopia border stand-off, and the aftermath of the Burundi crisis.

Acute *security problems* and armed conflicts continued in South Sudan, Somalia and Sudan (including Darfur, seemingly forgotten but still a war zone). International concerns with such problems persisted, as in Somalia, Darfur, South Sudan and Ethiopia (where, due to an Oromia-Somali Region 'border conflict' more than 800,000 people were displaced and hundreds killed), and these concerns were fed not least by the dramatic humanitarian consequences that followed. IGAD tried to further mediation in Eastern African conflict zones but with no substantial results.

Eastern Africa attracted increasing numbers of actors who envisaged for themselves a security role and/or a military facility on its soil. This seemed to be part of an emerging business model. China opened its first overseas military base near Obock in Djibouti on 1 August – a significant event, 90 years to the day since the founding of the Red Army. While described officially as a 'logistics hub', it was to be a full-fledged military base for around 10,000 personnel, equipped for communications monitoring and to resupply navy ships. Djibouti also hosted Japanese and Italian military bases, added to those of France (the oldest) and the USA. Russia also wanted to get involved but failed to reach a partnership agreement to share facilities with the Chinese. In addition, even India was considering opening a base in this most strategic Red Sea country, alongside its facilities in Madagascar and the Agaléga islands near Mauritius.

In February, the UAE, which had had a military facility in Eritrea since 2015, got permission for a base in Somaliland. Saudi Arabia could not stay behind and also planned a military presence in Djibouti. Elsewhere, France, a key foreign military power in Africa, had 4,000 troops for Operation Burhane in the Sahel. They had their air power and mission headquarters in Chad, plus five Reaper reconnaissance drones in Niger, special operations troops in Burkina Faso, a logistics hub in Côte d'Ivoire and a small presence in Gabon. French President Emmanuel Macron saw Africa as a key foreign policy priority.

The US kept some 4,000 troops in Camp Lemonnier in Djibouti, and about 800 in Niger. Special US operatives were present in Somalia (an estimated 500) to aid the Somali Federal Government against the Islamist terror movement al-Shabaab, which over the year killed more people than Boko Haram in Nigeria.

The AU's Mission in Somalia (AMISOM), with around 22,000 personnel, also continued to assist the Somali Federal Government in combating al-Shabaab. This movement offered no political way forward except rejection of the Somali political system and government, and persisted with constant violent attacks on government personnel, media, civilians and local NGO staff. Many bomb attacks occurred, creating hundreds of victims and causing huge damage, in a fruitless cycle of sabotage and bloodshed. A political solution did not seem in sight but a military solution was not reached either, due not least to AMISOM's limited mandate and unwise tactics.

After several years of the decline and near elimination of *piracy*, it suddenly increased again off the coast of Somalia. Twice as many incidents (54) compared with 2016 were recorded, including failed attacks, suspicious activities, (attempted) hijackings and kidnappings. The violent conflict in Yemen also continued to affect maritime space in the region, with a number of incidents occurring off its coast. Although these threats were expanding, shipping activity remained constant, with many more ships carrying armed guards. The hijacking on 23 March of the Comoros-flagged merchant tanker 'Aris 13' off the north-eastern coast of Somalia marked the first successful seizure of a merchant ship in five years. All this showed that insecurity remained high and that an underlying piracy infrastructure was still present, ready to be re-activated when conditions were right. A comprehensive, locally based maritime security approach remained a necessity.

While intensive donor-country relations with Eastern African nations were obvious, China's presence in the region also continued to grow in prominence; its ongoing economic activities and investments, and the opening of its military base in Djibouti have been referred to above.

As to *conflict configurations* in the sub-region, no major breakthroughs were reached on outstanding conflicts. The EAC and IGAD did their best but did not have sufficient influence on nations' elite group interests to solve them.

Burundi struggled with unresolved political and economic instability after the contested Nkurunziza presidential term extension and election, and its relations with Rwanda, Belgium, the EU and the UN remained fraught with tensions.

Rwanda tried to play an active role as AU and EAC trailblazer, helped by its relatively favourable economic growth trajectory and its peacekeeping troop contributions, but its bilateral relations with both Burundi and France remained strained.

Somalia and *Somaliland* presented quite different pictures with regard to security and conflict, with the latter largely peaceful and the former still caught in the violent turmoil of regional conflict and terrorist attacks by al-Shabaab. Somaliland, however, did not solve its border conflict with the Puntland Region around the territories of Sanaag and Sool, with troops on standby. Somalia's relations with Kenya remained tense; with Ethiopia they were much better. A London conference on Somalia was held in May, to give further impetus to institution building, peacemaking and economic development.

Kenya's two election rounds showed the fragility and unrest in its domestic politics, and in various peripheral regions, where violence and predation continued, beyond the control of the central government. Kenya kept a contingent of several thousand AMISOM troops in Somalia and lost dozens of its soldiers in al-Shabaab attacks on some of its bases.

Uganda still exercised its role as a major regional player and continued to be held in high esteem in African and international fora.

Tanzania strengthened its relations with Rwanda and Uganda, amid minor disputes with Kenya over trade issues. Relations with Western aid donors became more strained over their mounting ambivalence or dissatisfaction with President Magufuli's erratic and authoritarian governance style. Tanzania's cooperation with China was further intensified.

Compared with its African and Indian Ocean neighbours, *Seychelles* enjoyed domestic stability and few if any foreign policy problems. The country worked with fellow Small Island Developing States (SIDS) to address looming climate change issues.

The new *Comoros* government under President Assoumani determined that the country should aim to become an 'emerging economy', a goal that influenced both domestic and foreign policy. The president prioritised cooperation with France, but also intended to cement relations with Saudi Arabia as Comoros's principal partner in the Muslim world.

Sudan enjoyed improved relations with its neighbours and in the global domain, except with Egypt, and Khartoum aimed at a broader policy of 'normalising' its foreign relations. US sanctions (in place since 1997) were lifted in October, even though one precondition, an end to the Darfur war, was not really met. President al-Bashir's regime also remained an important partner for the EU on the migration issue. Al-Bashir skilfully managed to remain neutral in the Gulf crisis, in which Saudi Arabia and the UAE opposed Qatar.

As noted above, the violent conflict in *South Sudan* continued and deepened. A new IGAD-led initiative aimed at revitalising the peace process did not work and, in December, the conflict entered its fifth year, with very little prospect of a lasting resolution in sight.

Djibouti's international importance was very evident during the year, with quite a number of global players trying to get a foothold via a military base or other strategic interest. This gave President Ismail Omar Guelleh enough room to ignore domestic pressure from Afar and other opposition, continue autocratic policies and play foreign parties off against each other. Relations with Kenya and Ethiopia were good (although Ethiopian misgivings on high port fees were an issue). The new railway line between Addis Ababa (Ethiopia) and Djibouti City started commercial operations in November. Relations with Eritrea remained bad. In the Gulf crisis, Djibouti chose the side of Saudi Arabia.

Eritrea remained isolated in the region and unresponsive to criticism or calls for cooperation. The diplomatic crisis in the Arabian Peninsula and tensions between Egypt, Ethiopia and Sudan affected Eritrea's foreign relations. Qatar ended its role as a mediator in the Djibouti-Eritrean conflict, and relations with Sudan were somewhat tense, as shown in the Sudanese troop build-up along the border with Eritrea at the end of the year in response to human trafficking issues and suspected Egyptian support to Eritrea.

Ethiopia remained the crucial Horn of Africa power, as a major donor fund recipient, a main participant in the AMISOM forces in Somalia and other peace-keeping forces in Africa, and the location of the headquarters of the AU, ECA and other organisations such as IGAD, as well as because of its population size. Its relations with Kenya, Djibouti and Somaliland remained stable and cooperative. Tensions with Eritrea persisted. Domestic problems, however, were quite serious, leading to fears of instability in the wider region. International donors and diplomats urged the regime in Addis Ababa to ease tensions and tackle the country's social and political crisis.

Socioeconomic Developments

Eastern African *economic growth* was higher than that of other African regions, as measured by GDP increase: 5.4% on average. Ethiopia, Tanzania and Djibouti had the highest rates. Infrastructure investments were important again (though they raised public debt fairly rapidly), and so was the expansion of agriculture and services, and hesitant industrial production uptake was also seen. Educational levels rose in many areas, but social inequalities and governance issues, including corruption, persisted. On the scale of *multidimensional poverty* measurement, however, some the globally 'poorest regions' were still found in South Sudan, Ethiopia and Uganda. Food insecurity threats loomed large over the region. Most food and humanitarian aid was provided by USAID ($ 13.9 bn since 2008).

Major challenges for the local economies, which would continue to be largely agrarian for the near future, continued to be climate change and unpredictability, growing densities of population and agrarian activities, criminalisation of parts of the national economies, and pressure on water resources and pastoral areas due to large-scale investment schemes and peasant-pastoralist tensions. Legal systems were not well-equipped to deal effectively and fairly with land, water and other resource disputes. In the wake of growing economies, population densities and climate variabilities, environmental-ecological problems came to the fore, but were not effectively managed. The bias against investing massively in the agrarian sector and rural livelihoods was not overcome, despite it being well-known that no major non-oil economy ever made the developmental transition without capitalising the agricultural sector. Investments in expanding and scaling up functional agrarian systems, 'empowering' local farmers, improving context-specific irrigation, working on drought and heat resistant crops, and integrated agricultural techniques would be necessary, with social safety nets in place for the vulnerable. Some countries made progress here, but not enough to achieve a turn-around.

The sub-region was marked by one of the highest *population growth* rates in Africa, with an estimated annual average of 2.9%, indicating continued exponential growth. The overall fertility rate was 4.8, the population's median age was 18.1 years, and the total population in Eastern Africa's 13 countries reached around 317 m. There were no signs of a 'demographic transition', except in some of the largest cities, where birth rates dropped.

In the wake of population growth, *urbanisation* also accelerated across the region, but this did not lead to a decline in rural population numbers. Most cities were not equipped with sufficient facilities (including transport, sanitation and waste management) to deal with the rapidly increasing urban population numbers.

Government *investments in infrastructure, roads and new energy projects continued*, including the Lamu Port-South Sudan-Ethiopia Transport Corridor (LAPSSET) in Kenya. This project had a high price tag ($ 3.3 bn) and most major international investors gave up, but despite this – and the resulting delays – the project was pushed forward. The Mwambani Port and Railway Corridor (MWAPORC), centred in Tanzania, fared better, with Uganda joining in with proposed oil link connections.

Most *state budgets still showed substantial dependence on external funding*. For example, the overall ratio of aid to government budgets was 20.5%. Rwanda and Burundi received around 45% and 50% of their budgets, respectively, from aid, despite Rwanda's protestations that all dependence on foreign aid should be phased out, but Kenya only received 13%.

Remarkably, the *projected oil economy boom* in Uganda (with a 6.5 bn barrel reserve) and Kenya (750 m barrels reserve in the Turkana region, and more expected) did not materialise due to delays in pipeline construction, protracted bargaining about contracts, governance issues and stagnant world oil prices since the drop in 2014. Landlocked Uganda had long considered whether to opt for a pipeline to the coast through Kenya or through Tanzania, and in August decided for the latter, with a pipeline to be built for $ 3.9 bn. This cut short the idea of joining up with Kenya's pipeline, due to security concerns and delays caused by land disputes in northern

Kenya. Tanzania had also offered lower tariffs and other benefits. Kenya, counting on more oil finds, might still opt to build its own pipeline from Turkana region to the coast, in the framework of the LAPPSET corridor. Meanwhile, oil exports from South Sudan – the country's major source of income – remained at 130,000 b/d, down from 350,000 b/d before the start of the civil war in 2013. Persistent insecurity made oil companies desist from further investments. In general, politics and disputes between neighbours in Eastern Africa made oil and other trans-border investments anything but certain or secure.

State current account deficits continued to range widely, from 2% to 9% of GDP. Domestic tax revenue was still low, never beyond 50%. Surprisingly, the Somalia Federal Government had a budget surplus of $ 3.8 m, but this indicated underspending on necessary items such as education and security. The only other country with a surplus was Seychelles. South Sudan's deficit was significantly reduced from 2016, to 2.8%.

Inflation figures varied widely, from crisis rates in South Sudan (around 182%) and Sudan (34%) to low rates in Djibouti (3%), Seychelles (3.2%), Uganda (4.4%), Tanzania (5.3%) and, surprisingly, Somalia (1.5%). Ethiopia was also high, at 13.6%.

The great diversity of *socio-economic achievements* was reflected in the separate country data. In *Burundi*, the government struggled to restart economic growth and control the national budget. It had to introduce controversial measures to mitigate the effects of alarming economic conditions.

Rwanda felt the adverse effects of the drought that hit Eastern Africa, but was able to maintain growth. Despite all the president's plans of previous years, agriculture still remained the mainstay of the economy. The government made important progress in infrastructure development by increasing the number of households connected to electricity to over 35%, from 22% at the end of 2016. Economic performance remained strong, with a GDP growth of 5.1%.

Somalia and *Somaliland* had thriving private sectors but underdeveloped government investments due to a low revenue (tax) base and, in Somalia, insecurity and serious corruption. Somaliland fared better but had little access to global (capital) markets because of its unresolved political status.

Kenya suffered from the serious two-year drought, which sent food prices skyrocketing throughout the country. Alarming incidents of mass corruption, including the plunder of the National Youth Service, also damaged the economy.

Uganda's economy experienced a slowdown in growth, but was deemed basically sound. Various steps were taken towards the much delayed exploitation of oil and natural gas deposits. The country again received more South Sudanese refugees, and others arrived from the DRC.

Tanzania's indicators of macroeconomic performance continued to be good, with a solid 7.1% GDP growth rate. President Magufuli's economic nationalism and continuing severe liquidity problems weakened private sector initiatives, raising worries about a looming economic slowdown, added to by uncertainty over the government's strategic orientation.

The economic policy of the government of *Seychelles* was concerned with achieving more productivity-based growth, beyond tuna fish production and tourism. Several development plans were being implemented or refined.

Comoros registered 3.4% GDP growth, stimulated by government investments in public works (roads and a national hospital) and by private business (the tourism and hospitality sectors). The informal economy was substantial. Inflation was around 3%, but pressure was felt due to the generally high cost of living, including high electricity prices. Cash transfers from the diaspora (mainly in Marseilles, France) amounted to around 25% of GDP.

The socioeconomic situation in *Sudan*, still at war with itself (in Darfur and the Nuba mountains) remained very precarious. High inflation and repeated shortages of basic necessities fuelled social tensions in the capital and the regions. The state budget had a modest deficit and was biased towards the security apparatus at the expense of social services and education. Inflation was the second highest in the sub-region, at 34%. A widespread and acute watery diarrhoea epidemic was estimated to have killed some 1,000 people across the country.

South Sudan continued to experience a deteriorating economic situation, not helped much by slightly improving oil fortunes. Inflation was alarmingly high, at some 182% according to the IMF, but that was 50% less than in 2016 and the national budget was brought under control. The levels of underdevelopment and poverty, aggravated by famine conditions due to armed conflict and predatory activities in several areas, were stark.

Djibouti was affected by prolonged drought conditions, with a dire humanitarian situation for rural people (pastoralists) and some 200,000 people dependent on food aid. State revenues were healthy, due to the re-export business (notably, of course, from Ethiopia) and port fees from foreign bases and donors. The start of the new Djibouti-Ethiopian Railway's regular commercial operation connecting Djibouti's port with Ethiopia's capital Addis Ababa was delayed, but started in December. Some other large infrastructure projects did not progress as expected, either. The country's socio-economic inequality and the rural-urban divide were worrying.

Reliable economic data on *Eritrea* were lacking. The government tried to control all financial transactions by limiting cash transfers, but without providing adequate alternative financial instruments to handle payments. In December, it closed down hundreds of businesses as a punitive measure. The bulk of EU funds granted under the 11th EDF remained unused, for lack of feasible development projects.

Ethiopia's economy continued to grow, although foreign investment and tourism did not recover to the level before the 2016 crisis. Enormous economic and human damage was done by new clashes between ethnic groups erupting on the Oromo-Somali regional border, which led to the death of hundreds of people and hundreds of thousands being displaced.

On the World Bank's *Ease of Doing Business Index*, of 190 countries there were a few changes in the places of Eastern African countries, with Rwanda ranked at a remarkable 41st and Kenya at 80th. Somalia was lowest, on 190th (although doing business for foreigners might be quite difficult, it was not so for Somalis). South Sudan was 187th, Sudan 170th, Ethiopia 161st, Tanzania 137th and Uganda 122nd. Burundi sank again – 7 places, to 164th – the price of political authoritarianism and violent unrest. The report noted that overall a record number of reforms were made in SSA economies, making business easier in 36 of the 48 economies.

Much of the economic growth in the Eastern African region was stimulated by continuing FDI, to the tune of $ 7.5 bn (estimate; data were incomplete). FDI presented a mixed picture, however: there was an overall 4.5% increase over 2016, but it was volatile and unevenly divided, with more FDI inflows into Burundi, Tanzania and Uganda but less into Kenya and Rwanda. Despite its political problems and civil unrest, Ethiopia attracted $ 3.6 bn in FDI, the largest amount in Eastern Africa and second only to Egypt as Africa's prime destination.

While the ICT sector again saw much dynamism, with numerous start-ups and new business applications, an underestimated danger to Eastern African economies was cyber-crime and hacking. Because of their low investment in cyber-security in previous years, banks were particularly vulnerable to this new form of predatory business, but e-commerce operators, mobile service providers and telecom companies were also affected. Countries in the sub-region lost tens of millions each to cyber-crime scams.

Sub-regional Cooperation and Sub-regional Organisations

The *most important sub-regional bodies* in the region, apart from the AU as a continent-wide organisation, were still *IGAD* and the *EAC*.

On 27 March, an IGAD Summit of Regional Heads of State took place in Nairobi, aiming to develop durable solutions for the protracted Somali refugee situation in the Horn (there were 1 m IDPs in Somalia and 900,000 in neighbouring countries). Voluntary country-of-origin resettlement was one option discussed. Representatives of the UNHCR were present at this summit. Another meeting was held on 12–13 June: the 31st Extra-Ordinary Summit of the IGAD Assembly of Heads of State and Government, held in Addis Ababa. It was called by Ethiopia's Prime Minister Hailemariam Dessalegn to address the deteriorating security situation in South Sudan and follow up on the March meeting. It also appointed Ismail Wais (Djibouti) and Mohamed Ali Guyo (Kenya) as as IGAD's Special Envoys to South

Sudan and Somalia, respectively. But South Sudan's President Salva Kiir did not bother to attend. On 29 September, an informal ministerial meeting between EU ministers and IGAD foreign ministers was held in Brussels (Belgium) to discuss the multiple challenges affecting the security, stability and prosperity of the Horn of Africa, ranging from protracted conflicts and transnational crime to irregular migration and poor economic development; it ended with new pledges for better cooperation and new investment plans. The Somalia issue – which again took an inordinate amount of attention from EU and IGAD – was also discussed.

Regarding the EAC (with six member states), it emerged after an April meeting of a subcommittee of ministers of its member countries that a 'political federation' was unlikely to be achieved, and instead it was announced that the aim was to form a transitional 'confederation', i.e. a union of political units for common action in relation to other units. The EAC focused particularly on economic, regulatory and educational harmonisation issues. It was also announced that a common EAC passport would be issued as of January 2018, a year later than planned. On 20 May, during the EAC's 18th ordinary summit in Dar es Salaam, Uganda's President Museveni took over the chairmanship of the EAC from his Tanzanian counterpart John Magufuli, who urged Museveni to continue EAC cost-cutting measures and conclude a good EAC-EU EPA trade deal. A statement by the EAC Secretariat after its meeting in Arusha (Tanzania) on 28 July declared, just before the Rwandan presidential elections, that the EAC attached "... great importance to the promotion of democracy which will in turn guarantee political stability in the region". The head of the EAC's election observation mission to Rwanda said "... we as a Community are keen on free, fair and transparent elections in all the six Partner States". These were encouraging words but they had been heard many times before and had little effect on enhancing a level playing field or free campaigning for the Rwandan elections on 4 August. An article in the November issue of 'Foreign Affairs' even bemoaned the alarming decline of democracy in Eastern Africa, as all countries except two ('partly free') were rated by Freedom House as 'unfree'.

The *East African Legislative Assembly* (EALA), the 54-seat parliamentary/legislative body of the EAC founded on 28 November 2001 and based in Arusha, was not much in the news, but met several times, including in May. Among the bills approved were the EAC Community Youth Council Bill and the EAC Cross Border Trade in Professional Services Bill. An EALA committee also conducted public hearings on the EAC Sexual and Reproductive Health and Rights Bill in five member countries: Kenya, Uganda, Tanzania, Burundi and Rwanda. The five-year term of the EALA ended this year, and on 18 December the 4th Assembly was inaugurated after Kenya had offered its selection of new candidates (voted via the parliaments of the member states), the last country to do so. An EALA MP would receive a $ 13,500 monthly salary.

The *Eastern Africa Standby Force* (EASF), the regional force under the AU's African Peace and Security Architecture (APSA) umbrella, and composed of military, police and civilians mandated to enhance peace and security in the Eastern Africa region, held various mission planning courses, a field training exercise at Gebeit military base in eastern Sudan, and other events. Personnel were drawn from ten member states. It did not become fully operational and was not deployed during the year in any conflict in the sub-region.

Cooperation agreements between Eastern African countries and the EU and other donor partners continued relatively high levels of donor assistance, training and funding. Apart from already existing agreements (periodically renewed), the EU strengthened aid for employment investment schemes in Eastern Africa and kept up security cooperation.

The various other political-economic institutions in the Eastern African sub-region, including COMESA, ICGLR, IOC and IOAR, held meetings and events but these were generally of too little importance and impact to be discussed here. COMESA held its 37th Council of Ministers meeting on 3–4 November in Lusaka (Zambia), focusing, among other things, on a road map for deepening integration through the consolidation of the Free Trade Area, development of infrastructure, agriculture and industry, climate change adaptation and mitigation, gender mainstreaming and establishment of the Customs Union. Burundi had offered to organise the COMESA summit in Bujumbura in October, but COMESA Secretary-General Sindiso Ngwenya said the organisation rejected the offer because there was a "lack of an adequate vehicle pool, no relevant infrastructure and no reliable Internet infrastructure".

Continued *disagreements persisted on the use of the Nile waters*. Ethiopia (supported by Sudan) did not reach agreement with Egypt on the central issue of the impact of the Ethiopian Grand Renaissance mega-dam, which would decisively affect the water levels of the Nile and damage Egypt, especially while the huge reservoir in Ethiopia was being filled. No consensus was reached. A meeting of ministers of Egypt, Ethiopia and Sudan on 11 November in Cairo failed to approve an introductory report produced by the jointly selected French engineering consultants BRL Group and Artelia on the dam's effects on Egypt and Sudan; it appeared this time that Ethiopia and Sudan rejected it. Egypt's President Abd el-Fattah al-Sisi said again on 18 November that "... water to us is a question of national security.... a matter of life or death". A proposal by Egypt to Ethiopia on 26 December that the World Bank be asked to be involved in technical discussions/evaluations on the possible impact of the dam was not accepted. At a meeting of the *Nile Basin Initiative* (NBI) on 22 June in Entebbe (Uganda), Ethiopia had taken over the leadership of the NBI from Uganda. It would chair both the Nile Council of Ministers and the Nile Technical Advisory Committee of the NBI for the next year. On 18 July, the

EU announced it would allocate a grant of $ 15.8 m to the NBI for the stimulation of cooperation and the generation of data and information to sustainably manage and use the transboundary waters. On 23–25 October, the 5th Nile Basin Development Forum met in Kigali (Rwanda) for a kind of science and policy dialogue under the title 'Investing in Nile cooperation for a water-secure future', but no political decisions were taken there.

Burundi

Tomas van Acker

Compared with the previous two years, 2017 was a transition year for the CNDD-FDD government. The violence triggered by President Nkurunziza's pursuit of a third presidential term in 2015 had significantly scaled down. As Nkurunziza had both contained internal party dissidence and suppressed or side-lined various pockets of civic, political and armed opposition, the government and ruling CNDD-FDD elite started looking ahead again. Preparations for the long announced constitutional reform and the 2020 elections were the most notable indications of this shift. This is not to say that the crisis was over. The political landscape remained marked by severe tensions between the CNDD-FDD and the various opposition outfits. Political violence, while less intensive, continued to occur. The government had to introduce controversial measures to mitigate the effects of alarming economic conditions. And relations with Rwanda, Belgium, the EU and the UN remained fraught with tension.

 | DOI:10.1163/9789004367630_031

Domestic Politics

President Pierre Nkurunziza's efforts since the 2015 crisis to *re-establish order* in the ruling party and in the broader political environment proved successful. He consolidated the power of his loyalist networks of former rebel commanders within the 'Conseil National pour la Défense de la Démocratie – Forces de Défense de la Démocratie' (CNDD-FDD). The ability of these networks to deploy both the state's security apparatus and militant members of the party's own 'imbonerakure' (those who see from far) youth league, remained a key element in the party's power strategy. This resulted in *increased levels of control* over the state's institutions and over public life. With the CNDD-FDD's patronage system – one of its prime pillars of power – under pressure from adverse economic conditions, the party's legitimation and mobilisation strategies increasingly relied on *rhetoric and propaganda*. Throughout the country, up to the hill level (the smallest administrative entity), the CNDD-FDD spared no efforts to promote narratives that sought to delegitimise both its domestic and external adversaries, while highlighting the party's role as an instrument of 'divine will' and its historical struggle as a 'liberation movement'. These propaganda activities were coupled with the policy of participating alongside the population in the manual execution of public works.

Opposition parties continued to face the challenges imposed by the post-2015 context. The combination of administrative repression and violent intimidation made it impossible for most *opposition parties and politicians* to operate normally inside Burundi and publicly mobilise their members. With most of the important opposition parties either in exile, or split between a de facto popular wing and a de jure wing sympathetic to the CNDD-FDD, they had little impact on major domestic political proceedings. Despite facing similar challenges, there was little cooperation between the various opposition groups. In reaction to the incessant persecution of his followers, Agathon Rwasa, the unrecognised de facto leader of the biggest opposition group, the 'Forces Nationales de Libération' (FNL), which had seats in parliament as a member of the '*Amizero* y'Abarundi' coalition, took a more militant stance towards the government, but with little effect. The 'Conseil National pour le Respect de l'Accord d'Arusha et l'Etat de Droit' (CNARED), the platform of opposition parties and politicians in exile after the 2015 upheavals, started the year with an internal crisis. Several members who had not respected the platform's call to boycott talks in January with Benjamin Mkapa, the Tanzanian facilitator of the EAC-led mediation process (see below), were suspended. On 28 February, Charles Nditije, from the 'Union pour le Progrès National' (UPRONA) wing opposing the government, was elected to chair the platform. He succeeded Jean Minani ('Front for Democracy in *Burundi*' [FRODEBU] Niyakuri), who was in turn re-elected as chairman in November.

The *mediation initiatives* launched in response to the 2015 crisis did not manage to achieve a breakthrough. The main EAC-led process continued to suffer from a lack of credibility. Two sessions – the third and fourth round of talks – were organised in Arusha (Tanzania) in February and December. Facilitator Benjamin Mkapa was not able to find common ground. He was accused by CNARED of partiality after having stated in 2016 that Nkurunziza's third presidential term was not up for discussion. Nevertheless, CNARED participated in February. The most important stumbling block in this process was the government's constant refusal to share the table with CNARED as a political bloc. In February, the government withdrew its representatives just before the start of the session, claiming that it could not accept talking with people whom it deemed responsible for the 2015 failed coup d'état. In an attempt to break the deadlock, a two-day consultative meeting was organised in Helsinki in August by the Finnish NGO Crisis Management Initiative. While the government itself was not officially represented at this meeting, a CNDD-FDD delegation, led by ombudsman Edouard Nshimirimana, did talk with CNARED and opposition activists persecuted by the Burundian judiciary. However, this did not bring about a new dynamic. In December, Mkapa was again faced with the various parties' cemented positions, which made any meaningful progress impossible. With discussions focused on the modalities of the talks, pressing issues such as the constitutional reform initiative, the refugee crisis and the possibilities for opposition actors to be politically active in Burundi in view of the 2020 elections, were not properly dealt with. In the meantime, the chief mediator, Uganda's President Museveni, had expressed his disagreement with the EU sanctions against Burundi, which raised questions of his neutrality and further undermined the credibility of the process.

The preparations that were launched for the *process of constitutional reform* constituted a major source of tension between Nkurunziza loyalists and the opposition. The trajectory of popular consultations that was launched by the government and overseen by the National Commission for the Inter-Burundian Dialogue in response to the 2015 crisis came to an end. Media reports and testimonies from participants suggested that this process and its outcomes were tightly controlled by the authorities. An official account of all the findings of the consultation process was not made public. However, when on 12 May the Commission presented its final report to President Nkurunziza, its chairman declared that the need to amend the Constitution had emerged as a major proposition and that a majority of the participants had been in favour of doing away with presidential term limits. Opposition groups and activists, who objected that the outcome of the consultations had been orchestrated, argued that the political and security climate was not suitable to conduct a process of constitutional change. This was also the position of the EAC facilitator Mkapa and many of Burundi's international partners. It became clear that, rather than an uncertain parliamentary procedure, which had been unsuccessfully tried in 2014, the president preferred the *organisation of a referendum* so that the revision would be validated by the population.

In October, the commission appointed to draft the revised constitution presented its work to the council of ministers. While a draft bill detailing all the revisions was not published, news emerged that 77 articles would be revised. Among the most important proposed changes was the stipulation of a *seven-year presidential term limit* instead of the current five-year term, renewable once. In addition, the position of second vice president would be scrapped, and a prime minister, coming from the presidential party, would become head of the government. There were no indications that the proposed revisions would touch on the quota underpinning the ethnic power sharing provisions introduced by the Arusha Agreement. However, the absence of a publicly available draft bill reinforced fears among Nkurunziza's opponents that the spirit of the Arusha Agreement, which had brought ethnic peace to Burundi, could be eroded by the proposed amendments. On 12 December, Nkurunziza officially launched the preparations for the referendum, to be held in May 2018, warning that anyone who posed an obstacle to this process would be crossing a red line. The mandate of the Independent Electoral Commission (CENI) was extended, to prepare voter enrolment for both the 2018 referendum and the 2020 elections.

With the government and elected institutions halfway through their five-year mandates, the 2020 elections also appeared on the agenda. In addition to the CENI's voter enrolment, another measure taken by the government that aroused much controversy was the introduction of *citizen contributions to the funding of the 2020 elections*. With the 2015 crisis in mind, the government did not anticipate receiving much external funding from donors' electoral assistance programmes, but the measure was also in tune with the CNDD-FDD's rhetoric on the need to resist what it deemed neo-colonial meddling in sovereign matters by donors. The framework for these contributions from the population remained very vague. Introduced in August by the president, they were initially presented as a voluntary patriotic civil duty. However, on 11 December, the ministers of interior and finance issued an 'ordonnance', in which the exact amounts to be contributed were defined for various professional categories. In the case of civil servants, the contributions would be deducted from their salaries. For the highest income categories in the public sector, the contribution amounted to one month's salary. According to governance watchdogs and unions, these levies fell outside the regular taxation framework and amounted to a new levy on the population (see below). Citizens also questioned the voluntary nature of the contributions, as records were to be kept of those who did not comply.

Levels and frequency of *political violence* were less intense than in previous years, but there were, nevertheless, several violent incidents. On 1 January, Minister of Environment and Urban Development Emmanuel Niyonkuru, who was not considered a regime hardliner, was assassinated in Bujumbura in unclear circumstances.

During the night of 23 January, Mukoni barracks, in the Muyinga province, was attacked by a small group of unknown assailants. No one claimed responsibility, but it led to the arrest of dozens of military personnel and civilians. While the government claimed it was a criminal act rather than an attack against the army base per se, several elements of the former 'Forces Armées Burundaises' (FAB; the pre-Arusha Tutsi-dominated national army) from the base and from other regions were prosecuted in the weeks following the event. This was for several observers a further indication of divisions within the army, which had surfaced during the 2015 failed coup. These prosecutions prompted accusations by Burundian and international human rights groups of ethnic cleansing in the army.

The various attempts at *armed resistance* that had emerged after the failed coup in 2015 were not consolidated. Important divisions remained, both between and within the various groups, affecting their striking capacity and their credibility among Burundian constituencies opposed to the CNDD-FDD regime. The three groups, 'Résistance pour un État de Droit' (RED)-Tabara, 'Forces Républicaines du Burundi' (FOREBU) and 'Forces Nationales de Libération' (FNL)-Nzabampema, were mainly based in the South Kivu province of the neighbouring DRC. While it was difficult to attribute the recurring violent incidents to particular actors, it was clear that none of the three armed opposition groups were able to mount larger scale offensive operations inside Burundi. RED-Tabara, the group born out of the urban contestation movement and linked to the leadership of the Movement for Solidarity and Democracy, lost much of its momentum and was eclipsed by FOREBU, which consisted mainly of dissident Burundian military personnel who had organised themselves after the 2015 failed coup. In its August report, the UN Group of Experts on armed groups in the DRC stated that several RED-Tabara members had defected to FOREBU. The latter, according to the same report, was under the political guidance of Hussain Rajabu. FOREBU also recruited among Burundian refugees in the Lusenda camp in the DRC's South Kivu province. On 27 August, Jérémie Ntiranyibagira announced that FOREBU had changed its name to the 'Forces Populaires du Burundi' (FPB), and that a new leadership had been put in place. Ntiranyibagira replaced Godefroid Niyombare as leader of the new formation, with Edouard Nshimirimana second in command, in charge of operations. A spokesperson gave the reason for these changes as political differences between the various leaders. Niyombare, who had led the May 2015 failed coup attempt, denied that FOREBU had changed its name but confirmed the split. On 23 October, the FPB announced that Ntiranyibariga and Nshimirimana, with the other cadres, had disappeared in Tanzania and had been extradited to Burundi. There was no confirmation from the Tanzanian or Burundian authorities, and no further information about their fate.

On several occasions, combatants of the FNL faction led by Aloys Nzabempema, which had its bases in the Rusizi plain and the mountains of South Kivu in DRC, confronted the Burundian armed forces during their regular cross-border incursions into Burundian territory. Casualties were reported during incidents with the group around Gihanga, in the Rukoko forest reserve in Bubanza province, on 7 April and 16 May. An armed attack on 15 August against the convoy of the governor of Bubanza, who escaped unhurt, was also attributed to the FNL-Nzabampma.

Throughout the year and at various locations in the country, dead bodies, sometimes bound, were discovered on the streets, in gutters, in bushes and in rivers. In several cases, rights groups condemned the lack of proper investigation. There were regular armed attacks on opposition members, but a number of ruling party youth league activists were also killed. During December, a series of *hand grenade attacks* took place in several districts of the capital. In rural Burundi, too, there were several fatal incidents involving hand grenades. In most cases, the responsibility and motives behind these attacks remained unclear.

As in 2016, the *human rights situation* continued to cause severe tensions between the Burundian government and the UN. Several reports showed the same patterns of violent repression of various forms of political dissidence that had been seen in previous years. Intimidation, arrests, disappearances and killings of opposition party supporters were noted throughout the year. Again, FNL militants loyal to Agathon Rwasa were the prime targets. In many cases, they were accused of holding illegal political meetings. The few independent civil society organisations and human rights activists that remained in the country after 2015 continued to be vulnerable to persecution. In June, three local members of the NGO 'Parole et Actions pour le Réveil des Consciences et l'Evolution des Mentalités' (PARCEM) were detained in Muramvya province. In July, Germain Rukiki of the Association of Catholic Jurists of Burundi was arrested in Bujumbura. On 21 November, Nestor Nibitanga, associated with the 'Association Burundaise pour la Protection des Droits Humains', was arrested in Gitega. Several cases of 'popular justice' were recorded, in which often extremely disproportionate punishments were inflicted for petty crimes.

In a report presented to the UNSC in February, UN Secretary General A. Guterres denounced the persistence of human rights violations and deplored the *lack of will to investigate violations* on the part of the security services and 'imbonerakure'. The Burundian government rejected the report, authored by Jamal Benomar, the secretary general's special representative, whose replacement had been requested by Bujumbura in 2016. In September, the Commission of Inquiry on Burundi mandated by the UN Human Rights Council (UNHRC) in 2016 to follow up on previous investigations, presented its final report. Members of the Commission, presided over by Fatsah Ouguergouz, had been declared persona non grata and denied access to Burundi. Neither the Burundian government, despite its membership of the UNHRC, nor Burundi's official National Independent Human Rights Commission had replied favourably to the Commission's requests for cooperation, which collected much of its information among the Burundian refugee population in the region. After investigating human rights violations since April 2015, it noted the persistence of extrajudicial executions, arbitrary arrests and detentions, enforced disappearances, torture and cruel, inhuman or degrading treatment and sexual violence. It held the highest authorities of the state responsible and concluded that the abuses it had documented could qualify as *crimes against humanity* and therefore called for these alleged violations to be further investigated by the ICC, of which Burundi no longer wished to be member (see below). Unsurprisingly, this report was rejected by the Burundian government, too. Following the presentation of the report during the 36th session of the UNHRC in Geneva, *two resolutions on Burundi* were adopted. One, presented by the group of African countries, was supportive of Bujumbura's rejection of the report, and called for a new investigation, in cooperation with the Burundian government. It asked that cases of violations be treated by Burundian judicial institutions rather than being referred to the ICC. The second, backed by EU countries, called for a one-year extension of the mandate of the Commission of Inquiry. This much displeased the Burundian government, whose spokesperson stated that it would only allow UN experts on Burundian territory to provide technical assistance to the Burundian judiciary, not to investigate alleged crimes by themselves.

The *Truth and Reconciliation Commission* (TRC) was operational throughout the year. However, one year before the end of its mandate, only modest progress had been made. In addition to the collection of existing documents related to mass crimes, and work on the management of historical mass graves, TRC agents collected depositions in a limited number of communes and provinces. Its chairman, Mgr Nahimana, stated that by November, the TRC had worked in about half of the country's provinces and faced constraints in terms of both time and resources. Local observers reported that, in many places, there was only limited awareness of the TRC's work, and that the locally recruited agents in charge of the collection of testimonies did not always inspire confidence.

Several credible reports indicated an increased presence of *local 'imbonerakure'* divisions in the public sphere. These groups were implicated in various human rights violations. Despite strong international criticism and pressure, the 'imbonerakure' operated with growing self-confidence. On several occasions, they formally performed security duties in the public sphere. At a rally in Bujumbura, they publicly warned that they would retaliate if protests occurred again. They also played an increasingly important role as party vanguards, as shown in videos that surfaced on social media, where 'imbonerakure' members propagated the CNDD-FDD's narrative on the political crisis. The often-polarising language and songs they used on these public occasions were interpreted as hate speech and as calls to violence by many Burundians and observers.

Another issue that saw little progress was the *refugee crisis* caused by the 2015 unrest. By the end of the year, UNHCR reported that 428,531 Burundian refugees were registered in the region, the vast majority of whom had fled after the 2015 violence. While there was a campaign to repatriate refugees and there were significant return movements, other Burundians continued to flee, although at a considerably slower rate than in the previous two years. Aid agencies warned that support programmes for Burundian refugees remained seriously underfunded. On 15 September, at least 36 Burundian refugees, members of the persecuted Zebiya sect, were shot by soldiers of the Armed Forces of the DRC in the Congolese border town of Kamanyola, when a demonstration by refugees demanding the release of four members of their group arrested earlier got out of hand.

Foreign Affairs

Burundi's *diplomatic relations with key neighbours and important bilateral and multilateral partners continued to be tense* and marked by hostile rhetoric. The CNDD-FDD staged several mass demonstrations against the EU, Belgium and Rwanda, which it identified as the major sources of instability in Burundi and as a threat to the nation's sovereignty. The above-mentioned UN reports on the human rights situation, which the Burundian government dismissed as informed by a desire for regime change, produced a similar response. Apart from the rhetoric and propaganda, in some cases the Burundian government followed up with specific measures. After an earlier expression of distrust in 2016, it urgently demanded the replacement of the UN secretary general's special adviser Jamal Benomar, who was in charge of the UN's efforts to resolve the Burundi crisis. In April, the Burkinabé diplomat Michel Kafando was appointed to replace Benomar, to the satisfaction of both the Burundian government and the opposition. In a last-minute decision on 10 November, the Burundian authorities withdrew permission for the Belgian Embassy to organise its 'Belgian Week' festive and cultural activities in Bujumbura, which was widely interpreted as a further indication of the strained relationship between Bujumbura and Brussels.

On 23 October, the EU Council renewed for another year the *sanctions* it had put in place against four persons: three Burundian security officials involved in the repression of the 2015 protests and one dissident general implicated in the May 2015 failed coup attempt.

Amongst Burundi's neighbours in the region, both *Tanzania and Uganda* – countries that were hosting large Burundian refugee populations – showed support for Nkurunziza. In his inaugural speech on 20 May as new chairman of the EAC, Uganda's President Museveni – also chief mediator in the Burundi crisis on behalf of the EAC – spoke out clearly against the sanctions the EU had put in place, stating that approval of the EPA regional trade agreement hinged on lifting these sanctions. Relations with the *DRC* remained stable, despite an accidental confrontation between the two armies that had occurred when the 'Forces Démocratiques Nouvelles' were conducting an operation against Burundian rebels on Congolese territory late 2016. In July, Minister of Security Bunyoni was sent on a mission to Kinshasa, with the aim of brokering a deal with the DRC's President Kabila that would allow the Burundian armed forces to carry out operations against Burundian rebels on DRC territory. The group of experts noted the alleged implication of Burundian military personnel in arms smuggling operations in the Rusizi border area, which benefitted Mai-Mai fighters.

Relations with *Rwanda* remained strained. The Burundian government continued to blame Rwandan authorities for supporting and sheltering the plotters of the 2015 coup attempt and leaders of the armed opposition. In March, five Burundian MPs of the East African Legislative Assembly refused to join a meeting of that body in Kigali, citing security risks. In April, Burundi refused to let a WFP aid convoy enter the country from Rwanda, also on the pretext of possible security risks.

On the other hand, there were indications that *international actors* who had in previous years openly opposed Nkurunziza's third term and issued sanctions were adopting a more 'Realpolitik' approach when it became clear that Nkurunziza and the CNDD-FDD had been able to consolidate their power after the 2015 crisis. This change of attitude was perhaps most visible in the presence of various ambassadors and embassy representatives at the inauguration of the highly controversial constitutional reform process on 12 December.

On 27 October, the one-year period following Burundi's notification of its withdrawal from the Rome Statute came to an end, making Burundi the first nation to effectively leave the *ICC*. Regime supporters widely celebrated this move, which was in line with the government's position against what it deemed a hostile international order, complicit in the 2015 attempt at regime change. However, on 25 October, the day before Burundi's withdrawal from the ICC came into effect, the pre-trial Chamber of the ICC had authorised prosecutor Fatou Bensouda to start a 'proprio motu' investigation for alleged crimes against humanity committed by state agents and groups working on behalf of the state in Burundi between 26 April 2015 and 26 October 2017.

Socioeconomic Developments

Burundi's economy remained plagued by structural problems as well as by the consequences of the 2015 crisis and the aid sanctions that were imposed. *Economic growth stalled*, but picked up (0.5%) from two previous years of negative growth. Significant foreign currency shortages impacted on all levels of the economy, and drastically restricted imports. As in the previous years, this caused regular and long-lasting *fuel shortages*, resulting in severe problems for the transport sector in the capital, and also impacting on the cost of living and prompting speculative and parallel market practices. Imports and prices of medicines were also affected.

Inflation was high at 16.6 %, up more than 200% since 2016, and prices of several commodities skyrocketed, especially during the first months of the year. The government introduced a three-month de-taxation of certain staple foods from May to July and food prices had started to drop by the end of the year. The *problems in the energy sector* were also very tangible for Burundian families and economic operators. In addition to the regular power outages, the cost of electricity rose substantially. The state-owned provider REGIDESO explained this as a result of the purchase of electricity from a private supplier of thermal power to make up for the structural deficits in energy production. On the parallel market, exchange rates for the euro and dollar reached previously unseen heights.

The national *budget*, amounting to approximately $ 778 m, remained under pressure, with donor budget support programmes still on hold. The budget deficit was equal to 8.2% of GDP.

The government tried to mitigate the situation with *austerity measures and increased domestic revenue generation*. Again, these measures directly impacted the population, in the countryside as well as in the capital. Several new taxes were introduced, often on an ad-hoc basis. Civil servants in particular were expected to make various contributions for local public infrastructural works. In some cases, such as in the province of Kayanza, new taxes were imposed to pay for otherwise free administrative services to the population. The reform of the scholarship system for university students, which became a scholarship loan rather than an unconditional allowance, led to protests in the student community at Burundi University. Several students were arrested. On 13 December, the 2018 budget of $ 790.5 m was adopted by parliament. Austerity measures were maintained, and it was (unrealistically) foreseen that 81% of finance would come from internal revenue generation.

The economic crisis was aggravated by a severe *drought* and crop destruction by rains and pests. *Chronic malnutrition* remained the most pressing public health issue. In January, the government and the UN launched a humanitarian response plan for 3 m people in urgent need of assistance. In terms of public health, the year was also marked by a severe *malaria* epidemic, declared by the Ministry of Health on 13 March. Some 6.4 m cases were recorded, with a particularly high prevalence in the Northern and Eastern provinces, were many people contracted malaria several times during the year. The Ministry of Health reported 3,235 deaths from the disease. The outbreak, which had already started in 2015, and which public health activists claimed was declared too late, was contained by December. About 4,000 people had died from it. In October, the Global Fund, citing underperformance and poor financial management as reasons, announced that it would no longer entrust the management of its $ 72.3 m budget for 2018–20 to the Ministry of Health, but would instead redirect the funds through UNDP.

A number of major *economic projects* were announced. In Kabezi, Bujumbura Rural Province, the British company Rainbow Rare Earths launched its Gakara mining project, which it claimed had one of the highest grade rare earth deposits globally. Civil society watchdogs raised concerns regarding the Burundian government's lack of transparency in dealing with foreign mining companies. A presidential decree identified the site for the creation of a Special Economic Zone (SEZ), and a memorandum was signed with a private enterprise to develop the site. The SEZ would be constructed in the commune of Mutimbuzi, Bujumbura Rural Province. Close to both the airport and the border with the DRC, it was also one of the most chronically insecure places in Burundi. Other major economic projects that were announced included the renovation of the port of Bujumbura, in cooperation with the government of Japan.

Comoros

Simon Massey

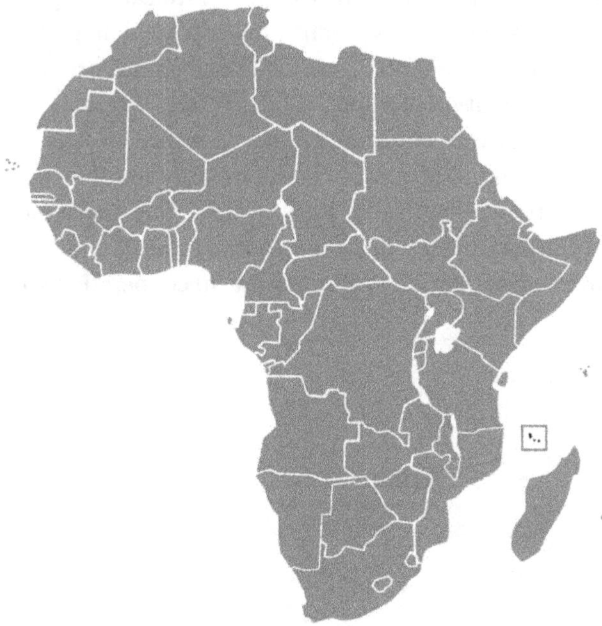

In his first full year in office since being re-elected president, Colonel Azali Assoumani drew on his political experience to consolidate his rule at home and renew relationships with bilateral partners and international organisations. A former coup leader, he had previously served as president of the Committee of State between 1999 and 2002, and then as president of the Union of Comoros between 2002 and 2006. Beyond short-term policies to drive down the high cost of living, the new government determined that Comoros should aim to become an 'emerging economy'. This goal influenced both domestic and foreign policy. Assoumani indicated that his government would be willing to consider revising the constitutional mechanism of the rotating presidency that he had introduced in 2002. In terms of foreign relations, Assoumani prioritised cooperation with France, whilst cementing relations with Saudi Arabia as Comoros's principal partner in the Islamic world.

Domestic Politics

Assoumani's priority was to be seen as delivering on the promises made during the presidential campaign, notably his *pledge to lower the cost of living*, and policies

 | DOI:10.1163/9789004367630_032

to cut the price to the consumer of electricity, gas, fuel and public transport were maintained. More fundamentally, he expressed the need for the government to adopt policies aimed at turning Comoros into an 'emerging economy'. The deeper reforms to the economy needed to realise this ambition, including the privatisation of state assets, required cross-party and inter-island support, as well as increased FDI and support from donors.

Driving forward reforms was undermined by the weak representation of Asoumani's party, the 'Convention pour le Renouveau des Comores' (CRC) in the *National Assembly*. The electoral cycle dictated that legislative elections be held a year before the presidential polls, but the 2015 elections had resulted in a fragmented National Assembly in which the CRC held only two out of 24 seats. The largest party, with eight seats, was the 'Union pour le Développement des Comores' (UPDC), the party of the previous president, Ikililou Dhoinine. The other main party, with seven seats, was 'Juwa' (meaning 'sun' in Shikomori), the party of Ahmed Sambi, who had held the presidency between 2006 and 2011. Sambi's support for Assoumani in the second round of the presidential elections was instrumental in his winning a close-run race and Juwa were rewarded with four posts in the government, including the Ministries of Justice and Foreign Affairs.

On 17 June a *cabinet reshuffle* replaced three Juwa members with Assoumani allies (the other Juwa member would be replaced later in the year), signalling an end to the alliance between Juwa and the CRC, and reigniting the *rivalry between Sambi and Assoumani.* One factor behind the breakdown of the alliance was the response of Sambi and Juwa to Assoumani's decision to sever diplomatic relations with Qatar. This decision was instigated by the dispute between Qatar and a Saudi-led coalition of Gulf States. The coalition lobbied Islamic-majority states in Africa to break diplomatic relations with Qatar and Assoumani acquiesced, but the decision to split with Qatar was severely criticised by Sambi and the outgoing minister of justice and defeated presidential candidate, Fahmi Said Ibrahim. The replacement of the four Juwa cabinet members proved a further obstacle to the government's legislative programme, with each new vote requiring the construction of a discrete alliance with the six parties and three independents represented in the National Assembly.

The *divided nature of Comorian politics* remained unchanged, explained by the chronic instability within the three islands of the Union stemming from an underlying ambivalence towards a shared Comorian national identity. Having first come to power following a coup d'état in 1999, Assoumani sought to address the enduring tendency towards separatism, or even re-attachment to France, on the part of Nzwani and Mwali by redrafting the Constitution to reassure the populations of the smaller islands by rotating the presidency every five years. The Comoros had endured over 20 coups d'état since independence from France in 1975 but, although the political instability continued, there had not been a successful coup since the introduction of the rotating presidency.

Throughout the year, however, there were indications that Assoumani, the architect of the *rotating presidency*, now considered the constitutional mechanism to have outlived its original purpose, the implication being that institutional stability was now embedded and secure. Formalising the break with Juwa, Minister of the Interior Mohamed Daoud confirmed that "revision of the rotating presidency and, hence, the Constitution is a possibility". Assoumani and other government spokespersons hinted that the continuity and quality of governance required to achieve the ambition of 'emerging economy' status was being held up by the wholesale change of government every five years as required by the existing constitutional mechanism.

Personal political aspirations also played a role in the mounting constitutional debate. If the current arrangement were to be revised, it would potentially allow Assoumani to stand for a further term as president. It would also upset the ambitions of politicians from Nzwani, including Sambi and other Juwa politicians, whose turn it would be to supply the president should the rotating presidency be retained.

The CRC lobbied the smaller parties for their support for constitutional reform in advance of a possible vote in the National Assembly. However, potentially the most influential instrument for progressing the reform of the rotating presidency was the Comorian national conference, the *assises nationales comoriennes*, a week-long national forum planned to open on 4 February 2018. This wide-ranging exercise in consultation had been proposed by civil society groups in 2014, but only received support from the government after the presidential election. Assoumani indicated that he would accept any policy recommendations made by the national conference since, "we must think of the future and the legacy that we will leave for our children". However, an alliance of opposition politicians accused him of seeking to take advantage of the conference to further his own agenda, notably the reform of the rotating presidency. This accusation was rejected by Assoumani, who pointed to the marginal role played by the CRC in the Steering Committee for the National Conference, the 'Commission de Pilotage des Assises Nationales' (CPAN), and that the functioning of the CPAN was under the observation of representatives from the international community, including the UN, the AU and the Arab League.

The importance of the *Comorian diaspora*, and notably the large Comorian community living in Marseilles, was underlined by a visit to the city by Assoumani while he was attending the One Planet climate change summit in Paris in mid-December. Assoumani described Marseilles, home to an estimated 80–100,000 people of Comorian descent, as the "biggest town in Comoros", expressing an intention to open an official Comorian consulate in the city. The World Bank estimated that remittances from the diaspora amount to about 21% of overall GDP and, whilst the diaspora were not yet able to vote directly in elections, political funding from diaspora sources was playing an increasing role in Comorian politics.

Foreign Affairs

As the former colonial power, *France* continued to be Comoros's most important economic, political and cultural partner. Yet, despite the closeness of the ties between the two countries – with about 100–150,000 Comorians resident in France, the French treasury guaranteeing the Comorian franc, and a defence treaty between the two countries – the question of whether the archipelago's fourth island, Mayotte, was Comorian or French remained seemingly intractable. From the Comorian perspective, France had reneged on the original rules of the Independence referendum in 1974 and opted to retain control of Mayotte. Since 2011, Mayotte had been a full department of the French republic. Moreover, since 1995, France had severely restricted visas for Comorians, leading to a crisis involving tens of thousands of migrants making the perilous sea crossing every year, many motivated by much higher living standards on Mayotte, but others simply seeking to visit family. Large-scale immigration from the other three islands of the archipelago was held by the native population of Mayotte to be responsible for critical pressure on the island's social services and for a steep rise in crime and insecurity.

The issue of irregular *migration from Comoros to Mayotte* was generally relatively under-reported in France. However, it made the headlines following a joke in bad taste made by the new French President Emmanuel Macron on 4 June. Overheard talking about categories of boats whilst visiting a sea rescue centre in Brittany, Macron remarked that "'kwassa kwassa' [the small fishing craft used to transport migrants in Comoros] don't do much fishing; they carry Comorians". Given the high death toll related to irregular migration between Nzwani and Mayotte, this remark was taken by many to be insensitive. Demonstrations by Comorian expatriates took place in France and Comoros, whilst Minister of Foreign Affairs Mohamed Bacar Dossar called for an apology. However, in an indication of the need to retain close relations with France, Assoumani later stated that the "hatchet had been buried" and that "this kind of clumsiness can happen". In December, Assoumani, together with his ministers for agriculture and foreign affairs, met Macron in Paris during the climate change summit, to discuss increasing trade and investment between France and Comoros.

A significant part of the sixth Comoros-France Joint Commission held in Moroni in mid-December was devoted to negotiating a 'roadmap' towards revision of the *visa arrangements* between Comoros and Mayotte/France. However, Assoumani's adoption of a pragmatic approach to the Mayotte impasse was underlined by a final declaration of the Commission, which prioritised deeper cooperation between the two countries rather than stressing the visa issue. The Joint Commission was also historic in that, for the first time since the establishment of an independent Comoros, the French delegation included two deputies and a senator from Mayotte. One of the deputies, Mansour Kamardine, a forthright supporter of maintaining a strict visa regime between Comoros and Mayotte, declared that "now is the time to start a virtuous circle towards the resolution of the territorial dispute", whilst accepting that "the full recognition by our neighbours and Comorian friends that Mayotte is French will take time".

Comoros's long-standing open-door policy, which had sought to maintain good relations across a spectrum of partners, was further eroded following the diplomatic *split with Qatar*. In January 2016, under pressure from Saudi Arabia, the Dhoinine government had officially severed diplomatic relations with Iran. In June 2017, the shift towards support for Saudi Arabia and its allies was further underlined by Assoumani's decision to sever relations with Qatar. Comoros also joined the Saudi-sponsored Islamic Military Alliance against Terrorism (IMAT). Attending a meeting of IMAT in Riyadh in late November, Minister of Defence Yousouf Mohamed Ali stated that Comoros stood "by Saudi Arabia in its declared positions against these groups and militias, including 'Hezbollah' and Iran's activity in conflict zones … we have clearly stated that we are severing our relations with Qatar". In a later interview, Assoumani candidly accepted that Comoros did not have the political muscle to equivocate between Saudi Arabia and Qatar and so had chosen to support the former, "a partner country for more than 40 years".

In mid-August, Comoros was admitted as the 16th member of *SADC* at the organisation's heads of state and government summit in Pretoria (South Africa). Enthusiasm on the part of the government for membership of an organisation that included the regional powerhouse South Africa was tempered by the scepticism of the Comorian business community. With Comoros already a member of COMESA, business leaders complained that the free trade provisions of that organisation had not in practice been applied in Comoros, and they remained unconvinced that the anticipated economic and financial benefits of SADC membership would materialise.

Socioeconomic Developments

Economic growth rose from a revised 2.2% in 2016 to an estimated 2.6%. This slight rise resulted from improvements in the supply of electricity, notably through the construction of new generators, as well as the commencement, albeit troubled, of competition in the telecoms sector.

The revised *inflation* rate for 2016 was 1.8%. The increase in oil prices throughout 2016–17 led to the inflation rate rising to an estimated 2.2% in 2017. In an interview with 'Al Watwan' newspaper, Governor of the 'Banque Centrale des Comores' (BCC) Younoussa Imani emphasised lower household costs for utilities, staple foods and telecoms as restraining factors on the rate of inflation. He cautioned, however, that the BCC's calculation of the inflation rate was restricted to prices in greater Moroni.

In February, the inauguration by Assoumani of an *electricity* plant on Ngazidja at Vwadju, the country's first industrial zone, raised hopes that decades of intermittent mains electricity might be at an end. The generating equipment, supplied by Caterpillar Power Systems, had the capacity to generate 18 MW of electricity 24 hours a day, enough to satisfy Ngazidja's current needs, estimated at 13 MW. The project cost CF (franc) 7 bn. Enhancement of the generation and supply of electricity on Nzwani and Mwali was also included in the project. In August, it was announced that the Abu Dhabi Fund for Development had agreed to fund a CF 4 bn project to install further Caterpillar generator sets, as well as new electricity transformers and medium- and low-voltage cables to upgrade the country's power grid across the archipelago.

Governor Imani of the BCC emphasised the importance of a reliable electricity supply for economic development, calling attention to the additional 1,600 new subscribers who had joined the national utility company, 'Gestion de l'Eau et de l'Electricité aux Comores' (MAMWE) since the completion of the new plant. He further claimed that dependable electricity meant that "the queues in front of workshops and bakeries caused by load shedding have disappeared" and that, in rural areas, numerous small industries involved in food processing had been revitalised.

However, potentially the most significant development in the energy sector was the announcement of confident forecasts for the exploitation of *geothermal energy* from the Karthala volcano on Ngazidja. The positive outcome of the initial exploration phase of the Karthala Geothermal Project was presented to the General Assembly of the International Renewable Energy Agency in January and a meeting of the Global Geothermal Alliance in February. The project received financial support from UNDP and the government of New Zealand, which led to an application for funding under the AU's Geothermal Risk Mitigation Facility. Karthala was estimated to have an upper capacity of 40 MW. Savings compared with the use of diesel-generated electricity were expected to amount to $ 20 m per year. By year's end, however, $ 27 m, or 60% of the overall cost of the initial exploration phase, still remained to be found.

On 23 January, the BCC announced funding for a project to resurface two main *coastal roads* on Ngazidja and Nzwani, with the aim of improving the transport of goods and people to support the agriculture, fishing and tourism sectors. Overall, 47 km of road would be resurfaced at a cost of € 24 m. The completion date was set for 2020 and the project would be co-financed by the BCC and EU.

Competition had been imposed on the *telecoms* sector by the sale of a second operating licence to the Madagascar-based firm Telecom Malagasy (Telma) in October 2015, bringing to an end the state monopoly held by Comores Télécom (Comtel). Telma had begun operating in December 2016 and rivalry between the two operators brought frustration for consumers throughout 2017. In particular, Comtel resisted inter-connectivity, meaning that Telma subscribers could not call Comtel subscribers and vice-versa. After a number of false starts and a visit to Assoumani by Xavier Niel, the co-owner of 'Le Monde' newspaper and a major shareholder in Telma, inter-connectivity was finally achieved in August. The continuing battle between the two operators was evident again in December, however, when Vice President for Telecommunications Abdallah Said Sarouma announced that he would expect Telma to double its workforce in the coming year to match the number of workers employed by Comtel.

Djibouti

Nicole Hirt

The political situation in Djibouti remained stable, and President Ismaïl Omar Guelleh and his 'Union pour la Majorité Presidentielle' (UMP) coalition dominated the political realm with little space for opposition or civil society activities. However, it seemed that Guelleh's son-in-law, Djama Elmi Okieh (dubbed 'Djama Speed'), was no longer a candidate to succeed him. The Afar-inhabited North, where the 'Front pour la Restoration de l'Unité et de la Démocratie' (FRUD) had been active in previous years, was relatively calm due to an Ethiopian military presence but, in October, a demonstration in Tajourah was violently dispersed by security forces. In August, China inaugurated its first naval base on African soil near the town of Obock, with a capacity to station up to 10,000 troops. The start of the new Djiboutian-Ethiopian Railway's regular commercial operation connecting Djibouti's port with Ethiopia's capital, Addis Ababa, was delayed, and some other large infrastructure projects progressed more slowly than expected. The country was affected by prolonged drought conditions, and the humanitarian situation remained dire, with 200,000 people dependent on food aid.

 | DOI:10.1163/9789004367630_033

Domestic Politics

President Ismaïl Omar Guelleh (widely dubbed IOG) remained in control of Djibouti's politics, the economy and the judiciary, and the UMP coalition continued to be the dominant political party. The military, the police and the security forces were also under the firm grip of the president, and the Guelleh clan's domination of all public affairs prevailed. The *political coalition* 'Union pour le Salut National', an umbrella of numerous small organisations, namely the 'Alliance Républicaine pour le Développement', the 'Union pour la Démocratie et la Justice', the 'Mouvement pour le Renouveau Démocratique et le Développement', the 'Parti National Démocratique', the 'Parti Djiboutien pour le Développement', the 'Mouvement pour le Développement et la Liberté' and the 'Centre des Démocrates Unifiés', continued to lack unity and did not pose any challenge to the president's rule. However, Guelleh's plans to make his son-in-law and minister of health, *Djama Elmi Okieh* (often dubbed 'Djama Speed'), his designated successor, received a severe blow in February when the latter fell out with his wife, Guelleh's youngest daughter Haibado, after an alleged affair with the female head of his ministry's human resources department. First Lady Kadra Mahamoud Haid played an important role in Djiboutian politics and was said to be pulling the strings in the background. She preferred Naguib Abdallah Kamil, a son from her first marriage with an ethnic Afar, as a candidate for her husband's succession. Naguib acted as Prime Minister Abdoulkader Kamil Mohamed's chief of staff.

In contrast to the remarkable political and economic agency of the female members of Guelleh's family clan, few *women* beyond the inner circle of power played a role in public affairs. Only seven, or about 10%, of National Assembly members were female and the only woman serving in the cabinet was Minister for Women and Family Affairs Moumina Houmed Hassan.

Djibouti's *political climate remained repressive*, and press freedom was very limited. There was only one newspaper, 'La Nation', which was under the control of the government, like the state-owned radio and television stations. The opposition Internet radio station 'La Voix de Djibouti' was not allowed to broadcast from inside the country but was based in France. Djibouti was ranked 172th out of 180 countries in Reporters Without Borders' press freedom report.

On 19 March, the leader of the '*Ligue Djiboutienne des Droits Humains*' (LDDH), Omar Ali Ewado, who had been arrested for prolonged periods in the past, was taken away by state security agents, who also harassed his family and pointed guns at his children. The reasons for his arrest were not known, and he started a hunger strike to protest against his detention. He was freed without charge on 27 March. On 27 October, the LDDH complained in a press release that a demonstration in Tadjourah (in the Afar-inhabited part of the country) initiated by young people who felt neglected by the government, had been violently dispersed by security forces who had fired life ammunition and made excessive use of tear gas, injuring various protestors.

In late February, the Dubai-based port operator *DP World* won an arbitration case against the government. The government had claimed that the company had bribed President Guelleh's arch-rival Abdourahman Boreh, the former head of Djibouti's port authority, but the loss of the case meant that the legal costs had to be borne by the state. The legal battle between Guelleh and Boreh, ignited by the two men's personal rivalries, had lasted for years and cost the country close to $ 100 m.

Tensions in the northern part of Djibouti, mainly around the town of Obock, the base of the *Afar resistance movement* 'FRUD-Combattant' (or 'FRUD armé'), under the leadership of Mohammed Kaddamy, remained high, and some clashes occurred in May. On 14 August, coast guards tried to prevent a boat with some 60 Eritrean refugees who were ethnic Afars heading for Obock from entering the port. This triggered a demonstration by the inhabitants, who saw the lives of the refugees in danger, and, after additional pressure from the local UNHCR office, the government gave in and hosted the Afar group from Eritrea at a refugee camp in Markazi.

Foreign Affairs

Djibouti maintained close relations with all neighbouring countries in the Horn of Africa except Eritrea, and was able to significantly strengthen its position as a strategically important player in the wider regional and international context. The small country played an active role in supporting *international anti-terrorism activities* in the region and the opening of the *Chinese military base* in August marked a new dimension in Djibouti's role as a host of international military facilities.

However, the country did not remain unaffected by the *diplomatic crisis on the Arabian Peninsula*, situated at a short distance across the Bab el-Mandeb. When Saudi Arabia, the UAE, Bahrain and Egypt cut diplomatic ties with Qatar in June, accusing the emirate of supporting regional terrorism, both Djibouti and Eritrea sided with the Saudi-led coalition and downgraded their diplomatic relations with *Qatar*. Consequently, Qatar ceased its mediation efforts between Eritrea and Djibouti initiated in 2010 and, on 14 June, withdrew its peacekeeping troops that were monitoring the contested border. Two days later, Djibouti accused *Eritrea* of occupying the contested territory, including Doumeira Mountain and Doumeira Island, and Foreign Minister Mahamoud Ali Yousuf declared that his country's troops had been put on alert. The government also lodged complaints with the UN and the AU. On 17 June, the AU Commission's Chairperson Moussa Faki Mahamat called for restraint and announced that a fact-finding mission would visit both countries. His call was echoed by the Ethiopian Ministry of Foreign Affairs. An effort by the AU to replace Qatar as a mediator was rejected by Eritrea. On 4 July, Eritrea's ambassador to the AU, Araia Desta, said his country would only accept mediation by Qatar. At the end of the month *China* offered its good offices as a mediator and suggested Chinese troops could monitor the contested borders, but Eritrea did not respond to this offer and the situation remained in limbo. The Somalia Eritrea Monitoring Group (SEMG) reported in a letter to the UNSC dated 6 November that Eritrea continued to support the armed resistance group 'FRUD armé' in the northern part of Djbouti. According to the SEMG, members of the group received training at the Anda'ali camp in Eritrea's Southern Red Sea Region, close to the border. It carried out raids and recruitment campaigns in Djiboutian locations and was involved in military encounters with Djiboutian and Ethiopian troops stationed in the area.

Djibouti's relations with *Ethiopia* remained close and their economies were closely linked to each other. Djibouti remained Ethiopia's only sea outlet and received parts of its energy supply from its larger neighbour. The Ethiopia Railway Corporation announced the start of commercial operations of the newly constructed electric railway connecting Addis Ababa with Djibouti for October and then for November, but test runs continued, and regular operation was further delayed. On 20 March, President Guelleh visited Ethiopia and met with Prime Minister Hailemariam Dessalegn. They stressed their countries' cordial relations and signed an agreement on extradition, mutual legal assistance in criminal matters and a memorandum of understanding on cooperation in the field of justice and legal training. In an interview with the 'Ethiopian Herald' on 15 March, Djibouti's ambassador to Ethiopia Mohamed Idriss Farah stressed that the two countries had commenced a process of economic integration with the aim of merging their immigration and customs services.

Djibouti continued to support the *AU peacekeeping mission in Somalia* (*AMISOM*), and Djiboutian soldiers contributed to the humanitarian component of the mission by distributing medicine to needy inhabitants of Belet Weyne, who were affected by a cholera outbreak. Relations with the unofficial government of Djibouti's neighbour *Somaliland* remained strong. On 9 June, Vice Minister Abdirahman Ismael Saylici travelled to Djibouti and met with the president, presumably to discuss the consequences of the diplomatic turmoil in the Arabian Peninsula. He was accompanied by the minister of state for planning and development.

Djibouti's prominent geo-strategic location made it an increasingly attractive host for a variety of *military bases*. On 1 August, *China* officially opened its first naval base on the African continent near the town of Obock. Beijing called the installation a logistics facility but, with a capacity of up to 10,000 troops, the base, which was operated by the Chinese People's Liberation Army Navy, was internationally perceived as a military outpost. The official aim of the mission was to support Chinese troops stationed in the Gulf of Aden, contribute to ongoing international operations, fight piracy and contribute to humanitarian operations. The

USA maintained its presence with about 4,000 troops and civilian staff at its base Camp Lemmonier, which also served as a planning base for targeted drone killings in the Horn of Africa and for a Navy Seals operation in Yemen carried out on 29 January against alleged al-Qaeda fighters.

The number of *French troops* stationed in Djibouti remained stable with 1,450 personnel, and the EU's anti-piracy operation Atalanta, which had been able to significantly reduce the prevalence of piracy in the region continued. In reaction to the presence of the Chinese navy, *Japan* decided to expand its Djiboutian base, and in November it leased an additional 3 ha from the government for this purpose. Saudi Arabian plans for yet another military base on Djiboutian soil did not materialise. On 28 April, the *Saudi Kingdom* and Djibouti signed a defence agreement, which confirmed Djibouti's position as a member of the Arab Coalition on Yemen and the Saudi-led Islamic alliance against terrorism. In an interview with the Saudi-sponsored news agency 'Al-Sharq al-Awsat' on 28 November, Djibouti's Minister of Defence Ali Hasan Bahdon stressed that his country welcomed a Saudi military base and that Saudi experts had arrived in the country to assess cooperation. However, he evaded the question of whether concrete steps had been taken towards the construction of the base. Relations with Saudi Arabia's ally, the *UAE*, were less cordial due to discords dating back to 2014, when President Guelleh had terminated the contract with Dubai-based port operator DP-World and had sued the company for corruption in a London arbitration court. In reaction to Djibouti's repudiation, the UAE had established close relations with Somaliland, where they leased the port of Berbera for a period of 30 years and sought permission to establish a military base.

Socioeconomic Developments

The government continued to rely heavily on FDI and the construction of *infrastructure projects* for development. China played a major role as a foreign investor, but progress was slower than anticipated. Construction of a $ 4 bn 700-km gas pipeline, intended to connect Ethiopia and Djibouti and financed by the Chinese POLY GCL Petroleum Group Holdings, fell behind schedule, allegedly due to complicated negotiations between the company and the Djiboutian government, as the Ethiopian minister of mines, petroleum and natural gas claimed in September. Construction did not start and plans to commence the export of Ethiopian gas to China after treatment at a Djibouti liquefaction plant were postponed to 2020. Another large infrastructure project, the 550-km fuel pipeline that was to be carried out by the South Africa-based Black Rhino investment company to connect Djibouti with central Ethiopia and to facilitate the flow of diesel, gasoline and jet fuel, was cancelled by the Ethiopian government due to a lack of funds. The Ethiopian Ministry of Transport argued that the newly constructed railway had the capacity to transport the fuel, so another large investment was not immediately necessary.

The government went ahead with its efforts to expand the *renewable energy* sector and specifically to exploit the country's high potential for geothermal energy. In July, it secured a $ 27 m grant from the Kuwait Development Fund for its Gale-Le-Koma geothermal project near Lake Assal, with a capacity of 15 MW. It was planned that the Djiboutian Geothermal Energy Development Office should carry out the construction work, which was seen as a contribution to the country's human resources development. The Swiss firm Green Enesys' *photovoltaic project* worth $ 390 m in the Grand Bara desert was not finalised. In 2015, the International Renewable Energy Agency had claimed that Djibouti could reach self-sustainability by 2020 because of its extraordinary variety of renewable energy sources and the government had confirmed its determination to reach this goal. For the time being, however, it still depended on electricity imports from Ethiopia, which planned to export 613,200 MWH to Djibouti in the fiscal year 2017/18. This was due to a rising demand for electric power as a consequence of new military installations and the lack of a coherent strategy to profit from wind, sun and geothermal energy sources.

The government's development agenda, *Vision Djibouti 2035*, had the ambitious aim of significantly improving the logistics capacity of the country, turning it into a commercial hub for East Africa and a middle-income economy. On 22 February, the IMF concluded its Article IV consultation with Djibouti and stated that the *economy had seen fast growth* of 6.5% in 2016, mainly because of the construction of new ports and the railway to Ethiopia. Growth for 2017 was projected at 7.1%. At the same time, *public debt* had risen sharply from 50% to 85% of GDP since 2014. As in previous reports, the IMF lamented that economic growth had not led to job creation and to rising incomes for ordinary Djiboutians and complained that 42% of the population remained poor. Almost one quarter (23%) lived in extreme *poverty*, with an unemployment rate of 39%. The nepotistic network around the president's family clan did not facilitate a more equal distribution of income, and TI's corruption report ranked Djibouti 122nd out of 180 countries. Consumer price *inflation* remained stable at 3% and the *fiscal deficit* narrowed to 3.8%, mainly due to increased income from re-export revenues. The Djibouti franc (Dfr) remained pegged to the US dollar at a rate of Dfr 177: $ 1 under a currency board arrangement. The IMF recommended that the competitiveness of the economy be improved by reducing costs of electricity, water and telecommunications rather than relying on the nominal exchange rate, and the World Bank stated in unusually unambiguous terms that infrastructure-led growth and mega-projects that increased the demand for foreign labour were unlikely to have a positive spill-over on job creation and poverty reduction. The Economic Intelligence Unit estimated that exports of goods and services amounted to $ 156 m compared with imports worth $ 755 m.

Djibouti's *tax system* was characterised by extensive tax exemptions for foreign investors, and the IMF demanded a thorough reform to generate resources for social spending and to initiate broad-based economic growth. The general *business environment* remained restricted, but Djibouti's rank in the World Bank's 'Doing Business' assessment improved to 154th (out of 190 listed countries) from 171st in 2016. On 3–7 December, the Chamber of Commerce hosted its first *international trade fair* under the motto 'Djibouti the Gateway to Africa'. Business enterprises from Canada, Japan, Yemen, Kenya, the UAE, Uganda and Ethiopia participated in the event, which promoted Djibouti's investment potential and its tourist attractions.

According to UNICEF, 200,000 people out Djibouti's close to 1 m population were affected by worsening *drought* conditions and in urgent need of *food aid* during the year. Some 20,000 *refugees* and migrants from Eritrea, Somalia, Yemen and Ethiopia aggravated the situation and were especially vulnerable because they lacked access to income generating activities. Only 65% of the rural population had access to safe drinking water. The school enrolment rate was also at a low of 65%, and only 61% of girls attended primary school. Just a quarter of the population had the opportunity to receive secondary *education*. The Global Hunger Index ranked the country 100th out of 119, and Djibouti's 2016 HDI ranking (latest available figures) was 172nd out of 188 countries, four places lower than in 2015.

Eritrea

Nicole Hirt

The State of Eritrea remained an autocratic political system with a heavily militarised command economy, and the open-ended national service that drove substantial numbers of the youth to flee the country remained in place. The human rights situation was worrying, and a crackdown on the very few remaining schools that offered religious education as part of their curriculum triggered the first student demonstration in Asmara since 2001. The young people protested against the arrest of a nonagenarian board member of the Islamic Al-Dia school, who had refused to accept government intervention in the school's curriculum. The diplomatic crisis in the Arabian Peninsula and tensions between Egypt, Ethiopia and Sudan affected Eritrea's foreign relations and led to the termination of Qatar's role as a mediator in the conflict with Djibouti and to a Sudanese troop build-up along its borders with Eritrea at the end of the year. The government tried to control all financial transactions by limiting cash transfers without providing adequate alternative financial instruments to handle payments. In December, it closed down hundreds of businesses as a punitive measure. The bulk of EU funds granted under the 11th EDF remained unused due to a lack of feasible development projects.

 | DOI:10.1163/9789004367630_034

Domestic Politics

Eritrea's autocratic political system was not reformed in any way, and the state remained under the firm rule of President Isaias Afewerki. The constitution that had been ratified in 1997 remained un-implemented, and plans to draft a new one seemed to have been dropped. There were no plans either to hold national elections in the near future, and the People's Front for Democracy and Justice (PFDJ) remained *the only political party*, with no other political organisations allowed. The cabinet of ministers met on 10 February, 8 September and 11 November, and discussed plans to improve education and health services as well as structural adjustments, including the revision of budgetary allocations to *priority development programmes* with the aim of expanding renewable energy and the electric power supply, and improving the supply of fuel, basic consumer goods and water for households, all of which had been in short supply for many years. As in previous years, there were *no major cabinet reshuffles* and most of the cabinet members were over 70 years of age. The post of minister of defence remained vacant, while Hagos Ghebrehiwet 'Kisha', PFDJ's head of economic affairs, retained his powerful position as economic adviser to the president and unofficial supervisor of the country's finances. Nesredin Bekhit, who was known for his notorious involvement in the contraband trade via the Sudanese border, remained minister of trade and industry, and Brigadier General Sebhat Ephrem retained his post as minister of energy and mining. Ms Leul Gebreab, previously head of the National Union of Eritrean Women, was appointed minister of labour and human welfare, replacing Salma Hassen. After the death of Eritrea's permanent representative at the UN, Girma Asmerom, in October 2016, his position was not filled by a replacement, but his former deputy Amanuel Giorgio acted as interim chargé d'affaires.

Presidential adviser and head of the ruling PFDJ *Yemane Gebreab*, who had been a key figure in representing the government to foreign policy makers and had acted as chief propagandist to the diaspora by delivering speeches at festivals and during seminars, was seriously injured on 5 July. He was reportedly attacked by Eritrean refugees with blunt weapons after holding a dinner at a PFDJ-owned restaurant in Rome with Eritrea's ambassador to Italy, Petros Fissehazion, and remained hospitalised for an extended period. While the Eritrean government remained silent about the incident, the Italian Ministry of Foreign Affairs confirmed the assault. According to Italian media, the suspected perpetrators were going to be charged with attempted murder.

Chief of Staff of the Eritrean Defence Forces Major General Philippos Weldeyohannes remained the strongman among the *military leadership*. Brigadier General Eyob 'Halibay' Fessahaye reportedly acted as leader of the Special Forces, a military elite group responsible for the president's personal security. Little was heard about Brigadier General Tekle 'Manjus' Kiflay, who was infamous for his involvement in human trafficking and smuggling, but it seemed that he retained his position as commander of the western military command zone and was in charge of border control. The 2012 rule of a compulsory *citizens' militia* that forced elderly people to carry guns and patrol their neighbourhoods remained in place, although prevailing passive resistance by the persons concerned prevented its firm implementation.

Ethiopian state media reported in March that almost 100 Eritrea-based 'anti-peace elements', namely members of the Eritrea-based wing of the *Oromo Liberation Front and Ginbot 7* had been captured while trying to cross the border into Ethiopia's northern Tigray region with the aim of committing acts of sabotage. However, reports by Ginbot 7 defectors who had voluntarily returned to Ethiopia indicated that only 280 fighters were left in Eritrea. Berhanu Nega, leader of Ginbot 7, spent most of his time touring the Ethiopian diaspora in the USA and Canada.

The appalling *human rights situation* did not improve, and civil liberties were non-existent. Eritrea changed places with North Korea and was placed second-lowest worldwide in Reporters Without Borders' *press freedom* ranking, with at least 11 journalists imprisoned without charge or trial. On 30 March, UNESCO awarded its Guillermo Cano World Press Freedom Prize to Swedish-Eritrean journalist Dawit Isaak, who had remained behind bars for 16 years. None of the surviving *members of the G15*, a group of prominent PFDJ officials who had been jailed after they had criticised President Isaias in 2001, demanding political reforms and national elections, had been brought before a court of law. *Religious freedom* was denied to followers of Jehovah's Witnesses and Pentecostal churches, and the permitted religious denominations, namely Orthodox, Catholic and Lutheran Christianity and Sunni Islam remained under close surveillance by government agents. Followers of unregistered churches were periodically rounded up and arrested in various parts of the country. In an attempt to *ban religious education*, the government cracked down on the three remaining schools in Asmara that provided religious education – the Catholic school at the Cathedral, the Orthodox school at Enda Mariam (the main Orthodox church) and the Islamic Al-Dia school, which served hundreds of students in the capital's Akria neighbourhood. Following the arrest of an elderly member of the school's board, Hajji Mussa Mohammed Nur, who had sharply criticised orders from the Ministry of Education to remove religion from the school's curriculum and had publicly declared his defiance, Asmara witnessed its first demonstration since 2001. On 31 October, a large crowd of students protested against the arrest of the nonagenarian and marched towards the Ministry of Education in downtown Asmara. The demonstration was dispersed by security personnel firing into the air with live ammunition. However, contrary to reports distributed by Qatar-based media outlets, there were no fatalities. Mobile phone videos documenting the rare event were widely shared on social media and provoked solidarity demonstrations by diaspora groups in many European and American cities. The demonstrators stressed Muslim-Christian solidarity against the government's interference in religious affairs and carried pictures of Hajji Mussa and the Orthodox Patriarch Abune Antonios, another prominent religious figure detained by the government.

Eritrea's *judicial system* remained in disarray and there was no rule of law. Most arrests and detentions, either for political reasons or for alleged criminal offences, occurred without formal juridical procedures. Since the closure of Eritrea's only university in 2006, there had been no formal possibility to study law, and so the country lacked qualified jurists and lawyers. Informal litigation based on customary law continued to be the basis of civil jurisdiction and conflict resolution, and there were no indications that the *civil and penal codes* introduced in 2015 were being implemented. *Corruption* remained endemic in the civil administration, which was mostly run by under-paid national service conscripts, as well as among high-ranking military personnel and PFDJ cadres. Conscripts regularly had to pay for holiday extensions and service exemptions, or to be smuggled over the border. TI's Corruption Perception Index ranked Eritrea as highly corrupt (164th out of 178 countries).

The mandates of the Special Rapporteur on the Situation of Human Rights in Eritrea and the Commission of Inquiry on Human Rights in Eritrea were not renewed beyond 2016, despite demands by several human rights organisations, and charges of crimes against humanity being committed by Eritrean government officials were not pursued by UN organisations or the ICC.

The *Eritrean diaspora* remained split between government supporters and opponents. However, the spontaneous demonstrations launched at several European, North American and Australian locations on the occasion of the arrest of Hajji Mussa in early November showed the widespread unease of many Eritreans abroad with the government's intervention in religious affairs.

Foreign Affairs

On 14 November, the UNSC extended the *targeted sanctions* imposed on Eritrea that had been in place since December 2009 (resolution 1907–2009) and December 2011 (resolution 2023–2011) for one year, with 11 votes in favour and four abstentions (Bolivia, Egypt, China and the Russian Federation). The UNSC urged the government of Eritrea to provide information concerning the fate of missing Djiboutian POWs and expressed concern over its support for regional armed groups.

Eritrea continued to place its port city Assab at the disposal of the *Saudi-led Arab coalition* against the Houthi rebels in Yemen. On 31 December, the Eritrean president travelled to Abu Dhabi and met with Crown Prince Sheikh Mohamed bin Zayed Al Nahyan, the deputy supreme commander of the UAE armed forces. As a consequence of the government's military alliance with Saudi Arabia and the UAE, relations with *Qatar* deteriorated sharply in the course of the diplomatic crisis in the Arabian Peninsula that evolved in June between Qatar and the Saudi Kingdom, the UAE and Bahrain. Ironically, both Eritrea and its foe Djibouti sided with the Saudi coalition and downgraded their relations with Qatar, which had been a close Eritrean ally and generous financial sponsor of the Isaias regime for many years. In response, Qatar resigned within days from its role as a mediator in the border dispute between the two countries. Qatar had been monitoring the Eritrean-Djiboutian border since 2010, but no progress had been achieved towards a rapprochement between the two governments and a demarcation of the contested border. The *AU* and *China* declared their readiness to step in as mediators, but Eritrea's ambassador to the AU Araia Desta insisted on 4 July that Qatar should remain the sole mediator in the dispute, despite the removal of its peacekeepers. This attitude was understandable against the background of China's close relations to the Djiboutian government as a host of its only military base in Africa, and the AU's perceived pro-Djiboutian bias, since the small country was a close ally of the AU's host, Ethiopia. No progress was made in the political stalemate between Eritrea and *Ethiopia*, but the situation along the contested border remained calm except for isolated shelling, mostly when Eritrean troops opened fire on refugees.

Eritrea's relations with *Egypt* remained close, since the al-Sisi government regarded the country as a strategic partner in its conflict with Ethiopia over the Nile waters. In mid-March, an Egyptian delegation visited Eritrea with the official purpose of discussing cooperation in the field of fisheries and was welcomed by President Isaias and his economic advisor Hagos 'Kisha' Gebrehiwot in person. On 20 March, Minister of Foreign Affairs Osman Saleh and presidential adviser Yemane Gebreab travelled to Cairo to continue the discussions and, on 6 May, the duo visited Egypt once again and met with Foreign Minister Sameh Shoukri, who stressed that cooperation with Eritrea was important due to the current challenges besetting the region. In late December, a complex diplomatic crisis evolved. Tensions between Egypt and Sudan increased over alleged Egyptian attempts to exclude the Sudanese government from the tripartite talks concerning the effect of Ethiopia's Renaissance Dam on the distribution of the Nile water. Egypt rejected these allegations, but a border dispute over the Halayeb Triangle further aggravated tensions between the countries.

To make matters worse, *Turkey*'s President Erdoğan visited Sudan on 24 December and proposed restoring the ancient Ottoman port of Suakin on the Red Sea coast. Two days later, Sudan's Foreign Minister Ibrahim Ghandour stated that the refurbished port would be able to service both civilian and military vessels, while Turkey stressed its intention to create a tourist attraction, even though Turkish Army Chief of Staff Hulusi Akar was a member of the Turkish delegation, tasked with discussing security cooperation. The Turkish move angered Egypt, which saw the reconstruction of the port on the strategically important Red Sea coast a short distance from the Arabian Peninsula as a provocation. Turkey, as well as Qatar, were considered to be supporters of the Muslim Brotherhood and therefore at odds with the Egyptian government.

The deteriorating *relations between Sudan and Egypt* had serious effects on Eritrea. On 30 December, the Sudanese government declared a six-month state of emergency in Kassala, Sudan's eastern province bordering Eritrea and a centre for smuggling and human trafficking with the involvement of Eritrean and Sudanese officials. Sudan feared a possible military build-up of Egyptian troops in Eritrea and started to deploy troops along its border with Eritrea with the official aim of clearing the region of illicit weapons.

While no official state visits of Eritrean delegations to Sudan took place, Foreign Minister Osman Saleh and his escort Yemane Gebreab visited *South Sudan* on 4 April, where they met President Salva Kiir in Juba. From 30 January to 1 February, they visited *Russia* and held talks with Foreign Minister Sergei Lavrov about economic cooperation and possible Russian investment in Eritrea's mining sector. In late August, the Israeli High Court decided that a plan of the Netanyahu government to offer Eritrean and Sudanese refugees in *Israel* the choice between deportation to Rwanda and indefinite imprisonment was unconstitutional. Nevertheless, the Israeli government continued its preparations to deport tens of thousands of persons branded 'illegal infiltrators' and decided on 19 November to close the semi-open Holot detention facility and to force refugees to make a decision between deportation and indefinite imprisonment in Israel. The decision was criticised as a violation of national and international law by Israeli pro-refugee activists and triggered international protests, including from prominent Jews in the United States.

The numbers of Eritreans reaching Europe via the Mediterranean decreased to about 8,000 individuals, probably an effect of the Khartoum Process, which had resulted in harsh measures against refugees en route from Sudan to *Libya*, and the deteriorating situation inside Libya, where Europe had empowered the local coast guards to apprehend refugees trying to reach Europe by boat and transport them back to Libyan detention centres, where they became victims of regular abuse and were subjected to appalling living conditions. Relations between the *EU* and Eritrea remained stable, but there were fewer efforts by European policymakers to court representatives of the Eritrean government. In late August, the Austrian head of the EU delegation in Asmara, Christian Manahl, was replaced by Josep Coll i Carbo, a Spaniard from Catalonia. On 20 December, the Dutch parliament passed a motion to close down the Eritrean embassy in the Netherlands in response to the protracted use of coercion to raise the 2% diaspora tax among diaspora Eritreans in the *Netherlands*.

Relations between the *USA* and Eritrea remained poor, and no ambassadors were exchanged. In October, the US put Eritrea on a sanctions list together with North

Korea, Russia and Syria for failing to combat human trafficking. This measure further limited access for Eritreans to American educational and cultural exchange programmes. Relations between Eritrea and *China* remained stable. On 11 November, Chinese ambassador to Eritrea Yang Zigang encouraged the Eritrean government to enhance its cooperation with his country in the economic field, stressing that the current level of mutual engagement left much to be desired.

Socioeconomic Developments

Eritrea's command economy remained under the control of the ruling PFDJ and the military leadership, and whatever was left of small business activities in the private sector came under even stronger scrutiny. The government's attempts to turn Eritrea's cash-based economy into a cheque-based economy continued, and families as well as businessmen were not allowed to withdraw sums exceeding ERN (nafka) 5,000 ($ 333) per month from their bank accounts. Due to the resulting limitation of bank notes in circulation, the *currency black market* rate gradually came to approximate the official exchange rate of ERN 15: $ 1, making it less attractive for diaspora Eritreans to use the informal 'Hawala' system to remit money to their relatives. However, *inflation* remained high at 8.9% according to the African Economic Outlook, which aggravated the population's dire economic situation. In an unusual move from mid-December, the government shut down 450 private businesses, including hotels and cafeterias, which made up the bulk of remaining private enterprises beyond the size of micro-businesses. The Ministry of Information justified the measures in an editorial published on 29 December by stating that the affected businesses had failed to use cheques and other unspecified banking systems for their transactions, and that cash transfers "are always fraught with security, social, economic and other avoidable pitfalls". The statement ignored the fact that Eritrea's *banking system* lagged decades behind international developments, and payments by debit or credit card or other methods of cashless payment were not in use in the country. The shut-down constituted another arbitrary measure taken by the ruling elite to secure total control over financial flows in the country with uncertain outcomes for its economic development.

In a report dated 3 February 2018, the government website shabait.com admitted that the 2017 *harvest* had been significantly lower than in 2016 due to low rainfall. In the Southern Region (Zoba Debub), the harvest amounted to only half of that in 2016; in the Central Region (Zoba Ma'akel), the harvest was down 41%. UNICEF indicated an increase in *malnutrition* rates in four out of six regions based on data from the Nutrition Sentinel Site Surveillance system and provided support to almost 58,000 children suffering from malnutrition. It also stressed that only half of the rural population had access to safe drinking water and that diarrhoea and measles outbreaks posed an additional threat to vulnerable children. The scarcity of consumer goods and fuel and shortcomings in the electricity supply in urban areas including Asmara continued.

The Warsay-Yikealo Development Campaign, introduced in 2002 as an *open-ended national service programme* to replace the original 18-month military and civil service, remained in place. Earlier promises to representatives of the international community that the length of the service would be reduced to its original 18 months were not kept. Male Eritreans aged 18–60 and women aged 18–27 were forced to work either for the military or for PFDJ-owned companies or in the public administration for a small remuneration that was not enough to maintain a family. The educational and health sectors continued to be run mainly by national service conscripts, who were often poorly motivated and not properly trained for their work as teachers or health personnel. As in previous years, thousands of young Eritreans opted to flee the country instead of doing national service for life. In November, UNHCR Ethiopia reported 22,700 new arrivals of Eritrean *refugees*, bringing the total numbers to almost 170,000. Sudan hosted 108,000 Eritrean refugees according to the UNHCR, excluding a high number of unregistered persons who tried to travel on towards Europe as quickly as possible via Libya or Egypt. In September, the UNHCR expressed its deep concern over ongoing deportations of Eritreans to their home country by Sudanese authorities. In August, more than 100 Eritreans, among them 30 children and 46 women, had been denied refugee status and accused of illegal infiltration after being arrested by the Rapid Support Forces, an infamous militia tasked to stop and detain refugees along the migration routes, which constituted a clear breach of international law. Deportations of Eritreans, with the exception of some prominent political figures, had been almost unknown before the initiation by the EU of the *Khartoum Process*, intended to curb migration from East Africa to Europe through improved migration management in the region.

The *National Indicative Program* (NIP) under the 11th EDF was signed by Eritrea and the EU early in the year. It had the ambitious aims of boosting the renewable energy sector in order to end the chronic electricity shortages and was also meant to improve governance and public financial management, modernise the financial sector, enhance economic planning and put Eritrea on a sound statistical basis. But it remained largely unimplemented. A PV mini-grid solar system, to be installed in the Southern Region at a cost of € 8 m, remained the only project announced under the NIP, and it was unclear whether any plans for the use of the remaining € 198 m existed.

The government continued to withhold statistical information and did not publish a national budget. Accordingly, *statistical data* remained unreliable and erratic. World Bank data indicated primary school enrolment had deteriorated to 39% in 2015 (the latest year for which figures were available), secondary school enrolment was at 25% and tertiary enrolment at 2.5%. Eritrea's *exports* depended heavily on copper and zinc produced by the Bisha mine, a joint venture between the Canadian Nevsun company and the Eritrean National Mining Company; the Colluli Potash mine in the Southern Red Sea region did not become operational. According to the African Economic Outlook, economic growth stood at 3.8% in 2016, down from 4.8% in 2015, and the current account deficit stood at –0.1%.

In July, UNESCO designated Eritrea's capital Asmara, known for its exquisite modernist buildings from the time of Italian colonisation, as a world heritage site. Most of the buildings constructed by futurist architects dated back to the 1930s and had been poorly maintained under the PFDJ government. However, the UNESCO decision did not result in the desired increase in tourism – according to the travel review website TripAdvisor, Eritrea was the least-reviewed country on earth in 2017.

Ethiopia

Jon Abbink

The one-party regime of the EPRDF (Ethiopian Peoples' Revolutionary Democratic Front) remained in place but appeared increasingly shaky, with country-wide contestation and political insecurity ongoing. Important ruling-party meetings were held toward the end of the year to deal with the crises. Ethiopia's economy continued to grow, although foreign investment and tourism did not recover to the level of before the 2016 crisis. Clashes between ethnic groups also continued, with a major new crisis erupting on the Oromo-Somali regional border, leading to hundreds of people being killed and hundreds of thousands displaced.

Domestic Politics

The one-party regime of the EPRDF remained in power during the year but cracks appeared and it became increasingly insecure as contestations, protests and clashes continued. Self-reflection and some disarray also emerged within the party itself over mismanagement and policy mistakes. The four constituent sub-parties – the Tigray People's Liberation Front (TPLF), the Southern Ethiopian

 | DOI:10.1163/9789004367630_035

People's Democratic Movement, the Amhara National Democratic Movement (ANDM) and the Oromo People's Democratic Organisation (OPDO) – developed somewhat different approaches to the country's problems during the year.

Although parliament, the ministries, the army, the security services and all important institutions remained under full EPRDF control, the differences within the ranks led to shifts and hesitant renegotiations of policy priorities, away from the TPLF as the undisputed centre. The performance of Prime Minister Hailemariam Dessalegn, designated as the party's crown prince by the former prime minister, Meles Zenawi of the TPLF, before his death, was seen as inadequate if not weak, but no immediate alternative was presented during party discussions. The fact that the Oromo and Amhara regions were the most affected by social unrest and demonstrations against land confiscations and repression of demands for social and economic reform meant that the leaders of the OPDO and ANDM wanted at least to be seen to be responding to the demands of the people in their own regions. There was emerging recognition of the seriousness of the protests, with persistent rumours that people in both regions were arming themselves and determined not to be walked over.

The year was thus one of *continued unrest* and multiple confrontations of protesters with police and army units and attacks on property; protests against abuse and lack of government accountability, notably in the provinces and the middle-sized towns, were frequent. Addis Ababa – strongly under regime control – remained largely silent. Hundreds of people were killed in repressive violence by army and militia forces. The official State of Emergency (SoE), in place since October 2016 and due to end in April, was extended by four months, until 4 August. It had led to a drop in public violence but not to the disappearance of discontent and grievances.

Under the SoE, *political and civil society activities* were more strongly monitored and restricted under auspices of the so-called 'Command Post', the authority with far-reaching powers to oversee the SoE's implementation, (re)establish law and order, and 'monitor possible abuses' by the authorities and armed forces. Local people complained that, while the SoE extended restrictions on the right of movement and expression, its proclamation had only formalised what had been the de facto situation for many years. The independent but severely curtailed *Human Rights Council* compiled a report indicating extrajudicial killings and masses of people arrested, and commenting on appalling prison conditions, including torture, supported by eye witness testimonies. The secretary of the SoE Command Post, Defence Minister Siraj Fegessa, noted in a statement that 11,352 suspects arrested under the SoE were to be released after 20 days of 'renewal training', in addition to the 9,800 prisoners already released in late 2016 (Unofficial figures for the numbers arrested/imprisoned were higher; some opposition members even claimed that an estimated 60,000 to 70,000 people had been imprisoned). In March, the Command Post said that 4,996 people had been charged with involvement in violence.

The armed forces generally acted with impunity; few if any court cases for abuse or unlawful killing or arrest were brought. Early in the year, more troops were sent to North Gondar (Amhara Region), including two regiments from the 13th and 32nd divisions, to quell local resistance.

Under the SoE rules, several bizarre measures were taken, such as, in January, the arrest of members of the Dorze people in the South, who were detained and accused of 'terrorism' because (as was the custom) they had carried swords during a traditional dancing ceremony. Also several community gatherings such as weddings and funerals were disturbed and broken up because of alleged breach of the rules prohibiting assembly in large groups.

Local civil rights organisations continued to suffer from great pressure, not to speak of international right groups, which had little if any space to move in the country. Intense surveillance continued, both electronically and otherwise, of opposition party supporters, journalists and critical bloggers; telephone tapping, electronic eavesdropping and personal *surveillance* were rampant, with the state's Information Network Security Agency having a central role. In a statement on 18 May, the high-level TPLF politician and advisor to the government Arkebe Oqubay, said '… the press in Ethiopia is as free as the press in Europe and the Ethiopian press is free to publish whatever it wants'. But they could not.

Only five new local Amharic magazines remained, treading carefully in fear of closure. Four *journalists* remained in prison; two more fled the country after intimidation by the security forces (Ermias Seyoum and Mesfin Zeleke of 'Yegna Press'). Also, paid informants were used by the security forces to report people suspected of criticism or opposition, who received unannounced 'visits' at home or in the workplace to intimidate them. Entry and searches of homes without a warrant were frequent. The news media and the Internet suffered from continued censorship and close monitoring. In the end, however, the 'information' gathered on the suspected subversive activities of these opposition voices was limited and did not uncover major anti-state activities or 'conspiracies'.

While the Command Post formally lifted provisions allowing the monitoring of media and communications on 15 March, these activities still continued. *Internet use and e-mail* were under surveillance and regularly cut off. For example, mobile access to the Internet was not possible in the first half of the year in Addis Ababa, parts of Oromia, Amhara and some other regions. Social media site access (all major applications) was irregular and interrupted. The net gain of this policy – except perhaps for information on religious extremists – was negligible. On 5 December, a report by Citizen Lab appeared, detailing the extent of cyber-surveillance and spyware used by the Ethiopian authorities to monitor even Ethiopian diaspora activists in the USA and elsewhere.

A major opposition figure, *Dr Merera Gudina*, of the Oromo Federalist Congress party, who had been arrested in December 2016, remained in prison, and

Hailemariam said that he 'would face justice'. Merera was denied bail and his court case dragged on through the year without much result.

While the number of mass *demonstrations* and violent incidents fell in the first half of the year, they did not stop completely. The 'restoration of law and order' under the SoE was superficial, as few if any of the underlying problems and grievances were addressed.

In the ruling party – and notably among OPDO and ANDM, and in the speeches of Hailemariam – a new *sense of urgency* about the crisis broke through toward the end of the year, with here and there even voices expressing fear of a permanent crisis or system breakdown, which would endanger the country's 'developmental path'. At a party congress in November, the TPLF experienced internal disagreements over how to respond to the unrest. Chairman Abay Woldu lost his position, and the vocal widow of Meles Zenawi, Azeb Mesfin, was removed from the TPLF Executive Committee and demoted.

Massive violence erupted on the regional border between Somali Region and Oromiya Region in October. This was the most severe crisis the country faced. The initial dispute was over local land demarcation between Oromo and Somali (sub-) communities. Already in late February and March, there had been weeks of confrontations with armed militia from the Somali Region, reportedly resulting in the death of more than 100 people in the border areas of the East Hararge, West Hararge, Bale and Guji zones of Oromiya Region. An agreement signed between the presidents of the two major regions on 21 April did not resolve the issues. Again in August and in September, major clashes broke out. With the Somali regional authorities and their armed forces allegedly taking the side of the local Somalis, a conflict erupted that saw hundreds of people killed, mostly Oromo, and tens of thousands of people driven out and displaced. No decisive federal action – either political or military – followed. The total number of IDPs reached about 500,000 towards the end of the year and led to an enormous crisis. The displaced Oromo fled further into Oromiya Region, where they had to be housed in make-shift camps or were quartered with other Oromo families in towns and villages. This led to serious tensions between the two regional state governments and within the EPRDF leadership. The Oromiya Region leadership was deeply dismayed and demanded action, trying to deal responsibly with the discord via high-level talks. As one of two regional states, the Somali Region 5 had at its disposal the 'Liyyu Police' (a special force), armed units that had been allowed to them by the late prime minister Meles Zenawi as a counter-force to the rebel Ogaden National Liberation Front and incursions from Somalia. Local Oromo came to see the unpopular leader of the Somali Region, Abdi Mohamud Omar (Abdi Illey), as the main culprit in the crisis; he was also accused of gross human rights abuses against the Somali people in his own region. No effective mediating structures existed to mitigate the conflict: a general problem in 'ethno-federal' Ethiopia.

Sporadic *armed clashes* were also reported from other parts of the country, as in the western Benishangul-Gumuz Region, where the armed Benishangul People's Liberation Movement claimed to have killed government soldiers in a battle in early January. In other places, regime forces also clashed with local protesters, such as in October-November in the towns of Borena, Qulubi, Babile, Aweday and Gulsum (in the east), when several people were killed. On 9–12 October, people took to the streets in the border town of Moyale, closing the road to Kenya. In Woldiya in northern Ethiopia, four people were killed by security forces during a football match when a clash erupted following ethnic insults between local Amhara supporters and the visiting team from Tigray. In early December, unknown members of the Mela ('Bodi') people attacked sugar plantation truck drivers, killing 13 of them, in response to continuing livelihood destruction and the high death toll among Bodi due road accidents caused by reckless driving.

In November, residents of the towns of Shakiso, Adola and Dima and also in the Guji Zone (in the south) protested against the extension of the local gold mining concession of the major entrepreneur Mohamed al Amudi, who they said 'never did anything for local communities'. Such cases showed that protests were contagious, expressing the deep, pent up grievances of people and generalising them.

Also in November, university *students* at Haromaya University protested against the authorities, demanding the abolition of surveillance ('spying') structures on campus. When no action was taken, thousands of students packed up and left the campus. In December, student protests spread to more universities, including those in Ambo, Nazreth/Adama, Bule-Hora, Asosa, Wolqite and Adigrat. Also in December, protests and clashes flared up in many places, with several deadly incidents in Shambu, Qellem, Wolqite, Chellenqo, and again in the Western Hararge area on the Oromo-Somali border, where dozens of people were killed and hundreds of homes burnt down.

In a remarkable move, a number of *Oromo and Amhara MPs boycotted the session of parliament* that started on 14 December, saying that they would not attend until the government addressed the political crises and the ethnic clashes in the country.

Various *'ethnic tensions'* also flared up in other parts of the country throughout the year. The settlement of around 20,000 Tigray-speakers in the Halaydagi area of Afar in January-February and earlier aroused protests from the local Afar people. After fights between the newcomers and the Afar, Ethiopian army troops came in on 3 February and killed four Afar in the Amibara district. Also in February, some 100 people of Borana Oromo and Somali ethnicity died in clashes in the Negele area, and thousands were displaced during February and March. In April in the town of Moyale, on the Kenya border, tensions led to killings between the Borana Oromo and Garri Somalis, who had effectively divided the town in two. In the last week of April, a violent border clash was reported between Afar and Amhara in Hadar locality in the North. Further clashes erupted between Buji, Koré and Guji peoples and among Oromo and Sidama (with some 5,000 Sidama driven out of Bale Zone in September).

There were also ongoing *incidents against Amharic-speakers* in various places, leading to discrimination, rioting and expulsion, often provoked by language imposition. This frequently happened in mixed ethno-linguistic cities such as Nazreth/Adama, Jimma and Debre Zeit/Bishoftu, which happened to be geographically in the post-1991 Oromiya Region. In Benishangul-Gumuz Region, rioting and displacement of Amhara-speaking people occurred. In some southern towns such as Zeway, there were riots and street killings of ethnic-minority workers from the Southern Region. In a repeat of 2016, another cross-border attack by Murle raiders from South Sudan in February led to the displacement of some 3,700 people in the Gambela Region, followed by several raids in early March, leading to the deaths of at least 22 local Anywak people.

Numerically *smaller ethnic minorities* in the country, such as in the Omo River Valley, continued to have a hard time surviving and defending their lands, culture and local economies vis-à-vis state policies and mega-projects. Many suffered displacement, land confiscation, pollution and human rights abuses.

Religious relations in Ethiopia saw no major public disturbances, although tensions on the local level frequently occurred, notably between Protestant-Evangelicals/Pentecostals on the one hand and Orthodox and traditional believers on the other. There were no major anti-government Muslim demonstrations as in 2011–14, but some Muslim activists/leaders were prosecuted and on 3 January the Ethiopian Federal High Court, in a questionable decision, sentenced 20 of them to prison terms ranging from four to five years, finding them guilty under the Anti-Terrorism Proclamation (652/2009) and for violating articles 32(1) (a) and 38(1) of the Penal Code of 2004 for 'trying to establish a state ruled by *shari'a* law and inciting violence'.

In February, government security forces abducted Abba Gebre Yesus, a monk from the famous, age-old Waldubba Orthodox Christian monastery, because he had frequently protested in public against the expropriation of monastery lands for a sugar plantation 'development' project, which had also led to graves being desecrated. In April, a further 38 monks from Waldubba were arrested when protesting against the sugar project. These actions against the monastery were also much resented by public opinion.

As a result of the interlocking crises and national policy challenges, *two important meetings* were held by the authorities at the end of the year: the first, on 10 November, a National Security Council meeting, discussing a highly critical document in Amharic ('Plan for stability based on analysis of the country's current situation'), and the second, the 36-member EPRDF Executive Committee's long meeting on 12–30 December, to review past policies and devise a future course. This intense meeting was to be a momentous one, the full results of which would only emerge in 2018. The final statement from the meeting repeated the usual rhetoric on stability, development and the need for 'good governance', and on the crucial role of the ERPDF, but also showed signs of self-criticism (of 'leadership failures') and some contradictions and disarray over the future course to take. This reflected the difference in views within the EPRDF on the course forward.

Foreign Affairs

Ethiopia remained the *crucial Horn of Africa power*, politically, as a participant in the AMISOM forces in Somalia and other peace-keeping forces in Africa, and because Addis Ababa was the 'diplomatic capital' of Africa, with the headquarters of the AU, the ECA and other organisations such as IGAD. Many diplomats visited the country and pressure was put on the regime in Addis Ababa to ease tensions, and 'solve' the social and political crisis.

Relations with *Kenya, Djibouti and Somaliland* remained stable and cooperative. With Djibouti, further economic ties were cemented, leading to even more integration. The new Addis Ababa-Djibouti electric railway contributed to this.

Tensions with *Eritrea* persisted, although Prime Minister Hailemariam indicated that he would renew an initiative to find a new opening to normalise relations.

Ethiopia kept at least 5,000 troops in *Somalia* (exact numbers undisclosed) as part of the AMISOM peacekeeping force, but seemed to want move more soldiers out, increasingly losing confidence in the weakly performing Somali Federal Government. With *Sudan*, relations were good, and the two countries were virtually unanimous against Egypt on the issue of the Blue Nile dam, while Sudan provided most of Ethiopia's fuel imports.

PM Hailemariam visited a number of countries to strengthen or expand political relations, discuss international relations and trade links or extract promises of investment. He was on state visits to Uganda on 2–4 March and to Rwanda on 27–29 April. He and his wife also visited Israel on 5–6 June, including the Western Wall in Jerusalem, and held talks with Israeli leaders. He was in Sudan on 15–17 August and in Qatar on 14–15 November.

Visits by foreign dignitaries to Ethiopia included that of Morocco's King Mohammed VI on 28–31 January, Singapore's Deputy Prime Minister Teo Chee Hean on 11 May, and India's President R.N. Kovind on a state visit on 4–6 October, when he signed a number of agreements on trade and other bilateral issues. *India* was the third-largest net foreign investor in Ethiopia, after China and Turkey. Egyptian Foreign Minister Sameh Shoukry was in Addis Ababa on 26 December to discuss the Blue Nile dam and its impact. IMF Managing Director Christine Lagarde was in the capital on 13–15 December, praising Ethiopia's economy and calling for the economic momentum to be sustained. She also visited the new Dukem industrial park. On 30 April, Somalia's new President Hassan Sheikh Mohamud visited Addis Ababa ahead of the London Somalia conference in May.

On 22 May, in an unexpected development, the former foreign minister of Ethiopia Tedros Adhanom was elected as chairman of *WHO*, despite his candidature being highly contested and even disputed by health experts. In the first job application interview, he had performed badly but, allegedly in the game of 'fair representation' of UN posts across member countries, he got the job.

Relations with the *EU* were marked by projects for development cooperation and commercial relations as well as concerns over migration. Under the EU Emergency Trust Fund for Africa, Ethiopia continued to receive funds to mitigate outmigration flows, to the tune of around $ 120 m, although this did not produce spectacular results. The EU's Foreign Affairs Representative Federica Mogherini, after meeting Hailemariam on 17 March in Addis Ababa, gave a typically lame statement on the situation in the country, not mentioning the political problems but only focusing on 'cooperation' and 'dialogue'.

The *Nile water dispute* remained deadlocked. The tension was with Egypt over the possible effects of the Ethiopian-built Grand Renaissance Dam in western Ethiopia on Nile water levels and thus on Egypt's water supply and agriculture (see below). On 11 November, a ministerial meeting of the tripartite committee of Egypt, Ethiopia and Sudan in Cairo on the dam failed to approve an introductory report by the jointly selected French engineering consultants BRL Group and Artelia on the dam's effects on Egypt and Sudan; it appeared Ethiopia and Sudan rejected it. Egyptian President Abd el-Fattah el-Sisi said again on 18 November that, although he regarded positively the developmental needs of "our friends and brothers in Ethiopia", "water to us is a question of national security.... a matter of life or death". A proposal by Egypt to Ethiopia on 26 December that the World Bank be involved in technical discussions/evaluations on the possible impact of the dam met with no response.

Ethiopia received a (first ever) visit from the Head of the *UNHCR Zeid Ra'ad Al Hussein*, on 2–4 May. He met with government officials to request that authorities grant UN staff access to the Oromia and Amhara regions to investigate the civil unrest and actions of the security forces. He inquired about the high number of detainees under the SoE and doubted that their rights provided for by the law would all be honoured. Other requests on the human rights situation, including that the UN special rapporteur on torture and other cruel, inhuman, or degrading treatment or punishment visit the country, were not granted.

Ethiopia, with a non-permanent seat in the UNSC since September 2016, presided it in September this year.

Socioeconomic Developments

The country's *economy continued to grow*. Figures from various sources were still not consistent, but the output of all three core sectors – agriculture, services, and trade and industry – increased and foreign investment continued, attracted by a cheap labour supply and government facilitation (such as tax breaks and infrastructural conditions). The private sector showed dynamism and initiative, despite bureaucratic and financial hurdles.

The Ethiopian *population* reached around 102 m, with a growth rate of 2.8%. The national fertility rate fell slightly, to 4.99 (children per woman). In the cities, but not in the countryside, some reduction in birth rates was visible.

Urbanisation surged ahead, with Addis Ababa as the main magnet, but also in other cities. The growth of the urban population was around 4.9%, well above average population growth. Ethiopia was 'catching up' in urbanisation compared with other African countries, and 20.5% of its population were now living in cities. This did not mean, however, that the countryside was emptying, because absolute numbers of the rural population also kept increasing steadily. Ethiopian cities struggled with problems of service provision and urban planning. On 11 March, a major disaster occurred when the Reppi (or 'Qoshe') garbage dump in Addis Ababa suddenly collapsed, killing some 115 people living nearby as they were buried under the rubble.

The overall economy grew by 7.5% and reached a *GDP* of $ 76.9 bn, with GDP per capita (current prices) at $ 830. Growth was below the government target of 11% annually (set in the Growth and Transformation Plan II, up to 2025). The *services sector* grew most strongly (with 14%), accounting for 39.3% of total GDP. Part of this was ongoing infrastructure spending (hydroelectric dams, railways, roads). *Agriculture* grew also, by 6.7%, but its share of GDP remained at 36%. Again a serious drought – by now a structural feature driven by gradual climate change – affected output. *Industry* grew by 10.5% and reached around 25% of GDP (AfDB figures). Tourism income recovered somewhat after the 2016 dip but not to the 2015 level, due to the persistent unrest.

The construction of the $ 5 bn *Blue Nile hydro-dam* continued and was 65% complete by the end of the year. A paper published in the academic journal 'GSA Today' confirmed Egypt's fears that the effect of the dam on the Nile flow – even if the reservoir were to be filled over a long period of 10–15 years – would be disadvantageous: reduction of the flow to Egypt could be as much as 25%, restricting fresh water supply and diminishing its ability to generate power. The authors also surmised that the restriction of Nile-borne silt from reaching the delta, combined with its sinking due to natural seismic compaction, could mean that parts of the delta surface now above sea level might be inundated by the end of this century. Although the benefits of the dam for Ethiopian energy production were obvious, the wider ramifications in the African region would make negotiations seem necessary. But these did not make headway during the year. The Gibe-3 dam in the Omo River was partly operational and brought Ethiopia's hydropower capacity to 3,822 MW.

The proven reserves of *natural gas* in the Ogaden of around 24.9 bn m³ remained unexploited, although a memorandum of understanding was signed in November between Ethiopia, Djibouti and China's Poly GCL for a gas pipeline to Djibouti port, i.e. for export, with production planned for 2019 (a project financed by the China Development Bank). Chinese drilling in the Hilal-7 gas field started in January.

Unemployment remained relatively high at 16.5%, with youth unemployment worse, at 23.3%, although authoritative official figures were not available and real figures were probably much higher. A $ 493 m 'Revolving Fund for Ethiopian Youth' was established by the government to stimulate youth entrepreneurship and job creation.

The interest of *foreign investors* kept pace, although with more caution because the ongoing protests, and threats of violence continued against foreign companies on expropriated lands without good neighbourly relations with local populations. The incidents, however, were not on the same scale as the 2016 violence. FDI picked up later in the year and amounted to $ 3.2 bn., some $ 400 m down from 2016. The number of foreign projects/enterprises reached about 800. While FDI thus went on steadily, it was not yet making a dent in the country's export economy, which was still largely driven by agriculture, coffee exports and (gold) mining.

The *national budget* announced in July (for the fiscal year 7 July 2017–7 July 2018) was $ 13.9 bn, 7.5% more than the previous year, but when annual inflation was taken into account the rise was virtually zero. The government's expectation was to meet 68% of the budget from domestic revenue (taxes), a somewhat optimistic idea, seeing that tax revenue fell by 10% and tax collection and administration were not in top shape. The public debt reached 60.3% of GDP, an increase of almost 4%.

Inflation remained relatively high, at 13.6% year on year (IMF figures) and there was ongoing depreciation of the local birr against the dollar (rate in December was Br 24: $ 1). In October, the government suddenly decided to devalue the birr officially by 15% against the dollar with the aim of reducing over-valuation and improving the economy's competitiveness. For the ordinary Ethiopian, life again became much more expensive. It also stimulated the *illicit outflow of foreign currency*; the sum leaving Ethiopia annually was estimated to be around $ 3 bn.

Ethiopia was one of the few countries in Africa that developed an *industrialisation policy*, with new industrial parks opened and under construction to house foreign and domestic enterprises. The process remained largely top-down. This model may have successes, notably in infrastructure development, but it also raises problems. In July, there was a relatively critical debate in parliament on the record of the Metals and Engineering Corporation, which was constructing large *sugar plantations*. Its chairman, Brigadier-General Kinfe Dagnew, had to face tough questioning and admitted mistakes. In November, a critical internal report was produced on the same subject, in which it appeared that mismanagement and serious waste of public funds had been rampant in the construction and management of the large-scale sugar plantations of the state Ethiopian Sugar Corporation (ESC) in southern Ethiopia. The report made waves even within the ruling party and would be discussed in parliament in 2018. There also were reports of bizarre import-export schemes involving sugar, whereby in one instance the ESC exported sugar to Kenya, but, because of a short-fall, it used imported sugar from abroad (via a Dubai company) to meet its contract and lost money on it: if they had sold the imported sugar in Ethiopia, the profits would have been much higher and responded to market demand. Asked why, one ESC official said: "We have this vision of being one of the top ten sugar producing and exporting countries by 2023 …" So this dogmatic 'vision' of the ESC forced it to manoeuvre itself into economically irrational if not absurd schemes to the detriment of public funds and sugar availability in Ethiopia itself. Such events were the logical result of a rigid state-led economic system that was overly dirigiste and thwarted private initiatives and proper market behaviour. In the past ten years, despite billions of investments in the 'sugar industry', the domestic sugar market saw continued shortages.

Two new *industrial parks* were opened, one in Meqele in Tigray and one in Hawassa in the South. The new 140 ha industrial park in Hawassa was expected to employ 60,000 workers at full capacity. It hosted 18 companies active in textiles (garment production) and apparel. In some industrial parks, however, complaints emerged of low pay, bad food and difficult labour conditions. There was relatively high labour turn-over.

In late October and early November, there were some *rare labour strikes*: in Hawassa's industrial park and in Zeway town against the lack of salary increase, and in Dessie town against dramatic tax hikes for small businesses. In March, there were teachers' strikes in Amhara Region (Gojjam, Gondar and Wollo) calling for salary rises.

On 11 January, the 752-km *Addis Ababa-Djibouti electric railway*, built by two Chinese companies, was officially opened on the Djibouti side, at the Nagad railway station. It had cost $ 4.2 bn (a Chinese loan) and replaced the old and derelict diesel-train line. Ethiopia's Prime Minister Hailemariam and Djibouti's President I.O. Guelleh were present at the ceremony. The trains were still operated by Chinese personnel.

The many *global indexes* that try to estimate the performance of countries on numerous economic and governance issues had measurement problems (different per country), but still indicated something. On the World Bank's Ease of Doing Business index, Ethiopia was placed 161st (of 190 countries), down from 159th in 2016. This reflected, among other things, the constant censorship and interruptions of the Internet. On the Heritage Foundation's Index of Economic Freedom, Ethiopia moved up one notch to 52.7 on a scale of 100, still below its highest ever mark of 54.5 in 2004 ('mostly unfree'). TI's Corruptions Perceptions Index figures put the country at a surprising 109th place out of 179 countries. More index figures could be added, but all pointed to a dynamic but strongly top-down managed unfree economy that was making no real structural progress. A final index figure: the HDI listed Ethiopia at 174th of 188 countries, still very low.

Ethiopia again received huge amounts of *donor development aid* in grants and loans (about $ 3.4 bn over the fiscal year July 2016-July 2017), as well as an estimated huge sum in remittances of $ 4.4 bn (6% of GDP, and perhaps more, due to much of it not being registered) from overseas Ethiopians – a sum almost double the country's total export revenue.

The annual IMF report (of December) on *debt* sustainability analysis raised the country's risk of external debt distress from 'moderate' to 'high'. This deterioration in the debt service-to-exports ratio suggested an increase in liquidity risks. Ethiopia spent some $ 1.2 bn to service its debts – slightly under half its export earnings. In September, there were signs that the country had trouble repaying the interest on the debt burden. Exports accounted for less than 20% of imports, meaning continuing trade deficits and foreign exchange shortages. Over the year, this shortage became more acute, hampering local business, despite the issuing of a $ 1.3 bn government bond in January. The annual *IMF Article IV consultation report* of 26 September had complimented Ethiopia for its continued GDP growth, poverty rate reduction and decline in the current account deficit from 9.1% of GDP in 2016 to 8.2%, but they recommended addressing "external imbalances" and "inadequate reserve buffers" (read: the alarming lack of foreign exchange), and limiting external borrowing so as not to accelerate the public debt.

Bribery and corruption remained a problem, and the government liked to be seen as acting against it. On 26 July, over 50 government officials and businesspersons were arrested on allegations of corruption and misuse of public funds valued at more than $ 181 m. Among the arrested were a brigadier general, a state minister and the head of the Legal Department at the Ministry of Finance and Economic Cooperation. The government also seized assets of more than 200 individuals as the investigation continued.

While the contested Grand Renaissance Dam on the Blue Nile showed that Ethiopia was able build a huge multi-billion-dollar project, it still could not feed its own people and called on the international community to do so. Again, *food insecurity problems* stalked the country. On 3 January, Ethiopia's National Disaster Risk Management Commission (NDRMC) said about $ 1 bn was needed to ward off a crisis and that 5.6 m. people needed immediate food assistance. In March, UN Secretary-General Antonio Guterres, during the 28th AU Summit, called on the 'international community' to provide $ 948 m to assist these people to ward off starvation. In a strange statement, he also called Ethiopia a "pillar of stability" – and that in a year that saw hundreds of people killed and thousands arrested, as well as a generally precarious socio-political situation. On 28 April, the NDRMC raised the number of those in need of food aid to 7.7 m.

The number of *IDPs and refugees* from surrounding countries was again substantial, testifying to the continued deep instability and political-economic misery of the Horn countries. In July, the International Organization for Migration (IOM) said there were 1,056,738 IDPs (including the displaced Oromo from the Hararge border areas with Somali Region, numbering 577,711). There were 367,557 other IDPs in Oromia; 52,523 in Afar; 28,954 in Tigray, 17,472 in Gambella, 8,921 in Amhara and 3,600 in Harar. Most of these IDPs were produced by conflict, but drought in the east also played a role and was responsible for 375,074 IDPs (according to the IOM). The refugee population was also substantial again: by 31 August, according to the IOM, the total was 852,721, with South Sudan (388,086), Somalia (252,036), Eritrea (161,941) and Sudan (42,967) being the major source countries. The UNHCR gave slightly different figures.

Environmental problems continued to be a grave challenge: erosion, land loss, salinisation and land fertility decline. One specific problem that came into the limelight was the water hyacinth disaster affecting Lake T'ana, the huge water reservoir in Amhara Region and source of the Blue Nile. This invasive species threatened to suffocate the lake and with it fisheries, navigation and water supplies to millions of people. Local authorities mobilised thousands of people to manually combat the rapidly spreading plant and studied other means to tackle it (such as the possible use of hyacinth eating insects such as the neochetina weevil).

Kenya

Nanjala Nyabola

Kenya was dominated by news related to the general election. Tension over the polls had built up throughout 2016 and finally came to a boil around the disputed August poll, which saw Uhuru Kenyatta declared the winner in questionable circumstances, immediately triggering protests and violent police reprisals. In the three days after the result was announced, the police killed at least 37 people in opposition strongholds in Nairobi and western Kenya. Tensions also spiralled in places like Laikipia, where the election reignited tensions over land ownership between the local communities and the significant community of European origin. The opposition filed a petition challenging the result, as was widely expected – all Kenyan multi-party elections except in 1962 and 2002 having been subject to legal review. The result of this petition was unprecedented: in a 4–2 vote, the Supreme Court annulled the August result, declaring that the elections had not been conducted in the spirit envisioned by the Constitution, returning Kenyans to the polls in November. Intrigues around the vote edged out equally important stories such as the calamitous two-year drought that sent food prices skyrocketing throughout the country, as well as increasingly alarming incidents of mass corruption, including the plunder of the National Youth Service.

 | DOI:10.1163/9789004367630_036

Domestic Politics

The central actor in this year's *general election* was the *Independent Elections and Boundaries Commission* (IEBC). Created by the 2010 Constitution to oversee the conduct of elections, the IEBC was plagued by accusations of partisanship and wrangling between senior staff members. Following intense pressure from the opposition and violent street protests, all sitting members of the IEBC had resigned in October 2016 to give way to a more representative membership, and replacement commissioners were appointed in January, leaving only six months to prepare for what was already a complicated election. The replacement commissioners soon received major criticism after several routine processes, including the verification and audit of the voter register, were inexplicably delayed and then rushed so as to hit the constitutional deadlines.

The election was further complicated by the requirement that it be digital by the standards set out by the Independent Review Commission (IREC, or the Kreigler Commission) in 2008. Given that the IREC was part of the political settlement after the 2008 election violence, there were legal and constitutional requirements that *digital technology* be incorporated into the IEBC's procedures. A French company, OT Morpho Safran, was contracted to provide electronic voter registration and identification systems, known as the EVID and the BVR systems, respectively. The opposition disputed the allocation of these contracts because they were single-sourced, i.e. there was no competitive tender and bidding process as required by law. Even so, the systems were rolled out and, for the first time, all Kenyans registered to vote were able to check the status of their voter registration through SMS or on the IEBC website, although there were several complaints that the system was faulty and delivered erroneous results across the country.

As in 2013, the two major *presidential candidates* were the incumbent, Uhuru Kenyatta, who led the Jubilee Party, and Raila Odinga, who led a coalition of parties known as the National Super Alliance (NASA) coalition. Another six candidates with smaller followings were also on the ballot and, for the first time since 2002, there were no women running for president. A record-breaking 16,259 candidates ran for 1,882 positions under the new devolution dispensation. According to the IEBC, Kenyatta won the August vote by 8.2 m votes to Odinga's 6.8 m.

The first indications of *election tension* arose in the context of the April primaries. The Kenya National Commission on Human Rights (KNCHR) reported that the primaries for all the major parties and some of the minor ones were conducted in an atmosphere of disorganisation and intimidation. KNCHR recorded at least 17 incidents of violence across the country, as well as instances of misuse of public property in support of specific candidates. There were also several cases of defection as candidates complained that their respective parties had already decided the outcome of the primaries before a vote had been conducted.

Several *high profile deaths* underscored the tense environment in which the 8 August election was going to be conducted. On 8 July, Cabinet Secretary for the Interior Joseph Nkaissery had a heart attack and died hours after chairing a security briefing on the upcoming election. An autopsy ruled out any foul play but his death raised tensions and speculation as Nkaissery had personally overseen much of the security arrangements for the election. Then, on 31 July, eight days before the vote, Chris Msando, acting head of ICT at the IEBC, was found dead about 20 km outside Nairobi. An autopsy revealed that he had suffered several severe cuts to his arm before being strangled to death. Msando's role was taken by the man he had replaced on the IEBC, who in turn had been suspended for failing to cooperate with the procurement department at the IEBC, raising further suspicions of foul play. Msando's murder remained unsolved. Similarly, on 19 August, Caroline Odiga, a deputy presiding officer in Siaya County, was found murdered in Sega trading centre. Her case also remained unsolved.

In the end, the August general election was *the most expensive election in the world*, costing $ 28 per person, but the great expense did not resolve the underlying political tension and lack of trust between key political figures or between the electorate and the IEBC. The IEBC estimated that it spent KES (shilling) 60 bn ($ 582 m) on the election overall, much of which went to foreign contractors who implemented the digital infrastructure including the EVID, BVR and Results Transmission System (RTS), although all these systems failed at some level, and Al Gurair, a Dubai-based firm that provided printed ballot papers for both elections. Days before the vote, the IEBC announced that the over 11,000, or just over one-third, of the polling stations would not be using the electronic systems owing to lack of 4G coverage – an issue that was highly disputed by voters.

Another notable development in this election was *the use of social media* for advocacy and accountability, as well as for the dissemination of hate speech. By the voting date, at least 10 m Kenyans were registered on the social media platform WhatsApp, as well as another 7 m on Facebook and 1 m on Twitter. This perhaps explained why Kenyatta's Jubilee party paid $ 6 m to the (now-defunct) data analytics and public relations UK corporation Cambridge Analytica to consult on their campaign. Similarly, Odinga's NASA paid an undisclosed amount to Aristotle Inc., a US firm, to perform the same function. The US consultants supporting this operation were summarily deported with only a day or two to the election. It also emerged that the Jubilee party spent an undisclosed amount retaining Harris Media Inc., which was responsible for a wave of US-style attack ads referring to Odinga as a "Lord of War" and promising an apocalypse should he be elected. Much of this was disseminated on WhatsApp before crossing over to more public facing platforms, but the National Cohesion and Integration Commission (NCIC) did not intervene.

In contrast, several voters used their presence on the app to disprove official election narratives, such as the absence of 4G in their various polling stations or to point out discrepancies between results announced on the RTS and those announced at polling stations. Citizen journalists also covered various cases of police violence, particularly in Mathare informal settlement in Nairobi and in Kisumu County on social media days before the local media broke the stories. It later emerged that the police prevented the media from accessing many of these locations and physically intimidated journalists who attempted to cover the events, even though citizen journalists had recorded and shared video and photographic evidence of police brutality. It was thus not until 17 August that the first reports of the violence appeared on traditional media.

However, social media were also used to disseminate information that amounted to hate speech. As a result, in July, with just a month left to the first election, the Communications Authority and the NCIC both issued guidelines that they claimed would prevent the dissemination of hate speech, but civil society argued that the guidelines were designed to restrict free speech. The NCIC also tried to pass regulations that would fine administrators of WhatsApp groups for producing or distributing hate speech, although it was unclear that these regulations were ever used. Despite these efforts, social media became a focal point for both hate speech and to counteract misinformation that was rampant in the traditional press.

The entire election would also have serious ramifications for the practice of *election observation* in general. Following the announcement of the result on 11 August, all the major election observation groups in the country, amongst them the EU, AU, the Carter Center and the EAC, signed off on the election as broadly free and fair. NASA went to court almost immediately to challenge the outcome and, during the court proceedings, lawyers for the IEBC and for Kenyatta relied heavily on the observer mission reports. Thus, when the *Supreme Court rejected the results of the poll*, it undermined the credibility of the observer missions, forcing several of them to backtrack on the reports they had issued, especially in the context of intense social media pressure from voters.

The Supreme Court handed down its decision on the presidential petition on 1 September, giving the IEBC 90 days to declare a *new election date* as dictated by the Constitution, and the IEBC settled for 26 October. The period between the elections was characterised by heightened tensions between Jubilee and NASA, several high profile violent incidents and unprecedented political behaviour. Significantly, Roselyn Akombe, a commissioner at the IEBC, fled the country and issued a statement in exile alleging high-level intimidation of commissioners and declaring that the IEBC could not conduct a free and fair election in these circumstances. At a press conference responding to Akombe's statement, IEBC Chair Wafula Chebukati agreed, although he declined to postpone the election.

Meanwhile, the opposition first produced an irreducible minimum list of alterations that they insisted needed to be made to the polling system before they would participate, including, for example, changing vendors for the EVID system. The

IEBC argued that it was too close to the election for these changes to be made and so, on 10 October, Odinga declared that he was withdrawing from the poll rerun. By an obscure provision of case law, this theoretically meant that the IEBC should call for fresh nominations, i.e. reset the electoral calendar. However, the IEBC declined and, although the Supreme Court agreed to hear a petition on the issue two days before the poll, there was no quorum on the bench for the case to be heard. As a result, Odinga and his followers called for a *boycott* of the new election.

The lack of a quorum at the court was directly attributable to several incidents. First the government declared 25 and 26 October public holidays. On 24 October, the day before the petition was to be heard, a driver and bodyguard of Deputy Chief Justice Philomena Mwilu were shot and killed. Mwilu did not attend court the following day. Justice Njoki Ndung'u told the court that she had taken a flight out of the city and would not be returning in time for the session, while Justices Ojwang and Wanjala did not offer reasons for their absence. As a result, the 26 October poll went on as scheduled.

Voter turnout in October was significantly lower than at the August poll, in part because of the boycott but perhaps also owing to anxiety over possible violence around the poll. Over 19 m Kenyans were registered to vote and, although over 15 m voted in August, only 7.6 m voted in October, according to IEBC figures. Only counties that corresponded to strongholds for Kenyatta and his running mate William Ruto registered voter turnout of over 40%, and in many polling stations, including in Nairobi, Mombasa and Kisumu, some polling stations had zero turnout. This extended the political uncertainty into the new year, perhaps best exemplified by the markedly low turnout nationwide at the country's Jamhuri day celebrations on 12 December.

Women's rights issues also arose in the context of the election. 2017 was a historic year because three women were elected governors around the country and Sophia Abdi Noor became the first Somali woman elected to office in Kenya in an open (i.e. not connected to the gender quota) election. However, several women candidates from across the country reported violence and intimidation by opponents and even by family members, who argued that women had no place in electoral politics. Similarly, HRW accused the police of perpetrating 65 sexual assaults between the 8 August vote and the 2 November swearing-in.

The election took place in an atmosphere of *self-censorship and intimidation of the traditional media*. At least two journalists were arrested in the course of their work. In April, Isaiah Gwengi was threatened and assaulted by police who he claimed were unhappy with his reporting of police brutality. And in the week before the election, Walter Menya was arrested for allegedly soliciting a bribe, although he argued that he was arrested because he refused to take the bribe and because he had published the details of a fundraising event for the Jubilee party where several senior civil servants illegally gave donations to the party. Journalists also argued that they were subject to violence from both the government and the opposition in the build-up to the election. In the chaotic days between the announcement of Kenyatta's victory on 11 August and the cancellation of the poll on 1 September, journalists also reported that the police prevented them from covering anti-government protests and alleged police violence in opposition strongholds. The main law used to prevent their access was the Firearms Act, which prohibits civilians from owning high calibre weapons and related artefacts without a permit. Although media organisations were theoretically exempt from some of these provisions, the police allegedly argued that Kenyan journalists wearing bulletproof vests and helmets would not be allowed to access the sites of violence. International journalists were seemingly exempt from these prohibitions, although some of them reported that the police deliberately damaged equipment while they were covering the protests and the aftermath.

Away from the election, the Somali terrorist group *al-Shabaab carried out attacks on the coast*, including sporadic incidents in mainland Lamu County. In July, Al Shabaab allegedly decapitated nine people near the Boni Forest on the Kenya-Somalia border, which the police had earlier identified as a major hiding place for the group. In August, another three decapitations occurred in the same area, and a third incident in September saw four civilians killed in the same way. Mariam el-Maawy, the principal secretary in the Ministry of Public Works, was shot in a roadside attack in September, becoming the highest profile victim of al-Shabaab in 2017.

At least *2,000 people were displaced* as a result of these attacks and, in response, the military, stationed in the area for several months, threatened to bomb the Boni Forest and urged all civilians living in the area to leave. As a result, local human rights groups accused the government of forced displacements. Meanwhile Coast Regional Police Coordinator Nelson Marwa accused senior politicians of instigating attacks to depress voter turnout in the county, consistent with patterns during the 1997 general election. Operation Linda Boni, the police-military operation to flush the group out of the forest, continued.

Al-Shabaab operations in north-eastern Kenya also continued. From January, there were regular attacks in Mandera town, with at least one attack reported almost every month until the end of the year. In March, five police officers were killed in an attack about 50 km from Mandera town. Notably, there was an increase in the use of improvised explosive devices throughout the region. In June alone, at least 40 people were killed in attacks staged by the group. In May, four civilians were killed in an attack in Liboi, Garissa County, and five police officers in Governor Ali Roba's personal security detail were killed in a similar attack in Mandera. By some measures, the group grew more brazen, including a day-time shooting into an Equity Bank branch in El Wak town in June that killed two civilians.

These attacks occurred against a backdrop of *increased spending on security*, leading to several questions about transparency within Kenya's defence sector. In

April, the government announced a KES 90 bn (approximately $ 820 m) military budget – over double the amount spent in neighbouring Ethiopia and by far the highest in the region. In January, President Kenyatta commissioned 525 armoured personnel vehicles – the last of a batch purchased through a police modernisation programme. Some were specifically purchased as part of the elections security programme but others were to assist in the broader conflict with al-Shabaab. In June, the government announced that it had acquired several 'mine resistant ambush protected' vehicles from China to help in the fight against al-Shabaab, who nevertheless still claimed responsibility for several successful attacks against the Kenyan Defence Forces (KDF).

Nature conservation was also a lightning rod issue. Laikipia county was at the epicentre of clashes between *pastoralist communities* like the Tugen and Samburu, and *sedentary communities* who had relatively recently moved into the province, notably the European immigrant owners of various nature reserves. The pastoralists claimed that they needed the pasture available in the reserves because of the searing drought in the country but the reserve owners argued that the pastoralists were a threat to the ecosystems established on these privately held lands. By 1 November, at least 22 people were confirmed killed and tens more injured in these clashes, as well as significant property damage at various sites. Meanwhile owners of the reserves alleged that local politicians had incited and armed groups to invade the farms and drive out reserve owners when it became known that the 99-year freehold leases on which the reserves were based would expire in 2017.

Foreign Affairs

The complicated election fuelled allegations of interference by major Western allies of the administration and at numerous points, diplomats in Kenya – particularly those of the EU, the UK and the US – did issue statements that some analysts argued amounted to interference. In August, the envoys endorsed the results of the August election and encouraged Odinga to seek restitution in the courts, only for the Supreme Court to annul the results of that election. In October, this coalition of diplomats threatened travel bans against anyone who derailed the vote, while also expressing concern about the late changes in the electoral law proposed by the Jubilee party.

In January, Foreign Minister Amina Mohamed ran for the position of *AU Chair*, hoping to succeed Nkosazana Dlamini-Zuma as the second woman to head the organisation. Kenyatta openly supported Mohamed's campaign, publicly hoping that it would increase the country's influence in the regional body, particularly after Kenya's successful push to change Africa's engagement with the ICC. The administration therefore dedicated huge amounts of public money to supporting

Mohamed's effort. Although she performed strongly in the early rounds of the vote she eventually lost in the second to last rounds to Mahamat Moussa Faki of Chad, allegedly failing to garner votes from regional neighbours like Uganda.

The KDF continued their operations in *Somalia* as part of the AU Mission in Somalia (AMISOM), despite growing concerns over funding shortages. In May, Kenyatta renewed his commitment to keep KDF troops in Somalia until "Kenya is secure". In January, Burundi's President Pierre Nkuruziza insisted that he would withdraw his troops from the country in the context of EU sanctions against him. However, after negotiations with the AU, Nkuruziza backtracked on this threat and the EU renewed its commitment to AMISOM in March by pledging € 120 m for troop salaries and allowances.

The government also continued a policy of 'voluntary' *returns of Somali refugees* from Daadab camp in Garissa County, despite the concerns of human rights groups that the returns were not fully voluntary. In February, the High Court declared that the government should stop the returns because they violated the principle of non-refoulement by returning refugees to a place where they would be exposed to harm. Despite this ruling, the returns continued with the support of UNHCR, even while refugees told AI that the main reason they took the option to return was that aid agencies had drastically reduced food rations to the camp, pushing them into significant debt. In defiance of the High Court ruling, by December, returns to Somalia from Daadab were continuing.

At the same time, Kakuma camp in Turkana saw an *influx of refugees* from South Sudan and Ethiopia amidst escalating political violence in both those countries. As tensions between Ethiopia's Oromo community and the state escalated, thousands of refugees crossed the border at Kakuma and in Moyale, while several hundred more made their way to Nairobi. Outside Kakuma, official support for these groups was sparse in the context of an increasingly hostile government policy against urban refugees.

Kenya's relationship with *South Sudan* remained complex. In January, two South Sudanese human rights activists went missing in Nairobi, their families claiming that they had been kidnapped by the South Sudanese regime. After a habeas corpus hearing, a Kenyan court declared that they were not in Kenyan custody. In May, four Kenyan aid workers were killed when their convoy was ambushed in Pibor, approximately 340 km north-east of Juba, an area under the control of rebel leader Riek Machar, although Machar's group, the Sudan People's Liberation Movement-in Opposition denied responsibility for the killings. In May, the Kenya Commercial Bank, one of the first Kenyan businesses to enter the nascent South Sudanese market soon after secession, closed several branches, citing hyperinflation.

There was diplomatic tension with *Tanzania* over allegations that the latter was hosting a server for Raila Odinga's election campaign. In July, media reports in Kenya said that Odinga's team had established back-up servers for their independent tallying of election results in Tanzania and in Germany, compelling the Tanzanian government to issue an official statement rejecting the claims. Meanwhile, Tanzania's official opposition party endorsed Uhuru Kenyatta's presidency, further signalling the tension between the two nations' ruling parties. In the end, Tanzania's President John Magufuli did attend the Kenyatta inauguration in November, signalling interest in moving past these tensions.

Socioeconomic Developments

Predictably, the uncertain election affected economic growth. For the first time in five years, *GDP growth contracted* to 4.9%, from an average of 5.5% in previous years. The treasury attributed the contraction to both the election and the prolonged *drought*, which lasted throughout the year, crippling agricultural production. In April, the government declared the drought a national emergency, with over 2.7 m people and 23 of 47 counties affected. By some estimates, food production at the coast fell by over 90% and the price of maize – the national staple – rose by a third. Counties in the north-east (Marsabit and Turkana) and those at the coast (Kilifi, Lamu, Tana River and Mombasa) were the worst affected. This drought pushed pastoralists into neighbouring countries in search of pasture, leading to low-level conflicts, particularly in South Sudan. No deaths were directly attributed to the drought, although millions of livestock died for lack of pasture.

Agriculture, which accounted for 31.5% of GDP, grew by only 1.6% compared with 5.1% in 2016. The Kenya Association of Manufacturers announced that several members were planning to cut back jobs due to the deteriorating *business environment*. As a result, the Kenya shilling weakened considerably against the US dollar to trade at an all-time low of KES 103.85: $ 1, while *inflation* rose to 8% from an average of 6.3% in 2016.

The *tourism* sector – Kenya's second largest source of income – was hit particularly hard by the electoral uncertainty, as both domestic and international tourism contracted. In Malindi, a popular destination for Italian tourists, occupancy at major hotels dipped to below 10% in the period between July and November. Industry experts also attributed the contraction to travel advisories by both the US and the UK, particularly warning against travel to the Lamu region.

Despite these challenges, the Treasury continued its commitment to *large-scale infrastructure projects*. In March, Cabinet Secretary for the Treasury Henry Rotich pledged just under KES 135 bn ($ 1.3 bn) to infrastructure related spending, most of which would be committed to roads. Still, the largest single budget item under this commitment remained the celebrated Standard Gauge Railway (SGR), which would receive just over half of the allocation pledged. The SGR, also known as the Madaraka express, was opened in May, symbolising deepening ties between Kenya and China. Built at a cost of $ 3.6 bn, far above the industry average, the SGR was financed primarily through loans from large-scale Chinese banks and would be run as a joint venture by the Kenyan and Chinese governments for five years. Supporters of the project pointed to the reduced cost of travelling between Kenya's two largest cities, but critics argued that the project was not financially feasible as it did not significantly lower the cost of sending cargo – the primary reason why the line was built. In addition, the SGR added considerably to Kenya's overall indebtedness. Similarly, there were concerns that the launch of the project was rushed to capitalise on the election as the trains that were received were not to the standard promised in project documents.

Developments along the *Lamu Port and South Sudan Ethiopia Transport corridor* continued. Dredging works for the construction of the Lamu port also continued, fuelling significant speculation over land, which grassroots activists linked to increased cases of murder on the mainland. Litigation against the developers included a case brought by fishermen organised under an umbrella group claiming that the project infringed on their cultural rights and denied them their livelihoods. Despite these complaints, the project received KES 1 bn ($ 9 m) from the NEPAD Development Infrastructure Project Preparation Facility to prepare the port for international investment. In September, the *Isiolo International Airport* opened to facilitate the export of 'miraa' (the stimulant Catha edulis Forsk.) from the highlands where it is grown to its primary market in Somalia.

Tensions over the *Lamu Coal Plant* also escalated as activists from the island maintained that it would be destructive to their ecosystem and livelihoods, though high-profile figures such as Deputy President William Ruto declared their support for the project. In February, the Energy Regulatory Council approved the construction of the plant, despite significant opposition and accusations that the permit approval process had been manipulated to push it through. Amu Power, the consortium of companies building the plant, received a capital injection of KES 206 bn (approximately $ 2 m) from China Power Global and promised that breaking ground on the plant would occur in October – it did not. Meanwhile, public opposition to the plant grew, including from outgoing Cabinet Secretary for the Environment Judy Wakuhungu, who officially declared her opposition to the plant in June.

In January, while doctors were still on a work stoppage carried over from 2016, *university lecturers went on strike* over unpaid salaries, bringing the higher education sector across 33 public universities to a standstill. The strike continued until March, when the government and the unions agreed on a new pay structure, but it resumed in early July as the government failed to implement its promises. In late July, the lecturers called off the strike, only to resume it in November, leading to severe disruptions in the academic calendar. Meanwhile, in early August secondary school teachers also announced that they would be going on strike, to protest against arbitrary transfers by the Ministry of Education.

Corruption remained a pressing issue. In May, the US government suspended $ 21 m in support for the Ministry of Health amidst reports of poor financial accountability and mismanagement. Significantly, details emerged of a complex scheme to short the market for *maize*, the country's main staple, in the context of the biting drought. Despite the drought, farmers in maize-producing regions complained that statutory boards had failed to purchase produce from them and that it was rotting in granaries. At the same time, the government announced a maize shortage and insisted that it was necessary to import maize to make up for it. Surprisingly, the imported maize appeared in Kenya days after the shortage was announced, raising questions about the unusual coincidence. The government claimed that the maize was imported from Mexico but the Mexican government denied this. In an interview, former minister for agriculture Kipruto arap Kirwa revealed that the maize shipment was part of an elaborate scheme involving distributing poor quality fertiliser from the National Cereals and Produce Board in order to depress production and allow the subsidised importation of maize. The scandal remained unresolved. At the same time, while the year had begun with promises that Cabinet Secretary Hasan Wario would face legal action over the debacle of mismanagement and corruption around the 2016 Olympics campaign, no such action was taken and Wario was appointed an ambassador soon after the election.

Sports remained a major unifying factor as Kenya hosted the International Association of Athletics Federations World under-18 Championships at the Kasarani stadium. The government waived ticket prices for the event and so it was the best-attended tournament in the event's history, with over 60,000 fans in the stands. The Kenyan team won 15 medals, including four gold, and came fourth overall. Former cabinet secretary for the interior Joseph Nkaissery, who had personally overseen the planning of the project, died before the event. In Rugby Sevens, the Kenya Lionesses had a remarkable run but failed to qualify for the World Cup after losing to South Africa in the finals of the Women's Rugby Africa Sevens Cup in September. The team did qualify for the Commonwealth Games, however, despite a scandal in which the Kenya Rugby Union claimed that it did not have the money to send the team to the Dubai Sevens Invitational for the first time since 2009.

It was also a mixed year in the *arts*. Film director Judy Kibinge made history as the first Kenyan director invited to join the Academy of Motion Pictures that distributes the Oscars every year, joining actress Lupita Nyong'o, who was invited shortly after she became the first Kenyan to win an Oscar in 2014. This signalled the growing significance of the film sector and also unfortunately triggered several high-profile clashes with the Kenya Film Classification Board, which many artists accused of hyper-censorship. Controversy also plagued Kenya's participation at the Venice Biennale – a centrepiece event of the global arts calendar – as the government failed to provide adequate funding for the invitees, while some participants received their visas from the Italian embassy only the day before the event. The

Nairobi National Museum also courted controversy by banning exhibitions by three of Kenya's leading visual artists – Michael Soi, Patrick Mukabi and Bertiers Mbatia – on the basis that their art was not suitable for children. The artists had been invited to exhibit as part of an International Day of Museums Celebration dubbed 'Speaking the Unspeakable' and commissioned especially by the Museum, to address the decline of publicly funded art spaces.

Rwanda

Yolande Bouka

The presidential elections dominated much of 2017. The ruling RPF consolidated its political power as President Kagame won 98.8 % of the vote. Rwanda's human rights record continued to be challenged by international human rights organisations and the UN. Rwanda was one of the leading troop and police contributing country to peacekeeping operations. Bilateral relations with both Burundi and France remained strained. The drought that hit Eastern Africa continued to plague Rwanda. The government made important progress in infrastructure development by increasing the number of households connected to electricity to over 35% from 22% at the end of 2016. Economic performance remained strong, with a GDP growth of 5.1%.

Domestic Politics

The Rwandan Patriotic Front (RPF) consolidated its hold on political power as President Paul Kagame won the *presidential elections* for the third consecutive time. These elections were to be a litmus test of Rwanda's political transition after

 | DOI:10.1163/9789004367630_037

being ruled by the same man since the end of the 1994 genocide. However, the RPF insistence on changing the constitution in 2015, which enabled Kagame to run and decisively win politically controlled elections in 2017 after 23 years in power, demonstrated the political elite's insecurity and raised important questions about the strength of the country's institutions and the sustainability of Rwanda's peacebuilding model beyond Kagame. While the electoral process was peaceful, several diplomatic missions and organisations expressed their concerns about irregularities, including the counting of ballots and vote tabulations.

The presidential elections took place under very *tight control of the political space*, with a poor human rights record and restrictions on freedom of speech, despite calls by international partners such as the United States to open political space and allow the democratic transition of power. The RPF government continued to be heavily criticised for stifling political opposition by controlling public speech and debate, and harassing and arresting members of the opposition. In May, for example, the government announced that candidates wanting to post campaign messages on social media networks needed to first submit the material 48 hours in advance to the National Electoral Commission (NEC) for approval. However, following national and international condemnation, the NEC reversed this ruling. Only two candidates were allowed to challenge President Kagame: Frank Habineza (Democratic Green Party of Rwanda) and Philippe Mpayimana (independent), who received 0.5% and 0.7% of the vote, respectively. Gilbert Mwenedata, another independent candidate, was disqualified from the presidential elections because the NEC rejected his candidacy, citing invalidity of his signatures. Controversial Catholic priest-turned-politician Thomas Nahimana also attempted to challenge Kagame but was denied entry to Rwanda in January for the second time in as many months.

While the Rwandan government received international accolades for having the highest percentage of *women* in parliament in the world, it had a mixed record for handling vocal female presidential challengers. During the election campaign, the most notable example was the treatment of *Diane Shima Rwigara*, a businesswoman and women's rights activist. Rwigara announced her candidacy for the presidency on 3 May. A few days later, nude photos, allegedly of Rwigara, were posted online. Several media sources accused Kagame's regime of being responsible. During her campaign, she vocally condemned Kagame's economic policy, brutal political repression and failure to address a growing famine. On 7 July, the NEC announced Rwigara's disqualification, citing her failure to collect enough qualifying signatures. After her candidacy was rejected, she launched the People Salvation Movement ('Itabaza') to advocate for open democratic processes and addressing basic needs of all Rwandans. In September, Rwigara was arrested on charges of inciting insurrection and forging electoral documents. She and her mother were held without bail while awaiting trial. Her arrest followed a pattern of intimidation of political opponents. She was the second female presidential candidate to be arrested ahead of presidential elections. Victoria Ingabire, who was arrested in 2010, remained in prison serving a 15-year sentence for "endangering state security" and "promoting ethnic divisionism". In November, the African Court on Human and Peoples' Rights found that Rwanda had violated the African Charter and the International Convention on Civil and Political Rights by denying Ingabire's right to an adequate defence, fair trial and freedom of expression. The court also suggested that the law prohibiting "minimisation of the genocide", under which Ingabire was convicted, posed a significant threat to freedom of speech in the country.

The government remained heavily criticised for its use of *arrest and detention to limit political debate*. In February, Violette Uwamahoro, a British national and the wife of a member of the banned Rwanda National Congress opposition group, went missing in Kigali. She had travelled from the UK to attend her father's funeral in Rwanda. While the authorities initially denied knowledge of her whereabouts, the police announced a month later that she was in their custody, charged with sharing state secrets, participating in the formation of an irregular armed group and committing offences against the established government or president. In March, a judge ruled that there was insufficient evidence against her, and she returned to the UK. On 26 September, eight leaders and members of the unregistered United Democratic Forces-Inkingi (FDU-Inkingi) party were charged with forming an irregular armed group and with offences against the president. Théophile Ntirutwa, the party's Kigali representative, was detained on 6 September and held incommunicado until 23 September. He was later charged with supporting an armed group.

Despite the RPF government's stated commitment to improving its *human rights* record, international organisations, such as HRW and AI, continued to document gross abuses perpetrated by the government. In July, HRW published a report detailing evidence of extrajudicial killings and enforced disappearances of petty criminals in western Rwanda by the military and the police force. In a subsequent report in October, the organisation offered testimony and evidence of unlawful detention, disappearances, torture and other human rights violations, mostly carried out by the military between 2010 and 2017. In the same month, the UN subcommittee on torture prevention suspended its seven-day visit to Rwanda, claiming that the authorities had obstructed them from accessing detention sites and prevented them from conducting private and confidential interviews, thereby compromising their fact-finding mission. In December, the UN released its findings and expressed its concerns over the government's practice of arbitrary detention and the reported torture and ill-treatment of detainees.

Following the elections, Kagame *reshuffled his cabinet* and created new ministries. Some of the new members included Edouard Ngirente, a man relatively unknown to the Rwandan political scene, who became the sixth prime minister since the genocide. Before his appointment, he had served as a senior economic advisor to the director of the World Bank. He replaced Anastase Murekezi, who had held the post from 2014 and was appointed chief ombudsman in the current administration. There were initially some concerns that Ngirente's arrival would lead to significant changes to the composition of the cabinet. However, the personnel changes were minimal, thereby allowing Kagame to seamlessly retain his influence over decision-making. Some of the structural changes to the cabinet included the division of the former Ministry of Natural Resources into two ministries: Environment, and Lands and Forestry. The former Ministry of Youth and ICT was also split into two: it was hoped that the creation of a ministry exclusively dedicated to ICT would increase the country's ICT penetration and thus improve labour productivity, creating an additional 1.5 m jobs by 2024 and enabling the economy's technological progress. Among the anticipated advancements were plans to make Rwanda cashless by 2024.

Women featured prominently in Kagame's new cabinet, accounting for more than half of the ministers appointed and Rwanda continued to be a world leader in the numerical representation of women in both legislative and executive branches of government. Indeed, 11 of the 20 ministers and two of the 11 ministers of state named were women, as well as five out of the six new cabinet members. A prominent female member of Kagame's cabinet since 2008, Louise Mushikiwabo remained as minister of foreign affairs and cooperation, now also responsible for EAC affairs, which were previously under the purview of the Ministry of Trade and Industry. Given Rwanda's ambition to lead regional and continental economic integration, Mushikiwabo was likely to continue to play a significant role in Rwandan diplomacy. Olivier Nduhungirehe, who was named minister of state, was to second her. Nduhungirehe was the Rwandan ambassador to Belgium between 2015 and 2017, and in that capacity had been a fierce and vocal supporter of the Rwandan government, often appearing in the media. His new high-level appointment was seen by many as a reward for his loyal service to the regime. Kagame continued to rely on a 'technocratic' cabinet to achieve his economic goals. Thus, only a few months after the formation of his new government, he removed Papias Musafiri and Jean Philbert Nsenginama as ministers of education and ICT, respectively. They were replaced by Eugène Mutimura, a former coordinator of the World Bank-supported African Centres of Excellence Project, and Jean de Dieu Rurangirwa, a former project coordinator at the Ministry of Finance and Economic Planning, who had provided consultancy services to the IMF on public-sector financial management.

The RPF maintained its commitment to seek accountability for crimes committed during the *1994 genocide*. In March, Pope Francis asked for forgiveness for the church's role in the genocide. For over two decades, the Rwandan government had sought official recognition of the role the Catholic Church had played in the execution of the genocide. The Pontiff's acknowledgment was a significant victory for genocide survivors and the Rwandan government, which was also seeking a similar apology from the French government. The Rwandan government continued aggressively to seek the extradition of genocide suspects around the world. In February, it signed an extradition treaty with the government of Malawi, and similar treaties with Zambia and Ethiopia in April. The government had consistently made use of such treaties to obtain custody of and prosecute genocide suspects and, in August, Jean Twagiramungu, a former teacher accused of planning and committing genocide in the former Gikongoro Prefecture, was extradited to Rwanda from Germany to stand trial. In Denmark, Wenceslas Twagirayezu was arrested in March and faced extradition as a suspected génocidaire. Once on Rwandan soil, genocide suspects were likely to be convicted and receive long sentences. In April, Rwanda's High Court convicted Bernard Munyagishari, whose case had been transferred from the International Criminal Tribunal for Rwanda to Rwanda in 2013, of genocide and crimes against humanity and sentenced him to life imprisonment. In December, Emmanuel Mbarushimana, extradited from Denmark in 2014, was found guilty on genocide charges and sentenced to life imprisonment. In July, Léopold Munyakazi, a university professor deported from the United States to Rwanda in 2016, was found guilty of genocide charges. The Intermediate Court of Muhanga sentenced him to life imprisonment in solitary confinement – a detention practice condemned by the UN Human Rights Committee as a violation of the prohibition of torture or other cruel, inhuman or degrading treatment. Some countries had been hesitant to extradite genocide suspects to Rwanda, expressing concerns over the country's human rights record and fair trial standards for genocide suspects. In July, for example, the UK High Court halted extradition proceedings for five Rwandan genocide suspects, citing risks that the suspects would be denied a fair trial.

Foreign Affairs

The Rwandan government remained a leading supporter of UN peacekeeping missions, with the RPF regime often explaining its continued engagement with peace and security initiatives in Africa by pointing to the devastating consequences of the failed UN intervention in 1994, which contributed to the genocide. Rwanda had deployed its first peacekeepers to the AU Mission in Sudan (AMIS) in 2004. Rwanda was now the sixth-largest *contributors of troops and police to UN missions*, with over 6,000 Rwandans deployed in various capacities, among them, 1,800 troops serving in the UN Mission in South Sudan (UNMISS). In August, Rwanda hosted a UN Peace Operations preparatory meeting in Kigali, where Minister of Defence James Kabarebe pledged more support to UN peacekeeping missions. In July, several Rwandese peacekeepers serving in the Rwanda Aviation Unit (RAU 5) in UNMISS received medals for their service. Deputy Special Representative of the Secretary-General (Political) Moustapha Soumaré specifically highlighted the contribution of the eight female Rwanda peacekeepers in the continent of 165, emphasising the need for more UN *female peacekeepers* to be deployed. Rwandan women serving as peacekeepers and police officers in UN missions were lauded for their contribution to peace and security and continued to promote Rwanda's image as a leader of in the promotion of women's empowerment and the Women, Peace and Security Agenda.

The RPF government also took several initiatives to position itself as a *leader on the African political scene.* It took a leading role in a series of events to showcase its peacebuilding and economic achievements as a model to export to other African countries. In July, at the AU Summit held in Addis Ababa (Ethiopia), Kagame was elected to serve as the head of the AU from the beginning in 2018 (one-year term). In 2016, Kagame had been selected to lead a team of experts and representatives of African governments to develop institutional reforms at the AU to promote the organisation's economic self-sufficiency and reduce dependence on foreign aid. In January, he published a report outlining a set of priorities against which the AU should realign its institutions. Rwanda worked to overcome the limitations of its small size and landlocked status by developing a series of regional and international treaties and alliances.

The Rwandan government also strove to reduce its dependence on Western donors and increasingly turned to the East for trade and development assistance. For example, in February, *India*'s Deputy Prime Minister Hamid Ansari undertook a three-day visit, the first time that an Indian dignitary of that level had visited the country. This visit followed a trip Kagame had made to India in January, when both leaders pledged to strengthen bilateral ties and economic exchange. During the February visit, Rwandan and Indian authorities signed a series of memorandums of understanding (MoUs) pledging to promote cooperation.

Rwandan efforts to increase bilateral cooperation also extended to countries in Africa. In April, Kagame visited *Djibouti* and signed five MoUs covering air services, visa waivers for diplomats and service passport holders, reciprocal promotion of investment, plans for a joint commission and greater ICT cooperation. During the visit, Kagame also expressed interest in developing a section of the land of the Port of Djibouti, highly sought after as a location at the crossroads of one of the busiest shipping routes in the world. While the possibility for Rwanda and Djibouti to become important trading partners was limited because of distance and transport challenges, these initiatives demonstrated the government's desire to ensure its connectedness to the rest of the continent and to overcome isolation.

Rwanda's *diplomatic activities* were mixed. Relations with *France* remained strained, despite a difficult September meeting at the UN General Assembly between Presidents Kagame and Macron to discuss mutual interests. Tensions between the two countries dated back to the 1994 genocide and their roles during this violent episode. Rwanda had accused the French government, then under President François Mitterrand, of having contributed to the genocide by providing political and military support to the Habyarimana regime and failing to prosecute genocide suspects living in France. The French government had accused the RPF of having shot down the plane that was carrying Presidents Habyarimana and Ntaryamira, resulting in the death of the two French pilots. The details of French and Rwandan actions before, during and after the genocide were still the subject of heated debate more than two decades on. While both countries re-established diplomatic relations in 2009, the relationship remained fragile. In June, three French-based NGOs filed a lawsuit against the French banking giant BNP Paribas, accusing it of being linked to transfers worth more than $ 1.3 m. between the National Rwanda Bank and the Swiss bank account of Willem Ehlers, a South African arms dealer. The money was said to have been used to purchase weapons, in violation of a UN arms embargo. In addition, in September, France's Constitutional Council denied a request from researcher François Graner to open former president Mitterrand's archives on the Rwandan genocide. Critics in France and Rwanda denounced the decision as a politically motivated attempt to hide France's role. The following month, the French Court of Appeal upheld a decision not to investigate two top French military commanders in Rwanda for complicity in the genocide. In December, the Rwandan government released an independent report from a year-long investigation into the possible role in the genocide of at least 20 French military and other officials.

Tensions with *Uganda* resurfaced openly. Presidents Kagame and Museveni had been critical regional allies for decades; in the 1980s, Kagame, then a refugee in Uganda, was a pivotal partner to Museveni during his campaign to remove Milton Obote from power. Museveni, in turn, provided military support to the RPF during the civil war. Over the years, Rwanda and Uganda had maintained close ties through political, economic and security cooperation. However, tensions started to emerge during the Second Congo War (1998–2003), sometimes leading them to engage each other militarily. Since then, foreign relations between the two countries had fluctuated, sometimes emerging in competition over the leadership and direction of economic integration within the EAC or opposing positions in the Burundi crisis. In October, Ugandan authorities arrested several top police officers on charges of colluding with Rwanda to repatriate refugees to their home country. They appeared before a military court, along with a Rwandan ex-army officer and a Congolese national. The suspects were accused of conspiring to kidnap Joel Mutabazi and another Rwandan security officer, Jackson Kalemera, in 2013, and handing them over to Rwandan authorities. Both Mutabazi and Kalemera were considered opponents by the Kagame regime. Kalemera was later tried in Rwanda and given a life sentence. Over the years, human rights organisations had reported many instances of Rwandan citizens seeking refuge in Uganda being illegally or secretly arrested and returned to Rwanda, where they often stood trial for 'treason' or for being a 'threat to national security'. For Uganda, the arrest of these senior officers in the security sector may have indicated tensions within the Ugandan political elite. For Rwanda, continued tensions reverberating in Ugandan politics had the potential to jeopardise ongoing efforts towards regional integration.

Tensions arising from the 2015 *Burundi* crisis continued to impact diplomatic relations. While the Rwandan government significantly decreased its engagement on Burundi, President Pierre Nkurunziza became increasingly hostile towards Kagame and his government. Burundi continued to accuse Rwanda of supporting rebels inside Burundi and Nkurunziza, in his New Year speech, threatened to cut off diplomatic relations if Rwanda did not apologise for meddling in Burundi since 2015. The continued tensions and instability thus remained a security concern for Rwanda and the continued influx of Burundian refugees put a lot of pressure on Rwanda's resources and infrastructure.

Meanwhile, in a continuation of the thawing of relations in 2016, Rwandan and DRC officials seized on a number of opportunities to continue to collaborate. In April, trade officials from both countries met in Bukavu (eastern Congo) to discuss and commit to stronger bilateral trade relations. The DRC continued to cooperate with Rwanda on the demobilisation of fighters for the Democratic Forces for the Liberation of Rwanda (FDLR), created in eastern Congo after the genocide and composed mostly of anti-Tutsi militia members and soldiers who had participated in the 1994 conflict. The group had since shrunk in strength, and many of its members were too young to have ever been involved in the genocide. The FDLR remained a source of instability in eastern DRC. In February, the infamous FDLR Brigadier General Cômes Semugeshi turned himself in and was repatriated to Rwanda. Hundreds of FDLR members, including women and youth, were sent back to Rwanda for demobilisation and reintegration. In addition to trade and security, Rwanda and the DRC also worked together on energy initiatives. In March, representatives from both countries met in Gisenyi to sign a Dutch-funded project on safe gas extraction. While the on-going collaboration between them was a good sign, given Rwanda and the DRC's history of military engagement since the end of the genocide, there remained on-going tensions at the border involving resurgent armed groups.

Rwanda found itself at the heart of debates about *cross-border migration*. It continued to host over 170,000 refugees, mostly from Burundi. While the government struggled to accommodate its current refugee burden, the Ministry of Foreign Affairs announced in November that it would be willing to offer refuge to 30,000 of the African migrants and refugees stranded in Syria, many while trying to reach Europe. That same month, Israel reportedly offered Rwanda and Uganda $ 5,000 per person to accept African migrants currently seeking asylum in *Israel*. This report came around the same time that President Netanyahu announced Israel's plans to open an embassy in Kigali and open air routes between the two countries to boost relations. Rwanda's stated willingness to welcome additional refugees from Syria and Israel raised important questions about the capacity of the Rwandan state to absorb more displaced people, given its current challenges and the weak international commitment to support refugees already in the region.

Socioeconomic Developments

Rwanda's development and *economic performance remained strong*, with a GDP growth of 5.1%, although it continued to show a downward trajectory, from 5.9% in 2016. While the manufacturing sector remained strong, production in other sectors such as agriculture, services and construction slowed. This was due to a combination of factors, such as the completion of large construction projects, policy adjustments to address external imbalances, and unfavourable weather conditions, which caused supply shocks in agriculture (which accounted for nearly 30% of GDP). Nevertheless, Rwanda's economic performance remained well above the growth average for the sub-region. Headline inflation fell below the central bank's 5% target, as food supply constraints and depreciation pressures receded, after peaking early in the year. With only four years remaining to the conclusion of its Vision 2020 plan, launched in 2000, the government maintained its commitment to its Second Economic Development and Poverty Reduction Strategy, which had been its consistent economic and development policy roadmap since 2013. Rwanda thus intensified investment in infrastructure development and private sector growth to transform the country from a low-income agriculture-based economy to a middle-income country.

The external *trade deficit fell* by over 20%, thanks to improved international prices and government policies. In order to counter a widening of the current account deficit, the government initiated an adjustment programme supported by the IMF, which promoted fiscal tightening by decreasing public spending and providing greater exchange flexibility. The government also accelerated the implementation of its 'Made in Rwanda' policy to encourage domestic production of certain goods, such as cement and rice. While these efforts led to an accumulation of foreign exchange reserves, the implementation of the EAC restriction on used clothing and business tax incentives also contributed to a drop in revenue mobilisation.

As in 2016, an increase in food prices drove up *inflation*, particularly in rural areas. An on-going drought, one of the worst in 60 years, hit much of Eastern Africa. In Rwanda, this resulted in a significant reduction in agricultural output. Eastern Rwanda received above-average rainfall during the September-December rainy season, but western Rwanda continued to experience rainfall deficits. With over 70% of the population still relying on subsistence farming, the resultant spike in food prices without a corresponding rise in wages made poor farmers particularly vulnerable to malnutrition. Rwandan authorities responded to the regional drought by launching a water resources mapping exercise to support irrigation and agricultural development.

Many development partners lauded Rwanda's approach to transforming the *agrarian and land sector* to reduce poverty and stimulate economic growth. The government continued to take great pride in its home-grown Green Revolution in SSA, which, according to government data, contributed to the drastic reduction of poverty and successful agricultural reform. However, some experts openly challenged the government's overly positive outlook. First, in May, the 'Review of African Political Economy' published a blog post challenging the quality and reliability of Rwandan agencies' poverty data. Then, in December, ten experts on agricultural development in Rwanda penned an article in 'The Conversation' discussing the negative consequences of government programmes for the poorest and most vulnerable.

Nevertheless, according to the *World Bank's Doing Business Index*, Rwanda ranked 41st out of 190 countries on ease of doing business, up from 56th the previous year. Rwanda remained one of the easiest countries to do business in Africa because of its implementation of a few reforms such as making it easier to pay taxes by establishing an online tax-filing platform, and improving investor protections and contract enforcement. The government also continued its fight against *corruption* and TI's annual survey listed Rwanda as the third-least corrupt country in SSA. This was the result of aggressive policies to punish petty graft. In June, the government dismissed 200 police officers implicated in such offences, a move approved during a cabinet meeting chaired by Kagame several days earlier. While corruption remained low, Rwanda's Bribery Survey still uncovered an increase in people reporting bribery incidents to 8.6% from 3.6% in 2016. As the country aimed to achieve 100% energy access for all Rwandans by 2024, the Rwanda Energy Group announced in September moves to reinforce its disciplinary committee.

Rwanda's economic policy continued to focus on *infrastructure development*. The 2017–18 budget announced in June again prioritised investment in infrastructure growth. Minister of Finance and Economic Planning Claver Gatete explained that priorities would be the construction of the Bugesera International Airport, improving and sustaining the quality of road networks, and the improvement and maintenance of road networks across the country. In January, the AfDB signed a $ 245 m agreement between Rwanda and Uganda for a road-building and improvement programme. In addition to roads, the government continued to focus on *electrification*. The number of households connected to electricity increased to over 35% from 22% at the end of 2016. In May, Rwanda inaugurated a methane-based power plant by Lake Kivu, which added 26 MW to the grid. In September, Symbion Energy and Highland Groups Holdings signed an agreement injecting $ 100 m in cash equity to upgrade and expand the Kibuye Power Plant 1, near Lake Kivu. Rwanda shares Lake Kivu with the DRC, and in recent years, both countries had taken steps to collaborate on energy initiatives in the region. In June, they signed an agreement to commission a feasibility study for the joint development of a plan to generate 200 MW of power from methane gas. Researchers had long been concerned about oil and gas exploration and extraction in Lake Kivu, which contains 60 bn m^3 of methane and 300 bn m^3 of carbon dioxide. Exploration and frequent seismic activity raised concerns about eruptions or explosions that could affect over 2 m people living along the shores.

Part of the government's effort to develop the private sector and the service industry was through the promotion of *tourism*, one the fastest growing sectors. The government continued to implement its MICE strategy (Meetings, Incentives, Conferences, Events, and Exhibitions). Rwanda hosted 169 meetings and conventions during the year, which injected $ 40 m into the economy. The International Congress and Convention Association ranked Rwanda the third-best destination for African business tourism. With the increase in conferences and conventions, the country also saw an increase in the number of gorilla trekking permits sold, despite doubling the charge from $ 750 to $ 1,500, thereby increasing government revenue from this activity.

Seychelles

Anthoni van Nieuwkerk and Jon Abbink

The Republic of Seychelles, the archipelago to the north-east of Madagascar made up of 115 islands (the main one being Mahé), remained generally stable politically and economically and had the highest per capita GDP per in Africa. The challenges and effects of climate change continued to place its economy at risk, as it relied heavily on high-end tourism and exports of tuna. To deal with this, Seychelles worked with fellow Small Island Developing States to address climate change issues. Regarding the economy, achieving more productivity-based growth remained Seychelles' key focus. Several development plans were being implemented or refined. Compared with its African and Indian Ocean neighbours, the Seychellois enjoyed domestic stability but faced some problems of unhealthy nutrition, sedentary lifestyles and substance abuse, coupled with educational and skills formation problems.

Domestic Politics

Politics in Seychelles was driven by an uneasy situation in which an *opposition coalition*, the Linyon Demokratik Seselwa (LDS), controlled the legislature and '*Parti*

 | DOI:10.1163/9789004367630_038

Lepep' (the People's Party) the executive. This came about when elections were held in September 2016 and the opposition coalition won the parliamentary elections for the first time. The coalition consisted of the Seychelles National Party, 'Lalyans Seselwa' (Seychellois Alliance), the Seychelles Party for Social Justice and Democracy and the Seychelles United Party. The LDS held 19 seats in the Sixth National Assembly, while Parti Lepep retained 14. This was the first time since the return of multi-party democracy in 1993 that Parti Lepep had not had a parliamentary majority. The next presidential election is due in 2020. The opposition's cohabitation with the ruling Parti Lepep was unprecedented and increased the likelihood of political gridlock, with fears of a negative impact on government service delivery, even though that did not happen in 2017.

President Danny Faure did not stand for the leadership of the governing Parti Lepep during its elective congress in June, saying he wished to separate party politics from his role as head of state. In his place, Vice President of the Republic Vincent Meriton was elected the party's president.

Civil and political rights were not under real threat in Seychelles, which was ranked 87th in the World Press Freedom Index, up five places from 92nd in 2016. Seychelles' strict defamation laws had not been used for years and there were few reports of abuses against journalists. However, the general-interest media practised a degree of self-censorship in order not to endanger their earnings from advertising, and newspapers took political sides, with the result that their reporting was slanted. The government's aim – to protect the country's image as a tourist paradise – meant that sensitive subjects remained off-limits.

The local lesbian, gay, bisexual, transgender and intersex group sought acceptance and respect from society and was officially registered, having been set up in 2016. They advocated for the laws of Seychelles to be reviewed to make them more inclusive. The first step had been taken in 2016 with the de-criminalisation of the act of 'sodomy' more than 60 years after its criminalisation in 1955. The local group was affiliated to a Lesbian, Bisexual, Gay and Transgender Coalition within the Indian Ocean and the Aids Rights Alliance of Southern Africa. *Human rights* issues in the political domain were not a problem, but there were persistent problems of rape (under-reported), sex trafficking and domestic violence, with police action relatively unsuccessful.

Foreign Affairs

The government continued to pursue pro-active '*oceans diplomacy*'. It participated in several high-profile multilateral platforms concerned with the interests of Small Island Developing States (SIDS). These included attending the summits of the AU,

SADC, the IOC and IORA. Seychelles hosted the WHO's 6th Conference of Ministers of Health of SIDS in the African Region.

President Faure was elected president for the year of *SIDS DOCK*, the SIDS initiative for renewable energy and sustainable development. It expanded its focus to help generate financial resources to help SIDS address adaptation to climate change, given the devastation caused by increasingly violent storms. This initiative was officially recognised by as a UN treaty organisation.

Foreign visits by Seychellois leaders were relatively few, as were foreign leaders' visitors to the islands. On 2 April, President Faure paid a visit to Kenya's President Uhuru Kenyatta in Nairobi and he joined other world leaders at the 25th meeting of the Commonwealth heads of government in London from 16 to 20 April. On 26–28 October, he paid a state visit to Mauritius. The president also attended the 'Our Oceans Conference' in Malta in October, when he committed Seychelles to collaboration in the areas of marine protected areas, sustainable fisheries, marine pollution, climate change, maritime security and sustainable blue economy. It was announced in February that Seychelles would create two huge new *marine parks* by 2020, covering about 30% of its waters (notably around the Aldabra archipelago). This would protect dolphins, coral, tuna and sea turtles, in return for a large amount ($ 22 m) of its national debt owed to the UK, France, Belgium and Italy being written off. Half of the protected area would be off-limits to fishing (evoking some protests by local fishermen).

Despite the decrease of Indian Ocean *piracy* in the past few years, Seychelles maintained its chairing of the Contact Group on Piracy off the Coast of Somalia and hosted the Regional Centre for Operational Coordination in the framework of the Regional Maritime Surveillance Mechanism with the support of the EU.

The government continued to pursue *bilateral relations* with selected countries and alliances, including its neighbours Mauritius, Madagascar, Comoros, Tanzania and Kenya, on matters relating to trade and maritime security. It also prioritised relations with the *EU*: the fifth Political Dialogue meeting focused on cooperation on 'Ocean Governance', including implementation of their Fisheries Agreement, commitment to the Paris Agreement on Climate Change and progress with the EPA. Shared maritime security interests included addressing the challenges of piracy, drugs and arms smuggling, human trafficking, illegal fishing and maritime pollution.

Socioeconomic Developments

The strong *tourism* sector continued to buoy the Seychelles economy. The number of visitors rose by 15% to reach a record high of nearly 350,000 (compared with a local population of 95,000), of whom around 50,400 were Germans. Seychelles successfully tapped new markets, including Russia and the Middle East (UAE) when established ones had come under pressure from the global crisis and its aftermath in the euro area. Tourism was estimated to contribute almost 30% of GDP, some $ 385 m, and provided some 26% of all employment.

On 31 October, the 2018 *national budget* was announced, to the tune of SCR rupee 7,951 m (= $ 586 m), an increase of 0.4% over 2017, with 40% of the total budget allocated to the education, health, family affairs and social sectors. The national budget set a target of a primary fiscal surplus of 3.0% of GDP, which was consistent with the government's goal of continuing to reduce its debt burden, which had continued to grow despite substantial, primary surpluses recorded in recent years.

Inflation rose to 3.2% year-on-year in July, but this reflected supply-side pressures from increases in regulated tobacco prices and tariffs. Food prices remained moderate (with inflation at about 2%). Private sector credit growth stood at 8.0% year-on-year at the end of the first quarter.

Poverty in Seychelles continued to be very low, with 2.5% of the population at the $ 3.10 per day (2011 PPP) line, and Seychellois had the highest average per capita GDP in Africa at an estimated $ 16,000, up from $ 15,410 in 2016. Seychelles' *human development attainment* remained high, as predicted by its national income, with a UNDP HDI score of 0.782 (ranking 63rd of 188 countries in 2016; a score published in 2017). Income inequality was significant, however, as measured by an income Gini coefficient of 46.8 for 2013 (the last year measured). Cross-country comparisons of inequality are difficult, but this measure indicated that income inequality in Seychelles was considerably higher than in Mauritius (Gini coefficient: 0.36), for example, and very much higher than for instance in Iceland (Gini coefficient: 0.27).

The *balance of trade* was sound: the merchandise trade deficit remained broadly stable, at about $ 450 m on a 12-month rolling basis through June. The Seychellois rupee depreciated slightly against the US dollar (by 1.2% through July), while gross official reserves remained little-changed, at $ 545 m in June (equivalent to 4.2 months of import cover).

Uunemployment stood at 4.5% (third quarter of 2016), indicative of a tight labour market in line with robust recent economic conditions. Youth unemployment was identified by the World Bank's Systematic Country Diagnostic (SCD) as a concern, since this was significant at about 14% (albeit not exceptionally high by international standards), with about half of all the unemployed aged 15–24. Furthermore, the low overall visible unemployment rate, of about 4%, was probably flattened by government employment in the large home-care programme (employing about 6% of the domestic labour force). The prison population remained large, equivalent to about 2% of the labour force. Income growth appeared increasingly concentrated amongst the most highly skilled. Rising demand for labour has been met by a surge in expatriate workers, their numbers measured by new and renewed Gainful Occupation Permits, which rose to 16,792 in 2016, an approximate doubling since 2014. Expatriates accounted for about one-quarter of the Seychelles' total workforce, and were employed mostly in construction and tourism. The small pool of local skilled labour and the high cost of external transport and energy presented a challenge in terms of deepening or diversifying sources of growth.

In view of the ongoing robustness of the tourism sector, the baseline *growth outlook* remained favourable, although the pace of real GDP growth of above 4% was expected to moderate itself to about 3.5% as construction linked to new tourism slowed (a moratorium on new permits for large hotels was extended recently to 2020). State land was no longer sold to foreigners, and the minister of finance announced in his 2017 budget speech that a property tax would be introduced on *land owned by foreigners*.

Seychelles remained highly vulnerable to exogenous shocks because of the significant *public debt* burden of approximately 70% of GDP, and Seychelles' very small, tourism- and import-dependent economy. Since the 2008 global debt crisis, however, the country had made major progress in reducing public debt and maintaining macroeconomic stability. The IMF Mission to Seychelles in September noted nothing alarming in its report, but called for a reduction in the economy's vulnerability over the long-term, and for improved resilience and inclusivity of growth.

The *banking* sector remained well capitalised, profitable and liquid, although the onshore sector continued to lack economies of scale, and interest-rate spreads were wide. The sovereign risk score remained at B. Seychelles was mentioned in the leaked 'Paradise Papers', which revealed the financial (double) dealings of global politicians, celebrities, corporate giants and business leaders.

The *World Bank strategy* regarding Seychelles was updated during the year with the aim of completing it by the end of the 2018 financial year. The strategy followed a recently completed SCD on the island nation, considered the first step in the preparation of the new strategy. The SCD identified Seychelles' growth challenges as "the 3Ps": *productivity* to sustain growth, which had hitherto been driven by high investment and expatriate labour; *participation* to revamp the education and social protection systems to maintain inclusion in a high-income economy; and *performance* to bring the efficiency and efficacy of state services and state owned enterprises (SOEs) into line with the needs of a high-income economy. Concurrently, the government was working on its National Development Strategy, which would be informed by sector strategy plans completed by the end of the year and was to be adopted in June 2018.

According to the World Bank's SCD, Seychelles faced a range of challenges, five of which were believed to require priority intervention. The first related to *shortfalls in the private sector enabling environment*. There was concern regarding the *business climate* in that Seychelles was only ranked 93rd in the World Bank's Ease of Doing

Business Report, and 129th out of 190 countries on enforcing contracts. Aspects of opening and operating a business were seen as difficult (e.g. in the vertically integrated tourism sector), and state capacity to regulate, monitor and evaluate strategically where productive resources should be allocated, was seen as limited. The historical dominance of SOEs had reinforced the high concentration of resources.

The second challenge related to *education and skills development*. It was believed that the system produced a large proportion of youth lacking in necessary academic or vocational skills and that there were insufficient opportunities for continuing education. The small University of Seychelles ('Unisey') introduced a new strategic plan for increasing the numbers and improving the quality of students and staff. Unisey would benefit from academic partnerships beyond Europe to bolster local expertise in SIDS governance, including much-needed managerial skills.

Social assistance was seen as the third challenge: it focused on the elderly and not on the youth, and it was not tied systematically to accessing economic opportunities for those who could work, which affected the structure of incentives.

Regarding macroeconomic and *fiscal policy stability*, there was the challenge to prioritise public expenditure within a consistent and sustainable macro framework, and to avoid the build-up of fiscal pressures and risks, including from SOEs. Public (government and SOE) spending efficiency was seen as a fifth challenge, relating to the capacity to track and monitor the adequacy of government programmes and sustain continuous improvements.

Additional challenges requiring intervention included the high cost and limited availability of credit; high electricity prices, particularly for businesses; limited job flexibility and labour market constraints; rising non-communicable disease prevalence that affected life expectancy (especially for men); the capacity to absorb environmental and global economic shocks and the financial and technical capacity to manage global economic and environmental risks, including the growing impact of climate change; high transport and other input costs; the need for transparency and accountability of public action; and finally scarcity of seasonal water and its management. President Faure referred to many of these challenges in his state of the nation address delivered on 14 February.

Somalia

Jon Abbink

Somalia remained a basket case of humanitarian emergency, political instability and violent confrontations, with here and there islands of urban investment, economic development and reconstruction. The Somali Federal Government remained a problematic outfit, not significantly expanding its political-territorial control or governmental authority over the country, marred by corruption, and still largely dependent on donor-funding, remittances, and AMISOM peace-keeping forces combatting al-Shabaab. This movement committed the worst car bombing in Somali history, with 512 people killed in a public slaughter in Mogadishu. The movement did not change its course or develop any constructive agenda for Somalia's societal or political future, and rejected any negotiations.

Elections in February yielded a new president, Mohamed Abdullahi 'Farmajo', a consensus figure who gained broad acceptance. A turn-around in the country's political and socio-economic fate was not achieved, however, and it was difficult to ascertain – apart from Somaliland, the independent part of Somalia in the north and doing relatively well – what Somalis really wanted, or how able or prepared they were to contribute to restoring their country.

 | DOI:10.1163/9789004367630_039

Domestic Affairs

An important political event was the *election of a new president*: Mohamed Abdullahi Mohamed 'Farmajo' (of the Marehan-Darod clan) became the new federal president of Somalia as a result of elections on 8 February (first scheduled for 2016). He had previously been prime minister from November 2010 until June 2011, and led the Tayo Political Party (established in 2012). A holder of dual Somali-USA citizenship, he had a good reputation and was popular, but the election itself was very contested and dubbed by some as 'selection', driven by moneyed interests, including foreign players such as Qatar; some $ 20 m allegedly changed hands in illegal vote buying and selling and other bribery. UN spokesman Stéphane Dujarric and the US State Department said it was credible that fraud and corruption had played a part in the electoral process, under which 135 clan elders chose an electorate of 14,000, which then in turn elected around 330 MPs and senators, who then voted on the presidency. Mohamed unexpectedly came top of a field of 24(!) candidates, including former president Hassan Sheikh Mohamed, former parliamentary speaker Sharif Hassan Sheikh Adan, and another former president, Sharif Sheikh Ahmed. President Mohamed was seen as a person of integrity and experience, gained, for example, when he was prime minister and through his public management career in the USA, and he proposed an anti-corruption agenda.

His choice of some of his close collaborators, however, was seen by some observers as somewhat dubious. On 23 February, he selected as *prime minister* the relatively young and inexperienced Hassan Ali Kheyre, a Norwegian – Somali dual national (of the Hawiye-Murursade subclan). He had been a Norwegian Refugee Council coordinator and executive of the British oil firm Soma Oil & Gas, a company plagued by rumours of fraud and other problems. His appointment was confirmed in parliament on 1 March. On 1 June at Villa Somalia, the presidential residence and national power centre, Mohamed announced as his *new chief-of-staff* Fahad Yasin Haji Dahir (of the small Reer Aw Hassan Kalweyne sub-clan); this was the third chief-of-staff in as many months since the presidential election). There were some concerns about him because of his history as a radical Islamist and former member of the Muslim Brotherhood-linked al-Islah and al-Ittihad al-Islami (in the 1990s), and allegedly an associate of people in the Islamist-terrorist movement Harakat al-Shabaab al-Mujahiddeen (al-Shabaab). Around 2005, Fahad Yasin had become a journalist for Al Jazeera in Somalia and he was also closely linked to leading political and financial Qatari networks active in Somalia.

On 11 January, the lower house of parliament (elected in late 2016) re-elected as its speaker, 71-year old Mohamed Osman Jawari. He won 141 votes from a total of 259 MPs.

Politics overall remained volatile, centrifugal and unstable, except in Somaliland. The usual problems of lack of professionalism, lack of political-administrative commitment, factionalism, and high levels of corruption in the security and military apparatus continued, confirming Somalia's shaky political status. Political freedoms, respect for civil liberties and a good independent justice system were precarious, and Somalia remained an 'unfree' country on the US Freedom House index.

The autonomy of some regions was consolidated, the most important among them being Puntland, Galmudug and Jubbaland. In Galmudug a crisis erupted on 10 January, when its president, Abdikarim Hussein Guled, lost a vote of confidence in the regional parliament while he was away on business in Mogadishu.

Relations between the various regional states remained tense, amidst outstanding territorial disputes. President Mohamed insisted upon their resolution within the framework of Somali federal unity. On 30 May, the new president of Galmudug, Ahmed Duale Haaf, signed a peace deal with his Puntland counterpart, Abdiweli Gaas, in the presence of Jubbaland's president, Ahmed Madhobe. It was meant to end a long-standing border conflict that had led to the death of at least 100 people in 2016. After a big meeting of leaders of Puntland, Jubbaland, Galmudug, Hir-Shabelle and Southwest regional states on 8–11 October in Kismaayo, *President Mohamed called for more unity* and cooperation among them and for work toward the resolution of disputes and the development of economic relations and administrative capacity-building, with ideas floated to provide a correspondingly larger share of the federal budget to the regions. An underlying concern was also to prevent further disunity of Somalia's political units vis-à-vis the ongoing diplomatic crisis in the Gulf Region. The regional states also asked to be given a more consultative role in foreign policy issues (referring to Art. 53 of the federal Constitution).

On 3 July, President Mohamed, in a speech commemorating the 57th anniversary of Somali Independence, called for unity talks with the Republic of Somaliland, but the country's leadership showed no eagerness for this. Although not without its internal problems, *Somaliland showed relative political stability*, with presidential elections on 13 November. There were three candidates: Muse Bihi Abdi of the ruling Kulmiye Party, Faisal Ali Waraabe of the For Justice and Development party (UCID), and Abdirahman Mohamed Abdillahi 'Irro' of the Wadani Party (the only three parties allowed). This election had been delayed from March. A public election debate between the candidates was held on 19 October in Hargeisa. The election proceeded peacefully, although there was a serious lack of interest among youthful Somaliland voters, reputedly fed up with what they saw as the 'clan-based politics' of the old guard (about 70% of Somalilanders are under 30). The election was won by Muse Bihi Abdi (a former air force pilot and Somali National Movement leader, of the Isaaq Habr Awal/Sa'ad Muse clan). An orderly transition of the presidency from Ahmed Mohamed Silanyo (Isaaq Habr Je'lo/Aaden Madoobe sub-clan) to Muse Bihi followed on 13 December.

Al-Shabaab, under the leadership of Ahmed Umar ('Abu Ubaidah/Diriyye', of the Dir-Bajimaal subclan) continued to be prominently present in rural regions of

South-Central Somalia and, despite many defections, recruited hundreds of new members, especially among poor and jobless youths, notably in Puntland this year, as well as from Muslim madrasas in north-east Kenya. In addition, villages under the control of al-Shabaab were regularly forced to give up their children for service in the movement.

AMISOM, the peace-keeping force under the AU and financed by the EU and the UN, continued to be active assisting the government against al-Shabaab. It comprised around 22,000 troops, from Uganda, Ethiopia, Djibouti, Kenya and Burundi, and was deployed in six sectors in South and Central Somalia. AMISOM was scheduled to withdraw in December 2020 and hand over all control to the Somali National Army (SNA). It announced a reduction of 1,000 troops, as well as handing over some functions to the SNA. But fears were that this scenario would not be realistic in view of the continued presence al-Shabaab and the extent of their territorial control. AMISOM secured the cities and main roads and slightly expanded its territorial grip during the year, but its hold was not deep or durable without effective Somali government institution-building or peace and reconciliation. On 27 January, al-Shabaab targeted a Kenyan AMISOM base at Kulbiyow on the Kenya-Somali border, killing an estimated 68 soldiers. A similar number of al-Shabaab militants were killed when the base was recaptured. This devastating attack closely resembled the El Adde base attack of 2016 and was not prevented, despite warnings by USA intelligence of an impending incident. On 12 February, Al-Shabaab killed 12 Somali soldiers, including two high-ranking army commanders, in an attack on the Afgoye-Wanlaweyne road near Mogadishu.

Al-Shabaab's hit-and run tactics, avoiding open battle but attacking selected army camps, media people, traditional clan elders, government offices and workers, markets and civilian gatherings, continued to claim many victims. AMISOM did not adopt the mobile 'guerrilla' warfare tactics in smaller units spread out over the country that were needed to pursue and defeat al-Shabaab in the rural hinterlands. AMISOM forces thus continued assisting the SNA in training and combat and allowed the government to expand and start new administration functions here and there, but did not achieve a turn-around in the fight against the terror movement, so that national security only marginally improved. This was remarkable, seeing that AMISOM troops were estimated to be more than double the number of al-Shabaab's. The SNA and AMISOM troops also allegedly transgressed their mandate in sometimes abusing and killing the wrong persons, as well as civilians. Al-Shabaab continued to succeed in its relentless reign of intimidation, abuse and terror, in which it was difficult to see a real political or societal programme, and they still called for an 'Islamic state' and again expressed loyalty to al-Qaida. This was not an attractive or workable prospect for the vast majority of Somalis, but al-Shabaab retained support by 'employing' jobless, penniless, uneducated youngsters (for a monthly allowance) or forcing parents in rural areas to hand over children for recruitment to their ranks. They also here and there acted as a judicial (Sharia) authority, mediating in disputes and conflicts and imposing their solutions. Upon the new president taking office in February, the movement immediately announced that it would continue fighting, especially targeting people around him. On 19 February, some days before the swearing in of the new president, al-Shabaab carried out a bomb attack on a Mogadishu market, killing 39 and injuring 50 people. When he took office, President Mohamed offered a truce and an amnesty deal for al-Shabaab in order to further national reconciliation, but this was rejected by them. In June, it was reported that former prominent al-Shabaab leader and Islamist radical Mukhtar Robow Abu Mansur, who had left al-Shabaab after a dispute with its then leader Ahmed Abdi Godane (who died in 2014), wanted talks with the Somali government. This led the US to remove him from its 'most wanted' list and he surrendered to government forces on 13 August.

Throughout the year, many al-Shabaab-orchestrated *terror attacks* occurred, mostly in the form of drive-by shootings and (car) bomb attacks, causing hundreds of deaths and leaving thousands of people injured and traumatised. They engaged in abductions for ransom, as when aid workers and local NGO personnel were kidnapped in September in Hiraan and Bay regions, and there were strong indications of the group seizing and trafficking women as sex slaves. With new contingents of local recruits, al-Shabaab was also active in north-east Kenya, perpetrating many attacks and killing dozens of people with roadside bombs and improvised explosive devices.

On 16 September, Mohamud Moallim Hassan Qoley, an army intelligence officer, was killed in a drive-by shooting, together with his bodyguard. A week later, on 23 September in Mogadishu, al-Shabaab militants shot and killed General Abdullahi Mohamed Sheikh Qururuh and a bodyguard as they walked home from a mosque. General Abdullahi was a senior officer at the SNA command and control headquarters, having served previously as deputy commander of army logistics. Such frequent killings and bomb attacks showed that security in Mogadishu did not improve during the year – rather the contrary. Equally, the number of attacks on rural area targets and army and AMISOM posts remained high, leading to hundreds of deaths during the year. By the end of the year al-Shabaab were on course to surpass their 2016 'record' of people killed, standing at 4,200.

The *most devastating terrorist bombing* occurred on 14 October, when a truck packed with explosives was detonated at Zoobe Junction in mid-Mogadishu, causing dreadful slaughter with 512 people killed and hundreds wounded and mutilated. The apocalyptic scene, with many victims unrecognisable, led to huge, angry demonstrations against al-Shabaab by the Mogadishu population. Then, on 28 October, another bombing in the capital, outside the Nasa Hablod Hotel 2, left 27 dead and many wounded. It showed again that Somali security forces had no effective answer to the politics of mass slaughter that al-Shabaab pursued. Just before the 14 October bombing, the Somali army chief and defence minister had resigned, his two positions being taken by General Abdi Jama Warsame and Mohamed Sheikh Mursal Abdirahma, respectively. On 26 October, Somalia's intelligence agency chief, Abdillahi Mohamed Sanbalooshe, wrote an Op-ed in the 'New York Times' complaining about the lack of international expert assistance to Somalia in technical training and handling forensic evidence related to terror bombings. Three days later he was dismissed.

On 11 February, the forces of the *Ahlu as-Sunna wal-Jama'a*, a moderate Sufi-oriented movement strongly opposed to al-Shabaab, declared their support for the new president and their readiness to align their forces with the Somali National Army. This was a statement against al-Shabaab terror and reinforced the cause of the Somali Federal Government.

In other parts of Somalia the attacks were less intense, but on 8 June al-Shabaab jihadists carried out a raid on Af-Urur military camp close to the Golis Mountains in Puntland, leaving at least ten soldiers dead. Al-Shabaab claimed it had killed 61 government soldiers. On 23 September, authorities in Puntland seized a *vessel from Yemen loaded with weapons*, including anti-aircraft machine-guns, AK47s, pistols and ammunition probably intended for Islamic State-allied Islamist militants in the Bari region.

The perennial centrifugal tendencies of Somalia's clan-based society thus continued to generate a *constant dynamic of conflict* and sustained the on-and-off local support for spoilers like al-Shabaab.

Somaliland remained much quieter, as did *Puntland*, although lethal skirmishes continued in the Galgala Mountains south of Bosaaso, where al-Shabaab loyalists continued to be active.

The *US kept special units operating in Somalia*, but the numbers were not known. On 4 May, one US Navy Seal soldier was killed and four wounded by al-Shabaab, in action at Darusalam village (Shabelle region). On 11 June, the US Africa Command said eight al-Shabaab fighters had been killed in an air strike in Sakow, Lower Jubbaland. On 5 September, these units again killed three suspected al-Shabaab terrorists during an airstrike in Bay Region, west of Mogadishu. On 21 November drone strikes allegedly eliminated some 100 al-Shabaab jihadists in their camp in the Leb-Adde hills in the Bay Region. US strikes also prevented a number of al-Shabaab car bombing attempts.

Foreign Affairs

The Somali Federal Government maintained good working relations with *Djibouti* and (to a lesser extent) with Kenya and intensified contacts with Saudi Arabia. Somalia had complex but good relations with *Ethiopia* (which had backed another candidate in the presidential elections) and, on 3 May, President Mohamed visited Addis Ababa for talks on security (AMISOM, the al-Shabaab threat and the neighbouring Ogaden region in Ethiopia), and regional relations.

On 26 September President Mohamed, accompanied by top officials including Foreign Minister Yusuf Garad Omar, paid a state visit to *Saudi Arabia* for talks on business relations, security and bilateral issues, thus also appearing to side with Saudi Arabia (and the UAE) in its dispute with *Qatar*. The Somali position remained unclear, however, and Mohamed did not openly distance himself from Qatar. This was delicate, as other Somali autonomous regions, such as Puntland, Southwest and Galmudug, had earlier indicated support for Qatar. Somalia and its disunited political elite remained vulnerable to divide-and-rule and financial politics by the Middle East powers as well as Turkey, whose involvement also contributed to disunity and factionalism.

On 28 November, President Mohamed was in Nairobi (*Kenya*) to attend the inauguration of the re-elected President Uhuru Kenyatta. He refused to meet Israeli Prime Minister Benjamin Netanyahu, who was also present, unlike his predecessor Hassan Mohamud, who had allegedly met with Netanyahu in 2016.

A *crisis in AMISOM* was averted in April, when AU Commissioner for Peace and Security Smail Chergui reached an agreement with the Burundi government to keep its peacekeepers in Somalia. The country had threatened to sue the AU over failure to pay its troops for almost one year.

On 13 June, *IGAD* appointed Kenyan national Mohamed Ali Guyo as its new envoy to Somalia, to further the organisation's mission to help the Somali government in its stabilisation efforts.

On 11 May, another *'London Somalia Conference'* took place, hosted by the UK government, and bringing together heads of state and government from East Africa and other key partners such as international organisations. Somaliland, however, was not present. The conference discussed plans for the recovery and rebuilding of Somalia and consolidating progress made since the Somali Federal Government was installed in 2012. The meeting yielded a new plan, the 'New Partnership for Somalia', partly linked to Somalia's National Development Plan of 2016.

In his speech to the *UN General Assembly* on 22 September, Prime Minister Hassan Ali Khayre, claiming progress in the battle against insecurity and al-Shabaab terror, pleaded for a lifting of the international arms embargo so that the gains made by the SNA could be consolidated.

Somaliland went its own way, and, while it did not make headway in its aim to get international recognition, it acted politically and economically as an independent power. In February, parliament voted to allow the construction of a *UAE military base* in the port of Berbera. Somaliland's neighbours had misgivings. The then president of Somaliland, Ahmed Mohamed Silanyo, said the base would help create jobs and training, and equipment would also be provided to Somaliland forces.

Plans to expand Berbera port for increased commercial traffic to and with Ethiopia were also on the agenda. In March, Somaliland confirmed a $ 442 m deal with UAE's Dubai Port (DP) World for the modernisation of Berbera port under a 30-year contract. The controversial deal, which also gave Ethiopia a share, was rejected by the authorities in Mogadishu. In June, Somaliland declared the suspension of all contacts with Qatar. Interestingly, on 21 March, Puntland's president, Abdiweli Mohamed Ali, said that DP World could also gain a concession to develop the port of Bosaaso.

The territorial conflict between *Somaliland and Puntland* (Sanaag and Sool regions) persisted and no progress toward a solution was made, either via the UN or via neighbouring Ethiopia. Armies in the area were kept on alert and the threat of war loomed.

Socioeconomic Developments

Again Somalia was not able to be self-sufficient; next to overseas remittances, it was kept alive by *massive donor support* (ODA and humanitarian aid) to the tune of $ 1.3 bn, equalling at least 20% of GDP (but an estimated drop of 11% in aid overall). Over 27% of it was provided by the US, and 31% by the EU and UK. The trade deficit was $ 2.1 bn, around 35% of GDP, the highest ever recorded.

The country's *economy continued to be largely informal*; national accounts were not easily quantified and again many different estimates circulated. The main economic sectors were livestock and livestock exports (40% of GDP), agriculture, construction, telecommunications, and remittance/money transfer companies (handling the largest share of national income: the approximately $ 1.6 bn of remittances from Somalis overseas). The government lacked the ability to collect domestic revenue effectively. Agriculture and animal husbandry remained the most important sectors. Economic growth, largely consumption-driven, was estimated at 2.4% (mainly agro-pastoral production, construction and telecommunications), which was at least 1% lower than in 2016. The agrarian sector (50% of export earnings) was hit again by drought, which also put about 6.2 m people at risk of food insecurity and shortages (i.e., half of the total population, mainly in the south). Industrial activity was negligible, with only minor contributions from fish canneries, sugar refining and textiles.

Together with the UN, the EU and the World Bank, the Somali government carried out a *Drought Impact and Needs Assessment* to ascertain the effect of the drought on the economy, analysing agriculture, water supply and sanitation, health and nutrition, food security, livelihoods, education and social protection. Damage was estimated at $ 3.25 bn, with total recovery needs of some $ 1.7 bn.

Somalia's *GDP* was an estimated $ 6.7 bn (or $ 17.4 bn in PPP), and external debt was around 75% of this sum. *Inflation*, however, was very low at 1.5%; a remarkable feat considering the lack of government control over currency supply (printing of the Somali shilling) and the exchange rate.

Youth unemployment ('youth' meaning under 30) stood at more than 50–60% and contributed to basic social and financial insecurity, migration flows and displacement, as well as violent extremism (as al-Shabaab paid 'salaries' to young recruits).

In February, the government launched the *National Development Plan* (NDP), finalised in October 2016. It aimed to address job creation, improve humanitarian conditions, develop economic growth strategies, receive and integrate Somali refugees returning from Kenya (as the largest refugee camps there would be closed), manage remittance flows, and develop social safety nets.

Under the *New Partnership Agreement*, reached between Somalia and the international community at the London Somalia Conference on 11 May, infrastructure investments and productive economic growth were set as targets. The AfDB would administer a new Multi-Donor *Somali Infrastructure Fund* (SIF), agreed upon during a meeting on Somalia on 25 May. The SIF would for three years (2018–20) prioritise energy, water and transport projects worth about $ 160 m (despite a funding gap of some $ 100 m). The *IMF* also assisted in devising and monitoring NDP strategies, including technical assistance ('institutional capacity-building') and currency reform in an economic landscape of forgery and counterfeit money, but it could not disburse new loans to the Somali government because arrears on previous loans were too large. A report on 8 February by the IMF on its Article IV consultations with the Somali government commended the economic and institutional restoration efforts made and tried to give a positive turn to a still very vulnerable and precarious economic situation in the country.

Piracy continued to be suppressed but had not gone away altogether, with a danger that it could return at any moment. The anti-piracy missions slackened off and at least five ships were hijacked off the coast of Somalia during the year, including the UAE oil tanker Aris 13 on 13 May – the first pirate hijacking in almost five years. On 12 April, Somali troops freed eight crew members of the MSV Al Kausar, an Indian vessel, held hostage since 31 March in Adalle village near Hobyo. Former pirates also moved into the human trafficking business.

Somaliland, being an independent entity that would not join Somalia in the foreseeable future, followed its own political and economic system and policies. Its GDP was about $ 1.9 bn (65% of it agriculture). There was slight economic growth but the rate was unknown. Like its southern neighbour, the country suffered from unemployment and drought: youth unemployment was estimated at 60%, and the drought was the worst in years, affecting some 1.5 to 2 m people (over 30% of the population).

Environmental problems continued to be felt but were hardly acted upon: deforestation (through charcoal production), erosion, overgrazing, pollution, wildlife depletion, the deleterious effects of the ongoing fighting, and sea pollution, including by foreign vessels, continued. Local initiatives to address these issues could not compensate for the lack of national policy and capacity to tackle the issues.

Migrants, refugees and IDPs remained present in the Somalias in large numbers. An estimated 1.1 m people in Somalia had been displaced by drought or fighting. The Somaliland port of Bosaaso was again a transit point for migrants to Saudi Arabia and Yemen. As of 25 September, international donors had made available $ 1.1 bn for humanitarian operations in a country that seemed forever stuck in crisis.

South Sudan

Daniel Large

Conflict continued and deepened in South Sudan during the year. The government combined official declarations of a ceasefire with ongoing military campaigns and an abortive, controversial National Dialogue initiative. As new rebel groups formed, armed opposition remained fragmented, despite some efforts to achieve greater unity. Declarations of famine in two parts of Unity State in February highlighted the consequences of the fighting and the impact of the deliberate counter-insurgency government policy. South Sudan continued to experience a deteriorating economic situation, not helped much by slightly improving oil fortunes. High numbers of IDPs and refugees fleeing to neighbouring countries continued to be registered, inseparable from the fighting patterns. Despite a new IGAD-led initiative aimed at revitalising the peace process, the conflict entered its fifth year in December with very little prospect of any real, lasting resolution in sight.

Domestic Politics

Conflict continued and worsened over the year. In late April, IGAD's Joint Monitoring and Evaluation Commission, the body charged with overseeing implementation

 | DOI:10.1163/9789004367630_040

of the August 2015 Agreement on the Resolution of the Conflict in South Sudan (ARCSS), admitted that the security situation had collapsed. It proved exceedingly hard to oversee the terms of the 2015 deal, amidst constant government obstruction, such as in July, for example, when government forces prevented a monitoring team from the Ceasefire and Transitional Security Arrangements Monitoring Mechanism from accessing Kajo Keji.

Thomas Cirillo Swaka, an ethnic Bari, resigned in February as deputy chief of staff of the Sudan People's Liberation Army (SPLA), and in March formed a new armed rebel movement, called the National Salvation Front, opposing President Salva Kiir's rule. Defections from the Sudan People's Liberation Movement In Opposition (SPLM-IO) followed, amidst continued opposition splintering. In May, seven opposition groups, including Riek Machar's SPLM-IO and Cirillo's National Salvation Front, announced they would form "a united front on common strategic and operational issues" as a means to oust Kiir's government. Further *fragmentation of rebel groups* continued nonetheless. In June, for example, a former South Sudanese law maker, Abraham Majak Maliab, formed another new opposition movement, the Popular Front for Democratic Reform and Pan-African National Guard.

On 22 May, President Kiir declared a unilateral *ceasefire* and promised to release political prisoners. The initiative met with criticism from the UN, the US and the UK, as further fighting was reported in Ayaci county, Eastern Equatoria State, and in Yei, Central Equatoria State. The government renewed its commitment to restore a permanent ceasefire in October. However, there was little relation between such claims and the reality of *ongoing military campaigns*. Heavy fighting between SPLA-IO and government forces continued in July around Mathiang in Upper Nile State, just north of the opposition's headquarters in Pagak. The government claimed its unilateral ceasefire did not include the Pagak area. Kiir issued a decree in November approving a 90-day extension of the state of emergency in parts of Bahr al Ghazal region, including the so-called Gogrial, Tonj, Wau and Aweil East States.

Efforts to pursue a *National Dialogue*, which had been announced in 2016, continued on a stop-start basis amidst uncertainty and controversy. In March, Paride Taban, the former bishop of the Catholic Diocese of Torit, resigned as co-chair of the National Dialogue Steering Committee. In April, the initiative was postponed due to lack of funding and, in May, the government put it on hold after the steering committee failed to reach a quorum. South Sudan's judges and justices declared a nationwide strike in May after negotiations with the government failed. The strikers demanded better working conditions and the resignation of the chief justice. In November, a Supreme Court judge resigned, complaining that a lack of independence from the executive had turned the judiciary into a "mockery".

In an unexpected move, *the SPLA's Chief of General Staff, General Paul Malong, was dismissed* by President Kiir on 10 May and replaced by General James Ajongo. After leaving Juba for Aweil, his home base in northern Bahr el Ghazal, the same day, Malong's exit provoked concern that he might rebel. However, he subsequently returned to Juba on 13 May for reconciliation talks, and was placed under house arrest. There later followed a standoff before Malong was allowed to leave South Sudan for Kenya in November.

In May, Uganda convened a *meeting of SPLM factions* in Kampala, involving the SPLM (in government), the SPLM-IO faction led by Taban Deng Gai and the SPLM-Former Political Detainees (FD). Machar's SPLM-IO faction was not included. The meeting was unsuccessful in achieving the reunification of the party. The SPLM-FD declined to sign, stating that the proposed agreement was not inclusive. In July, and again under the auspices of Uganda's President Museveni, three SPLM factions signed the Entebbe Declaration to activate the 2015 Arusha Agreement on the reunification of the SPLM. The SPLM-IO quickly denounced the initiative.

Inter-communal clashes continued in various parts of the country, adding further layers of insecurity to an already fragmented conflict. A three-month state of emergency was declared in July, covering parts of Gogrial, Tonj, Wau and Aweil East to contain the growing clashes between clan-based militias. The government announced that the SPLA would be given further powers to address the situation, while citizens' rights would be suspended. At least 18 people were killed and more than 30 wounded in clashes between the Apuk and Aguok communities in the Gogrial area, Warrap State.

In a *crack-down on media reporting*, the government's Media Authority suspended local operations of Al-Jazeera in Juba after it reported on the SPLA-IO and the situation in Kajo Keji. In May, authorities released a UN-Miraya FM radio journalist, George Livio, who had been detained without charge since August 2014. The Court of Appeal ruled the National Security Service's wiretapping system 'unconstitutional'. In June, the Media Authority banned some 20 foreign journalists from South Sudan for "unsubstantiated and unrealistic stories". In July, claiming the outlets "disseminate subversive material", the government blocked website access for South Sudanese users to at least four independent media outlets (Sudan Tribune, Radio Tamazuj, Nyamilepedia and Paanluel Wel). The head of state television was arrested for not broadcasting a presidential speech. After clashes between government and SPLA-IO troops near Kaya, Central Equatoria, at least 19 were killed, including an American freelance journalist, Christopher Allen.

The situation for *civil society groups* continued to be difficult, amidst ongoing intimidation and repression. The executive director of the Unity Cultural and Development Center, an NGO in Wau, was detained by security officials without charge for two weeks. Pressure on international agencies continued. Despite previous such attempts, which met with heavy criticism, the government increased registration and licensing fees for NGOs in May. The new order increased the fees for international NGOs from $ 600 to $ 3,500.

In December, South Sudan's *conflict entered its fifth year* but, unlike the initial extent of the fighting that had broken out in Juba in December 2013, it now engulfed a far greater area of the country. Unsurprisingly in this context, South Sudan topped the Fragile States Index for 2017 (published by the Fund for Peace). Fighting continued, despite the efforts of the IGAD-led High Level Revitalization Forum (see below), which resulted in a December Agreement on Cessation of Hostilities, Protection of Civilians and Humanitarian Access signed by the government, SPLM-IO and others on 21 December. Government and SPLA-IO clashes in Unity State were reported just hours after the agreement theoretically came into effect.

Foreign Affairs

In January, President Kiir visited *Egypt* and met in Cairo with President al-Sisi, whom he thanked for supporting South Sudan against UNSC efforts to impose an arms embargo. Egypt's desire for support against Ethiopia's Grand Renaissance Dam was also part of the discussions.

The role of *Uganda* continued to be important, and in multiple ways. In April, First Vice President Taban Deng met Uganda's President Yoweri Museveni to discuss bilateral relations and the situation in South Sudan. A second round of consultations between SPLM factions in Uganda ended in June, and mandated Museveni to consult further with other opposition groups. In July, President Kiir visited Kampala, where he met Museveni and some former political detainees for 'SPLM-reunification consultations'. Later, Rebecca Nyandeng announced she had reconciled with Kiir. The SPLA-IO accused Uganda of mounting airstrikes against one of their outposts in Thochdeng, Upper Nile State. Uganda's role involved direct engagement with the government and opposition groups. In November, Sudan's President al-Bashir paid a state visit to Kampala, where he discussed South Sudan with Museveni.

In April, South Sudan signed a trade and economic cooperation agreement with *Turkey*. The Turkish Cooperation and Coordination Agency became more active and finished building an education facility in Juba in December.

Relations with *Sudan* remained important. In May, the UNSC reduced the UN Interim Force for Abyei (UNISFA), warning that it might withdraw support for the Joint Border Verification and Monitoring Mechanism force; in November, however, UNISFA's mandate was extended until 15 May 2018. In July, the planned meeting of Sudan and South Sudan's Joint Political and Security Committee, scheduled to be held in Juba shortly after Eid al-Fitr, was postponed. Kiir visited Khartoum and met al-Bashir in early November. Following Sudan's October announcement that it would open a humanitarian corridor to deliver aid to South Sudan, Sudan's Defence Minister Ahmed Awad Ibn Auf and his South Sudanese counterpart, Kuol Manyang, agreed to open four border crossings.

Regional diplomatic efforts to restart some kind of peace process continued. The 31st Extra-Ordinary Summit of the *IGAD* Assembly of Heads of State and

Government on South Sudan, took place on 12 June in Addis Ababa (Ethiopia), but was not attended by Kiir. Chaired by Ethiopia's Prime Minister Hailemariam Dessalegn, the summit discussed the security and humanitarian situation in South Sudan and reiterated that full implementation of ARCSS was the only way forward. IGAD announced it would convene a High-Level Revitalization Forum. In July, IGAD's Council of Ministers held its 58th Extra-Ordinary Session on the situation in South Sudan and, again, condemned the continued violence. It called for a cessation of hostilities and for inclusive negotiations to take place in Juba. On 21 December, the IGAD-led High Level Revitalization Forum concluded its first phase with an Agreement on Cessation of Hostilities, Protection of Civilians and Humanitarian Access, signed by the various parties to the conflict, including the South Sudanese government and the SPLM-IO. Clashes between government and SPLA-IO forces in the Koch area, Unity State, were reported just hours after the agreement came into effect.

Although a planned visit by Pope Francis to South Sudan was postponed for security reasons, there were *visits by other foreign political figures*. China's former ambassador to Sudan and ambassador to the China-Arab States Cooperation Forum visited Juba in April for talks. German Foreign Minister Sigmar Gabriel visited Juba in July, and urged South Sudan's leaders to use peaceful means to resolve the conflict. In September, and the UK's Minister for Africa Rory Stewart also visited and appealed to the government to take the lead and bring an immediate end to the on-going civil war.

Relations with the *US* deteriorated. In September, the US Department of the Treasury imposed economic sanctions on three officials for their alleged roles in destabilising South Sudan and 'enriching' themselves through corruption: General Malek Reuben Riak Rengu, the army's deputy chief-of-staff in charge of military procurement; Minister of Information and Broadcasting Michael Makuei Lueth; and Paul Malong Awan, the former SPLA chief of general staff. Three South Sudan-based companies owned or controlled by Malek Reuben Riak Rengu were also sanctioned. The government urged the US to rethink the 'unfortunate' sanctions. In November, Canada also imposed sanctions on the same three South Sudanese officials. In late October, America's Ambassador to the UN, Nikki Haley, visited Juba and issued a severe warning to President Kiir, saying the US had lost trust in the government. In December, further vindicating criticism of the government's high level of impunity, Kiir promoted three generals (Marial Chanuong, Santino Deng Wol, and Gabriel Jok Riak), who were facing UN sanctions over alleged human rights violations.

Opposition leaders and groups continued to pursue international diplomacy of their own in order to promote their causes. Efforts to involve the South Africa-based Riek Machar in peace talks continued, as other opposition groups sought to mobilise international support. In October, Ethiopia's and Sudan's foreign ministers, Workneh Gebeyehu and Ibrahim Ghandour, met Machar in South Africa to discuss IGAD's attempts to revitalise the peace process. Taban Deng criticised IGAD's separate consultations, saying they undermined the Transitional Government of National Unity. Also in October, opposition faction leaders – including Lam Akol, leader of the National Democratic Movement; Thomas Cirillo, chairperson of the National Salvation Front; and Gabriel Changson Chang, leader of the Federal Democratic Party – visited the US.

Socioeconomic Developments

The economic situation worsened. The IMF concluded its Article IV consultation with the Republic of South Sudan in March and called on the government to restore 'fiscal discipline'. In May, South Sudan's biggest bank, the Kenya-based KCB Group Plc, announced it would shut down five branches due to hyperinflation and a dollar shortage. Kenya's Equity Bank Group also closed seven of its 12 branches in South Sudan.

South Sudan's *budget for 2017–18*, which was passed by parliament in August, totalled SSP (pound) 46.5 bn ($ 300 m), an increase of over 30% from the 2016–17 budget. According to a Ministry of Finance 2017–18 report released in September, four government agencies – the National Security Service, Defence, the Ministry of Finance and Economic Planning, and the Office of the President – accounted for over 77% of total operating expenditure. Officially, the government made efforts to implement its Fiscal Stabilisation Measures Action Plan but in reality it was hard to work out actual expenditure and debt levels or how much the government had accepted from oil companies in advance payments.

The *budget crisis affected public expenditure*, and the government struggled to pay civil servants and the military. In November, Kiir ordered the Ministry of Foreign Affairs to reduce diplomatic staff in order to save money. South Sudan temporarily stopped issuing passports in November, when its German passport technology provider, Muhlbauer, shut down the system over unpaid bills. In December, the government tacitly removed subsidies on fuel, a move many attributed to the scarcity of hard currency. Despite the economic crisis, however, the government reportedly spent millions of dollars buying Israeli surveillance drones and security cameras to fight crime in Juba.

The rate of *inflation* officially decreased but remained very high. The National Bureau of Statistics reported that the annual Consumer Price Index increased by 102% from September 2016 to September 2017 however, this excluded the second-largest city, Malakal. The exchange continued its steep decline, from SSP 18.5: $ 1 in December 2015 to SSP 70: $ 1 in August 2016, and SSP 172: $ 1 in August 2017.

Oil production fell to about 120,000 b/d (compared with a peak of 350,000 b/d before Independence in 2011), with Petroleum Minister Ezekiel Lul Gatkuoth seeking to reach production of 150,000 b/d by December. Oil prices rose slightly from $ 43 per barrel in 2016 to about $ 55.

Uncertainty surrounded the state of South Sudan's arrangement with Sudan concerning the 2012 deal on *oil exports*. In November, the government reportedly agreed to pay Sudan the outstanding export fee debt of $ 262 m for transferring oil through Sudanese territory. However, in the face of official acknowledgement that the government would probably not be able to honour the renewed 2012 agreement and "make full payments to Sudan", South Sudan appeared to be deeper in debt. In December, Deputy Finance Minister Mou Ambrose Thiik stated that South Sudan owed Sudan $ 1.3 bn from the 2012 deal; he was fired shortly afterwards.

The government continued *efforts to stimulate the oil sector* by seeking to attract new companies and pushing existing operators. The sector continued to be affected by violence, including abductions of oil workers, such as in March, when three foreign oil workers were abducted in the Adara oilfield in Upper Nile state by the SPLA-IO. In March, the government granted a Nigerian company, Oranto Petroleum International Ltd, a licence to explore block B3 and be a 90% shareholder in the block, with the state-owned Nile Petroleum Company (Nilepet) holding the remaining 10% stake. The government and Equatorial Guinea announced a new oil partnership. In April, the government announced it was ready to reopen negotiations over drilling rights to oil blocks B1 and B2 following a breakdown of talks with Total, Tullow Oil and the Kuwait Foreign Petroleum Exploration Company.

South Sudan's fuel shortage worsened amid reports of *massive corruption* in the state-owned Nilepet; indeed, South Sudan was ranked the second-most corrupt country after Somalia in TI's Corruption Perception Index, i.e., 179th out of 180 countries. Nilepet's managing director James Thelweng was dismissed, and replaced by Chol Deng Thonin in August. The organisers of South Sudan's first international oil conference in Juba in October hailed the event as a success, but it failed to attract any big energy companies – or President Kiir.

Levels of *food insecurity* remained severe over the year, aggravated by fighting. This was graphically demonstrated in February, when famine was declared in the rebel-held Unity State counties of Leer and Mayendit, where some 100,000 people faced starvation. The declaration led to an escalated humanitarian response in the affected areas, and the famine status was lifted in June. An estimated 6 m people across the country experienced crisis or emergency levels of food insecurity from June to July, amidst what FAO called a 'dire' situation.

The number of *IDPs and refugees* fleeing South Sudan increased. Refugee flows followed patterns in the fighting: government offensives in January in Upper Nile caused many Shilluk to flee to opposition-held areas or to Sudan; fighting near the opposition stronghold of Pagak in Jonglei caused many to flee to Ethiopia; government counter-insurgency operations in the Equatorias caused an exodus to Uganda. In March, UNHCR Grandi warned that Uganda was at breaking point, as the numbers of refugees there could surpass a million before mid-2017. In April, Bidi Bidi became the world's largest refugee camp. In July, Archbishop of Canterbury Justin Welby visited South Sudanese refugees in northern Uganda. At the end of the year, with IDPs within South Sudan totalling some 1.9 m, UNHCR had recorded a total of 668,192 new refugee arrivals during the year. Most were in Uganda (1,037,898), Sudan (772,715), Ethiopia (421,867), Kenya (111,612) and the DRC (88,970).

Conditions for *humanitarian aid* operations worsened, despite First Vice-President Taban Deng Gai's positive speech to the UN General Assembly in September that claimed otherwise. In April, the government appeared to halt its plan to increase *work permit fees* for foreigners but in October again announced that it would increase the cost of work permits for foreign workers from $ 100 to $ 4,000. The UN recorded the highest number of humanitarian access incidents reported by aid agencies in a year (1,159) in South Sudan. Some 30 aid workers were killed, including six between Juba and Pibor in March, the deadliest attack on humanitarian workers since the conflict broke out in 2013. UN Under-Secretary-General for Humanitarian Affairs and Emergency Relief Coordinator Stephen O'Brien condemned the culture of impunity in South Sudan when he visited in August, and called for an immediate end to violence.

Mandated in the summer of 2016 by the UNSC to protect Juba, the 4,000-strong *Regional Protection Force* finally deployed in August as the UN Mission in South Sudan (UNMISS) continued to struggle to undertake peacekeeping amidst conflict. The Japanese Self-Defense Force completed its withdrawal, ending a five-year mission. In May, British troops arrived to provide engineering and medical support to UNMISS, and General Frank Mushyo Kamanzi from Uganda assumed his position as the new UNMISS commander. In October, reporting to the UNSC, the UN peacekeeping chief Jean-Pierre Lacroix offered a dire appraisal of the situation in South Sudan and called on its leaders to "bring the country back from the impending abyss".

Sudan

Jean-Nicolas Bach and Clément Deshayes

Sudanese internal politics remained tense, both within the regime and in its relations with many sectors of society. Within the regime, President Omar al-Bashir announced the formation of a new government emerging from the 'National Dialogue'. But the composition of and participants in this Government of National Accord (or Consensus) were far from representing a solid basis for peaceful political competition. Tensions also remained very high within many segments of society, particularly student movements and (armed) groups in peripheral regions. Hundreds of political prisoners remained in jail.

Tensions reached their peak in Darfur in May, when a joint attack was launched by rebel groups based in Libya (SLA/Minni Minawi) and South Sudan (SLA/Transition Council). They were repelled but the attack sent a message to the international community that the Darfur war was not over. An end to the war was one of the preconditions raised by the US in 2016–17 for lifting its sanctions on Sudan, imposed back in 1997. The negotiations during the year and the eventual lifting of the sanctions in October made 2017 a very important year. Sudan had a broader policy aimed at normalising Khartoum's foreign relations. Thus, al-Bashir's regime remained an important partner with the EU regarding migration policies (it hosted a thematic

 | DOI:10.1163/9789004367630_041

meeting of the Khartoum Process) and skilfully managed to remain neutral towards the Gulf crisis, in which Saudi Arabia and the UAE opposed Qatar.

The socioeconomic situation remained very precarious. High inflation and repeated shortages of basic needs fuelled social contestation in the capital and the regions. The state budget remained unbalanced and biased towards the security apparatus at the expense of social services and education. A widespread and acute watery diarrhoea epidemic probably killed some 1,000 people across the country.

Domestic Politics

After a very tense end of 2016 marked by strong social conflicts, 2017 started with the last jolts of the *general strike* of November and December 2016. Several *political leaders and activists were arrested* at the beginning of January, while those arrested in November-December 2016 remained in jail. The political atmosphere eased following two events that occurred at the end of January: the release of some of the political detainees and the return to Sudan, on 25 January, of *Sadiq al-Mahdi* – former prime minister of the elected government overthrown by the 1989 coup. He led one of the most prominent opposition parties, the National Umma Party. His return put an end to a period of political exile that had started in August 2014, after a one-month detention by the National Intelligence and Security Services (NISS). The return of al-Mahdi came after the cessation of hostilities between the regime and the armed movements – some of them allied with the National Umma Party within the broader Sudan Call.

Following the conclusion of the *National Dialogue* process during the autumn of 2016, President Omar al-Bashir dissolved the Sudanese government on 3 March and appointed Lieutenant General Bakri Hassan Saleh as prime minister, the first prime minister of Sudan since the abolition of the position after the 1989 coup, in which he had been deeply involved. Bakri had previously been first vice president of the Republic and a member of al-Bashir's inner circle. The *government of National Accord (or National Consensus)* was announced during May. But it was quite a disappointment for the political actors involved in the National Dialogue. The extensive government of 31 ministers and more than 40 secretaries of state was very similar to the previous one, with the exception of the inclusion of the Popular Congress Party (PCP), which had been in opposition since it had its separation from the National Congress Party (NCP) in the late 1990s. Key positions were still held by NCP politicians and many other positions were distributed as a 'reward' for the groups who had agreed to participate in the National Dialogue. In addition, 65 parliamentary seats were created specifically for participants in the National Dialogue. Most of the opposition had, however, boycotted the National Dialogue and were very critical of the new government. Even voices of NCP allies showed their frustration concerning the non-implementation of the National Dialogue recommendations and the minor role granted to their parties. And, despite the nomination of Bakri Hassan Saleh and his increasing authority as the regime's number two, power again remained greatly concentrated in the hands of al-Bashir.

This continuing greater *concentration of power* in the president's hands was obvious in the reform of the *Rapid Support Forces* (RSF), a paramilitary force under control of the NISS and originally recruited from among the Darfuri Arab militias, and more specifically among the Rizeigat tribe of the leader of the RSF, Brigadier General Mohamed Hamdan Dagalo, known as Hemeti, a former Border Guard commander and Janjaweed militia leader. The RSF had been accused by several NGOs of violating human rights and of numerous crimes against the population of Darfur and South Kordofan and had more recently been used to control and reduce the number of migrants going to Libya. In January, new legislation integrated the RSF into the Sudan Armed Forces – undoubtedly to be understood in the context of normalisation of Sudan's external relations with foreign partners (see below). In May, a great ceremony was held in order to mark the completion of training by 11,438 new RSF recruits – officially extending the force to 17,357 soldiers.

The RSF and other affiliated groups, as well as rebel movements, were largely responsible for continued *great insecurity* in conflict areas and especially in *Darfur*. The rebel groups still active in Darfur did not control large territories, with the exception of the Sudan Liberation Army/Abdelwahid Nur (SLA/Nur), which was in control of areas in the Djebel Marra. The Justice and Equality Movement (JEM) and the Sudan Liberation Army/Minni Minawi (SLA/MM) were mainly operating from bases in South Sudan and Libya. The process of fragmentation of these groups went on, with various factions splitting off, new alliances of local warlords forming, and some groups making agreements with the regime. There was also an increase in the number of groups allied to nobody, but involved in racketeering and theft. Three Darfur rebel groups (the Sudan Liberation Movement [SLM]/Justice, SLM/Unity and JEM/Jali) announced the creation of the Sudan Liberation Force Alliance (SLFA) in July, while the SLM/Second Revolution had signed a peace treaty with the government in January. Despite the intervention of the army and the RSF and the arrest of tribal leaders, numerous clashes between Arab tribal groups occurred during the year and were very deadly especially in South Darfur. Contrary to official declarations, the situation had not improved in Darfur in 2016. The security situation was still of great concern, and conditions inside the IDP camps remained alarming, due to the lack of aid, facilities and sufficient food, and the presence of militias. The few attempts made by IDPs to return to their original homes, encouraged by the authorities, failed because armed groups had moved onto their land.

In the two other areas of conflict, *the Blue Nile and the Nuba Mountains*, the military situation remained stable, and a more or less respected ceasefire was ongoing. But the split in the main rebel group, the Sudan People's Liberation Movement

North (SPLM-N), weakened its position. Tensions started in March, when the Deputy Chairman Abdelaziz el-Hilu resigned and the Nuba Mountain Liberation Council (NMLC), a branch of the SPLM-N, called for the replacement of Malik Agar, chairman of the SPLM-N, and Yassir Arman, its general secretary. The NMLC and more generally the SPLM-N in the Nuba Mountains accused Agar and Arman of abandoning the issue of self-determination for the Nuba Mountains. Agar and Arman were dismissed and replaced by Abdelaziz el-Hilu, and most of the military commanders took the side of el-Hilu, including commanders of the Blue Nile area. These tensions led to a split of the movement, the delay of the negotiations started in Addis Ababa (Ethiopia) under the umbrella of the AU, and a unilateral ceasefire announced by el-Hilu in August.

Broadly speaking, the *opposition groups were increasingly divided*. The division of the Sudan Call went on: the members of the National Consensus Forces (e.g. the Sudanese Communist Party and the Sudanese Ba'ath Party, who had left the Call in 2016) continued to denounce the strategy of negotiation with the regime promoted by the Umma Party. Members of Darfur rebel groups, such as the SLA/MM and the JEM, agreed to go to Germany to participate in peace talks. But the SLA/Nur rejected the talks. In addition, the split within the SPLM-N further weakened the position of the Call and the alliance of the rebel group within the Sudan Revolutionary Front (SRF). Meanwhile an opposition political party, the Sudanese Congress Party led by Omar el Digeir, was quietly active in the streets and in the media; it came to be particularly targeted by the NISS and large numbers of its leaders and activists were arrested.

Student movements experienced harsh repression. Conflict on university campuses was at a very high level throughout the year, especially among Darfuri students. Following a new cycle of tensions, many universities expelled Darfuri students involved in political or cultural activities, and the NISS frequently arrested students and political and association leaders. This repression and the targeting of Darfuri students, denounced in an AI report in January, strengthened tensions at universities. Every week or two, incidents, demonstrations and public speeches occurred in different universities. Two events were particularly significant. The first was the passing of a death sentence on a Darfuri student involved in the Sudanese Congress Party at Khartoum University. He was accused of killing a policeman during a demonstration. The sentence shocked students, especially Darfuris, and was perceived by many to be politically motivated. Demonstrations took place in Khartoum to protest against the verdict. The second event was the mass resignation of around 1,500 students at Bakht el-Rida University in White Nile. They started a march to Khartoum, demanding the release of ten students accused of killing two policemen in a demonstration in May, and the return of students dismissed from the university. The march was stopped by the NISS in Sheikh el-Yagout village, where a number of opposition and association leaders joined in to express their support for the students. In addition, several organisations denounced the "targeting of Darfuri students", including the Darfur Bar Association and the Darfur Relief and Documentation Centre, which in September released a report called 'The political assassination of students from Darfur'.

Press freedom was severely restricted by the government, and journalists and newspapers probably faced more difficulties than in 2016. The NISS, which was responsible for censorship, frequently seized newspaper print runs, causing major financial losses. Independent newspaper such as 'El Jerreeda', 'El Watan', 'El Tayyar' and 'Akhir Lahza' were specifically targeted. Several journalists and editors-in-chief were arrested because of their work. Reporters Without Borders continued to rank Sudan 174th out of 180 countries on its index of press freedom.

The year was also marked by the *death of Fatima Ibrahim Ahmed* in England, on 12 August. She was the first woman to hold a seat in the Sudanese parliament (in 1965). She founded the Union of Sudanese Women in 1952 and joined the Sudanese Communist Party a few years later. Her husband, a famous trade union leader, had been executed under former president el-Nimeiry in 1971. Her funeral in August in Khartoum was an important gathering of the opposition.

Foreign Affairs

There were about 2,3 m *IDPs* in Sudan, mostly originating from western and southern regions, and 924,810 *refugees* and asylum seekers, most of whom (772,715) were from South Sudan (UNHCR 2018 data). Sudan also hosted about 111,000 Ethiopian citizens, 13,000 Eritreans and probably between 200,000 and 300,000 Syrians (no official figures available). Sudan remained a transit country for most migrants (79%), as revealed by a study conducted by the Organization for International Migration. Sudanese citizens for their part continued leaving the country for to economic and political reasons: the UNHCR estimated that there were 580,000 Sudanese refugees in neighbouring countries, while Sudanese became one of the largest groups of asylum seekers in Europe, and the largest in France, after the dismantling of camps in northern France.

The Sudanese government remained an important partner for the *EU* as part of the EU's broader strategy to reduce migration flows toward Europe. The so-called *Khartoum Process* remained a key component of the EU-Emergency Trust Fund for Africa (EU-ETF), along with the Rabat Process on its south-western border and the 2016 EU-Turkey Agreement on its eastern border. A Khartoum Process meeting, the 'Thematic meeting on the development benefits of migration and addressing root causes of irregular migration and forced displacement', was held on 22–23 November in Khartoum, gathering representatives of East African states and international partners involved in the Process. On this occasion, Sudanese representatives underscored the historical and normal nature of the movement of people and raised the question of the conditions needed for these movements to become profitable for everyone, opening a different perspective from the current tendency to systematically criminalise and attempt to control migrants towards Europe. The complex causes of migration being relatively well-known, international institutions remained focused on fighting 'illegal migration', 'smuggling and trafficking'. A representative of the UNHCR declared that the great majority (74%) of migrants from the Horn of Africa were leaving for political reasons, compared with only 20% from West Africa.

Throughout the year, the EU was systematically accused by numerous media and human rights organisations such as HRW of 'sponsoring', through this Khartoum Process and the EU-ETF, the Sudanese authoritarian regime and its former Janjaweed militias, now operating as border guards or RSF along the borders to control migration. Such accusations were to be treated with caution as there was no evidence of any direct funding of Sudanese institutions by EU agencies. The EU-ETF only aimed at sponsoring intermediary agencies implementing border control or migration 'management' programmes, including the German agency GIZ ('Better Migration Management' programme), the French CIVIPOL (acting for the French Ministry of Interior, operating from Sudan notably through their ROCK programme) and Expertise France (also operating from Sudan as a leader of the EQUIP-Sudan education programme), the British Council (another implementing partner of the Better Migration Management programme, tasked with 'awareness raising'), the International Organization for Migration, the UN Office on Drugs and Crime, and the Italian Department of Public Security, but there is no doubt that these policies aimed at reducing migration flows toward Europe.

These migration issues appeared deeply connected to regional and internal politics when, at the end of September, the RSF intercepted armed militias accused of organising human trafficking and killed 17 men and 'freed' the migrants. It later appeared that these militias where border guards under the authority of one of the most influential Darfur leaders, Musa Hilal. Tensions increased as Abdellah Razikall, a close ally of Musa Hilal, was arrested in November, and especially when Musa Hilal himself was eventually captured by the RSF in December (see the report of the UN Monitoring Group on Darfur, 28 December 2017). By the end of December, Musa Hilal was still under house arrest in Khartoum.

These events occurred in the line with increasing *tensions between the government and Darfuri leaders*. Khartoum notably intensified its campaign of arms collecting in Darfur throughout the year, provoking local resistance, and newly trained RSF recruits (see above) were to be used to secure regions such as Darfur. In May, tensions were exacerbated when a joint offensive from opposition movements (SLA/MM based in Libya) and South Sudan (SLA/Transition Council) was launched against Sudanese security forces – the first offensive of this size since 2015. The insurgents were repelled but demonstrated the persistence of the armed conflict and the volatility of the region – a message to be considered in the context of ongoing negotiations between Khartoum and the US government for the lifting of US sanctions.

These historic negotiations on lifting the *US sanctions*, imposed on Sudan since 1997, continued, and led to the easing of the embargo by the administration just before Barack Obama left office in January. The lifting of the remaining sanctions was conditioned on Sudanese cooperation in five policy tracks: Sudan's disengagement from the South Sudanese conflict; improvement of the security situation in Darfur, the Blue Nile and South Kordofan; Sudan's assistance in fighting the Lord's Resistance Army; its engagement in fighting terrorist groups; and the facilitation of access for humanitarian agencies to the affected Sudanese regions. No conditions were imposed with regard to human rights or political transition. The definitive decision was expected in July, but the administration of the new US President Donald Trump finally postponed its decision until 6 October, when Sudan was eventually removed from the list of states under US embargo.

Just a month before, on 24 September, President Trump's administration had also removed Sudan from the list of states whose citizens were barred from entering the United States. The controversial Executive Order ('Protecting the Nation from Foreign Terrorist Entry Into the United States') was initially issued on 27 January and aimed at freezing the entry of citizens from six countries, including Sudan (Syria, Libya, Iran, Somalia, Yemen). However, Sudan was not removed from the US list of state sponsors of terrorism, and the US administration expressed the need for political improvements in Sudan and a move toward a 'transition' as a sine qua non for the deepening of relations between the two countries. International sanctions from the ICC were maintained against individuals related to crimes committed in Darfur, including President Omar al-Bashir.

Sudan became involved in the so-called '*Qatar* crisis', which affected Horn of Africa geopolitics in general. Shortly after President Trump's visit to Riyadh, rising tensions among countries of the Gulf Cooperation Council reached their peak when Saudi Arabia, followed by the UAE, Bahrain and Egypt, cut diplomatic relations with Qatar and announced an economic ban on the latter from 5 June. While Turkey supported Doha materially and diplomatically, Saudi Arabia and the UAE urged Horn of Africa states to take a clear stand on the crisis. Unlike other East African states, Khartoum adopted an original position by not taking part: as a longtime ally of Qatar, Khartoum managed not to cut diplomatic relations. Among other things, Doha had supported Sudan when it took sides with Iraq in the 1991 Gulf War, had been strongly involved in the peace process in Darfur and had supported Sudan financially after South Sudan's Independence in 2011. At the same time, Khartoum was able to maintain relations with the powerful *Saudi Arabia*, and increased the number of its troops contributing to the Saudi-led coalition fighting in Yemen, unofficially estimated at at least 2,000. Further tension involving the Gulf countries and *Turkey* arose in late December, when a visit by Turkish President Recep Tayyip Erdoğan confirmed Sudan's agreement with Turkey's plan to upgrade Suakin, the Sudanese port on the Red Sea coast. This decision was strongly criticised by Cairo, Asmara and the UAE, which accused Turkey of planning a military base on the Sudanese coast.

There was no major change of attitude concerning the *Grand Ethiopian Renaissance Dam* on the Blue Nile, started in 2011. Ethiopia confirmed its intention to start filling the artificial lake by 2018 and Sudan maintained its opposing stance alongside Ethiopia. The Tripartite group (Egypt, Ethiopia and Sudan) made no significant progress concerning any understanding on the dam's impacts on Sudan and Egypt, or on the issue of delaying the filling of the lake. The dissemination of the second report elaborated by the French company BRL was postponed, but diplomatic relations were not cut. Representatives of the countries met to discuss the issue, as in January, when the three countries' leaders al-Sisi, al-Bashir and Hailemariam met on the occasion of the AU Summit in Addis Ababa.

Socioeconomic Developments

Although the intensity of social struggles decreased, the year witnessed a number of *strikes and demonstrations*, as in previous years. Throughout the year incidents of sectoral or localised social conflicts took place. The dock workers of Port Sudan went on strike against the privatisation of the docks and the arrest of one of their leaders. Doctors also protested and sometimes went on strike for various reasons: lack of material and human resources and attempts to suppress news on the cholera/water diarrhoea outbreak. Localised conflicts concerning teachers took place – about delays in paying salaries, or the lack of security in certain areas. The question of insecurity was also the cause of protests, the first for years, by shop owners and merchants in the Darfuri Suq.

The project to build two *new dams at Kejbar and Dal* in Northern State was still creating fear and anger among the Nubian community. These new dams would be constructed mainly by Chinese companies and financed by Saudi Arabia in exchange for the use of agricultural land. They would flood numerous Nubian villages, agricultural land and historical sites. The issues of *land and access to water* remained the trigger for many localised conflicts and the effect of the increasing *gold-mining* activities led to ongoing, substantial discontent among the population. Concerned citizens denounced the use of chemicals like cyanide, which had dangerous health effects on the inhabitants of the area and their livestock, and was a cause of land and water pollution. Other conflicts erupted around the question of the use of land by mining companies and the question of redistribution of the profits and benefits of extractive activities. Several demonstrations took place in Northern State, Nile State and South Kordofan. In the last, riot police killed a secondary school student during a demonstration in Kologi.

Reconfiguration of *trade unions*, started in 2016 with the creation of the Central Committee of Sudanese Doctors, continued, with the reform of the historical El Gezira and El Managil Farmers Association. The authorities responded by arresting most of the leaders of the Farmers Association.

Sudan continued to grapple with *major economic readjustments* since the secession of South Sudan. The economic situation was still very challenging since the loss of oil income and revealed how poor had been the state's preparations to deal with the consequences. Economic growth, however, remained positive with a *rise in GDP* of around 3.4%, according to the government, and 3.25% according to IMF projections. The problem of the unreliability of government economic figures remained because of the lack of transparency and faulty methods of data collection.

The rate of *inflation* remained very high, reaching an annual 34.1%, according to the Sudanese Central Bureau of Statistics. Economists such as Hamid Eltigani, professor at the American University in Cairo, disputed this and estimated the annual inflation rate to be close to 50%. The IMF attributed the high inflation to loose fiscal and monetary policies. Related to inflation, *the dollar rate remained very fluid*, impacting the price of imported goods and the external (import-export revenue) imbalance. The dollar rate on the *informal market* increased from SDG (pound) 17 in February to SDG 30 at the end of December, alongside the official customs rate, which was raised from SDG 6.7 to SDG 18 in December, causing a doubling of prices. The main blowback of this would be seen in 2018. The government tried unsuccessfully to control inflation and was planning to bring it down to 19.5% in 2018. The lifting of US sanctions in October appeared to have a negative impact on inflation and the dollar exchange rate. To combat the disparity between the official and black market rates, the authorities tried to repress currency dealers, but with a very limited effect on the rate.

As a result of the high dollar rate, long years of sanctions and a major imbalance of exchange, Sudan had very low foreign exchange reserves and remained dependent on funding by Gulf States. Foreign currency reserves were only equal to one-and-a-half months of imports of goods and services. Nevertheless, the *trade deficit* seemed to be narrowing and would probably fall to 3% of GDP, according to the IMF, as compared with 6.1% in 2016.

Many international organisations and NGOs pointed out the *imbalance in the state budget* between security matters and social services such as education and health. The state planned to spend only SDG 5.3 bn (3%) on education and health, while the official budget was SDG 14 bn for the Ministry of Defence, SDG 4.3 bn for the security services, SDG 3 bn for the RSF and SDG 6.3 bn for the Ministry of Interior, of a total budget of SDG 96.2 bn. The 2018 State budget, presented in December, went in the same direction, with an increase in the budget for the NISS and the RSF while the proportion of expenditure allocated to health and education remained the same. According to the IMF, the state budget represented 8.6% of GDP and income from taxes (mainly on VAT) 5%. The oil revenue brought in only 0.8% of GDP (compared with 2% in 2013). The low level of taxes compared with other African countries remained too low for public accountability and the regime was under pressure to find other sources of income, as oil had been in the past and gold was today.

Sudan continued its development of *gold mining*, an easy cash resource. According to the Sudanese Ministry of Minerals, 103 tonnes of gold were extracted – a significant increase on the 93 tonnes in 2016, and Sudan became the ninth-largest gold producer in the world and the third in Africa, after South Africa and Ghana. Around 450 local and international gold-mining companies were operating in Sudan in various areas, mainly in Nile State, Northern State, River Nile, East/South Kordofan, South Darfur and North Darfur. New guidelines were applied from March. Private prospectors had to sell a minimum of 50% of the gold they mined to the Central Bank of Sudan, as gold had recently become the state's main source of hard currency. In a report by Sudan Democracy First Group (SDFG), the mining sector was denounced as corrupt. Following a report by the UN Panel of Experts, the SDFG estimated that around $ 4.5 bn worth of gold was smuggled from Sudan to the UAE during the year. Sudan was still ranked 175th out of 180 countries on TI's Corruption Perception Index.

Regarding *access to goods and services*, it was a difficult year. The population faced major inequalities in access to basic services such as electricity and clean water. The proportion of the population that had access to these services increased (35% of the population had access to electricity in 2015), but war-torn and marginalised areas were still largely excluded, despite the efforts of various organisations. The quality of services also remained very unequal, with good access to water and electricity in the centre of Khartoum and other major cities, while in other areas electricity was available for only a few hours a day and water was untreated. Thus, while range and accessibility seemed to be increasing, quality remained very uneven.

Inflation and the high dollar exchange rate made *imported goods* or processed goods based on imported products or food almost inaccessible. Alongside inflation, *shortages* continued in various areas during the year. Shortages of wheat forced bakeries to close their doors several times in areas like Kassala and Gedaref. Shortages of cooking gas, petrol and drinking water impacted various parts of the country, including Khartoum. Rumours of 'organised shortages' and speculation by businessmen close to the regime created tensions. Farmers and opposition parties accused some businessmen of buying crops at very low prices and storing them so as to stimulate shortages and raise prices. However, it was also the case that in some areas sorghum, the basic staple of the major part of the population, was not harvested because prices were so low. Crops rotted in the fields in the area of Gedaref, for example, because farmers said that they would lose money by selling them.

According to the government, national *unemployment* stayed at a very high level, reaching 19% in July.

Sudan was also shaken by a public health crisis in the form of a *cholera/watery diarrhoea outbreak*. NGOs and doctors tried to sound the alarm when they noted cases of cholera. According to doctors and local doctors' organisations, the beginning of a cholera epidemic was seen in the south of Sudan, in Blue Nile State, and then reached several other areas, such as White Nile, Northern State, Khartoum and IDP camps in Darfur. The Ministry of Health initially denied any outbreak, before finally acknowledging that an epidemic of watery diarrhoea was indeed occurring. A battle on numbers then followed this crisis. The Ministry of Health and WHO kept refusing to talk about cholera but declared in October that 35,000 people had been affected by 'acute watery diarrhoea' and almost 1,000 had died. Doctors of the National Epidemiological Corporation explained that it was a cholera outbreak and according to their data (July), 23,930 cases had been registered, and 930 had succumbed. In October, the minister of health declared Sudan free of watery diarrhoea, but this statement was contested.

Tanzania

Kurt Hirschler and Rolf Hofmeier

President Magufuli, in his second year in office, ever more vigorously pursued an authoritarian leadership style that significantly narrowed the previously existing democratic space and curtailed critical public debate. The freedoms of assembly and of expression of opposition voices were frequently restricted by state authorities, political rallies were banned outside of election periods, many opposition politicians were repeatedly arrested, interrogated and intimidated, critical media were closely scrutinised and the state organs showed an increasing intolerance of any dissenting opinion. Despite a noticeable deterioration in the general political climate, the stability of the political system was not under threat and the dominant long-ruling CCM ('Chama cha Mapinduzi' / Revolutionary Party) was able to control all spheres of public life and still enjoyed the unwavering support of the majority of the population. Magufuli further consolidated his grip on the CCM, despite continued discontent within party ranks. On the surface, the situation in semi-autonomous Zanzibar remained relatively calm, but the long-standing confrontation between the CCM and the opposition CUF did not vanish. Neighbourly relations with Rwanda and Uganda were strengthened, amid minor disputes with Kenya over trade issues. Relations with Western aid donors became more strained

 | DOI:10.1163/9789004367630_042

over dissatisfaction with Magufuli's erratic governance style, while cooperation with China was further intensified. Indicators of macroeconomic performance continued to be good, with a solid 7.1% GDP growth rate, but uncertainty over the government's strategic orientation of stressing economic nationalism and continuing severe liquidity problems weakened private sector initiatives, raising worries about a looming economic slowdown.

Domestic Politics

The Magufuli administration continued to drastically change the country. The *fight against corruption and fraud*, negligence and indiscipline in the public sector, and embezzlement and waste of public funds remained high on the government's agenda. The government demonstrated its willingness to *stop the culture of impunity* and to take strong action, even against prominent people. As in 2016, numerous public servants were sacked on allegations of corruption, fraud, misuse of funds or alleged underperformance in office, among them Minister of Energy and Minerals Sospeter Muhongo, who was forced to resign in late May for failing to supervise the mining sector, after Magufuli had received the first of two investigation reports that had concluded that mining companies had understated the value of their exports (see Socioeconomic Developments). In mid-June, two key suspects in the *Tegeta Escrow case* were arrested and charged with economic sabotage. In mid-September, Air Tanzania's former managing director and former chief finance officer were sentenced to six years in jail or a fine of TSh (shilling) 35 m for causing the national airline a loss of almost $ 1 m through fraudulent deals in 2007. Two officials from the Ministry of Energy and Minerals were brought before court in mid-September and accused of causing a $ 1.1 m loss in tax revenue by undervaluing an export-bound consignment of diamonds that had been seized at Dar es Salaam airport.

After detecting more than 16,000 so-called ghost workers and removing them from the public sector payroll in 2016, the president fired almost 10,000 civil servants in May after a verification process found that they had forged academic certificates. However, several of those affected insisted that they held authentic certificates and appealed against their dismissals. Given the shortage of civil servants in some crucial sectors such as justice, health and education, the decision to fire 10,000 people was received with some reserve. In February, the Tanzania Commission for Universities threatened to expel more than 7,000 students on the grounds that they lacked the required qualifications. They were given one week to prove their academic credentials.

In its *drive to put the country in order*, the Magufuli administration went against anything it perceived as "wrong, immoral, inappropriate, dangerous or obstructive" to the government's efforts to develop and industrialise the country. However, most measures aimed at punishing individual misbehaviour and not at bringing about structural or procedural reforms. The efforts to promote *better work ethics, discipline* and a *result-oriented civil service* were not always successful, with some of the measures even being counterproductive. The president's spontaneous and frequently erratic decisions led to an *atmosphere of fear* in some parts of the civil service, where decision-makers were reluctant to decide anything because of a constant threat that any 'wrong' decision could immediately cost them their job. On the other hand, some politicians and civil servants acted over-zealously. Several office-holders overstepped their constitutional competences by issuing directives or ordering arrests, which they were not legally entitled to do, and with complete disregard for legal procedures.

The government's efforts to *contain smuggling and abuse of illicit drugs* took a strange twist in mid-February, when Dar es Salaam Regional Commissioner Paul Makonda presented a list of 97 names of people allegedly involved in the use of and trade in illegal drugs. The list included prominent politicians, among them the leader of the strongest opposition party CHADEMA (Party for Democracy and Progress), Freeman Mbowe, well-known artists, leading business people and religious leaders. In a series of televised press conferences, Makonda named suspects and summoned them to police stations, where they were interrogated and had to undergo a drugs test. Some of those on Makonda's list rejected the accusations and threatened to sue him for defamation. Makonda's actions aroused strong criticism from members of parliament and Information Minister Nape Nnauye, who considered the public naming of suspects unlawful. In mid-March, Makonda, accompanied by armed police, stormed a TV and radio station late at night and (unsuccessfully) demanded that they broadcast a video-clip in which one of his critics was accused of illegitimate and immoral behaviour. Following a public outcry, Nnauye set up a team to investigate the issue, which in its report harshly condemned Makonda's action as an attack on media freedom. The following day, Magufuli, who had backed Makonda throughout the entire affair, sacked Nnauye and replaced him with former justice minister Harrison Mwakyembe.

The government's quest to clean up the country also saw a further crackdown on people accused of *practising or promoting homosexuality*, which was illegal in Tanzania but never aggressively persecuted. In February, Health Minister Ummy Mwalimu announced that 40 privately-run health centres would be stopped from providing HIV/AIDS related services, accusing them of promoting homosexuality. In mid-September, 20 people undergoing training in HIV/AIDS education programmes were arrested in Zanzibar on allegations of being implicated in homosexuality. One month later, 13 people were arrested in a Dar es Salaam hotel for allegedly promoting homosexuality. This arrest seemed to be politically motivated rather than being part of the government's campaign against homosexuality. The group, including an acclaimed human rights lawyer from South Africa, had convened for a legal consultation on the possibility of mounting a court case against the government's HIV/AIDS policies. Dozens of men suspected of being gay were reportedly detained and taken to hospitals to undergo forced anal examinations.

In yet another arena of his campaign against 'immorality', Magufuli told a public rally on 22 June that he would never allow *pregnant school girls* to return to government schools after giving birth. Magufuli's statement contradicted his party's 2015 election manifesto and the Education Ministry's long-standing efforts. During the parliamentary budget debate in mid-May, the Parliamentary Social Services Committee, together with the opposition, had urged the education minister to accelerate preparations for the already signalled guidelines for the re-entry policy. Magufuli's statement caused an outcry within and outside Tanzania. Although the president and Home Affairs Minister Mwigulu Nchemba threatened to deregister NGOs that campaigned for allowing teenage mothers to return to school, and to fire all head teachers who failed to comply with the orders, on 29 June, a group of 26 Tanzanian NGOs jointly called on the government to reconsider its decision. The pan-African women's organisation Femnet set up an online petition and numerous people used social media platforms to criticise the president's statement. On 6 July, at least 22 global and African human rights organisations jointly stated their support for the 26 Tanzanian NGO's concerns and demands. On 3 August, the African Commission on Human and People's Rights, together with other AU human rights institutions, criticised Magufuli's statement and urged the government not to undermine the girls' right to education and equality. Obviously unimpressed by the criticism, the government pursued its fight against teenage mothers. On 11 December, Mwanza Regional Commissioner John Mongella directed that all pregnant school-girls be arrested and taken to court in order to prevent other school-girls from having love affairs and to force them to reveal the names of those who had impregnated them.

The *human rights situation deteriorated significantly*. The opposition's opportunities to exercise their legal rights were severely limited by the prolonged presidential directive to ban politicians from political activities outside of their respective constituencies until the next elections in 2020. Provisions of the proposed *new Political Parties Act* sought to permanently institutionalise the presidential directive. The Magufuli administration intensified its drive to *clamp down on the opposition* with a strategy of demoralisation through constant harassment and frequent short-term arbitrary arrests, interrogations and court charges. About 400 members of the leading opposition party CHADEMA, but also from the small ACT (Alliance for Change and Transparency)-Wazalendo party, including MPs and the party leadership, were temporarily arrested and interrogated by security forces for conducting political activities outside their constituencies, criticising the president or talking for longer than their allotted time during a rally or disputing government data on economic growth, and other charges. One of the most outspoken opposition politicians, CHADEMA's chief whip in parliament Tundu Lissu, was arrested six times and his residence invaded and searched several times by the police. In February, Lissu announced that he would stand for election as president of the Tanganyika Law Society, the country's bar association. Justice Minister Mwakyembe thereupon threatened to deregister the association, but Lissu was nevertheless elected on 18 March. On 7 September, Lissu sustained life-threatening injuries in an attempt on his life, when unknown assailants fired about 30 bullets at his car. He was rushed to Dodoma General Hospital and later flown to a hospital in Nairobi (Kenya), where he slowly recovered. Nobody was arrested, and the government turned down demands from CHADEMA to request the US for assistance with the investigation.

Assaults and abductions by 'unknown assailants' became a new but increasing phenomenon. In April, three local singers were reportedly abducted and tortured by unknown individuals, before being released. Journalist Azory Gwanda disappeared on 21 November in unclear circumstances and continued to be missing. Journalists and media associations started campaigns to urge the authorities to intensify their investigations and bring the journalist back.

In August, the police claimed victory in the so-called *Kibiti killing case*. Since 2014, more than 40 people, mainly police officers and local political leaders (mainly from CCM) but also ordinary citizens, had been mysteriously killed in Kibiti, Mkuranga and Rufiji Districts of Coast Region. The reasons behind the killings remained unclear, but the security forces assumed a criminal background. The police finally raided a forest camp and killed 13 suspects in early August. In September, a person suspected of being the mastermind behind the killings was caught and shot by police in Dar es Salaam. However, the abduction in November of journalist Azory Gwanda, who was researching the Kibiti killings, indicated that the case was not yet solved.

The government and administration imposed *extreme restrictions on suspected dissidents* and intimidated or arrested politicians, civil society activists, journalists, lawyers, musicians and ordinary people, thus creating a widely-felt atmosphere of fear. The space for NGOs shrank significantly. They were threatened with deregistration by the administration, the president and ministers; their staff and supporters were intimidated and temporarily arrested, and their activities were blocked by police or civil servants. A popular local rapper was arrested in March for mocking the president, but – on Magufuli's personal order – was released the following day. *Media freedom and freedom of expression* were severely curtailed. Four newspapers were temporarily banned, for "sedition", "threatening national security" or publishing "false information". Leading politicians, including the president, warned the media not to "overextend their freedom". Several journalists were temporarily arrested or intimidated by the authorities. Maxence Melo, managing director and co-founder of the popular online forum and whistle-blower website JamiiForums, faced juridical harassment throughout the year. He had been arrested but granted bail in December 2016 under the Cybercrimes Act of 2015 for refusing to reveal the identities of anonymous whistle-blowers. In January, Mike William Mushi, another JamiiForums founder, was also charged in court. But some ordinary citizens were also charged, or remanded for several hours or days without charge, after posting messages critical of the government on social media or WhatsApp groups.

In September, the government tightened *control on social media* and introduced the *Electronic and Postal Communications (Online Content) Regulations*. Some of its provisions posed a further threat to the freedom of expression. It was aimed at controlling content on social media and imposed enormous fines on individual users and online providers. All digital media platforms, including online forums and blogs, were required to be registered with the Tanzania Communications Regulatory Authority, which had the right to deny registration or to deregister a website, forum or blog. Bloggers and forum providers were to be held responsible for any content posted on their sites and had to block anonymous users, identify sources of contents and cooperate with law enforcement officers. Tanzania fell ten places in the World Press Freedom Index of Reporters without Borders – making a total drop of 22 places since 2015.

The growing intolerance of criticism, political opposition, public debate, expressions of dissent, media freedom, violations of the rule of law and of the separation of powers, disrespect for due procedures, and the dramatic narrowing of the democratic space provoked *increasing criticism* from various angles. The new communication regulations were widely criticised in the media and by civil society organisations. In mid-January, three local human rights and media organisations lodged a petition in the East African Court of Justice to challenge the *Media Services Act of 2016*. Somewhat surprisingly, bishops of several churches also criticised the authoritarian streak, but were immediately threatened with deregistration of their churches by the home affairs minister. In a speech delivered in late August to the African Leadership Forum in South Africa, Magufuli's immediate presidential predecessor *Jakaya Kikwete* called upon African ruling parties to view opposition parties not as enemies, but as partners in fostering democratic principles based on the rule of law. In Tanzania, Kikwete's words were widely understood as advice to Magufuli to reconsider his clampdown on the opposition. Several NGOs continued to demand the resumption of the *constitutional reform process*, while the government clarified that this was not on its list of priorities.

Notwithstanding the accusations that democracy and the rule of law were being undermined, opinion polls indicated that *Magufuli still enjoyed wide popular support*. In mid-June, the NGO Twaweza published the results of an opinion poll, which indicated a 71% approval rate for Magufuli from the 1,805 respondents. Although this rate was significantly higher than Magufuli's election result of 58%, it was a sharp decline of his popularity compared with the 96% he had polled in a similar

Twaweza survey in June 2016. Respondents approved his fight against corruption and improvements in public service delivery.

The opposition was further weakened by prominent *defections to the ruling CCM*, after politicians received offers from the party or the government, among them the ACT-Wazalendo former chief advisor and its chairperson and 2015 presidential candidate. In October, ten senior ACT leaders announced their collective defection. In late November, Magufuli appointed one of the formerly fiercest critics of CCM, former CHADEMA presidential candidate Wilibrod Slaa, as ambassador to Sweden. At parliamentary and lower levels, too, numerous politicians quit the opposition and joined CCM, where they were rewarded with government or party posts.

By-elections for local councils on 26 November in 43 wards across the country were marred by irregularities and *unprecedented violence*, which left dozens of people injured, some seriously. Observers from the Legal and Human Rights Centre (LHRC) reported excessive use of force by the security forces, arrests and abductions of party leaders, representatives and voters and attacks with machetes, beatings and torture. The violence indicated the dramatically increased level of intolerance and hatred between the two main political parties. Later, the authorities imposed a TSh 60 m ($ 27,000) fine for airing "seditious information" on five TV stations that had broadcast the LHRC report. CCM won all but one of the contested seats.

The leadership wrangle in Zanzibar's main opposition party, the *Civic United Front* (CUF) escalated further. Since 2016, the party had been split into two factions, one led by the former chairman Ibrahim Lipumba, the other by the former secretary-general Seif Shariff Hamad. In July, Lipumba stripped eight MPs affiliated with the Hamad faction of their party membership, so that they automatically lost their seats in parliament. They were replaced by eight other legislators, sworn in in September. In November, the eight ousted MPs demanded their reinstatement, after the High Court ruled that their expulsion from the party was unlawful.

Magufuli's leadership was widely supported by his *ruling CCM* and the dissent that existed was hardly expressed openly. He further strengthened his control over the party when on 11 March the CCM's National Executive Committee (NEC) *expelled 18 senior party members* and issued strong warnings to four others for "unethical conduct". This was widely understood as a measure to purge the party of supporters of the influential former prime minister, Edward Lowassa, who had defected to the opposition in the run-up to the 2015 elections. The *party structures were radically streamlined* at an extraordinary National Congress on 12 March, attended by more than 2,300 delegates. The NEC was reduced from 388 to 163 members and the Central Committee from 34 to 24. Various party organs were reduced in size and the frequency of their meetings was minimised. Several party positions were removed and multi-leadership posts were prohibited. According to CCM chairman Magufuli, the reforms were aimed at strengthening party efficiency, reducing costs and dependency on rich business people, and bringing "the party back to the people".

Foreign Affairs

Maguful pursued his *low-profile and business-oriented foreign policy*. As in 2015 and 2016, he skipped several high profile international meetings, where Tanzania was represented by the vice president or ministers. As a reflection of the intensifying alliance with *Uganda*'s President Yoweri Museveni, several joint infrastructure and trade projects were launched and agreements on cooperation in trade, electrification and health care signed. The most significant infrastructure project was the construction of a crude oil pipeline from western Uganda to the port of Tanga, which had originally been planned to be built through Kenya. The opening of a one-stop border post was intended to partly divert Uganda's imports and exports from Kenya to Tanzania.

Relations with *Kenya* remained difficult due to ongoing trade disputes. Both countries blocked several products from the other country or imposed duties. In October and November, the Tanzanian government seized and auctioned 4,000 cows belonging to Kenyan Masai herders. The authorities blamed the influx of 18,000 cows from neighbouring countries for environmental destruction. In early November, Tanzanian authorities seized 6,400 one-day-old chickens, allegedly smuggled from Kenya, and burnt them to death on suspicion that they could spread bird flu.

During his tenure as *EAC chairman*, which ended on 20 May, Magufuli introduced his cost-cutting measures to the regional body. According to him, the secretariat alone had reduced its expenditure by more than 25%. But no solution was found to the conflict over EPA trade deals with the EU. Kenya and Rwanda wanted the EPAs to be signed whereas Tanzania rejected them.

Magufuli condemned the ICC decision to investigate alleged human rights abuses in *Burundi*, saying it would interfere with the EAC's efforts to restore peace, which, however, did not progress. The Burundi peace dialogue mediator, former Tanzanian president Benjamin Mkapa, was accused of taking sides with Burundi's President Nkurunziza. According to UNHCR, Tanzania was hosting about 360,000 Burundian refugees by the end of October.

Holding the SADC Troika chair until August, Tanzania was involved in trying to find a solution to the conflicts in the *DRC*. In April, Foreign Minister Mahiga led a SADC mission to the DRC to assess the political and security situation. The mission stressed the need for peaceful and transparent elections and called for the establishment of a government of national unity in the DRC. On 7 December, at least 14 Tanzanian UN *peacekeeping soldiers were killed* and more than 40 injured in a rebel attack in North Kivu.

After eight Tanzanians were arrested and charged with espionage in *Malawi* in January, Foreign Minister Augustine Mahiga and Malawi's President Peter Mutharika agreed to revive talks to resolve the long-standing misunderstandings between the countries, resulting from the simmering *Lake Nyasa/Lake Malawi border conflict.*

During a two-day official visit on 22–23 January, *Turkish President Erdoğan* signed nine agreements with Magufuli on cooperation in defence, economic development and health. Magufuli asked for a loan to help finance a stretch of the proposed new standard-gauge central railway line. Erdoğan urged Tanzania to shut a number of schools allegedly linked to the Gülen movement, but the targeted schools denied any link to the movement. Only one week after Erdoğan's visit, a Turkish-Portuguese consortium was awarded the tender for the construction of 205 km of the new railway line. The tender had previously been awarded to Chinese companies, and the Chinese government had agreed a $ 7.6 bn loan but Magufuli had suspended the contract over irregularities shortly after assuming office, and fresh bids were invited.

Despite the dispute over the railway project, *cooperation with China* intensified. China had become Tanzania's largest trading partner and second biggest investor after the UK. During the CCM national congress, the ruling party stressed its close traditional links with the Communist Party of China. Chinese Foreign Affairs Minister Wang Yi visited Tanzania on 9–10 January and promised support for Tanzania's industrialisation drive and to upgrade the TAZARA railway. On a return invitation, Mahiga travelled to China on a four-day official visit in December and met several potential investors.

India remained an important partner for investment and trade, with Tanzania being among India's five top investment destinations.

Tanzania was among the several countries accused of violating the *UN sanctions against North Korea*, allegedly having entered into a military-related contract with a North Korean firm. Mahiga, however, denied the accusations, explaining that Tanzania had ceased military cooperation with North Korea in 2014.

On 25 April, Tanzania expelled the *head of the UNDP mission* in the country for the allegedly deteriorating performance of her office. The media, however, linked the dismissal to her criticism of the controversial Zanzibar elections.

Although *Western donors* were increasingly concerned about the authoritarian drive, they lauded the government for improvements in education, public service delivery and the fight against corruption, waste of public funds and mismanagement, and continued to fund development projects.

Socioeconomic Developments

According to most standard indicators, *macroeconomic performance* was again quite satisfactory, generally in line with the strong continuous growth trend since the early 2000s. Tanzania remained in the top group of the fastest-growing and most consistently performing economies in Africa, although it was still characterised by a very low level of material wealth for the vast majority of the population (almost half living below the international poverty line). In the latest *HDI*

(March 2017, data for 2015), Tanzania was ranked 151st (out of 188 countries) in the 'low human development' category. The (nominal) *average per capita income* was estimated to be around $ 1,000 per year – thus close to attaining the government's declared goal of achieving the status of a 'lower middle-income country'. The *average per capita income* (in PPP terms) was calculated at about $ 2,500. In the World Economic Forum's new 2018 Inclusive Development Index, Tanzania was rated 48th of 74 listed emerging economies and in top position among SSA countries.

Tanzania's economy continued to show remarkable resilience in a difficult global setting, its low level of outward trade openness somewhat shielding it from negative external repercussions. The *GDP growth rate* was estimated at 7.1%, better than foreseen throughout the year, but close to the government's original target and consistent with the growth trend over more than a decade.

Climatically, it was a rather mixed year. Due to prolonged *drought* conditions early in the year, the government had to admit problems of food security for sections of the population, causing steep increases of food prices. Subsequent favourable rainfall then eased the situation for the rest of the year.

The *agricultural sector* again performed poorly, with a growth rate of just above 2%. The main *drivers of growth* were communications, tourism and other services sectors, while mining activities encountered unforeseen problems and manufacturing industries continued to be hampered by difficulties in obtaining credit and a slowdown of demand due to a general shortage of liquidity throughout the economy. Existing expectations of a faster and more fundamental transformation of the economy, linked with prospects for substantial natural gas production and export of liquefied natural gas, remained somewhat elusive, since full commercial exploitation did not appear realistic before sometime in the 2020s.

Headline *inflation* was again successfully contained at close to the 5% target, at an average rate of 5.3% for the year and a low of 4.0% in December. A prudent monetary policy thus again met its desired target. For a second consecutive year, the *exchange rate* of the shilling to the dollar remained unusually stable throughout the year, reaching TSh 2,230: $ 1) at year's end. This was largely the result of a tight liquidity situation in the domestic banking system and above all of a further strongly improved balance of payments situation. The *structural trade deficit*, which had been significantly lowered in 2016 to $ 2.8 bn, was contained at that level (provisionally estimated $ 2.9 bn), principally as a result of a further reduced import bill of an expected $ 7.9 bn. This fall was mainly due to a decline in the import of capital goods (resulting from reduced investments) and a lower oil bill. Export earnings also declined to about $ 5.0 bn, mainly due to reduced mineral exports. On balance, two-thirds of Tanzania's import needs were thus covered by its own export earnings. The *services account* again improved significantly (by 39%) to a new record surplus of $ 1.9 bn, largely resulting from tourism as the main foreign exchange source. These achievements contributed to another reduction of the *current-account deficit* to about 3%, the lowest level in recent history. Gross *foreign exchange reserves* grew strongly to $ 5.9 bn by the end of December, sufficient to cover 5.4 months of imports of goods and services. Since the debt reductions in the early 2000s, the *external debt* had again been increasing rapidly in recent years, reaching a new high of $ 19.2 bn at year's end (from $ 17.2 bn in 2016). The composition of external debt remained practically unchanged (around 80% owed by the state, 20% by the private sector); 47% of the debt was owed to multilateral agencies and under 10% to bilateral donors, while the remainder was composed of commercial debts and export credits. Several observers warned of the trend towards more borrowing, but a debt sustainability analysis by the IMF concluded that Tanzania remained at low risk of external debt distress. Under somewhat mysterious conditions, the government obtained a $ 500 m syndicated loan from Crédit Suisse in August, but the long-envisaged issue of a eurobond again did not materialise.

IMF missions visited Tanzania in April and December to conduct the sixth and seventh reviews of the programmes under the extended current *Policy Support Instrument* (PSI). Macroeconomic performance was judged to have been satisfactory and most quantitative targets under the PSI were met, though implementation of structural measures and budget implementation (particularly in development spending) were considered lagging. Identifying a mixed economic performance, the IMF viewed the outlook as subject to emerging risks and warned that various indicators, particularly private sector concerns about the authorities' enforcement of rules, suggested a weakening of economic activity.

On 8 June, Finance Minister Philip Mpango submitted the *budget for the fiscal year 2017–18* to parliament. Total expenditure was budgeted at TSh 31,712 bn (about $ 14.2 bn), a seemingly realistic increase of only 7.3% over the 2016–17 budget, whose ambitious goals had proved very difficult to implement. 38% of the total budget was earmarked for development expenditure, while, under previous governments, well over 70 % had always been allocated for recurrent expenditure. The focus was clearly on infrastructure projects and on laying the foundations for industrialisation. The revenue forecast was composed of tax and non-tax revenue (63%), domestic and external non-concessional borrowing (24%) and external financing from development partners (13%). Only 3% was cautiously expected to come in the form of general budget support, since donor countries showed increasing reluctance to provide such generous untied aid. The fiscal deficit was expected to be reduced to 3.8% of GDP.

The *2016–17 budgetary outcome* was marked by the achievement of most domestic revenue targets, but by continued external financial shortfalls. The government strongly emphasised efforts to widen the tax base and curb tax evasion, restrict leakages and wastage of government resources and control public expenditure. Domestic revenue collection thus increased to 15.3% of GDP. The fiscal deficit turned out at 1.7% of GDP, the lowest level in seven years and less than planned. This was primarily the result of serious under-execution of budgeted development expenditure (62% execution rate), a rigorous slashing of recurrent expenditure and a further build-up of government arrears (around 6% of GDP) to contractors, suppliers and public servants. A verification exercise to determine the genuineness of all pending claims took much longer than expected and the unresolved arrears issue remained a serious economic problem throughout the year, since it negatively affected many businesses and sharply reduced liquidity. *Budget execution* during the first half of 2016–17 was again problematic and remained behind set targets: while somewhat lagging tax collection was still expected to catch up, an execution rate of 59% for development expenditures demonstrated clearly the government's inability to achieve its ambitious development goals and left the credibility of the budget exercise in doubt.

The *2nd Five-Year Development Plan 2016/17–2020/21* provided the medium-term framework for the government's goal of transforming Tanzania into a semi-industrialised middle-income country by 2025. Magufuli consistently emphasised the build-up of modern *infrastructure* and faster *industrialisation* as his overarching developmental orientation. Recurring uncertainties about the government's concrete intentions and Magufuli's often erratic directives (regarding both projects and personnel) led, however, to a widely-felt atmosphere of insecurity, particularly with respect to private-sector business activities. A growing negative business sentiment was observed not only by the IMF and the World Bank, but also by all domestic business institutions and spokespersons, although the government repeatedly stressed its unequivocal support for private-sector activities. Magufuli expressed the view that the 1990s privatisation of former parastatal enterprises had been a mistake and declared the intention to repossess the firms (about 200) that had remained dormant in private hands. A new form of *economic resource nationalism* thus clearly gained ground in Magufuli's pronouncements. Some activities seemed strangely reminiscent of the authoritarian state-led economic strategies during Tanzania's socialist past under Julius Nyerere. The anti-corruption and harsh revenue-generation drives, coupled with problems in the banking sector (sharp increase of non-performing loans), contributed significantly to a widely-felt credit and liquidity squeeze and a slow-down of private sector activities. All this culminated in a strange mismatch between continued good macroeconomic indicators and low-key business sentiment. In the Global Competitiveness Index 2017–18, Tanzania nevertheless obtained a slightly higher score, ranking 113th (up from 116th) out of 137 countries; the World Bank's Doing Business Report 2018 showed a score at 137th (down from 132nd).

Unforeseen attention turned on the *mining sector* throughout the year. On 3 March, the government, suspicious of having long been deceived about true values and desiring to force mining companies to introduce a higher level of in-country beneficiation, announced an immediate *ban on the export of all unprocessed minerals*. The main addressee was Acacia Mining, the largest operator (three *gold mines*). Two commissions of enquiry were subsequently tasked to investigate this complex issue and to recommend fundamental changes to mining legislation. In July, three mining laws were passed that drastically changed the relationship between the government and foreign mining companies. The dispute with Acacia escalated when an outrageous tax bill for $ 190 bn was slapped on the company in July. After acrimonious discussions, an agreement was reached in October with Acacia's Canadian parent company Barrick Gold, which included a $ 300 m compensation payment to the government, a 16% government equity stake in Acacia and an equal share in all future profits. In September, *raw diamonds* from the Williamson mine were confiscated, and Magufuli ordered the construction of a wall around the area of artisanal *Tanzanite mines* near Arusha. Magufuli was exuberantly praised in parliament for his strong defence of the national interest against international mining giants, but no nationalisation was planned.

Several major *infrastructure projects* were either launched or approved for future execution. In August, Magufuli and President Museveni of Uganda laid the foundation stone for the construction of a $ 3.6 bn *pipeline* for the export of Ugandan oil via Tanga port. The construction of the first section (Dar es Salaam-Morogoro) of a new *electrified standard-gauge railway*, paid for from Tanzania's own resources, started in April; an agreement for the second section up to Dodoma was subsequently concluded. In December, the government, after a period of uncertainty, finally approved a joint venture between Oman and China for a $ 10 bn project to build a major new port and a special economic zone near Bagamoyo; the government withdrew its own envisaged participation due to non-availability of funds. Nevertheless, important expansion works were taking place at Dar es Salaam's port. A government decision to pursue the long-discussed Stiegler's Gorge mega-project (2,100 MW *hydropower* in Rufiji Basin) met strong resistance from environmentalists, with finalisation being many years away. Two new *natural gas power plants* in Dar es Salaam, built and financed by Japan, greatly relieved the hitherto often precarious electricity availability. Over 50% of Tanzania's installed grid capacity of 1,400 MW now already came from natural gas. After long delays, an agreement was finally concluded between the National Development Corporation and a Chinese company for the exploitation of substantial coal (Mchuchuma) and iron ore (Liganga) deposits in the south-west.

Uganda

Volker Weyel

The aftermath of the 2016 presidential and parliamentary elections having only just died down, Ugandans were already presented with a foreshadowing of the 2021 vote. An apparently personal initiative by an MP to scrap the constitutionally-enshrined age limit for the office of president was hotly debated. The plan led to public protest and violent scenes even in parliamentary chambers, but eventually became law. It provided an opportunity for the incumbent to extend his tenure for the foreseeable future. The already toxic political atmosphere deteriorated, with political opponents, civil society organisations and the media bearing the brunt. Uganda ended its military presence in the CAR, where remnants of a former Ugandan insurgency had taken refuge, but had largely withered away. On the whole, though, the regional environment hardly improved. Burundi's crisis still loomed and Kenya had to come to terms with its botched elections. More South Sudanese fled to Uganda from internal strife in their homeland, and new refugees arrived from the DRC. Uganda still exercised its role as a major regional player and continued to be held in high esteem in African and international fora. The economy experienced a slowdown of growth, but was basically sound. Various steps were taken towards the effective exploitation of the oil and natural gas deposits.

 DOI:10.1163/9789004367630_043

Domestic Politics

The state apparatus, including the security forces, remained under the firm control of President Yoweri Kaguta Museveni, head of state and government since early 1986, with the National Resistance Movement (NRM) continuing to be the main political party. Guesses about who might one day succeed to the 'throne' provided some sort of entertainment. Two opposition parties, the Forum for Democratic Change (FDC) and the Democratic Party (DP), became suspicious that a constitutional change benefiting Museveni was in the offing and started a campaign called 'Togitwatako' ('Don't touch it'). Eventually, an NRM backbench MP tabled a private member's bill aimed at *scrapping the constitutional age limit for presidential candidates* – currently a minimum of 35 and a maximum of 75 at the time of election. This provision would have made the 1944-born Museveni ineligible to run in the next presidential election due in 2021.

The opposition mobilised its supporters to protest against the move and intense debate even took place within the ruling party. Mainly FDC MPs took the protest to parliament, which met in a tense atmosphere on 21 September, its buildings surrounded by army and police forces. Opposition members disturbed the proceedings in an attempt to thwart debate on the subject, and the introduction of the motion was postponed. On 27 September, Speaker Rebecca Kadaga suspended 24 opposition MPs (plus a junior minister, for entering parliament with a gun) for three consecutive sittings, leading to mayhem. Plainclothes police and army personnel on the orders of the inspector-general of police intervened to evict the suspended MPs. The security operatives, looking not only for the suspended MPs but also for a few other oppositionists, assaulted and led away a number of members; some ended up in hospital. Afterwards, the meeting resumed and the bill was presented by Raphael Magyezi. The brawl in parliament produced violent scenes that went viral internationally via news and social media (and led to a ban of live TV broadcasts covering the subject). The homes of three opposition MPs were attacked with grenades hurled by "unknown assailants".

The bill had its first reading on 3 October in the absence of the opposition, which boycotted the meeting. On 5 October, parliament went into recess and MPs were later given UGX (shilling) 29 m each, corresponding to about $ 8,000, ostensibly to enable them to hold consultations in their constituencies. This 'facilitation' was returned by some MPs, including opposition leader Winifred Kiiza. The mood prevailing in a number of places was such that some proponents of the change feared for their personal safety and called off public meetings. As usual, protests launched by the opposition were declared to be in contravention of the Public Order Management Act of 2013 and thus illegal. Ruthless use of force was applied by the police, which led to the death of a youngster on 18 October in the Western town of Rukungiri.

The 10th Parliament hit rock bottom when the bill was modified in order to compensate the MPs for their actual loss of credibility as well as for possible loss of seats in the next election. Ultimately the bill as it was put to the vote provided for the *abolition of the age limit clause* (removing both the 75-year maximum and 35-year minimum age limits for candidates) for the president and for local council chairpersons, while at the same time *re-introducing the presidential term limit*, which had been eliminated in 2005. No president would now be able to serve for more than two terms, with the provision to be applied from the 2021 elections onwards. At the same time, the constitutional change extended the legislative period from five to seven years, to be applicable with immediate effect to the current parliament and local councils. This provision was apparently added after several MPs made their approval of the age limit proposal contingent on the extension of their own tenure by two years. On this basis, 317 of the 434 MPs voted for the bill, 97 voted against (including a number of independent and NRM MPs) and two abstained. Thus the two-thirds majority required was obtained, amounting in fact to almost three-quarters. The bill passed on 20 December and was signed into law by the president exactly one week later. Museveni rubbished all talk of his intention to become 'life president', but was now legally given the opportunity to offer himself as candidate for two more five-year terms, beginning in 2021 – or even for seven-year terms, as he preferred (though such plans would be subject to a referendum).

Despite Kadaga's order to the contrary, security operatives had again been present when parliament took its decisive vote. It also emerged that the Christian chapels below the assembly hall were used as sort of stand-by room for them, the desecration drawing a harsh reaction by the Catholic archbishop of Kampala.

Another envisaged constitutional amendment also became the subject of heated debate in parliament and of public distrust. The intention was to ease the compulsory acquisition of private *land* for development purposes such as road construction. The government tabled the bill in parliament on 13 July, but it faced stiff opposition from various quarters and made no headway during the year.

At the beginning of the year, parliament still took its watchdog role seriously. Controversy arose over the August 2016 *payment of bonuses*, authorised by the president and totalling UGX 6 bn (about $ 1.8 m at the time), to 42 government officials, including the attorney-general, his deputy and the permanent secretary in the Ministry of Finance, in appreciation for their role in the successful conclusion of a protracted international arbitration case with Heritage Oil over capital gains taxes. On 22 June, parliament adopted a report by its Committee on Commissions, Statutory Authorities and State Enterprises recommending that the 42 beneficiaries of this "presidential golden handshake" refund the money, but they did not do so.

The *Anti-Terrorism (Amendment) Act, 2017*, assented to by the president on 13 May after being passed by parliament on 5 April, further amended the definition of terrorism and adjusted provisions on financing of terrorism. The *National*

Biotechnology and Biosafety Bill, 2012 was passed on 28 June and again, after the president refused to sign it, on 4 October. On 21 December, it once more reverted to parliament for reconsideration, the president citing concern over the possible effects of genetically modified organisms on indigenous crops and livestock. On 18 July, parliament granted leave to MP Bernard Atiku to prepare a private member's bill on the prevention and prohibition of *human sacrifice*. Atiku pointed out that ritual killings and human sacrifice practices were on the rise, with mainly children being the victims: "Since 2009 about 219 cases of ritual murders have been reported from different parts of the country."

Widespread dissatisfaction among youth and townspeople led to the advent of a newcomer on the political scene. In a by-election for a constituency near Kampala on 29 June, called because the court found irregularities in the 2016 ballot, the popular singer Robert *Kyagulanyi* Ssentamu, better known by his stage name Bobi Wine, stood as an independent and took 77.7% of the vote, beating NRM, FDC and other candidates. He soon became a competent and outspoken critic of government.

The main opposition party, the *FDC, elected a new president* at a delegates' conference in Kampala on 24 November. The incumbent, General Mugisha Muntu (rtd), lost to Patrick Oboi Amuriat by 41.1% to 57.6% of the vote. Underlying was disagreement about strategies, four-times presidential contender and former party president Kizza Besigye favouring furious 'defiance' action in contrast to Muntu's moderate approach. Amuriat, a former MP from Teso, toed Besigye's line. The faction of the Uganda People's Congress (UPC) headed by James Akena, son of Milton Obote, continued its struggle for control of Kampala's Uganda House, owned by the Milton Obote Foundation. Akena was sacked from the Foundation's board in October; subsequently, a general meeting of the Foundation was prevented by a court injunction sought by Akena.

The Universal Periodic Review on *human rights* carried out by the UN Human Rights Council in November 2016 in Geneva was concluded on 16 March. The majority of the 226 recommendations made by the Council members were accepted, frequently being uncontroversial or rather general in nature, such as to intensify "efforts to combat all forms of violence against women and girls". Among the suggestions rejected by Uganda was the amendment of the "Public Order Management Act, 2013, and the Non-Governmental Organizations Act, 2016, to ensure free assembly and association in line with international human rights standards" or the ratification of the International Convention for the Protection of All Persons from Enforced Disappearance. The next review was to take place in November 2021.

Uganda had been among the first countries to embrace the *APRM process* created in 2003. From 2004, it underwent the various stages of this evaluation, and the first peer review was concluded in 2008. In May, it presented its second Country Self-Assessment Report and at the end of October a group of about 20 experts came for two weeks and paid visits to all regions.

In a follow-up to the electoral campaign for the 2016 polls, there were complaints about broken promises. In view of the fact that many girls do not attend school during their menstrual period, the president had promised them *free sanitary pads*, but the First Lady and Education Minister Janet Museveni indicated in February that there was no money for the pads in her ministry's budget. This statement, considered widely as uncaring and arrogant, backfired in a most embarrassing way. *Stella Nyanzi*, a controversial academic who in 2016 had publicly undressed in a row over her non-fulfilment of teaching duties at the renowned Makerere Institute of Social Research, started a campaign to collect money to buy pads for school girls. This was soon supported by the opposition and many civil society activists, and eventually also by parliamentarians who, in "a Corporate Social Responsibility (CSR) drive" dubbed 'Keep a Girl in School', collected money for reusable sanitary towels, which were distributed to some primary schools in the North. Nyanzi's cyber-harassment of Janet Museveni and badmouthing the president as "a pair of buttocks" on social media earned her a charge to answer and a month in prison before she was released on bail.

Incidences of *corruption* included State Minister for Labour Herbert Kabafunzaki being trapped on 7 April soliciting a UGX 5 m ($ 1,400) advance for a UGX 10 m bribe from the tycoon who owned the new Pearl of Africa hotel to quash a case of alleged sexual harassment. The most conspicuous reference to a high-ranking Ugandan involved in corruption, however, was made abroad: in November, the US Department of Justice charged a Chinese and a Senegalese national under the Foreign Corrupt Practices Act for allegedly having paid a $ 500,000 kickback to Foreign Minister Sam Kutesa for procuring "business advantages" for a Chinese firm in the oil business.

The 2016 tragedy in the *Mountains of the Moon*, the Rwenzori range (see *Africa Yearbook 13*), did not find a comprehensive political or legal appraisal. Imprisoned Rwenzururu king Wesley Mumbere in February was released on bail, but not allowed to visit his home region.

NGOs and the media faced rough times, often amounting to more than just low-level harassment. The premises of ActionAid were searched by the police in September and its accounts were blocked for almost a quarter of a year. A number of break-ins occurred in offices of other NGOs, and no culprits were apprehended. Directors and editors of the tabloid 'Red Pepper' were arrested on 21 November and the paper had to close. The charge referred to treason and offensive communication; an article published the previous day had insinuated that Museveni was "plotting to overthrow Kagame", the Rwandan president. The electronic media experienced a number of interventions by the Uganda Communications Commission (UCC). Kanungu Broadcasting Services had to cease operations because of a political programme deemed to promote insecurity. All radio and TV stations were directed by UCC to transmit live the president's New Year message on 31 December.

The *Uganda Police Force*, now largely seen as an instrument to quell civic unrest but as less capable of dealing with everyday issues of citizens' safety, including the threat posed by criminal gangs and a spate of murders of women in the metropolitan region, was beset by internal strains. Senior police officer Andrew Kaweesi, together with his driver and his bodyguard, was murdered by unknown assailants on 17 March, giving rise to various theories, including that it was an inside job. The force also suffered from tensions with the various intelligence agencies, the antagonism between Inspector-General Kale Kayihura (in place since late 2005 and re-appointed for three years in May) and Security Minister Henry Tumukunde being common knowledge. Close confidants of Kayihura were paraded before an army court martial on 27 October to answer charges of having (four years earlier) illegally returned Rwandan refugees to their home country. The presence of auxiliary forces such as the 'crime preventers', the use of the 'Boda Boda 2010' goons (an unofficial motorcycle-taxi drivers' pro-government militia who even beat schoolchildren mistakenly suspected of demonstrating against the age-limit scheme) and the alleged links of some police officers to organised crime, led to Kayihura's credibility being questioned. There was also an outcry about cases of torture in police custody, specifically in the special operations centre at Nalufenya, near Jinja. In May, the president had to point out publicly that "the use of torture is unnecessary and wrong".

In January, a major reshuffle in the higher ranks of the *Uganda People's Defence Forces* (UPDF) was effected by their commander-in-chief, phasing out more members of the bush war old guard in favour of younger officers. Chief of Defence Forces General Edward Katumba Wamala was appointed minister of state for works; his army position went to freshly-promoted General David Muhoozi, previously commander of the land forces, and that post was given to Peter Elwelu, a division commander (who had led the ill-fated operation in the Rwenzori range in 2016) promoted from brigadier to major-general. Another notable decision by the president was to relieve his son, Major-General Muhoozi Kainerugaba, of the headship of the UPDF's Special Forces Command (SFC) and make him senior presidential advisor for special operations. Proscovia Nalweyiso, who had joined the guerrillas in 1982, was promoted from brigadier to major-general, the first woman to hold that rank in East Africa.

Military permeation of the state continued. When medics in government hospitals went on strike, Museveni deployed military doctors to replace them. The UPDF also were employed to control fishing on Lake Victoria, i.e. to prevent immature fish being caught, a practice that had led to depletion of fish stocks. Military intelligence in some cases effectively took over police functions, and SFC soldiers were among the security operatives who were deployed in parliament during the age limit debate.

The national *football* team, the Uganda Cranes, having qualified to take part in the Africa Cup of Nations for the first time since 1978, were defeated by Egypt

(0:1) in their second group match on 21 January and were thus prematurely forced out of the tournament. Despite a 1:0 win over Egypt in Uganda's Mandela National Stadium on 31 August (losing the return on 5 September in Alexandria 0:1), they missed qualification for the 2018 FIFA World Cup.

2017 saw the deaths of several prominent Ugandans: Jack *Maumbe Mukhwana*, a founding member of NRM and its antecedents, died on 27 February; the 1939-born left-winger hailed from Bugisu. Jehoash *Mayanja Nkangi*, a former prime minister of Buganda kingdom and in 1980 founder of the Conservative Party, born in 1931, died on 6 March; he had held various ministerial portfolios in Museveni's government, including finance. The head of the three-man Presidential Commission of the 1980 interregnum, Joel Hunter *Wacha-Olwol*, hailing from Lango and born in 1923, passed away on 2 May. Former DP national chairman Boniface Muyogoma *Byanyima*, a descendant of the kings of Buhweju (territory annexed to Ankole by the colonial power in 1901) born in 1920, died on 16 May. He was the father of Winnie Byanyima, Oxfam International's executive director, and the father-in-law of Kizza Besigye and had fostered the young Museveni. The former DP president John *Ssebaana Kizito*, born in 1934 and hailing from Buganda, died on 3 July. He had served as a minister under Museveni, stood against him as a presidential candidate in 2006 and was twice elected mayor of Kampala. A founding member and later national chairman of UPC, the minister of state for local government under 'Obote II', Edward *Ruran-garanga*, born in 1932 in Ankole, died on 31 July.

Foreign Affairs

Uganda's stand in international fora followed in principle the position jointly agreed in the caucuses of African states and developing countries, although it became apparent that ultimately the *perceived national interest* was decisive. So, in the 21 December UN General Assembly vote on resolution ES-10/19 dealing with the Jerusalem issue, Uganda abstained, thus avoiding entry into the bad books of the US Trump administration (which in a 9 October National Day message by Secretary of State Rex Tillerson had praised Uganda as "a key partner with shared interests in promoting regional security and economic growth"). Notable flexibility had earlier been demonstrated by Speaker Kadaga. In Tehran, she attended the 22–23 February 6th 'International Conference in Support of the Palestinian Intifada'. She also paid a visit to Iran's President Hassan Rouhani with a view to strengthening bilateral cooperation in the areas of trade and investment. In Jerusalem, speaking at a seminar for heads of African parliaments taking place from 5–7 December in the Knesset, Kadaga referred to the 1976 Israeli raid on Entebbe airport to rescue the passengers of a hijacked plane. She described this as a binding factor for the two countries and called for Israeli investments in agriculture, manufacturing and the mining sector.

Another kind of collaboration between Israel and Uganda (plus Rwanda), according to media reports, concerned the deportation of African migrants (mainly originating from Eritrea or Sudan) from Israel to the two East African countries, with a price tag for every case. Uganda and Rwanda denied the existence of such deals.

Internationally, Uganda continued to play a *respected role*. With effect from January, the chairman of the Uganda Human Rights Commission, Med S.K. Kaggwa, started his one-year term as chairman of the Jeddah-based Independent Permanent Human Rights Commission of the OIC (of which Uganda had been a member since Idi Amin's days). Executive Director of Oxfam International Winnie Byanyima was chosen to be a member of the independent Global Commission on the Future of Work launched by the ILO on 21 August. In early December, she was appointed for a second five-year term to head Oxfam International, having initiated its restructuring, including the relocation of its headquarters to Nairobi. In New York on 5 December, the Assembly of States Parties of the ICC elected Solomy Balungi Bossa, a former judge at the International Criminal Tribunal for Rwanda, as judge on the ICC, a body which in 2016 had been branded by her country's president as "a bunch of useless people". Museveni nevertheless received ICC president Silvia Fernández de Gurmendi on 1 March, as well as, once again, ICC-indicted Sudanese leader Omar al-Bashir on 13 November for a two-day visit. Calls to arrest him were ignored; a High Court decision on 15 November, referring to al-Bashir's 2016 visit, stated that Uganda was still awaiting UNSC sanctions for failing to arrest him, so it would be "unnecessary to issue an immediate arrest warrant".

Other *prominent visitors* to Uganda included UN Secretary-General António Guterres and UNHCR Filippo Grandi in June, the UK's Foreign Minister Boris Johnson in March and Germany's Foreign Minister Sigmar Gabriel in August, and Archbishop of Canterbury Justin Welby, also in August. The Aga Khan, a major economic and humanitarian player in East Africa as well as being a spiritual leader, was special guest at the celebration of the 55th anniversary of Independence on 9 October, held in Bushenyi.

Some visits were connected to the major crisis that brought Uganda into the international limelight throughout the year. South Sudanese escaping the chaos at home continued to arrive, making Uganda the leading host of refugees in Africa and one of the five top receiving countries worldwide. At year's end, according to the Office of the Prime Minister, the number of *refugees and asylum seekers* stood at 1,395,146, close to three-quarters of them from South Sudan (1,037,898), 242,406 from the DRC, 40,634 from Burundi, 37,193 from Somalia, 15,260 from Rwanda and 21,755 from elsewhere. Most of the South Sudanese were put up in West-Nile subregion, the largest settlements being at Bidibidi and Imvepi. Uganda's hospitality was applauded internationally, but the pressure on host communities increased and the financial and logistical strains became apparent, with international assistance lagging behind. Uganda was one of the pilot countries of the Comprehensive Refugee Response Framework crafted by the UNHCR, aimed at the inclusion of refugees in the local communities right from the start. A Solidarity Summit, co-hosted by Guterres and Museveni, was held on 22–23 June in Kampala. Donor pledges announced during the meeting amounted to $ 358 m, far below the $ 2 bn hoped for.

The first *Nile Basin* Heads of State summit was held in Entebbe on 22 June but, apart from Museveni as the host, Egyptian President Abdel Fattah el-Sisi and Ethiopian Prime Minister Hailemariam Desalegn, it was only attended by less prominent representatives. They failed to achieve progress in the controversy over the distribution of the river's water.

Oil-rich *Equatorial Guinea* caught the interest of the Ugandan president. It became known that UPDF instructors had been sent to train its national army in late 2016 and President Teodoro Obiang Nguema Mbasogo came for a state visit in April, with Museveni making a return visit in August.

The one-year-chairmanship of the *EAC* was once more handed to Museveni, in May. The grave conflicts in two member states, South Sudan and Burundi, persisted. Kenya saw a questionable election, but this time it had no serious repercussions on landlocked Uganda. Relations with Tanzania were cooperative, and those with Rwanda plagued by strong subliminal mistrust, with the Kigali government expecting a tougher stand against opponents who lived in Uganda.

The leitmotif of relations with the *DRC* was cooperation in the field of security. Former M-23 fighters cantoned in Bihanga military camp had not yet been repatriated, but many left of their own accord. A number had allegedly been recruited to quell opposition to President Joseph Kabila in December 2016. The insecurity in the DRC also found expression in a 7 December attack on MONUSCO troops that killed 15 Tanzanian peacekeepers and five Congolese soldiers. It was attributed to the Allied Democratic Forces (ADF), a former Ugandan Islamist rebel group that had established itself among the violent operatives who thrived in eastern DRC. Though the role of ADF was disputed, on 22 December the UPDF started attacks on ADF camps, using its long-range artillery and air-force and acting with DRC consent. It claimed that more than 100 rebels were killed. The Kinshasa and Kampala governments had a joint interest in smooth oil exploration activities, largely conducted by the French company Total in the border area. In March, the military training programme in mountain warfare conducted by French instructors in the Rwenzori range had been extended. At the close of the year, several thousand refugees from the DRC's Ituri province entered Uganda, many crossing Lake Albert.

UPDF operations as part of the AU Regional Task Force (AU-RTF) against the remnants of the *Lord's Resistance Army* (LRA) in the CAR ceased. In May, US Army Special Forces ended their involvement, and Uganda withdrew its 2,500 troops in

August. South Sudan also wound up its AU-RTF participation. While the LRA had become irrelevant to Uganda, it continued to be a threat to civilians in the CAR and the DRC.

With more than 6,000 soldiers, the UPDF continued to be the biggest troop-contributor to the 2007-incepted AU Mission in Somalia (*AMISOM*). In December, it embarked on a gradual reduction of its troop strength as foreseen by the UNSC in its 30 August Resolution 2372, extending AMISOM's mandate until 31 May 2018. UPDF successes in fighting al-Shabaab were accompanied by losses; on 30 July, for example, 12 soldiers were killed by the militia. The Somalia assignment allowed the UPDF not only to achieve combat experience but also to be supplied with large quantities of weaponry, largely from the US. Visiting generals from the US National Defense University were received by President Museveni on 18 February at State House, Entebbe. The US Africa Command (*AFRICOM*) provided joint exercises and training facilities, including a course for officers at the US Army Joint Readiness Training Center in Fort Polk, Louisiana, in March.

Socioeconomic Developments

Uganda was commended "for its growth and poverty reduction achievements over the past three decades" by *IMF* Managing Director Christine Lagarde, on 28 January, concluding a visit to the country. Challenges were also noted by the IMF on 7 July, when its Executive Board completed the eighth review of its Policy Support Instrument (PSI), which was devoted to advice and monitoring. The board stated "that growth has recently moderated" and welcomed the government's "focus on promoting growth through planned infrastructure and oil sector investments", but also recalled the need "to foster inclusive and stronger growth". While the government expressed interest in a successor PSI, another non-financing tool approved on 14 July by the board found application in Uganda: the Policy Coordination Instrument (PCI) enabling countries "to signal commitment to reforms and catalyze financing from other sources". An IMF team visiting from 23 October to 3 November initiated discussions for a three-year macroeconomic programme under the PCI.

Real *GDP growth* in the financial year 2016/17 (which ran from July 2016 to June 2017) missed the 5.5% target; it reached 4%, down from 4.8% in the period before. Per capita income, according to Finance Minister Matia Kasaija, grew "at only 2% annually compared with population growth of 3% per annum". For 2017/18, a 5% GDP growth was projected.

Inflation remained within the 5% target range. The calendar year's average headline inflation (including food crops, fuel and electricity) stood at 5.6%, slightly higher than the rates recorded for 2016 (5.5%) and 2015 (5.4%). Core inflation eased to 4.4% from 5.9% in 2016. The *exchange rate* of the national currency against the dollar saw some ups and downs during the year, but it closed at virtually the same amount at year's end as end-2016 (UGX 3,635.1: $ 1 compared with UGX 3,610.5: $ 1). The *central bank rate* (i.e., the lending rate to banks) which stood at 12% at end-2016, was lowered in stages, reaching 9.5% in October. International *reserves* were able to cover about five-and-half months of imports.

The *2017/18 budget* was read by Minister Kasaija on 8 June; it bore the heading 'Industrialization for Job Creation and Shared Prosperity'. Parliament had approved it on 31 May. Total foreseen expenditure amounted to UGX 29,008 bn, corresponding to $ 8.1 bn. The increase from the 2016/17 appropriation of UGX 26.3 trn to UGX 29 trn was 10%, but in dollar terms only meant a minor change (from $ 7.9 bn to $ 8.1 bn). Domestic sources were to finance 75.5% of the budget, the external financing for projects consisting mainly of loans. Leaving aside interest payments, expenditure was directed in the first place to infrastructure (works and transport, UGX 4.6 trn), followed by education (UGX 2.5 trn), energy (UGX 2.4 trn) and health (UGX 1.8 trn). Security spending (including the external intelligence service) came next, the amount on the record (UGX 1.5 trn, about $ 410 m) being slightly less than in the 2016/17 allocation. Budget implementation proved challenging. As pointed out by the IMF team in early November, parliament "did not approve some of the government's revenue enhancing measures, while additional expenditure pressures have given rise to a supplementary budget". This led to a widening of the overall fiscal deficit and an increase of financing needs.

In May, the *World Bank* resumed funding, which had been stopped in 2016 over the sexual exploitation of local women by road construction workers, as well as over poor project performance. Minister Kasaija acknowledged the importance of giving "social and environmental issues due attention".

Valorisation of the *oil and natural gas deposits* proceeded, albeit slowly. On 9 January, British-Irish Tullow Oil announced its intention to transfer its Uganda interests to French Total for $ 900 m. China's CNOOC then exercised its pre-emption rights, acquiring 50% of these interests. After government approval, completion of this farm-down was expected by mid-2018. Then the French and the Chinese companies would each have a 44.1% stake in the oil reserves so far discovered. The decision as to who would build the oil refinery in Hoima district was still pending. The foundation stone for the crude oil pipeline from Hoima to Tanga was laid in the Tanzanian port by President Magufuli of Tanzania and President Museveni on 5 August, with construction expected to last three years and to cost $ 3.6 bn. The 1,445-km underground pipeline would be the longest electrically-heated pipeline worldwide.

In view of Uganda's own peripheral *gold-extraction*, it was undocumented flows, largely from the DRC, that still appeared to feed the country's gold exports. Local production was carried out by artisanal miners; about 20,000 of them were evicted from their open-pits in Mubende district by army and police in August to stop unregulated mining. The African Gold Refinery, set up in Entebbe by Belgian and Ugandan investors to refine gold to 99.9% purity, was officially opened by the president on 20 February.

The most prominent *strikes* during the year were those by medical doctors in public hospitals (over remuneration and the dearth of essential supplies) and officers in the justice system. Traders in Kampala in April protested against the influx of Chinese competitors.

While local leaders, including the king of Bunyoro, called on people to 'produce many children', the Uganda Bureau of Statistics sent a different message. In its analytical report on the *2014 census* presented in December, it stated: "Intensification of family planning and reproductive health programmes is necessary."

Corruption, as described by Minister Kasaija, not only "held back projects and programmes in some sectors" but also "hampered service delivery". The level of corruption encountered in the country's public sector again placed Uganda 151st out of the 180 states and territories covered by TI's 2017 Corruption Perceptions Index. It once more lagged significantly behind Rwanda (at 48th) and again did worse than Tanzania (103rd) and Kenya (143rd), but outshone Burundi (157th) and South Sudan (179th).

PART 6

Southern Africa

Henning Melber

Two of Africa's longest-serving presidents announced their retirement within three months of each other: Eduardo dos Santos, who had ruled Angola since 1979, and Robert Mugabe, who had been in power in Zimbabwe since 1980. The extent to which their demise from power would create a new dynamic in both domestic and regional politics remained to be seen. In general, governance and socio-economic trends showed little to no improvement in most countries. The peace dividend attributed to the sub-region for quite some time seemed not to have shown the expected improvements for ordinary people.

Elections, Democracy and Human Rights

After 38 years in power, president Eduardo dos Santos stepped aside in *Angola* for health reasons to make room for a younger man, while retaining the presidency of the governing 'Movimento Popular de Libertação de Angola' (MPLA). After elections on 23 August, in which the MPLA maintained a clear majority with 61% of the votes and 150 out of 220 seats in the National Assembly, João Lourenço (born 1954), became the new head of state on 26 September. Considered a person of integrity, he was not known for indulging in the obscene luxury of the 'oiligarchy'. He seemed determined to build new trust in the MPLA government and, during the remainder of the year, dismissed more than 250 higher-ranking officials in government and the public service, including the military. Under dos Santos, massive repression could no longer stop a rising tide of popular protest. It became increasingly clear that change was urgently needed. Dos Santos, however, remained in charge of the party, and it remained to be seen how far Lourenço could indeed be the new broom to sweep clean some of the dust in the long run.

The scenario was similar in neighbouring *Zimbabwe*, when the peaceful transfer of power in Angola was followed rather unexpectedly in mid-November by a gentle military coup. Since Independence in 1980, the former jewel of Africa had been under the increasingly authoritarian rule of Robert Mugabe, who at 93 had no thoughts of retirement. Shortly before the intervention of the military, the Zimbabwe African National Union-Patriotic Front (ZANU-PF) nominated him as candidate for the upcoming presidential election. But he pushed his luck when he tried to install his wife, Grace, as his successor and began forcing her competitors out of the way. On 6 November, he dismissed his long-time confidant Vice President Emmerson Mnangagwa, who had been his loyal deputy for decades and was widely considered

 | DOI:10.1163/9789004367630_044

the 'crown prince'. This turned out to be the mistake that cost Mugabe the presidency. Under the command of Mnangagwa's close ally, General Constantino Chiwenga, the Defence Forces intervened on 15 November and put the president and his wife under house arrest. After a few days of negotiations and increased pressure from his own party to oust him by means of a vote of no-confidence and impeachment in parliament, Mugabe was finally forced to step down and announced his resignation on 21 November. The military intervention was declared a "corrective measure" but not a putsch, and both SADC and the AU were at pains to work out how to deal with the removal from office of an elected president. In the end, a quick return to pseudo-civilian government allowed the regional and continental African bodies to ignore their own rules and remain passive. On 24 November, Mnangagwa (dubbed 'the crocodile'), who had returned from his short stay abroad two days before, was sworn in as the country's new head of state. Some celebrated him as a saviour in the first moments of euphoria following the long-awaited removal of Mugabe, but evidence was growing that Mnangagwa did not offer an alternative to the authoritarian and repressive character of Zimbabwe's political system. The cabinet he appointed on 30 November included several high-level military officers who had initiated the coup, and the army seemed to remain more than ever in control of politics and the state.

General elections took place for the third time in five years on 3 June in *Lesotho*, after the governing coalition under Prime Minister Phakalitha Mosisili collapsed following a lost vote of confidence in February. Despite fears of a coup, the elections were conducted peacefully and an opposition alliance led by Tom Thabane was voted into power. But the assassination of the commander of the army, Khoantle Motsomotso, on 5 September was a warning sign and a reminder that the country's defence force would remain a powerful if not decisive factor in the political sphere and in ultimate charge of state affairs, keeping political stability a remote goal.

While not on the brink of collapse, the policy situation was unusually rough in *South Africa* with regard to the battle for the leadership of the governing African National Congress (ANC). Two representatives of different factions were fighting to succeed the embattled President Jacob Zuma as the head of the party at the 54th Elective Conference on 16–20 December: Zuma's deputy, former minister of foreign affairs Cyril Ramaphosa, and Zuma's ex-wife and former minister of home affairs, Nkosazana Dlamini-Zuma, who had returned to domestic politics from her position as chairperson of the AU Commission in Addis Ababa (Ethiopia). The latter was widely considered Zuma's insurance policy to avoid prosecution for abuses of office. Ramaphosa, on the other hand, who had been a trade union leader before making a fortune in the private sector and especially the mining industry, was seen by many, particularly outside the ANC, as the person who could put an end to Zuma's intrigues, manipulations and mismanagement, which had escalated to corruption and so-called state capture on an unprecedented scale. After tense campaigning and similar fierce battles at the conference, Ramaphosa won the inner-party election by only a narrow margin. The result showed that Zuma and his cronies still wielded considerable influence: half of the six top ANC leadership positions fell into the hands of Zuma loyalists and indicated that Ramaphosa would have to plan carefully in order not to rock the boat and risk party unity.

Politics in *Zambia* were tense too. Though a comparatively young generation of political leaders was in power, all was not well. The political system seemed fragile, with fast changing governments, and the authoritarian leanings of President Edward Lungu of the Patriotic Front caused growing turmoil. The fact that his rival, Hakainde Hichilema of the United Party for National Development, was cut from the same cloth was further stoking the potential for violence. In their embittered battles, Lungu accused Hichilema and some of his close followers of treason for not making way for a presidential motorcade in April. While Hichilema was detained under arrest, South Africa's leader of the official opposition Democratic Alliance was refused entry to the country in May to attend Hichilema's court hearings. The accused were finally acquitted in August.

Despite being firmly governed by the former liberation movement, the South West African People's Organisation (SWAPO), *Namibia* faced some domestic policy problems too ahead of the party's congress in November, which was overshadowed by bitter factional rivalry. The campaigning of three different factions for the party's leadership positions (of which two formed an alliance against the faction under the acting president and head of state) ended in hitherto unequalled amounts of dirty laundry being washed in public, including accusations of instigating tribalism. In the end, President Geingob's 'Team Hage' emerged largely unscathed and secured an unexpectedly clear mandate from the more than 600 delegates. Geingob and his entourage were elected to all the party leadership positions and the central committee and politburo did not include any dissenting voices worthy of note. As a result, the dominant party faction ended the year in firm control of all party-political offices.

In *Mozambique*, President Filipe Nyusi used his authority to appoint higher-ranking office bearers, gradually strengthening his influence and reducing that of his predecessor Armando Gubueza. While rumours of a coup d'état were rampant in *Madagascar*, President Hery Martial Rajaonarimampianina survived a chronic crisis that was marked by continued distrust, institutional incapacity and political stalemate. *Mauritius* faced a transfer of political power in the office of the prime minister from the father Sir Anerood Jugnauth to his son Pravind Jugnauth on 23 January. Although challenged in terms of its constitutionality, the country maintained its lead position for the continent in terms of good governance.

Little of note took place in terms of domestic policy in *Malawi*, despite the usual criticism of lack of good governance and the degree of corruption under the presidency of Peter Mutharika and the Democratic Progressive Party. Similarly, despite continued protests by civil rights groups and trade unions, King Mswati III remained in firm control of *Swaziland*. In almost usual contrast, political stability was maintained largely undisturbed, despite increasing signs of contestation over government, in *Botswana* during the last full year in office of President Ian Khama, who started to prepare for the hand-over to his successor.

The *Bertelsmann Foundation Transformation Index* (BTI 2018), based on aggregated assessments for each country between 2007 and 2017, painted an almost gloomy picture on governance indices and sub-titled the regional overview as "a lost decade". While top ranking Mauritius and Botswana continue to receive good marks for their democracy status (8.50 and 8.20, respectively), they recorded a decline in several of the four criteria (elections, assembly rights, freedom of expression and civil rights), as did the next ranked South Africa and Namibia with aggregate scores of 7.60 and 7.50, respectively. They were followed by Malawi (6.45), Zambia (6.00), Lesotho (5.60), Madagascar (5.35), Mozambique (4.48), Angola (4.20) and Zimbabwe (3.83). Only in Botswana was transformation management classified as 'very good', while Mauritius, South Africa and Malawi were classed as 'good' in governance. But, as the report noted: "despite all positive aspects, it is symptomatic of the entire region that even these well governed countries show significant shortcomings with regard to policy coordination, anti-corruption policy and the efficient use of resources".

In contrast and from a slightly different perspective, the Mo Ibrahim Foundation's *Ibrahim Index of African Governance* (IIAG) 2017, published in December, presented trends for 2006 to 2016 differently, albeit with similar negative overall results for the sub-region. In terms of general tendencies, only Namibia (ranked overall for 2016 as 5th out of 54 countries on the continent) and Zimbabwe (40th) recorded "increased improvements". Swaziland (34th) was classed as having "slowing improvements". Mauritius (1st), Lesotho (15th), Zambia (16th), Malawi (18th) and Angola (45th) were judged to show "warning signs"; South Africa (6th) and Madagascar (32nd) were "bouncing back", but Botswana (3rd) and Mozambique (23rd) recorded "increasing deterioration". Interestingly, while many of the countries scored rather well over the ten-year period, their record for the five-years 2012–16 showed "warning signs" (Mauritius, Lesotho, Zambia, Malawi and Angola).

Based on 2017 data, Freedom House's *Freedom in the World* report (2018) highlighted civil and political rights in the world and in some cases its findings deviated remarkably from those of the BTI and IIAG. Classified as 'most free' in the sub-region (with an aggregate score out of 100) were Mauritius (89), South Africa (78), Namibia (77) and Botswana (72). Lesotho (64), Malawi (63), Madagascar (56), Zambia (53) and Mozambique (52) qualified as 'partly free'. Trailing behind as 'not free' were Zimbabwe (30), Angola (26) and Swaziland (16). Notably, Zimbabwe was downgraded from 'partly free' to 'not free' for the year "due to the process by which elected president Robert Mugabe was compelled to resign in November under pressure from the military".

BTI, IIAG and Freedom House used different methodological approaches and criteria, producing at times considerably different results for the ranking of individual countries. While their classifications should be viewed with caution, they suggested that the tendency towards improvements in democracy and governance indices had in general slowed down. The states in the sub-region – while still comparing favourably overall with other parts of the continent – failed by and large to make good use of the peace dividend most of them had enjoyed for quite some time.

In the annual *World Press Freedom Index* presented by Reporters Without Borders for 2018 with an assessment of the situation in 180 countries for 2017, Namibia, after several consecutive years of decline, finally lost to Ghana the distinction of having the best score for African countries, while most other states – with the exception of Mozambique – recorded modest improvements or kept the same place in the rankings. The survey ranked the states in the sub-region as follows: Namibia (26th/-2), South Africa (28th/+3), Botswana (48th/0), Madagascar (54th/+3), Mauritius (56th/0), Malawi (64th/+6), Lesotho (68th/0), Mozambique (99th/-6), Zambia (113th/+1), Angola (121st/+4), Zimbabwe (126th/+2) and Swaziland (152nd/0).

Socioeconomic Developments

Generally, the sub-region's economies continued battling with the consequences of previous periods of serious drought, which impacted on a variety of sectors beyond agriculture mainly, but not only, in South Africa and Namibia, where there was slow, if any, recovery. By mid-year, due to an overall recovery in agricultural production, food security had improved for large parts of the population in most countries but remained generally tense and precarious. The SADC Secretariat published in August reports from the annual dissemination forum in Johannesburg (10–14 July) on the Regional Vulnerability Assessment and Analysis. It recorded a 28.2% increase in *cereal production* to 43.3 m tonnes for the 2017/18 marketing year, with harvest increases in Lesotho (ninefold), Zimbabwe (quadruple), Swaziland (triple) and South Africa (double) as top performers. *Food insecurity* had as a consequence declined most in Zambia (by 92%), Malawi (87%), Mozambique (84%), Botswana (79%), Swaziland (75%) and Zimbabwe (74%), while it had increased by 9% in Namibia.

During the year, the *water shortage* in Cape Town as a prominent international holiday destination made headlines, and not only in South Africa. The dire situation culminated in water restrictions, which, as usual, impacted the most vulnerable population groups more than others. At the same time, it directed attention to one spectacular case, while the more general challenges of coping with a resource in decline in many parts of South Africa and the wider region remained largely ignored.

The decline in commodity prices due to negative trends on the world market continued to affect several of the natural resource-based economies. The AfDB estimated in its *regional economic outlook* an average economic growth rate for the year of a modest 1.6%, which made Southern Africa the worst performing regional bloc on the continent. The average regional inflation rate was calculated at 9.4%, a small decline from 10.5% in 2016. Sluggish growth rates, high unemployment and tight fiscal constraints remained a challenge for most economies. The fiscal deficit was estimated as having increased to an average of 5% for the sub-region, contrasting negatively with the 3% norm prescribed in the convergence criteria. The low economic growth rate in South Africa negatively affected neighbouring economies, as did the continued economic stagnation in Angola, in particular as regards the Namibian economy. The international financial rating agencies responded to growing debts and liquidity impasses in South Africa and Namibia with negative adjustments to their credit ratings.

Worst hit by economic decline was *Namibia*, which slid into its most dramatic economic crisis to date. The recession, in combination with overspending by the government, almost bankrupted the state. Many grand reform plans remained unfulfilled and large disparities in income were evident. President Geingob's Harambee Prosperity Plan, announced with great fanfare at the beginning of his term in office, had not yet delivered any meaningful improvements for the living conditions of ordinary people.

Changes in governments also impacted on economic policies. President Lourenço surprised many in *Angola* and abroad by mounting an unexpectedly ruthless attack on corruption at the highest levels of government. Even the dos Santos dynasty, particularly Eduardo dos Santos's four children, who, thanks to their father's protection, had manoeuvred their way to the control levers of important state-owned companies, were not spared. Isabel dos Santos, believed to be the richest African woman, was removed as the head of Sonangol, the state oil group. Numerous ministers and other senior officials did not escape unscathed either. Lourenço announced a grace period for transferring funds back home from tax havens, the total amount estimated to add up to $ 30 bn. After the grace period, he threatened, all cases of embezzlement and tax evasion would be dealt with by the judiciary. Lourenço's actions sent a clear signal, at least symbolically. However, it remained to be seen how serious would be the clean-out of the institutions of government – and what scope for action the established elite would allow him.

The change of government enforced by the military in *Zimbabwe* also fuelled hopes and expectations that the new President Mnangagwa would be able to create a more positive investment climate to attract foreign investment. Among his first announcements was his intention to compensate former commercial farmers for the expropriation of their property during the fast track land reform, obviously in a move to regain investors' confidence.

Continued high inequality also fuelled the *land issue* in both Namibia and South Africa. A long-announced second national land conference for Namibia was postponed several times due to financial constraints and lack of a coherent policy, while a Landless People's Movement emerged as a political party in the making to challenge the SWAPO policy and claim restitution rights for local population groups. Concern over skewed land distribution was also a policy matter at the governing ANC's elective conference in December, where delegates adopted a resolution that in specific cases expropriation without compensation would be feasible. In contrast, predominantly Afrikaans-speaking white farmers mobilised in South Africa against farm killings, which they claimed amounted to genocide.

Mozambique continued to be rocked by *corruption scandals*. As a former 'donor darling', the country lost the trust of the donor community. The discovery of $ 2 bn in 'hidden debt' cost the government its reputation – and the flow of ODA declined considerably. Cases of alleged large-scale corruption also remained a major issue in Botswana, Malawi and Mauritius, while South Africa was marred by chronic embezzlement through political office bearers as well as higher-ranking officials in the civil service and state-owned enterprises, dubbed 'state capture'. TI's Corruption Perception Index 2017 singled out Malawi as a state, that continued "to decline significantly". The overall rankings for the sub-region's countries did not show any improvements. Using 100 as the maximum score for non-corruption, they were rated in the following order (with rank out of 180 countries, followed by score, in brackets): Botswana (34th/61), Namibia (53rd/51), Mauritius (54th/50), South Africa (71st/43), Lesotho (74th/42), Swaziland (85th/39), Zambia (96th/37), Malawi (122nd/31), Mozambique (153rd/25), Madagascar (155th/24), Zimbabwe (157th/22), Angola (167th/19).

The World Bank's *Doing Business Report* 2017 ranked the sub-regional countries out of a total of 190 states as follows: Mauritius (49th), Botswana (71st), South Africa (74th), Zambia (98th), Lesotho (100th), Namibia (108th), Swaziland (111th), Malawi (133rd), Mozambique (137th), Zimbabwe (161st), Madagascar (167th) and Angola (182nd), with the regional average rank of all SADC states at 120th.

Sub-regional Organisations

All 12 countries in the sub-region were members of *SADC* (whose 16 member states also include the DRC, Seychelles, Tanzania and, since August, the Comoros). An *Extraordinary Summit* was held under the chairmanship of King Mswati on 18 March at the Lozitha Royal Palace in Swaziland. It approved the resolutions of the Strategic

Ministerial Retreat on Regional Integration, which was held on 12–14 March under the theme: 'The SADC we want'. It discussed the situation in the DRC and Lesotho but remained largely observant and even expressed words of approval to the Congolese government under President Kabila, who continued to delay any elections. It extended the contracts of the SADC Executive Secretary Stergomena Lawrence Tax, and the Deputy Executive Secretary for Regional Integration Thembinkosi Mhlongo, for a further four-year term.

The *37th Ordinary SADC Summit* was held on 19–20 August in Pretoria. It appointed Jacob Zuma and Hage Geingob, respectively, as the chairperson and deputy chairperson of SADC, and Eduardo dos Santos and Edward Lungu, respectively, as chairperson and deputy chairperson of the SADC Organ on Politics, Defence and Security Cooperation. With any changes in office (such as the later replacement of Jacob Zuma and Eduardo dos Santos) their successors would take over the position during the remaining year in office. Among many other things, the summit urged member states to implement projects that were in line with focus areas of agro-processing, mineral exploitation, energy, pharmaceuticals, boosting skills for enhancing regional integration, and creating a mechanism for the involvement of the private sector. The summit directed that a regional Natural Gas Committee should be established to promote the inclusion of gas in the regional energy mix for industrial development, admitted the Union of Comoros as a new member of SADC, and noted that the assessment of Burundi was a work in progress. The situation in Lesotho and the DRC were matters of special concern and were addressed in the final communique.

On 16 August, the *SADC People's Summit* opened in Johannesburg. The forum, established for NGOs and social movements, assembled over 1,000 delegates from SADC countries, who focused mainly on human rights issues. It included the 2nd Permanent People's Tribunal, which discussed with local communities the exploitation of land, eco-systems, labour and organisations by big corporates with the support or endorsement of governments. Members of the *SADC Democracy Forum* protested during the summit outside of the venue, demanding the resignation of the heads of state in the DRC, Swaziland, Zambia and Zimbabwe.

Following major energy supply crises in previous years, SADC's Southern African Power Pool (SAPP) recorded for the first time in a decade surplus capacity in regional *energy production*. By September, the surplus generation capacity was estimated at 2,616 MW, and SAPP anticipated a continued positive trend, which would benefit economies and ordinary people in the sub-region.

On 16 November, SADC Chairperson Jacob Zuma called an emergency meeting on *Zimbabwe* in response to the soft coup by the military. It was attended by the ministers responsible for foreign or external affairs from the SADC Troika member states (Angola, Tanzania and Zambia) and the SADC Council Chairperson Maite Nkoana-Mashabane, who was also South Africa's minister of international relations and cooperation. In line with the overall cautious approach, SADC did not ultimately decide on any condemnation of the unlawful intervention by the Zimbabwean army to replace president Robert Mugabe, who was forced to resign against his will. The official phrasing created was that Mugabe resigned as provided by the Constitution. The inauguration of his successor, Emmerson Mnangagwa, was attended by several presidents and former presidents of SADC member states. Following the assassination of the army commander, Khoantle Motsomotso, in *Lesotho* on 5 September, SADC deployed on 3 December a 258-strong regional force to the country, composed of soldiers from Angola, Malawi, Namibia, South Africa, Tanzania, Zambia and Zimbabwe.

SACU, the oldest existing customs union in the world, continued with Botswana, Lesotho, Namibia, South Africa and Swaziland as its members. Apart from Botswana, they were also in a Common Monetary Area with their currencies pegged to the South African rand. SACU had for years maintained a fragile balancing act, reconciling the different interests of its members. Its performance had declined, limiting the revenue that the most dependent smaller countries received from the pool and enhancing a precarious fiscal balance for the annual budgets of Botswana, Lesotho, Namibia and Swaziland. The revenue shares distributed to member countries in 2016/17 were 20% for Botswana, 6% for Lesotho, 18% for Namibia, 50% for South Africa and 7% for Swaziland. In early December, the SACU Council of Ministers determined the following payments for the 2018/19 financial year: Botswana R (rand) 19.4 bn, Lesotho R 5.5 bn, Namibia R 17 bn, Swaziland R 5.8 bn, South Africa R 43 bn. South Africa, which contributed over 90% of the income shared within SACU, continued to demand a revised revenue sharing formula, which it considered not to its benefit. Renegotiating the stakes might further limit the financial transfers to the smaller economies, adding more pressure on foreign currency accounts as international reserves. The 5th *SACU Summit* was held on 23 June in Lozitha (Swaziland). It reconfirmed the intention for SACU to remain operational but agreed to discuss a new road map reviewing the agreement entered into in 2002, which should address the differing expectations of the member states. How the dissatisfaction among them could best be resolved remained a matter of speculation.

In anticipation of the consequences of *Brexit*, a joint statement by the UK and SACU following a meeting of SACU member state trade ministers with the British minister for trade policy on 19 July in Johannesburg stressed the British intention to avoid any interruption of trade between the partners by continued exchange relations with the SADC EPA, of which all SACU states were also members. This was another reminder that the sub-region's economic situation was to a large extent vulnerable, due to its world market dependency, and linked to global shifts and trends not only in commodity prices but also in trade relations.

Angola

Jon Schubert

Long-time president, José Eduardo dos Santos, stepped down after 38 years in power. He was succeeded by João Lourenço in the August elections. Although the ruling party continued to dominate politics after contested election results, this was a momentous change that brought about fresh political dynamics toward the end of the year. Nonetheless, the economic crisis persisted, which also reduced Angola's diplomatic clout, and the overall human rights situation remained dire.

Domestic Politics

Domestic politics were dominated by the *general elections* held in August, the country's third since the end of the war in 2002, and the first in which President dos Santos would not be the top candidate of the ruling Popular Movement for the Liberation of Angola ('Movimento Popular de Libertação de Angola'; MPLA). Under Angola's 'hyperpresidentialist' system, the head of the list of candidates of the party or coalition with the most seats in parliament automatically becomes president, with the second name on the list tapped for the vice-presidency. Accordingly, much

 | DOI:10.1163/9789004367630_045

of the political debate turned around the candidates' lists and the candidates' rankings, especially for the ruling MPLA, where a move up or down the candidates' list indicated their respective standing and influence within the party.

Early in the year, several associations of 'organised' civil society announced that they would hold street rallies to persuade the president to change his mind and run in the elections. In the end, however, the MPLA fielded Defence Minister *João Lourenço* as its top candidate, followed by Minister of Territorial Administration Bornito de Sousa. This meant that de Sousa was both in charge of overseeing the running of the elections and a candidate but, while opposition parties and civil society noted and challenged this, de Sousa's place on the list remained unchanged.

The other main question regarded dos Santos's future role and whether Lourenço would bring anything new, as dos Santos would stay on as the *party president* for the foreseeable future. Dos Santos also issued a number of decrees before the elections that would ensure his continued influence over the security apparatus, promoting a number of officers to higher grades with consequent higher salaries. Similar decrees were also issued to ensure dos Santos's lifelong immunity as 'emeritus president', and to lock in his latest appointments in state-owned companies beyond his stepping down. Lourenço himself was widely seen as a dos Santos loyalist. He had regained the president's trust after being cast out into political insignificance in 2002, when he made his ambitions to succeed dos Santos clear. He was a party stalwart with liberation struggle credentials, and, as a former army general, was respected among the armed forces. He was also, as Angolan observers noted, "not known for his intellectual capacities", and overall a somewhat lacklustre candidate, or so it seemed, although, unlike some of his party comrades, he enjoyed a reputation for relative probity. His wife, Ana Dias Lourenço, by contrast, was a respected economist, having served as Executive Director for Africa at the World Bank.

The *MPLA campaign*, running under the slogan "Correct what is bad, improve what is good", made full use of the resources of the state to spread its message. But it failed to ignite much enthusiasm, partly because the failings of previous administrations were never clearly identified. Still, Lourenço tried to present himself as accessible, making use of Facebook, and soon earning the nickname 'JLo' from the population. Nonetheless, the overall mood among Angolans and Angola-observers was one of cautious scepticism, and the dominant overall impression was that Lourenço would not bring about much change.

Opposition parties, by comparison, were hampered by their lack of funds, public visibility and opportunities to campaign. According to the second-largest opposition party, the Broad Convergence for the Salvation of Angola – Electoral Coalition ('Convergência Ampla de Salvação de Angola-Coligação Eleitoral'; CASA-CE) in Luanda in May, advertising agencies had refused to take on their poster campaign, having had been forbidden to accept the commission, lest the provincial government take away the agency's billboard concessions in public space. By contrast,

João Lourenço toured the country in his capacity as defence minister, using state assets to campaign. During the official campaign period, a civil society association also tallied the airtime given to political parties and found that of the 500 minutes the team had monitored, 332 had been given to the MPLA, 21 minutes to CASA-CE, 17.6 minutes to the third-largest opposition party, the Social Renewal Party ('Partido de Renovação Social'; PRS), and a mere 13.5 minutes to the largest opposition party, the National Union for the Total Liberation of Angola 'União Nacional para a Libertação Total de Angola'; (UNITA).

In parliament, the MPLA's dominance also marginalised opposition parties. In May, the largest opposition party, UNITA, introduced a draft bill on local elections, which were stipulated by the 2010 constitution but had been delayed ever since. However, the MPLA faction decided the topic needed to "mature" more so that a consensus could be reached and voted against further discussion of the bill.

In February, parliament approved a bill that would criminalise *abortion*, with the abstention of UNITA, CASA-CE and the PRS. This, however, led to the mobilisation of civil society, led by a small group of feminist activists in Luanda, who organised a protest march. The mobilisation proved successful, to the point where regime-affiliated women (including Isabel dos Santos) offered their material support. The police, usually quick to crack down on any unauthorised demonstration, also held back and cleared the streets for the demonstrators. The protest persuaded parliament to reopen discussions on the bill, though not to shelve it entirely. As a test case for mobilising the population across social classes and sectors around a common, 'apolitical' issue, the campaign was a relative success.

Other *demonstrations* were less successful in that respect. A small rally against Bornito de Sousa's candidacy as vice president for the MPLA in Luanda in February, for example, was blocked by the police, with police dogs being set loose on the activists. In April, seven demonstrators were sentenced to 45 days in prison for "resistance to authorities" when they tried to protest against irregularities in the electoral registration process. Subsequent demonstrations against irregularities in the preparation of the electoral process were also swiftly impeded.

Further *human rights violations* included extra-judicial killings, among them those of two youths in the diamond-producing town of Cafunfo, Lunda Norte, in February. They had taken part in a demonstration against the abduction of the local sovereign, King Mwanangana Malembe Yavo Samuel, by a group allied to the competing Queen Mwakafunfo, who had been accompanied by police agents. Another demonstration in Cuango, Lunda Norte, in June was also stopped by the police, who used live ammunition, killing one bystander and wounding several demonstrators. In the oil-producing enclave province of *Cabinda*, human rights defenders deplored the high level of unemployment, lack of freedom of expression, increased deforestation by oil companies and the overall securitisation of the province, which remained one of the world's most heavily militarised areas. In May, guerrillas aligned with the Front for the Liberation of the Cabinda Enclave ('Frente de Libertação do Enclave de Cabinda') posted a video displaying four police agents they had kidnapped in a raid, saying they would be treated as prisoners of war. The authorities denied the attack ever took place, saying the situation in Cabinda was "stable". The investigative news site 'Maka Angola' also reported various cases of summary killings of youths by the police's Criminal Investigation Service in Luanda's outlying neighbourhoods.

While President dos Santos was away in Spain for medical reasons, as in previous years, *preparations for the elections* continued. The electoral roll was completed by the end of March. At the end of May, the Constitutional Court found faults in the candidates' lists of all parties save the MPLA. UNITA, by contrast, had to remove 11 "insufficient" candidates from its lists, CASA-CE 63 candidates, and PRS 73. The nominally independent, but MPLA-dominated, National Electoral Commission ('Commissão Nacional Eleitoral'; CNE) contracted a Portuguese and a Spanish firm to supply the election materials and carry out the electronic vote-counting. Opposition parties contested this, citing alleged irregularities in the previous two elections in which these companies had played a central role. The CNE acknowledged the need for discussion, but the contracts were maintained. In the last phase of campaigning, a UNITA communal secretary was killed in Caála, Huambo province, when a visiting UNITA delegation was attacked, allegedly by MPLA supporters. A pre-election poll – Angola's first – carried out by a Brazilian consultancy firm at the government's request, gave the MPLA 38% of the vote, followed closely by UNITA with 32%, and CASA-CE with 26%.

Elections took place on 23 August and were relatively calm and orderly, despite reports of widespread abstentions (20%) and targeted voter disenfranchisement, with voters turning up at polling stations only to hear they had been registered at a different place, often kilometres away. On the evening of election day, the MPLA announced its "qualified victory", with 63% of the vote. The following day, the CNE declared "provisional results", giving the MPLA a 61% majority, a number more or less fabricated out of thin air: none of the provincial results had been counted and parallel counting by the opposition indicated substantial opposition gains in key urban areas. The opposition electoral commissioners on the CNE immediately rejected the results, but to little effect. Opposition claims to the Supreme Court were, unsurprisingly, dismissed, though the *final results* acknowledged opposition gains, most notably in Luanda's two most populous municipalities and in Cabinda.

The MPLA thus still held a majority of 150 seats in the 220-strong *National Assembly* (25 fewer than in 2012), followed by 51 for UNITA (19 more than before) and 16 (up 8) for CASA-CE. The PRS lost one seat and was left with two, while the decline of the historic first liberation movement, the National Front for the Liberation of Angola ('Frente Nacional de Libertação de Angola') continued, leaving the party with only one seat. Opposition parties initially threatened to boycott parliament, but soon took up their seats – a move that might have been spurred on by the acquisition of a fleet of 250 Lexus LX 570 luxury SUVs, one for every MP, at a cost of $ 312,000 each. Following the elections, UNITA's president, Isaías Samakuva, announced his decision to step down from the party leadership in 2018, while Abel Chivukuvuku resigned his seat in parliament to concentrate fully on leading CASA-CE.

Lourenço was sworn in on 26 September. The initial composition of the *Cabinet* and appointments of provincial governors promised more of the same. However, after a short lull, Lourenço in the remaining months of the year swiftly proceeded to dismiss and replace over 250 figures in government and administration, including some key dos Santos loyalists, earning him the epithet "implacable exonerator". *Notable dismissals* included General Manual Hélder Vieira Dias 'Kopelipa', dos Santos's formidable head of the Presidency's security office, General Zé Maria, head of military intelligence, National Police Commander Ambrósio de Lemos, the infamous "roving ambassador" Luvualu de Carvalho, and Valter Filipe, the governor of the National Bank, who was replaced by José de Lima Massano, a renowned economist who had held the position until 2015.

In mid-November, Lourenço's moves to curb dos Santos's influence culminated in his *dismissal of Isabel dos Santos* from her post at the helm of the state oil company Sonangol. She had been appointed as CEO of Sonagol in mid-2016 by her father, officially on the strength of her track record as "Africa's first woman billionaire", to restructure the company, which was in deep crisis following the drop in world oil prices. Not only did she fail to turn Sonangol around, continuing to milk its revenues for the benefit of her own business empire and pushing the company to the "brink of bankruptcy", but her appointment also proved deeply unpopular among the population and the ranks of the MPLA. She was replaced by Carlos Saturnino, the former head of Sonangol E&P, who had himself been dismissed by Isabel dos Santos ten months earlier.

One of the areas where Lourenço's presidency also had unexpected and very immediate effect was in the *media*. In March, critics lamented the inequality of space and airtime allocated on public media (television, radio and daily newspaper), citing the lack of coverage of UNITA's 51st anniversary rally on 11 March in contrast with the broad and sympathetic coverage given to dos Santos's visit to the Laúca dam in Malanje province on that day. In July, the Constitutional Court rejected a UNITA submission to rule as unconstitutional the new media law, announced by the president in January. Journalists from independent weeklies were also routinely impeded from access, intimidated or detained. In April, the Angolan bishop's conference, also decried the "lack of political will" to extend beyond Luanda the coverage area of 'Rádio Ecclesia', the Catholic Church's broadcaster and one of the few independent stations. However, in one of his first speeches following the elections, Lourenço stated that public media should be unbiased and serve all Angolans, not just the interest of one party. Almost overnight, public media started running news items that, though not overtly critical of the government, admitted that some things were perhaps not quite as perfect as had till then been claimed. A few weeks later, Lourenço replaced the board of directors of the 'Jornal de Angola', thereby formalising this new spirit. More importantly, he also cancelled an existing contract that the public TV channel TPA2 and the regime-affiliated, private channel Zimbo had with Semba Communications, a production company owned by two of dos Santos's other children.

Lourenço gave other signals indicating a *change in style* from dos Santos, stopping his motorcade at red lights and queuing in line at a fast food restaurant like an ordinary citizen, which Angolans remarked upon very favourably. Also, official celebrations of Independence Day were staged in the municipality of Matala, in the southern province of Huíla, rather than in Luanda at the national stadium. When Lourenço's plane touched down in the provincial capital, Lubango, an MPLA welcome committee, including the party's women's and youth wings, was waiting for him, waving party flags. Lourenço, however, refused to disembark until they all had left, saying he was here as president for the entire country, not of the party.

Large-scale and petty *corruption* persisted. In May, the Luanda collective taxi drivers' association complained that, despite an overhaul of the traffic police in the previous year to curb bribe-taking by traffic agents, the police had only "changed tactics", and now negotiated bribes at the police station rather than on the streets. At the other end of the economic spectrum, the Angolan Sovereign Wealth Fund ('Fundo Soberano de Angola'), headed by President dos Santos's son José Filomeno 'Zénú' dos Santos, was also mired in controversy. The Panama Papers revealed that the fund had paid out $ 90 m in management fees to the Mauritius-based QG Investments Africa Management, an asset management firm owned by Jean-Claude Bastos de Morais, a close friend of Zénú's. In addition, the controversial Porto Caio project, a new deep-water port in Cabinda province initiated by Bastos, also led to the forced expulsion of 300 families of fishermen from their homes in July. The leaks then revealed that of that $ 41 m had been paid out in dividends to QG Investments Ltd in the British Virgin Islands, and Bastos held shares in many of the ventures his company had recommended to the Fund. At year's end, no investigations had started in Angola. In other instances, however, Lourenço made more serious moves than his predecessor to tackle illicit enrichment by regime figures, most notably when he announced on 13 December that Angolans who held undeclared assets abroad would have a period of grace during which they could repatriate the money, no questions asked, to invest it for the country's benefit; after that, he warned, authorities would take steps to seize the assets.

This was followed by the nomination of General Hélder Fernando Pitta Grós as *Procurator-General* of the Republic, replacing João Maria de Sousa, who had held the post for ten years. Pitta Grós then swiftly announced the creation of a commission of inquiry to investigate allegations of extrajudicial killings by police agents;

under the previous procurator general, most citizen complaints had been dismissed as unsubstantiated. Such moves further bolstered Lourenço's popularity, which at the end of the year was much higher than before the elections, with even opposition politicians giving him the benefit of doubt for the time being.

Foreign Affairs

Relations with the neighbouring *DRC* grew tense, due to an influx of more than 20,000 refugees from *Congo*, displaced by conflicts in the Kasaï provinces. In April, the governor of Lunda Norte, Ernesto Muangala, denied reports that Angolan police officers had been killed by Congolese rebels and said the borders were secure and no Angolan troops were involved in the conflicts across the border. In May, however, the Angolan army moved infantry, artillery and tank units to its north-eastern border, as a "preventive measure" according to army sources. In December, reports emerged of human rights violations resulting from the government's crackdown on illegal Congolese immigrants in the Lunda provinces. More importantly, Congolese businesses also complained about Angolan products "flooding" the domestic market, as Angolan sellers were undercutting their prices to get access to dollars. Finally, although Angola had in 2016 successfully mediated between DRC President Kabila and the opposition over the delayed elections, there were signs that Angola's patience was running out. In August, Sindika Dokolo, President dos Santos's Congolese-Danish son-in-law, very visibly called upon Kabila to step down, meeting with the prominent DRC opposition politician Moïse Katumbi.

South Africa stressed in March the need to further reinforce the important commercial exchange between the two countries, despite trade having dropped by 75% in 2016 because of the economic crisis. In November, Lourenço's first state visit was to South Africa, during which five agreements were signed. Most important among these was one for visa-free travel for nationals of the two countries, an agreement that had been mooted for years without advancing, but which, to the joy of many Angolans and South Africans, took effect on 1 December. Lourenço also travelled to Zimbabwe, as part of the *SADC* mediation team following the ousting of Robert Mugabe. The virtually irreplaceable Minister of Transport Augusto Tomás visited *Zambia* with a view to reviving construction of the Lobito Transport Corridor to link the two countries by rail.

Relations with *Portugal* remained somewhat ambivalent. A money-laundering investigation into the affairs of one of dos Santos's daughters, Welwitschea José 'Tchizé' dos Santos, was shelved in February. However, charges were filed against Vice President Manuel Vicente for allegedly paying an $ 810,000 bribe to a Portuguese magistrate to stop an earlier corruption investigation. Spending by Angolan tourists in Lisbon reached new heights, making Angola Portugal's most important non-European source of tourism income. After Lourenço's election, Portugal's President Marcelo Rebelo de Sousa immediately flew to Luanda to congratulate his counterpart. Although this was criticised by pro-democracy activists in both countries, it underscored the continued importance of the ties between the two countries. De Sousa's affable manner, shown on TV footage as he chatted with ordinary people in the streets and emerged from the waters off Luanda's Ilha in his swimming trunks, also very much endeared him to the Angolan population at large.

Relations with *Brazil* also remained important, with the new government seeking to reinforce cooperation in the non-oil sectors, the second Angolan television series premiering on 'TV Brasil', and Angolan kuduro singer Titica performing at Rock in Rio. The Angolan Development Bank also approved the financing of an under-water fibre-optic cable linking the two countries across the South Atlantic.

China remained one of Angola's most important partners, partly because Angola was China's second-largest supplier of crude oil. China made a $ 600 m loan towards the construction of the new deep-water port in Cabinda (see above), though the chairman of the Angola-China Industrial and Commerce Association said in May that the number of Chinese businesses in Angola had fallen by about three-quarters in the wake of the oil price crisis. Even so, the Bank of China opened a branch in Luanda in May and, in September, China sent a special envoy to congratulate Lourenço on his election, stressing China's commitment to advancing bilateral ties.

In May, Lourenço (then still defence minister) visited his *US* counterpart James Mattis to sign a memorandum on strategic partnership. Commercial exchanges were dominated by oil, though various court cases overshadowed the usual state of affairs: in July, Halliburton agreed to pay $ 29.2 m under the Foreign Corrupt Practices Act for violating federal anti-bribery rules in its business dealings in Angola; in November, SBM Offshore USA Inc agreed to pay a $ 238 m penalty for bribery schemes over ten years in five countries, including Angola. In May, Cobalt International filed a demand in the International Court of Arbitration for $ 2 bn compensation from Sonangol for breach of agreement. The dispute was settled in December, with Sonangol agreeing a $ 500 m payout.

In April, Lourenço (then still defence minister) visited *Spain* with a view to reinforcing cooperation in military and security matters. *Germany* also strengthened its military cooperation with Angola in April, in the areas of peacekeeping, intelligence and humanitarian missions. *France* signed a cooperation agreement through the French Development Agency in May, paving the way for a $ 545 m funding envelope together with the World Bank and the Angolan government for projects in the areas of water, energy and agriculture. *Russia* launched Angola's first commercial telecommunications satellite on 27 December. Communication was lost immediately after the launch but was restored two days later. In February a cooperation agreement was signed with the *UK* with a view to reinforcing the existing partnership and expanding commercial exchanges. In December, the UK also announced the extension of its land mine clearing support.

Socioeconomic Developments

With oil prices fluctuating between $ 40 and $ 50 per barrel, compared with the pre-2014 price of $ 100, Angola ended the year as Africa's *second-largest oil producer*, with an average production of 1.6 m b/d. In September, the Soyo LNG plant also resumed full production capacities, after several years of recurring interruptions due to technical failures. Despite these higher output levels, the economy was still largely beset by the crisis it entered in 2015, with around half of government expenditure earmarked for *debt servicing*. The National Bank kept the kwanza relatively stable against inflationary pressures, but only thanks to strict currency controls. Even the doubling of the National Bank's euro sales to domestic markets in April did little to alleviate the *foreign exchange shortage*. For example, in July, the Emirates airline announced that it was immediately abandoning its concession to the national carrier TAAG, owing to the difficulties it faced in repatriating profits because of the lack of foreign exchange. Several other international airlines also reduced or suspended their operations in Angola for the same reason and, in April, even foreign diplomats complained about currency shortages to the Ministry of Foreign Affairs. Many Angolans resorted to buying consumer goods such as cars, motorcycles or household appliances in Angola for kwanza, and reselling them abroad for hard currency.

As a result of the high demand and low supply of foreign exchange, the kwanza (AOA) was officially traded at around AOA 165: $ 1 over the year, though street rates, after peaking at around AOA 500: $ 1 in January, fluctuated between AOA 350 and AOA 450 during the year. Thus, while GDP grew by between 1.3% and 2.3%, depending on the source of estimates, the Angolan economics weekly 'Expansão' estimated that, despite a salary adjustment in July, Angolans had lost 48% of their purchasing power since the onset of the crisis, with a drop of 20.8% in 2017 alone. Generally, the economy remained largely *import-dependent*, which, in combination with the dollar scarcity, resulted in shortages and rising prices. This also made Luanda, again, the world's most expensive city for expatriates, according to consultancy firm ECA International.

In May, the Ministry of Commerce estimated that Angola only produced 2% of the goods it needed, with the remaining 98% having to be imported. Ambitious projects to improve this situation through state investments in large-scale *agriculture* projects across the country were, as in previous years, announced by both the outgoing and the incoming administration, though any tangible effects remained to be seen.

The *banking sector* remained plagued by discoveries of high amounts of 'bad debt', loans given out with little to no guarantees to MPLA luminaries throughout the years of high oil revenues. In March, a Portuguese newspaper revealed that General Kopelipa had transferred $ 300 m from the failing Banco Espírito Santo Angola to its Dubai parent bank, while in April Switzerland froze CHF (franc) 160 m originating from the same bank under suspicions of money laundering. BPC bank, also teetering on the verge of failure with € 2.6 m worth of bad loans on its books, had also handed out generous credits to MPLA figures, as leaks in July revealed.

The *cement* sector witnessed shortages after a dispute over fuel: in July, the Kwanza-Sul Cement Fabric (FCKS), complained that Sonangol had halted heavy fuel oil deliveries to the company for clinker production. Deliveries stopped, according to the owners, after they had refused to offer Isabel dos Santos shares in FCKS. As CEO of Sonangol, while she was also the owner of the rival producer Cimangola, she had installed a mechanism whereby FCKS would have to buy all heavy fuel oil from Cimangola. After Lourenço's election, the reform commission for the oil sector decreed that cement companies could buy heavy fuel oil directly from the Luanda refinery, thereby resolving the shortages. In November, the government announced the opening of a tender for a fourth telecommunications licence, in a bid to diversify the mobile phone market, hitherto dominated by UNITEL, also owned by Isabel dos Santos, and Movicel, owned by a consortium of army generals.

In February, the Australian company Lucapa Mining announced the discovery of a 227-carat *diamond* at its Lulo diamond mine, the second-largest ever found in Angola. State mining company SODIAM announced after Isabel dos Santos's dismissal from Sonangol that it would divest its shares in the Swiss-based jewellery maker di Grisogono, controlled by Isabel's husband Sindika Dokolo, "for reasons of public interest and legality". Although a wind of change did start blowing after Lourenço's election, the couple's business interests continued to dominate many sectors of the economy. In February, for example, Isabel's drink distribution company SOBIDA opened a new *beer production and bottling* plant, after which the company would start producing the very popular Portuguese Sagres beer in Angola. Sindika Dokolo took over the former building of the National Assembly in downtown Luanda in order to develop cultural activities there.

Problems with *rubbish collection* continued, with residents of various municipalities in Luanda and other provincial cities such as Lubango reporting that they were "drowning" in mountains of uncollected refuse and demanding that local administrations tackle the problem. Although the 'rubbish tax' introduced in 2016 yielded daily revenues of about $ 10,000 in Luanda, the rubbish collection company dismissed workers who had been striking to demand the payment of salary arrears.

In March, the World Bank approved a $ 200 m loan to improve *water delivery* to 950,000 people in nine provincial cities. In April, the Public Luanda Water

Distribution Company ('Empresa Pública de Águas de Luanda'; EPAL) opened its new headquarters in the Talatona business district. The glass-panelled building was initially reported to have cost $ 700 m to build, and would, according to EPAL's CEO, give more "dignity" to the company. Following outcries on social media, given the poor state of water supply to Luanda residents, the company clarified a few days later that the construction costs had been $ 7 m – while rainfall in March claimed 11 deaths in a single night and left 250 families homeless. Similarly, daily electricity outages remained the norm for most of the capital's residents.

March saw the publication of a survey carried out among faculty in eight *higher education* institutions, in which 60% of respondents stated that academic freedom was not protected and 33% said they felt they could be persecuted or killed for carrying out their research with scientific rigour. Teacher and faculty strikes recurred throughout the year to protest against salary arrears and poor teaching conditions. In primary schooling, though legally free of charge, parents reported having to pay up to € 300 per month to secure study places for their children and students in Uíge province also reported the persistence of demands for sexual favours in exchange for better grades.

The *health* system remained underfunded. In January, health authorities warned of a cholera outbreak in Luanda. In February, WHO officially declared the devastating yellow fever outbreak of 2016 over, though it recommended vaccination efforts be kept up for at least six more months. In March, the Catholic bishops publicly denounced the "scandalous and glaring" lack of drugs and "endemic dehumanisation" of patients in hospitals. Along with slightly raising the 2018 budget allocated to health to 7.4% of government spending, the new government gave some signals of wanting to improve the situation: in November, the trial started of three employees at the Ministry of Health, accused of embezzling $ 2 m from a Global Fund grant to combat malaria. New Minister of Health Sílvia Lutucuta also dismissed the health inspector-general and the administrative managers of the two largest public hospitals. Even so, Angola ranked as the worst of all Lusophone countries, according to a WHO report published in December, with only 36% of the population having access to adequate health services.

In February, the opening match of the national football championship between Santa Rita de Cássia and Recreativo do Libolo at the 4th of January Stadium in Uíge resulted in a tragedy when, shortly after the start of the game, additional fans tried to enter the stadium, resulting in a rush that led to 17 deaths and injuries to over 60 people. On a more positive note, the Ministry of Public Administration, Work and Social Security, announced in March that it had concluded the disbursement of a total of $ 26.5 m to former Angolan *contract workers* in the German Democratic Republic, who had been clamouring for the payment of outstanding salaries and pensions since their return to Angola after the fall of the Berlin Wall. Also, in July, UNESCO added the historical centre M'banza Kongo to its list of *world heritage* sites, in culmination of a candidacy that had been initiated in 2014. M'banza Kongo, the capital of the Kongo kingdom, had been an important seat of government and one of the largest cities in Africa in the 15th century, when the first Portuguese explorers reached it. Following the conversion of King Afonso I to Catholicism in 1516, M'banza Kongo became an important ecclesiastical centre with several schools; SSA's first ambassador to the Vatican was sent from there in 1608.

In other news, one of President dos Santos's younger children, Eduane Danilo dos Santos, made headlines when he posted on Instagram a picture of a wristwatch he had just purchased for $ 500,000 in a charity auction at the Cannes Film Festival. Danilo's youthful age of 26 even gave the celebrity auctioneer, the US actor Will Smith, reason to pause and wonder aloud how this young man had that kind of money to spend. Following the huge outcry in Angola, Danilo communicated that he had not bought a watch, but rather a series of photographs for his own (hitherto unknown) charity 'Espírito de Criança' (Child's Spirit), and that he intended to promote, alongside HIV/AIDS research, art and culture in Angola.

Botswana

David Sebudubudu

The domestic political landscape remained stable throughout the year. This being the last full year of President Ian Khama's presidency, his government maintained its priority areas – job creation, eliminating poverty, improving funding for education, eradicating mother-to-child transmission of HIV, and combating corruption. A major domestic development was the conclusion of opposition cooperation talks. The country's foreign policy continued unchanged, and there were no major changes on the socio-economic front.

Domestic Politics

Although this was the last full year of Ian *Khama's Presidency*, the domestic political scene remained stable. This was a rare achievement in Africa and one worthy of celebration and recognition, given that some analysts had suggested in 2008 that he would not vacate the Presidency at the end of his term in office owing to his military background.

 | DOI:10.1163/9789004367630_046

Frosty relations continued between the Botswana Democratic Party (BDP) government and some *trade unions*, particularly the Botswana Federation of Public Sector Unions (BOFEPUSU). On 23 January, friction and dissonant relations between the Botswana Public Employees Union (BOPEU) and BOFEPUSU resurfaced, with BOPEU's president openly disparaging BOFEPUSU for reiterating the support it had given to the opposition alliance, the Umbrella for Democratic Change (UDC), in the 2014 general elections; a decision that BOPEU opposed. BOPEU, perceived in some quarters to be sympathetic to Khama, withdrew from BOFEPUSU. On 31 January, BOFEPUSU urged its members to continue to be spirited "in the fight for liberation" from BDP rule. The BDP failed to embrace a proposal from its secretary general, Botsalo Ntuane, that called for a review of its relations with unions. This proposal was echoed by BOFEPUSU on 31 January, claiming that this was necessary if the party wanted to rule past 2019. Interestingly, BOPEU suspended its president in September, pending an audit.

On 30 January, reports suggested that the opposition *UDC collaboration talks*, which included the Botswana Congress Party (BCP), had failed. It was reported that the Botswana Movement for Democracy (BMD) and the Botswana People's Party (BPP) had abandoned the talks. Contrary to these reports, however, the opposition concluded its talks in February and the BCP was embraced as part of the UDC. The four parties that formed the alliance were allocated seats as follows: Botswana National Front (BNF) 22, BCP 17, BMD 14 and BPP 4. The BNF was allocated the presidency of the UDC, the BCP and BMD held the two vice presidencies, and the BPP took the chair. The conclusion of opposition talks that included the BCP was a major development in domestic politics. However, media reports immediately suggested divisions within the opposition grouping, related in part to the UDC vice presidency. It was reported that the BMD and its leader Ndaba Gaolatlhe wanted only one vice presidency, which he would occupy – a proposal that the BCP opposed. Interestingly, on 8 February, the BPP president, Motlatsi Molapise, noted that his party was querying the number of constituencies allocated to it. The BPP also publicly denounced the BCP's membership of the UDC, which caused openly stated discontent within the BCP. Media reports also suggested an uneasy relationship between the BCP and the BMD.

The *BDP* Youth League held its elective congress in Tsabong on 10 February, amid allegations of inequity. The party also held its 55th National Council in Gaborone on 24 March, to evaluate its policies and those of the government; President Khama appealed for harmony. On 7 July, the BDP held its 37th elective congress in Tonota, where Vice President Mokgweetsi Maisi was re-elected as chairman of the party. Mpho Balopi and Shaw Kgathi were elected secretary general and deputy secretary general, respectively. Satar Dada was elected treasurer and Jagdish Shah deputy treasurer. Moyo Guma, Slumber Tsogwane, Ngaka Ngaka, Machana Shamukuni and

Ponatshego Tshiping were elected onto the executive committee as additional members, while Botsalo Ntuane, Tebogo Masire, Tshekedi Khama, Velamina Brooks and Ms Goitse Phori were appointed to the executive committee by President Khama. The BDP maintained is widely publicised recruitment of members throughout the year, particularly from opposition parties.

The *BCP*, meanwhile, on 20 March, brought a case against the Independent Electoral Commission (IEC) concerning the electronic voting machines that had been introduced through a contentious 2016 amendment of the Electoral Act. At year's end, the court was yet to make a determination on the matter. In July, the BCP held its conference in Francistown. Following the inclusion of the BCP in the UDC, BCP members of parliament were recognised in August as *UDC members of parliament*. In the wake of the 2016 amendment of the Electoral Act referred to above, in December an amendment bill was introduced that proposed a Voter Verifiable Paper Audit Trail. A by-election in the constituency of Tlokweng was held on 13 May and won by Kenneth Segokgo (UDC). In August, the UDC registered a new symbol with the IEC for the 2019 general elections. In July, the BNF also held its party conference in Kang. Although Botswana had remained resolute in support of the ICC, the UDC suggested in February that it would pull out of the ICC in line with the position adopted by the AU.

The *BMD factional divisions* that centred on Sydney Pilane's disputed return to the party continued. On 27 April, it was reported that the party's Chairman Nehemiah Modubule and Secretary General Gilbert Mangole had been beaten by party activists associated with the party's president, Ndada Gaolathe. Modubule and Mangole were linked to Pilane's doubtful membership and return. In May, the BMD suspended seven members, including Gaolathe and its vice president, Wynter Mmolotsi, for taking part in a youth congress in April at Ramotswa, which was deemed illegitimate by the party's National Executive Committee (NEC) because it had been deferred. The seven members opposed their suspension and failed to appear at the disciplinary hearing. Six of them were expelled from the party on 21 June ahead of the party's elective congress in July. In June, there were fears that some constituencies might send dissident representatives to the congress because of divisions within the party between the two opposing factions. The Modubule and Mangole faction was perceived in some quarters to be working against efforts to ensure opposition cooperation, as they were identified with Pilane, who was considered a source of instability in the party. Consequently, in July the BMD held a volatile congress in Bobonong after members aligned to the Gaolathe faction tried to force their way into the congress premises; some party members were injured in the process. Consequently, the Gaolathe faction held a concurrent congress at a different venue in Bobonong, resulting in the two factions presenting two parallel NECs, each declaring itself legitimate. Efforts to invalidate the Bobonong congress and calls for a re-run were unsuccessful. Calls for a re-run of the BMD congress resonated even outside the party, including in the Botswana National Front Youth League, which put pressure on the UDC's NEC to address the BMD brawl. The competing BMD factions presented themselves before the UDC NEC in September, in an effort to resolve the impasse, with the faction associated with Pilane accusing Gaolathe of violating the party's constitution. The UDC proposed 'power sharing' between the two factions but the Gaolathe faction preferred a re-run of the congress.

The upshot was that the Gaolathe faction declared the *formation of a new party* – the Alliance for Progressives (AP) – on 20 September. With the departure of the Gaolathe faction from the BMD, the UDC NEC decided that the BMD should put in place an interim leadership to allow the party to hold a fresh elective congress before the end of January 2018 as the NEC that had been elected in July was not considered legitimate. The BMD accepted this proposal. The UDC also decided that the BMD NEC that was in place before the volatile congress would steer the party to a fresh congress. The party held another congress on 2–3 December, to elect its NEC – and all those who had been elected at the July congress in Bobonong were returned unchallenged. Pilane was elected as party president. This legitimised the new NEC with the UDC, and Pilane became one of the two UDC vice presidents, the other being the BCP party president, Dumelang Saleshando. Meanwhile, ruptures were reported throughout the year between members of the UDC, and reports suggested that the BPP had vowed to maintain its membership of the UDC only if the BCP was not a part of it. On 25 November, the BPP suspended its chairman, Richard Gudu, and an additional member of the Central Committee, Peter Kuchwe, for participating in a UDC meeting and press briefing without party approval.

Disputes between the government and trade unions persisted. On 4 April, the High Court annulled a 3% 2016/2017 financial year salary increase announced on 30 March 2016 for non-unionised public service employees and those that were not members of the Public Service Bargaining Council (PSBC), as well as a 4% 2017/2018 increment announced in March, without involving the PSBC. The court contended that it was illegal for the government to adjust its employees' salaries or conditions of services without reference to the PSBC, although the announcements were consistent with previous court decisions. In April, BOPEU challenged these decisions in court, calling for the suspension of BOFEPUSU from the PSBC for failing to meet the requirements of the PSBC constitution, including for an inspection of membership and unpaid subscriptions. This challenge was unsuccessful. Following these court cases, BOFEPUSU criticised the government for its reluctance to go back to the PSBC. The government argued that there was a need to include non-compliance on the PSBC agenda, and as well as stating that the schedules of its representatives were tight so that they were not available for PSBC meetings. Ultimately, following years of tension between the government and BOFEPUSU, the latter ended its membership of the PSBC on 28 April, saying it would rejoin the PSBC in 2019. This termination of membership allowed BOFEPUSU members to benefit from the disputed salary increments and, after this withdrawal, the government agreed to pay the increments to BOFEPUSU members from 1 June. BOFEPUSU, which had supported the UDC in the 2014 elections, was hoping for a change of government in 2019. Interestingly, the Court of Appeal decided that the government's decision to increase salaries outside the PSBC diminished the standing of trade unions.

Despite its respected status, issues affecting the *judiciary* continued to arise. In February, BOFEPUSU criticised the president of the Court of Appeal, Justice Ian Kirby, for averring that "'the term, Executive-minded' is often used by parties, unions or interest groups who have been unsuccessful in litigating a case against government, to describe the judge who wrote their judgment". In March, President Khama set aside the 2015 suspension of four High Court judges and a tribunal that he had appointed to investigate them, after they tendered an apology to him and the Chief Justice. One of the four, Key Dingake, had openly disparaged "executive minded judges". In February, the High Court ruled that the re-appointment of six judges of the Court of Appeal by the president after they had served a fixed term was illegal. He declared Section 4 of the Court of Appeal Act unlawful, and granted six months for corrective measures to be put in place so that the appointment of the six judges could be normalised. The case, which was brought by one of the trade unions, led to a near crisis. On 1 June, the Court of Appeal affirmed that Section 4 of the Court of Appeal Act was unlawful. However, it decided that judges of the Court of Appeal could serve beyond one fixed-term contract. Interestingly, in May the Judicial Service Commission (JSC) wanted four other judges, Gaolapelwe Ketlogetswe, Lot Moroka, Godfrey Nthomiwa and Tshepo Motswagole, to tender an apology to Chief Justice Maruping Dibotelo for signing a petition in 2015 calling for his impeachment and thus "undermining" him. The four judges declined to apologise and were unsuccessful in challenging the JSC in court, when the Chief Justice opposed their application. The four judges appealed the decision in November. In December, the dispute was brought to a close after they withdrew the petition and the attendant court case. Another four judges apologised separately. In all, 12 judges had petitioned the Chief Justice in 2015 but issues relating to this petition were sustained throughout the year – causing ripples within the judiciary, and attracting negative publicity. Meanwhile, media reports suggested that Judge Lot Moroka was being investigated by the Directorate of Intelligence and Security Services (DISS) and the auditor general for "staying [in a hotel] more than 14 days and … entertaining his family". Moroka was presiding over a case in which the opposition BCP was challenging the adoption of the electronic voting machine, to be used in the 2019 general elections.

On 19 April, the Court of Appeal invalidated President Khama's refusal to appoint Omphemetse Motumise as a *High Court* judge in line with a 2015 recommendation of the JSC. On 17 October, Khama confirmed his appointment, which would come into effect from 1 January 2018. This confirmation followed a Statutory Notice by the Law Society of Botswana requesting Khama to implement the decision of the Court of Appeal and demonstrated that Khama was unwilling to appoint Motumise. On 23 November, the Court of Appeal annulled a High Court decision that permitted civil servants to vote in party primary elections. Following this case, on 6 December, the BDP set party primaries in constituencies held by the opposition for January 2018 after they had been suspended in October pending a final determination of the case by the Court of Appeal. On 12 December, the High Court decided that a transgender woman would be allowed to change her records in the registry to be identified as a female rather than a male – evidence that issues affecting minorities remained a public issue.

Allegations and issues of *corruption, maladministration and money laundering* continued in the private media, with the state media maintaining its deafening silence. The matters raised included the long-standing and widely publicised 'Kgosi affair'; Khato Civils and its executive chairman, Simbi Phiri, who successfully brought a legal challenge to have his accounts unfrozen; and allegations of money laundering and possible corruption in the awarding of contracts by Minister of Land Management Water and Sanitation Services Prince Maele. The other major scandal that was widely reported in December was on the P (pula) 250 m (although some initial reports put it at P 326 m) missing from the National Petroleum Fund (NPF), for which Bakang Seretse, then managing director of Kgori Capital, Kenneth Kerekang, a former director of energy, and Botho Leburu, a director of Khulaco Management Services, were investigated and charged by the Directorate on Corruption and Economic Crime (DCEC) for money laundering. Reports suggested that Seretse's company had been responsible for managing the NPF from January 2016. The P 250 m was transmitted following a request by the director of the DISS, Isaac Kgosi, for use by the DISS to build "fuel storage tanks, before being diverted for alleged purchase of military hardware in Israel". No charge was laid against Kgosi, despite his reported involvement in the misappropriation of NPF funds. Furthermore, and disturbingly, the media reported that Minister of Resources, Green Technology and Energy Security Sadique Kebonang "sold three houses to Seretse for P 15 m …", suggesting a possible conflict of interest, but President Khama failed to sack him. In August, some senior officials of the DCEC, including Director General Rose Seretse, were redeployed; she was replaced on 1 September by Victor Paledi, a former deputy commissioner of police. Media reports suggested that their removal had to do with disclosures to the media of some high profile investigations the DCEC was conducting. As part of raising awareness on issues of corruption, Botswana celebrated the UN International Anti-Corruption Day in Gaborone on 11 December, when President Khama cautioned on the dangers posed by corruption. On 14 December, he commenced his farewell tour of the country ahead of his last day in office as president, 31 March 2018.

Foreign Affairs

Consistent with President Khama's *upfront policy*, on 19 January, Botswana expressed its disapproval of the decision of Gambia's President Yahya Jammeh not to concede defeat, and declared its non-recognition of his presidency and government forthwith. On 7 April, Botswana deplored the spiralling conflict and human rights abuses in Syria. It declared its disapproval of USA's withdrawal from the Paris Agreement on Climate Change on 2 June and its recognition of Jerusalem as the capital of Israel on 7 December. On 31 July and 30 November, Botswana condemned North Korea for carrying out ballistic missile tests and, on 3 May and 3 August, criticised Venezuela for "the continuing deterioration of democracy, governance as well as the rule of law". On 11 October, Botswana expressed its disagreement with a declaration of independence by the Spanish region of Catalonia, while on 13 October it applauded the Palestinian National Liberation Movement (Fatah) and the Islamic Resistance Movement (Hamas) for entering into a peace accord. On 16 October, Botswana denounced terrorist attacks in Somalia, and urged concerted efforts to contain terrorism. On 14 November, Botswana condemned the spiralling humanitarian catastrophes facing the Rohingya people in Myanmar, which it regarded as 'ethnic cleansing', and called for a cessation of violence and human rights violations.

Botswana preserved its *foreign relations*. Vice President Mokgweetsi Massi visited Japan on 16–20 January, attended the 6th TANA High level Forum on Security in Africa in Ethiopia on 22–23 April, and led the Botswana delegation to the 72nd session of the UN General Assembly on 17 September. Masisi also led Botswana's delegation to the 28th session of the Assembly of Heads of State and Government of the AU in Addis Ababa (Ethiopia) on 30–31 January. As expected, President Khama decided not to attend the 28th AU summit, at which Botswana's Minister of Foreign Affairs and International Cooperation Pelonomi Venson-Moitoi stood unsuccessfully as a candidate for the critical position of AU Commission chairperson. It was reported that some SADC states did not support her candidacy, although she had been recommended as the Southern Africa regional candidate in 2016. On 3 October, Zimbabwe's President Robert Mugabe blamed Khama for Venson-Moitoi's failure, an accusation that Botswana rebuffed on 5 October.

President Khama attended the 37th SADC ordinary summit for Heads of State and Government in Pretoria (South Africa) on 18 August. He visited Germany on 6 March, Mozambique on 24–26 April, Sweden on 19–21 June, the USA and Chile from 30 July to 2 August, Malta on 1–4 October and Zambia on 24 October. He attended the inauguration of Zimbabwe's President Emmerson Dambudzo Mnangagwa on 24 November, and that of Kenya's President Uhuru Kenyatta on 28 November. Minister Venson-Moitoi attended the 16th session of the Africa-Nordic Meeting of Foreign Ministers, led the Botswana delegation to the 5th summit of Heads of State and Government of Africa and the EU on 29–30 November, and attended the 106th session of the Council of Ministers of the ACP on 4–7 December. On 18 March, she also led the Botswana delegation to the SADC extraordinary summit of Heads of State and Government in Lozitha (Swaziland).

Several *high-level visits* took place during the year. Zambian President Edgar Lungu visited on 6–7 February and attended Botswana's Independence celebrations on 30 September; former US President George W. Bush and his wife visited on 4–5 April, Mozambican President Filipe Jacinto Nyusi on 24–26 April, and the minister of external relations of the Federative Republic of Brazil on 8–10 May. Zimbabwe's President Robert Mugabe, Kgosi Letsie III of Lesotho and former presidents Thabo Mbeki of South Africa, Armando Guebuza of Mozambique, and Sam Nujoma and Hifikepunye Pohamba of Namibia attended the funeral of Botswana's second president, Ketumile Masire, in Kanye on 29 June. South African President Jacob Zuma visited on 17 November to attend the 4th session of the Botswana-South Africa Bi-National Commission.

In August, the Tibetan spiritual leader, the *Dalai Lama* decided not to participate in a widely publicised Ubuntu Conference, organised by the Mind and Life Institute, a few days before it took place in Gaborone, citing his health. Another expected speaker who also withdrew a few days before was Botswana's former vice president, Ponatshego Kedikilwe. Botswana had pledged to extend "the normal courtesies" to him and President Khama had announced that he would meet him during the visit. As expected, the Dalai Lama's visit was opposed by China, but the government insisted that the visit was private.

Socioeconomic Developments

There were no major changes on the socio-economic front and the government maintained its key priority areas. GDP growth was estimated at 4.7% (up from 4.3% in 2016). The *2017/2018 budget* projected revenue at P 57.2 bn, while expenditure stood at P 59.5, but expenditure increased to P 61.9 bn following supplementary funding, thus increasing the deficit to P 2.42 bn from the projected P 2.35 bn. The government announced that the budget shortfall had arisen largely because of the need to provide for water and power projects and to sustain the Economic Stimulus Programme. On 18 May, it was reported that the government had secured a loan of P 1.5 bn from the World Bank to fund the Emergency Water Security and Efficiency Project, which was projected to cost P 1.6 bn. The main sources of revenue for the 2017/2018 budget were customs and excise at 29.8%, and followed by minerals at 28.6%, and non-mineral revenue at 21.6%. The country maintained steady foreign reserves, but with a decline to P 73.7 bn in December from P 76.8 bn in December 2016.

Inflation was contained within the Bank of Botswana target of 3–6 %, reported at 3.1% and 3.2% in January and December, respectively. The country also maintained a positive business environment, and this was affirmed by *positive credit ratings* by renowned agencies, securing A-/A-2 from Standard & Poor's and A2 from Moody's. In the World Economic Forum's 2017/2018 Global Competitiveness Index, Botswana was placed 63rd of the 138 countries assessed, compared with 64th in the 2016/2017 Index.

Despite this positive economic outlook, *socio-economic challenges* – poverty, unemployment, HIV/AIDS and inequality, persisted – calling for innovative strategies for tackling them for the sake of the country's stability. In order to cushion those adversely affected by social risks, the government maintained its social programmes for various groups, as in previous years. The government reported that unemployment had fallen to 17.7% in 2016 and, according to the results of a survey released by Statistics Botswana in January 2018, the poverty rate had fallen to 16.3% in 2015/2016 from 19.3% in 2009/2010. There were no reports of changes in inequality while the government declared in November that 308,067 people infected by HIV were receiving treatment, in line with the 2016 Treat All project. Mother-to-child transmission was put at 1.4% at the end of 2016. All these efforts were in line with government's commitment to eliminate AIDS by 2030 and the UNAIDS 90–90–90 target by 2020.

Lesotho

Roger Southall

The seven-party coalition government led by Prime Minister Phakalitha Mosisili, which had led the country since the February 2015 general election, lost a vote of no confidence in February. This followed the breakaway from the government by Monyane Moleleke, hitherto deputy leader of Mosisili's Democratic Congress (DC), in January, and his formation of a new party, the Alliance of Democrats (AD). Rather than resign, Mosisili advised King Letsie III to dissolve parliament. However, in the June election that followed, the All Basotho Convention (ABC) emerged as the largest party. Its leader, Tom Thabane, subsequently put together a new coalition composed of the ABC, the Basotho National Party (BNP), the Reformed Congress of Lesotho (RCL) and the AD and resumed the post of prime minister, which he had held prior to the 2015 election. One of the principal tasks of the new government was seen as the implementation of reforms to the security sector. However, the assassination of the army commander, Khoantle Motsomotso, by two senior officers in September indicated that the new government would face an uphill task in removing the Lesotho Defence Force (LDF) from the political arena.

 | DOI:10.1163/9789004367630_047

Domestic Politics

Mosisili's seven-party coalition, formed in 2015, had always been based upon fragile foundations. Its stability had been brought into question in November 2016 when it had emerged that Moleleke had forged an agreement with Thabane to oust Mosisili as prime minister, and to form a new coalition government. Subsequently, after Moleleke had been suspended from the DC in December 2016, he announced the formation of the AD in January. In effect, this constituted the externalisation of his *Lirurubele* faction from the DC, leaving Mosisili's *Lithope* faction as the core of that party. The *split within the DC* prompted the return of Tom Thabane on 12 February. He had fled to South Africa in June 2015 following the murder, by members of the LDF, of Brigadier-General Maaparankoe Mahao, whom he had appointed commander of the army prior to his defeat in the election of that year. He claimed he was risking his life by returning. Declaring that Mosisili no longer commanded a majority in parliament, he vowed to defeat him in a *vote of no confidence*.

The vote on 1 March resulted in Mosisili's defeat and Thabane backing Moleleke's bid to become Prime Minister. However, Mosisili declined to stand down, and urged the King to call a new election, which he did on 7 March, despite opposition objections. Lesotho's third *general election* in five years took place on 3 June. It was conducted peacefully, to the relief of Basotho citizens, for the campaign had been punctuated by fears that the LDF would stage a coup were the elections to be won by the opposition alliance led by Thabane.

The ABC leader had pledged to strip the army of political protection and carry out the reforms of the security sector that had been called for by the Phumaphi Commission. This had been appointed, under prompting by SADC to investigate the assassination of Mahao and to explore the deeper causes of Lesotho's chronic instability. However, its recommendations that individuals implicated in the murder of Mahao be suspended and prosecuted, and that a raft of reforms of the Constitution and the security sector be implemented had been consistently blocked by Mosisili.

Although the LDF denied any malicious intent, and the elections passed off in an orderly fashion, groups of armed soldiers hovered around a number of voting stations. The soldiers claimed that they had been brought in to assist the Independent Election Commission (IEC), but it was help that the IEC had not requested and had not wanted. An IEC spokesperson remarked to reporters that some voters had felt intimidated.

Be that as it may, the *election result* was to the liking of neither Mosisili nor the LDF. Mosisili's DC lost 17 seats, in its attenuated state after the defection of Moleleke, while Thabane's ABC, having marginally improved on its performance in the 2015 election, emerged as the largest party, with 46 seats in the 120 seat National Assembly, compared with the 30 for the DC and 11 for its ally, the Lesotho Congress of Democracy. Moleleke's AD followed up with nine seats, another new party, the Movement for Economic Change, won six, the BNP five, and the Popular Front for Democracy three, with five other parties taking one seat each, while a further 18 parties(!) won no seats at all. The results in a further three constituency seats, which recorded wins for the ABC, were declared null and void because the candidates had died during the election campaign.

Thabane's *coalition*, composed of the ABC, AD, BNP and RCL, together held 62 of the National Assembly's 120 seats. This was a narrow majority that could easily be overturned by the defection of the partners, or factions within the individual parties – a real danger, given the short lives of recent governments. Indeed, there remained widespread concern, even after Mosisili had conceded defeat, that he would continue to do his best to frustrate security sector reforms from behind the scenes by using his influence with the army.

Unsurprisingly, there was a major flurry of alarm when Thabane's estranged wife was murdered the day before the incoming prime minister's formal *inauguration*, which was endorsed by the attendance of South Africa's Deputy President Cyril Ramaphosa (along with a sizeable security detail). There were clear indications that Thabane would be taking over a deeply divided country. Mosisili had chosen not to make an exit speech, and the inauguration was boycotted by a number of members of the opposition. The tense state of affairs was made painfully clear by Thabane's refusal to accept a military security detail following his election, and opting for his own security arrangements.

Prior to his election, Thabane had floated the idea of demilitarising Lesotho's *security framework*, citing the particular example of Costa Rica as a country that had transitioned to an alternate defence arrangement whereby measures had been put in place to ensure strong civilian control over the army, the army had taken on a developmental role, and monies previously spent on the military had been diverted to spheres such as health and education. He combined this with explicit indications that the size of the army should be reduced.

As Prime Minister, Thabane was soon making commitments to improving the lot of Lesotho's impoverished population: ending hunger, reducing crime, clamping down on violence against women, and so on. However, it was not long before he was to be accused by the opposition of launching a 'reign of terror'. A long statement of *allegations by the opposition parties* was issued on 15 September, presenting a litany of complaints. These included accusations that Thabane had intervened to quash police investigations into the murder of his estranged wife, having removed the police commissioner from his post within a week of coming into office and replaced him with a retired police officer, who had disbanded the investigation team. It was also alleged that a female police officer, Senior Inspector Lerato Motseki, who had indicated that investigations into the murder of Lipolelo Thabane were progressing, was stripped naked by seven of her male colleagues and subjected to a beating. Police officers were further accused of beating up mourners at a funeral, who had been wearing blankets associated with the opposition; one of them was later found dead, with his body mutilated seemingly to remove evidence of bullet wounds. Tseliso Mokhosi MP, the former minister of defence, was also said to have been so tortured and mistreated by the police that he fled the country following his release after questioning.

Further complaints were that the new government had shut down a radio station, 'Mo-Afrika FM Radio', because it had broadcast news unwelcome to the authorities, only allowing it back on air following an order from the High Court; that there had been a succession of dismissals from key posts – the head of the police, the National Security Service (NSS) and the Correctional Service, along with the unconstitutional removal of the president of the Court of Appeal – followed by the appointment of Pheello Ralenkoane, who had stood at a candidate for the BNP in the recent elections, as the new director of the NSS; that many students had not received their stipends from the National Manpower Development Secretariat, which fomented a state of unrest in tertiary education institutions; and that, as a result of "intimidation, humiliation and suppression of the Opposition", the leader and deputy leader of the LCD (Mothetjoa Metsing MP and Tselios Mokhosi MP respectively), along with the deputy leader of the DC, Mathibeli Mokhothu MP, who was also the official Leader of the Opposition in parliament, had been forced to flee the country.

The various individual complaints that the opposition document listed suggested that the new government was unlikely to prove less intolerant than its predecessor, despite Thabane's explicit commitment to opening up political space. The opposition allegations were backed to some extent by AI, which in September declared that Thabane's first 100 days in office had fallen short in tackling the deeply entrenched culture of impunity for past *human rights* violations.

Ten days before the publication of the opposition's document, Lesotho had been rocked by *fears of yet another coup*, with the gunning down of the new commander of the army, General Khoantle Motsomotso on 5 September. He was assassinated by two fellow officers, Brigadier Bulane Sechele and Colonel Tefo Hashatsi, known as fervent supporters of former army boss Tlali Kamoli. Both had been under criminal investigation for the assassination of Mahao, and they in turn were killed by Motsomotso's bodyguards as they attempted to flee his compound. Given the internal divisions within the army and the opposition's resistance to external intervention, the quest for political stability in Lesotho remained as elusive as ever.

Foreign Affairs

Mosisili's relations with SADC were rendered increasingly tense, first, by the promotion of some 32 officers in the days running up to the election, and second, by the leak of a letter in which the LDF had sought permission from the authorities to be allocated 22 pieces of land around the country. This was seen as an attempt by the army to place soldiers in strategic locations, from which they would be able to intimidate voters or unleash a reign of terror if the elections were won by the opposition alliance. The fears they generated were sufficient to prompt stern warnings from SADC, and notably from South Africa, that any military intervention or attempted theft of the election by Mosisili would not be tolerated.

Following his election, Thabane therefore looked for strong *backing from SADC* to implement the Phumpahi Commission's recommended reforms. Nonetheless, the thrust of the opposition's complaints published on 15 September seemed to be directed at calling into question Thabane's efforts to bring about reforms of the security sector. In particular, the opposition called for the establishment of a joint multi-party security mechanism in which both government and the opposition would be represented, and objected to any notion of bringing in 'foreign troops' (i.e. from SADC) to supervise reforms within the security sector.

The latest assassinations resulted in a flurry of *action by SADC*. Angola's Minister of Foreign Affairs Georges Rebelo Chikoti arrived in Maseru on 6 September, the day after the murder of General Khoantle Motsomotso, to assess the situation ahead of a larger SADC team, which arrived a few days later. Subsequently, on 15 September, a SADC summit committed to the deployment of a contingency force, including military and intelligence officers and civilian experts, to determine the size and nature of a more extensive deployment of personnel. This was followed by a decision to deploy a force of 1,200 military personnel and security experts in the near future. President Jacob Zuma of South Africa appealed to political actors to work together to bring about peace and stability, observing that SADC could not be expected to be involved in Lesotho's internal affairs forever. In many ways, SADC's involvement was a re-run of earlier events, for it had sought to implement reforms designed to remove the army from the political arena following the disputed 1998 election.

Socio-Economic Developments

During the year, the country's energies were almost completely absorbed by the volatility of the political situation. The *budget*, presented by the new Finance Minister Moeketsi Majoro on 19 July, was officially devoted to "pursuing fiscal sustainability within the context of political instability and insecurity". However, it amounted to little more than a repetition of the woes that had afflicted Lesotho's economy for years. Growth was minimal, at just over 2% for 2016/17; the balance of payments had deteriorated following a drop in receipts from SACU, stagnant remittance incomes, an inability to generate internal revenues and popular pressures for upward wages.

The minister pointed to the risks of growing indebtedness, and Lesotho's dependence upon imports and failure to increase exports.

Despite affirmations that the government was implementing a more stringent *fiscal strategy* aimed at returning Lesotho to a sustainable fiscal path, the budget included targeted revenue for the fiscal year of M (maluti) 12,808 m, a predicted shortfall of M 720.9 m, and predicted current expenditure of M 12,359 m. A total appropriation of M 17,423 m (inclusive of capital expenditure) was therefore heavily dependent upon a reduction of government financial reserves and borrowing. Foreign financial and other support, notably favourable continued access to the US market for textile exports under the AGOA scheme, was widely depicted as dependent upon the government's ability to implement the security reforms required to bring about peace and stability.

Madagascar

Richard R. Marcus

Continued institutional fragility, downward economic pressures, poor governance, and increased opacity added to the political spiral for another year. President Hery Martial Rajaonarimampianina struggled to find wins he could boast of. Popular support could at best be considered anaemic. The private sector was showing signs of impatience with reforms. A notable handful of close advisors were accused of corruption and political space became taken up with preparations for the 2018 presidential elections. The opposition and international community alike levelled accusations that changes were meant to delay elections and invalidate the candidacy of Rajaonarimampianina's predecessors. A political vacuum emerged amidst significant fracturing. Rajaonarimampianina's electoral prospects were poor; Ravalomanana and Rajoelina remained the leading challengers but with narrow support. The way forward on the electoral code and constitution had the potential to further undermine political stability and the population had entered a state of malaise.

 | DOI:10.1163/9789004367630_048

Domestic Politics

Each year of Rajaonarimampianina's presidency had been replete with fears of a *coup d'état* and 2017 was no different. The level of government incompetence combined with political fissures and economic stagnation exceeded those that had existed when Marc Ravalomanana had been overthrown in March 2009. Yet Madagascar was structurally different from coup-riven countries in Africa. Military leadership is part of the civil service, embedded in the existing political dynamic, and continued to benefit from patterns of rent-seeking. A coup was thus only possible if an external financier supported a marginalised military faction. Rumours of such funds being floated grew throughout the year, but at no point materialised.

There was a minor *cabinet reshuffle* on 25 August with Minister of Industry and Private Sector Development Armand Tazafy and Minister of Commerce and Consumer Affairs Nourdine Chabani switching jobs, and Minister of Transport Benjamina Ramarcel Ramanantsoa promoted to presidential special projects. However, the significant change was the return of Henry Rabary-Njaka, a longstanding confidant of the president, as minister of foreign affairs. A partner in a Paris law firm specialising in business rights, he had served as presidential chief of staff (2014–15) and secretary general of the president's party, New Forces for Madagascar (HVM). While not welcomed by the international community, the move was seen as further securing a tight circle around the president.

Corruption remained a significant issue. TI, with an office in Antananarivo, ranked Madagascar 155th of 180 countries in its 2017 Corruption Perceptions Index, with a score of 24 (well below the regional average of 32 and a drop from 26 in 2016, 28 in 2015 and 32 during the transitional – and illegitimate – presidency of Andry Rajoelina). TI also stated that more than half of the Malagasy population thought corruption had increased. The World Bank's Country Policy and Institutional Assessment, Bertelsmann Foundation, and the Varieties of Democracy Project all similarly found increases in corruption, pointing to it as a significant cause for concern. A number of members of Rajaonarimampianina's inner circle were ensnared in scandals. Most notable was the *Claudine Affair*. Claudine Razaimamonjy, a close advisor of the president, was arrested on 3 April for misappropriation of public funds, favouritism, falsification of public documents, abuse of function, and money laundering for activities related to 13 communes. At her hearing, Razaimamonjy claimed that the charges brought by the 'Bureau Indépendant Anti-Corruption' (BIANCO) were politically motivated and "the beginning of an operation to overthrow the Rajaonarimampianina regime". The international community, led by US Ambassador Robert Yamate, largely applauded the legal process, while press commentators were quick to point out the unusual strength shown by BIANCO and the perception of weakness shown by Rajaonarimampianina in being unable to protect someone hitherto deemed untouchable.

The Claudine Affair drove a deeper wedge between the executive and the *judiciary*. In early July, magistrates went on strike in order to protest against mounting government efforts to intervene in judicial processes at multiple levels. SeFaFi (a human rights NGO) released a report on 7 October supporting the judicial action and criticising government opacity. These events compounded existing tensions over the unconstitutional unwillingness of the president to allow the establishment of the High Court of Justice.

The struggle with *institutional reforms* continued. Social sector institutions remained weak and lacked vertical accountability. High-rent sectors such as mining, despite having strong legal codes, saw continued poor enforcement and accountability. Trust in the National Assembly waned. Both transparency and accountability were victims undermined by fiscal policy, investment and political processes. Nowhere was this clearer than with regard to the Electoral Code and the Constitution. In September, President Rajaonarimampianina ordered a review of the 2010 Constitution of the Fourth Republic, viewed by many as a flawed document, both self-contradictory and uninterpretable in key areas. The Electoral Code also has recognised flaws such as the voter registration system, registration transparency and accountability, and cost of access. Workshops on reform held in August included the Independent National Electoral Commission (CENI), political parties, civil society organisations and government. With no agreement, the government took unilateral control of the process, creating a closed inter-ministerial committee. While constitutional and Electoral Code reforms were viewed as a necessity, the timing and nature of efforts were broadly viewed as aimed at benefiting Rajaonarimampianina rather than rectifying structural concerns. Specifically, the opposition saw these as efforts to invalidate the candidacies of his leading opponents, Marc Ravalomanana of the 'Tiako I Madagasikara' (TIM) party, and Andriy Rajoelina, of the Mapar party, and delay elections. These accusations were heightened when, on 26 October, the inter-ministerial committee held a meeting where Prime Minister Mahafaly refused to set up a legal framework but formally opposed the draft law championed by the CENI. Should the effort to use the Electoral Code fail, Rajaonarimampianina hinted that he would try to invoke Article 25(4) of the African Charter on Democracy, Elections and Governance, which bars perpetrators of unconstitutional change, in order to block Rajoelina from running in 2018, and citing Ravalomanana's conviction in absentia in the February 2009 murder of protestors by presidential guards, in order to block his candidacy.

Law 2016–029 *Code of Communication* had been passed on 14 July 2016 but its impacts were first widely felt in 2017. While the intention was to ensure the quality of reporting, journalists argued that it would be used to trump up charges of false news and defamation to spread fear of fines and worse. Private media had long been tied to individual politicians with a conflation of ownership and patrimony with political reporting. In 2017, President Rajaonarimampianina enjoyed the support of such outlets as SkyOne TV and SkyOne Radio, Le Citoyen and Akon'nyMadagasikara, Dream'on, Dream'in, On Air, AZ Radio, I-BC, AZ Tele, La ligne, de mire, Triatra, La Depeche and La Chasse aux infos. L'Express de Madagascar, Ao Raha and Radio Television Analamanga also supported the president but the future remained unclear as they were owned by the former appointed mayor of Antananarivo and potential presidential candidate Edgar Razafindravahy. The Malagasy Broadcasting System (owned by Marc Ravalomanana), Viva radio and television networks (owned by Andry Rajoelina), and the Midi Madagasikara newspaper group were consistently critical.

Civil society has been historically weak and has frequently experienced vertical divisions between politically captured leaders and constituencies, undermining the efficacy of civil society organisations. The FFKM (Council of Christian Churches) has nonetheless managed to play an important mediating political role as part of a broader pattern of *church-led reconciliation* dating to the period of the monarchy. Its political role, most notable in the 1992 conflict, gathered steam again starting in January. The leader of the Lutheran Church, Pastor David Rakotonirina, did not attend an event with the president at Iavoloha Palace. Bishop Odon Arsène Razanakolona (Catholic Church), Monsignor Samoela Lala Ranarivelo (Episcopalian Church) and Pastor Irako Ammi Andriamahazosoa (Protestant Church) attended but showed little deference. The FFKM emerged as renewed powerbroker, challenging the president's move to an inter-ministerial committee on electoral reform and efforts to delegitimise the candidacies of Ravalomanana and Rajoelina.

Zafy Albert, president of Madagascar from 1993 to 1996, died on 13 October at the age of 90. His presidency had been stormy and he was ultimately impeached on charges of corruption. Yet, he was remembered for his role in the creation of Madagascar's Third Republic and his influence as an elder statesmen and leader of the National Reconciliation Committee. Many of those close to him had since been jockeying to inherit his political legacy in advance of elections, most notably former prime minister Jean Omer Beriziky.

Governance indicators (Mo Ibrahim Index, V-Dem, World Bank and Freedom House) indicated modest gains over the previous five years. However, key areas, including accountability and access to healthcare and education had continued to deteriorate and progress remained far short of the aspirations that came with the return to a democratic process. Moreover, the starting point was low, with Freedom House giving a total freedom rating of 56/100, comparable to Bhutan and Guatemala. Progress had been slow and political entrepreneurs had learned to profit on the sidelines, making it very difficult to promote change and leading to criticism from international organisations. Heading into 2018, Madagascar appeared on the brink of a crisis marked by distrust, institutional incapacity and political stalemate.

Foreign Affairs

ODA dropped slightly to 6.5% of GNI, according to 2016 figures. The World Bank remained the largest donor at $ 212 m, followed by the US ($ 134.7 m), the EU ($ 80.8 m) and France ($ 77.8 m). During the political crisis (2009–13), international donors overwhelmingly discontinued direct work with the government, shifting funding to education, health, humanitarian aid and other areas where direct support was most feasible. In 2017, access to social services remained a priority for both multilateral and bilateral doors, but improving governance and fostering economic recovery continued to grow in importance. The World Bank's funding priorities were coordinated with the government's new national development plan. For their parts, the US concentrated efforts in humanitarian areas, as well as health, water and environmental change, and the EU focused on social sectors, local authorities and non-state actor support, food security, gender issues, democracy and human rights, climate change adaptation, and environment. In addition to foreign aid, *France* remained Madagascar's largest trading partner (with total imports and exports amounting to € 974 m), its leading customer (taking 22% of the country's exports), and its leading source of tourists (approximately 50%). The *IMF* Executive Board completed its second ECF review with an announcement on 6 December. The general position was that the economic programme as supported by the ECF was strong, owing to success in meeting key medium term fiscal objectives for regulatory reform, revenue performance, and international reserves. This warranted dispersal of $ 44.5 m.

Turkey's President Recep Tayyip Erdoğan visited on 25 January, creating warmer relations. While the governments agreed on exchanges of electronic media programs, diplomatic training and financial assistance to the armed forces, the new closer relations raised questions in parts of the international community about Madagascar's relationship with a leader broadly accused of leading his country away from greater transparency and accountability. While Rajaonarimampianina sought to develop relations with *China*, particularly in extractive resource sectors, Madagascar faced challenges in paying its bills to some Chinese companies, such as the China Harbour Engineering Company, stoking concerns.

Foreign relations are often viewed in Madagascar in terms of the opportunities created for individuals and 2017 saw significant efforts by advisors close to Rajaonarimampianina to court foreign investors for his 2018 campaign. Rajaonarimampianina used the occasion of a *state visit to Paris* on 28 June to meet with a French strategic intelligence and lobbying organisation to support his 2018 campaign run. Rajoelina spent significant portions of the year in France, where he courted support. Ravalomanana returned to Paris and Denmark in late May and was in Montreal on 19–22 June accompanying his wife in connection with her work as mayor of Antananarivo. All such moves raised questions about mingling public, party and private activities.

Madagascar's permanent representative at the *UN* was Zina Andrianarivelo-Razafy. UNICEF, UNDP and other agencies were intensively involved in humanitarian efforts, including $ 20 m in cyclone relief in March, food airlifts in March and April, and plague monitoring through the year starting with the August outbreak. UN Under-Secretary General Haile Menkerios visited in early October in an effort to stave off political turmoil and stressed the need to hold elections in 2018. While he appeared as standard bearer for the international community, Menkerios had been UN Special Envoy to Madagascar during the political crisis, perhaps undermining some of his ability, and that of the UN agencies, to influence outcomes.

Socioeconomic Developments

The IMF forecast that GDP would rise to between 4.1% and 5.1% in 2018. Yet, GNI had fallen from $ 440 m in 2014 to $ 400 m in 2016 (most recent data), possibly implying a drop in capital transfers. Madagascar continued to remain *vulnerable to economic shocks*. The country's 0.512 on the UNDP HDI made it 158th out of 186 countries on the list, according to the most recent data (2016). Expenditure on public health and education remained a low at 1.5% and 2.1% of GDP, respectively. Some 64.3% of the population lived in rural areas according to World Bank data. According to UNDP, 78% of the population were living on under $ 1.90 per day, 90% on under $ 3.10 per day (purchasing power parity), and 86% remained vulnerable. The level of child labour remained high, with nearly a quarter of 5–14-year-olds working. The HDI reflected that the richest quintile of the population averaged 9.8 years of schooling compared with 1.7 years for the poorest quintile. The rural poor were far less likely to learn reading, writing, mathematics and other critical skills and had become trapped in a poverty cycle. Similar stagnation was also notable in gender development with a World Bank's Country Policy and Institutional Assessment score (2016) of 4.0, comparable to Azerbaijan, Lesotho and Uzbekistan, and rates for women in adult literacy were consistently below the average. Literacy overall had dropped from over 70% in 2000 to 64.7% in the most recent measure (2015), and in equality of opportunity.

While there were modest gains in the economy and greater regulatory stability, the impacts were not felt by the population overall. *Agriculture* remained the main source of income for 80% of the population; the fall in rice production (the food staple) by 20% compared with 2016 was catastrophic for many. While there was a widespread assumption that rice prices were manipulated as part of a political game in which poverty became an electoral tool, the increase in rice prices combined with increased commodity prices drove inflation up to 9%.

Madagascar saw an outbreak of *pneumonic plague* first reported 23 August. While vector-borne bubonic plague, affecting the lymph nodes, has been endemic and public health facilities have been attuned, pneumonic plague, based in lung tissue and highly infectious, has been uncommon. By the time it was brought under control on 20 November, 2,267 cases and 195 deaths had been reported. There was significant criticism of the government's early response and accusations that this was another sign of government incapacity. The WHO intervention team classified the event as a Grade 2 emergency and joined the inter-ministerial team in creating surveillance, community engagement, case management, communications and logistics.

Madagascar has long been the world's largest producer of *vanilla*, producing approximately 75% of world supply, but 2017 was an historically bad year with a harvest of only approximately 1,500 tonnes (a fall of 20%), which drove prices to near record highs of $ 550/kg at year's end. The 1,500% increase in vanilla prices in 2014–17 was a boon to large producers, but local farmers received more modest benefit. The high price drove some buyers to purchase artificial vanilla and others out of the market altogether. The pattern was similar to that of 2004, when the drop to nearly 10% of value year on year led to severe impacts on local populations. In that time rent-seeking in both the vanilla sector and the illicit rosewood sector, sharing overlapping labour and commodity pools in the north eastern Sava region, made potential vulnerability all the greater.

There was some *progress* in areas such as customs reform, financial resilience and social inclusion. Rajaonarimampianina did not ultimately succeed in building more private sector confidence, but he did successfully encourage external investment. High vanilla prices and surging investment in mining bolstered GDP, offering new opportunities and a workable budget profile. The government worked particularly hard to court Chinese investment, going so far as to send officials from the Ministry of Mines to take part in a seminar in Beijing from 7 to 27 June in an effort to increase Sino-Malagasy mining relations.

The World Bank's *Doing Business Index* ranked Madagascar 162nd of 190 countries, a slight improvement over 2016, driven by increases in the potential to obtain credit. Core areas such as electricity supply, resolving insolvency and enforcing contracts remained troublingly low. *Extractive resource industries* continued to be a bright spot for private sector activities. With a long history of artisanal mining, there were more than 100,000 jobs in the sector but they provided low incomes and accounted for less than 1% of GDP. World Bank projections pointed to continued increases in chromium, nickel, cobalt, ilmenite and zirsill, and possibly zircon and iron ore. Mining could account for as much as 14% of GDP by 2025, equivalent to an increase in GDP of $ 554 m per year, from $ 10 bn in 2016 to $ 16.5 bn, heralding significant and long-term royalties, corporate taxes and other financial windfalls. On the other hand, nascent projects such as Tulear Sands and Wisco demonstrated the high social risks. Local populations near the Ranobe mine of Tulear Sands, for instance, originally welcomed the potential jobs but then became angry and disillusioned, and accused the owners (Australian mining company World Titanium Resources Ltd) of not supporting its commitments, stealing land rights, destroying rural livelihoods and cultural landscape, and resorting to lies. Demonstrations against the company took place in Andaboly, Tulear, on 4 June. The challenge was how to ensure that massive profits by a small number of companies – Kraoma, Ambatovy, QMM, Sakoa, Toliara Sands, and Wisco – would translate into gains not only in GDP but for ailing social and job sectors, and reduce soaring wage gaps and intransigent poverty.

Malawi

George Dzimbiri and Lewis Dzimbiri

President Mutharika and his allies continued to face numerous criticisms over poor governance and the involvement of one of his key ministers in a scandal popularly known as 'Maizegate'. The anger worsened as the president continued to shield his former cabinet minister of agriculture, who was allegedly involved in the affair. The year also witnessed by-elections in three constituencies and three local government wards. The opposition Malawi Congress Party (MCP) won in five of the six and the governing Democratic Progressive Party (DPP) in just one. Electricity outages dominated the year, as the Electricity Generation Company of Malawi only managed to generate half of the power needed, leading to persistent, longer and more intensive load shedding in most parts of the country. For the first time in more than six years, inflation remained in single digits at 9.3% during the second quarter of the year, resulting in banks narrowing the interest rate gap. There were various kinds of industrial action, particularly strikes in both private and public sector organisations, calling for wage increases, other benefits and improved working conditions.

 | DOI:10.1163/9789004367630_049

Domestic Politics

Intra-and inter-party conflicts characterised the domestic scene. *Intra-party conflicts* were noticeable in both the ruling DPP and opposition parties. On 17 January, President Peter Mutharika said some DPP members from the northern region would have to leave the party if they were not ready to work with the current leadership because they were pushing for the removal of the regional governor, Kenneth Sanga. The president said this in Mzuzu during a meeting held at a tourist lodge, aimed at uniting two factions of the party that had emerged in the region.

The *opposition* MCP was also beset by internal conflicts. On 10 February, its National Executive Committee fired the outspoken Salima North West MP, Jessie Kabwila, from her post as MCP publicity secretary and veteran Lilongwe Mapuyu South MP, Joseph Njobvuyalema, from his post as deputy director of internal affairs. The meeting resolved to re-instate James Chatonda Kaunda as first deputy secretary general. During October, tension started simmering in the Alliance for Democracy (AFORD) ahead of the party's convention scheduled for 16 December in the Central Region. There were disagreements between the party president, Enock Chihana, and the Revamp AFORD Movement (Ramo), a grouping that had been at the centre of activities to resuscitate the party. Chihana had threatened to fire all party members affiliated to Ramo, accusing the pressure group of overstepping its mandate and thus dividing the party.

Inter-party conflicts became a typical feature of the year. On 12 January, the DPP accused the leader of the opposition, Lazarus Chakwera, of plotting against the government to push for a subsidised maize price in Agricultural Development and Marketing Corporation (ADMARC) depots. In his statement, the acting DPP secretary general, Francis Mphepo, claimed that Chakwera and others would easily incite violence because of 'Maizegate', but Chakwera laughed off the claims and accusations as mere propaganda. In a related development, on 14 January, the Umodzi party president, John Chisi, had denounced President Mutharika for shielding cabinet ministers suspected of involvement in corruption and misappropriation of public resources. Chisi was speaking in response to the dubious procurement of maize from Zambia by ADMARC. Mutharika also came under pressure because of his seeming inaction over the alleged theft of K (kwacha) 236 bn from the government. The perennial allegations that seven members of Mutharika's cabinet were among those who had stolen the money resurfaced and occupied newspaper headlines. On 16 January, DPP and MCP supporters clashed in Chiradzulu district during memorial prayers for Reverend John Chilembwe. The violence started when some DPP supporters intimidated MCP supporters dressed in party colours accompanied by Chakwera, their party president. The DPP accused the MCP supporters of encroaching on their territory. On 26 March, Uladi Mussa, the president of the former ruling party, the People's Party (PP), called on Mutharika to resign within 30 days because of high levels of nepotism and tribalism, favouritism and ill-will in dealing with corruption, tax on water, university fee rises and the increase in the maize price. The government responded that the PP had no moral ground for accusing Mutharika of corruption because the country had experienced higher levels of corruption when the PP was in government. On 26 September, the DPP was accused of unleashing terror against MCP supporters when they were competing for the Nsanje Lalanje parliamentary seat. On 27 September, some people believed to be DPP sympathisers, invaded the MCP constituency removing flags and harassing MCP supporters. The MCP regional chairperson for the south, Peter Simbi, said he had been informed that the DPP had brought these people from Ndirande, Bangwe and Nancholi townships in Blantyre to terrorise the constituency. On 18 November, Mutharika attacked Chakwera in parliament, suggesting that the MCP leader was mentally unstable and should undergo psychiatric assessment. The president was responding to Chakwera's attack on his opening address to the 47th session of parliament on 10 November.

The government was also in conflict with civil society organisations (CSOs) over various *governance and corruption* issues. On 19 January, the NGO gender coordination network criticised Mutharika for not including women on the newly appointed ADMARC board. In early January, Mutharika had appointed James Masumbu as chair of the all-male board, which included Stain Singo, Paramount Chief Gomani, Jafali Mussa, Ken Ndanga and Chancy Gondwe, among others. Mutharika also appointed a new University of Malawi board, which included Professor Jack Wirima as chair and Press Corporation Chief Executive Officer George Partridge and Justice Duncan Tambala as members.

On 9 February, Mutharika fired Minister of Agriculture, Irrigation and Water Development George Chaponda as leader of the house in parliament over his involvement in the maize procurement scandal, 'Maizegate', to pave the way for investigations. Chaponda was replaced as leader of the house by Minister of Local Government and Rural Development Kondwani Nankhumwa. However, he retained his position as minister of agriculture, irrigation and water development and some CSOs, the Malawi Law Society and other citizens were not happy with this. They eventually, held a nation-wide demonstration on 17 February to force Mutharika to dismiss Chaponda from this position too. On 2 March, CSOs organised demonstrations aimed at petitioning Mutharika to deal with corruption at the highest level.

On 26 November, the Malawi Electoral Support Network and 16 other CSOs pressured the government to keep to its word and put the *Electoral and Local Government Amendment Bill* on the agenda for the current parliamentary session. The six proposed laws were missing from the Order Paper, but in an evasive statement Minister of Justice and Constitutional Affairs Samuel Tembenu said he would table them. The CSOs' demand came after the Public Affairs Committee (PAC), a grouping of faith-based non-governmental and human rights organisations, petitioned Mutharika and Speaker Nankhumwa to table the bills by 30 November, threatening to mobilise nation-wide street protests if nothing was done. On 29 September, after the discovery that the government was forcing some state agencies to fund its party's activities, CSOs appealed to the DPP to desist from this abuse of power.

The main parties, the DPP, PP UDF and MCP, prepared for *by-elections* held on 17 October, when the MCP candidate Lawrence Sitolo won the Nsanje Lalanje constituency with 8,775 votes, ahead of the DPP's Gladys Ganda with 5,453 votes and the independent candidate Winnie Wakudyanaye with 194. In Lilongwe City South East, MCP candidate Ulemu Msungama won with 6,722 votes, followed by the DPP's Reuben Ngwenya with 3,597. Ellen Kadango and Christopher Manja received 311 and 891 votes, respectively. Sosten Gwengwe, was declared the winner in Lilongwe Msozi North Constituency with 10,015 votes, defeating the DPP's Bruno Daka (2,559 votes). In Ndirande Makata Ward, MCP candidate Thom Litchowa was declared the winner with 969 votes against 910 for the DPP's Thom Lita, 363 for Ishmael Chilambo of the UDF and 114 for the PP's Mathews Shawa. In Mtsiriza Ward, MCP candidate Frank Zikaola got 921 votes compared with 825 for Julio Benedicto Jumbe of the DPP and 169 for the UDF. In Mayani North Ward, a DPP candidate won the seat with 2,390 votes against 1,690 for the MCP candidate and 219 for the UDF candidate.

Various *legislative bills* kept parliament busy. On 10 January, the vagrancy law, which had stirred excitement in various quarters, was annulled: a panel of three judges, Michael Mtambo, Zione Ntaba and Slivester Kalembera, sitting in the High Court in Blantyre, declared Section 184 (1c) of the penal code, which punished rogue and vagabond behaviour, unconstitutional on the grounds that the law was too broad and gave the police too much power to arrest perceived criminals. On 8 February, Mutharika assented to the National Parks and Wildlife Act, which a development minister of natural resources energy and mines said would help clean up Malawi's image with respect to the ivory trade and other wild life crimes. On 8 February, members of parliament also passed the Financial Crime Bill, which was aimed at avoiding the negative consequences of using weak laws to deal with money laundering and terrorist financing offences. On 15 February, Mutharika assented to this bill as well as to the long awaited Access to Information Bill, which would enable citizens to access government information in line with constitutional provision. The government had previously attempted to water down the bill, which had led to a protracted war of words between the government and CSOs. On 15 February, parliament raised the marital age from 16 to 18 years.

On the Mo Ibrahim Governance Index, Malawi fell to 18th out of 54 African nations. The report showed that, overall, Malawi had remained stagnant over the decade with regard to good *governance and accountability* indicators.

Foreign Affairs

On 29 January, Mutharika left for the AU heads of state summit in Addis Ababa (Ethiopia). Speaking at his departure, Mutharika said that he would present Malawi's case under the topic 'Harnessing the Demographic Dividend through Investments in the Youth'. On 5 February, the governments of Malawi and Tanzania signed a joint permanent Commission of Cooperation agreement amid the long-standing wrangle over the ownership of *Lake Malawi*. The agreement had been arrived at through discussion by a three-member committee comprising three former presidents, Joachim Chissano of Mozambique, Thabo Mbeki of South Africa and Festus Mogae of Botswana.

Malawi continued to enjoy good relations with other countries and international agencies and received *international financial support*. On 11 January, the Royal Norwegian Embassy made a grant of K 2.3 bn through Save the Children to implement an inclusive education project to keep learners in school. On 17 February, the United States government donated $ 4.6 m (about K 3.3 bn) for humanitarian food assistance. A press release from the US Embassy said the donation was in response to the report by the Malawi Vulnerability Assessment Committee, which estimated that 6.7 m people needed food assistance to alleviate suffering. On 4 March, the EU disbursed € 560 m (about K 431 bn) towards programme support over the coming six years. The funding was meant to support growth in Malawi through collaboration with government and other stakeholders to develop programmes focused on addressing private sector needs. On 8 March, the Global Fund gave Malawi close to $ 450 m (about K 323 bn) to support tuberculosis, AIDS and malaria programmes that promoted access to free medicine. On 16 March, DfID announced that it would stop supporting the Farm Input Subsidy Programme from July, thereby depriving the programme of about £700,000 (about K 630 m). DfID had been a key partner of the government in the programme since its inception in 2005. On 26 March, the governments of Malawi and the People's Republic of China signed an agreement under which China would donate $ 15 m (about K 11 bn) for the construction of five community colleges. The two governments also signed a three-year $2.2 m (about K 1.6 bn) agreement for disaster relief and office equipment. On 23 March, Germany gave the Ministry of Education, Science and Technology 7.4 m primary school textbooks valued at K 4 bn to help improve the quality of education.

Socioeconomic Developments

On 24 January, the *World Bank* gave hope that Malawi would finally access budgetary support amounting to $ 80 m before the end of the 2016/2017 financial year. The news came after the visit of World Bank Vice-President for Africa Makhtar Diop, who expressed confidence in the success of Malawi's public finance management reforms. In the 2015/16 financial year, the government had not met conditions for receiving budgetary support from World Bank and the EU, but Diop believed that important progress had been made on public finance management, especially in auditing of accounts and reconciliation.

On 26 January, Malawi was downgraded in TI's *Corruption Perception Index*: out of 176 countries assessed, Malawi slumped from 120th in 2015 to 112th in 2016, with an unchanging score of 31 points out of 100. The 2016 results showed that, despite the score shifting marginally from 37 to 31 since 2012, the country's rating over the previous four years had followed a consistent downward trend, reflecting the perception of the general public that corruption had worsened.

The *local currency* (kwacha) remained stable against the US dollar. It appreciated against the Zambian kwacha in January, but depreciated against sterling, the euro, the Japanese yen, the Chinese yuan and the South African rand in the review month. Inflationary pressures eased in January as headline *inflation* decelerated by 1.8% to 18.2% in December 2016. The 12-month average inflation rate in January 2017 stood at 21.3%, marginally down from 22.0% recorded in a comparable period in 2016, as a result of a drop in food inflation by 3.3% to 21.1% and in non-food inflation by 0.4% to 15.0%. On 15 September, Malawi's inflation as measured by the Consumer Price Index hit single digits at 9.3% for the first time in more than six years, according to the National Statistics Office. The drop in inflation compelled the Reserve Bank of Malawi to reduce the bank rate from 22% to 18% in July, triggering commercial banks to reduce their lending rates to 25% from 27% from 7 September. Gross official reserves were estimated at $ 605.2 m in January, compared with $ 602.7 m in December 2016. Prospective import coverage remained constant at 2.9 months.

On 19 May, Minister of Finance, Economic Planning, and Development Goodall Gondwe presented the 2017/2018 *national budget*, which was pegged at K 1,297.2 bn (K 1.3 trn), an increase of 26.1% on the 2016/2017 revised budget of K 977.8 bn. This represented a 13.5% increase at current prices, but a decline in real terms. Total revenue and grants were projected to increase by 13.3%, a slight reduction. Grants were projected to decline by 8.4% and domestic revenue to increase by 17.0%, remaining at the same level in real terms.

Charges for *public utilities* continued to increase. The Electricity Supply Commission of Malawi (ESCOM) and the three water boards, Blantyre, Lilongwe and Northern Region, increased their tariffs in September. Water charges rose by 10% and electricity by 2.5%. In July, the cost of living in Malawi's four cities, Lilongwe, Zomba, Blantyre and Mzuzu, rose by about 2.7% compared with June due to increases in the prices of food and non-food items. According to a Centre for Social Concern report, the average cost of living for a household of six in the four cities rose to K 120,500 from about K 117,000, and Blantyre had the most expensive basic needs basket at K 131,500, followed by Lilongwe at K 124,500 and Zomba at K 112,500.

Tobacco earnings fell by $ 276.4 m, representing an 18% drop, as a result of over production, which allowed buyers to offer lower prices. During the 2016/2017 season, farmers produced 195 m kilos of tobacco, compared with 193 m produced and sold the previous year. High rejection rates and low prices affected sales. On average, a tobacco leaf was fetching $ 1.50 on all the auction floors during the first few days but as the time progressed prices fell to $ 1.00. Buyers and tobacco authorities expressed concern over the presence of non-tobacco materials in tobacco bails, a perennial occurrence in recent years.

Electricity outages were a regular phenomenon. ESCOM reduced supply by over 60%, which prompted a drastic load shedding programme that saw some areas having no power for over 24 hours. ESCOM attributed the situation to low water levels in Lake Malawi. Fluctuating levels of water in Lake Malawi and the Shire River were regularly given as explanations for constant electricity blackouts throughout the year.

The *child mortality* rate had fallen by 73% over 24 years: during September, for example, the number of children who died before the age of five had been reduced to 64 per 1,000 live births, compared with 234 in September 1992. The success was attributed to the work of community health workers in awareness campaigns on hygiene, child care, preventive healthcare and other primary healthcare activities among villagers.

Labour disputes escalated in all sectors of the economy. On 16 January, members of staff at Mzuzu University turned down a 10% salary increase offered by the University's Council in a closed meeting on 10 January in an attempt to end a three-month stalemate that had led to closure of the institution when lecturers went on strike. On 8 February, employees of the judiciary laid down tools following the government's delay in paying their housing allowances approved by the National Assembly in 2012 but still not implemented. On 16 March, academic staff at Chancellor College vowed not to call off their strike unless their employer, the University of Malawi Council, addressed their grievances. Lecturers at Chancellor College, a constituent college of the University of Malawi, alongside their colleagues at the Polytechnic, Kamuzu College of nursing and the College of Medicine, wanted salary disparities between similar grades at the four colleges to be resolved. On 28 March, academic and non-academic staff of the University of Livingstonia went on strike, warning that they would only return to work if their conditions of service were improved and three of their top managers were fired. The employees demanded the immediate dismissal of Vice-Chancellor Professor Yohane Nyasulu, Registrar Peter Kayira and Finance Officer Francis Kumwenda, as well as a 60% salary increase, re-introduction of overtime allowances and adherence to conditions of service. In a related development, employees at the Lilongwe University of Agriculture and Natural Resources went on strike on 19 September to push the institution's management to implement a 20% salary increase. The president of the University Workers' Trade Union said they had resumed the strike after the university management failed to give them feedback by September 9 after they had raised grievances in May following a 40% salary increase for academic staff of the University of Malawi, one of the four public universities in Malawi.

Road accidents increased during the year: statistics from the Directorate of Road Traffic and Safety Services (DRTSS) showed that 1,791 people had died in 694 road accidents, a rise from 1,112 deaths in 962 accidents in 2016. According to the DRTSS, drunk driving topped the list of causes of accidents, followed by speeding and reckless driving. Of those who died, 919 were males and 282 female. The Central Region registered 562 deaths in 477 accidents, followed by the Southern Region with 235 deaths in 206 accidents, the Eastern Region with 174 deaths in 159 accidents and the Northern Region with 151 deaths in 120 accidents.

Mauritius

Tor Sellström

After a disputed transfer of power from Prime Minister Anerood Jugnauth to his son Pravind in January, the domestic political situation stabilized, although Mauritius continued to be plagued by high-level cases of corruption. Brexit and the termination of the EU sugar protocol called for foreign trade and policy adjustments, while the government cautiously and successfully navigated the mounting rivalry between India and China. A major diplomatic breakthrough was achieved at the UN on the issue of the Chagos archipelago. With modest GDP growth, an ambitious development model was launched, focusing *inter alia* on expansion of infrastructure. Overall, Mauritius maintained a leading position in Africa regarding governance and socio-economic development. Having no armed forces, the country was not involved in any military conflict.

Domestic Politics

On 23 January, Sir Anerood Jugnauth stepped down as *prime minister* and handed over executive power to his son, Pravind Jugnauth, in the latter's capacity as leader

 | DOI:10.1163/9789004367630_050

of the ruling Alliance Lepep's (People's Alliance) major coalition party, the Militant Socialist Movement. Dubbed 'the *papa-piti* (father-son) deal', the constitutionality of the dynastic succession was strongly contested. The leader of the Mauritian Social-Democratic Party, Xavier-Luc Duval – who until the end of 2016 had served as deputy prime minister – called for general elections, arguing that the electorate had not been consulted. Similarly, Roshi Bhadain, the cabinet minister for good governance, stated that "a mafia gravitates around the government". He resigned with immediate effect and launched a new political party, the Reform Party. On 1 March, in a rare political comment, Cardinal Maurice Piat, bishop of the capital city, Port Louis, expressed the opinion that the Mauritian political parties acted as 'clans', with the primary objective of clinging to power. Despite the criticism, the *papa-piti* deal was upheld. In addition to the premiership, Pravind Jugnauth assumed responsibility for the ministerial portfolios of home affairs and external communications, as well as finance and economic development.

Mauritius continued to be plagued by *nepotism* and *corruption*. The case of alleged money-laundering against former Prime Minister Ramgoolam, leader of the Labour Party, remained on the agenda. Although he had been cleared of most charges, a final verdict was expected in early 2018. Another high-level case of money-laundering was revealed on 13 September, when Prime Minister Jugnauth requested the attorney general (and member of the cabinet), Ravi Yerrigadoo, to step down for allegedly having transferred gambling proceeds to private bank accounts abroad. Evidence of financial impropriety involving *President Ameenah Gurib-Fakim*, which first surfaced in February, finally gathered strength towards the end of the year. Gurib-Fakim – Africa's only female head of state – was accused of abuse of power and inappropriate financial links to an Angolan banker suspected of setting up a foundation (Planet Earth Institute) in Mauritius to mask illicit activities. As early as April, the leaders of the opposition parties sent an open letter to Gurib-Fakim calling on her to resign. These hugely consequential allegations of corruption against the president caused considerable embarrassment and were likely to further tarnish the reputation of Mauritius as a jurisdiction of substance on the eve of the 50th anniversary of its Independence on 12 March 2018.

Scheduled parliamentary elections were to be held in 2019. In the meantime, many observers paid particular attention to the *by-election* held in the urban constituency of Quatre Bornes in mid-December, which was seen as an important indicator of the opinion of the electorate. The outcome was a victory for Arvin Boolell of the opposition Labour Party, but the election was marred by a low turnout, with almost 45% of the registered voters choosing to abstain.

Local elections were held on 13 February on the distant, semi-autonomous island of *Rodrigues*, the easternmost populated land of Africa. The winner was the veteran politician Serge Clair and his 'Organisation du Peuple de Rodrigues' (OPR), which took ten of the 12 directly contested seats in the local assembly, with two seats going to Nicolas Von Mally's 'Mouvement Rodriguais' (MR). Allowing for proportionally allocated seats, the final result was ten to the OPR, a member of the ruling Alliance Lepep, and seven to the MR, which was not represented in the national parliament in Port Louis.

Foreign Affairs

Since Independence in 1968, Mauritius' foreign policy had been largely consensual and no major international re-alignments took place under Pravind Jugnauth's leadership. Traditionally guided by economic considerations, Jugnauth Jr continued to pursue the consolidation of the small island republic as *a financial centre* and *a trade, transport and communications hub* between Europe, Asia and Africa. During the year, Brexit and the removal of European reference prices and production quotas on cane sugar were of short-term concern in relations with the UK and the EU, while the growing rivalry between India and China in the Indian Ocean represented both challenges and opportunities. Under its 2012 'Africa Strategy', Mauritius' footprint on the continent was strengthened. Last but far from least, a diplomatic breakthrough was achieved when the UN General Assembly in June asked the International Court of Justice (ICJ) for an advisory opinion on the separation and continued colonisation of the *Chagos archipelago* by the UK since the time of Mauritius' Independence.

The *Brexit* negotiations between the UK and the EU were followed with keen interest. Representing around 12% of foreign sales, the UK remained, alongside France, Mauritius' leading export market, with textiles and clothing, sugar and seafood as major items. Similarly, almost 150,000 British holidaymakers per year accounted for more than 10% of all foreign tourists visiting the island. A post-Brexit weakening of the British economy would have a significant impact, making Mauritian goods more expensive in the UK and Mauritius less attractive as a tourist destination. Against this background, after the June 2016 British referendum the government had introduced a 40% reduction of freight costs by the national carrier Air Mauritius, focusing on other markets than the UK. The policy was expanded during the year to cover products such as fruit, flowers and vegetables in addition to textiles and clothing. Various marketing initiatives to launch Mauritian goods and consolidate its tourism industry were also taken. Targeting tourists from the Netherlands, Germany, Scandinavia and Eastern Europe, the Dutch airline KLM started regular flights to the country in October. Finally, the Mauritian government and business community remained confident that the UK government's undertaking to protect the interests of Commonwealth member states would be upheld and that a separate trade deal between all the parties could be reached before the scheduled Brexit divorce in 2019.

Of more immediate concern was the future of Mauritius' *sugar exports* after the termination in September of the EU's sugar protocol, which had allowed Mauritius and other sugar-exporting ACP countries to sell raw sugar to the EU market at fixed prices and in agreed volumes. Although the industry's contribution to the Mauritian economy had fallen considerably over the previous decade – representing less than 2% of GDP – the export of cane sugar remained significant, with more than 90% of production going to the EU. The importance of cane cultivation was underlined by the fact that around one-third of production was contributed by some 30,000 small growers. At year's end, it was still too early to assess the overall impact of the expiry of the EU protocol. In comparison with other cane exporters, however, Mauritius was well placed to meet the challenge. As a global pioneer in bagasse-based produce to the public electricity grid, which reduced its dependency on imported petroleum, the Mauritian sugar industry had largely adjusted to the scheduled external shock by gradually increasing its competitiveness in energy generation. In addition, after a comprehensive reform in 2005, it had successfully diversified into ethanol production and moving up the value chain by exporting refined, rather than raw, sugar.

Mauritius continued to boost its ambitions as an *Indian Ocean hub* by deepening its political, economic and security links with India, while at the same time partnering with China with a view to strengthening the latter's commercial relations with Africa. As the rivalry between the two Asian giants increased in the region, the chosen path was not without complications, but the small island state, located at the intersection of Indian and Chinese geopolitical interests, continued to benefit from the attention separately extended by each of the two big powers.

Mauritius, often called 'Little India' on account of the majority population of Indian origin, further consolidated relations with *India*. In February, it was announced that Indo-Mauritian citizens could apply for identity cards as Overseas Citizens of India, allowing for visa-free travels, work and study permits, residence status and the right to own property in India. Indian FDI statistics published at the same time showed that the May 2016 amendment of the double taxation avoidance agreement between the two countries had not had the negative impact that many had predicted. On the contrary, between April and December 2016, Mauritian FDI into India had amounted to no less than $ 12.8 bn, or more than one-third of the total. Mauritius thus maintained its position as the leading FDI source, ahead of Singapore, with investment flows amounting to $ 7.1 bn, and Japan, with $ 4.2 bn. On his first trip abroad, in May Prime Minister Jugnauth paid an official visit to his Indian counterpart Narendra Modi in New Delhi. The high point of the visit was the signing on 27 May of agreements on maritime security and a credit line of $ 500 m from India to Mauritius. Worthy of note was that the security cooperation arrangement was concluded only two weeks after Mauritius – but not India – attended the significant 'One Belt, One Road' summit meeting on the Chinese initiative for a combined overland and maritime silk road between China and Europe, held in Beijing.

Under the new *maritime security agreement*, existing cooperation in Mauritius' Exclusive Economic Zone was expanded, notably with regard to the Mauritian coast guard, which already included deputed Indian naval personnel. At the signing ceremony, Prime Minister Modi characterised India and Mauritius as "frontline states of the Indian Ocean" joined in the fight against piracy, human trafficking, illicit fishing and other forms of illegal exploitation of marine resources. Most observers, however, viewed the security agreement in the light of India's strategy to contain China's growing military presence in the western Indian Ocean, under the so called 'string of pearls' policy, including its first ever overseas naval base in Djibouti, fully operational in 2017, as well as port facilities in Sri Lanka, Pakistan and Seychelles. To this end, India had established a communications intelligence unit in Mauritius and was in the process of setting up a second unit in Madagascar. The cooperation with Port Louis also covered the two distant Mauritian islands of *Agaléga*, situated around 1,000 km north of Mauritius and with a small population of 300 people, where India financed the expansion of a runway and a jetty.

The Indian credit of $ 500 m was extended to finance major infrastructural developments, notably the metro express project in the greater metropolitan area of Port Louis, but also the construction of social and low-income housing units. During his visit to India, Jugnauth also discussed the signing of a comprehensive economic and partnership agreement with his Indian host.

Relations with *China* deepened during the year. Chinese Foreign Minister Wang Yi visited Mauritius in February and in mid-May his Mauritian counterpart, Vishnu Lutchmeenaraidoo, took part in the 'One Belt, One Road' summit meeting in Beijing, where bilateral discussions took place on the signing of a free trade agreement. More significant in the African context was that the parties explored the feasibility of a joint financial services centre for *cooperation with Africa*, as well as the extension of Mauritius' air connections between China and the African continent. Promoting Mauritius as an important gateway for Chinese investments, the government invited China to establish partnerships with Mauritian enterprises within the framework of the business parks and special economic zones that were being established by Mauritius in several African countries.

Such ventures were developed during the year in Ghana, Madagascar and Senegal, enhancing bilateral cooperation in various sectors, including trade, investment and capacity building. Under the *Mauritius-Africa Fund*, a free trade zone was set up in Côte d'Ivoire and in June Pravind Jugnauth announced the establishment of joint commissions with additional African countries, among them Ethiopia, Kenya and Zambia. In the case of Kenya, the cooperation included so called 'bush and beach tourism', i.e. package tours for overseas holidaymakers combining wildlife with seaside.

Mauritius' most important diplomatic achievement took place on 22 June, when the UN General Assembly requested the ICJ to give an advisory opinion on the pre-Independence separation of the *Chagos archipelago* by the UK. It had subsequently been turned into the British Indian Ocean Territory (BIOT) and the island of Diego Garcia into a US military base. The resolution was a triumph for Sir Anerood Jugnauth, who, in his capacity as minister mentor and sole survivor of the 1965 constitutional conference, led the Mauritian UN delegation. The recorded vote was 94 in favour to 15 against, with 65 abstentions. While many expected a different outcome, India voted in favour and China abstained. Calling for withdrawal of the draft resolution, the UK declared that sovereignty would revert to Mauritius only when the archipelago was no longer required for defence purposes.

Socioeconomic Developments

GDP growth was estimated at 3.9%. Although this was positive in an African context, the diminishing competitiveness of the export-oriented manufacturing sector vis-à-vis lower-income countries, coupled as it was with an ageing population, inadequate human capital development and a general lack of innovation, was threatening future growth and Mauritius' ability to sustain inclusive socioeconomic development. Against this background, the government launched a new development model – '*Vision 2030*' – to jumpstart a new phase of high growth with shared prosperity. The aim was to make Mauritius a high-income country by 2023, increasing per capita income from around $ 9,800 to $ 13,600. Within the comprehensive strategy, a plan for the period 2017/18–2019/20 was launched to provide short- to medium-term directions and sub-targets against which progress could be measured.

In addition to the financial services sector, ICT and the ocean-based 'blue economy', the *tourism industry* continued to grow for a fourth successive year, with the number of international visitors increasing by 5.2%. Arrivals from France accounted for the largest number, or 20.4%, with those from the UK (11%) in second place. The number of Chinese tourists fell by 8.1%, but holidaymakers from India increased by 4.4%, overtaking the number from China. The government's objective was to receive 1.6 m tourists by 2019/20. To this end, discussions opened on the construction of a second terminal at Port Louis airport, which would raise its capacity to 4.5 m passengers per year.

The largest infrastructure project was the *metro express* between the metropolitan area of Port Louis and the central town of Curepipe. Financed by India, contracts were awarded in July to the Mumbai-based firm Larsen & Toubro. Despite initially sparking controversy and social protests by transport sector workers and residents facing compulsory acquisition of their properties along the planned route, construction started in September, and the metro was expected to be fully operational in two years. With regard to Mauritius' ambitions to become a true Indian Ocean maritime hub, the expansion of the *container terminal* in Port Louis was completed in October, increasing its capacity to handle up to 750,000 TEUs.

Several of the *social welfare reforms* announced in 2016 were implemented, notably the introduction of nine-year schooling and the extension of subsistence allowances to more than 8,000 families under the plan to combat pockets of poverty. To further arrest inequality, in June Prime Minister Jugnauth introduced a solidarity level on high income earners, as well as a pledge that water would be made available to all households on a round-the-clock basis by 2019. As regards *gender equality*, Mauritius continued to show little progress, ranking 20th in Africa and 112th in the world on the World Economic Forum's Global Gender Gap Report.

Generally, Mauritius maintained a leading position in Africa with regard to *governance* and *socio-economic achievement*. It remained within the UNDP 'high' category for human development, ranking second after Seychelles. It was classified number one on the Ibrahim Index of African Governance, ahead of its Indian Ocean neighbour, and surpassed South Africa as the highest-ranked African country on the World Bank's ease of doing business list. On TI's Global Corruption Perceptions Index, Mauritius dropped to 54th place globally and 6th in Africa.

Mozambique

Joseph Hanlon

Recession and stalemate characterised the year. The hidden $ 2 bn debt was the key issue, with the IMF and donors demanding information on how the money had been used, and the government and ruling party Frelimo flatly refusing to say. After the crisis of 2016, the economy stabilised, but the sharp devaluation of 2016, the withholding of some aid and loans, and a fall in investment kept the economy in recession, with the government resorting to heavy domestic borrowing and not paying its bills. A ceasefire in the low-level war between the government and the armed opposition party Renamo held throughout the year, and talks continued without a settlement. Two-and-a-half years after his election, President Nyusi finally won control of Frelimo at the party congress in September, which allowed him to move forward.

Domestic Politics

The $ 2 bn secret loan dominated for second year in a row. In 2016, it had been revealed that secret loans had been arranged in 2013/14 under President Guebuza (in post 2005–15). In 2016, IMF Managing Director Christine Lagarde told the BBC that, in keeping loans secret, the Mozambique government was "clearly concealing corruption". It is widely believed that senior Frelimo figures had benefitted. The loans had been arranged by Crédit Suisse and the Russian bank VTB for three new companies set up by the security services ('Serviço de Informações e Segurança do Estado'; SISE). Unusually, all the money had gone directly to Privinvest, a Beirut and Abu Dhabi-based company, and none to Mozambique. Exactly what Privinvest was supposed to supply had never been revealed, but it appeared to be fishing boats, patrol boats and other military equipment and coastal protection services. Donors and the IMF had forced President Filipe Nyusi to agree a forensic audit by Kroll Associates, but SISE refused to cooperate. Government guarantees for the loans had been signed by the then finance minister and National Treasury director, but in January a report was released by the administrative tribunal and government auditor ('Tribunal Administrativo'; TA) saying that the guarantees were "a violation of the constitution and budget law" because they were over the limit authorised by parliament. The report also noted that "the government has not made any mention of the final uses of these loans". Senior figures clearly knew about the loans and Nyusi, in his capacity as defence minister, knew that equipment was being purchased. It was revealed in April that he had taken an active part in setting up one of the three companies, ProIndicus. Thus, at highest level, too many people were compromised, and the need for unity meant that they had to be kept inside the party and protected.

The Executive Summary of the *Kroll audit report* was released on 24 June by the attorney general's office ('Procuradoria Geral da República'). Despite having been refused essential information, it documented major misconduct, and showed that no one had clean hands. Kroll suggested that the contractor, the Privinest Group, "had a role in structuring the projects [and] introducing Crédit Suisse as a lender". All of the loan, after fees were deducted, went directly to Privinvest. Kroll concluded that Privinvest had overcharged Mozambique by at least $ 700 m. Kroll had not been given the information needed, and was unable to provide even quite basic information on where the money had gone or how it had been used. The head of the three companies, António Carlos do Rosário, a SISE official, repeatedly refused to supply information on the grounds that it was "classified" or for "national security" reasons. Kroll could not explain a complete inconsistency about $ 500 m of the loan, which had been included in the government budget under the heading of security rather than as fishing equipment. Rosário told Kroll it had been used for military equipment, while Privinest insisted no weapons had been delivered. Fees to the organising banks, VTB and Crédit Suisse, totalled $ 200 m. Kroll noted that "Crédit Suisse imposed a number of 'preceding conditions' that needed to be met before it would approve the loan financing, including the requirement to have the loan agreement approved by the Bank of Mozambique and checked by the Mozambique Administrative Court and that the 'operation' needed to be reported to the

IMF. Documentation suggested that these conditions were 'overcome' so that no court or Bank of Mozambique approval was required and no reporting to the IMF was needed." Kroll could not figure out how this had happened.

Under President Joaquim Chissano (in post 1986–2005), the *military* had been kept relatively weak so as to prevent any possible coup, but Guebuza had used some of the secret loans to re-equip and build up the military and security services. In the on-going war with Renamo, senior retired military figures, some of whom had fought against Renamo in the 1982–92 war, were opposed to any concessions to Renamo. They could not be bypassed, and there were some people who did not want to move on either the secret debt or Renamo. Frelimo's *unity-at-all-costs position* had two aspects that tended to balance each other. Senior figures were protected, no matter what they did, but consensus decision-making put pressure on people not to resist majority views. This, in turn, created space for a new leader such as Nyusi to reshape the party, buying off and shifting recalcitrant senior members. His struggle to gain control over the Frelimo party and thus the government had led to infighting and delays, and the two dominant issues carried over from 2016 – the $ 2 bn secret debt and the low-level war with Renamo – continued unresolved. But there was movement, and Nyusi won control of Frelimo at the September party congress.

Lacking full *control of the party*, Nyusi looked to men of the Chissano generation, who were relatively old but had no loyalty to Guebuza. On 30 January, Nyusi named Lagos Lidimo as *director general of SISE*, replacing Gregório Leão, who had been appointed by Guebuza in 2005. After the 1992 peace accord, Chissano had appointed Lidimo as chief of staff of the new joint army. He had been forcibly retired by Guebuza in 2008. Thus, the new head of SISE was hostile to Guebuza – and this led to the release of more information to the Kroll auditors. Lidimo was already ill when he took up the post and was replaced in late October (after the party congress) by Julio dos Santos Jane, who had been named police commander by Nyusi in March 2016. Two other key defence people loyal to Nyusi had been kept in post until the congress, but Graca Chongo was seriously ill and finally retired as armed forces chief of staff, while the deputy commander of the national police, Jose Weng San, died just after the congress following a lengthy illness. Nyusi moved slowly to *curb Guebuza allies*. At the beginning of the year, the Council of Ministers imposed a ban on logging, and extended it on 4 April, in an effort to end illegal logging and wood exports, which cost the country $ 150–200 m per year. This was a major victory for one of Nyusi's closest allies, Land, Environment and Rural Development Minister Celso Correia, and was clearly aimed at a very senior Guebuza ally who had been identified for more than a decade as controlling the illegal trade. The Frelimo Political Commission, the party's most powerful body and effectively also in control of key government decision, had until the September party congress been dominated by Guebuza loyalists. They were replaced by three of Nyusi's ministers and three people who had been ministers under Chissano but not Guebuza. A *minor cabinet reshuffle* on 12–13 December saw Guebuza ally José Pacheco – who had lost his seat on the Frelimo Political Commission – moved from the Ministry of Agriculture to become foreign minister. Agronomist Higino Marrule became agriculture minister. Max Tonela moved from Industry and Trade to Minerals and Energy, while Ragendra de Sousa was promoted from deputy minister to minister of industry.

Afonso Dhlakama, the head of *Renamo* (the main parliamentary opposition party, but also maintaining an armed force in the bush, mainly near Mount Gorongosa in the centre of the country), called a new-year ceasefire, which was extended three times and then made indefinite on 4 May. The ceasefire was unilateral but, in a 2 January telephone press conference, Dhlakama said he had received assurances from Nyusi that the defence and security forces would stop their attacks. In accepting the ceasefire, the government immediately stopped running armed convoys through the area of Renamo attacks, and in April withdrew troops close to Dhlakama's base on Gonongosa. Negotiations between small teams continued in secret with no formal statements and by the end of the year there were only assurances that a settlement would be announced early in 2018. Nyusi said that he and Dhlakama were talking regularly on the telephone. They met on 6 August near the Renamo base in the bush of Gorongosa, where Dhlakama had been living since late 2015. On 13 December, Nyusi went to the Chitengo camp in Gorongosa National Park and Dhlakama was in his Satungira base on Mount Gorongosa, but they only spoke on the telephone. Protocol and status still mattered. "I never lost any elections. I was always robbed and Renamo knows this. I consider myself president since 1994," Dhlakama said in an interview published in the daily 'O Pais' on 28 December, "I consider myself above the President of the Republic." From statements on both sides late in the year, it appeared that Dhlakama had won his two main demands. First, provincial governors were appointed by the president, and Dhlakama wanted them appointed by the party that won the most presidential votes in the province. Following strong resistance, Dhlakama moved to proposing elected governors. But both Frelimo and Renamo leaders were unhappy with the prospect of elected mayors building an independent power base and no longer being controlled by the party, and thus there appeared to be agreement on party appointments. Second, Dhlakama wanted his military forces to be integrated into the army and wanted a form of joint command. This was initially resisted by many inside Frelimo, but after the congress Nyusi appeared to have gained enough authority to opt for a return to the Chissano-style weak army, and thus the integration of senior Renamo officers was less of an issue.

Corruption was a growing problem. In January, criminal investigation was removed from the remit of the police and a new Criminal Investigation Service was established under the attorney general's office. In January, Attorney-General ('Procuradora-Geral') Beatriz Buchili was sharply critical of the previous Criminal

Investigation Police, for failing to investigate kidnappings. She presented her annual report to parliament on 19–20 April. The report noted "with concern cases of corruption that are highlighted by the greedy and excessive manner in which they were practised, as well as by the amounts and status of the people involved". Three people had been charged and had their bank accounts frozen in the case of an $ 800,000 bribe paid in 2009 by the Brazilian aircraft company Embraer to sell two planes to LAM, the national airline, with the amount being added to the price of the planes. Buchilli did not name the three, but they were named in other documents and the press as José Viegas, then head of LAM, Mateus Zimba, then Mozambique head of Sasol, and Paulo Zucula, then minister of transport under Guebuza. They were finally arrested on 6 December, held in prison overnight, charged, and released on a total bail of $ 240,000. On the $ 900,000 in bribes paid by Odebrecht to win the contract for the white elephant Nacala airport, Buchilli promised prosecutions. Many senior officials "feel very comfortable with arbitrary behaviour, abuses, illegalities and injustices", the ombudsman ('Provedor de Justiça'), José Abudo, told parliament in his annual report on 25 October.

The *mayor of Nampula*, Mahamudo Amurane, was assassinated on 4 October, the Mozambican Day of Peace and Reconciliation. Amurane had been elected in the 2013 municipal elections on the Mozambique Democratic Movement (MDM) ticket, but a bitter dispute between Amurane and the MDM national leadership followed. The assassination was never explained and no one was arrested.

An armed group of Mozambican *Islamists* occupied the town of Mocímboa da Praia, Cabo Delgado, on 5 October; two police, 14 raiders and one community leader were killed in the subsequent fighting over two days. On 12 October, police units on the road from Mocímboa to Palma were attacked, with one member of the riot police and three attackers killed. Sporadic fighting continued in the three districts of north-eastern Cabo Delgado near the Tanzanian border: Nangade, Palma and Mocimboa da Praia. At least 300 people were arrested. On 17 December, a convoy of riot police ('Unidade de Intervenção Rápida'; UIR) going from Mocímboa da Praia to a base in the village of Mitumbate was ambushed and the UIR national director of reconnaissance was killed. Two helicopters and a navy ship shelled the village of Mitumbate on 23 and 24 December, causing at least 50 casualties. According to Mocímboa da Praia residents, the Islamist group wanted to impose Sharia law, ban the sale of alcohol and remove secular monuments and Christian crosses. Residents, including local Muslim leaders, said they had been warning the authorities repeatedly, but the authorities, at least in public, denied that there was a threat.

Foreign Policy

The $ 2 bn secret loan continued to negatively affect foreign relations with members of the donor community. In early January, the Swedish ambassador and the

IMF resident representative met with Nyusi to say that cooperation with Kroll was inadequate. Within days, the head of SISE was replaced and more information was released. The completion of the report was postponed three times, from February until May. But senior figures were not named, and Kroll said it could not account for more than half of the $ 2 bn. The government promised to publish the report, but only released a summary, while the full report was eventually leaked. The government had hoped in vain that some additional information and good conduct of the economy would appease the donors. The IMF, backed by the G14 group of budget support donors, demanded information on where the money had gone, and "accountability" – key people were to be named and their role explained, although they did not necessarily need to be prosecuted. On 20 July, William Murray from the IMF Communications Department said that the Fund noted that only a summary had been published. "One of our main conditions is that we want to see full publication of this audit report.... There are information gaps, in particular on the use of the loan proceeds. We want to see those information gaps closed." In July, former budget support donors, the World Bank and Japan all said that the Kroll forensic audit was insufficient to allow a resumption of direct funding to the government. The IMF confirmed on 13 October that there would be no further "engagement" with Mozambique until it provided more information on the secret debts, and that it did not expect a new programme in 2018. Ambassadors and senior IMF officials were personally offended by having been lied to and demanded public shaming, which Frelimo and Nyusi were not prepared to offer. "We cannot see, in the short and medium term, the return of direct external support to the State Budget," admitted the Bank of Mozambique's Monetary Policy Committee on 26 October. In year-end messages, both Nyusi and Bank of Mozambique Governor Rogério Zandamela were open about the fact that the *economic crisis* had been caused by the sudden cut in budget support and aid, but both argued that Mozambique was successfully resisting the donor strike and would not give in.

At the beginning of the year, it was revealed that the US Securities and Exchange Commission (SEC) was investigating the banks involved in the sale of the *Ematum bonds*, Crédit Suisse, VTB and BNP Paribas. The SEC was involved because a number of US firms had acquired the bonds. Financial watchdogs from Switzerland and Britain were also looking into Crédit Suisse's and VTB's involvement. In November, it was reported that the US Justice Department and Federal Bureau of Investigation (FBI) were also investigating the role of the three banks. The FBI was looking at whether the banks had facilitated improper payments to senior Mozambican officials, and the Justice Department was also examining whether the banks had helped Mozambican officials to borrow more than the country's economy could reasonably repay.

Brazil's treasury was paying Mozambique's corrupt bills because Mozambique was not repaying loans to the Brazilian Development Bank (BNDES) for two major contractors caught up in the *lava jato* (car wash) scandal – Odebrecht and Andrade

Gutierrez. Both were now considered in default, so the Export Guarantee Fund paid $ 22.4 m to BNDES in December, according to 'Folha de São Paulo'. One non-payment was for Nacala airport, won by Odebrecht through a bribe, but completed and now an unused white elephant. The other was the Moamba Major dam project, paralysed after the Brazilians halted work because of Andrade Gutierrez. Ironically, the dam was urgently needed to provide water to Maputo, but in January Mozambique's TA said the contract had been given to Gutierrez without a tender process and without the required review of the contract by the TA. A subcontractor of Gutierrez on the dam, Infra Engineering Mozambique, was owned by three senior Frelimo figures.

Mozambique was among the 128 countries that supported the 21 December resolution at the UN General Assembly which effectively demanded that the United States withdraw its recognition of *Jerusalem* as the capital of Israel. US President Donald Trump said he would cut aid from countries that voted for the resolution.

Turkish President Recep Tayyip *Erdoğan* visited Maputo with a 150-member delegation on 24 January. He offered Turkish investment in exchange for Mozambique combatting "terrorist cells". He wanted 24 Turkish business people expelled and the closure of the highly respected Willow schools in Maputo and Matola, which were run by Fethullah Gülen. Mozambique refused Erdoğan's offer.

Mozambique ordered missiles and communications equipment from *North Korea*, as well as refurbishment of Soviet-era military equipment in violation of UN sanctions, according to UNSC expert panel reports published on 27 February and 5 September.

Pigeon pea may seem an obscure crop, but in *India* it is known as dhal. Fear of a dhal shortage was so great that in July 2016 Narendra Modi had made the first ever visit to Mozambique by an Indian prime minister, primarily to promote pigeon pea production and exports. Up to 2 m peasants produced 300,000 tonnes of pigeon pea in 2017 because they believed they had a guaranteed market, but in India there was a boom in production far beyond any expectations. On 5 August, the Indian government imposed an import ban, and Mozambican peasants could not sell their crop.

Socioeconomic Developments

GDP growth fell from 6.6% in 2015 to only 3.1%, and it was only that high because of an increase in global prices and export volumes of two key exports, aluminium and coal, the World Bank reported in its *Mozambique Economic Update*. The biggest hit came from donors: "On budget donor grants and project lending is estimated to have narrowed to 3.8% of GDP in 2017, down from 9% of GDP in 2015." The report continued: "The fallout from revelation of $ 1.4 bn in previously undisclosed borrowing has had severe consequences on Mozambique's economy, extending well beyond the nominal burden of the additional debts." Mozambique was becoming a "two-speed economy", with growth in the capital-intensive resource extraction sector with low employment generation. Consumption at the top 1% was 15.3 times as much as the median, according to the 2017 expenditure survey.

The *economic crisis* caused by the secret debt and partial donor withdrawal had reached its worst at the end of 2016 and eased in the first half of 2017. In 2016, the currency devalued dramatically, from Mt (méticals) 45: $ 1 to Mt 78: $ 1, but by mid-2017 it had recovered slightly, to Mt 60: $ 1, where it remained for the rest of the year. The government continued cutting spending, borrowing domestically, and not paying its bills either to domestic suppliers or to repay the secret debt. The World Bank noted in July that government had been unable to sell bonds even at an interest rate of 28.3%. By the end of the year, the government's domestic debt exceeded $ 1.6 bn, half of it treasury bills and bonds, and the other half other Bank of Mozambique debt. The World Bank also noted that a dramatic drop in *government spending*, from 39% of GDP in 2014 to 30% in 2016, was caused entirely by cuts in investment. Government wages remained at 11.3% of GDP, but capital expenditure was almost halved, from 15.1% of GDP in 2014 to 8.5% in 2016; the most significant cut was in government-financed investment, down 8.3% of GDP to just 3.4%, but donor-supported investment was down as well, from 6.8% of GDP to 5.1%.

On 26 October, the Bank of Mozambique Monetary Policy Committee pointed to "the difficulties that the public sector has in mobilizing resources to finance its expenditures" and said that an indication of the shortage of money was that domestic public debt had risen by $ 46 m in just two months, from $ 1,608 m on 10 August to $ 1,654 m on 25 October. The 2018 budget, released in October, included substantial cuts. Hiring of new teachers would fall from 8,300 to only 2,200 in 2018. Spending on education and health would increase but spending on agriculture would fall by 27% and spending on water and public works would be halved, because of cuts in *aid*. Bank of Mozambique Governor Rogério Zandamela said on 26 October, "We can live without aid, but it will be a difficult life. It requires fiscal reforms to be much deeper than what we had in mind." No payments on the $ 2 bn commercial secret debt were included in the state budget, Prime Minister Carlos Agostinho do Rosário told parliament on 29 November. Interest rates remained high, and the base rate was 19.5% at the end of the year.

Imports had fallen by 38%, from $ 7.4 bn in 2015 to $ 4.5 bn in 2016 (excluding foreign funded mega projects), according to trade data published on 8 November by the National Statistics Institute. Vehicle imports had fallen by 74%, and food and clothing each by 31%. South Africa remained the largest supplier, providing 31% of imports, but this represented a fall of 45% in 2016. Imports from China fell by 40%. *Exports* had remained steady, falling only 2.5%, from $ 3.4 bn in 2015 to $ 3.3 bn in 2016. Mozambique had become a resource economy, with coal, electricity, aluminium and gas the main exports. Tobacco was the only major agricultural export.

On 5 December, the Council of Ministers announced that high-ranking officials would have their *perks cut* substantially, saving the government $ 120 m in 2018, according to Economy and Finance Minister Adriano Malaeiane. Cutting the extravagant rent subsidy would save $ 18 m; government cars would be smaller and officials would lose the right to buy subsidised personal cars. Fuel and mobile telephone subsidies were reduced and the bonus for academic degree holders was cut. Local media noted, however, that the cuts came after a spending spree, with an estimated $ 12 m spent on luxury cars and $ 9 m on a presidential jet; media also pointed out that in 2010, after the riots caused by price rises, the government had approved a similar austerity package but had never implemented it. The lowest non-agricultural *minimum wage* for civil servants was set at $ 61 per month, the lowest since 2006. Minimum wages from 1 April 2017 were approved and announced by the Council of Ministers on 18 April. The minimum for teachers was $ 116 per month and for doctors $ 712. Fuel subsidies were cut sharply and bread subsidies were stopped on 1 April.

Organised crime continued. One tonne of *ivory* from Mozambique was seized in Sihanoukville Port, Cambodia, on 5 December, and 763 kg of ivory – 85 pairs of tusks – was stolen from the locked warehouse of the Cabo Delgado provincial forest and wildlife service in April, indicative of a growing ivory trade that had shifted to Mozambique after crackdowns in Tanzania. Eight people were jailed for stealing $ 1.2 m from the army between 2010 and 2015; they had worked in the wages sector of the army command and had put the names of friends and relatives on the payroll. Setina Titosse, former chair of the government's Agricultural Development Fund, was jailed for 18 years for organising a $ 5.6 m fraud, in which money for fake projects was paid to individuals, many of whom were also convicted. The prosecution was based on a lengthy investigation by the Central Office for the Fight against Corruption.

More than 2,400 officials failed to make their *asset declaration*, in violation of the 2012 Law on Public Probity. Lucia do Amaral, chair of the Reception and Verification Commission (CRV) which implemented the law, told a Maputo seminar on 21 December that 7,056 officials were obliged to declare their assets on taking office but the CRV had so far only received declarations from 4,454 officials. Those required to declare their assets included members of the central and provincial governments, parliament and the provincial assemblies, judges, prosecutors, members of the board of the Bank of Mozambique, and managers of public institutions, public funds, and companies that were owned by the state or where the state had a holding. The declarations are not public.

The first three contracts for the use of Mozambique's share of *natural gas* production in Cabo Delgado were announced on 30 January – to Shell to use gas to produce liquid fuels (diesel, naphtha and kerosene), to the Norwegian company Yara to produce fertilizer, and to the London-registered GL Energy Africa to generate electricity. But movement was slow on the development of the $ 20 bn onshore gas liquification plant; the lead company for Area 1, which would use the plant, Anadarko, had still not been able to make enough advance sales of gas. Exxon-Mobil bought 25% of the Area 4 gas block off Cabo Delgado for $ 2.8 bn. This provided a windfall capital gains tax payment of $ 350 m shortly before the end of the year, which eased financial problems. Financing for the floating gas liquification plant for Area 4 was agreed in December, with $ 4.7 bn coming from a consortium of 15 banks and $ 3.2 bn from the concession companies themselves. All the project's liquefied natural gas would be bought by UK oil major BP when the plant comes on stream in 2022.

After three years of negotiation, on 30 March, the Brazilian mining giant Vale agreed the sale of part of its assets in Mozambique to the Japanese company Mitsui, for $ 770 m. Mitsui was purchasing 15% of Vale's holding in its open cast *coal mine* at Moatize, Tete, and half of Vale's participation in the Nacala Logistics Corridor, which consisted of the new coal terminal at the northern port of Nacala-a-Velha, and the railway from Moatize to Nacala, which crosses southern Malawi. Plans for a new *railway line* from coal mines in Tete to a new offshore port at Macuse, just north of Quelimane, moved a step forward. The route would be only 500 km, half the distance to the port of Nacala, and with falling coal prices the cost of domestic transport became significant. The project now involved the Portuguese company Mota Engil, the China National Complete Engineering Corporation, and Thai Moçambique Logistica.

The dream of *biodiesel* was over: Almirante Dima, deputy national director of hydrocarbons, said on 5 April that biofuel could only be economically viable when oil cost more than $ 100 a barrel. No new large plantation, either state or private, had succeeded in Mozambique since Independence in 1975. In January, the Procana sugar project failed for a second time. TSB, the third largest-sugar company in South Africa, admitted it had given up on a plan for a sugar plantation for ethanol on 37,000 ha in Massingir, Gaza province. TSB had been allocated the land in 2012 after another sugar project on the same land, Procana, had collapsed in 2008. The Portuguese pulp and paper company Portucel, with one of the largest land concessions in Mozambique (356,000 ha), said on 9 February that it planned to "permanently … scale down" its operation and had written down the value of its Mozambique project by € 49 m.

Police said that between February and April they had expelled over 4,000 *artisanal miners* from the Namanhumbir area of the northern province of Cabo Delgado. The Namanhumbir rubies were officially exploited by Montepuez Ruby Mining Ltd, 75% owned by the British company Gemfields, on a concession covering 33,600 ha.

According to first results of the August *national census* announced on 29 December, Matola was now Mozambique's biggest city; it had more than doubled in size in a decade and had a population of 1,616,267. Maputo came second with 1,101,170, giving the capital area (Maputo plus Matola) a population of 2,717,437. The population of Maputo city had actually fallen by 10,468 in the previous decade. Five other cites had populations of over 300,000: Nampula (743,125), Beira (533,825), Chimoio (372,821), Quelimane (349,842) and Tete (305,722). Population growth in Mozambique in the previous decade had jumped to 3.5% per year, compared with 2.4% in the decade before, and was now one of the highest in Africa. The World Bank noted that 45% of the population was under 14 years old and that women bore an average of 5.9 children.

"Because we are a resilient people, we can, with all pride and without fear, affirm that the State of the Nation is challenging but encouraging," Nyusi said on 20 December. And in an 18 December statement, Zandamela said that, in 2017, there had been "a gradual return to the normality of the economic and financial indicators, which had deteriorated substantially in the previous year." A joint civil society report released on 19 December disagreed and said, "The State of the Nation was good for the top leaders of the country, but bad for the rest of the population."

Namibia

Henning Melber

This was a year of mixed performance. Politically, President Hage Geingob managed convincingly to consolidate his party base at the congress of the South West African People's Organisation (SWAPO), warding off attacks on his leadership. This could be seen as stabilising the dominant party system and avoiding distracting interruptions from within. But attacks between competing factions displayed hitherto unprecedented divisions among the first- and second-generation of leaders in the former liberation movement, which had been in power since Independence in 1990. Ethnic-regional animosities bordering on tribalism also reached new proportions, not least in connection with disputes over land policy. Economically, the country remained in recession and continued to face a fiscal crisis. This required a reduction of the budget, with negative consequences for services and employment as there was less investment in public works and social expenditure was more limited. The promise of prosperity for all, a trademark under the Geingob administration, remained a remote dream. Internationally, Namibia's image was dented by its continued emphasis on close ties with North Korea and by being categorised as a tax haven by the EU. Further downgrading by international financial rating agencies was considered by government to be motivated by hostile intentions.

 | DOI:10.1163/9789004367630_052

Domestic Policy

The dismissal of Deputy Minister of Land Bernardus Swartbooi in December 2016 continued to fuel conflicts over the *land policy*. Frustrated over what was perceived as a biased redistribution of land through the Ministry's resettlement policy, which was accused of giving preference to beneficiaries from other regions of the country over residents who expected to receive land rights, Swartbooi was central in the establishment of a Landless People's Movement (LPM). Now a SWAPO backbencher in the National Assembly, he continued to harshly criticise and insult his former minister in parliament. At the end of July, he was finally dismissed from the party and stripped of his seat. This provoked demonstrations by his followers in the Southern region, during which, for the first time since Independence, SWAPO regalia, symbols and membership cards were publicly burned. At the end of the year, there were growing signs that the LPM might be a party in formation that could compete at the next parliamentary and presidential elections expected in late 2019.

The *land issue* also remained a matter of controversy in the wider context of the redistribution and restitution of ancestral land. While the government announced that a long promised second *land conference* following the first national land conference of 1991, originally scheduled for 2016 and re-scheduled for September, had been postponed for a second time to 2018, the LPM held a land conference in September. On 19 September, SWAPO MPs prevented the tabling of a motion by a member of an opposition party to discuss the allocation of land under the government's resettlement programme. Requests to disclose a list of all beneficiaries so far were ignored but demands for a land audit increased as a prerequisite for an informed discussion at a future national land conference.

Three days ahead of his 76th birthday, President Geingob declared at a press conference on 31 July that he would not enter a *party-political election campaign* for the forthcoming SWAPO Congress but that, if the party and his health permitted, he would be available for another term in office as head of state for 2020–2025. However, the subsequent fierce competition for the votes of delegates nominated for the party congress indicated anything but a relaxed atmosphere over the issue of who should be the party president and by implication the party's next candidate for state president at the next national elections. During the electoral process in the regions, which decided a large number of the almost 800 delegates who would vote in the party's leadership election at the congress in late November, dissent and conflicts were even fought out in court. The party headquarter interfered in the nomination and election procedures on several occasions and overruled local decisions. Geingob and his close follower, SWAPO Secretary General Nangolo Mbumba were accused of meddling in local and regional affairs, abusing their alleged authority and twisting party rules. The appointment of delegates to the party congress became a battlefield of hitherto unprecedented proportions.

The party's central committee decided on 12 August that Geingob, who was the acting party president, would not be the sole candidate for the presidency at the congress, thereby ruling on earlier controversies: in 2015, Geingob had claimed to be the duly elected party president but was confirmed only as interim president after former state president Hifikepunye Pohamba resigned. When Geingob replaced Pohamba as head of state, the latter had handed Geingob the position of deputy party president, and he had since then run both offices. But the party constitution made no provisions for such a transfer and, with the central committee's decision, the *fight for control of SWAPO* took on new dimensions for post-Independence history. On 15 October, the central committee endorsed the nominations of two other 'old hands' from the first struggle generation, Nahas Angua and Jerry Ekandjo, as candidates for the party presidency. Like Geingob, who campaigned as 'Team Hage' (also dubbed Team Harambee), they formed their own teams and entered the contest with Pendukeni Ivula-Ithana and Helmut Angula, respectively, as challengers to Netumdo Nandi-Ndaitwah for the party vice presidency. The positions of secretary general and deputy secretary general were also contested by candidates of the three teams, although Angua and Ekandjo soon formed a strategic alliance as Team SWAPO. The campaign turned bitter and nasty, with accusations and counter accusations of betrayal, tribalism and incompetence, as well as personal insults, which tested party unity to its limits.

The 6th SWAPO Congress to elect the new *party leadership* finally took place on 23–27 November in a tense atmosphere. While many predictions of the outcome had pointed to a neck-and-neck race, the result was a sweeping victory for Team Hage and a crushing defeat for all the other contenders. Out of the 766 delegates, 574 voted for Hage Geingob as president and 552 for Netumbo Nandi-Ndaitwah as vice president, while Sophia Shaningwa garnered 523 votes as secretary general and Marco Hausiku 545 votes as her deputy. Not only did Team Hage take all four positions by a convincing majority, but the elections for members of the party's central committee also eliminated most of the candidates from the other two teams in favour of Geingob followers. Similar control was achieved over the party's politburo. As a consequence, Geingob was not only confirmed as the party's next presidential candidate for the national elections, but also consolidated his influence over the party organs. Members of the dissenting factions were sidelined completely and faced irrelevance.

On 4 November, the official *political opposition* party, the Democratic Turnhalle Alliance (DTA), changed its name to the Popular Democratic Movement (PDM). As the party leader McHenry Venaani explained, this was one indicator of a broader party transformation. The name DTA had remained associated for many among the electorate with a pro-South African party created prior to Independence. An Afrobarometer survey of five countries in the region under one-party dominance published during the year revealed surprisingly conflicting results. While only 24%

of respondents declared they were closed to any opposition, 52% believed that the opposition could be a serious alternative for the country. At the same time, in all five countries, the opposition was least trusted to be able to meet socio-political priorities.

Matters of *good governance* remained contested. A draft bill on whistleblowers tabled in parliament on 16 February was widely considered an anti-whistleblower bill and became a matter of controversy. It suggested that confidential information could only be released "in good faith", while "false disclosure" would be punishable by a fine of up to N$ 100,000 or imprisonment for up to 20 years. This stoked fears that investigative journalism could be punished. An amended version was passed by the National Assembly on 6 June and finally signed into law by Geingob on 6 October. The punishments it stipulated were considerably reduced, but still remained restrictively high with maximum penalties for "false reporting" set at a fine of N$ 30,000 or ten years' imprisonment. In early December, the local Institute for Public Policy Research released a damning report on the lack of transparency and accountability in both government and private institutions. Access to information, it concluded, "remains a thorny political and governance issue". In response, the Ombudsman confirmed that this assessment reflected his own experience. In late November, his office had presented a report entitled "A Nation Divided", which concluded that racism and racist discrimination remained alive. It strongly criticised the continuing discrimination against same-sex relations and expressed concerns over growing animosities motivated by tribalism and the lack of initiatives to reduce gender-based violence. Notwithstanding such concerns, Namibia retained its place as fifth of all African countries in the annual Mo Ibrahim Index of African Governance, released on 20 November, and the first gay parades took place undisturbed in Namibian cities in December.

Foreign Affairs

In contrast to his numerous overseas trips in previous years, President Geingob only made one extended visit abroad, to the USA on the occasion of the opening of the UN General Assembly session in September, which he combined with other events promoting Namibia. In early April, former President George W. Bush had visited Namibia.

Geingob emphasised that he was limiting his travel to shorter *Africa-related trips* mainly as a cost saving measure. On 28 January, while attending the annual AU Summit of Head of States in Addis Ababa (Ethiopia), he signed up to the *APRM*. At the Summit, Namibia voted against Morocco's readmission to the AU and continued to call for independence for West Sahara in line with the position taken before as a matter of principle. Geingob undertook *state visits* on 26–28 April to Zimbabwe and on 11–13 July to Botswana. On 19–20 August, he attended the 37th *SADC* Heads of State Summit in Pretoria (South Africa), where he was elected to be the SADC Deputy Chairperson. On 26 September, he attended the inauguration of President Lourenco in Angola.

Brazil's foreign minister visited on 7–8 May. On 31 August, the secretary general of the Commonwealth Secretariat paid a courtesy visit to State House. The "all-weather-friendship" with *China* continued to thrive. Deputy Prime Minister and Minister of International Relations and Cooperation Netumbo Nandi-Ndaitwah paid an official visit to China on 10–13 April and a delegation of the National Committee of the Chinese People's Political Consultative Conference visited in early November. Geingob acknowledged China's continued support in the provision of military hardware and software at the commissioning ceremony for two donated naval vessels on 27 October at Walvis Bay, when he applauded "the commitment of the Chinese Liberation Army to render support to the NDF [Namibian Defence Force] in terms of training of military personnel and supplying of military equipment". China's economic engagement was a major contributing factor to the close bilateral relations (for further details, see below under 'Socio-economic Developments').

Relations with *North Korea* received critical international attention. There was evidence of the continued presence of North Korean companies and workers, tasked with the construction of an ammunition factory nearby the capital and the headquarters of the Ministry of Defence, as well as the maintenance of public buildings such as State House and the Heroes Acre, the Independence Museum and a military museum. These ongoing activities were considered as a violation of the sanctions imposed by the UNSC. On 22 and 25 August the USA and Japan, respectively, announced sanctions against Chinese and Namibian firms that continued to collaborate with North Korean contractors to execute work in Namibia. On 13 September, Deputy Prime Minister and Minister of International Relations and Cooperation Netumbo Nandi-Ndaitwah announced ahead of the opening of the UN General Assembly in New York that all contracts with North Korea had been terminated and invited the sanctions committee to carry out a fact-finding mission, while also stressing Namibia's historically good relations with North Korea. A report broadcast by CNN in late October, however, accused the government of continued violation of the sanctions, quoting the coordinator of the UN Panel of Experts as accusing Namibia of misleading investigators during an earlier visit and of since then being in non-compliance with the obligation to provide convincing evidence that the collaboration had ended. In an official statement on 24 October, the Foreign Ministry rejected the accusations and renewed the invitation to the UN Panel of Experts. On 25 October, the minister of information declared in parliament that the CNN journalist had misled the foreign minister by not declaring upfront that the interview he was granted would refer to ties with North Korea. He reiterated that Namibia had stopped doing business with the North Koreans, who he insisted nevertheless remained friends. The Speaker of Parliament added that Namibia would not allow itself to be bullied.

On 5 December, the *EU* for the first time released a blacklist of 17 countries declared to be tax havens. It would be linked to EU legislation so that the jurisdictions implicated would not be eligible for funding except for development aid. It included Namibia for its lack of response to earlier inquiries. An infuriated finance minister declared on 6 December that the listing was "unjust, prejudiced, partisan, discriminatory and biased", and based merely on a misunderstanding in communication. While he dismissed any immediate negative consequences as unlikely, this slur on Namibia's reputation was certainly not in the country's interest.

Socioeconomic Developments

Economic constraints were far from over. A financial liquidity crisis continued to hamper fiscal policy and limited investments to stimulate the local economy, which was still bearing the scars of the drought and the collapse of state funds in 2016. The *annual budget* was tabled in the National Assembly on 8 March. Revenue for the financial year was projected at N$ 56.43 bn, with expenditure at N$ 62.54 bn, equivalent to 36.6% of GDP. Current expenditure on salaries in the public sector alone amounted to more than half of the budget, and this was considered untenable and unsustainable. But the bloated civil service was justified as an investment in social stability and peace, given the high level of unemployment. Finance Minister Calle Schlettwein reconfirmed a new fiscal strategy. Its declared priority was the stimulation of economic growth rather than poverty reduction, despite all the official rhetoric about a pro-poor policy. Again, budget allocations for the educational sector topped the list at close to N$ 12 bn, followed by military and security expenditure at N$ 10.7 bn. This made Namibia the 12th-highest state for the proportion of defence expenditure to GDP.

In a ministerial statement on 7 June on the state of the economy in the regional context, Schlettwein conceded that the state had been unable to pay outstanding bills on time and stressed that only the loan of N$ 10 bn in local currency obtained in late 2016 from the AfDB had prevented a catastrophe, while the economic environment remained vulnerable. Despite such constraints, fiscal discipline remained a matter of concern. Several critical accounts released during October by the auditor general for the financial year 2015/16 lamented the fact that many ministries and government agencies had overspent their annual budget allocations without authority or explanation.

In his *mid-year budget review* (MYBR), Schlettwein had to adjust already modest projections downward further, estimating economic growth for 2016/17 at 1.1% (instead of a forecast 1.3%) and the revised budget deficit at 6.9% (instead of

6.3%). He put public debt as a ratio of GDP at 38.3% (instead of 39.1%), with a projected peak in the mid-term future anticipated to be 44.2%. Revenue projections indicated further downward pressure, while suggestions that spending could be contained were considered unconvincing by local economists. Schlettwein had also projected a modest economic growth rate of 1.6%, but actual performance turned out to be worse. With the sluggish growth rates at year's end, Namibia had entered a full-scale *recession*, as was confirmed by the IMF's Article IV Mission annual assessment at a media briefing on 13 December. The head of the mission stressed that the growth of the government's wage bill required policy intervention.

Financial rating agencies maintained their sceptical prognoses. Despite claims by both the finance minister and the president that the economy was gradually recovering and getting back on track, Moody's on 11 August downgraded the long-term senior unsecured bond and issuer rating to junk status, while maintaining its negative outlook for the country's economy. Finance Minister Schlettwein in a lengthy response reacted with disappointment and dismissed the highly influential signal as the result of a poorly conducted assessment that drew "speculative conclusions". As a result of the MYBR, Fitch Ratings on 20 November also downgraded the country's long-term foreign currency Issuer Default Rating from BBB – to BB+, which translates into junk status, but with a "stable outlook". This prompted Schlettwein to note a positive trend, since Fitch's prognosis was more optimistic than Moody's, although the Fitch downgrade cemented the sub-investment grade rating. The expected result would be an increase in debt servicing costs and a negative impact on foreign investment rates, both likely to contribute to less money being available for capital investments and add to pressure on the labour market, where youth unemployment was estimated to be close to 40%. As some minor consolation, Namibia went up in the World Bank's Doing Business Report for 2018 released on 31 October from 108th to 106th of 190 countries.

In mid-year, the 5th *National Development Plan* (NDP 5) for 2017/18 to 2021/22 was presented. It was announced as a complementary measure to the Harambee Prosperity Plan introduced by Geingob at the beginning of his term in office as a blueprint for development until 2020. NDP 5 was set out as a roadmap towards a declared goal of rapid industrialisation. It defined four integrated pillars for sustainable development: economic progress, social transformation, environmental sustainability, and good governance. It explicitly linked to Agenda 2030, the SDGs, COP21 and the AU's Agenda 2063 and promised binding, data-based measurement and control of success.

In February, the minister of *fisheries* announced a controversial fishing quota for pilchards of 14,000 tonnes, going against strong concerns of experts, who warned that the biomass was rapidly approaching complete depletion and was facing total extinction in Namibian waters due to overfishing. In mid-December, however, the cabinet endorsed the minister's decision to introduce a three-year moratorium on pilchard fishing, considered by experts as too little too late and a measure that would be unable to restore sustainability. The current stock was estimated at only 1% of the historic population. Lack of transparency in the management of the marine ecosystem and sloppy control of the real catches were criticised as major factors limiting the protection of natural resources off the coast, which were closely interrelated. As a result of the diminished pilchard stock, populations of seabirds, gannets and penguins had also shrunk because of the lack of food.

Tourism remained a growth sector despite the overall economic decline and the rising crime rate, and an increase in reported attacks on tourists further dented the country's image. The UK, Canada and Germany rated Namibia as a high-risk travel destination, which was a cause of concern to the Hospitality Association of Namibia, afraid of losing out on a highly competitive market. However, Chinese tourists, who had started to visit African destinations in large numbers, contributed to an overall increase in visitors, while a considerable decline in visitors from Angola who were registered as tourists was counted as a result of that country's ailing economy.

By 2017, *Chinese investment* in Namibia stood at $ 5.3 bn, of which $ 5.2 bn was spent on uranium mining. The Husab *uranium* mine became the largest single Chinese government investment on the continent to date, with an input of $ 4.6 bn. As one of the largest known uranium deposits in the world it had a production potential of 15 m lb of uranium oxide per year. Anticipated to become fully operational during 2018, it would set Namibia among the top producers on the world market. However, while the government applauded the economic investments, workers complained about working conditions and low wages. Tax evasion by Chinese businesses seemed widespread and was another subject of complaint and, towards the end of the year, the Chinese embassy began to offer an introduction to the Namibian tax system. As the ambassador declared: "We will continue to promote education campaigns among Chinese citizens to raise their awareness to abide by the law." In general, however, the massive presence of Chinese companies and citizens, not least in the construction and retail sectors, aroused strong feelings among ordinary Namibians, bordering on xenophobia. Another major bone of contention was dubious financial transactions, suspected to be money laundering, as well as the scale of organised poaching (including rhinos, pangolins and other endangered species), in which Chinese were extensively involved. Some of those who faced trial were released on bail and escaped justice by leaving the country.

A 2016 *Labour Force Survey* released mid-year showed that the population stood at 2.3 m, of whom 36.4% were under 15 years old. Of the 63.6% (1.48 m) of over-15s, more than 450,000 (30.6%) were classified as economically inactive. Of the remaining 1 m who were economically active, 66% (676,000) were considered employed. The agriculture, forestry and fishing sectors combined remained the largest employer, with 20.1% of the labour force (compared with 29.5% in 2014).

But agriculture suffered from the devastating consequences of the 2015/16 drought and saw a loss of almost 90,000 jobs, more than half of those employed since 2014. While urban employment increased by 6.3%, rural employment fell by 18.8%. Critics alleged that the re-definition of 'economically active' had deliberately cut the number of 'unemployed' to present a more favourable picture. End-of-year examination results in schools were once again disappointing and illustrated an ongoing *educational crisis*. Almost 61% of the more than 22,000 full-time Grade 12 learners who took the Namibia Senior Secondary Certificate exams failed to qualify for admission to tertiary institutions.

At the annual staff meeting of the Office of the President on 27 February, Geingob declared that, by creating a new narrative that set a vision, he was "dealing in hope". He had dubbed 2018 a "year of reckoning", and added in his New Year message on 31 December that it would also be a "year of hope" and "a year of shared prosperity", and shared prosperity is certainly something many Namibians continued to hope for when entering the new year.

South Africa

Sanusha Naidu

The year began with spill over effects of unresolved issues and more complex anxieties about the 'State of the Nation'. The country's political, economic and social landscape was still shaking from ambiguities and contradictions around the Zuma presidency, further downgrades relating to the country's credit rating status, an economy that seemed to be teetering on the brink of collapse and an international relations agenda and identity that appeared to be hollowing out. The ANC's policy conference in June and its elective conference in December became the focus of every public debate and discussion forum among scholars and the general populace. Their outcomes had significant implications for the polity of the state in terms of governance and renewal, underlining the country's transformation agenda.

Domestic Politics

In usual fashion, the year begun with the African National Congress (ANC) delivering its customary *January 8 Statement*, marking the celebration of the birth of the organisation. Dubbing 2017 'The Year of Oliver Tambo', the leadership of the

 | DOI:10.1163/9789004367630_053

ANC saw this as an opportunity to invoke the struggle credentials and character of this stalwart party icon, to deepen the ANC's unity and advance the process of self-correction. Some analysts described this as the rebranding of the party, which was struggling to keep its head above water. But, as behaviour and evidence throughout the year indicated, highlighting Tambo's image and philosophy failed to renew the party's principles and values.

On 9 February, President Jacob Zuma delivered the 10th *State of the Nation Address* (SONA). Amidst what had become a highly securitised event, and what ordinary South Africans had come to accept as the new normal of mayhem, the 10th SONA provided little insight into the country's affairs or the progress the Zuma administration had made in the previous 12 months, nor did it present any substantive or coherent outlook towards where the country was heading. The speech was insipid and underpinned by a litany of catchphrases pulled from previous years' SONAs and platitudes that inspired little confidence among the general public in the governance and management of the country's political and socio-economic affairs. Radical Economic Transformation was introduced as part of the renewal of the government's game plan, though the framework for how it would be implemented remained obscure.

The real state of the nation became clear outside the National Assembly (NA) with the use of pepper spray and water cannons. The ejection of the Economic Freedom Fighters (EFF) from the NA had become a feature of Zuma's SONA for the past three years. This time around, the pandemonium that raged outside of the NA received more attention, with Zuma delivering his address to only his party members in parliament, almost empty opposition benches and the media and visitors in the gallery. In what had become known as the tragedy and farce of SONA, the EFF were expelled for challenging Zuma's credibility and legitimacy. When they refused to leave the chamber, the Speaker asked security to remove them from the house. Scuffles broke out between EFF members and security personnel, who some observers said were not the parliamentary protection services but rather riot police dressed as waiters. The brute force used by these security personnel led to the Democratic Alliance (DA), United Democratic Movement (UDM) and the Congress of the People (COPE) objecting and exiting the NA.

Towards the end of March, rumours were circulating that Zuma was going to institute another *cabinet reshuffle*. Some analysts argued that he needed to expedite the nuclear deal that had allegedly been done with the Russians and that the reshuffle was really about this and other outstanding deals and tenders that needed to be completed. This was to be Zuma's 11th cabinet reshuffle since taking office in May 2009. After meeting with the ANC National Executive Committee (NEC) and the party's top six, Zuma announced in the late hours of 30 March that he was restructuring his cabinet to bring in younger ministers to create more efficiency around the transformation agenda. Mainstream media and senior political analysts saw the move as a way for him to surround himself with loyalists and remove members of the South African Communist Party from his government, but also to embed his and his network's control of the state structure. This view was reinforced with the announcement that Finance Minister Pravin Gordhan and his deputy, Mcebisi Jonas, were both dismissed from the cabinet. Gordhan and Jonas were recalled while on an international investment visit to the UK talking to key investors and re-instilling confidence in the South African economy. Gordhan, who had become an outspoken critic of and activist against state corruption and had tried to tighten the purse strings of government during his time as finance minister, would inform the public through an interview with 'Business Day' that it was "absolute nonsense that his sacking by Zuma had been prompted by an intelligence report." He also disputed allegations in the intelligence report that he had had meetings with individuals to undermine the country during the investment road-show in London. According to Gordhan, the report was based on "manufactured information".

Malusi Gigaba replaced Gordhan as finance minister and Sifiso Buthelezi became his deputy. Other ministers who did not survive the reshuffle included Tina Joemat-Pettersson and Derek Hanekom. For the most, part old faces remained but were shifted to different portfolios. The real intention was, as some analysts put it, "to capture the National Treasury". There were mixed *reactions to the reshuffle*. At the party level, Deputy President Cyril Ramaphosa and Secretary General Gwede Mantashe voiced their dissatisfaction. But the party's communications centre issued a statement noting that the ANC was satisfied with Zuma's explanations. The public and civil society groups expressed their anger and disapproval not just of the reshuffle but also of the removal of Gordhan and Jonas, which was seen as a final straw in entrenching the capture of state resources. Support for Gordhan poured in from all quarters through rallies, marches, public platforms, discussions on radio and television talk shows, and letters to the newspapers. Even days before the impending reshuffle, the head of the Ahmed Kathrada Foundation, in paying respects to the struggle icon who had passed away after battling a long illness, had acknowledged Gordhan's integrity and moral character as a model for all public servants. The DA, as the official opposition, applied to the courts to have the swearing in of new ministers set aside. The court dismissed this application, but the High Court ordered Zuma to provide reasons, to be placed on record, for firing Gordhan. Legal experts were quick to point out that the judiciary could not do more than that or overturn the president's decision, because that would be seen as encroachment on the separation of powers.

In March, the Constitutional Court extended for 12 months the contract for Cash Pay Services (CPS) to administer *social development grants* on behalf of the Department of Social Development. The ruling did not validate the contract between the Department and the parent company of CPS, Net1 (which the Constitutional Court declared invalid), but was made because the Department had failed to finalise a new payment system by 1 April. The Chief Justices, in delivering their judgement, were scathing of Social Development Minister Bathabile Dlamini and her department for not abiding by the court's earlier ruling. In June, the Constitutional Court ordered that an enquiry be established to set out the role and responsibilities of the Minister of Social Development. The background to this was that Black Sash, a social justice organisation, had brought a case against the minister and the Ministry in March, asking the Court to assume a supervisory role in the payment of the social grants, following statements by the South African Social Security Agency (SASSA) and the Ministry that payments could not be disbursed by 1 April as ordered by the Constitutional Court in a previous ruling in 2015. At the time of the 2015 ruling, SASSA had agreed that it would have a new service provider in place and that there would be no disruption of the payment system. In reviewing the application, the chief justices indicated that, following their 2015 November ruling when they had declared the contract with CPS invalid, they could not assume such a role again. Instead, they ordered an enquiry into the role and responsibilities of the social development minister. This decision followed an earlier ruling when the Court had asked Minister Dlamini to explain why she should not be held "personally liable for the costs incurred from a (previous) application relating to the social grant debacle". The enquiry, which was supposed to have been instituted 14 days from the court ruling, was pushed forward to January 2018. The social development saga around the disbursement of the social grants remained in the spotlight. By December, the Ministry had signed a service agreement with the South African Post Offices (SAPO). This was considered a breakthrough, and confirmed what most civil society groups had argued, that the SAPO was the state channel that should have been originally contracted to administer the disbursement of the grant.

Alongside the social grant crisis, South Africans were confronted with another tragedy, the case of the 144 known (the number could be higher) psychiatric patients who died in the *Life Esidimeni* hospital catastrophe. Uncovered in 2016 by an investigative programme on the television news channel, eNCA, the Life Esidmeni crisis exposed in public hearings during the year how health care services in Gauteng had been manipulated and become part of the wider context of state rot and resource exploitation. The exposé revealed that the level of capture and manipulation of state tenders and contracts had percolated throughout the country's provincial and local levels, making the concept of South Africa as a rentier state much more real. In short, Section 27, an NGO working on the rights of the poor and marginalised through socio-economic litigation, highlighted the reasons for closing down the Life Esidimeni hospital, according to the former provincial Member of the Executive Council (MEC) for Health, as two-fold: 1) to save money and 2) to deinstitutionalise responsibility.

The *Healthcare Ombudsman*, Prof Malegaparu William Makgoba, was tasked to provide a report on the crisis. The final report, which dealt with only 94 deaths, was released in February. The main conclusions were as follows: the 27 NGOs to which patients were transferred were not properly licensed to care for mentally ill patients nor did they have the competency, structural capacities or proper facilities and resources to provide the specialised care needed for such patients; all the patients in the care of these NGOs died unlawfully; and the decision to close the Esidimeni facility and transfer the patients to NGOs was made rashly and without due diligence and was chaotic in its implementation, with little or no respect for human dignity, care and human life. In concluding his report, the Ombudsman noted that the crisis showed gross human rights violations and infringed the Constitution, the National Health Act and the Mental Healthcare Act. The Ombudsman also recommended that the Gauteng premier needed to consider the suitability of Qedani Dorothy Mahlangu to continue as MEC for health. The report further advised that the Gauteng Mental Marathon Project, under which the crisis took place, be disbanded.

Following the Ombudsman's report, an *arbitration council* was established, led by former Chief Deputy Justice Dikgang Moseneke. The arbitration officially began in October and was to last for three weeks. However, given the depth and nature of what had occurred, the process continued until the end of the year and looked likely be finished in early 2018. The evidence heard led one commentator writing in the 'Daily Maverick' to describe testimony presented by family members of the victims, government officials, provincial bureaucrats and NGOs (particularly Section 27) as pointing to "government culpability". The arbitration allowed family members of the deceased patients to finally hear the truth about the circumstances around the catastrophe, see who should be held responsible for the crisis and challenge provincial officials and the NGOs involved to at least acknowledge liability, after avoiding the issue. The question that remained was whether the findings of the arbitration would be appropriate to the scale of the Esidimeni crisis.

Racism continued to expose fault lines in society. Racially motivated killings and slurs remained a blight on South Africa's democratic project. Leading political figures also stoked the fires. In March, Western Cape Premier Helen Zille, a former leader of the DA, tweeted: "For those claiming the legacy of colonialism was ONLY negative, think of our independent judiciary, transport infrastructure, piped water etc." This not only landed her in hot water with her party but also led to an outrage on Twitter and within the broader public. In April, the party's Federal Legal Council recommended the leadership to take disciplinary action against Zille. The outcome was a formal disciplinary hearing with a press briefing in June, at which Zille made a public apology and noted that she would be stepping back from all political party activities, except for her position as premier. The press briefing was the result of heated protracted exchanges between Zille and the DA leadership, which some interpreted as Mmusi Maimane (Zille's successor as party president) stepping out of the former leader's shadow.

Tensions also reached a high in the *state security* cluster, with a High Court ruling in March that declared unlawful Berning Ntlezema's appointment as head of the special crimes unit, the Hawks. Ntlezema challenged the ruling and reported for work as the head of the Hawks with access to the unit's resources. The Hawks also came under criticism for what some analysts described as 'going rogue' regarding the Ntlezema saga. Eventually in September, Ntlezema announced his retirement after an unsuccessful court appeal, not without controversy and mudslinging between Police Minister Fikile Mbabula, and Ntlezema in the interim. The security cluster remained a contested space with the acting police commissioner, Khomotso Phalane, accused in June of interfering in investigations related to corruption and money laundering led by the Internal Police Investigative Directorate (IPID). Despite Phalane claiming his innocence, he eventually stepped down after what he claimed was "constructive engagement" with Mbabula. Paul O'Sullivan, a private forensic investigator and a renowned corruption buster, was accused by Phalane of being behind the investigation against him. Phalane accused the IPID of being captured by O'Sullivan. In December, O'Sullivan launched a R (rand) 193 m lawsuit against the state in response to his arrest in October 2016, claiming compensation for malicious prosecution and the trauma he suffered.

Throughout the year, the clouds of *state capture* continued to loom over the country's domestic landscape. In July, the investigative journalist centre, Amabugane, released hundreds of thousands of emails and other documents revealing a trail of how the Gupta family had orchestrated the capture of state resources. Dubbed the Gupta email leaks, then later *#Guptaleaks*, the emails and documents had been compiled over a period of several years. They constructed a detailed framework of the actors involved and the intensity at which capture of state resources had taken place from the national to local government levels, and from influencing political decision making to allegedly laundering millions of rand by setting up corporations and subsidiaries that channelled money out of the country into overseas accounts.

The #Guptaleaks also reverberated internationally, implicating overseas companies complicit in the Guptas' alleged criminal activities. These included the UK PR firm Bell Pottinger, the auditors KPMG, global consultancy firm McKinsey and software giant SAP. In November, Amabugane, together with the online news platforms 'Daily Maverick' and 'News 24', opened emails and documents up to public access. In addition, a group of academics produced a report published as 'The Betrayal of the Promise', whose analysis revealed significant drivers of state capture and assessed how it had become systemic at various levels of the state. The conclusion was that state capture had entrenched itself in the most basic structures of local government, making the concept of a rentier state a reality. On a lighter note, 'state capture' was included as a term in South Africa's lexicon.

Zuma's popularity with the electorate continued to falter. In April, and with the *#ZumaMustFall* hashtag continuing on Twitter and other social media platforms, a mass gathering of people across South Africa took place to demonstrate discontent with the head of state. This was just the beginning of what was to become a tumultuous year for Zuma's presidency of both of the ANC and the Republic. In the same month, opposition parties – the DA, EFF and UDM – wrote to the speaker of the NA requesting a debate on a *motion of no confidence* against Zuma in light of the March reshuffle. The debate was set for 18 April and saw terse discussions emerge over ANC MPs, who were encouraged to vote with their conscience and not be guided by blind loyalty to the party.

The process around the motion of no confidence became a long drawn out issue, with opposition parties approaching the Constitutional Court in May with an *application for a secret ballot* on the basis that ANC MPs were instructed not to vote with other political parties and that an open ballot would disadvantage them if they did. In addition, the speaker of the NA declared that she did not have the power to initiate such a process. Ruling on the matter at the end of June, the justices of the Constitutional Court noted that there was no clarity in the Constitution on "when a secret or open ballot is appropriate" and so the speaker had the power to make that decision on the basis of best practice. While the UDM tried to push the Court to set a date for the motion and order the speaker to implement a secret ballot, the Court refrained from doing so on the ground that this was judicial overreach and would compromise the separation of powers.

Following the ruling, the speaker of the NA set the date for the motion for 5 August, but the issue of the secret ballot was still unresolved. A day before the motion, the speaker announced that the motion would be conducted by secret ballot. Analysts and commentators gauged the speaker's decision in light of her being unable to defy a decision made by the Constitutional Court, which had previously held her accountable for parliament's inertia on the former public protector's report on Zuma's private residence, Nkandla, which had disclosed publicly funded upgrades that he was supposed to repay. But there were also murmurings of internal tensions within the ANC as the leadership battle heated up in the run-up to the Elective Conference in December. In the end, the final tally was 177 yes votes versus 198 against. The numbers indicated that between 31 and 40 ANC MPs had broken ranks and voted in favour of the motion. Although *Zuma survived this fifth motion of no confidence*, it was a turning point in the ANC, and opposition parties saw it as the tide turning against Zuma.

In October, the Supreme Court of Appeal dismissed Zuma's and the National Prosecuting Authority's application to appeal against a High Court decision which ruled that the 2009 decision to drop the 'spy tape charges' against him was irrational. The High Court decision meant that the head of the National Directorate of Public Prosecutions (NDPP), Shaun Abrahams, had to start putting together a state prosecution that would involve 16–18 charges consisting of 783 counts of corruption, fraud, money laundering and racketeering related to Zuma's alleged involvement in the multi-billion rand *arms deal*. This ruling and the appeal decision were unprecedented in South Africa's democratic history, not only because they involved a sitting head of state, but also because they created a legal precedent for future presidents of the Republic.

Zuma's legal battles continued. One newspaper described 2017 as Zuma's annus horribilis. In December, the North Gauteng High Court rejected his application to have the 2016 State of Capture Report by the former public protector, Thuli Madonsela, to be reviewed and set aside. In a separate court application brought by three civil society groups, Corruption Watch, Freedom under Law and the Council for the Advancement of the South African Constitution, the North Gauteng High Court ruled that the appointment of Shaun Abrahams was unlawful. The Court's judgement noted that, because of Zuma's conflicted position as a result of the pending corruption charges against him, Deputy President Cyril Ramaphosa should assume all duties, oversight and responsibilities relating to the NDPP for the duration of Zuma's term in office. Towards the end of the year, the Constitutional Court found that the NA had failed in its duty to hold Zuma to account for not upholding the Constitution in the Nkandla affair. In delivering their judgement, the majority of the Constitutional Court justices also instructed parliament to initiate the process of developing rules for the impeachment of a president. This aspect of the decision was disputed by Chief Justice Mogoeng, who argued that it was judicial overreach and undermined the separation of powers to instruct the legislature on what its duties, responsibilities and rules should be.

Alongside all of this, the DA was grappling with its own governance challenges. In the *Nelson Mandela Bay Metro Municipality*, the DA's coalition government was showing cracks amid tensions between the mayor, Athol Trollip (DA), and his deputy, Mongameli Bobani of the UDM. Corruption allegations appeared to be the central issue, though the UDM and EFF suggested that this was Trollip's attempt to exert the DA's control over Metro. In August, Bobani was removed by a motion of no confidence, which led to the UDM threatening to leave the coalition unless their member was re-instated. While other parties in the coalition with the DA, such as COPE, supported the motion, arguing that Bobani was driven by ambition and not the requirements of office, the EFF saw it as DA bullying tactics by Trollip and the leader of the UDM responded by saying that the DA had "gone rogue".

In September, the DA instituted an internal inquiry led by its chief whip in the NA, Johnny Steenhuis, to examine the leadership style and management behaviour of its mayor in the *City of Cape Town*, Patricia de Lille. This report was in response to complaints regarding de Lille's aggressive governance style. The DA kept quiet about the content of the report. For several weeks, de Lille asked to be informed of the allegations and whether she was being formally charged. In December, the DA required her to provide reasons as to why she should stay in her position as mayor, since as they claimed she had brought the party into disrepute and had acted in a less than creditable way. In response, de Lille questioned the allegations, especially as they seemed to be broad and vague, and asked that there be some formal inquiry so that she could prepare a rejoinder based on the evidence and within a legal framework.

The *ANC's 5th Policy Conference* took place from 30 June to early July and provided a strategic platform for the race for the much coveted presidency of the party. Despite the leadership trying to shut down any talk of factions contending for the top job, it was difficult to close those divisions. The conference emerged with three broad focus areas as the party's policy vision for the next five years: Organisational Unity; Radical Socio-Economic Transformation and Inclusive Ownership. Deputy President Cyril Ramaphosa got drawn into the Radical Economic Transformation debate, which was being pursued by the Zuma camp as their battle-cry towards the election of their candidate (Nkosana Dlamini-Zuma) at the elective conference.

The year closed with the *ANC's 54th Elective Conference*, held on 16–20 December in Nasrec, Johannesburg. It turned out to be a fiercely contested affair. Two main factions aimed for control of the party. Ramaphosa became ANC president but had to accept that the top six as well as the NEC consisted of individuals that were from both factions. Analysts saw this as a litmus test of Ramaphosa's ability to handle power balance in the party, especially by exerting influence and leverage around what he termed 'The New Dawn' for the ANC and the country.

Foreign Affairs

As in 2016, foreign affairs remained overshadowed by domestic politics. The year began with the annual World Economic Forum in Davos (Switzerland) and the bi-annual AU summit in Addis Ababa (Ethiopia). At the 28th AU summit, South Africa was confronted with the issue of Morocco and *Western Sahara*. Earlier in January, the leader of the Saharawi Democratic Republic (Western Sahara) had visited Pretoria in what media believed was an attempt to lobby for support against the re-admission of *Morocco* to the AU. While an official noted that the Zuma presidency was not opposed to Morocco's re-entry, the sense was that it would create an asymmetrical balance of relations in the AU in favour of Rabat. With 39 out of 54 member states voting in favour of Morocco's readmission, South Africa found itself in a minority group with the likes of Algeria. Some analysts saw the Morocco-South Africa tension as about more than Western Sahara. It was argued that, while the Morocco question showed South Africa's weakening diplomatic status at the AU, it also signified that Pretoria's fault lines on the continent were being exposed. Despite still maintaining Western Sahara's right to self-determination, the Zuma government announced in a surprise move in November that it was re-establishing relations with Morocco. The shift in the government's attitude and stance, following

13 years of icy relations, was seen as Pretoria trying to influence Morocco on the Western Sahara issue. But it also brought into focus the emerging strength of Rabat's political and economic positioning within the AU and across the continent.

In February, South Africa's continued attempts to withdraw from the *ICC* were blocked by a ruling in the Pretoria High Court, which declared that the withdrawal was unconstitutional and invalid without the approval of parliament. Determined to go ahead, Justice Minister Michael Masuthu tabled a bill in parliament in December that proposed repealing the implementation of the Rome Statute, which would effectively enable South Africa's withdrawal from the ICC.

At the ANC's Policy Conference in July, a proposal was submitted by the party's Western Cape Branch, to either downgrade or sever formal relations with *Israel.* Writing in the 'Mail and Guardian', economist Peter Draper argued that adopting such proposal would significantly affect four sectors of the South African economy: trade, technology, tourism and investment. The reasoning for the proposal suggested that it was partly motivated by the issue of Palestine. In December, at the ANC's Elective Conference, a decision was taken to downgrade relations with Israel. It appeared that the decision of American President Donald Trump to recognise Jerusalem as Israel's capital played a critical role, especially with regard to the way the US tried to pressurise the Africa, Latin America and Asia bloc in the UN into supporting its proposal by threatening to withhold financial aid.

In August, South Africa assumed the chair of *SADC*. Looming large on its agenda were the Comoros Archipelago's application for membership, the conflict in the DRC, and the peace initiative in Lesotho. A special SADC envoy was appointed for the DRC, while the SADC Preventive Mission for the Kingdom of Lesotho was launched on a six-month basis. Comoros was admitted as the 16th member of the bloc.

The major test for South Africa's SADC chair was the political crisis that emerged in *Zimbabwe* in November. With the Zimbabwean military announcing that it had seized control of the country's capital and President Robert Mugabe confined to his residence, it became apparent that his reign was coming to an end. Rumours abounded that the Zuma administration was aware but chose to remain silent. As SADC chair, South Africa responded through diplomatic channels, by sending two special envoys to address the situation. Some analysts saw the SADC intervention as limited since it seemed that it could do little to prevent the military from extending its control, despite the general disapproval of military coups on the part of both SADC and the AU. It became apparent that SADC's diplomatic response did little to change the domestic political situation in Zimbabwe.

South Africa's relationship with Zimbabwe was further complicated by allegations of an attack by *Grace Mugabe* on a model in Sandton in August. In a court battle, Mugabe accused the model of attacking her first. While the incident drew media attention, focus turned to the diplomatic implications. South Africa's foreign ministry, the Department of International Relations and Cooperation (DIRCO) was caught in the cross fire of what became a diplomatic embarrassment. At the centre of the issue was whether Grace Mugabe had been in South Africa on an official visit or in her personal capacity. This would inform the South African government's response to the situation. It seemed that DIRCO, when considering the circumstances surrounding the incident, had decided to grant the Zimbabwean First Lady diplomatic immunity so that she could leave the country. This brought mixed reactions. A Zimbabwean newspaper reported that she had been in South Africa on a personal visit for a scheduled medical appointment. In light of this information, there was a public outcry that the South African government had erred in its judgement and provided her with a 'getaway pass'. A more discerning analysis from the Africa Desk editor of the 'Mail and Guardian' pointed out that the Zuma administration had to consider the implications the incident would have for bilateral relations, given their vested political and economic interests, not to mention the large Zimbabwean expat community in South Africa. And the SADC dimension could not be overlooked, either. The incident remained a stain on South Africa's foreign policy landscape since there was a looming court battle to determine whether Mrs Mugabe should have been granted diplomatic immunity.

In October, South Africa assumed the Chair of *IORA*, which it saw as an opportunity to tie in the broader objectives of IORA's blue economy programme and Pretoria's Operation Phakisa. South Africa would seek to leverage its position and advance cooperation and linkages between the IORA's and Africa's maritime security codes, protocols and strategies. While South Africa saw itself as the anchor state in performing this bridge-building role, it would also have to navigate the geostrategic interests in the region of other partners, especially China, India and the United Kingdom.

Overall, South Africa's international relations appeared to be informed by the country's domestic political landscape. In June, Mrs Dlamini-Zuma returned to South African after serving one term as the *AU Commission Chairperson*. Her tenure had seen mixed results. A Nigerian commentator writing in 'Pambazuka News' described her term in office as one in which: "She only cared about ambitions at home. She just didn't care about the African." On the other hand, those closer to home noted that she had faced challenges that were in existence long before she took up the position. But it was difficult to shift the perception in parts of the continent that Dlamini-Zuma had been marking time in Addis Ababa before returning to run for the presidency of the ANC and ultimately of the Republic. This was evidenced by her being appointed as a member of parliament in November and being endorsed by President Zuma as his preferred candidate at the ANC Elective Conference.

Socioeconomic Developments

According to official figures released by Stats South Africa, the *economy grew* by 1.7%, exceeding expectations and the projections made by the National Treasury, which had forecast 1%. Much of the growth seemed to be due to a partial revival in the agricultural sector, which appeared to bounce back after grappling with the impact of a drought. In terms of sectoral contributions, the agricultural, forestry and fisheries sector showed a 21.9% year-on-year improvement in the first nine months of the year, and registered a 44.2% rise in the third quarter, the biggest quarterly jump in 20 years. There were also positive signals in mining, with a solid 4.4% rise over the year; transport and storage rose by 1.2% and finance and real estate by almost 1%. Manufacturing, the centrepiece of the country's industrialisation programme, declined by 1.2%.

Despite this general improvement, *unemployment* remained high. This was indicative of a sluggish economy, which, even though it created 123,000 new positions, could not generate more sustainable levels of employment opportunities for the many new job seekers who entered the market. By the end of the third quarter, the unemployment rate stood at 27.7%, with a staggering youth (15–34-year-olds) unemployment level of 38.6%, 10.9% above the national average.

The South African Reserve Bank (SARB) cut *interest rates* in July by 0.25 basis points to 6.75% to boost activity in the economy. For consumers, this was a welcome reprieve alongside an *inflation* rate that remained on target. With inflation falling from 6.6% in January to 4.8% by the end of October, the SARB was able to keep the bank repo rate at a fixed percentage. Household consumption also increased by 1.4% in the first nine months of the year, which assisted in boosting domestic economic activity.

With the forecasts for economic growth projected at less than 2% for 2018 and 2019, the government undertook a series of measures to boost economic activity and investment confidence. During the *Medium Term Expenditure Budget* speech in October, Finance Minister Malusi Gigaba announced plans for the partial sale of the state's stake in the country's national telecommunications company, Telkom. Gigaba also hinted that the state might undertake more privatisation efforts to help address the budget deficit, which was forecast to widen to 4.3% for the fiscal year 2017–18.

The economy continued to be affected by *policy uncertainty*. Zuma's cabinet reshuffle in March, and in particular the dismissal of Pravin Gordhan, caused shockwaves in the South African financial market. Following a rally against the US dollar, rumours of Gordhan's imminent removal as finance minister led to the rand slumping by almost 2% against the dollar. Moreover, as investors became nervous, the banking sector saw its market share closing at over 7% down, with around

R 86 bn of its market capitalisation wiped out, while the bond market was also severely impacted.

The most significant consequence of the cabinet reshuffle was the warning signs of *credit rating agencies* downgrading South Africa's sovereign credit status to junk. Agencies such as S&P and Fitch cautioned that Gordhan's removal would signal a negative shift in policy direction, which would adversely affect the country's fiscal outlook and public finances, and potentially weaken its governance standards. Such warnings seemed to go unheeded. In November, S&P Global Ratings downgraded South Africa's long-term local currency rating to 'BB+' or junk from a 'BBB-' stable outlook. The decision came a week after the Fitch rating agency had also downgraded the country to junk status, but with a stable outlook. Moody's Investor Service, however, chose a more cautious approach, stating that they had placed South Africa's 'Baaa' long-term insurer and unsecured bond ratings on review for a downgrade. The consequences of a downgrade by all three global rating agencies would have created an economic avalanche: inflation would have skyrocketed overnight; the cost of borrowing and government debt would have escalated; taxes would have increased; large amounts of capital would have left the country; and government social development expenditure would have been at risk. While it may appear that the South African economy escaped this fate, it was not out of the woods. For the South African economy to self-correct and move itself out of junk status, it would need to undertake pragmatic policy planning and political coherence and stability, at least in the short to medium term.

In February, the deputy president announced details of the *national minimum wage*, set at R 3,900 per month for a 45-hour week and R 3,500 for a 40-hour week. It was envisaged that it would be implemented by May 2018. The Congress of South African Trade Unions supported the programme and it was agreed that this would assist in regulating and stabilising workers' incomes, especially domestic and farm workers, who needed to have a fixed income. The national minimum wage, however, did not detract from the growing and widening *inequality gap*. Oxfam released a report in January indicating that the richest 1% in South Africa owned 42% of the wealth and that the total net wealth of just three of the country's billionaires was equivalent to that of the bottom 50% of the country's population.

South Africa's growing *poverty and inequality gap* was further illustrated by the National Income Dynamic Study, which showed that 29% of the population (over 55 m people) were trapped in extreme poverty; over the past several years 3 m South Africans had become impoverished; four-fifths of the rural population were living below the poverty line; there was a lack of intergenerational income mobility, with 95% of children born to parents in the bottom of the income distribution quintile occupying the same place in the distribution; and 10% of the population owned 90–95% of the country's wealth.

Underlying the poverty and inequality landscape was the growing sense of frustration among the poor and economically marginalised regarding the slow pace of *service delivery programmes* by the government. The number of service delivery protests was the third-highest since 2004. Gauteng topped the list of provinces, recording more than 13% of protests, followed by the Eastern Cape, KwaZulu Natal and North West. Anger aroused by state corruption, enrichment by the political elite and a sense of abandonment by the ANC-run government fuelled the violent nature of the service delivery protests. The protests were also aggravated by police reaction, which as one commentator noted "adds another layer of violence … further destabilising the already vulnerable relationship between communities and authority figures".

The year ended with the *Steinhoff scandal*, which highlighted the opacity of South Africa's private sector. In December, the Viceroy group released an incriminating report on the alleged accounting and financial irregularities and practices of the Steinhoff multinational corporation. The report disclosed that, under the leadership of its former CEO Markus Jooste, the company's earnings had been artificially inflated. This caused ripples on the Johannesburg Stock Exchange, which saw Steinhoff's shares lose 80% of their value, or some € 10 bn. The impact of the report exposed to risk the Public Investment Corporation (PIC), the South African government's asset fund, which invests the government employees' pension fund. Through the PIC's investment in Steinhoff, the pension fund lost about R 12 m. The Steinhoff crisis not only revealed the callous nature of South Africa's private sector but also made clear that private sector corruption should be treated in the same way as state fraud and corruption. The Steinhoff issue also laid bare the inner workings of the 'Stellenbosch mafia', a specific business related conglomerate, which is considered an insular network of financial capital related networks operated by white Afrikaans-speaking members.

Swaziland

Marisha Ramdeen

The Kingdom of Swaziland, ruled by King Mswati III since 1986, remained a country with a small population of approximately 1.3 m people. With the highest rate of HIV/AIDS in the world, the people continued to experience severe food shortages, medical shortages and unemployment. The ongoing drought exacerbated the situation as it affected the agricultural and industrial sectors, further raising unemployment and poverty levels. Excessive use of force by the police continued to contravene human rights laws, and the welfare and protection of children came under the spotlight during the year. The reinstatement of the AGOA trade agreement, together with renewed programme support from the EU, brought fresh hopes of increased trade and development.

Domestic Politics

Pro-democracy groups made calls for regime change, while the country geared itself up for *national elections* due in 2018. For example, the International Union of Socialist Youth called on governments, regional bodies and multilateral organisations

 | DOI:10.1163/9789004367630_054

to pressurise the Swazi regime to introduce multi-party elections. The Swaziland Solidarity Network also called on governments and activists across Africa to support the campaign for freedom in Swaziland ahead of a 'Mobilising International Solidarity for the Democratisation of Swaziland' conference that took place in July in South Africa. The People's United Democratic Movement, the largest opposition group in Swaziland, stated that they would not contest the national elections in 2018. As part of its voter education tour, Swaziland's Elections and Boundaries Commission (EBC) called for an end to ritual killings around voting time. The EBC was concerned about reports of people mysteriously disappearing across Swaziland as there had been evidence of ritual murders in past elections.

Strikes and protests also took place throughout the year. In January, approximately 100 non-academic staff at Limkokwing University in Mbabane protested about working conditions and short-term contracts. Nurses engaged in strike action over the severe shortages of medical drugs. A bus protest against a corrupt police official and a student protest over the late payment of grants took place during February. In October, members of public sector unions such as the National Public Service and Allied Workers Union, the Swaziland National Association of Teachers and the Swaziland Democratic Nurses Union protested to call for salary increases.

Governance indices reflected a poor *human rights record*. In November, the Mo Ibrahim Foundation released its Index of African Governance, in which Swaziland came 50th out of 54 African countries, with a score of 48.9 out of 100 in a range of four areas of governance and a score of 24.6 out of 100 in participation and human rights. Human rights abuses were evident in the excessive use of force by the Swazi police. In February, police fired warning shots during the bus protest to disperse crowds as well as firing live rounds during the student protest. Police also exercised severe force during the public service workers' strike. There was growing concern both locally and internationally about the level of police control, given that 35% of the entire Swazi government workforce was assigned to security-related functions. The US State Department's 2017 Human Rights Report on Swaziland reported that, while there were "mechanisms in place to investigate and punish abuse and corruption, there were few prosecutions or disciplinary actions taken against security offices accused of abuses". The police were accused of spying at a Pensioners' Association meeting, for example. This had been an ongoing occurrence in previous years and distrust of the police continued to grow. Anti-religious policies were implemented in contravention of civil liberties. The Swazi Ministry of Education introduced a ruling that the only religion to be taught in public schools would be Christianity. Print and technological *media censorship* continued throughout the year. It was reported that two journalists from the Swaziland's state-controlled television almost lost their jobs for covering the protest march by public sector workers calling for salary increases.

Gender discrimination continued. According to a UNICEF report in October, one in three females suffered some form of sexual violence during their childhood, one in four experienced physical violence and three in ten experienced emotional abuse as children. Discriminatory laws against women and girls remained prevalent. Married men continued to enjoy more privileges and status than their wives. For example, the Swazi Customary Law and Marriage Act specifies that "married women require the consent of their husbands to enter into certain contracts, including accessing credit from financial institutions". In August, the Southern African Litigation Centre, and Swaziland's Women and Law in Southern Africa Swaziland went to court to challenge these discriminatory laws. The case was ongoing at year's end.

Foreign Affairs

The *EU* and the government met in February to review the performance of their cooperation in 2016 and to plan key priorities for 2017 and beyond. The review indicated satisfaction with Swaziland's cooperation with the EU, which fell within the Cotonou Partnership, a treaty between the EU and the ACP countries. As part of the *EPA* ratified in October 2016, the EU would support two new programmes related to education and training with a total value of E (elangeni) 45 m for the period 2017/18. A Water Harvesting Small Earth Dam Project with a total value of E 42 m was also approved for the next five years, which was to construct 75 small dams and reservoirs to respond to the drought situation and promote water accessibility. These programme estimates were endorsed by the EU delegation in December 2016 and January 2017, when the partners also signed a new Financing Agreement worth € 5 m in support of capacity strengthening and technical cooperation for the government and non-state actors.

In March, King Mswati made a business visit to *India* accompanied by his ministers of foreign affairs, trade, economic planning, health and agriculture. It was reported that talks with the Indian government included plans to revive the Ngwenya Mine, which had collapsed in 2014.

A joint meeting was held in Swaziland in June for the *SADC* ministers responsible for education and training, science, technology and innovation to review the progress and implementation of on-going programmes and initiatives in their respective sectors, particularly in relation to the regional priority agenda.

Swaziland continued with *claims for land* in parts of South Africa. The state-owned newspaper 'The Observer' reported that the Border Determination Special Committee, appointed by King Mswati, aimed to recover all the Swazi land lost during the colonial era, which extends as far as Pretoria and the Limpopo province. The claim also applied to parts of Mozambique.

King Mswati addressed the *UN General Assembly* in September. The key issues he raised included commitments to the Sustainable Development Goals (SDGs); pledges for assistance with drought relief; and support from educated facilitators and the international community for the SADC University of Innovation and Technology, which would produce skilled manpower and provide solutions to meet the skills gap. King Mswati also declared the intention that Swaziland would be free of AIDS by 2022, highlighted malaria eradication efforts, and recalled that Swaziland had been elected Chair of the African Leaders Malaria Alliance during the AU summit in January. In closing, he called for the participation of *Taiwan* in the UN, stating that the country had demonstrated commitment and aligned itself with the UN's priorities.

In December, US President Donald Trump endorsed the re-admission of Swaziland into *AGOA*, and the country's eligibility for trade benefits in 2018. Swaziland had been suspended from AGOA in January 2015 after it reportedly failed to meet five benchmarks, including: the full passage of amendments to the Industrial Relations Act; full passage of amendments to sections 40 and 97 of the Industrial Relations Act relating to civil and criminal liability of union leaders during protest actions; and establishing a code of good practice for the police during public protests. The failure to respect workers' rights, including freedoms of assembly, association and expression, also contributed to its removal from the list of beneficiaries.

South Africa's African National Congress called for Swaziland to be referred to SADC for abuse of human rights and suppression of dissent and political activity. In 2004, Swaziland had ratified the UN International Covenant on Civil and Political Rights and its progress report had been due in 2005. In view of the failure to submit this report, the Human Rights Committee scheduled a review of the kingdom in July.

Socioeconomic Developments

Swaziland continued to be classified as a lower-middle-income country, but its income distribution was highly skewed, with an estimated 20% of the population controlling 80% of the nation's wealth. Swaziland had the world's highest *HIV* prevalence rate, with more than one-quarter of the adult population infected by HIV/AIDS.

In terms of its *exports*, sugar and soft drinks concentrates were the largest foreign exchange earners. Other exports included wood pulp and cotton. Mining had declined in importance in recent years and the only iron ore mine had closed in 2014, but coal, gold and diamond mining, and stone quarrying, continued on a small scale. South Africa continued to be Swaziland's most important trading partner, accounting for 90% of imports and 60% of exports. Swaziland continued to rely heavily on the sugar industry and Coca-Cola's concentration plant contributed about 40% to the country's GDP. Many casual labourers in the sugar industry earned around $ 5 a day. Real *GDP growth* declined to an estimated 1%, down from 1.3% in 2016. According to the AfDB's Economic Outlook, growth was sluggish, particularly in the wholesale and retail trade, but also in financial services, where output was hindered by reduced government spending due to ongoing fiscal challenges. In spite of progress in the agricultural sector following the El Niño-induced drought of 2015, livestock production fell. The manufacturing sector improved, driven mainly by investment in textiles. Construction activity decreased due to limited fiscal space, which stalled the implementation of public projects.

Unemployment and poverty rates remained high. Unemployment stood at 40%, and two-thirds of the population survived on less than a dollar a day. In September, UNICEF released its Swaziland Humanitarian Situation Report, which outlined the severity of the drought and its consequences. A study by the National Disaster Management Agency indicated that total revenue lost due to the 2016 drought stood at $ 296 m, which represented 7% of Swaziland's GDP in 2016. Apart from the lost revenue, the drought also created severe food shortages. One in three people were in need of emergency food assistance, with 640,000 potentially affected by some degree of *food insecurity*. The consequent increased level of malnutrition, particularly in children, was further exacerbated by the collapse of the school feeding scheme.

Following a year of *anti-Indian sentiment*, private and public schools were forced to conduct lessons in Siswati. The government also ordered schools to provide religious education only in Christianity. Other religious groups slammed this, saying that it fuelled intolerance. Swazi schools opened for the new school year with new religious education textbooks that referred only to the Bible. Schools were obliged to submit their religious studies syllabi at the start of each term to show that they contained no Islamic or Jewish references. Criticism was particularly strong from the Muslim community, which made up one-tenth of the population. People with albinism were also victimised and targeted by witchdoctors, who used body parts to make spells that they claimed brought good luck.

The health sector faced *severe shortages of medical drugs*, which led to a strike by nurses. $ 18 m was owed to drug companies in May and delivery of medicines was suspended until bills were paid. The Ministry of Health, with support from WHO, conducted a sensitisation workshop for technical officers and senior officials on the SDGs to provide a platform for senior health systems technical officials, policy makers and key stakeholders to review, discuss and coordinate efforts towards attaining the health SDGs. At an HIV conference held in Paris in July, a Swazi Health Ministry official indicated that the rate of new infections had been halved in the last five years as a result of boosting access to antiretrovirals.

In the *education* sector, the government approved a Ministry of Education and Training decision to introduce school fees, effectively ending free primary education, which had been available in the country since 2005. The Swaziland National Association of Teachers criticised the decision as a violation of the right to primary education guaranteed in the country's Constitution.

In September, following the annual *Umhlanga or Reed Dance* ceremony, King Mswati picked his fourteenth wife; about 40,000 young women participated in the event. The 'Business Insider' reported that King Mswati was the third-wealthiest king in Africa with an estimated $ 200 m.

Zambia

Edalina Rodrigues Sanches

Zambia became increasingly authoritarian under Patriotic Front (PF) President Edgar Lungu, who had been elected in a tightly contested presidential election in 2016. The runner-up, the United Party for National Development (UPND), engaged in a series of actions to challenge the validity of the results. The UPND saw 48 of its legislators suspended for boycotting Lungu's state of the nation address and its leader, Hakainde Hichilema, was arrested on charges of treason after his motorcade allegedly blocked Lungu's convoy. Independent media and civil society organisations were under pressure. A state of emergency was declared after several arson attacks. Lungu announced his intention to run in the 2021 elections and warned judges that blocking this would plunge the country into chaos. The economy performed better, underpinned by global economic recovery and higher demand for copper, the country's key export. Stronger performance in the agricultural and mining sectors and higher electricity generation also contributed to the recovery. The Zambian kwacha stabilised against the dollar and inflation stood within the target. The cost of living increased. The country's high risk of debt distress led the IMF to put off a $ 1.3 bn loan deal. China continued to play a pivotal role in Zambia's

 | DOI:10.1163/9789004367630_055

economic development trajectory. New bilateral cooperation agreements were signed with Southern African countries.

Domestic Politics

The controversial results of the August 2016 *presidential elections* heightened political tensions for most of the year. Hakainde Hichilema, the UPND presidential candidate since 2006, saw the PF incumbent Lungu win the election by a narrow margin and subsequently contested the results, alleging that the vote was rigged. The initial petition to the Constitutional Court was rejected because the 14-day petition period expired before lawyers could begin their arguments. The UPND subsequently appealed to the High Court and stated that the party would not recognise the legitimacy of Lungu's victory until its electoral petition against the results was heard in court. For his part, Lungu accused his rivals of trying to overturn the election results.

On 17 March, President Lungu delivered the *state of the nation address* to the National Assembly. He declared Zambia to be a Christian nation and highlighted values of national unity, peace and sovereignty and the roles that each and every individual should play to safeguard national values and principles. Patriotism, namely the defence of Zambian economic interests (particularly regarding the exploration of natural resources), was also strongly emphasised. The UPND legislators boycotted the event on the grounds that they could not listen to someone whose election was the subject of a petition in the High Court. This was the second time they had boycotted parliament, the first being on 30 September 2016 at the official opening of National Parliament. On that occasion, their actions were referred to the Committee on Privileges, Absences and Support Services, which subsequently asked the speaker to reprimand them. This time, the committee decided to suspend the 48 UPND legislators who boycotted the address for 30 days. National Assembly Speaker Patrick Matibini found them guilty of breaking parliamentary rules and challenged them to resign on moral grounds if they did not recognise that there was a legitimately elected government. The *suspension of UPND legislators* triggered further polarisation, and many considered the decision unlawful and undemocratic. In fact, most of the parliamentarians who were suspended (46 of the 48) challenged the speaker's decision in the Lusaka High Court and asked for a judicial review.

In April, Hakainde Hichilema and five of his collaborators were arrested on *charges of treason* for disobeying police orders to give way to the presidential motorcade in what was seen as an attempt to put the life of the president in danger. Critical remarks on Hichilema's detention came from all quarters of civil society, including religious leaders and international organisations. Deprose Muchena, AI's regional director for Southern Africa, publicly criticised the detention of Hichilema and his followers, describing them as victims of a "cynical ploy to silence all political opposition".

Throughout the detention period, the Zambian authorities put considerable pressure on Hichilema's supporters. This included *obstructing attendance at his trial*; Mmusi Maimane, the leader of South Africa's main opposition party, the Democratic Alliance, was prohibited from entering the country to attend. When interviewed on this issue, Maimane stated that he simply wanted "to stand side-by-side with someone who has been fighting for the rule of law" and referred to the charges as "an affront to democracy across the region" that was clearly politically motivated. The Lusaka High Court also barred international media outlets from covering the trial by withdrawing their accreditations. Hichilema was eventually released in August amid speculation that the charges against him and his collaborators had been dropped after a deal was negotiated by the Commonwealth.

On 5 July, after a series of arson attacks, President Lungu declared in a nationally televised address that he had decided "to invoke article 31 [leading] to a *state of public emergency*". He cited several fires, including one that had burnt down the main market in the capital Lusaka, and described them as "premeditated acts which if left unchecked could have serious consequences". Lungu also alleged that supporters of the UPND were behind the attacks. The National Assembly approved the emergency powers on 11 July and extended the state of emergency for a period of 90 days. Under the emergency declaration, police could prohibit public meetings, close roads, impose curfews and restrict movement. Opposition members of parliament (MPs) boycotted the vote by exiting the chamber, leaving only the 85 members of the president's majority party to pass the measure. Through its president, Linda Kasonde, the Law Association of Zambia (LAZ) stated that the executive branch should have been reluctant to invoke Article 31, despite such power being given to the president under the Constitution, and that the state of public emergency could not extend beyond three months, as there was no power of extension under Article 31. The International Press Institute expressed concern over the imposition of emergency powers and comments made by the inspector general of police that some publications could be closed while the 90-day state of emergency was in place. Bishop Simon Chihana, president of the International Fellowship of Christian Churches, declared: "This is a clear sign of dictatorship – just because of a fire at a market and you declare a state of emergency?"

Independent media and civil society organisations were under pressure. There was an ongoing campaign to silence 'The Post' editor Fred M'membe, who faced legal charges for refusing to hand over houses, books and other property owned by 'The Post' after the closure of the newspaper in 2016. The 'Mast Newspaper' saw its printing press confiscated by the police on suspicion that it belonged to 'The Post'. LAZ's president, Linda Kasonde, came under attack when reports showed that she had previously worked for Hakainde Hichilema. Lewis Mwape, executive director of the Zambia Council for Social Development (ZCSD), and five other leaders of civil society organisations were arrested and charged with standing against a corrupt tender process in which 42 fire tenders were acquired for $ 1 m each. This was promptly condemned by many civil society organisation platforms and networks, including the African Monitor, the Africa Working Group, and the International Forum of National NGO Platforms.

Opposition political parties' activities were often undermined. In August, Savior Chishimba, leader of the United Progressive Party and a fierce critic of Lungu, was detained for allegedly defaming the president. Chishimba was released one week later. In October, UPND members were arrested in Luwingu for allegedly holding an indoor meeting without a police permit, which prompted criticism from civil society organisations such as the ZCSD. As in previous years, *floor crossing and infighting* continued to weaken opposition political parties, particularly the Multi-Party Democracy (MMD) and the Rainbow Party (RB). In the MMD, conflict over leadership resumed between the Nevers Mumba faction and the Felix Mutati faction. Mumba had been declared the legitimate party president by the court in 2016, following a lawsuit he filed against the Mutati faction, which elected the latter as party president. However, the party never came together to support one leader. As this continued to trigger infighting, most senior officials crossed over to either the UPND or the ruling PF. In the RB, over 500 members were reported to have joined the ruling PF, citing leadership failure by Wynter Kabimba. Kabimba was the PF's former minister of justice and secretary general, and he along with other senior PF members had founded the RB in 2014. The two main parties also suffered some internal turbulence. Former Copperbelt Minister Mwenya Musenge was expelled from the PF for disagreeing with President Lungu over Hakainde Hichilema's detention. He later formed the National Democratic Congress. Former UPND Bweengwa MP Highvie Hamududu officially launched a new political party called the Party for National Unity.

Zambia opened public discussions on whether to leave the *ICC*. This was in response to the AU Summit's adoption of an 'ICC withdrawal strategy'. An unprecedented 16 countries, including Zambia, submitted reservations on this decision. The consultation process was undertaken in March, in collaboration with some civil society organisations in 31 districts of Zambia, which were sampled for public sittings. The results from the sample of individual citizens indicated that 9.0% of individuals were of the view that Zambia should withdraw from the ICC, while 90.1% were against it. With regard to civil society organisations and institutions, 0.9% were of the view that Zambia should withdraw from the ICC while 98.2% were against.

Lungu announced that he would stand in the *next general election*, due in 2021. This raised controversy, as the Constitution states that a president can only serve for two five-year terms. His bid to run in the election was challenged in court by the opposition, who argued that he was serving his second and final term. Lungu had first been elected president in January 2015 after the death of Michael Sata and had been re-elected in 2016, but it remained unclear whether that would count as two terms under the law. In reaction to the criticism, Lungu warned the judges against blocking him from running, saying that a judicial intervention like the one in Kenya could plunge the country into chaos. Zambia's opposition legislators abandoned parliament to protest against Lungu and accused him of not respecting the separation of powers between the executive and the judiciary and of trying to intimidate the judges.

According to Freedom House ratings, Zambia was 'partly free' in terms of respect for political rights and civil liberties, 'partly free' in net freedom, and 'not free' in press freedom. Public satisfaction with *regime performance* had decreased, according to Afrobarometer surveys. Comparing the 2012 and 2017 surveys, the proportion of Zambians that evaluated the last election as free and fair fell from 78% to 60%, satisfaction with democracy decreased from 78% to 49%, and the proportion of those who considered the country to be democratic dropped from 76% to 59%. The surveys also showed that "Zambians stand by their firm commitment to democratic ideals, reiterate solid support for institutional checks and balances, and strongly reject one-man rule."

Foreign Policy

China continued to be a strategic trade and investment partner. Zambia was currently China's second-largest investment country in Africa, as China had invested heavily in modernising roads and other infrastructure. In March, President Lungu met with Tian Guoli, president of the Bank of China, and Yang Youming, the Chinese ambassador to Zambia, at State House and urged Chinese investors to partner with local private companies to foster economic growth in the country. The Bank of China would help finance the construction of 2,000 homes for Zambian military personnel, who faced a critical housing shortage. The K (kwacha) 1.5 bn ($ 157 m) project would be financed by the Development Bank of Zambia with support from the Industrial and Commercial Bank of China. In June, Lungu met with Wang Yong, the Chinese state counsel in charge of China's economy, and his delegation at State House. Wang Yong's visit was aimed at strengthening economic investments. As result of this meeting, Zambia and China signed two economic and technical cooperation agreements worth RMB (yuan) 450 m for the expansion of the Levy Mwanawasa Hospital and the construction of an international conference centre in Lusaka to enable Zambia to host the AU summit in 2022.

Lungu's international trips continued to raise controversy and criticism because of their cost, but they were justified by the government as being key for the country's development strategy and economic recovery. Throughout the year, most of his overseas visits sought to boost mainly bilateral ties with *Southern African countries*. On 6–7 January, Lungu visited Ghana for the inauguration of President Nana Akufo-Addo. Between 27 and 31 January, he attended the 28th AU Heads of State meeting in Addis Ababa (Ethiopia), followed by a visit to Botswana (6–7 February), where Lungu joined Zimbabwean President Emmerson Mnangagwa and Botswana's leader Seretse Khama Ian Khama to evaluate progress on the construction of the Kazungula Bridge, which would connect eight SADC countries. From 28 February to 5 March, he visited Israel, where he met with Prime Minister Benjamin Netanyahu to open the door for further cooperation, and he was in Swaziland on 17–19 March to attend the SADC summit.

On 17–18 May, Lungu attended the AU C10 Summit held in Malabo (Equatorial Guinea), and on 15 June he attended the inauguration ceremony of Lesotho's President Tom Thabane. On 4–6 July, Minister of Agriculture Dora Siliya and Minister of Finance Felix Mutati visited Kenya to discuss agricultural trade. Kenya and Zambia eventually signed an agreement on trade in agricultural commodities that would allow Kenya's private dealers to import maize and sugar on more convenient terms. In this new arrangement, the Zambian government removed 10% of the additional tax on maize exported to Kenya to enable a fast-track movement of the commodity.

In August, Lungu attended the inauguration of Rwandan President Paul Kagame and on 19–20 August he participated in the SADC summit in Pretoria (South Africa). In September, he attended the 72nd session of the UN General Assembly and the inauguration of Angola's new President João Manuel Gonçalves Lourenço. On 18 October, he travelled to the Republic of the Congo to attend the Great Lakes Region Summit. By the end of the year, Lungu had also visited Egypt (14 November), Zimbabwe for President Emmerson Mnangagwa's inauguration (24 November), and Kenya for President Uhuru Kenyatta's inauguration (28 November).

This was also a year in which several leaders paid *visits to Zambia*. On 19 June, Rwandan President Paul Kagame arrived in Lusaka for a state visit aiming at fostering a closer partnership and more cooperation, particularly with regard to imports and exports. Trade between the two countries was on an upward trend, with imports from Zambia growing from $ 2.8 m in 2015 to $ 11.6 m in 2016. As one of the means to promote interaction between the citizens of the two countries, flights by the national carrier RwandAir were increased to seven a week. The two heads of state witnessed the signing of three bilateral agreements: an air services agreement, a MoU on defence and security cooperation, and an extradition treaty between the two nations.

South African President Jacob Zuma came as a guest of honour to officially open the 91st Agricultural and Commercial Show, held from 2 to 7 August. The show was organised under the theme 'The Promotion of a Green Economy'. Two months later, he visited Zambia again to officially open the Oliver Reginald Tambo National Heritage site in Lusaka as part of a celebration of Tambo's legacy and the centenary year of the struggle. The visit was also expected to strengthen bilateral ties between the two Southern African countries, which share a long history of friendship. They shared economic ties that amount to at least R (rand) 30 bn and Zambia was among South Africa's top trading partners in the region. The two countries had signed 21 agreements and MoUs over previous years, including cooperation in the field of agriculture, which enabled them to share agricultural development experiences, capacity building and skills development programmes (among other areas of cooperation).

Socioeconomic Developments

Zambia experienced *economic growth* of 3.8% to 4%, up from 3.6% in 2016, underpinned by improved global conditions for growth and the easing of domestic constraints. The strong global demand for commodities, particularly from China, contributed to supporting the recovery of metal process prices, particularly copper, which accounted for 77% of Zambia's exports. Having declined between the first and third quarters of 2016, *exports* grew by 14% between the fourth quarter of 2016 and the third quarter of 2017, driven by increased copper prices. *Imports* also increased by 4% between the fourth quarter of 2016 and third quarter of 2017. This was driven by consumer goods (13% growth), raw materials (24%), and intermediate goods (85%). The kwacha was more stable than in 2016. It strengthened by 10.3% between January and the end of July. However, between August and November, the local currency came under renewed pressure and depreciated by 11.9%. *Inflation* stood within the Bank of Zambia's (BoZ's) medium-term target range of 6–8%. Internally, stronger performance from the agricultural sector, higher levels of electricity generation, and higher mining outputs helped economic growth. The mining industry performed better and was expected to grow by a yearly average of 5.5% between 2017 and 2021, which contrasted positively with the average decline of 5.4% experienced between 2012 and 2016. Maize production reached a record high of 3.7 m tonnes, up 27% from 2016, and electricity production increased from 3 m MW in the fourth quarter of 2016 to 3.69 m MW in the third quarter of 2017, according to Lungu's address to the nation on occasion of the New Year.

However, the year was distressing for many households. According to the Jesuit Centre for Theological Reflection (JCTR) 'basic needs basket', the national monthly average *cost of living* increased from K 3,471 in 2016 to K 3,511. Government policy measures such as the removal of fuel and electricity subsidies, which resulted in subsequent tariff hikes, were major factors. People's ability to afford the high cost of living was also compromised by on-going high unemployment rates (particularly among youth) and few economic opportunities. In addition, the JCTR's 'basic needs basket' identified increases in prices of kapenta, fish, mealie meal and charcoal as major contributing factors.

In October, Minister of Labour and Social Security Joyce Simukoko stated that the government would soon make an upward adjustment to the *minimum wage* in its efforts to improve conditions of service for workers countrywide. The minimum wage had not been revised since 2012.

Fiscal imbalances and the accumulation of *debt* continued to present a challenge to the ability of monetary policy to achieve its objectives, according to the BoZ. Debt sustainability was at the core of Zambia's discussions with the IMF over a $ 1.3 bn loan and economic programme. Finance Minister Felix Mutati stated that the government had submitted a proposal in May and was waiting for the IMF board to meet in August to make a decision on whether to bail out the country.

In June, the government launched as new *economic blueprints* the Economic Stabilization and Growth Program (ESGP) and the Seventh National Development Plan (7NDP) for 2017–21. The ESGP aimed at restoring macroeconomic stability and creating conditions for sustained growth, with a heavy emphasis on public financial management: enhancing resource mobilisation, refocusing public spending on core public sector mandates, scaling up social protection programmes, strengthening accountability and transparency in the use of public resources, and restoring budget credibility were its key points. The 7NDP offered a broad parameter for the government's development agenda. It had five pillars, namely: (i) economic diversification and job creation, (ii) poverty and vulnerability reduction, (iii) reducing development inequalities, (iv) enhancing human development, and (v) creating a conducive governance environment for a diversified and inclusive economy.

In September, an IMF Debt Sustainability Analysis assessed Zambia to be at high risk of *debt distress*, indicating that there were heightened vulnerabilities associated with public debt. The current value of public and publicly guaranteed external debt as a share of GDP was 34.5%. Though this value was lower than in 2016 (37%), it was expected to increase dramatically in the coming years and to reach 44.3% in 2021. In December, the *IMF* clearly stated for the first time that much of the anticipated $ 1.3 bn loan deal with the Zambian government had been postponed. IMF Communications Director Gerry Rice confirmed that negotiations were on hold due to extensive borrowing by the PF government.

The government announced that Zambia was set to re-launch an airline carrier in partnership with Ethiopian Airlines. The long-awaited national airline would operate as *Zambia Airways 2014* Ltd, as a successor to the defunct Zambia Airways, liquidated in 1994. Since then, Zambia had had no national airline. According to Transport Minister Brian Mushimba, the government would be the majority shareholder in the partnership.

Zimbabwe

Amin Y. Kamete

The removal of President Robert Mugabe in what has been dubbed a 'soft coup' was the biggest story of the year. Before Mugabe's resignation, factional struggles in the Zimbabwe African National Union-Patriotic Front (ZANU-PF), in which his wife, Grace Mugabe, was the key player, dominated the news for most of the year. Away from ZANU-PF, the opposition remained divided and bickered constantly. While foreign relations with the usual friends remained good, there was very little improvement in relations with Western countries and multilateral lenders. Arguments about 'illegal' Western sanctions and human rights abuses persisted. Though some indicators improved, the economy showed no sign of significant improvement with cash shortages being one of the major challenges.

Domestic Politics

The year started quietly. The major developments in domestic politics related to justice. On 1 February, *#ThisFlag* activist and cleric Pastor Evan Mawarire was arrested by state security agents at Harare airport on his return from the US. He had spent

 | DOI:10.1163/9789004367630_056

six months outside the country. Mawarire was at the heart of the protests that had rocked Harare in 2016. He was charged with organising demonstrations and inciting violence. He was freed on bail by the High Court on 8 February. On the same day, the Constitutional Court dismissed a case against President Mugabe lodged by Promise Mkwananzi, a leading activist of the pressure group *#Tajamuka*. Mkwananzi had accused the ageing leader of violating the Constitution during the violently repressed protests in 2016. In the landmark case, Mkwananzi had asked the court to decide whether repressive actions by Mugabe had violated the Constitution.

In May, the Pan-African research group *Afrobarometer* released the results of a survey that claimed 64% of Zimbabweans trusted President Mugabe and that 56% of Zimbabweans approved of the government's management of the country. The report also indicated that at least 36% distrusted opposition parties. The survey showed that 50% of adult Zimbabweans trusted the Zimbabwe Electoral Commission (ZEC). Opposition parties disputed the survey's results, which were given very wide coverage by the state-controlled media.

There was some activity in government's response to cybercrime but opposition parties claimed this was an attempt to clamp down on criticism. In May, it was reported that Zimbabwe was one of the countries hit by the WannaCry ransomware, a massive cyber-attack that hit computers in 104 countries. In the aftermath of the attack, on 17 May, Information and Communication Technology Minister Supa Mandiwanzira announced that the government would speed up the finalisation of the *Computer Crime and Cybercrime Bill*. Opposition parties expressed concern that the real intention behind the bill was to abuse the law to criminalise criticism of the president. This seemed to have been confirmed in August, when it was reported that the government was finalising the new cybercrime bill to criminalise false information posted on the Internet, revenge porn, cyber-bullying and online activity against the government, among other activities. Mandiwanzira said that the Cyber Crime and Cyber Security Bill would soon go to parliament, and was expected to be fast-tracked into law before the end of the year.

ZANU-PF *succession struggles* escalated. The main factions were 'Team Lacoste', aligned to Vice President Emmerson Mnangagwa, and 'Generation 40' ('G40'), aligned to Grace Mugabe. The factional struggles intensified during Presidential Youth Interface Rallies, which were organised by the ZANU-PF youth league ostensibly as occasions for Robert Mugabe to interact with the youth. The idea was to take the interface rallies to all ten provinces. The rallies started on 2 June with the Mashonaland East rally, which took place in Marondera. Commentators and Mnangagwa allies interpreted these rallies as being held to bolster the G40 faction as a strategy to advance Grace Mugabe's presidential ambitions. This appeared to be the case as the star of these rallies was undoubtedly Grace Mugabe. She used the rallies to attack Team Lacoste in general and Mnangagwa in particular. On 29 July, at the 5th Youth Interface Rally in Chinhoyi, Grace Mugabe launched a scathing attack on the Lacoste faction, accusing it of plotting against her husband and persecuting G40-aligned ministers. She singled out Higher and Tertiary Education Minister Jonathan Moyo, claiming that he had been falsely accused of corruption, although these charges continued to haunt him for most of the year.

Grace Mugabe's public statements on succession suggested that the factional struggles were heating up. On 27 July, *Grace Mugabe* challenged the president to name his preferred successor. This was the first time she appeared to contradict her husband. Though her stated reason for this naming was to end deepening divisions over the future leadership of the ruling ZANU-PF, it could also have been a sign that the succession battle was intensifying. She told a ZANU-PF rally that Mugabe had rejected her advice to name a successor, and hence her public challenge. This was a public contradiction of her own statement in February, when she stated that Mugabe should run 'as a corpse' in the 2018 election if he died before the vote. In an apparent reference to Mnangagwa, Mrs Mugabe warned associates of her husband from the period of the liberation struggle that they were also too old to take power. This was a rebuttal to those who were insisting that Mugabe should step down because his advanced age.

At the 6th Youth Interface Rally for Matabeleland South, held in Gwanda on 12 August, Vice President *Emmerson Mnangagwa* was rushed to hospital after falling ill. This incident exposed the rifts in ZANU-PF and worsened the relationship between Mugabe and his deputy. It later emerged that he had ingested poison. Official sources close to the vice president, however, downplayed social media claims that Mnangagwa had been poisoned. Rumours on social media linked his sudden illness to the ice-cream that had been served at the rally, and which was sourced from Mugabe's company, Gushungo Dairy Estate. On 14 August, Mnangagwa was airlifted to South Africa for medical attention after his health reportedly took a turn for the worse. Mnangagwa's illness fuelled suspicions that the poisoning was an assassination attempt. Mugabe and the G40 faction mounted spirited attempts to downplay the poisoning allegation. Grace Mugabe's outbursts and her angry public response to the rumours of food poisoning demonstrated how sensitive she was to the allegations, but her sensitivity and anger only fuelled the rumours of an assassination attempt on Mnangagwa. As the ZANU-PF succession wars reached a tipping point, Vice President Phelekezela Mphoko, then Acting President in the absence of Mugabe, and his counterpart Emmerson Mnangagwa openly traded accusations. On 30 September, Mnangagwa publicly told a memorial gathering that he had been poisoned. In a hard-hitting statement released on 3 October, Mphoko accused Mnangagwa of undermining Mugabe's authority and trying to destabilise the country by fanning ethnic tensions for political ends. In a rebuttal on 4 October, Mnangagwa said Mphoko had no authority to comment on his health issues and pointed out that Mphoko was "neither competent nor privileged to comment on my health because he is neither my doctor nor my employer".

President Mugabe showed the same sensitivity to the speculations about Mnangagwa's poisoning. On 1 September, at the 7th Presidential Youth Interface Rally in Gweru, he castigated some elements that he accused of peddling false allegations that Mnangagwa had fallen ill after eating ice cream from his dairy company. Mugabe claimed that Mnangagwa's South African-based doctor had briefed him on his deputy's ailment and ruled out food poisoning. On 5 October, Mnangagwa again said he had been hospitalised because he had been poisoned. This escalated the succession battles and was met with another angry outburst by Grace Mugabe, who insisted she had no reason to kill Mnangagwa because she was "the wife of the president". The relationship between Mugabe and his deputy never recovered. Grace Mugabe intensified her public attacks on Mnangagwa in the presidential interface rallies and at many events that she attended.

On 30 August, a *Grace Mugabe solidarity march* took place in Harare. The turnout was not as high as anticipated and Mnangagwa's Lacoste faction was blamed for sabotaging it. War veterans, who continued their criticism of Mrs Mugabe, and opposition parties poured scorn on the march. There was talk that Mugabe's wife was angling to be one of the vice presidents in place of Mnangagwa, which was seen as a path to the presidency. Suspicions of a *dynasty* in the making intensified when Mugabe's daughter, Bona Mugabe-Chikore, received two appointments in May in quick succession. On 24 May, she was appointed to the unpopular Censorship Board in a move that was interpreted as being intended to stifle criticism of President Mugabe. On 27 May, she was named as a board member of the new state-run Empower Bank.

In an explosive presentation to the *ZANU-PF politburo* on 19 June, Higher and Tertiary Education Minister Jonathan Moyo alleged that Mnangagwa and his Lacoste loyalists were aiming to succeed Mugabe through a number of schemes. On 4 October, Mnangagwa responded to the politburo, accusing Moyo of being a CIA agent working to destroy ZANU-PF from within. In a lengthy report, Mnangagwa claimed that Moyo was working with Western diplomats and officials against ZANU-PF. Mnangagwa reportedly accused Moyo and his G40 faction counterpart, Minister of Local Government, Rural Development and National Housing Saviour Kasukuwere, of secretly conniving to reduce Mugabe's powers by challenging ZANU-PF's 'one centre of power' principle and leaking confidential information to the press.

In what was interpreted as a reflection of the factional struggles in ZANU-PF, on 9 October, Mugabe announced a shock *cabinet reshuffle.* He dropped three ministers and reassigned ten others. Suspicions that this was an expansion of intra-party factionalism were given credence when Mugabe took the Ministry of Justice from Mnangagwa and gave it to Central Intelligence Organisation director-general Happyton Bonyongwe. Those axed from the cabinet included Priscah Mupfumira (Public Service), Tshinga Dube (War Veterans) and Abednico Ncube (Rural Development), all of whom were believed to be sympathetic to Mnangagwa. Patrick

Chinamasa, a high profile Mnangagwa ally, was reassigned from the Finance and Economic Development Ministry to a new ministry, the Ministry of Cyber Security, Threat Detection and Mitigation. Zimbabweans jokingly referred to him as 'Minister of WhatsApp'. On 7 October, Mugabe had warned of the reshuffle, saying it was targeted at underperformers, but there was strong belief within ZANU-PF that Mugabe wanted to weaken Mnangagwa by getting rid of his allies.

In the last quarter of the year, the Presidential Interface Rallies continued and Grace Mugabe's *public attacks and humiliation of Mnangagwa* at the rallies intensified. The factional battles came to a head during the 9th Interface Rally in Bulawayo on 4 November. During her speech, Grace Mugabe was booed by what her allies claimed were people hired by Mnangagwa. She was visibly angry, and so was President Mugabe who, for the first time, publicly threatened to fire Mnangagwa the next day. In an indication of Mrs Mugabe's power, on 10 November, four people appeared in court on charges of undermining President Mugabe's authority after his wife was heckled at the Bulawayo rally. The Bulawayo rally was seen as marking the beginning of the end for Mnangagwa and Team Lacoste and the ascendency of Grace Mugabe to the presidency.

On 5 November, Grace Mugabe 'interfaced' with indigenous churches at Rufaro Stadium in Harare. In her speech, she launched her longest and most vitriolic attack on Mnangagwa. In her publicly broadcast speech, she gloated over her husband's threat to fire Mnangagwa, hinting that the end was near for the vice president. Obviously referring to Mnangagwa, Mrs Mugabe told the rally that "the snake must be hit on the head". On 6 November, *Mnangagwa was removed from his post* as vice president. Media, Information and Broadcasting Services Minister Simon Khaya Moyo announced that Mnangagwa had displayed "traits of disloyalty" and that his "conduct in discharge of his duties" was "inconsistent with the responsibilities". Mnangagwa was also expelled from the ruling party. The sacking made it more likely that Grace Mugabe was on the way to being vice president and then president of Zimbabwe. On 6 November, the ZANU-PF youth league endorsed Grace Mugabe as the right candidate to occupy the vice presidency ahead of the extraordinary congress set for December. In what seemed to be a choreographed speech at the ZANU-PF politburo meeting on 8 November, the second vice president, Phelekezela Mphoko, urged President Mugabe to quickly appoint Mnangagwa's successor, saying that he was "now lonely". Mphoko said Mugabe should not be afraid or ashamed to appoint his wife as vice president, insisting that the people had "identified the one they want".

In what was to be the beginning of a fast-moving chain of events, in an unprecedented move on 13 November, *General Constantino Chiwenga*, the commander of the Zimbabwe Defence Forces warned that the military would not hesitate to step in to end purges against former liberation war fighters in ZANU-PF. This was a clear response to the sacking of Mnangagwa. Chiwenga, a political ally of Mnangagwa, said ZANU-PF had been hijacked by people who had not fought in the 1970s liberation war – a clear reference to the G40 faction and Grace Mugabe. Chiwenga reminded "those behind the current treacherous shenanigans that, when it comes to matters of protecting our revolution, the military will not hesitate to step in". His statement was read out at a news conference attended by the army top brass but the state-controlled press and public broadcaster ignored it. Responses were quick. On 14 November, a statement issued by the ZANU-PF youth league, and read by Secretary for Youth Kudzanayi Chipanga, condemned Chiwenga, telling him to first account for the $ 15 bn missing from the country's diamond sales, as he, together with Mnangagwa, presided over the country's diamond revenues. The youth league said they were ready to die for Mugabe. Jonathan Moyo used Twitter to contemptuously dismiss Chiwenga's warning. On the same day, through its Secretary for Information Khaya Moyo, ZANU-PF called Chiwenga's statement "treasonous". Khaya Moyo said Chiwenga's utterances did not represent the rest of the command element and were meant to disturb national peace and stability, stating that "the gun seeks to overreach by dictating to politics and norms of constitutionality".

In the early hours of 15 November, army soldiers deployed in central Harare, taking control of state television, surrounding government ministries and sealing off Robert Mugabe's official and private residences. This was the beginning of what was later to be termed a *'soft coup'.* At 1:26 am, Major General Sibusiso Moyo appeared on state television and declared that the army was taking what he called "targeted action" against the "criminals" around Mugabe "who were committing crimes that are causing social and economic suffering … in order to bring them to justice". The army spokesman insisted that this was not a takeover of the government but a move by the army "to pacify a degenerating political, social and economic situation" which, if not addressed, would cause violent conflict. Several government ministers linked to the G40 faction were reported to have been arrested. It later turned out that the G40 members arrested were Finance and Economic Development Minister Ignatius Chombo, and the combative ZANU-PF Secretary for Youth, Kudzanayi Chipanga. Mugabe and his wife were effectively under house arrest. Moyo, Kasukuwere and Patrick Zhuwao, the three most prominent members of Grace Mugabe's G40 faction skipped the country and Vice President Mphoko was also abroad.

Thousands of people celebrated the army takeover and urged Mugabe to step down. With police nowhere to be found, people could gather and march without police repression. They tore down pictures of Mugabe and marched to his office and residence. On 17 November, President Mugabe made his first public appearance since being confined to his house. He presided over the graduation at the Zimbabwe Open University as its chancellor. His wife was not with him and there were rumours that she had left the country, though these turned out to be false. *Negotiations,* mediated by Jesuit priest Fidelis Mukonori were reportedly going on behind the scenes to persuade Mugabe to step down. It was reported that he had insisted that he could not resign to legitimise a coup. On 16 November, Mugabe was pictured smiling as he took part in talks with an army general and South African government ministers at State House.

The 'soft coup' had widespread public backing, especially in Harare. The Zimbabwe National Liberation War Veterans Association called for a huge turnout in support of the military takeover. On 17 November, at least eight out of ten ZANU-PF provinces voted for Mugabe to resign as president and party secretary, for Grace Mugabe to be fired from the party and for Mnangagwa to be reinstated as a member of the Central Committee. Mnangagwa had by then left the country, reportedly fearing for his life, and was reported to be in South Africa. Groups opposed to Mugabe backed the military, with #ThisFlag leader Pastor Evan Mawarire urging people to turn up for the solidarity march planned for 18 November. On 19 November, Mugabe was expected to resign in a national address on live television but, when he did address the nation, he did not announce his resignation. Instead, in a rambling 30-minute address, he offered no concessions. There was speculation that he had swapped speeches. ZANU-PF warned it would seek to impeach him if he failed to resign by midday on 20 November. After the speech, the ZANU-PF chief whip announced that parliament would proceed with impeaching Mugabe on 21 November.

On 21 November, parliament heard charges in Mugabe's *impeachment proceedings.* MPs cheered as they listened to allegations against him, including that he had "allowed his wife to usurp constitutional power" and that he was "of advanced age". The impeachment motion was introduced by ZANU-PF and seconded by the opposition MDC and crowds gathered outside parliament in support of the proceedings. On 21 November, *Mugabe resigned.* In a letter read out by the speaker of parliament, he said the decision was voluntary and he had made it to allow a smooth transfer of power. The news halted the impeachment hearing. MPs and crowds celebrated and ZANU-PF said former vice president Mnangagwa would succeed Mugabe. On 24 November, *Mnangagwa was sworn in as president* in a packed National Sports Stadium, having returned to Zimbabwe two days before.

On 30 November, the newly inaugurated President Mnangagwa named a *new cabinet* comprising new and old faces. Some of the old faces were Patrick Chinamasa (Finance and Economic Development), Obert Mpofu (Home Affairs) and Kembo Mohadi (Defence, Security and War Veterans). Among the new faces were key figures from the military. They included Major General Sibusiso Moyo (Foreign Affairs) and Air Marshal Perrance Shiri (Lands, Agriculture and Rural Resettlement). Opinion was divided on the new cabinet, with the opposition dismissing it as being made up of "dead wood". The *ZANU-PF extraordinary congress* was held on 15 December, trimmed down to one day of business on a reduced budget. On 18 December, Police Commissioner-General Augustine Chihuri, seen as a member of the G40 'cabal', was retired as the commissioner general of the Zimbabwe Republic

Police. Deputy Commissioner Godwin Matanga was appointed as acting commissioner general. Like many Zimbabweans, the opposition cheered the firing of the unpopular Chihuri. On 23 December, Mnangagwa appointed now-retired army boss Constantino Chiwenga and Kembo Mohadi as vice presidents of ZANU-PF and, on 27 December, they were appointed as Zimbabwe's new vice presidents.

Foreign Affairs

Relations with most African and Asian countries and organisations remained good. There was little change in relations with OECD countries and major multilateral organisations. ZANU-PF and the government continued blaming Zimbabwe's economic woes on 'illegal' *Western sanctions.*

Zimbabwe continued to be an active and enthusiastic participant in *SADC* affairs but, unlike in previous years, was not the centre of attention. Mugabe attended the 37th Heads of State and Government Summit in Pretoria (South Africa) on 19–20 August. For the second year running, Zimbabwe was not on the agenda. Mugabe was not accompanied by his wife, whose absence was possibly due to her having been accused of assault (see below).

Relations with *South Africa* remained friendly, but they were tested. On 14 August, Gabriella Engels, a 20-year-old model, claimed *Grace Mugabe* had assaulted her with an extension cord at a Sandton Hotel in Johannesburg on 13 August and there was speculation that Grace Mugabe could face prosecution. Diplomatic immunity could only be granted if she had been in the country on official business, but reports were that this was a private health-related visit. On 16 August, it was reported that she was seeking diplomatic immunity. Acting National Police Commissioner Lesetja Mothiba stated that the position of the police was that she should go to court. Police Minister Fikile Mbalula said Grace Mugabe was due to appear in court but she did not attend, fuelling speculation she may have returned to Zimbabwe. South African police put border posts on red alert to prevent her fleeing. On 18 August, South Africa granted her diplomatic immunity, allowing her to avoid prosecution. The decision was widely condemned, but she returned to Zimbabwe on 19 August.

While relations with most of Africa were good, relations with *Botswana* continued to be frosty. On 3 October, Mugabe mocked Botswana's President Ian Khama for his unenthusiastic attitude towards campaigning for Botswana's Foreign Affairs and International Cooperation Minister Pelonomi Venson-Moitoi to become AU chairperson. Botswana said it would not respond to Mugabe's jibe due to his advanced age. On 7 November, Khama used social media to take another sly dig at Zimbabwe and Mugabe following the sacking of Mnangagwa, suggesting that Grace was responsible.

Zimbabwe maintained good relations with *China*. On 20 January, Chinese Ambassador Huang Ping commended the fruitful relations between the two countries and reiterated that his country had contributed to the economic growth of Zimbabwe, as evidenced by the number of successful projects that were underway. Huang mentioned the completion of the Victoria Falls International Airport refurbishment, the commencement of the construction of the Zimbabwe Parliament Building and the Kariba South Hydro Power Station Extension. After the removal of Mugabe, China's role in the 'soft coup' came under scrutiny. Less than two weeks before the events, the then army chief Constantino Chiwenga visited Beijing for a meeting with Chinese Defence Minister Chang Wanquan on 5 November. Amid speculation, China's Foreign Ministry insisted the meeting was a "normal military exchange as agreed by the two countries". There was speculation that Chiwenga was seeking China's support for a move against Mugabe. Whatever China's role in the coup, Beijing's priority was ensuring friendly bilateral relations that would allow commercial development in Zimbabwe to continue, regardless of who was in power.

Relations with *Russia* remained strong. On 29 May, Vice President Mphoko arrived in Russia for the 21st St Petersburg International Economic Forum, where Zimbabwe was expected to strengthen economic and investment ties with Russia. Mphoko was accompanied by a high-powered delegation comprising Industry and Commerce Minister Mike Bimha, Mines and Mining Development Minister Walter Chidhakwa and Finance and Economic Development Minister Patrick Chinamasa. Russia had shown keen interest in the country's industries and private sector investors were expected to visit the country to follow up on deals discussed on 3 June in St Petersburg.

There was no major shift in relations with the *EU*. On 24 February, following an annual review, the European Council adopted a decision extending EU restrictive measures against Zimbabwe. The measures continued to apply to President Mugabe, his wife and Zimbabwe Defence Industries. The EU also introduced an exception to its arms embargo, allowing for the export of certain explosive substances solely for use in civilian mining and infrastructure projects. On 5 June, the EU extended a $ 2.6 m grant to Zimbabwe to help improve human rights protection. The grant marked the resumption of EU direct development assistance to Zimbabwe after the bloc imposed sanctions in 2002. The fund was intended to support the rule of law through justice sector reforms and increase access to justice for all. The grant came under the framework of the 11th EDF signed between Zimbabwe and the EU in 2015. In October, Zimbabwe's agricultural sector received a boost after the EU made over $ 7 m available towards funding the training of agricultural extension workers as part of efforts to improve sustainable farming.

Relations with the *United Kingdom* did not change much. On 6 October, President Mugabe claimed Britain was open to dialogue with his regime after a meeting with Conservative MP Sir Nicholas Soames in Harare. The meeting was criticised by the opposition. On 29 November, UK Foreign Secretary Boris Johnson said that Britain could take steps to stabilise Zimbabwe's currency system and extend a bridging loan to help it clear World Bank and AfDB arrears, but such support depended on "democratic progress".

Relations with the *US* did not improve. On 16 January, President Barack Obama extended for another year sanctions that were targeted at members of Mugabe's inner circle, the military top brass and associated companies accused of undermining democracy. The opposition welcomed the extension. The Zimbabwean government was optimistic that relations with the US would improve after Donald Trump became president but, by September, nothing had changed. In his address to the UN General Assembly on 21 September, Mugabe called Donald Trump a "giant gold Goliath" who threatened to make other countries "extinct". Mugabe urged Trump to "blow your trumpet" in a way that would promote peace and the self-determination of countries, and not their extinction.

Relations with *multilateral organisations* were mixed. In May, Zimbabwe secured a syndicated loan put together by the African Export-Import Bank (Afreximbank) that would enable it to clear $ 1.7 bn of arrears with the World Bank and the AfDB. On 7 July, the IMF released the annual Article IV consultation report on Zimbabwe. It noted that, while many of the country's underlying strengths remained, some of its industrial and agricultural base had been eroded. The dollarised economy faced difficulties of diminishing net capital flows and an acute cash shortage. The IMF noted that, with re-engagement with creditors delayed, access to external financing was limited. Zimbabwe was yet to reach a deal with the World Bank and other foreign lenders over clearing arrears and implementing reforms. In July, the AfDB launched three projects worth $ 26 m that had been approved by the Bank's Board of Directors. On 23 September, Afreximbank signed a memorandum of understanding with the Reserve Bank of Zimbabwe (RBZ) for a $ 600 m nostro stabilisation facility. In December, the RBZ exchange control division approved and registered the bank's $ 600 m loan facility from Afreximbank.

Socioeconomic Developments

There were no significant changes in the country's economic challenges. *Economic indicators* did not improve much and deflationary pressures continued. RBZ figures showed that the December consumer price index for all items was 99.5%. The annual inflation rate was 3.5%, compared with –0.9 in 2016. According to Economist Intelligence Unit (EIU) estimates, real GDP growth stood at 2.9%, a rise from 0.6%, in 2016. The EIU put the nominal GDP at $ 17.2 bn, up from $ 16.6 bn in 2016. The current account balance was –$ 1.47 bn, compared with –$ 1.28 bn in 2016. Total international reserves rose to $439 m from $407 m in 2016. According to the 2017 budget statement, Zimbabwe's public debt stood at $ 13.58 bn or 74.9% of GDP. Of this, $ 7.55 bn (41.6% of GDP) was external debt.

Zimbabwe's performance in several key *world rankings* did not change significantly. In the World Bank's Ease of Doing Business Report, the country was ranked 159th, four places up from 2016. The World Economic Forum's Global Competitiveness Report 2017–18 ranked Zimbabwe 124th out of 137 economies, compared with 126th the previous year. In the 2016 Human Development Report, Zimbabwe was indexed at 0.516 and ranked 154th.

The country faced several *humanitarian challenges*. There were multiple hazards, including drought, floods and outbreaks of cholera and typhoid. According to post-harvest assessments and the July report of the Vulnerability Assessment Committee (ZimVAC) 1.1 m people were projected to be 'food insecure' during the peak hunger period of January to March 2018. This was a decrease from 4.2 m people projected during the same period in 2017. There was a decrease in the global acute malnutrition prevalence from 4.4% in 2016 to 3.2% in 2017. Thirty-seven districts were affected by flooding caused by torrential rains during the period February to April. The government responded by declaring a state of disaster and launched a humanitarian appeal. The country also experienced the escalation of a protracted typhoid outbreak, which increased in severity during January to March. Harare later experienced a resurgence of typhoid and, between October and December, 2,032 typhoid cases were confirmed, though no deaths were reported. A total of six cholera cases including three deaths were reported.

On *demographic indicators*, according to estimates, the death rate stood at 10.2 per 1,000 people. Due to the deteriorating economic situation, the flow of Zimbabweans out of the country in search of better economic opportunities persisted. UN estimates put the net migration rate at 8.5 migrants per 1,000 people. Average life expectancy for the total population was 64 years. The infant mortality rate was estimated at 32.7 deaths per 1,000 live births. The literacy rate remained above 90%, making Zimbabwe the leader in Africa.

On *HIV* prevalence, UNAIDS figures showed that 1.3 m people were living with HIV. The prevalence rate among adults aged 15–49 was estimated at 13.5%. Adults aged 15 and over living with HIV numbered some 1.2 m. HIV incidence was 3.03%. Deaths due to AIDS were estimated at 30,000. The coverage of adults and children receiving antiretroviral therapy was 75%.

The *education and health* delivery systems continued to experience problems with staffing, equipment and funding. Health and education personnel continued to constitute a substantial part of the brain drain. Industrial action and threats of industrial action arising out of salary disputes were a constant feature throughout the year, further compromising these sectors, and delays in paying salaries and annual bonuses did not help boost morale. As in 2016, Primary and Secondary

Education Minister Lazarus Dokora generated controversy with his zeal for an endless raft of reforms.

According to the Confederation of Zimbabwe Industries (CZI), the *manufacturing sector* recorded 5.5% growth in volume output compared with 2016, while the weighted average capacity utilisation fell from 47.4% to 45.1%. The level of capital investment in the sector grew. This helped explain the growth in capacity that was not being fully utilised. The CZI survey showed that there was increased demand for foreign currency, attributable to increased production output as more firms imported raw materials.

On 7 December, Finance and Economic Development Minister Patrick Chinamasa presented the *2018 national budget* with the theme 'Towards a New Economic Order'. Chinamasa proposed a $ 5.7 bn budget, with revenue projected at $ 5.1 bn. The economy was projected to grow by 3.7% in 2018. The budget deficit was expected to be $ 1.7 bn, much higher than the originally projected amount of $ 400 m. The 2018 budget deficit was projected at $ 675.8 m. Employment costs were $ 3.3 bn and capital expenditure was $ 1.2 bn, translating to 5.5% of GDP. The import bill was still relatively high, with imports estimated to rise to $ 6.8 bn, from $ 6.4 bn in 2016, despite a sharp drop in food imports.

www.ingramcontent.com/pod-product-compliance
Lightning Source LLC
LaVergne TN
LVHW080114011026
849160LV00013B/1102